Lecture Notes in Computer Science   14813

Founding Editors

Gerhard Goos
Juris Hartmanis

The series Lecture Notes in Computer Science (LNCS), including its subseries Lecture Notes in Artificial Intelligence (LNAI) and Lecture Notes in Bioinformatics (LNBI), has established itself as a medium for the publication of new developments in computer science and information technology research, teaching, and education.

LNCS enjoys close cooperation with the computer science R & D community, the series counts many renowned academics among its volume editors and paper authors, and collaborates with prestigious societies. Its mission is to serve this international community by providing an invaluable service, mainly focused on the publication of conference and workshop proceedings and postproceedings. LNCS commenced publication in 1973.

Osvaldo Gervasi · Beniamino Murgante ·
Chiara Garau · David Taniar ·
Ana Maria A. C. Rocha ·
Maria Noelia Faginas Lago
Editors

Computational Science and Its Applications – ICCSA 2024

24th International Conference
Hanoi, Vietnam, July 1–4, 2024
Proceedings, Part I

 Springer

Editors
Osvaldo Gervasi 🅘
Mathematics and Computer Science
University of Perugia
Perugia, Perugia, Italy

Chiara Garau 🅘
Department of Civil and Environmental
Engineering and Architecture
University of Cagliari
Cagliari, Italy

Ana Maria A. C. Rocha 🅘
Algoritmi Research Centre
University of Minho
Braga, Portugal

Beniamino Murgante 🅘
School of Engineering
University of Basilicata
Potenza, Italy

David Taniar 🅘
Faculty of Information Technology
Monash University
Clayton, VIC, Australia

Maria Noelia Faginas Lago 🅘
Department of Chemistry, Biology
and Biotechnology
University of Perugia
Perugia, Italy

ISSN 0302-9743   ISSN 1611-3349 (electronic)
Lecture Notes in Computer Science
ISBN 978-3-031-64604-1   ISBN 978-3-031-64605-8 (eBook)
https://doi.org/10.1007/978-3-031-64605-8

This Springer imprint is published by the registered company Springer Nature Switzerland AG
The registered company address is: Gewerbestrasse 11, 6330 Cham, Switzerland

If disposing of this product, please recycle the paper.

Preface

These two volumes (LNCS volumes 14813–14814) consist of the peer-reviewed papers from the 2024 International Conference on Computational Science and Its Applications (ICCSA 2024) which took place during July 1–4, 2024. In addition, the peer-reviewed papers of the 55 Workshops, the Workshops proceedings, are published in a separate set consisting of 11 volumes (LNCS 14815–14825).

The conference was held in a hybrid form, with some participants present in person, hosted in Hanoi, Vietnam, by the Thuy Loi University. We enabled virtual participation for those who were unable to attend the event, due to logistical, political and economic problems, by adopting a technological infrastructure based on open source software (jitsi + riot), and a commercial Cloud infrastructure.

ICCSA 2024 was another successful event in the International Conference on Computational Science and Its Applications (ICCSA) conference series, previously held in Athens, Greece (2023), Malaga, Spain (2022), Cagliari, Italy (hybrid with few participants in presence in 2021 and completely online in 2020), whilst earlier editions took place in Saint Petersburg, Russia (2019), Melbourne, Australia (2018), Trieste, Italy (2017), Beijing, China (2016), Banff, Canada (2015), Guimaraes, Portugal (2014), Ho Chi Minh City, Vietnam (2013), Salvador, Brazil (2012), Santander, Spain (2011), Fukuoka, Japan (2010), Suwon, South Korea (2009), Perugia, Italy (2008), Kuala Lumpur, Malaysia (2007), Glasgow, UK (2006), Singapore (2005), Assisi, Italy (2004), Montreal, Canada (2003), and (as ICCS) Amsterdam, The Netherlands (2002) and San Francisco, USA (2001).

Computational Science is the main pillar of most of the present research, industrial and commercial applications, and plays a unique role in exploiting ICT innovative technologies, and the ICCSA conference series have been providing a venue to researchers and industry practitioners to discuss new ideas, to share complex problems and their solutions, and to shape new trends in Computational Science. As the conference mirrors society from a scientific point of view, this year's undoubtedly dominant theme was the machine learning and artificial intelligence and their applications in the most diverse economic and industrial fields.

The ICCSA 2024 conference is structured in 6 general tracks covering the fields of computational science and its applications: Computational Methods, Algorithms and Scientific Applications – High Performance Computing and Networks – Geometric Modeling, Graphics and Visualization – Advanced and Emerging Applications – Information Systems and Technologies – Urban and Regional Planning. In addition, the conference consisted of 55 workshops, focusing on very topical issues of importance to science, technology and society: from new mathematical approaches for solving complex computational systems, to information and knowledge in the Internet of Things, new statistical and optimization methods, several Artificial Intelligence approaches, sustainability issues, smart cities and related technologies.

We accepted 53 full papers, 6 short papers and 3 PhD Showcase papers from 207 submissions to the General Tracks of the conference (acceptance rate 30%). For the 55 workshops we accepted 281 full papers, 17 short papers and 2 PhD Showcase papers. We would like to express our appreciation to the workshops chairs and co-chairs for their hard work and dedication.

The success of the ICCSA conference series in general, and of ICCSA 2024 in particular, vitally depends on the support of many people: authors, presenters, participants, keynote speakers, workshop chairs, session chairs, organizing committee members, student volunteers, Program Committee members, Advisory Committee members, International Liaison chairs, reviewers and others in various roles. We take this opportunity to wholeheartedly thank them all.

We also wish to thank our publisher, Springer, for their acceptance to publish the proceedings, for sponsoring part of the best papers awards and for their kind assistance and cooperation during the editing process.

We cordially invite you to visit the ICCSA website https://iccsa.org where you can find all the relevant information about this interesting and exciting event.

July 2024

Osvaldo Gervasi
David Taniar
Beniamino Murgante
Chiara Garau

Welcome Message from Organizers

After the very hard times of COVID, ICCSA continues its successful scientific endeavors in 2024, hosted in Hanoi, Vietnam. This time, ICCSA moved from the Mediterranean Region to Southeast Asia and was held in the metropolitan city of Hanoi, the capital of Vietnam. Hanoi is a vibrant urban environment known for the hospitality of its citizens, its rich history, vibrant culture, and dynamic urban life. Located in the northern part of the country, Hanoi is a bustling metropolis that combines the old with the new, offering a unique blend of ancient traditions and modern development.

ICCSA 2024 took place in a secure environment, allowing for safe and vibrant in-person participation. Combined with the active engagement of the ICCSA 2024 scientific community, this set the stage for highly motivating discussions and interactions regarding the latest developments in computer science and its applications in the real world for improving communities' quality of life.

Thuyloi University, also known as the Water Resources University, is a prominent institution in Hanoi, Vietnam, with a strong reputation in engineering and technical education, particularly in water resources and environmental engineering. In recent years, the University has expanded its academic offerings to include computer science, reflecting the growing importance of technology and digital skills in all sectors. This year, Thuyloi University had the honor of hosting ICCSA 2024. The Local Organizing Committee felt the burden and responsibility of such a demanding task and put all necessary energy into meeting participants' expectations and establishing a friendly, creative, and inspiring scientific and social/cultural environment that allowed for new ideas and perspectives to flourish.

Since all ICCSA participants, whether informatics-oriented or application-driven, realize the tremendous advancements in computer science over the last few decades and the huge potential these advancements offer in coping with the enormous challenges of humanity in a globalized, 'wired,' and highly competitive world, the expectations for ICCSA 2024 were high. The goal was to successfully match computer science progress with communities' aspirations, achieving progress that serves real, place- and people-based needs and paves the way towards a visionary, smart, sustainable, resilient, and inclusive future for both current and future generations.

On behalf of the Local Organizing Committee, I would like to sincerely thank all of you who contributed to ICCSA 2024.

Nguyen Canh Thai

Organization

ICCSA 2024 was organized by Thuyloi University (Vietnam), the University of Perugia (Italy), the University of Basilicata (Italy), Monash University (Australia), Kyushu Sangyo University (Japan), the University of Minho (Portugal), and the University of Cagliari (Italy).

Honorary General Chairs

Norio Shiratori	Chuo University, Japan
Kenneth C. J. Tan	Sardina Systems, UK

General Chairs

Nguyen Canh Thai	Thuyloi University, Vietnam
Osvaldo Gervasi	University of Perugia, Italy
David Taniar	Monash University, Australia

Program Committee Chairs

Beniamino Murgante	University of Basilicata, Italy
Chiara Garau	University of Cagliari, Italy
Ana Maria A.C. Rocha	University of Minho, Portugal
Bernady O. Apduhan	Kyushu Sangyo University, Japan

International Advisory Committee

Jemal Abawajy	Deakin University, Australia
Dharma P. Agarwal	University of Cincinnati, USA
Rajkumar Buyya	Melbourne University, Australia
Claudia Bauzer Medeiros	University of Campinas, Brazil
Manfred M. Fisher	Vienna University of Economics and Business, Austria
Pierre Frankhauser	University of Franche-Comté/CNRS, France
Marina L. Gavrilova	University of Calgary, Canada

Sumi Helal	University of Florida, USA & University of Lancaster, UK
Bin Jiang	University of Gävle, Sweden
Yee Leung	Chinese University of Hong Kong, China

International Liaison Chairs

Ivan Blečić	University of Cagliari, Italy
Giuseppe Borruso	University of Trieste, Italy
Elise De Donker	Western Michigan University, USA
Maria Noelia Faginas Lago	University of Perugia, Italy
Maria Irene Falcão	University of Minho, Portugal
Robert C. H. Hsu	Chung Hua University, Taiwan
Yeliz Karaca	University of Massachusetts Medical School, Worcester, USA
Tae-Hoon Kim	Zhejiang University of Science and Technology, China
Vladimir Korkhov	Saint Petersburg University, Russia
Takashi Naka	Kyushu Sangyo University, Japan
Rafael D. C. Santos	National Institute for Space Research, Brazil
Maribel Yasmina Santos	University of Minho, Portugal
Anastasia Stratigea	National Technical University of Athens, Greece

Workshop and Session Organizing Chairs

Beniamino Murgante	University of Basilicata, Italy
Chiara Garau	University of Cagliari, Italy

Award Chair

Wenny Rahayu	La Trobe University, Australia

Publicity Committee Chair

Elmer Dadios	De La Salle University, Philippines
Nataliia Kulabukhova	Saint Petersburg University, Russia
Daisuke Takahashi	Tsukuba University, Japan

Shangwang Wang　　　　　　Beijing University of Posts and
　　　　　　　　　　　　　　　Telecommunications, China

Local Organizing Committee Chairs

Doan Quang Tu　　　　　　　Academy of Military Science and Technology,
　　　　　　　　　　　　　　　Hanoi, Vietnam
Ho Sy Tam　　　　　　　　　Thuyloi University, Vietnam
Le Quang Tuan　　　　　　　Thuyloi University, Vietnam
Nguyen Huu Quynh　　　　　Thuyloi University, Vietnam
Ta Quang Chieu　　　　　　　Thuyloi University, Vietnam

Technology Chair

Damiano Perri　　　　　　　University of Perugia, Italy

Program Committee

Vera Afreixo　　　　　　　　University of Aveiro, Portugal
Vladimir Alarcon　　　　　　Northern Gulf Institute, USA
Filipe Alvelos　　　　　　　University of Minho, Portugal
Debora Anelli　　　　　　　Polytechnic University of Bari, Italy
Hartmut Asche　　　　　　　Hasso-Plattner-Institut für Digital Engineering,
　　　　　　　　　　　　　　　Germany
Ginevra Balletto　　　　　　University of Cagliari, Italy
Socrates Basbas　　　　　　Aristotle University of Thessaloniki, Greece
David Berti　　　　　　　　ART SpA, Italy
Michela Bertolotto　　　　　University College Dublin, Ireland
Debnath Bhattacharyya　　　Koneru Lakshmaiah University, India
Sandro Bimonte　　　　　　CEMAGREF, TSCF, France
Ana Cristina Braga　　　　　University of Minho, Portugal
Tiziana Campisi　　　　　　Kore University of Enna, Italy
Yves Caniou　　　　　　　　Lyon University, France
José A. Cardoso e Cunha　　Universidade Nova de Lisboa, Portugal
Rui Cardoso　　　　　　　　University of Beira Interior, Portugal
Leocadio G. Casado　　　　University of Almeria, Spain
Mete Celik　　　　　　　　Erciyes University, Turkey
Maria Cerreta　　　　　　　University of Naples Federico II, Italy
Mauro Coni　　　　　　　　University of Cagliari, Italy

Florbela Maria da Cruz Domingues Correia — Polytechnic Institute of Viana do Castelo, Portugal

Roberto De Lotto — University of Pavia, Italy

Marcelo De Paiva Guimaraes — Federal University of Sao Paulo, Brazil

Frank Devai — London South Bank University, UK

Joana Matos Dias — University of Coimbra, Portugal

Laila El Ghandour — Heriot Watt University, UK

Rafida M. Elobaid — Canadian University Dubai, United Arab Emirates

Maria Irene Falcao — University of Minho, Portugal

Florbela P. Fernandes — Polytechnic Institute of Bragança, Portugal

Paula Odete Fernandes — Polytechnic Institute of Bragança, Portugal

Adelaide de Fátima Baptista Valente Freitas — University of Aveiro, Portugal

Valentina Franzoni — University of Perugia, Italy

Andreas Fricke — University of Potsdam, Germany

Raffaele Garrisi — Centro Operativo per la Sicurezza Cibernetica, Italy

Maria Giaoutzi — National Technical University, Athens, Greece

Salvatore Giuffrida — University of Catania, Italy

Teresa Guarda — Universidad Estatal Peninsula de Santa Elena, Ecuador

Sevin Gümgüm — Izmir University of Economics, Turkey

Malgorzata Hanzl — Technical University of Lodz, Poland

Maulana Adhinugraha Kiki — Telkom University, Indonesia

Clement Ho Cheung Leung — Chinese University of Hong Kong, China

Andrea Lombardi — University of Perugia, Italy

Marcos Mandado Alonso — University of Vigo, Spain

Ernesto Marcheggiani — Katholieke Universiteit Leuven, Belgium

Antonino Marvuglia — Luxembourg Institute of Science and Technology, Luxembourg

Michele Mastroianni — University of Salerno, Italy

Hideo Matsufuru — High Energy Accelerator Research Organization, Japan

Alfredo Milani — University of Perugia, Italy

Fernando Miranda — Universidade do Minho, Portugal

Giuseppe Modica — University of Reggio Calabria, Italy

Louiza de Macedo Mourelle — State University of Rio de Janeiro, Brazil

Nadia Nedjah — State University of Rio de Janeiro, Brazil

Paolo Nesi — University of Florence, Italy

Rajdeep Niyogi — Indian Institute of Technology Roorkee, India

Suzan Obaiys — University Malaya, Malaysia

Marcin Paprzycki — Polish Academy of Sciences, Poland

Eric Pardede   La Trobe University, Australia
Ana Isabel Pereira   Polytechnic Institute of Bragança, Portugal
Damiano Perri   University of Perugia, Italy
Massimiliano Petri   University of Pisa, Italy
Telmo Pinto   University of Coimbra, Portugal
Maurizio Pollino   ENEA, Italy
Alenka Poplin   Iowa State University, USA
Marcos Quiles   Federal University of São Paulo, Brazil
Humberto Rocha   University of Coimbra, Portugal
Marzio Rosi   University of Perugia, Italy
Manna Sheela Rani Chetty   Koneru Lakshmaiah University, India
Lucia Saganeiti   University of L'Aquila, Italy
Tamie Salter   Citizen Alerts Inc., Canada
Francesco Scorza   University of Basilicata, Italy
Marco Paulo Seabra dos Reis   University of Coimbra, Portugal
Jie Shen   University of Michigan, USA
Chien Sing Lee   Sunway University, Malaysia
Francesco Tajani   Sapienza University of Rome, Italy
Rodrigo Tapia-McClung   Centro de Investigación en Ciencias de
                                          Información Geoespacial, Mexico
Eufemia Tarantino   Polytechnic of Bari, Italy
Sergio Tasso   University of Perugia, Italy
Ana Paula Teixeira   Universidade do Minho, Portugal
Maria Filomena Teodoro   IST ID, Instituto Superior Técnico, Portugal
Yiota Theodora   National Technical University of Athens, Greece
Carmelo Torre   Polytechnic of Bari, Italy
Giuseppe A. Trunfio   University of Sassari, Italy
Toshihiro Uchibayashi   Kyushu University, Japan
Marco Vizzari   University of Perugia, Italy
Frank Westad   Norwegian University of Science and Technology,
                                          Norway
Fukuko Yuasa   High Energy Accelerator Research Organization,
                                          Japan
Ljiljana Zivkovic   Republic Geodetic Authority, Serbia

Additional Reviewers

Michal Abrahamowicz   McGill University, Montreal, Canada
Lidia Aceto   Università del Piemonte Orientale, Italy
Marco Baioletti   University of Perugia, Italy
Birol Ciloglugil   Ege University, Turkey

Maria Danese	National Research Council, Italy
Alexander Degtyarev	Saint Petersburg State University, Russia
Alexander Derendyaev	Institute for Information Transmission Problems, Russia
Joana Dias	University of Coimbra, Portugal
Ivan Gerace	University of Perugia, Italy
Alessandra Marra	University of Salerno, Italy
Giovanni Mauro	University of Campania Luigi Vanvitelli, Italy
Paolo Mengoni	Hong Kong Baptist University, China
Marco Reis	University of Coimbra, Portugal
Cristiano Russo	University of Napoli Federico II, Italy
Valentino Santucci	University for Foreigners of Perugia, Italy

Workshops

1. *Advances in Artificial Intelligence Learning Technologies: Blended Learning, STEM, Computational Thinking and Coding (AAILT 2024)*
2. *Advanced and Innovative Web Apps 2024 (AIWA 2024)*
3. *Advanced Processes of Mathematics and Computing Models in Complex Computational Systems (ACMC 2024)*
4. *Advances in Information Systems and Technologies for Emergency Management, Risk Assessment and Mitigation Based on the Resilience Concepts (ASTER 2024)*
5. *Advances in Web-Based Learning 2024 (AWBL 2024)*
6. *Blockchain and Distributed Ledgers: Technologies and Applications (BDLTA 2024)*
7. *Computational and Applied Mathematics (CAM 2024)*
8. *Computational and Applied Statistics (CAS 2024)*
9. *Cyber Intelligence and Applications (CIA 2024)*
10. *Computational Methods, Statistics and Industrial Mathematics (CMSIM 2024)*
11. *Computational Optimization and Applications (COA 2024)*
12. *Computational Astrochemistry (CompAstro 2024)*
13. *Computational Methods for Porous Geomaterials (CompPor 2024)*
14. *Workshop on Computational Science and HPC (CSHPC 2024)*
15. *Cities, Technologies and Planning (CTP 2024)*
16. *Sustainable Digital Circular Economy (DiCE 2024)*
17. *Evaluating Inner Areas Potentials (EIAP 2024)*
18. *Econometrics and Multidimensional Evaluation of Urban Environment (EMEUE 2024)*
19. *Environmental, Social, Governance of Energy Planning (ESGEP 2024)*
20. *Ecosystem Services in Spatial Planning for Resilient Urban and Rural Areas (ESSP 2024)*
21. *Ethical AI Applications for a Human-Centered Cyber Society (EthicAI 2024)*
22. *14th International Workshop on Future Computing System Technologies and Applications (FiSTA 2024)*

23. *Geographical Analysis, Urban Modeling, Spatial Statistics (Geog-An-Mod 2024)*
24. *Geomatics for Resource Monitoring and Management (GRMM 2024)*
25. *International Workshop on Information and Knowledge in the Internet of Things (IKIT 2024)*
26. *Regenerating Brownfields Enhancing Urban Resilience Appeal (INFERENCE 2024)*
27. *International Workshop on Territorial Planning to Integrate Risk and Urban Ontologies (IWPRO 2024)*
28. *MaaS Solutions for Airports, Cities and Regional Connectivity (MaaS 2024)*
29. *Development of Urban Mobility Management and Risk Assessment (MAINTAIN 2024)*
30. *Multidimensional Evolutionary Evaluations for Transformative Approaches (MEETA 2024)*
31. *Building Multi-dimensional Models for Assessing Complex Environmental Systems (MES 2024)*
32. *Models and Indicators for Assessing and Measuring the Urban Settlement Development in the View of Zero Net Land Take by 2050 (MOVEto0 2024)*
33. *4th Workshop on Privacy in the Cloud/Edge/IoT World (PCEIoT 2024)*
34. *Scientific Computing Infrastructure (SCI 2024)*
35. *Downscale Agenda2030 (SDGscale 2024)*
36. *Socio-Economic and Environmental Models for Land Use Management (SEMLUM 2024)*
37. *Ports of the Future - Smartness and Sustainability (SmartPorts 2024)*
38. *Smart Transport and Logistics - Smart Supply Chains (SmarTransLog 2024)*
39. *Smart Tourism (SmartTourism 2024)*
40. *Sustainable Evolution of Long-Distance Freight Passenger Transport (SOLIDEST 2024)*
41. *Sustainability Performance Assessment: Models, Approaches, and Applications Toward Interdisciplinary and Integrated Solutions (SPA 2024)*
42. *Specifics of Smart Cities Development in Europe (SPEED 2024)*
43. *Smart, Safe and Health Cities (SSHC 2024)*
44. *Smart and Sustainable Island Communities (SSIC 2024)*
45. *From Street Experiments to Planned Solutions (STEPS 2024)*
46. *Sustainable Development of Ports (SUSTAINABLEPORTS 2024)*
47. *Theoretical and Computational Chemistry and Its Applications (TCCMA 2024)*
48. *Transport Infrastructures for Smart Cities (TISC 2024)*
49. *From Structural to Transformative-Change of City Environment: Challenges and Solutions and Perspectives (TRACE 2024)*
50. *Transport and Digital Multiscale Sustainable Network for Circular Economy (TransNet 2024)*
51. *Temporary Real Estate Management: Approaches and Methods for Time-Integrated Impact Assessments and Evaluations (TREAT 2024)*
52. *Urban Regeneration: Innovative Tools and Evaluation Model (URITEM 2024)*
53. *Urban Space Accessibility and Mobilities (USAM 2024)*
54. *Virtual Reality and Augmented Reality and Applications (VRA 2024)*
55. *Workshop on Advanced and Computational Methods for Earth Science Applications (WACM4ES 2024)*

Sponsoring Organizations

ICCSA 2024 would not have been possible without the tremendous support of many organizations and institutions, for which all organizers and participants of ICCSA 2024 express their sincere gratitude:

Springer Nature Switzerland AG, Switzerland (https://www.springer.com)

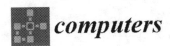

Computers Open Access Journal (https://www.mdpi.com/journal/computers)

Thuyloi University, Hanoi, Vietnam (https://en.tlu.edu.vn/)

University of Perugia, Italy (https://www.unipg.it)

University of Basilicata, Italy (http://www.unibas.it)

Monash University, Australia (https://www.monash.edu/)

Kyushu Sangyo University, Japan (https://www.kyusan-u.ac.jp/)

University of Minho, Portugal (https://www.uminho.pt/)

University of Cagliari, Italy (https://en.unica.it/en)

Venue

ICCSA 2024 took place on the main campus of Thuyloi University in Hanoi, Vietnam.

Plenary Lectures

Harnessing Artificial Intelligence for Enhanced Spatial Analysis of Natural Hazard Assessments

Prof. Dr. Biswajeet Pradhan

Director - Centre for Advanced Modelling and Geospatial Information Systems (CAMGIS), School of Civil and Environmental Engineering, Faculty of Engineering and IT, University of Technology Sydney, Australia

Abstract. In the realm of natural hazard assessments within spatial domains, the advent of Artificial Intelligence (AI) represents a paradigm shift, revolutionizing the way we conceptualize, model, and interpret environmental risks. This keynote address illuminates the profound impact of AI technologies, particularly machine learning algorithms and data-driven approaches, in reshaping our understanding and prediction capabilities concerning natural disasters.

By assimilating and scrutinizing vast spatial datasets, AI-driven models offer unparalleled accuracy and efficiency, facilitating timely and precise hazard assessments. Real-time processing of geospatial information not only enables rapid predictions but also forms the cornerstone of proactive disaster management strategies. Furthermore, AI's capacity lies in its adeptness at deciphering intricate spatial patterns inherent to natural hazards, unraveling subtle cues and previously unnoticed correlations within the data fabric.

This keynote delves into how AI's nuanced interpretation, coupled with advanced algorithms, elevates hazard modeling, providing deeper insights into the spatial dynamics of environmental risks. By augmenting traditional methodologies and revealing hidden patterns, AI fosters comprehensive risk assessments, fostering informed decision-making processes. The fusion of AI and natural hazard assessments in spatial domains heralds a more resilient approach to disaster preparedness and response.

Join us in embracing this transformative era, where AI's sophisticated modeling techniques and precise spatial interpretations converge, heralding proactive and effective mitigation strategies amidst the ever-evolving landscape of environmental challenges.

Short Bio. Distinguished Professor Dr. Biswajeet Pradhan is an internationally established scientist in the field of Geospatial Information Systems (GIS), remote sensing and image processing, complex modelling/geo-computing, machine learning and soft-computing applications, natural hazards and environmental modelling. He is the Director of the Centre for Advanced Modelling and Geospatial Information Systems (CAMGIS) at the Faculty of Engineering and IT at the University of Technology, Sydney (Australia). He was listed as the World's Most Highly Cited Researcher by the Clarivate Analytics Report for five consecutive years, 2016–2020 as one of the world's most influential minds.

He ranked number one (1) in the field of "Geological & Geomatics Engineering" during the calendar year 2021–2023, according to the list published by Stanford University Researchers, USA. This list ranks the world's top 2% most highly cited researchers based on Scopus data. In 2018–2020, he was awarded as World Class Professor by the Ministry of Research, Technology and Higher Education, Indonesia. He is a recipient of the Alexander von Humboldt Research Fellowship from Germany. Between 2015–2021, he served as "Ambassador Scientist" for the Alexander Humboldt Foundation, Germany.

Professor Pradhan has received 58 awards since 2006 in recognition of his excellence in teaching, service and research. Out of his more than 850 articles (Google Scholar citation: 70,000, H-index: 129), more than 750 have been published in science citation index (SCI/SCIE) technical journals. He has authored/co-authored ten books and thirteen book chapters.

Software Engineering Research in a New Situation

Prof. Carl K. Chang

Professor Emeritus, State University of Iowa, USA

Abstract. With the rise of Generative Artificial Intelligence (GAI), epito-mized by Large Language Models (LLMs), a profound shift has unfolded in software engineering research. In this presentation, I will traverse my four-decade journey in software engineering research, focusing on situational awareness in the era of the Internet of Things (IoT). I have wit-nessed the turbulence brought forth by the AI community that demands changes in our approaches. Meanwhile, owing to the pervasiveness of ser-vices computing, services became the first-class citizen in modern-day software engineering methodologies.

I argue that situational awareness must permeate the entire lifecycle to consistently deliver software services that align with the dynamic needs of users and the ever-evolving environments. I will elucidate this argu-ment by reviewing the Situ framework, offering a comprehensive illus-tration of my perspective. Furthermore, I will outline my vision regarding the formidable research challenges considering the rapidly shifting land-scape dominated by an irresistible and profoundly disruptive generative AI tsunami.

Short Bio. Carl K. Chang is a former department chair and Professor Emeritus of Computer Science at Iowa State University. His research interests include requirements engineering, net-centric computing, situational software engineering and digital health. Chang was the 2004 President of the IEEE Computer Society. Previously he served as the Editor-in-Chief for IEEE Software (1991–1994), and as the Editor-in-Chief of IEEE

Computer (2007–2010). He was the 2012 recipient of the Richard E. Merwin Medal from the IEEE Computer Society. Chang is a Life Fellow of IEEE, a Fellow of AAAS, and a Life Member of the European Academy of Sciences (EurASc).

Interpretability and Privacy Preservation in Large Language Models (LLMs)

Prof. My Thai

University of Florida (UF) Research Foundation Professor
Associate Director of UF Nelms Institute for the Connected World

Abstract. Large Language Models (LLMs) have transformed the AI landscape, captivating researchers and practitioners with their remarkable ability to generate human-like text and perform complex tasks. However, this transformative power comes with a set of critical challenges, particularly in the realms of interpretability and privacy preservation. In this keynote, we embark on an exploration of these pressing issues, shedding light on how LLMs operate, their limitations, and the strategies we can employ to mitigate risks. We begin by examining the interpretability in LLMs, which often function as enigmatic "black boxes." Their complex neural architectures make it challenging to understand how they arrive at specific outputs. This lack of transparency raises questions of trust and accountability. When deploying LLMs in real-world applications—whether for chatbots, content generation, or decision-making—it becomes crucial to demystify their decision paths.

We will use explainable AI (XAI) to offer faithful explanations, from the black-box to white-box models, and from feature-based [1, 2] to neuron circuits-based [3, 4] explanations. By visualizing attention mechanisms, feature importance, and saliency maps, we empower users to comprehend LLM predictions. XAI not only fosters trust but also encourages responsible utilization of LLMs.

We next turn our attention to one of the utmost concerns and challenges: data privacy. LLMs process vast amounts of data, raising risks of data leakage, model inversion, the right to be forgotten, and inadvertent exposure of sensitive information. Furthermore, the integration of LLMs into diverse applications also significantly brings these challenges to the next level [5].

This talk explores strategies to protect privacy, including differential privacy, federated learning, and data encryption.

Short Bio. My T. Thai is a University of Florida (UF) Research Foundation Professor, Associate Director of UF Nelms Institute for the Connected World, and a Fellow of IEEE and AAIA. Dr. Thai is a leading authority who has done transformative research in Trustworthy AI and Optimization, especially for complex systems with applications to healthcare, social media, critical networking infrastructure, and cybersecurity. The results of her work have led to 7 books and 350+ publications in highly ranked international journals and conferences, including several best paper awards from the IEEE, ACM, and AAAI.

In responding to a world-wide call for responsible and safe AI, Dr. Thai is a pioneer in designing deep explanations for black-box ML models, while defending against explanation-guided attacks, evident by her Distinguished Papers Award at the Association for the Advancement of Artificial Intelligence (AAAI) conference in 2023. At the same year, she was also awarded an ACM Web Science Trust Test-of-Time award, for her landmark work on combating misinformation in social media. In 2022, she received an IEEE Big Data Security Women of Achievement Award. In 2009, she was awarded the Young Investigator (YIP) from the Defense Threat Reduction Agency (DTRA), and in 2010 she won the NSF CAREER Award. She is presently the Editor-in-Chief of the Springer Journal of Combinatorial Optimization and the IET Blockchain Journal, and editor of the Springer book series Optimization and Its Applications.

References

1. Vu, M., Thai, M.T.: PGM-explainer: probabilistic graphical model explanations for graph neural networks. In: Advances in Neural Information Processing Systems (NeurIPS) (2020)
2. Nguyen, T., Lai, P., Phan, H., Thai, M.T.: XRand: differentially private defense against explanation-guided attacks. In: AAAI Conference on Artificial Intelligence (AAAI) (2023)
3. Vu, N., Nguyen, T., Thai, M.T.: NeuCEPT: learn neural networks' mechanism via critical neurons with precision guarantee. In: IEEE International Conference on Data Mining (ICDM) (2022)
4. Conmy, A., Mavor-Parker, A., Heimersheim, S., Garriga-Alonso, A.: Towards automated circuit discovery for mechanistic interpretability. In: Advances in Neural Information Processing Systems (NeurIPS) (2023)
5. Vu, M., Nguyen, T., Jeter, T., Thai, M.T.: Analysis of privacy leakages in federated large language models. In: International Conference on Artificial Intelligence and Statistics (AISTATS) (2023)

Contents – Part I

Geometric Modeling, Graphics and Visualization

Advanced and Emerging Applications

Urban and Regional Planning

Contents – Part II

PHD Showcase Papers

Short Papers

Computational Methods, Algorithms and Scientific Applications

A Multi-centrality Heuristic
for the Bandwidth Reduction Problem

João Maues[1], Israel Mendonça[3], Glauco Amorim[2],
Sanderson L. Gonzaga de Oliveira[4], Ana Isabel Pereira[5,6],
Diego Brandão[2(✉)], and Pedro Henrique González[1]

[1] System Engineering and Computer Science Program, Federal University of Rio de
Janeiro, Rio de Janeiro, Brazil
{jvmaues,pegonzalez}@cos.ufrj.br

[2] Department of Computer Science, Federal Center for Technological Education of
Rio de Janeiro, Rio de Janeiro, Brazil
{glauco.amorim,diego.brandao}@cefet-rj.br

[3] School of Advanced Science, Kumamoto University, Kumamoto, Japan
israel@cs.kumamoto-u.ac.jp

[4] Department of Science and Technology, Federal University of São Paulo,
São Paulo, Brazil
sanderson.oliveira@unifesp.br

[5] Research Centre in Digitalization and Intelligent Robotics (CeDRI),
Instituto Politécnico de Bragança, 5300-253 Bragança, Portugal
apereira@ipb.pt

[6] Laboratório Associado para a Sustentabilidade e Tecnologia em Regiões de
Montanha (SusTEC), Instituto Politécnico de Bragança, 5300-253 Bragança, Portugal

Abstract. The Bandwidth Minimization Problem for Sparse Matrices is
a well-known NP-Hard problem critical in numerous significant scientific
applications. The Cuthill-McKee algorithm, a heuristic based on degree
centrality for minimizing bandwidth, is a common solution approach.
One can integrate other centrality measures into the Cuthill-McKee
method or similar algorithms. This work explores the impact of utilizing these diverse centrality measures on the performance of the Cuthill-
McKee heuristic. It introduces a novel multi-centrality constructive algorithm designed as an alternative for practical applications emphasizing
efficient execution for large linear systems. The results demonstrate clear
advantages of considering multiple centrality measures over solely degree
centrality. This approach notably enhances the heuristic's effectiveness,
offering significant improvements in solving complex bandwidth minimization problems.

Keywords: Bandwidth Reduction Problem · Graph Centrality ·
Cuthill-Mckee method

1 Introduction

Solving large-scale sparse linear systems, represented by $Ax = b$, where A is an
$n \times n$ sparse matrix, x is the unknown vector of dimension n, and b is a known

O. Gervasi et al. (Eds.): ICCSA 2024, LNCS 14813, pp. 3–15, 2024.
https://doi.org/10.1007/978-3-031-64605-8_1

vector of dimension n, plays a crucial role in various scientific and engineering fields. Many simulations in science and engineering require solving extensive sparse linear systems, often representing the highest computational cost. For instance, as discussed by Kaveh [16], in structural mechanics problems, linear systems of real-world problems account for 30% to 50% of computational costs, reaching up to 80% in comparison to nonlinear systems in structural optimization problems.

The challenge of the Bandwidth Minimization Problem (BMP) traces back to the 1950s when structural engineers initially examined steel frameworks using computers [3]. By concentrating all non-zero elements within a slim band around the main diagonal and employing a reordering matrix, efficiency gains in operations like inversion and determinants can be achieved, resulting in time savings [3]. Bandwidth reduction heuristics aim to place non-zero coefficients of a sparse matrix as close as possible to the main diagonal. Figure 1 illustrates an example application of a bandwidth reduction heuristic to a matrix.

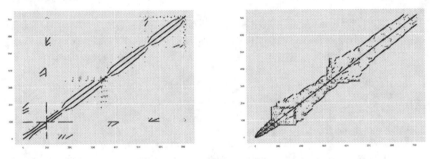

Fig. 1. Example of how a sparse matrix instance behaves before and after bandwidth reduction using the Cuthill-McKee algorithm for such reduction.

The Cuthill-McKee method [4] stands out as the most classical heuristic for bandwidth reduction. Another highly effective algorithm to solve this problem and considered by many researchers to be the state of the art of PMB is DRSA [21]. However, current metaheuristics used to optimize this problem face a computational cost challenge during execution.

Many heuristics and metaheuristics have been developed to achieve higher bandwidth reductions [2]. Recent research has not found in the literature in-depth studies evaluating the impact of combinations of various centrality measures. This article studies different centralities on bandwidth reduction in sparsely populated matrices commonly used in the literature. It presents a new multi-centrality constructive algorithm designed as an alternative for practical applications with efficient execution for large linear systems. Until the present work, we found no in-depth studies in the literature evaluating the impact of using combinations of different centrality measures to guide the choice of vertex labeling in the BMP. Therefore, this work aims to carry out a comprehensive study on the impact of different centralities on bandwidth reduction in sparse matrices commonly used in the literature. Furthermore, it proposes a multi-centrality heuristic designed as an alternative for practical applications emphasizing efficient execution to help solve large linear systems.

We organized the remaining structure of this article as follows. Section 2 presents a detailed description of BMP and a formulation. Related works are presented in Sect. 3, followed by the description of the proposed method and its components in Sect. 4. Section 5 describes computational experiments and their results. Finally, Sect. 6 presents the conclusions and future works.

2 Problem Description and Mathematical Formulation

We mathematically formulate the problem using as a base the formulation that can be found in [6]. Let a graph $G = (V, E)$, where V is the set of vertices and E is the set of edges, let $n = |V|$. A labeling f of G assigns integers $1, 2, ..., n$ to the vertices of G. The bandwidth of a graph G with labeling $f : V \rightarrow \mathbb{N}$ is defined as:

$$B_w(f) = \max_{\{u,v\} \in E} |f(u) - f(v)| \tag{1}$$

The bandwidth reduction problem aims to find a labeling f that minimizes $B_w(f)$. Suppose $A = [a_{ij}]$ represents the incidence matrix of a graph V. The bandwidth reduction problem aims to identify a permutation of rows and columns that maintains all non-zero elements of A within a band as close as possible to the main diagonal. This understanding of the problem emerges in practical applications aimed at solving non-singular systems of linear algebraic equations in the form $Ax = b$ [1].

3 Relevant Related Work

The literature review uses Scopus, a bibliographic database specializing in academic journal articles, to explore the BMP with the following search string: "bandwidth reduction of sparse matrix". The problem studied in this article has two relevant factors as its objective: the highest reduction in bandwidth in a favorable execution time. Focusing on these characteristics, Table 1 aims to highlight the most significant studies in the literature that address BMP, identifying the main methods used as proposed solutions to this challenge.

Table 1. Most promising heuristic methods for bandwidth reduction.

Heuristic	Year	Bandwidth reduction	Cost
Cuthill-McKee [4]	1969	low	low
RCM [7]	1971	low	low
FNCHC [18]	2007	reasonable	high
VNS-band [19]	2010	high	high
KP-band [17]	2011	low	low
DRSA [21]	2015	high	high
RBFS-GL [9]	2018	low	low
ACHH [11,12,14]	2020	high	low
FNCHC+ [8,10]	2022	high	reasonable

A study focused on low computational cost heuristics conducted in [13] concluded that the Variable Neighborhood Search metaheuristic in [19] demonstrated better effectiveness in bandwidth reduction for instances from the SuiteSparse matrix collection [5], surpassing low-cost heuristics. FNCHC stood out as the second-best in this set but achieved the best results in 12 instances in a smaller set. Although the VNS-band achieved superior results, it incurred a considerably higher computational cost.

Finally, the latest relevant work related to the BMP was carried out in [14], presenting an ant colony hyperheuristic approach as a new and promising method for optimizing bandwidth in large-scale matrices. The study compared its effectiveness with low-cost heuristics. Results based on a wide range of sparse matrix instances indicate that the proposed approach has the potential to be more effective and efficient than existing low-cost heuristics in optimizing bandwidth for large-scale matrices.

Another relevant point to note in Table 1 is the case of the state of the art, the DRSA [21], but its execution times are higher than VNS-band [8,10,14]. Despite having a high bandwidth reduction rate, in practice, it does not make sense to use it, as the resolution of linear systems without such methods is usually faster.

4   Multi-centrality Heuristic Algorithm

This section presents the Multi-centrality Heuristic method (MCH), which combines a multi-start constructive heuristic with a multi-centrality approach in choosing vertex labeling for the bandwidth reduction problem. Section 4.1 introduces the Multi-centrality Constructive Algorithm. The second subsection explains how we selected the centralities to contemplate the heuristic proposal.

4.1   Multi-centrality Constructive Algorithm

The proposed Constructive Heuristic aims to generate a high-quality solution computationally efficiently through iterative restarts to explore various solutions effectively in the quest for an optimal solution. In Algorithm 1.1, we construct a vertex sequence q using depth-first search to obtain a high-quality solution and label them as follows: 1, 2, ..., n. Following the labeling order according to the centrality, from the lowest to the highest at the current neighborhood level. The idea is based on an observation that adjacent vertices should have close labels in a good solution (with a small maximum bandwidth), as explained in the constructive approach proposed in [19]. In this specific algorithm, we add extra relevance by ordering vertices according to their centrality. Additionally, our procedure should allow us to generate different solutions in different restarts. To achieve this, we introduced randomness to select the first vertex.

Algorithm 1.1: Multi-centrality Constructive Algorithm

Data: Graph A, *ArrayCentrality*

1 $centrality \leftarrow randomChoice(ArrayCentrality)$;
2 **for** $i \leftarrow 1$ **to** $|V|$ **do**
3 | $mark[i] \leftarrow$ false;
4 **end**
5 $k \leftarrow RandomInt(1, |V|)$;
6 $mark[k] \leftarrow$ true;
7 $q[1] \leftarrow k$; $ql \leftarrow 1$; $f[k] \leftarrow 1$; $l \leftarrow 1$;
8 **while** $l < |V|$ **do**
9 | $r \leftarrow 0$;
10 | **for** $il \leftarrow 1$ **to** ql **do**
11 | | $i \leftarrow q[il]$;
12 | | **for** $jl \leftarrow 1$ **to** $|A[i]|$ **do**
13 | | | $j \leftarrow a[i, jl]$;
14 | | | **if** *not* $mark[j]$ **then**
15 | | | | $r \leftarrow r + 1$; $s[r] \leftarrow j$;
16 | | | **end**
17 | | **end**
18 | **end**
19 | $q \leftarrow sorted(q, lambda(x) : centrality[x])$;
20 | $j^* \leftarrow 0$;
21 | **for** $jl \leftarrow 1$ **to** ql **do**
22 | | $j \leftarrow q[j^*]$; $l \leftarrow l + 1$; $f[j] \leftarrow l$; $j^* \leftarrow j^* + 1$;
23 | **end**
24 | $q \leftarrow s$; $ql \leftarrow r$;
25 **end**
26 **return** f

Vertices for breadth-first search are placed in levels as follows: the first level contains only vertex k (randomly selected), and label one is assigned to it ($f(k) \leftarrow 1$); vertices adjacent to k are in the second level ordered in decreasing order, with labels 2, 3,... The third level contains vertices not included in previous levels but connected to vertices in the second level, and so on, with the labeling order always following the centrality values of each vertex.

Suppose there are n_i vertices in level i. The method randomly chooses a centrality to order the vertices q. The labeling process then takes place by the sequence of ordered vertices.

In addition, Algorithm 1.2 was implemented with a multi-start control feature to execute Algorithm 1.1. It takes as input a graph, the maximum number of iterations max_{iter}, and a list of centrality dictionaries, where each dictionary is constructed having a vertex linked to a centrality value at the vertex in question. Then, it runs the multi-start algorithm max_{iter} times, utilizing the calculated list of centrality as a parameter. The algorithm's objective is to perform multiple initializations (multi-start) of the main algorithm, possibly varying the centrality measure used, to explore different initial solutions and improve the chances of finding a high-quality solution.

Algorithm 1.2: Multi-start Centrality Heuristic

Data: Graph A, int max_{iter}, List $ArrayCentrality$
1 $f_{sol} \leftarrow inf$;
2 **for** $k \leftarrow 1$ to max_{iter} **do**
3      $f \leftarrow$ ConstructiveCentralities(A, $ArrayCentrality$)
4   **if** $f < f_{sol}$ **then**
5         $f_{sol} \leftarrow f$
6   **end**
7 **end**
8 **return** f_{sol}

This algorithm combines the flexibility of multiple random calls for the initial choice of the first vertex to be labeled by the algorithm with the diversification provided by selecting different centrality measures. The idea is that diversified centralities can guide the construction of the solution in various ways, exploring several aspects of the graph's structure.

The combination with the constructive algorithm proposed in [19] aims to find good-quality solutions while maintaining an acceptable runtime for practical use in sparse linear systems resolutions.

4.2 Selecting Centralities

Before conducting the experiments, it was essential to identify the centralities most pertinent to bandwidth reduction. Thus, the methodology adjusted the Cuthill-McKee algorithm, detailed in [4], by modifying the criteria for selecting the labeling order based on various centralities from existing literature. It aimed to assess the impact of each centrality on the bandwidth reduction.

We implemented each selected centrality with two labeling orders: one from the lowest to the highest degree (Smallest) and another from the highest to the lowest degree (Largest). Based on the highest reduction, Table 2 outlines the implementation choices for each centrality.

Table 2. Bandwidth Reductions by Centrality.

Node	Centrality	Reduction(%)
A	Smallest Closeness	52.90
B	Smallest Degree	51.96
C	Smallest Katz	46.84
D	Smallest Harmonic	50.58
E	Largest Eigenvector	50.09
F	Smallest Betweenness	51.03

Table 3. Heatmap of the correlation between centralities.

Correlations	A	B	C	D	E	F
A	1					
B	0.97	1				
C	0.89	0.88	1			
D	0.93	0.91	0.94	1		
E	0.92	0.91	0.94	1	1	
F	0.96	0.97	0.86	0.89	0.89	1

We analyzed the relationship between bandwidth reductions among the algorithms. The correlation was calculated for each pair of results obtained from the implemented algorithms, as shown in Table 3. Typically, a correlation exceeding 0.7 is considered high, but in this study, we focused on correlations higher than or equal to 0.8.

To investigate these correlations, we represent a graph, as illustrated in Fig. 2. In this graph, each vertex V represents an implemented centrality, and an edge E is established between two vertices if the correlation between their corresponding values exceeds the desired correlation threshold, as shown in Table 4. After formulating the problem for the specified correlations, we approach the minimum dominating set problem as described in [22] and solve a binary integer programming problem, where the chosen vertices are the solution to the problem in question.

The highest reduction potential emerged from a correlation of 0.9, involving vertices representing the highest eigenvector centrality and the lowest degree centrality. Consequently, opting for other combinations was deemed unnecessary to avoid redundancy and ensure the implementation of a high-quality solution to the problem.

5 Computational Experiments

We divided this section into three distinct subsections. The introductory subsection outlines the details of the implementation and tuning parameters. The last

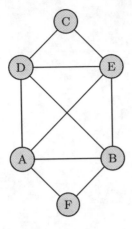

Fig. 2. Graph G with nodes V

Table 4. Correlations edge

Edge	Correlation
AB	0.97
AD	0.93
AE	0.92
AF	0.96
BD	0.91
BE	0.91
BF	0.97
CD	0.94
CE	0.94
DE	1.00

two sections comprehensively analyze the principal considerations of the algorithm proposed in this work, establishing insightful comparisons with existing literature.

5.1   Implementation Details and Parameters Tuning

We implemented the proposed method in Python 3.9.12 and executed it ten times for each instance on an Intel Core 11th generation processor, i7, with a frequency of 2.80 GHz and 16.0 GB of RAM. The matrices used in this work for comparison were the same as those used by Mladenovid et al. [19]. We used a set of 43 instances from the SuiteSparse Matrix Collection [5] to assess the effectiveness of each implemented algorithm in bandwidth reduction.

Before experimenting, it was essential to establish a maximum iteration parameter first. This parameter could not be too low as it would test a few restart solutions. Furthermore, it could not be too high as it would increase the computational cost of the method. After evaluating a few possibilities, we established $max_{iter} = 100$.

5.2   MCH1 × MCH2 × MCH3

After choosing the parameters and centralities of the algorithm, we implemented three versions of MCH to understand which centralities would perform best, as presented and discussed in this subsection. Using the proposed methodology of constructive multi-start by centralities presented in this study, the initial versions developed were as follows. The constructive method Version 1 (MCH1) uses degree centrality in its implementation. In contrast, the constructive method Version 2 (MCH2) employs the centrality of eigenvectors as the basis for your vertex labeling decision. The Version 3 (MCH3) construction method implements a random call approach with both centralities.

Thus, we executed each version 10 times for each instance; initially, Version 3 showed apparent superiority over the other versions, as shown in Table 3. Then, to evaluate the statistical significance of the differences in the values of the best solutions between the three implemented versions, a two-to-two hypothesis test was performed between the best bandwidth reduction values for each version. Given that the data did not fit a normal distribution and the methodology paired the measurements from the experiments, the non-parametric Wilcoxon Signed Rank Test was used [15,20]. This test allows the rejection of the null hypothesis at a significance level denoted by θ, with a probability of $(1 - \theta) \times 100\%$. This study considered a significance level of $\theta = 0.05$. The formulated hypotheses are as follows:

- Null Hypothesis (H0): The median difference is zero.
- Alternative Hypothesis (H1): The median difference is not zero.

The null hypothesis requires no differences in the values of the best solutions between each implemented version and the absence thereof. We expect to observe positive and negative differences if the null hypothesis is valid. However, the methodology rejected the null hypothesis because the p-value is 0.005, lower than θ. It indicates more positive differences than negative ones, corroborating the conclusion that Version 3 outperforms the other versions.

5.3 Multi-centrality Heuristic × Methods Published in the Literature

After conducting the initial experiments and the execution time was favorable, we sought to measure algorithms in the literature that had a time of less than 0.5 sec to compare the results obtained by the proposed methodology with low-cost heuristics. In addition to these initially implemented algorithms, the constructive component of the VNS-band metaheuristic proposed in [19] was implemented for comparison purposes.

The results presented in Table 5 highlight the execution times associated with the heuristics developed in this work and other important ones in the literature. Although Cuthill-McKee presents the lowest average execution time (0.03 s), suggesting effectiveness in only one specific instance, it obtained the worst overall result in bandwidth reductions, as shown in Table 5.

Table 5. Comparison of times between heuristics in seconds.

Heuristic	Average time(s)
Cuthill-McKee	0.03
VNS Constructive	0.16
MCH	0.29
GPS	31.80
FNCHC	146.20
VNS-band	157.33

The VNS constructive component, with a bandwidth value of 11, still presents relevant performance and an average execution time of 0.16, indicating efficiency in finding solutions in a favorable time in performance and demonstrating better consistency in instances with a high value of N (nodes), as shown in Table 5.

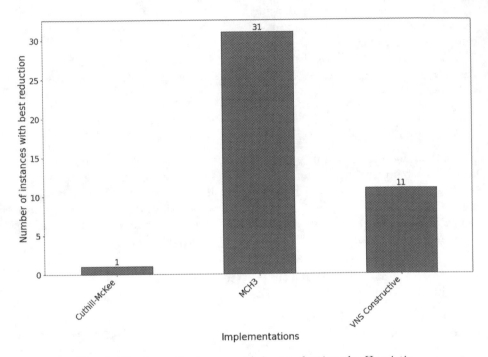

Fig. 3. Number of instances with best reductions by Heuristic.

The VNS-band, FNCHC, and GPS heuristics have higher execution times, with VNS-band and FNCHC standing out with 157.33 and 146.20 s, respectively. Despite having a high power of bandwidth reduction, these approaches may be less efficient when the resolution time of a linear system is shorter than the execution time of such heuristics.

Versions 1, 2, and 3 showed a low variation in the execution times, with values of 0.41, 0.42, and 0.29, respectively. From a practical point of view, they proved to be heuristics that behave more consistently and are competitive in terms of efficiency.

In summary, analysis of execution times reveals performance variability between heuristics. While Cuthill-McKee is good in a single case, other heuristics, such as Version 3 and Constructive VNS, demonstrate broader consistency across different scenarios. Heuristics with higher times, such as VNS-band, FNCHC, and GPS, may be less suitable when the resolution time of a linear system without reduction is already shorter than the execution time of these heuristics.

6   Conclusions and Future Works

The research presented in this work focuses on developing and evaluating a new multi-centrality constructive algorithm for bandwidth minimization in sparse matrices. By introducing the use of centrality measures in the algorithm, the study aims to increase the efficiency and effectiveness of bandwidth reduction techniques for large linear systems through computational experiments and comparisons with traditional heuristics such as Cuthill-McKee.

Our computational experiments reveal that strategies implemented within a relatively simple construction procedure can outperform known algorithms used in practice for bandwidth reduction, such as Cuthill-McKee. In particular, the reset procedure based on random centrality choices confirms the benefit of encouraging diversification of this study. Thus, the additional diversification results in satisfactory quality solutions. One can use the approach in practice for the bandwidth reduction problem, combined with the fact that constructive heuristics consume considerably less computer time.

Based on the results presented in this work, a possible direction of study is the implementation of hybrid versions of the VNS-band. An additional approach would be to implement a machine learning classification model in the instance preprocessing, allowing for analysis of the behavior of reductions with different centrality strategies per instance class. This comprehensive approach not only enriches the understanding of the performance of different centralities but also offers valuable insights by exploring the nuances of the approach proposed in this work.

Acknowledgement. The authors would like to thank the following Brazilian Agencies: CAPES and the National Council for Scientific and Technological Development - CNPq. DB thanks Fundação Carlos Chagas Filho de Amparo à Pesquisa do Estado do Rio de Janeiro (FAPERJ) for the financial support through the grants E-26/210.798/2024. Additionally, the authors are grateful to the Foundation for Science and Technology (FCT, Portugal) for financial support through national funds FCT/MCTES (PIDDAC) to CeDRI, UIDB/05757/2020 (DOI: 10.54499/UIDB/05757/2020) and UIDP/05757/2020 (DOI: 10.54499/UIDB/05757/2020) and SusTEC, LA/P/0007/2020 (DOI: 10.54499/LA/P/0007/2020).

References

1. Marti, R., Laguna, M., Glover, F., Campos, V.: Reducing the bandwidth of a sparse matrix with tabu search. Eur. J. Oper. Res. **135**(2), 450–459 (2001). https://doi.org/10.1016/S0377-2217(00)00325-8. https://www.sciencedirect.com/science/article/pii/S0377221700003258. Financial Modelling
2. Chagas, G.O., Gonzaga de Oliveira, S.L.: Metaheuristic-based heuristics for symmetric-matrix bandwidth reduction: a systematic review. Procedia Comput. Sci. **51**, 211–220 (2015). https://doi.org/10.1016/j.procs.2015.05.229. https://www.sciencedirect.com/science/article/pii/S1877050915010376. International Conference on Computational Science, ICCS 2015

3. Chinn, P.Z., Chvátalová, J., Dewdney, A.K., Gibbs, N.E.: The bandwidth problem for graphs and matrices—a survey. J. Graph Theory **6**(3), 223–254 (1982). https://doi.org/10.1002/jgt.3190060302. https://onlinelibrary.wiley.com/doi/abs/10.1002/jgt.3190060302

4. Cuthill, E., McKee, J.: Reducing the bandwidth of sparse symmetric matrices. In: Proceedings of the 1969 24th National Conference (1969). https://doi.org/10.1145/800195.805928

5. Davis, T.A., Hu, Y.: The University of Florida sparse matrix collection. ACM Trans. Math. Softw. **38**(1), 1–25 (2011)

6. Garey, M.R., Johnson, D.S.: Computers and Intractability: A Guide to the Theory of NP-Completeness (Series of Books in the Mathematical Sciences), 1st edn. W. H. Freeman (1979). http://www.amazon.com/Computers-Intractability-NP-Completeness-Mathematical-Sciences/dp/0716710455

7. George, J.A.: Computer implementation of the finite element method. Ph.D. thesis, Computer Science Department, Stanford University, CA, USA (1971)

8. Gonzaga de Oliveira, S.L.: An evaluation of heuristic methods for the bandwidth reduction of large-scale graphs. Revista Pesquisa Operacional **43**(e268255), 1–22 (2023)

9. Gonzaga de Oliveira, S.L., Bernardes, J.A.B., Chagas, G.O.: An evaluation of reordering algorithms to reduce the computational cost of the incomplete Cholesky-conjugate gradient method. Comput. Appl. Math. **37**, 2965–3004 (2018)

10. Gonzaga de Oliveira, S.L., Carvalho, C.: Metaheuristic algorithms for the bandwidth reduction of large-scale matrices. J. Comb. Optim. **43**, 727–784 (2022)

11. Gonzaga de Oliveira, S.L., Silva, L.M.: Evolving reordering algorithms using an ant colony hyperheuristic approach for accelerating the convergence of the ICCG method. Eng. Comput. **36**, 1857–1873 (2020)

12. Gonzaga de Oliveira, S.L., Silva, L.M.: Low-cost heuristics for matrix bandwidth reduction combined with a Hill-Climbing strategy. Rairo - Oper. Res. **55**(4), 2247–2264 (2021)

13. Gonzaga de Oliveira, S.L., Bernardes, J.A.B., Chagas, G.O.: An evaluation of low-cost heuristics for matrix bandwidth and profile reductions. Comput. Appl. Math. **37**(2), 1412–1471 (2018). https://doi.org/10.1007/s40314-016-0394-9

14. Gonzaga de Oliveira, S., Silva, L.: An ant colony hyperheuristic approach for matrix bandwidth reduction. Appl. Soft Comput. **94**, 106434 (2020). https://doi.org/10.1016/j.asoc.2020.106434. https://www.sciencedirect.com/science/article/pii/S1568494620303744

15. Hettmansperger, T.P., McKean, J.W.: Robust Nonparametric Statistical Methods. CRC Press (2010)

16. Kaveh, A.: Structural Mechanics: Graph and Matrix Methods. Research Studies Press (2004)

17. Koohestani, B., Poli, R.: A hyper-heuristic approach to evolving algorithms for bandwidth reduction based on genetic programming. In: Bramer, M., Petridis, M., Nolle, L. (eds.) Research and Development in Intelligent Systems XXVIII, pp. 93–106. Springer, London (2011). https://doi.org/10.1007/978-1-4471-2318-7_7

18. Lim, A., Rodrigues, B., Xiao, F.: Int. J. Artif. Intell. Tools **16**, 537–544 (2007)

19. Mladenovic, N., Urosevic, D., Pérez-Brito, D., García-González, C.: Variable neighbourhood search for bandwidth reduction. Eur. J. Oper. Res. **200**, 14–27 (2010). https://doi.org/10.1016/j.ejor.2008.12.015

20. Pratt, J.W.: Remarks on zeros and ties in the Wilcoxon signed rank procedures. J. Am. Stat. Assoc. **54**, 655–667 (1959). https://api.semanticscholar.org/CorpusID: 120225998
21. Torres-Jimenez, J., Izquierdo-Marquez, I., Garcia-Robledo, A., Gonzalez-Gomez, A., Bernal, J., Kacker, R.N.: A dual representation simulated annealing algorithm for the bandwidth minimization problem on graphs. Inf. Sci. **303**, 33–49 (2015)
22. West, D.B.: Introduction to Graph Theory, 2 edn. Prentice Hall (2000)

Exact Algorithms for Weighted Rectangular Covering Problems

Ryoya Umeda[1]([✉]), Wei Wu[2], Yannan Hu[1], and Hideki Hashimoto[3]

[1] Tokyo University of Science, 1-3 Kagurazaka, Shinjuku-ku, Tokyo 162-0825, Japan
1423504@ed.tus.ac.jp
[2] Shizuoka University, 3-5-1 Johoku Naka-ku, Hamamatsu, Shizuoka 432-8561, Japan
[3] Tokyo University of Marine Science and Technology, 2-1-6 Etchujima, Koto-ku, Tokyo 135-8533, Japan

Abstract. Given n points on a 2-dimensional plane and t types of rectangles of different sizes and weights, the weighted rectangular covering problem (WRCP) aims to cover all the points with rectangles so as to minimize the total weight of the used rectangles. The WRCP is known to be NP-hard and can be solved in $O(n^6 2^n)$ time. In this paper, we first propose a new algorithm that improves the running time to $O(\min\{n^5 2^n, tn^3 2^n\})$. We then consider a special case where each rectangle has zero width or height, in other words, we are given weighted line segments. For the weighted line-segment covering problem (WLSCP), we show that it is still NP-hard and can be solved in $O(tn2^n)$ time. We also consider the WLSCP with unit-length line segments and show the problem can be solved in polynomial time.

Keywords: rectangular covering problem · dynamic programming · minimum cost flow · NP-hardness

1 Introduction

This study focuses on the 2-dimensional *weighted rectangular covering problem* (WRCP), where we are given n points on a 2-dimensional plane and t types of rectangles, each having width, height, and weight. The WRCP asks to cover all the points by the given rectangles in an arrangement parallel to the x and y axes, and the objective is to minimize the total weight of the used rectangles. The WRCP is known to be NP-hard in the strong sense and can be solved by a dynamic programming algorithm in $O(n^6 2^n)$ time proposed by Porschen [5]. In this study, we propose a new method also based on dynamic programming, but with a better running time of $O(\min\{n^5 2^n, tn^3 2^n\})$.

We then consider a special case of the WRCP, the *weighted line-segment covering problem* (WLSCP), where points should be covered by given weighted line segments, which can be treated as rectangles having zero widths or heights. For the WLSCP, we first prove its NP hardness, and then design an algorithm with a time complexity of $O(tn2^n)$. For the special case where all the points are placed on integral coordinates and each line segment has a unit length (length of 1), we show this WLSCP is polynomially solvable.

2 Weighted Rectangular Covering Problem

In this section, we describe the weighted rectangular covering problem, and introduce an exact algorithm proposed by Porschen [5]. For this problem, we propose a new dynamic programming algorithm with a better running time.

2.1 Problem Definition

We are given a set of points $P = \{1, 2, \ldots, n\}$, each point i with coordinates (a_i, b_i), and a set of rectangle types $R = \{1, 2, \ldots, t\}$, each rectangle type r with width w_r, height h_r, and weight c_r. We assume that all input values are non-negative integers. The weighted rectangular covering problem (WRCP) aims to place rectangles with types in R on the plane to cover all the given points, such that the total weight of the used rectangles is minimized. In this paper, we assume that there are enough rectangles of each type, and each rectangle must be placed without rotation and each edge of the placed rectangle must be parallel to either the x-axis or the y-axis. For input values t and n, we assume that

$$t \leq n^4. \tag{1}$$

The following Lemma shows that Assumption (1) is natural.

Lemma 1. *Given an instance with $t > n^4$, there exists an optimal solution using at most n^4 types of rectangles.*

Proof. For any four points $i, j, k, l \in P$, if there exists a type $r\ (\in R)$ such that a type-r rectangle can cover all these four points, we use r'_{ijkl} to denote the type with the smallest weight among the types that can cover the four points. Obviously, set $R' = \{r'_{ijkl} \mid i, j, k, l \in P\}$ has at most n^4 elements. For any rectangle whose type is not in R', let i', j', k' and l' be the leftmost, rightmost, uppermost, and lowermost points covered by the rectangle, and we can replace this rectangle with a rectangle of type $r'_{i'j'k'l'}$ without increasing the weight. Therefore, any feasible solution can be transformed to a solution only using rectangle types in R' without increasing the total weight. ∎

In this study, we use $A = \{(x_1, y_1, r_1), (x_2, y_2, r_2), \ldots, (x_k, y_k, r_k)\}$ to represent a solution with k rectangles, where $r_j \in R$ is the type of rectangle j and $(x_j, y_j) \in \mathbb{R}^2$ indicates its bottom-left coordinates. Tuple (x_j, y_j, r_j) is called the placement of rectangle j. A point i with coordinates (a_i, b_i) is covered by a rectangle placement (x_j, y_j, r_j) if and only if

$$x_j \leq a_i \leq x_j + w_{r_j} \qquad \text{and} \qquad y_j \leq b_i \leq y_j + h_{r_j}$$

hold.

The rectangular covering has been investigated from 1980s. For the WRCP, Fowler et al. [2] demonstrated its NP-hardness, and Porschen [5] proposed an exact algorithm with time complexity of $O(n^6 2^n)$. We first in Sect. 2.2 introduce Porschen's algorithm, and then in Sect. 2.3 propose an improved method with a better running time.

2.2 Porschen's Algorithm

In this section, we introduce the exact algorithm based on dynamic programming (DP) by Porschen [5]. Let $f_j(S)$ be the minimum weight required to cover a set of points S ($\subseteq P$) using at most j rectangles, $W(A)$ be the total weight of solution A, and $C(S)$ be the set of feasible solutions to the subproblem in which the point set to be covered is S. Then, $f_j(S)$ can be formally defined as

$$f_j(S) = \min\{W(A) \mid A \in C(S), |A| = j\}.$$

For each subset S, $R(S)$ is defined as a subset of rectangular types, each can cover all the points in S, that is,

$$R(S) = \left\{ r \in R \mid \max_{i \in S} a_i - \min_{i \in S} a_i \le w_r \text{ and } \max_{i \in S} b_i - \min_{i \in S} b_i \le h_r \right\}.$$

The boundary value $f_1(S)$ for each S can be computed as

$$f_1(S) = \begin{cases} 0 & \text{if } S = \emptyset \\ \min_{r \in R(S)} c_r & \text{otherwise.} \end{cases} \tag{2}$$

Algorithm 1. A method to generate $G(S)$.

1: $G(S) = \emptyset$.
2: **for** $(p_l, p_r, p_t, p_b) \in S^4$ **do**
3:     $S' \leftarrow \{p \in S \mid a_{p_l} \le a_p \le a_{p_r} \text{ and } b_{p_b} \le b_p \le b_{p_t}\}$.
4:     $G(S) \leftarrow G(S) \cup \{S'\}$.
5: **end for**

To perform dynamic programming, Porschen's method first generates $G(S)$ by Algorithm 1 using $O(|S|^5)$ time. Based on $f_1(S)$ and $G(S)$, $f_j(S)$ can be computed by the following recurrence formula:

$$f_j(S) = \min_{S' \in G(S)} \{f_1(S') + f_{j-1}(S \setminus S')\}. \tag{3}$$

The basic idea is that an optimal solution to the subproblem corresponding to $f_j(S)$ is able to be separated into one rectangle covering points in S' and the other $j - 1$ rectangles covering points in $S \setminus S'$. Each $f_j(S)$ can be computed in

$O(n^5)$ time, because the size of $G(S)$ is bounded by $O(n^4)$, and the computation of $S \setminus S'$ takes linear time. Value $\min_{j=1}^{n} f_j(P)$ is the optimal value to the WRCP.

The framework of the algorithm proposed by Porschen is shown in Algorithm 2. Time to compute all values of $f_1(S)$ in Step 1 is bounded by $O(tn2^n)$, while all the other steps require $O(n^6 2^n)$ time in total. With Assumption (1), the overall running time of this algorithm is $O(n^6 2^n)$.

Algorithm 2. Porschen's algorithm.

1: Compute $f_1(S)$ for each $S \subseteq P$ according to (2).
2: Generate $G(S)$ using Algorithm 1.
3: **for** $j = 2, 3, \ldots, n$ **do**
4:     Compute $f_j(S)$ for each $S \subseteq P$ based on the recurrence formula (3).
5: **end for**
6: **return** $\min_{j=1}^{n} f_j(P)$.

2.3 Proposed Method

In this section, we propose a new algorithm also based on DP but different from the method described in Sect. 2.2.

In Algorithm 1, we introduced a construction method to generate candidates $G(S)$ for solving the subproblem $f_j(S)$. In this section, we propose a new construction method in Algorithm 3 that reduces the number of elements in $G(S)$ to $O(t|S|^2)$ if $t < |S|^2$.

For every combination of $(p_l, p_b) \in S^2$ and $r \in R$, Algorithm 3 adds to $G(S)$ the sets of points that are covered by a rectangle r with its bottom-left coordinates at (a_{p_l}, b_{p_b}). By selecting the more efficient construction method (i.e., better one between Algorithm 1 and Algorithm 3), the size of $G(S)$ can be bounded by $O(\min\{|S|^4, t|S|^2\})$.

Algorithm 3. A new method to generate $G(S)$.

1: $G(S) = \emptyset$.
2: **for** $(p_l, p_b) \in S^2, r \in R$ **do**
3:     $S' \leftarrow \{p \in S \mid a_{p_l} \le a_p \le a_{p_l} + w_r \text{ and } b_{p_b} \le b_p \le b_{p_b} + h_r\}$.
4:     $G(S) \leftarrow G(S) \cup \{S'\}$.
5: **end for**

We design a new DP method, in which we consider a new type of subproblem. Let $f(S)$ be the minimum weight to cover the point set S ($\subseteq P$) without any constraint on the number of rectangles. Note that this definition simplifies the definition of $f_j(S)$ in Porschen's algorithm by omitting the number of rectangles. Value of $f(S)$ can be computed recursively as follows:

$$f(S) = \min\left\{ f_1(S), \min_{S' \in G(S)\backslash\{\emptyset,S\}} f(S') + f(S \setminus S') \right\}. \tag{4}$$

Value of $f(P)$ implies the optimal value of the problem.

The pseudocode of the proposed approach is shown in Algorithm 4. The boundary conditions of the new approach are the same, that is, computing $f_1(S)$ according to (2). We enumerate S lexicographically to ensure that when solving a subproblem of $f(S)$, all the corresponding subproblems have been solved.

We analyse the time complexity of Algorithm 4. In Step 1, we obtain all values of $f_1(S)$ in $O(tn2^n)$ time. Step 2 takes $O(n \min\{|S|^4, t|S|^2\})$ time to generate $G(S)$. In the loop from Step 3 to Step 5, each $f(S)$ is obtained in $O(n \min\{|S|^4, t|S|^2\})$ time. Considering the enumeration of set S, the loop of Steps 3–5 is the bottleneck of this algorithm, which implies that the overall time complexity of our new exact algorithm is $O(\min\{n^5 2^n, tn^3 2^n\})$.

Algorithm 4. A new dynamic programming approach.

1: Compute $f_1(S)$ for each $S \subseteq P$ according to (2).
2: Generate $G(S)$ using the one with the better running time between Algorithm 1 and Algorithm 3.
3: **for** $i = 0, 1, \ldots, 2^n - 1$ **do**
4:    Construct S by binarizing i.
5:    Compute $f(S)$ based on (4).
6: **end for**

---

3   Weighted Line-Segment Covering Problem

In this section, we consider the weighted line-segment covering problem (WLSCP), which can be treated as a special case of the WRCP when every given rectangle type has width or height of zero (i.e. $w_r = 0$ or $h_r = 0$ holds for each $r \in R$).

For the WLSCP, we first prove that it is NP-hard in Sect. 3.1, and then propose an exact algorithm in Sect. 3.2.

3.1   Complexity Analysis

We extend the idea of Fowler [2] to prove the NP-hardness of the WLSCP.

Theorem 1. *The WLSCP is NP-hard in the strong sense.*

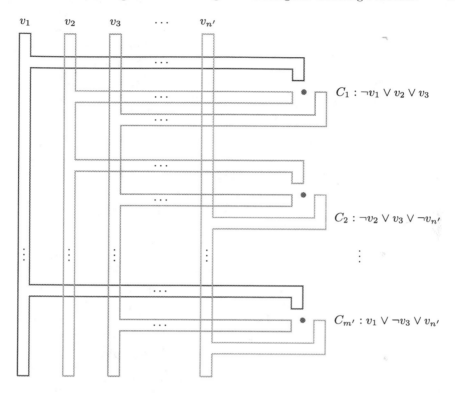

Fig. 1. A schematic overview of the constructions used in the proof of Theorem 1. (Color figure online)

Proof. We prove NP-hardness by a polynomial-time reduction from 3-SAT which is known to be NP-complete in the strong sense. We are given a 3-SAT formula Φ with n' variables $v_1, v_2, \ldots, v_{n'}$, and m' clauses $C_1, C_2, \ldots, C_{m'}$. A literal is either a variable (a positive literal) or the negation of a variable (a negative literal). A clause is a disjunction of literals (or a single literal). Each clause is a disjunction of at most three literals, where a literal is either a variable or the negation of a variable.

We transform the 3-SAT formula Φ to a WLSCP instance I_Φ with only two types of line segments:

$$t = 2; \quad w_1 = 0, h_1 = 3, c_1 = 1; \quad w_2 = 3, h_2 = 0, c_2 = 1.$$

We first show how to set the points in the WLSCP instance. Figure 1 presents an overview of the construction. We call each line in the figure a *wire*, which is a linear arrangement of a set of points in the WLSCP such that any pair of consecutive points on the wire can be covered by a single line segment, while every type of line segment can only cover up to two points on the wire. Each variable in 3-SAT corresponds to a cycle (a colored cycle in Fig. 1) containing an even number of points. If the cycle of variable v_i consists of $2\gamma_i$ points, then the minimum number of line segments required to cover the cycle is γ_i, and there are only two coverings which achieve this minimum, one representing $v_i =$ true, and the other representing $v_i =$ false. Figure 2 represents a portion of a wire, illustrating an example of the correspondence between two assignments and Boolean values. Note that no points located on the intersection of any two cycles (see Fig. 3). This property ensures that no line segment can cover three points in the intersection region.

We describe how to represent clauses and how to set up *clause points* (red points in Fig. 1 and Fig. 4), which are not belong to any cycle. For each clause in the formula there is a clause point located in a region, where the three variable cycles corresponding to the literals in the clause are brought into close proximity (see Fig. 4a). The cycles are arranged so that the clause point can be covered "for free" if at least one of the three wires is in the state corresponding to the literal in the clause (Fig. 4c). If none of the literals satisfies the clause, then an extra line segment is needed to cover the clause point (Fig. 4b). Because the distance between any two consecutive points in the cycle can be flexibly adjusted in the range of 2 to 3 (Fig. 5), all the above construction requirements can be easily satisfied.

Using such a transformation, if the formula Φ is satisfiable, then no additional line segments are needed to cover the clause points, which implies that the optimal value to the WLSCP is $\sum_{i=1}^{m'} \gamma_i$. Otherwise, if the formula Φ is unsatisfiable, the optimal value to the WLSCP is greater than $\sum_{i=1}^{m'} \gamma_i$.

By generating all the variable cycles in compact, γ_i can be bounded by $O(m'n')$, which implies that the size of instance I_Φ is bounded by polynomial with respect to m' and n', and the transformation can be done in polynomial time. ∎

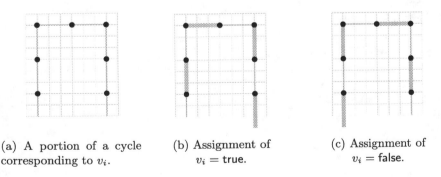

(a) A portion of a cycle corresponding to v_i.

(b) Assignment of $v_i =$ true.

(c) Assignment of $v_i =$ false.

Fig. 2. The correspondence between two assignments and Boolean values.

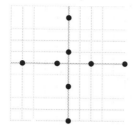

Fig. 3. No point lies at the intersection of any two cycles.

3.2   Exact Algorithm

In this section, we propose an exact algorithm for solving the WLSCP with time complexity of $O(tn2^n)$.

We first consider a special case of the WLSCP where $b_i = b_j$ holds for every pair $i, j \in P$, that is, all points are placed on a line parallel to the x-axis. We call this special case 1-dimensional WLSCP (1D-WLSCP), and we show that it can be solved in $O(n \log n + tn)$ as follows. We first sort the points by their x-coordinate values and assume that the points are numbered in non-decreasing order of x-coordinate values, that is,

$$a_1 \leq a_2 \leq \cdots \leq a_n. \tag{5}$$

Then, we show that the 1D-WLSCP can be solved by a straightforward DP approach. We define s_{ik} as

$$s_{ik} = \begin{cases} 0 & \text{if } a_1 \geq a_i - w_k \\ \max\{j \in P \mid a_j < a_i - w_k\} & \text{otherwise.} \end{cases}$$

We first compute s_{ik} for all the pairs of (i, k). This computation can be performed in $O(tn)$ by using two-pointer technique [4]. Consider a subproblem of the 1D-WLSCP in which the point set are given as $\{1, 2, \ldots, i\}$, and we use $g(i)$ to denote the optimal value. By setting boundary condition

$$g(0) = 0,$$

$g(i)$ for $i = 1, 2, \ldots, n$ can be computed by using the following recurrence formula:

$$g(i) = \min_{k \in R}\{g(s_{ik}) + c_k\}. \tag{6}$$

The optimal value to the 1D-WLSCP is $g(n)$, which can be computed in $O(tn)$ time. Considering the sorting process, the overall time complexity of this algorithm is $O(n \log n + tn)$. The correctness of the algorithm can be easily demonstrated through induction, as $g(i) \leq g(i+1)$ holds for any $i \in \{0, 1, \ldots, n-1\}$.

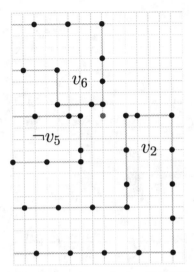

(a) The portion of the WLSCP instance that represents a clause, e.g., $v_2 \vee \neg v_5 \vee v_6$.

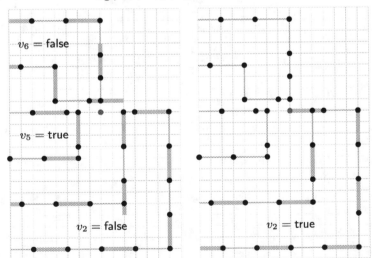

(b) The covering when $v_2 =$ false, (c) The covering when $v_2 =$ true. $v_5 =$ true, and $v_6 =$ false.

Fig. 4. Relationship between covering and clause.

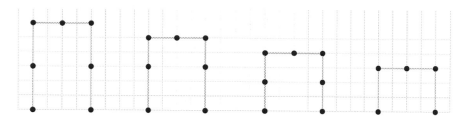

Fig. 5. Flexibility in cycle design.

Note that another variant of 1D-WLSCP with $a_i = a_j$ for every pair $i, j \in P$ can also be solved by a similar approach.

Based on the DP method for the 1D-WLSCP, we design the following divide-and-conquer method for the WLSCP. Let S be a subset of P, and we consider two subproblems $\mathbf{P_v}(S)$ and $\mathbf{P_h}(P \setminus S)$ of the WLSCP. In the subproblem $\mathbf{P_v}(S)$ (resp. $\mathbf{P_h}(P \setminus S)$), the point set is S (resp. $P \setminus S$) and the line-segment types are limited to those with $w_r = 0$ (resp. $h_r = 0$). Figure 6 shows an example with 24 points, where S is the subset containing all the black points in the middle subfigure. Both $\mathbf{P_v}(S)$ and $\mathbf{P_h}(P \setminus S)$ can be further divided into several 1D-WLSCPs, which can be solved by the proposed DP method. Thus, the optimal value $g_v(S)$ of the $\mathbf{P_v}(S)$ (resp. $g_h(P \setminus S)$ of the $\mathbf{P_h}(P \setminus S)$) can be obtained in $O(|S|t)$ (resp. $O(|P|t - |S|t)$) time, and the total time to solve both $\mathbf{P_v}(S)$ and $\mathbf{P_h}(P \setminus S)$ is bounded by $O(tn)$. Note that combining the optimal solutions to $\mathbf{P_v}(S)$ and $\mathbf{P_h}(P \setminus S)$ forms a feasible solution to the WLSCP. The proposed algorithm enumerates all the subsets of P and outputs the solution with the minimum weight as follows:

$$v_{\text{alg}} = \min_{S \subseteq P}\{g_v(S) + g_h(P \setminus S)\}. \tag{7}$$

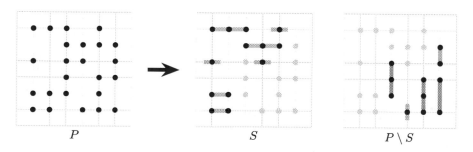

Fig. 6. An example of the partition of P into S and $P \setminus S$.

Let v^* be the optimal value to the WLSCP. To show the correctness of the proposed method, we first observe that the covering (corresponding to v_{alg}) obtained by the algorithm is feasible, and hence v_{alg} is a valid upper bound on the optimal value v^*. Consider an arbitrary optimal covering A^* of the WLSCP, in which S^* is the point set covered by vertical line segments in A^*. Because

$$v_{\text{alg}} \le g_{\text{v}}(S^*) + g_{\text{h}}(P \setminus S^*) \le v^*$$

holds, v_{alg} is also a valid lower bound on the optimal value v^*. Therefore, we have $v_{\text{alg}} = v^*$, and the proposed algorithm is correct.

By lexicographically enumerating subset S, the WLSCP can be solved in $O(tn2^n)$ time, which is faster than directly applying the algorithms for the WRCP in Sects. 2.2 and 2.3.

4 Weighted Line-Segment Covering Problem with Unit-Length Line Segments

In Sect. 3.1, we proved that the WLSCP, in which the length of every line segment is 3, is NP-hard. In this section, we investigate the case when every line segment has a unit length, that is,

$$R = \{1, 2\}; \quad w_1 = 0, h_1 = 1; \quad w_2 = 1, h_2 = 0. \tag{8}$$

For the *weighted line-segment covering problem with unit-length line segments* (WLSCP-UL), we show that it is reducible to the *minimum cost flow problem* (MCFP).

In the MCFP [1], we are given a directed graph $G = (V, E)$ with a source vertex $v_{\text{s}} \in V$ and a sink vertex $v_{\text{t}} \in V$. Each edge $(i, j) \in E$ has an associated cost c'_{ij} that denotes the cost per unit flow on that edge. We assume that the flow cost varies linearly with the amount of flow. We also associate with each edge $(i, j) \in E$ a capacity u_{ij} that denotes the maximum amount that can flow on the edge and a lower bound l_{ij} that denotes the minimum amount that must flow on the edge. The MCFP aims to send an amount of flow q from source v_{s} to sink v_{t} with a minimum total cost.

Given a WLSCP-UL instance with n points ($P = \{1, 2, \ldots, n\}$), we construct a directed graph for the MCFP with $n + 4$ vertices:

$$V = P \cup \{v_{\text{even}}, v_{\text{odd}}, v_{\text{s}}, v_{\text{t}}\}.$$

We divide the vertices $1, 2, \ldots, n$ into the following two subsets:

$$V_{\text{even}} = \{i \mid i \in P, \ a_i + b_i \text{ is even}\},$$
$$V_{\text{odd}} = \{i \mid i \in P, \ a_i + b_i \text{ is odd}\}.$$

The edge set E are set as follows:

$$E = E_{\text{s}} \cup E_{\text{even}} \cup E_{\text{odd}} \cup E_{\text{match}} \cup E_{\text{t}} \cup \{(v_{\text{s}}, v_{\text{even}}), (v_{\text{even}}, v_{\text{odd}}), (v_{\text{odd}}, v_{\text{t}})\},$$

where

$$E_{\mathrm{s}} = \{(v_{\mathrm{s}}, j) \mid j \in V_{\mathrm{even}}\},$$
$$E_{\mathrm{even}} = \{(v_{\mathrm{even}}, j) \mid j \in V_{\mathrm{odd}}\},$$
$$E_{\mathrm{odd}} = \{(i, v_{\mathrm{odd}}) \mid i \in V_{\mathrm{even}}\},$$
$$E_{\mathrm{match}} = \{(i, j) \mid i \in V_{\mathrm{even}}, j \in V_{\mathrm{odd}}, |a_i - a_j| + |b_i - b_j| = 1\},$$
$$E_{\mathrm{t}} = \{(i, v_{\mathrm{t}}) \mid i \in V_{\mathrm{odd}}\}.$$

Figure 7 shows an example of the graph construction.

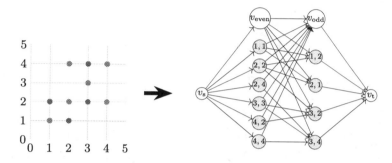

Fig. 7. An example of the reduction from WLSCP-UL to MCFP.

For each edge (i, j), c'_{ij}, u_{ij} and l_{ij} are set as

$$c'_{ij} = \begin{cases} \min\{c_1, c_2\} & \text{if } (i,j) \in E_{\mathrm{even}} \cup E_{\mathrm{odd}} \\ c_1 & \text{if } (i,j) \in E_{\mathrm{match}} \text{ and } |a_i - a_j| = 0 \\ c_2 & \text{if } (i,j) \in E_{\mathrm{match}} \text{ and } |b_i - b_j| = 0 \\ 0 & \text{otherwise;} \end{cases}$$

$$u_{ij} = \begin{cases} n & \text{if } (i,j) \in \{(v_{\mathrm{s}}, v_{\mathrm{even}}), (v_{\mathrm{even}}, v_{\mathrm{odd}}), (v_{\mathrm{odd}}, v_{\mathrm{t}})\} \\ 1 & \text{otherwise;} \end{cases}$$

$$l_{ij} = \begin{cases} 1 & \text{if } (i,j) \in E_{\mathrm{s}} \cup E_{\mathrm{t}} \\ 0 & \text{otherwise.} \end{cases}$$

The flow amount q sent from v_{s} to v_{t} is set to $q = n$.

The rationale for this transformation is that the non-zero edge flows in E_{match} represent line segments covering two points, while the non-zero edge flows in $E_{\mathrm{even}} \cup E_{\mathrm{odd}}$ correspond to line segments used to cover only one point. The setting of l_{ij} ensures that all the nodes are covered. A flow from v_{s} to v_{t} corresponds to a covering of the WLSCP-UL with the same cost. Thus, using the above transformation, the optimal value of MCFP coincides with the optimal value of WLSCP-UL.

There are various algorithms [3] for the MCFP with polynomial time. Hence, the problem WLSCP-UL can also be solved in polynomial time.

Theorem 2. *The WLSCP-UL is solvable in polynomial time.*

For the WLSCP with one type of vertical line segment and one type of horizontal line segment, we showed that the problem is NP-hard if both line segments have length of 3 units, and polynomial-time solvable if both line segments have length of 1 unit. Whether the problem can be solved in polynomial time when involving line segments with length 2 is an intriguing question that remains unanswered in this study.

5 Conclusion

In this paper, we studied the weighted rectangular covering problem (WRCP), which requires to cover n points on a 2-dimensional plane by t types of weighted rectangles. For the WRCP, there exists an exact algorithm [5] with time complexity of $O(n^6 2^n)$. We proposed a new exact algorithm based on dynamic programming with a better running time of $O(\min\{n^5 2^n, tn^3 2^n\})$. We then considered a special case of the WRCP, the weighted line-segment covering problem (WLSCP), in which rectangles are given as horizontal or vertical line segments. For the WLSCP, we proved that it is NP-hard in the strong sense, even if there are only one horizontal type and one vertical type of line segments with length of 3 units. To solve the WLSCP, we proposed an exact algorithm with time complexity of $O(tn2^n)$. For the WLSCP with unit-length line segments, we showed that the problem can be solved in polynomial time by reducing it to the minimum cost flow problem.

Future research could be devoted to determining whether the WLSCP is NP-hard when line segments with length 2 units are involved. Designing approximate and heuristic algorithms for the WRCP and WLSCP would also be a good direction.

References

1. Ahuja, R.K., Magnanti, T.L., Orlin, J.B.: Network Flows. Prentice Hall, Hoboken (1993)
2. Fowler, R.J., Paterson, M.S., Tanimoto, S.L.: Optimal packing and covering in the plane are NP-complete. Inf. Process. Lett. **12**(3), 133–137 (1981)
3. Fredman, M.L., Tarjan, R.E.: Fibonacci heaps and their uses in improved network optimization algorithms. J. ACM **34**(3), 596–615 (1987)
4. Kravchenko, S.A., Sotskov, Y.N.: Optimal makespan schedule for three jobs on two machines. Math. Methods Oper. Res. **43**, 233–238 (1996)
5. Porschen, S.: On rectangular covering problems. Int. J. Comput. Geom. Appl. **19**(04), 325–340 (2009)

Clinical Factors to Investigate Survival Analysis in Cardiovascular Patients

Najada Firza[1,3]([⊠]) [iD], Rossana Mancarella[2] [iD], Francesco Domenico d'Ovidio[1] [iD],
and Dante Mazzitelli[1] [iD]

[1] Department of Economics and Finance, University of Bari "Aldo Moro", Largo Abbazia Santa Scolastica, Bari, Italy
najada.firza@uniba.it
[2] Agenzia Regionale per la Tecnologia e l'Innovazione ARTI Puglia, Bari, Italy
[3] Catholic University Our Lady of Good Counsel, Tirana, Albania

Abstract. Cardiovascular diseases are one of the leading causes of mortality worldwide; however, the management of patients with this pathology within hospital facilities has not been uniquely realized.

Through appropriate statistical methods (i.e., survival analysis, Cox regression, and logistic regression), we have tried to illuminate the survival and length of stay of patients with cardiovascular diseases in hospitals. The results obtained classify the clinical factors into risk variables (which reduce survival) and protective variables (which prolong survival) and are linked to the long stay of this particular category of patients.

The aim of this work is to analyze the variables responsible for long stays in patients with cardiovascular diseases to monitor the health of patients and better manage the financial resources of health facilities in relation to this problem.

Keywords: Logistic Regression · Cox Regression · Long Hospital Stay (LOS) · Cardiovascular Diseases (CVD)

1 Introduction

Cardiovascular diseases (CVD) are the leading cause of death in Italy and Europe [1]. The Global Burden of Disease (GBD) study estimates that there were 17.8 million deaths due to CVD [2] worldwide in 2017, which is expected to reach 23.6 million by 2030 [3]. Consequently, CVD is associated with a consistently high number of hospital admissions, a long hospital stay (LOS), and increased mortality rates [4]. All this means that there is an increase in healthcare costs for hospitals [5]. Accordingly, the Italian National Health System dedicates many resources to the prevention, diagnosis, and treatment of these diseases.

Obviously, many variables lead a patient to an LOS, and numerous studies state that an LOS depends on risk factors, socio-demographic variables, the clinical situation at the time of admission, the treatment in hospitals, the development of complications, and so on.

O. Gervasi et al. (Eds.): ICCSA 2024, LNCS 14813, pp. 29–45, 2024.
https://doi.org/10.1007/978-3-031-64605-8_3

Many studies have investigated the causes associated with a prolonged LOS. These factors have a broad spectrum concerning physiological and clinical aspects and lifestyle: female sex, New York Heart Association (NYHA) functional class [6], low left ventricular ejection fraction (LVEF), concomitant community-acquired infection, arrhythmias, cerebrovascular diseases, dementia, hyponatremia, polytherapy, pressure ulcers, chronic alcohol consumption, peripheral edema, the development of renal failure, the presence of social problems that require special intervention, and concomitant acute medical problems that require specific treatments, just to name a few [7–9].

Regardless of risk factors and the presence of comorbidities, generally, a longer hospitalization is also linked to suboptimal clinical outcomes.

The present research aims to quantify the main factors influencing the length of stay in hospitals, not only to monitor the health risk of these patients, but also to effectively use the resources of facilities. Accordingly, this work considered two representative samples of patients with at least one CVD admitted to hospitals in the Puglia Region, in the last period with available data (2009–2014). We used survival methods (i.e., Cox regression and logistic regression) to explore the length of patients' stays, highlighting factors related to mortality and an LOS. Using more recent data, results could change in some way, but the methodological innovation will remain.

In fact, the ability to identify hospitalized CDA patients at risk of prolonged hospital stays could be assessed by healthcare professionals. A risk stratification for an LOS can help provide good opportunities for patient care by identifying patients who need special attention and certain interventions, such as education and specific therapies [10].

Reducing the LOS of hospitalized patients has been considered a primary strategy for deploying resources efficiently [10]. This study can help improve the treatment of CVD patients while enhancing their clinical outcomes and reducing the costs associated with healthcare.

2 Materials and Methods

2.1 Study Design and Data Collection

The data analysed was collected by the Apulian Regional Health Agency (AreS-Puglia) at the administrative level. The agency continuously monitors data quality. IBM SPSS 22 software was used for the data analyses.

The original database, which contained over 4 million records registered over a period of 6 years, was obtained from the complete registration of hospital discharge cards (HDC) for all patients admitted to Apulian hospitals between 2009 and 2014. The data were confidential and under the responsibility of AreS-Puglia, and were granted to us solely for statistical analysis in aggregate form.

The *Semi-parametric Cox Regression model* and the *Logistic Regression model* are the methods used in this work. These methodologies were chosen by the authors over other methodologies because they are known in the literature to resolve issues regarding survival analysis. (see Sect. 2.3 and 2.4).

For our research, we investigated a sub-population in the original database consisting of patients who were admitted to hospitals in Puglia during the specified time period and had at least one diagnosis related to cardiovascular diseases (Category IX of the International Classification of Diseases, 9th Revision, codes I00 to I99). The sub-population in question consists of over 1,300,000 HDC, with almost 1,150,000 being ordinary hospitalizations.

According to Table 1. Distribution of the outcomes of hospitalizations for cardiovascular diagnoses in Puglia, 2009–2014.), over 96% of patients hospitalized for cardiovascular diagnoses in Puglia survived from 2009–2014, despite a slightly increasing mortality trend.

Table 1. Distribution of the outcomes of hospitalizations for cardiovascular diagnoses in Puglia, 2009–2014.

	Observed Data			%		
Year	Surviving	Dead	Total	Surviving	Dead	Total
2009	229161	6496	235657	97,2	2,8	100,0
2010	242011	6563	248574	97,4	2,6	100,0
2011	223147	6810	229957	97,0	3,0	100,0
2012	198833	7302	206135	96,5	3,5	100,0
2013	191884	7242	199126	96,4	3,6	100,0
2014	183684	7583	191267	96,0	4,0	100,0
Total	1268720	41996	1310716	96,8	3,2	100,0

2.2 Differential Sampling

Two representative samples were randomly extracted from the entire population to demonstrate the robustness of the results and provide a concrete example for comparison. Of course, robustness should be confirmed by both clinical relevance and statistical significance of the analyses. Additionally, the age factor divided by class was used in the second sample to investigate possible relationships with LOS and confirm the other factors in the Cox model. We analyzed Sample I, which represents approximately 0.10% of the population (with over 11,000 hospitalizations), and Sample II, which represents approximately 0.6% of the population (with over 6,000 hospitalizations).

Table 2. Distribution of the outcomes of hospitalizations for cardiovascular diagnoses in Puglia in the two samples, 2009–2014., highlights two randomly extracted samples from the dataset of 1,310,716 admissions recorded in public and private hospitals in Puglia from 2009 to 2014. The admissions had at least one diagnosis related to cardio-circulatory diseases.

It is important to note that the dynamics of deaths in Table 1. Distribution of the outcomes of hospitalizations for cardiovascular diagnoses in Puglia, 2009–2014., should not cause alarm. It is necessary to highlight the increasingly frequent recourse, first to a day hospital and then to outpatient services, for the treatment of milder pathological forms (thus avoiding hospitalization and, consequently, detection through HDC). Below, we must also mention the aging Apulian population, which is more exposed to potentially fatal cardiovascular events.

The relevance of the present research lies in the proportion of hospital deaths in the observed population, which should not be excessive, and the maintenance of this condition in the extracted samples. This ensures good representativeness while maintaining temporal dynamics Table 2. Distribution of the outcomes of hospitalizations for cardiovascular diagnoses in Puglia in the two samples, 2009–2014., confirms these conditions, despite random variations. Therefore, the two determined samples can be used as a reference for analyzing hospitalizations.

Table 2. Distribution of the outcomes of hospitalizations for cardiovascular diagnoses in Puglia in the two samples, 2009–2014.

	Sample I data					Sample II data				
Year	Surviving	%	Dead %		Total	Year	Surviving %		Dead %		Total
2009	1969	96,8	66	3,2	2035	2009	1123	96,6	40	3,4	1163
2010	2040	96,3	78	3,7	2118	2010	1204	97,6	29	2,4	1233
2011	1944	96,9	63	3,1	2007	2011	1112	96,1	45	3,9	1157
2012	1741	96,1	70	3,9	1811	2012	983	95,1	51	4,9	1034
2013	1658	95,9	71	4,1	1729	2013	865	96	36	4	901
2014	1569	95,6	73	4,4	1642	2014	863	95,1	44	4,9	907
Total	10921	96,3	421	3,7	11342	Total	6150	96,2	245	3,8	6395

The aim of this study is to investigate whether specific hospitalisation variables affect the length of stay. This is logical when considering the diseases and required interventions. However, other hospitalisation-related variables may also significantly influence hospitalisation duration. The study analyses the main characteristics of hospital stays, with a focus on the impact of patient mortality.

The analysis does not include day hospital admissions or day surgery, nor does it cover outpatient or emergency room care that does not require admission.

Patient data includes personal information such as gender, age, and residence, as well as the length of hospital stay. Additionally, recorded are characteristic elements of hospitalization, such as the health facility where it occurred, the admission and discharge ward, and any transfers. Clinical variables, such as diagnosis, diagnostic procedures, interventions, and admission outcomes, are documented.

2.3 Semi-parametric Cox Regression Model

The survey methodology is a duration analysis performed through some of the best-known techniques concerning survival analysis. In particular, we used Cox's semiparametric model to identify variables that influence the duration of hospitalization, reducing any confounding effects. The variable response is the duration of hospitalization, considering deaths that logically determine the interruption of hospitalization for reasons opposite to those desirable (i.e., the discharge of patients for at least a partial recovery).

In the biomedical field, the Cox model is one of the best-known and most important models for survival analysis under the hypothesis of proportional risks over time. It is called "semiparametric" because no assumptions are made about the form of the survival function and, therefore, about the risk function. In this model, however, the influence of explanatory variables (or prognostic factors) on risk, itself, is parameterized. Its theoretical foundations start from the concept of the risk function, whose general estimate (with events of interruption, default, or death, generically indicated with di and not necessarily equispaced in time) is given in a group of n statistical units with r distinct times of interruption according to the following:

$$\widehat{H}_k(t) \cong \sum_{i=i}^{k} \frac{d_i}{n_i} = \sum_{i=1}^{k} \widehat{q}_i, \text{ with } t_k \leq t \leq t_{k+1} \text{ and } k = 1, 2, \ldots, r,$$

where r < n and n_i equal the number of units that survived until event d_i [11].

The Cox model [12] was created to verify, through a sample, the influence that some characteristics, both quantitative and qualitative (i.e., explanatory variables or "prognostic factors"), possessed by the sampled units can have on survival times.

It defines $h_i(t)$, the hazard function at time t (for $t \geq 0$), for any unit with certain values of prognostic factors and $h_0(t)$ the risk function (baseline function) at time t for any unit having prognostic factors with a zero value. This condition implies that quantitative factors are rescaled so their minimum value is zero and that qualitative factors are defined with zero indicator variables corresponding to basic modalities often assumed to have the least risk [13]. That said, assuming that at any moment the risk function $h_i(t)$ is proportional to the function $h_0(t)$ at a rate of the parameter ψ, the Cox model is expressed by the following formulation:

$$h(t) = \psi h_0(t) = \exp(\beta) \, h_0(t), \ \beta \in IR.$$

Notably, $\psi = h(t)/h_0(t)$ represents the default risk at time t of any statistical unit with respect to another unit belonging to the base group, for which it is called the *relative risk*, or *risk ratio*. Of course, if $\psi < 1$ (and, therefore, $\beta = \ln\psi < 0$) the default risk for said unit is smaller than for the unit belonging to the base group. The opposite is true if $\psi > 1$ and $\beta > 0$ [14].

Now, we explicitly consider a variable X relative to a prognostic factor, with determinations x_i taking the value 0 if the unit belongs to the base group. For the generic individual of the sample, the previous formulation becomes as follows:

$$h_i(t) = \psi(x_i)h_0(t) = \exp(\beta x_i)h_0(t), \beta \in IR.$$

Logically, if the survival of the sampled units is affected by several factors, this model is generalized as follows:

$$h_i(t) = \exp(\beta_1 x_{1i} + \beta_2 x_{2i} + \ldots + \beta_m x_{mi})h_0(t), \beta_j \in IR.$$

Cox's model assumes that:

- The explanatory variables have a multiplier effect on the risk. That is, the link function is exponential. This assumption is generally plausible when the risk ratio is ψ positive;
- The relationship between the risk functions of individuals with different values of prognostic factors is constant between the layers identified by the factors;
- The invariance over time of the values of explanatory variables: If this does not happen, it means that it is no longer legitimate to record the values of prognostic factors (or a set of them) only at the beginning of the study. However, there is also a model for non-time-independent covariates.

Consequently, it is always advisable to check in advance at least for the absence of the stratification effect. That is, survival data should be classified according to the levels of the factors, with all the subgroups (strata) defined based on all the J combinations of the levels of factors so individuals in the same stratum are characterized by the values of the same explanatory variables. In the case of quantitative covariates, a preliminary reduction into classes must be performed.

In each subgroup, the survival function is estimated with the Kaplan–Meier method [11]. The points—t, $\ln \widehat{H}_j(t)$—are reported in a Cartesian reference, where.

$j = 1, 2..., J$ identifies the subgroup where the analysis takes place.

If the diagrams (one for each value of j) obtained by joining the points t, $\ln \widehat{H}_j(t)$ appear parallel, then the risks of the various groups can be considered perfectly proportional.

Cox's model, however, is robust enough to provide reliable results even when the parallelism of the lines is not perfect. At most, it may be sufficient to verify that they do not intersect, except possibly at the extremes [15].

In our work, we used the Kaplan–Meier method [16] to identify variables that are significant for Cox regression. Subsequently, with the forward stepwise method that was validated through a backward stepwise elimination procedure, the statistically significant variables were validated for Cox regression ($p < 0.05$).

2.4 Logistic Regression Model

In order to compare and confirm the results obtained with the Cox model, a logistic regression analysis was also used in this work.

Generally, in epidemiological studies, it is assumed that the baseline is characterized by healthy subjects.

Accordingly, the "of interest" event is death. The variable Y of the model is defined as a function of a set of predictive, categorical, and/or quantitative variables:

$Y = f(X_1, X_2,..., X_k)$.

In the case of a Bernoullian answer with the average $E(Y) = p$, where p is the probability of success, however, the classical linear relation:

$E(Y) = b_0 + b_1 x_1 + b_2 x_2 + ... + b_k x_k$.

the following transformation is conducted:

$$g(E(Y)) = a + b_1 x_1 + \cdots + b_k x_k$$

where the function g is given by: $g(p) = \log \frac{p}{1-p}$ [17].

The probability of success is given by $p = \frac{exp^{a+b_1x_1+\cdots+b_kx_k}}{1+exp^{a+b_1x_1+\cdots+b_kx_k}}$.

As for the interpretation of the coefficients within the equation of the logit model, consider that each coefficient b is the logarithm of the odds ratio conditioned to the value assumed by the predictive x:

$$\frac{p|x+1}{1-p|x+1} = \exp(b)\frac{p|x}{1-p|x}$$

The logit model was first used with variables that were significantly relevant for a correlation with the outcomes of the analysis. Subsequently, with the forward stepwise method, validated through a backward stepwise elimination procedure, the statistically significant variables for logit regression ($p < 0.05$) were selected. The selection criterion for the progressive insertion and eventual removal of predictive variables is based on the test of the difference in the likelihood of subsequent models, while the subsequent interpretation of the model is usually based on the Wald index bj/SE(bj) [18].

3 Results and Discussion

In this paper we considered it mandatory to combine the results paragraph with the discussion paragraph because the multitude and detailed specificity of the results obtained had to be discussed simultaneously so as not to confuse the reader and lead him into misunderstandings about the research carried out.

3.1 Use of the Semi-parametric Cox Regression Model in Sample I

To identify the possible explanatory variables to include in the model, a preliminary analysis used the Kaplan–Meier method [16]. The graphic results of this analysis are reported conclusively only for prognostic factors significantly influencing the duration of hospitalization (except deaths). The prognostic factors that produced roughly parallel risk and survival curves (thus implying roughly proportional risks) and that were therefore included in the Cox model are listed below, divided by categories [19].

a. Cardiovascular diagnostic CCS.

  96. Heart valve diseases.
  98. Essential hypertension.
  100. Acute myocardial infarction.
  107. Cardiac arrest and ventricular fibrillation.
  108. Congestive heart failure, not from hypertension.

b. CCS of cardiovascular interventions and procedures.

  44. Coronary artery bypass.
  47. Diagnostic cardiac catheterization and coronary arteriography.
  48. Listing, reviewing, replacing, or removing cardiac pacemakers or an automatic defibrillator.
  54. Other vascular catheterizations, excluding the cardiac category.

c. Nosological classifications (besides cardiovascular diseases).

1. Infectious and parasitic diseases.
2. Neoplasms.
13. Diseases of the musculoskeletal system and connective tissue.
16. Injuries and poisoning.
17. Symptoms, signs, undefined conditions, and other factors influencing the state of health.

d. Operative classifications (other than cardiovascular interventions).

8. Operations of the blood and lymphatic system.
14. Operations of the musculoskeletal system.

All the "non-clinical" characteristics of hospitalizations are not proportional or even time dependent, in some cases [20].

As seen in Table 3. Prognostic factors for the analysis of cardiovascular patients' hospital stays, Cox model.), the model was quite significant when it was obtained by applying the objective variable "duration of hospitalization" with the forward stepwise technique concerning the aforementioned prognostic factors. The probability of exclusion was $\alpha = 0.05$. The maximum loglikelihood test ensures, in fact, an almost infinitesimal probability ($p < 0.0000001$) that the relationships identified in the model are due to chance.

The effects of individual prognostic factors are also all statistically significant, some exceptionally. The variables that increase the probability of "risk" (of short hospitalizations, unfortunately, including deaths) by reducing "survival," that is, the duration of hospitalization, are as follows:

– CCS of cardiac arrest (a "risk" more than 25 times higher than the lack of diagnoses in this classification) [21];
– A diagnosis belonging to the nosological category "Symptoms, signs, undefined conditions, other factors influencing the state of health" (probability 1.8 times greater than the absence of one of these diagnoses);
– Non-cardiac vascular catheterization surgery (1.75 times greater probability than cases without interventions);
– CCS of congestive heart failure, not from hypertension (probability almost 1.6 times greater than its lack).

These conclusions are drawn, of course, from the last column of the table, which depicts the proportionality parameter $Exp(\beta) = \psi$ (also called the "odds ratio").

Some prognostic factors, presenting negative coefficients, protect patients from the risk of short hospitalizations (or death) and, hence, are statistically connected to long hospitalizations.

Table 3. Prognostic factors for the analysis of cardiovascular patients' hospital stays, Cox model.

Prognostic factors	β	SE	p-values	EXP(β)
Diseases of the heart valves	−1,143	0,286	<0,001	0,319
Essential hypertension	−0,730	0,168	<0,001	0,482
Cardiac arrest and ventricular fibrillation	3,234	0,108	<0,001	25,385
Congestive heart failure, not due to hypertention	0,463	0,125	<0,001	1,589
Diagnostic cardiac catheterization, coronary arteriography	−0,837	0,284	<0,005	0,433
Insertion, review, replacement, removal of cardiac pacemaker or automatic defibrillator	−1,417	0,582	<0,020	0,242
Other vascular catheterization, excluding cardiac cathegory	0,560	0,188	<0,005	1,750
Diseases of the musculoskeletal system and connective tissue	−0,826	0,266	<0,005	0,438
Symptoms, signs, undefined conditions, other factors influencing the state of health	0,594	0,125	<0,001	1,811

Going from the most connected factor to the least regarding the duration of hospitalization, these factors are listed in their order of relevance, as follows:

- The insertion, revision, replacement, or removal of a cardiac pacemaker or automatic defibrillator. (Compared to those who do not undergo interventions of this type, the probability of short hospitalizations is reduced to less than a quarter);
- CCS of heart valve diseases (a third-less probability compared to those without these diseases);
- Interventions of diagnostic cardiac catheterization or coronary arteriography and diagnoses of the nosological category diseases of the musculoskeletal system and connective tissue reduce almost equally the probability of short hospitalizations (43–44% compared to cases without these factors);
- CCS of essential hypertension also significantly reduces (to less than half) the probability of short hospitalizations.

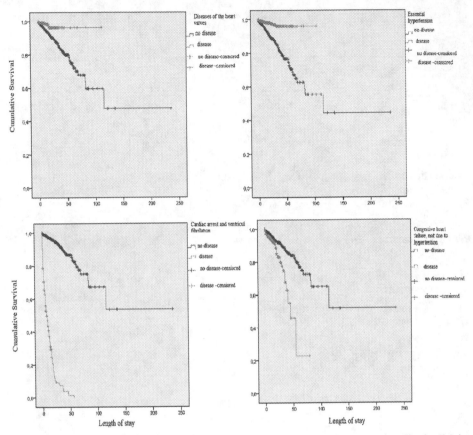

Fig. 1. Prognostic factors for the cardiovascular patients' hospital stays using Kaplan-Meier estimators.

We now observe the effects of notable prognostic factors on hospitalization times using graphs derived from the Kaplan–Meier estimators (Fig. 1) used to identify variables entitled to be included in the Cox model [22].

First, hospitalizations for diseases belonging to the CCS "Heart Valve Diseases" last up to 100 days, with high survival and a very concentrated distribution of deaths in the first month.

Approximately the same observations can be made concerning the pathologies belonging to the CCS (Fig. 1) "Essential Hypertension" and (Fig. 2) the interventions of "Diagnostic Cardiac Catheterization, Coronary Arteriography" (whose hospitalizations do not exceed 50–60 days). The dynamics related to the other prognostic factors are completely opposite, particularly for hospitalizations concerning the CCS (Fig. 1) of "Cardiac Arrest and Ventricular Fibrillation" (the duration curve of which is very steep, with many deaths concentrated in the first 10 days of hospitalization but never exceeding 55 days).

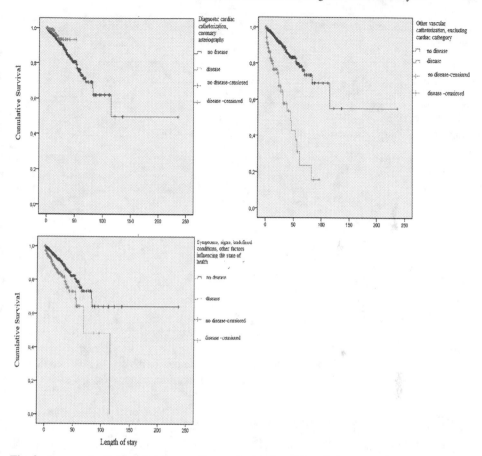

Fig. 2. Prognostic factors for the cardiovascular patients' hospital stays using Kaplan-Meier estimators.

3.2 Use of Logistic Regression Model in Sample I

Table 4. Prognostic factors for the analysis of cardiovascular patients' hospital stays, Logistic regression model.), demonstrates the results of a logistic regression model of the status variable (surviving/deceased) from the same variables considered in the previous Cox model to understand the role of censorship (more specifically, deaths) within this model [23].

If we compare the two methods, Table 3. Prognostic factors for the analysis of cardiovascular patients' hospital stays, Cox model.) makes evident that, concerning simple death events, the interventions of insertion, revision, replacement, or removal of a cardiac pacemaker or an automatic defibrillator, as well as diseases of the musculoskeletal system and connective tissue lose any statistical significance. Meanwhile, the other prognostic factors increasing the risk of death are much more relevant.

Conversely, "protective" factors have slightly lower effects in their odds ratio; however, they generally vary little from those of the Cox model. It can, then, be assumed that

Table 4. Prognostic factors for the analysis of cardiovascular patients' hospital stays, Logistic regression model.

Prognostic factors	B	SE	p-values	EXP(β)
Diseases of the heart valves	−1,290	0,261	<0,001	0,275
Essential hypertension	−0,881	0,169	<0,001	0,414
Cardiac arrest and ventricular fibrillation	5,388	0,201	<0,001	21,867
Congestive heart failure, not due to hypertention	1,184	0,147	<0,001	3,266
Diagnostic cardiac catheterization, coronary arteriography	−0,981	0,266	<0,001	0,375
Other vascular catheterization, excluding cardiac cathegory	3,015	0,205	<0,001	20,388
Symptoms, signs, undefined conditions, other factors influencing the state of health	1,368	0,148	<0,001	3,926

the structure of the latter model is only partially influenced by trends in hospital deaths and that its results are sufficiently reliable to discern prognostic factors.

3.3 Experimental Procedure in Sample II

The cardio–circulatory disease variables initially included in the Cox model are as follows:

- Total number of diagnoses and procedures (procedures include both examinations and interventions);
- Variables related to subjects, such as sex and age classes;
- Variables concerning the type of hospital admission (in the case of surgical or medical hospitalization).

Once the likelihood tests were verified, it was found that the p-value was highly significant (p = 0.0001). In fact, the individual variables highlighted in Table 5 are all very significant (with the least significant variable being p = 0.005).

The variables that most increase the probability of death during hospitalization are as follows:

- Cardiac arrest (deaths more than 16 times greater than the lack of it);
- Non-cardiac vascular catheterization surgery (2.9 times higher probability);
- Acute cerebral vascular disease (2.38 times higher probability);
- Essential hypertension and hypertension with complications are relevant factors for lengthy hospital survival.

Table 5. Prognostic factors for the analysis of cardiovascular patients' hospital stays, Cox model.

Prognostic factors	B	SE	p-values	EXP(β)
Age (classes)	0,287	0,055	<0,001	1,332
Essential hypertension	−0,800	0,209	<0,001	0,450
Hypertension complications/ secondary hypertension	−0,588	0,178	0,001	0,555
Cardiac arrest and ventricular fibrillation	2,780	0,150	<0,001	16,112
Acute cerebrovascular disease	0,870	0,173	<0,001	2,387
Infectious and parasitic diseases	0,603	0,214	0,005	1,827
Diseases of the respiratory system	0,408	0,138	0,003	1,504
Other vascular catheterization, excluding cardiac cathegory	1,069	0,244	<0,001	2,912

Starting from the results described here, it is appropriate to observe how the effects of significant prognostic factors induced in hospitals remain in survival times. To do this, we will use Kaplan–Meier estimators [24], which are not constrained to fixed-time subintervals.

Therefore, they allow comparisons between modes of flexible prognostic factors using survival curves relative to the subjects who detect such rules. The first prognostic factor for which we cite the graph of the survival function (Fig. 3) is the age group [25].

The graph (Fig. 3) highlights that the hospital stays of patients suffering from cardiovascular diseases, distributed by age group, differ in two groups:

- Short- and medium-duration hospitalization (1–1 80 days) for the age groups 57–67, 68–77, 78–83, and > 84. Older patients are also likelier to die in the first 60 days.
- Long stay (180–365 days), which is part of the age groups < 44 and 45–56. We can add that people younger than 44 have more chance of survival than other classes from the first month of hospitalization; this probability increases over time compared to other patients. It was found that between 80 and 130 days of hospitalization, the likelihood of living increases for the 57–67 age group compared to the age group 45–56.

Concerning patients suffering from cardiovascular diseases who have cardiac arrest and ventricular fibrillation (Fig. 3) as their main diagnosis, we can reinforce the predictions of the Cox method (16 times greater probability of death). Namely, patients with such a diagnosis have a much higher probability of death than patients without such a diagnosis. We can add that the sample combined with cardiac arrest has a maximum hospital stay of 125 days (instead of months).

Regarding (Fig. 4) noncardiac vascular catheterization surgery (2.9 times higher probability), these patients have shorter hospital stays (maximum 140 days) and greater chances of death, up to 44 days of hospitalization.

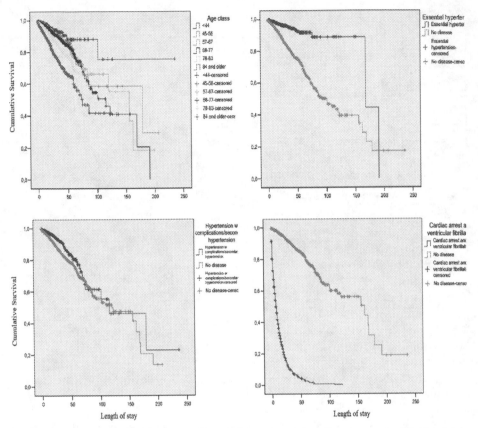

Fig. 3. Prognostic factors for the cardiovascular patients' hospital stays using Kaplan-Meier estimators.

Acute cerebral vascular disease patients (Fig. 4) are 2.4 times likelier to die. Patients with this disease die more frequently in the first 65 days. The situation of mortality greatly lessens as time progresses. The longest hospital stay for this type of diagnosis is 210 days.

However, patients with infectious and parasitic diseases are 1.8 times likelier to die in hospitals than patients without these issues. The most deaths occurred between the first and twentieth days of hospitalization. The duration of hospitalization in this circumstance reached 244 days.

Last, patients with respiratory diseases (Fig. 4) were likely to die 1.5 times more often than patients who do not have the disease. They die more between the first and the 54th days. Finally, such hospitalizations can last 247 days.

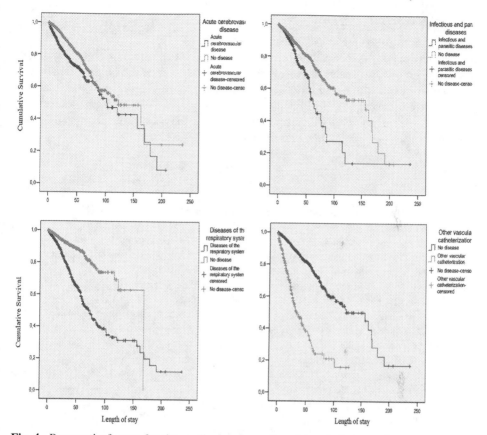

Fig. 4. Prognostic factors for the cardiovascular patients' hospital stays using Kaplan-Meier estimators.

4   Conclusion

The aim of this study was to statistically determine whether clinical and non-clinical factors impacted the duration of hospital admissions for cardiovascular diseases in Puglia between 2009 and 2014 (last year of free-use data).

The significant results described here are all related to diagnostic categories or interventions, particularly for the important nosological category of prognostic factors. It is worth noting that literature suggests a strong link between longer hospitalizations and less successful clinical interventions.

The analysis of both samples confirmed the clinical relevance and statistical significance of three prognostic factors: essential hypertension, cardiac arrest and ventricular fibrillation, and other vascular catheterization (excluding cardiac category). This demonstrates the robustness of the results.

In the analysis, we also included the 'age class of patients' factor in a second representative sample to investigate whether hospital admissions for this diagnostic category allow for more choices that are less dependent on clinical motivations. We conducted further analysis of data parallel to that presented in Sample I to verify the duration of hospitalizations following this diagnostic category.

This work provides tools and information to recognise symptoms that exacerbate the mentioned diagnoses. It aims to prevent the worst outcomes and to prepare for serious emergencies and acute interventions for certain age groups and disease combinations. Based on these epidemiological results, it is appropriate to expect Apulian hospitals to activate intervention identification protocols for the six diagnoses mentioned in this work and for the age groups at greatest risk (68–77, 78–83, and > 84).

References

1. Wilkins, E., et al.: European Cardiovascular Disease Statistics 2017. European Heart Network, Brussels (2017)
2. Roth, G.A., et al.: Global, regional, and national age-sex-specific mortality for 282 causes of death in 195 countries and territories, 1980–2017: a systematic analysis for the Global Burden of Disease Study 2017. Lancet **392**, 1736–1788 (2018)
3. Centers for Disease Control and Prevention). The Burden of Chronic Diseases and Their Risk Factors—National and State Perspectives; CDC: Washington, DC, USA (2004)
4. Moriyama, H., Kohno, T., Kohsaka, S., Shiraishi, Y., Fukuoka, R., Nagatomo, Y., et al.: Length of hospital stay and its impact on subsequent early readmission in patients with acute heart failure: a report from the WET-HF Registry. Heart Vessels **34**(11), 1777–1788 (2019). https://doi.org/10.1007/s00380-019-01432-y
5. Timmis, A., et al.: European society of cardiology, on behalf of the Atlas Writing group, European society of cardiology: cardiovascular disease statistics 2021. Eur. Heart J. **43**(8), 716–799 (2022). https://doi.org/10.1093/eurheartj/ehab892
6. New York Heart Association, New York Heart Association. Criteria Committee. Nomenclature and criteria for diagnosis of diseases of the heart and great vessels. Little, Brown Medical Division (1979)
7. Wright, S.P., Verouhis, D., Gamble, G., Swedberg, K., Sharpe, N., Doughty, R.N.: Factors influencing the length of hospital stay of patients with heart failure. Eur. J. Heart Fail. **5**(2), 201–209 (2003). https://doi.org/10.1016/S1388-9842(02)00201-5
8. Formiga, F., Chivite, D., Manito, N., Mestre, A.R., Llopis, F., Pujol, R.: Admission characteristics predicting longer length of stay among elderly patients hospitalized for decompensated heart failure. Eur. J. Intern. Med. **19**(3), 198–202 (2008). https://doi.org/10.1016/j.ejim.2007.09.007
9. Mitani, H., Funakubo, M., Sato, N., Murayama, H., Rached, R., Matsui, N., et al.: In-hospital resource utilization, worsening heart failure, and factors associated with length of hospital stay in patients with hospitalized heart failure: a Japanese database cohort study. J. Cardiol. (2020). https://doi.org/10.1016/j.jjcc.2020.05.010
10. McPherson, K.: Length of stay and health outcome. Br. Med. J. (Clin. Res. Ed.) **288**(6434), 1854–1855 (1984). https://doi.org/10.1136/bmj.288.6434.1854
11. Kaplan, E.L., Meier, P.: Nonparametric estimation from incomplete observations. J. Am. Stat. Assoc. **53**, 457–481 (1958). Tripepi, G., Catalano, F.: (2004)
12. Cox, D.R.: Regression models and life-tables (with discussion). J. Royal Stat. Soc. B **34**, 187–220 (1972)
13. Cox, D.R.: Partial likelihood. Biometrika **62**, 269–276 (1975)
14. Delvecchio, F.: Analisi dei tempi di sopravvivenza. Dipartimento di Scienze Statistiche dell'Università di Bari, Appunti a uso degli studenti (2001)

15. Cox, D.R., Snell, E.J.: Applied Statistics: Principles and Examples. Chapman & Hall, Londra (1981)
16. Kaplan-Meier analysis. Giornale Italiano di Nefrologia **21**(6), 540–546. Van Dijk, P.C., Jager, K.J., Zwinderman, A.H., Zoccali, C., Dekker, F.W.: The analysis of survival data in nephrology: basic concepts and methods of Cox regression. Kidney Int. **74**(6), 705–709 (2008)
17. Berkson J.: Application of the logistic function to bio-assay. J. Am. Stat. Assoc. **39**(227), 357–365 (1944). https://doi.org/10.2307/2280041
18. Lenz, S.T.: Alan Agresti (2013): Categorical data analysis. Stat Papers **57**, 849–850 (2016). https://doi.org/10.1007/s00362-015-0733-8
19. Provenzano, F., Tripepi, G., Zoccali, C.: How to measure effects in clinical research (corrected). G. Ital. Nefrol. **27**(3), 296–300 (2010)
20. Almashrafi, A., Elmontsri, M., Aylin, P.: Systematic review of factors influencing length of stay in ICU after adult cardiac surgery. BMC Health Serv. Res. **16**, 318 (2016). https://doi.org/10.1186/s12913-016-1591-3
21. Barili, F., et al.: An original model to predict Intensive Care Unit length-of stay after cardiac surgery in a competing risk framework. Int. J. Cardiol. **168**, 219–225 (2013). https://doi.org/10.1016/j.ijcard.2012.09.091
22. Cox, D.R., Snell, E.J.: The Analysis of Binary Data, 2nd edn. Chapman and Hall, London (1989)
23. Hosmer, D.W., Lemeshow, S.: Applied Logistic Regression, 2nd edn. Wiley, New York (2000)
24. Goel, M.K., Khanna, P., Kishore, J.: Understanding survival analysis: Kaplan-Meier estimate. Int. J. Ayurveda Res. **1**(4), 274–278 (2010). https://doi.org/10.4103/0974-7788.76794
25. Marschall, A., et al.: Pacemaker therapy in the elderly and very elderly: comorbidity-burden vs age, as prognostic factors for excess of length of in-hospital stay, complications and mortality. Euro. Heart J. **42**(Supplement_1), October 2021. ehab724.2820.https://doi.org/10.1093/eurheartj/ehab724.2820

A Study on Different Parameters Affecting Overall Cost of Global Content Distribution Services in Metropolitan Cloud Network

Semanto Mondal[(⊠)] and Rajib Chandra Ghosh

University of Naples Federico II, Naples, Italy
`{s.mondal,r.chandraghosh}@studenti.unina.it`

Abstract. Due to the advancement of technology and the internet, every digital component is connected which results in a tremendous increase in digital content. To make digital content respectively multimedia content available to potentially large and geographically distributed consumer populations, Global Content Distribution Networks are used. In the era of cloud, several cloud providers provide cloud services to their users by optimizing cloud-based content delivery. There are different factors associated with a cost-effective model such as content delivery cost, computation cost, and storage cost associated with the cloud network [1]. In this study, we have tried to analyze different parameters that can affect the overall cost and performance of different Global Content Distribution services such as the capacity of resource blocks and, the addition of edge computing by applying different network constraints such as flow conservation constraints, flow chaining constraints, communication and computation capacity constraints, maximum delay constraints. We have also tried to experiment with the effect of different network infrastructures on the overall cost of four different Content Distribution services for different service graphs.

Keywords: Global Content Distribution Network (GCDN) · Edge Computing · Service Graph · Network Optimization

1 Introduction

In less than fifteen years, Content Delivery Networks (CDNs) have become key actors in the value and supply chain of the Internet. The main objective of these cloud networks is to maintain Quality of Service (QoS) and quality of Experience (QoE) while maintaining lower cost as well as minimal delay which can be utilized in the field of cloud gaming, content delivery, as well as on-demand video [2, 3].

Cloud networks can be designed with centralized as well as distributed computation resources. With the help of wired as well as wireless network connectivity different digital devices such as servers are connected. In the centralized network all the computation is performed centrally after that the content is delivered to the end users who might reside in a geographic location far away from the original servers. Here several problems arise For example when large content is transferred to a longer distance itneeds a larger capacity

© The Author(s), under exclusive license to Springer Nature Switzerland AG 2024
O. Gervasi et al. (Eds.): ICCSA 2024, LNCS 14813, pp. 46–64, 2024.
https://doi.org/10.1007/978-3-031-64605-8_4

of the communication channel as well as overall delay also increases significantly. To overcome this problem distributed computation resources such as Edge Computing come into the picture. Caching can also be used to reduce the delivery cost. In services like Professional Video on Demand (e.g.; Netflix), and User Generated Video on Demand (e.g.: Facebook) caching near the user end can be utilized to reduce both usage of resources as well as delay in the network [4]. Other techniques such as computation offloading which refers to the process of transferring the computational task to the computation node from the parent node to make the computation process faster as well as to minimize the resource allocation in the parent node [5, 6, 7].

In this paper, we have tried to minimize the overall cost by using different network infrastructures, by changing the network capacity which resulted also into a change in resource allocation block as well as by changing caching and computation rates. Figure 1 shows the overall workflow of the project for different services:

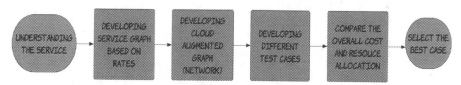

Fig. 1. Overall Workflow

2 Formulation of Cloud Network Flow Optimization

In order to formulate the optimization problem, we leverage the recently proposed cloud network flow optimization framework [8, 9, 10, 11]. The goal is to optimize the configuration of a service over a cloud network. The service is described by a service graph $R = (I, \mathcal{K})$ where I is the set of service functions and $\mathcal{K}$ the set of commodities. In addition $g : \mathcal{K} \to \mathcal{O}$ refers to a mapping function that maps each commodity to a specific information object. The cloud network is also described by a directed graph $G = (V,E)$ with V vertices and E edges representing the set of nodes and links in the cloud network. The target is to minimize cost and latency.

$$min \left(\sum_{(u,v)\epsilon \varepsilon^a} y_{uv} w_{uv} + \sum_{k\epsilon K^d} l_T^k \right) \tag{1}$$

Equation (1) is the objection function where $(u, v)\epsilon \mathcal{E}^a$ defines the set over which the minimization is performed [10]. Here, $\mathcal{E}^a$ represents the set of edges in the network. y_{uv} Represents the number of allocated resource blocks from node u to v and w_{uv} represents the cost associated with each resource block for transmitting content from node u to v. Here l_T^k is the total delay for the destination commodities and $l_T^k \leq L^k$ where L^k is the maximum delay constraint per destination commodity. The function aims to minimize the total cost as well as the delay of content distribution over the network considering the following constraints.

$$\sum_{v\epsilon\delta^-(u)} f_{vu}^k = \sum_{v\epsilon\delta^+(u)} f_{uv}^k \ \forall u\epsilon V, \ k\epsilon K \tag{2}$$

Equation (2) is the flow conservation constraint which states that, for a specific content type K, in a node u the total incoming flow is equal to the total outgoing flow in other words what goes in is that comes out [8, 9].

$$f_{pu}^k = f_{up}^l \forall u \in V, \ k \in K, l \in X(k) \tag{3}$$

Equation (3) is related to the chaining constraint [10] which states that for every vertex u, and every pair of content types k and l associated with u, the flow of content from vertex p to vertex u for content type k is equal to the flow of content from vertex u to vertex p for content type l. $\forall u \in V, k \in K, l \in X(k)$; this part of the constraint states that the equality holds for all vertices u in the set of vertices V, for all content types k in the set of content types K, and all content types l in the set X(k).

$$f_{su}^k = \begin{cases} 1, & \text{if } k \text{ is sourced at node } s(i.e. \forall k \in K^s) \\ 0, & \text{otherwise} \end{cases} \tag{4}$$

Equation (4) is the source constraint which states that the content type k originating from source vertex s must follow a specified path to reach vertex u to avoid any sort of bypass of content.

$$f_{ud}^k = \begin{cases} 1, & \text{if } k \text{ is requested at node } d(i.e. \forall k \in K^d) \\ 0, & \text{otherwise} \end{cases} \tag{5}$$

Equation (5) is related to destination constraints which ensures that for every content type k associated with the destination vertex d, there is exactly one unit of flow from the vertex u to the destination vertex d.

$$f_{uv}^k R_k \leq f_{uv}^o \ \forall (u, v) \in \mathcal{E}^a, k \in K, o = g(k) \tag{6}$$

$$\sum_{o \in \mathcal{O}} f_{uv}^o = f_{uv} \tag{7}$$

Equation (6) is related to the actual flow constraints [9] and ensures that the flow of commodity k through the edge (u,v), does not exceed the flow of the corresponding object o through the same edge considering k is mapped to object o using mapping function g(k) and Eq. (7) ensures that the summation of object flow over edge (u,v) is equal to the total flow.

$$f_{uv} \leq y_{uv} c_{res}; y_{uv} \leq c_{uv} \ \forall (u, v) \in \mathcal{E}^a \tag{8}$$

Equation (8) is the communication capacity constraint [9] which states that the total flow on a link (u,v) or an edge is less or equal to the total allocated rate (where the rate is equal to the number of resource blocks multiplied by capacity per block) and number of allocated resource block should be less or equal to the maximum possible resource block for the link or edge (u,v).

$$l^k = \sum_{(u,v) \in \mathcal{E}^a} l_{uv}^k f_{uv}^k \ \forall k \in K \tag{9}$$

$$l_T^k = l^k \ \forall k \in K^s \tag{10}$$

$$l_T^k \geq l^k + l_T^l \ \forall k \in K \backslash K^s, l \in X(k) \tag{11}$$

$$l_T^k \leq L^k \ \forall k \in K^d \tag{12}$$

Equations (9), (10), (11) and (12) are related to the delay constraints which set the lower and upper bound to the allowed total delay for delivering any content type or stream of k [9].

$$f_{uv}^k \in \{0, 1\}, f_{uv} \in \mathbb{R}^+, f_{uv}^o \in \mathbb{R}^+, y_{uv} \in \mathbb{Z}^+ \ \forall (u, v) \in \mathcal{E}^a, k \in K, o \in \mathcal{O} \tag{13}$$

Equation (13) is related to the domain of the variables. $f_{uv}^k \in \{0,1\}$ This is related to discrete flow which does not allow splitting of the content flow and maintains a specific path from source to destination. f_{uv} And f_{uv}^o are the flow variables can take any positive real numbers whereas y_{uv} is the resource allocation variable that belongs to any positive integer [9, 10].

We have used the LpProblem class from a Python library named PuLP using liner programming where all the above-mentioned constraints are used to develop the final optimization model which optimizes the cost of different services in different networks. All the constraints are utilized to optimize the overall cost of the model and to understand how different parameters such as resource block capacity, the total number of resource blocks, location of processing, the addition of computation node at the access layer, and transmission rate affect the overall performance of the cloud network.

3 Cloud Augmented Graph and Service Graph Implementation

Three different networking scenarios have been implemented to test different cases and to provide a general conclusion. All these scenarios are for a single metropolitan area with a single core node and multiple edge and access nodes. The communication cost is set at 100 whereas the computation in and computation out costs for the computation nodes are set to 1 and 10 respectively. The overall cost of different networks is compared for varying rates as well as the capacity of the resource block.

In the first network of Fig. 2, there are single communication node in the core and 3 communication nodes in both the edge and access layer. Each communication node in the edge layer is having 3 computation nodes. Source nodes are located both in the core and access layer whereas destination nodes are located only at the access layer. There are no computation nodes in the access layer.

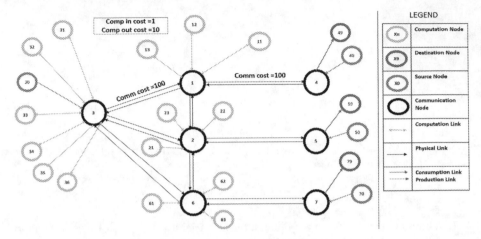

Fig. 2. Cloud Augmented Graph-1

The second network that is Cloud Augmented Graph-2 in Fig. 3 is the extended version of the network one that is also for a single metropolitan area having a single communication node in the core layer and 4 communication nodes in the edge layer. Each communication node of the edge layer has 4 communication nodes residing in the access layer. Here also there are no computation nodes in the access layer and all of these computation nodes belong to the Core and Edge layer.

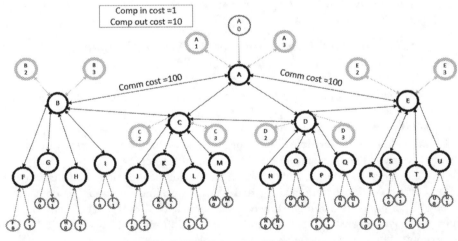

Fig. 3. Cloud Augmented Graph-2

Cloud network-2 is further extended to cloud network-2A in Fig. 4 where two main modifications have been implemented. The first one is, that now in all layers communication nodes have only one computation node which will be responsible for both caching and processing and the second one is, that computation nodes are also integrated with the communication nodes of the access layer.

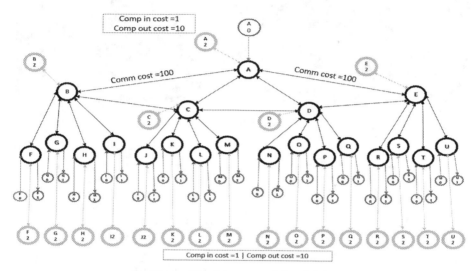

Fig. 4. Cloud Augmented Graph-2A

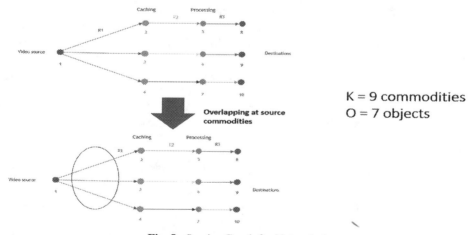

K = 9 commodities

O = 7 objects

Fig. 5. Service Graph for Network-1

Figure 5 is the service graph for network-1 where there are 9 commodities and 7 objects. Here a single source and 3 destinations are considered. R_1, R_2, R_3 are the rates associated with caching and processing.

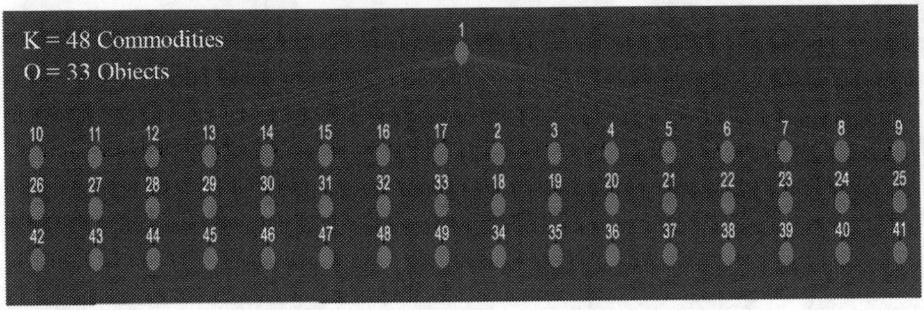

K = 48 Commodities
O = 33 Objects

Fig. 6. Service Graph for Network-2 & 2A

Figure 6 represents the service graph for both network-2 and 2A having 48 commodities and 33 objects also has a single source along with 16 destinations.

4 Professional Video on Demand (e.g.: Netflix)

In professional video-on-demand cases, users can watch the content whenever they want. Netflix and YouTube are good examples of these services. Video that the user accesses frequently can be cached near to the user so that next time when any other users are accessing the same content the delivery cost as well as time should be minimized.

Here in this service, the general consideration is that the rate before caching is smaller than the rate after caching. Source functions are located at the core node and the destination functions are at the access nodes. So, we have decided the rate as follows: $R_1 < R_2$, $R_1 = 15$, $R_2 = R_3 = 50$. For all the services the cost associated with the communication link is set to 100 per resource block, 1 for computation in and 10 for computation out. The maximum allowable delay is set as $L^k = 100$.

For cloud network-1 we have considered two different cases as shown in Table 1 in terms of communication link capacity and total amount of resource blocks:

Table 1. Cases for Cloud Network-1 for all services

Case-1	Case-2
Capacity per resource block = 5 Mbps	Capacity per resource block = 50 Mbps
Number of resource blocks = 200	Number of resource blocks = 20
Total capacity of communication link = 1 Gbps	Total capacity of communication link = 1 Gbps

For cloud network-2 we have considered two different cases as shown in Table 2 in terms of communication link capacity and total amount of resource blocks:

Table 2. Cases for Cloud Network-2 & 2A for all services

Case-1	Case-2	Case-3
Capacity per resource block = 5 Mbps	Capacity per resource block = 50 Mbps	Capacity per resource block = 200 Mbps
Number of resource blocks = 200	Number of resource blocks = 20	Number of resource blocks = 5
Total capacity of communication link = 1 Gbps	Total capacity of communication link = 1 Gbps	Total capacity of communication link = 1 Gbps

Table 3 shows the comparison concerning different cases for network 1. Whereas Figs. 7 and 8 show the content flow and allocation of resource blocks as well as the total amount of cost for different links. Due to the increase in resource block capacity, caching got overlapped which resulted in a reduction of overall content delivery cost from 4026 to 727.

Table 3. Performance Comparison on Coud Network-1

Case-1 (5 Mbps)	Case-2 (50 Mbps)
Total Cost = 4026	Total Cost = 727
Total number of resource blocks used 51	Total number of resource blocks used 26
Caching is redundant and at Edge	Caching is overlapped at the core
Total number of links used 22	Total number of links used 18

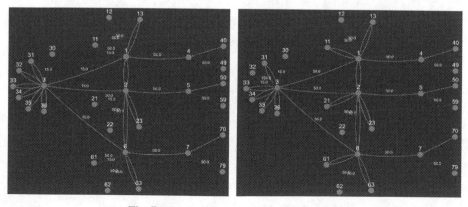

Fig. 7. Content flow graph for cases 1 and 2

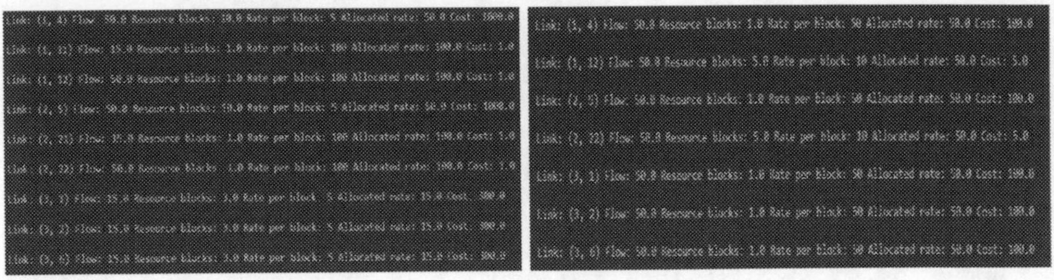

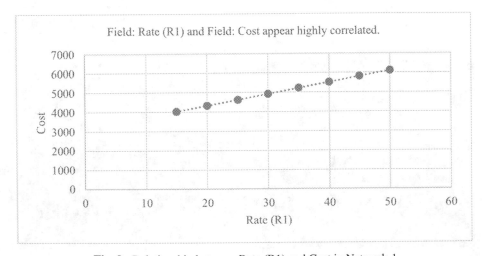

Fig. 8. Allocated resource block and cost per link for cases 1 and 2

Table 4. Rate (R1) vs Cost for communication resource block capacity $= 5$ Mbps in Network-1

Rate (R1)	Cost	Caching
15	4026	Edge
20	4326	Edge
25	4626	Edge
30	4926	Edge
35	5226	Edge
40	5526	Edge
45	5826	Edge
50	6114	Core

Fig. 9. Relationship between Rate (R1) and Cost in Network-1

Based on Table 4 as well as Fig. 9 it is clear that, if we keep the capacity of the communication resource block constant and change the rate (communication, consumption and production), with the increase of the rate (R) the overall cost of the network also increases linearly.

In general, when we increase the communication link capacity while keeping the cost the same as smaller resource blocks, caching is done with overlapping near the source that is at the core because it reduces the total number of resource block usage. On the contrary, if we fix the channel capacity to a particular value and chance R1 which is the rate before caching, we can observe that, at some point when R1 = R2 where R2 is the rate after caching, then automatically caching gets overlapped and happens at the core instead of happening at the edge redundantly. The cost remains the same from core to the edge for both catching at the core and edge, but usage of computation resource block reduces when caching is done at the core with overlapping. As a result, to optimize the cost caching moved from edge to core without increasing the channel capacity.

Table 5. Performance Comparison on Coud Network-2

Case-1 (5 Mbps)	Case-2 (50 Mbps)	Case-2 (200 Mbps)
Total Cost = 17692	Total Cost = 2492	Total Cost = 2489
Total number of resource blocks used 200	Total number of resource blocks used 48	Total number of resource blocks used 45
Caching is redundant and at Edge, and Processing is at Edge	Caching is redundant and at Edge, and Processing is at Edge	Caching is overlapped at the core; Processing is at the Edge
Total number of links used 53	Total number of links used 53	Total number of links used 47

Table 6. Performance Comparison on Coud Network-2A

Case-1 (5 Mbps)	Case-2 (50 Mbps)	Case-2 (200 Mbps)
Total Cost = 6496	Total Cost = 2492	Total Cost = 2489
Total number of resource blocks used 92	Total number of resource blocks used 48	Total number of resource blocks used 45
Caching is redundant and at Access, Processing is at Access	Caching is overlapped and at Edge, Processing is at Edge	Caching is overlapped at the core; Processing is at the Edge as well as the core
Total number of links used 69	Total number of links used 45	Total number of links used 47

Tables 5 and 6 show the comparison of different cases for networks 2 and 2A. For both networks 2 and 2A, we can visualize from the table that for higher capacity total number of resource allocation blocks is reduced due to overlapping of caching at a single node instead of redundant overlapping at different nodes. It is also clear that an increase in communication resource block capacity from 5 Mbps to 50 Mbps results in a significant reduction in cost whereas 200 Mbps couldn't reduce the cost predominantly.

5   Professional Live Video (e.g.: IPTV)

In professional Live Video, the consideration is that there will be one broadcasting channel that broadcasts the content like a live football match and there will be multiple users watching the content from a single metropolitan area. Here the rate before caching function is the same as the rate after caching function and the rates are considered as follows: $R_1 = R_2$, $R_1 = R_2 = 15$, $R_3 = 55$. Source functions are located at the core and destination functions are located at the access layer. The rate after processing is higher than before processing why because here we are considering that there might be some personalized content such as advertisements could be added to the original content as a result the rate should be higher.

Table 7. Performance Comparison on Coud Network-1

Case-1 (5 Mbps)	Case-2 (50 Mbps)
Total Cost = 4008	Total Cost = 1004
Total number of resource blocks used 42	Total number of resource blocks used 17
Caching is overlapped and at Core	Caching is overlapped and at Core
Total number of links used 18	Total number of links used 18

Table 8. Performance Comparison on Coud Network-2

Case-1 (5 Mbps)	Case-2 (50 Mbps)	Case-2 (200 Mbps)
Total Cost = 19288	Total Cost = 4088	Total Cost = 2475
Total number of resource blocks used 212	Total number of resource blocks used 60	Total number of resource blocks used 40
Caching and processing are at the edge, caching is redundant	Caching and processing are at the edge, caching is redundant	Caching is overlapped at the core; Processing is at the Edge
Total number of links used 53	Total number of links used 53	Total number of links used 47

From Tables 7, 8, 9 and Fig. 10 it is visible that if the rate is higher than the individual resource capacity then the usage of resource blocks increases, and overlapping can't reduce the cost. Whereas if the capacity of the communication resource block increases it allows overlapping resulting in a reduction of usage of both links and communication and computation resources as a result we can observe a reduction in overall cost.

Likewise, in professional live video case based on Table 10 as well as Fig. 11 in case of professional live video, if we keep the capacity of the communication resource block constant and change the rate (communication, consumption, and production), with the increase of the rate (R) the overall cost of the network also increases linearly.

For professional live video, we have considered that the commodities before and after caching belong to different objects. We have also tried to check the effect of making

Table 9. Performance Comparison on Coud Network-2A

Case-1 (5 Mbps)	Case-2 (50 Mbps)	Case-2 (200 Mbps)
Total Cost = 6496	Total Cost = 2496	Total Cost = 2385
Total number of resource blocks used 92	Total number of resource blocks used 52	Total number of resource blocks used 41
Caching is redundant and at Access, Processing is at Access	Caching is redundant and at Access, Processing is at Access	Caching is overlapped at the core; Processing is at the Edge
Total number of links used 69	Total number of links used 69	Total number of links used 63

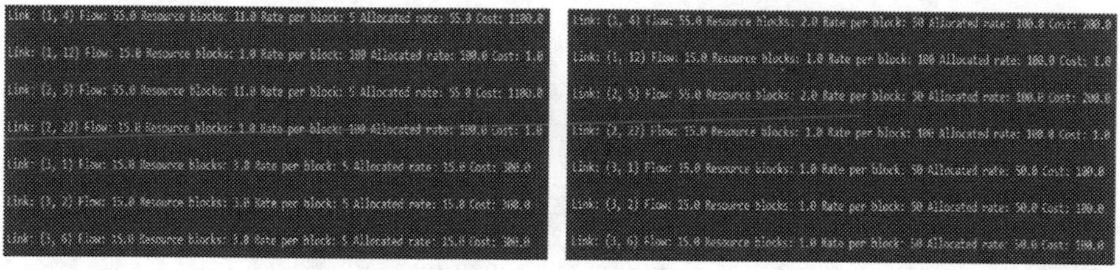

Fig. 10. Allocated resource block and cost per link for cases 1 and 2 in network 1

Table 10. Rate (R3) vs Cost for communication resource block capacity = 5 Mbps in Network-1

Rate (R3)	Cost	Caching
15	2052	Core
20	2382	Core
25	2712	Core
30	3042	Core
35	3372	Core
40	3702	Core
45	4032	Core
50	4362	Core
55	4692	Core

commodities before and after caching as the same object in network 2. In that case, the total number of commodities is 48 and the total number of objects is reduced to 18. The commodities after processing still belong to different commodities because after caching different personalization can be done on the content such as adding personalized advertisement or promotional content. Even though in network 1 caching is happening at the core in case 1, in case 2 caching is happening at the edge when the total number of objects is 33. In Network-1 each access node has a single destination whereas in

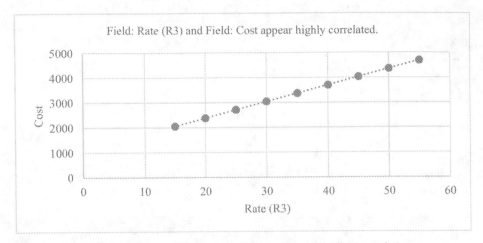

Field: Rate (R3) and Field: Cost appear highly correlated.

Fig. 11. Relationship Between Rate (R3) and Cost in Network-1

network-2 there are 4 destinations in each access node. From Fig. 12 it is clear that the communication rate of content from core to edge will be 60 if caching is happening at the core whereas it becomes 15 if caching is happening at the edge.

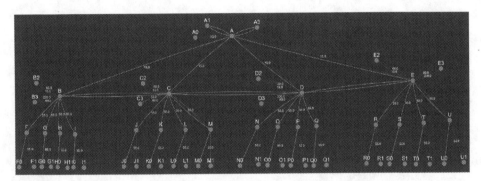

Fig. 12. Content flow graph in network 2

Referring to Fig. 13 when commodities after caching belong to the same object as well as commodities before caching belong to the same object too then caching gets overlapped and moved to the core. The communication rate of content flow from the core to the edge is 15. To reduce overall resource allocation caching overlaps at the core on the contrary processing is at the edge and redundant because these belong to different objects. The overall cost gets reduced from 19288 to 19255 for case 1.

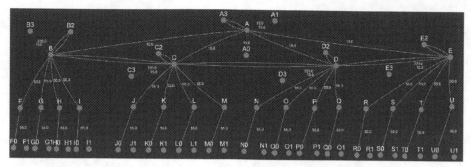

Fig. 13. Content flow graph in network 2 when commodities before and after caching belong to the same object

6   User Generated Video on Demand (e.g.: Facebook)

In general, users generate content on different social media platforms, and other users using the same platform can view this content. Facebook, Twitter, Instagram, and TikTok are a few examples of these services where users can watch the content generated by the other user. The content can be cached to the CDN servers near the user and the user can watch this content whenever they want as they result these videos are known as video on demand.

In this case, the rate before caching is smaller than the rate after caching. The source and destination are both located at the node associated with the access layer. The rates are set as follows: $R_1 < R_2$, $R_1 = 15$, $R_2 = R_3 = 50$.

Table 11. Performance Comparison on Coud Network-1

Case-1 (5 Mbps)	Case-2 (50 Mbps)
Total Cost = 4056	Total Cost = 734
Total number of resource blocks used 51	Total number of resource blocks used 14
Caching is redundant and at the edge	Caching is overlapped and at the edge
Total number of links used 22	Total number of links used 18

Table 12. Performance Comparison on Coud Network-2

Case-1 (5 Mbps)	Case-2 (50 Mbps)	Case-2 (200 Mbps)
Total Cost = 17932	Total Cost = 2732	Total Cost = 2647
Total number of resource blocks used 197	Total number of resource blocks used 47	Total number of resource blocks used 45
Caching and processing are at the edge, caching is redundant	Caching and processing are at the edge, caching is redundant	Caching is overlapped at the edge for the last 8 destinations, Processing is at the Edge
Total number of links used 52	Total number of links used 52	Total number of links used 47

Table 13. Performance Comparison on Coud Network-2A

Case-1 (5 Mbps)	Case-2 (50 Mbps)	Case-2 (200 Mbps)
Total Cost = 6416	Total Cost = 2612	Total Cost = 2612
Total number of resource blocks used 89	Total number of resource blocks used 45	Total number of resource blocks used 45
Caching is redundant and at Access, Processing is at Access	Caching is overlapped, and Processing is at both access and core	Caching is overlapped, and processing is at both access and core
Total number of links used 69	Total number of links used 50	Total number of links used 50

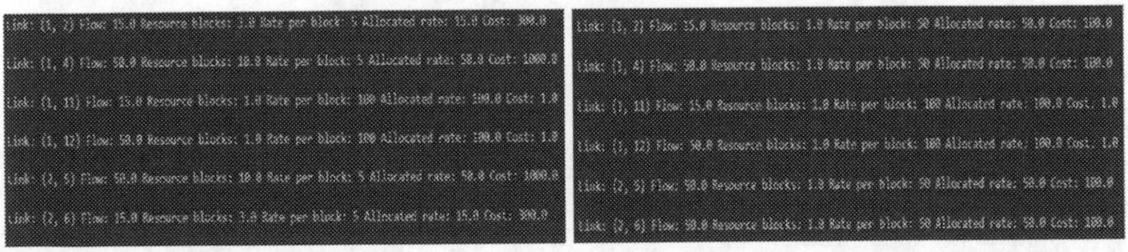

Fig. 14. Allocated resource block and cost per link for cases 1 and 2 in network 1

From Tables 11, 12, 13 and Fig. 14, it can be stated that when we increase communication resource capacity from 5 Mbps to 50 Mbps we can see a significant drop in cost due to overlapping and reduced amount of resource block allocation. Whereas if we increase the communication link capacity further to 200 Mbps we can't see much reduction in cost. So, for this case, 50 Mbps capacity is more suitable meaning case-2 is more appropriate than case-3 and case-1.

7   User Generated Live Video (e.g.: Facebook Live)

This service follows similar methodologies to professional live video. In services like Facebook Live, the user can go live and start sharing video content whereas other users can watch this content live. We have designed this service for a single metropolitan area where there will be a single source who can produce live content and multiple users can watch this content. So, this is a single source-multiple-destination scenario.

Here the rate before caching function is the same as the rate after caching function and the rates are considered as follows: $R_1 = R_2$, $R_1 = R_2 = 15$, $R_3 = 55$. Both source functions as well as destination functions are located at the access layer. Like professional live video service, the rate after processing is higher than before processing why because here we are considering that there might be some personalized content such as advertisements could be added to the original content as a result the rate should be higher.

Table 14. Performance Comparison on Coud Network-1

Case-1 (5 Mbps)	Case-2 (50 Mbps)
Total Cost = 4345	Total Cost = 1034
Total number of resource blocks used 52	Total number of resource blocks used 17
Caching is redundant and at the edge	Caching is overlapped and at the edge
Total number of links used 20	Total number of links used 18

Table 15. Performance Comparison on Coud Network-2

Case-1 (5 Mbps)	Case-2 (50 Mbps)	Case-2 (200 Mbps)
Total Cost = 19528	Total Cost = 4328	Total Cost = 2715
Total number of resource blocks used 212	Total number of resource blocks used 60	Total number of resource blocks used 39
Caching and processing are at the edge, caching is redundant	Caching and processing are at the edge, caching is redundant	Caching is overlapped at the edge; Processing is at the Edge
Total number of links used 52	Total number of links used 52	Total number of links used 46

From Table 14 and Fig. 15 for network-1 it can be stated that when we increase communication resource capacity from 5 Mbps to 50 Mbps we can see a significant drop in cost due to overlapping and reduced amount of resource block allocation. Whereas from Tables 15 and 16 it's clear that increasing the communication link capacity further to 200 Mbps from 50 Mbps reduces the cost significantly for networks 2 and 2A. So, for this case 50Mbps capacity is more suitable meaning case-2 is more appropriate than case-1 for network 1 on the contrary case-3 is more suitable for both network 2 and network 2A.

Table 16. Performance Comparison on Coud Network-2A

Case-1 (5 Mbps)	Case-2 (50 Mbps)	Case-2 (200 Mbps)
Total Cost = 6416	Total Cost = 2616	Total Cost = 2564
Total number of resource blocks used 89	Total number of resource blocks used 51	Total number of resource blocks used 35
Caching is redundant and at Access, Processing is at Access	Caching is redundant and at Access, Processing is at access	Caching is overlapped at edge and access; Processing is at both access and edge
Total number of links used 68	Total number of links used 68	Total number of links used 45

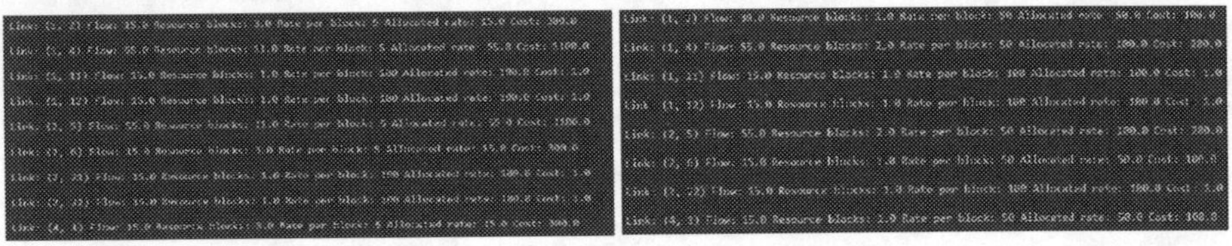

Fig. 15. Allocated resource block and cost per link for cases 1 and 2 in network 1

8   Overall Comparison for Network 2 & 2A

Cloud Network 2A is the modified version of Cloud Network 2. The main difference is that, in a cloud network 2A computation node is also added to the access layer along with the core and edge. A comparison has been made concerning the communication resource block, computation resource block, total cost, and maximum delay for destination commodities for four different services with respect could augmented graphs 2 and 2A. From these comparisons we can answer the following research questions:

RQ1: Weather increase in capacity reduces total delivery cost considering different rate requirements.

RQ2: Whether adding a computation node at the access layer reduces the overall cost of the network.

From the dual axis plots in Figs. 16 and 17, we can answer both the research questions that we proposed earlier. We have considered the data of professional live video service to generate the below plots. According to the plot in Fig. 16, as communication block capacity increases, both the cost and resource allocation reduce. Alongside, Fig. 17 demonstrates that in cloud network 2A the cost is less compared to that of cloud network 2 for different communication block capacities.

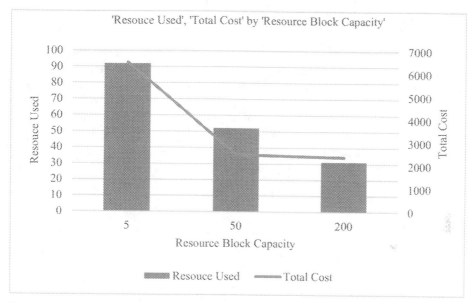

Fig. 16. Total Resource Used and Total Cost vs Resource Block Capacity in Professional Live Video

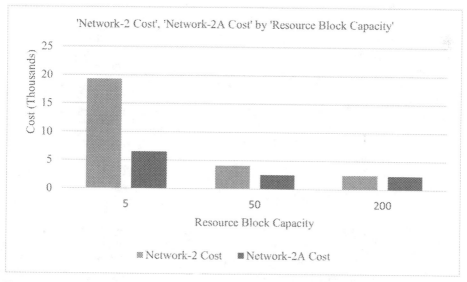

Fig. 17. Total Cost in Network 2 and 2A for different Communication Block Capacity in Professional Live Video

9 Conclusion

As the utilization of resources increases the overall delivery cost also increases. An increase in capacity reduces the usage of resources hence reducing the overall costs whereas an increase in rate for constant resource capacity linearly increases the cost. Overlapping reduces the use of links, which reduces the overall usage of resources as a result of overall cost reductions but to achieve this the capacity of resources should be large enough based on the requirements. For a larger network, adding a computation node at the access layer reduces the overall cost. The work focuses on a single metropolitan area which can be extended to multiple metropolitan areas using the same optimization concepts in future work.

References

1. Balasundaram, S.R., Banu, S.: Cost effective approaches for content placement in cloud CDN using dynamic content delivery model. Int. J. Cloud Appl. Comput., 01 July 2018
2. Llorca, J., Sterle, C., Tulino, A.M., Choi, N., Sforza, A., Amideo, A.E.: Joint content-resource allocation in software defined virtual CDNs. In: 2015 IEEE International Conference on Communication Workshop (ICCW), London, UK, pp. 1839–1844 (2015)
3. Cai, Y., Llorca, J., Tulino, A.M., Molisch, A.F.: Compute - and data-intensive networks: the key to the metaverse. In: 2022 1st International Conference on 6G Networking (6GNet), Paris, France (2022)
4. Llorca, J., Tulino, A.M., Varvello, M., Esteban, J., Perino, D.: Energy efficient dynamic content distribution. IEEE J. Sel. Areas Commun. 33(12), 2826–2836 (2015)
5. Prerna, D., Tekchandani, R., Kumar, N.: Device-to-device content caching techniques in 5G: a taxonomy, solutions, and challenges. Comput. Commun. 153, 48–84 (2020). ISSN 0140-3664
6. Lin, H., Zeadally, S., Chen, Z., Labiod, H., Wang, L.: A survey on computation offloading modeling for edge computing. J. Netw. Comput. Appl. 102781 (2020)
7. Jiang, C., Cheng, X., Gao, H., Zhou, X., Wan, J.: Toward computation offloading in edge computing: a survey. IEEE Access 7, 131543–131558 (2019)
8. Barcelo, M., Llorca, J., Tulino, A.M., Raman, N.: The cloud service distribution problem in distributed cloud networks. In: 2015 IEEE International Conference on Communications (ICC), London, UK, pp. 344–350 (2015). https://doi.org/10.1109/ICC.2015.7248345
9. Barcelo, M., Correa, A., Llorca, J., Tulino, A.M., Vicario, J.L., Morell, A.: IoT-cloud service optimization in next generation smart environments. IEEE J. Sel. Areas Commun. 34(12), 4077–4090 (2016)
10. Feng, H., Llorca, J., Tulino, A.M., Raz, D., Molisch, A.F.: Approximation algorithms for the NFV service distribution problem. In: IEEE INFOCOM 2017 - IEEE Conference on Computer Communications, Atlanta,GA,USA, pp. 1–9 (2017)
11. Poularakis, K., Llorca, J., Tulino, A.M., Tassiulas, L.: Approximation algorithms for data-intensive service chain embedding. In: Proceedings of the Twenty-First International Symposium on Theory, Algorithmic Foundations, and Protocol Design for Mobile Networks and Mobile Computing (Mobihoc 2020). Association for Computing Machinery, New York, NY, USA, pp. 131–140 (2020)

Fluid Simulation with Anisotropic Pressure Segregation and Time-Dependent Tensor Fields

Arthur Gonze Machado[1] 🆔, Emanuel Antônio Parreiras[2] 🆔,
Gilson Antônio Giraldi[2] 🆔, and Marcelo Bernardes Vieira[1](✉) 🆔

[1] UFJF - Universidade Federal de Juiz de Fora, Departamento de Ciência da
Computação, Juiz de Fora, MG, Brazil
arthur.gonze@ice.ufjf.br, marcelo.bernardes@ufjf.br
[2] LNCC - Laboratório Nacional de Computação Científica, Av. Getúlio Vargas, 333,
Quitandinha, Petrópolis, RJ, Brazil
emanuel1@ice.ufjf.br, gilson@lncc.br

Abstract. We propose a mathematical and computational model to
address an anisotropic incompressible fluid transport problem. Our
method aims to modulate the pressure and viscosity terms using a symmetric positive-definite second-order tensor field that can vary both
spatially and temporally. We introduce an anisotropic projection step
designed to accumulate and adjust pressure as the tensor field changes
over time. This step relies on a velocity update scheme that ensures the
divergence-free nature of the velocity field even as the tensor field varies
through time. Also, we propose a novel tensor-based particle advection
scheme based on the Explicit Integration following the Velocity and Acceleration Streamline (X-IVAS) method, implemented within an extended
Marker-and-Cell (MAC) grid. Our method is unconditionally stable and
presents suitable accuracy for designing incompressible fluid behavior.
The experimental results show how anisotropic tensor fields modulate the
pressure field, thereby influencing the behavior of the fluid flow.

Keywords: Anisotropic Pressure Segregation · Fluid Simulation ·
Incompressible Navier-Stokes · Time-Dependent Tensor Fields

1 Introduction

Even with significant advancements in Machine Learning in the last decade, simulating fluids still heavily relies on numerical methods. The computational costs
involved in these methods are well known, and their use has numerical errors
that need evaluation. Therefore, the Navier-Stokes equations are often simplified
according to the objectives of each problem [17]. These assumptions and simplification may introduce several limitations and may not accurately capture all the

M. B. Vieira—Supported by UFJF, FAPEMIG grant APQ-00080-21, CAPES, and
Grant Productivity Research Scholarship Level 2 CNPq (307645/2023-1).

O. Gervasi et al. (Eds.): ICCSA 2024, LNCS 14813, pp. 65–82, 2024.
https://doi.org/10.1007/978-3-031-64605-8_5

details of a physically accurate fluid flow. These limitations are often acceptable on determined applications, i.e. generating visual effects or simulating an overly controlled specific scenario. In this work, we assume that the fluid density is constant. Therefore, we are interested in solving a version of the incompressible Navier-Stokes equations.

The incompressibility constraint is an important simplification for Computational Fluid Simulation. Physically accurate fluids indeed change their density, e.g. sound wave propagation. But in the macroscopic context, these perturbations in the fluid density are so small that they are irrelevant for several fluid flow applications. In this work, we propose a method that allows for compressible effects, plugged into an incompressible fluid computational method.

Assuming that the fluid flow is isotropic makes the Navier-Stokes equations less difficult to analytical or numerical solutions. The isotropic flow assumes that fluid properties, e.g. viscosity, are considered to be uniform in all orientations. We are interested in the anisotropic modulation of pressure and evaluating its effects on fluid flow. In this sense, tensor fields are an important mathematical tool used to simulate anisotropic fluid flow effects. Also, it can emulate surface tension, porous walls, and fluid phase transitions. Applications of this approach can be used for scientific data visualization and Visual Effects (VFX).

The "Explicit Integration following the Velocity and Acceleration Streamline" (X-IVAS) method has proven to be a fitting solution for our challenges [7,9]. Unlike other methods, X-IVAS is a P2 Fractional-Step method [6] that incorporates pressure in the advection step by accumulating it throughout the simulation. This accumulated pressure is then transformed into kinetic energy, reducing the numerical dissipation of the momentum. It uses a pressure segregation scheme, which is the process of uncoupling the computation of the pressure from the velocity [2,3,14].

The purpose of this work is to develop a mathematical and computational model that can address anisotropic incompressible fluid transport based on symmetric second-order positive-definite tensor fields. Our model modulates and deviates the pressure and viscosity terms through a tensor field that can change temporally and spatially (Sect. 3.2). Also, we aim to adapt the X-IVAS method within its pressure segregation scheme to obtain anisotropic fluid flow (Sect. 3.3). The original X-IVAS method assumes an isotropic fluid flow, prompting us to propose an adaptation for anisotropic pressure segregation, thereby achieving anisotropic fluid flow. We provide examples of tensor fields varying in time to modulate fluid flow. One of them uses a fluid property to construct a constantly evolving tensor field. We build the experiments upon existing models presented in the works of [12,16,19] further advancing the understanding and application of our tensor-based X-IVAS method.

The main contributions of this paper are 1) A novel tensor-based pressure correction method. We propose a new anisotropic projection step to accumulate and adjust pressure as the tensor field changes in time; 2) A velocity update scheme that guarantees that it remains divergence-free as the tensor field varies in time; 3) A tensor-based anisotropic particle advection scheme based on the X-IVAS method in Marker-and-Cell (MAC) grid.

2   Related Works

The development and improvement of numerical methods and models that can accurately capture the complexities of anisotropic fluid flow behavior are not new to the CFD research topic. Modeling turbulence is one of the main approaches to simulating anisotropic fluid flow. Turbulence is a fundamental problem of fluid dynamics that remains a formidable challenge for science. It appears in many physical phenomena and engineering problems. This topic has been a challenge for over 150 years as discussed by [10].

Recent contributions on anisotropic fluid flow for animations are presented by [12,16,19]. In [16], a symmetric positive-definite second-order tensor field is coupled to the incompressible Navier-Stokes equations. This tensor field rigidly conforms the fluid flow to behave according to its anisotropy. The authors proposed an anisotropic pressure correction scheme and a tensor-velocity term coupled to the advection step. This tensor field transforms the velocity and the pressure gradient over the projection step, enforcing the fluid flow to the tensor orientation. A centered grid was used to store the fluid quantities. The computation method to solve this novel numerical scheme was created over the [18] contributions. The work of [19] took a step further improving this approach to a 3D domain with custom numerical and computational methods. Finally, [12] proposed a numerical method to account for the multiple degrees of freedom of a 3D domain. A MAC grid with multiple points of reference was used to greatly improve the numerical accuracy. This numerical accuracy allows the usage of many different configurations of the tensor field to influence the fluid flow.

Advancements in machine learning and neural networks have also made a significant impact on CFD research. Neural networks have been applied to fluid flow problems such as turbulence modeling, flow control, and flow prediction. This research front allows an efficient and suitable accurate solution to the governing Partial Differential Equations (PDEs). Some notable works include the development of Physics-Informed Neural Networks (PINNs) [15]. These networks receive direct information about the underlying governing equations for training. There is also the application of CNNs for solving these PDEs on an image-based training approach without the need for labeled data [5]. These recent advancements in both anisotropic fluid flow modeling and the application of neural networks to CFD hold great potential for advancing our understanding of complex fluid phenomena, improving simulation accuracy, and enabling efficient design optimization in a wide range of engineering applications.

3   Proposed Method

Our novel method enables pressure segregation while considering time-dependent tensor fields. This section addresses the challenge of incorporating the temporal variations of the tensor field into the pressure segregation process [2,3,14].

The main mathematical fact that supports this work is given by [4]. Any vector field $\mathbf{u}(\mathbf{x})$ can be uniquely decomposed from two arbitrary tensor fields

T and **S** that are symmetric positive-definite dyadics in $\mathbb{R}^3$. This decomposition can be performed by solving the **ST**-Poisson equation:

$$\nabla_{\mathbf{S}} \cdot \nabla_{\mathbf{T}} \mathbf{p}(\mathbf{x}) = \nabla_{\mathbf{S}} \cdot \mathbf{u}(\mathbf{x}),$$

where $\mathbf{p}(\mathbf{x})$ is a vector field with continuous second derivatives, $\nabla_{\mathbf{S}}$ and $\nabla_{\mathbf{T}}$ are the **S**-Gradient and **T**-gradient terms, respectively. We refer to [4,19] for more details. As proposed by [16,19], we set $\mathbf{S} = \mathbf{I}$ to obtain the **T**-Poisson equation:

$$\nabla.\nabla_{\mathbf{T}} \mathbf{p}(\mathbf{x}) = \nabla \cdot \mathbf{u}(\mathbf{x}), \tag{1}$$

3.1   Navier-Stokes Equations with Tensor Fields

Our approach utilizes a prediction-correction anisotropic pressure segregation method. This method is coupled with a time-dependent positive-definite second-order tensor field to solve the incompressible Navier-Stokes equations. Our primary goal is to solve the model proposed by [16] that accounts for the anisotropy of a symmetric positive-definite second-order tensor field. The ensuing mathematical formulation is:

$$\rho \frac{\partial \mathbf{u}}{\partial t} + \rho(\mathbf{u} \cdot \nabla)\mathbf{u} = \mu \nabla \cdot (\mathbf{T}\nabla\mathbf{u}) - \mathbf{T}\nabla\mathbf{p} + \mathbf{f}, \tag{2}$$

restricted to:

$$\nabla \cdot \mathbf{u} = 0. \tag{3}$$

The tensor field plays a crucial role in our fluid simulation as it not only influences diffusive forces but also affects the pressure gradient force. Our interest lies in the modulation of the forces represented on the right-hand side (RHS) of Eq. 2 that act on the fluid.

The key point of this work is how to deal with pressure segregation under the influence of a tensor field. Local variations in pressure can drive fluid motion, causing the fluid to accelerate or decelerate. Consequently, this process is a conversion of kinetic pressure to kinetic energy (velocity). Conversely, in incompressible fluid dynamics, spots with a non-null divergence of the velocity can result in the conversion of kinetic energy into kinetic pressure. Numerically, the conversion of velocity into pressure occurs in the projection step. The reverse is performed in the advection step, by the pressure gradient term. Our main interest is how to perform both conversions through a second-order positive-definite tensor field. The conversions must be carefully performed to avoid the introduction of artifacts in the simulation and keep it stable.

As shown by [16], and [13], the tensor transformed pressure can be discarded throughout the simulation and still reflect the influence of the tensor field. However, as shown in this work, a properly accumulated anisotropic pressure estimation can open several possibilities to modulate and deviate the fluid.

In summary, this work proposes to use the tensor field to intermediate the exchange between kinetic pressure and kinetic energy, and vice versa, through a tensor pressure segregation based on the anisotropic Helmholtz decomposition. It is admitted that the tensor field varies in time, which makes the problem even more challenging. This is discussed in the next section.

3.2 Anisotropic Helmholtz Projection and Varying Tensor Fields

Let us consider the anisotropic Helmholtz decomposition, denoted by Eq. 1. It shows how a vector field $\mathbf{u}(\mathbf{x})$ can be decomposed as a scalar $\phi(\mathbf{x})$ and a vector $\mathbf{u}'(\mathbf{x})$ field, subject to the tensor field $\mathbf{T}(\mathbf{x})$. Now suppose that the vector field smoothly varies in time as $\mathbf{u}(\mathbf{x}, t) = \mathbf{u}_t$, and the tensor field smoothly varies as $\mathbf{T}(\mathbf{x}, t) = \mathbf{T}_t$. The anisotropic Helmholtz decomposition at any time t is defined as (Eq. 1 with $\mathbf{S} = \mathbf{I}$):

$$\mathbf{u}_t = \nabla_{\mathbf{T}_t} \phi_t + \nabla \times \mathbf{a}_t,$$
$$\mathbf{u}_t = \nabla_{\mathbf{T}_t} \phi_t + \mathbf{u}'_t,$$
$$\mathbf{u}'_t = \mathbf{u}_t - \nabla_{\mathbf{T}_t} \phi_t, \tag{4}$$

where $\mathbf{u}'_t$ is a divergence-free vector field concerning the standard coordinate system and is subject to the tensor field $\mathbf{T}_t$. It can be obtained by solving the $\mathbf{T}$-Poisson equation (Eq. 1):

$$\nabla \cdot \nabla_{\mathbf{T}_t} \phi_t = \nabla \cdot \mathbf{u}_t.$$

Assume that $\{\mathbf{u}'_0, \mathbf{u}'_1, \cdots, \mathbf{u}'_n\}$ represents a divergence-free vector field finite sequence until an arbitrary n-th vector field. Each arbitrary vector field $\mathbf{u}_t$ is the addition of the previous divergence-free vector field $\mathbf{u}'_{t-1}$ to an arbitrary vector field $\delta\mathbf{u}_t$ as:

$$\mathbf{u}_t = \mathbf{u}'_{t-1} + \delta\mathbf{u}_t, \tag{5}$$

whose anisotropic Helmholtz decomposition is:

$$\nabla \cdot \nabla_{\mathbf{T}_t} \delta\phi_t = \nabla \cdot \left(\mathbf{u}'_{t-1} + \delta\mathbf{u}_t\right),$$
$$\nabla \cdot \nabla_{\mathbf{T}_t} \delta\phi_t = \nabla \cdot \delta\mathbf{u}_t, \tag{6}$$

where $\delta\phi_t$ refers to the decomposition of the incremental vector field $\delta\mathbf{u}_t$. This equation means that we only need to decompose the increment $\delta\mathbf{u}_t = \mathbf{u}_t - \mathbf{u}'_{t-1}$ to find the divergence-free vector field $\mathbf{u}'_t = \mathbf{u}_t - \nabla_{\mathbf{T}_t} \delta\phi_t$ in the sequence. Therefore, the equation:

$$\mathbf{u}'_t = \mathbf{u}'_{t-1} + [\delta\mathbf{u}_t - \nabla_{\mathbf{T}_t} \delta\phi_t], \tag{7}$$

is sufficient to define the whole sequence, given a divergence-free initial vector field $\mathbf{u}'_0$ such that $\mathbf{u}_0 = \nabla_{\mathbf{T}_0} \delta\phi_0 + \mathbf{u}'_0$.

Now, consider the corresponding scalar field sequence $\{\delta\phi_0, \delta\phi_1, \cdots, \delta\phi_n\}$ as defined by Eqs. 6 and 7. In this work, the main problem is to find the accumulated scalar field:

$$\begin{cases} \phi_n = f_{\mathbf{T}_0}(\delta\phi_0) + f_{\mathbf{T}_1}(\delta\phi_1) + \cdots + f_{\mathbf{T}_{n-1}}(\delta\phi_{n-1}) + \delta\phi_n, \\ \nabla_{\mathbf{T}_n} \phi_n \text{ is } \mathbf{T}_n\text{-solenoinal,} \end{cases} \tag{8}$$

i.e., our problem is to find operators $f_{\mathbf{T}_t}(\cdot)$ that transform the intermediary scalar fields $\delta\phi_t$, that is the solution for the t-th element subject to $\mathbf{T}_t$, into scalar fields $f_{\mathbf{T}_t}(\delta\phi_t)$ that are decomposition solutions subject to the last tensor field $\mathbf{T}_n$.

For example, suppose the tensor fields are constant in t with $\mathbf{T}_i = \mathbf{T}$. The solution, in this case, is straightforward with the identity operator $f_{\mathbf{T}_t}(\delta\phi_t) = \delta\phi_t$, resulting in the accumulation $\phi_n = \delta\phi_0 + \delta\phi_1 + \cdots + \delta\phi_n$ and the $\mathbf{T}_n$-irrotational total gradient $\nabla_{\mathbf{T}}\phi_n = \nabla_{\mathbf{T}}\delta\phi_0 + \nabla_{\mathbf{T}}\delta\phi_1 + \cdots + \nabla_{\mathbf{T}}\delta\phi_n$. Since all decompositions in the series are subject to the same tensor field $\mathbf{T}$, they admit the application of the linear operator $\mathbf{T}$ directly into a simple summation of all incremental scalar field solutions.

However, if the tensor fields vary along the sequence, the solution of Eq. 8 is not trivial. Equation 7 shows that all elements in the sequence are coupled by the anisotropic Helmholtz decomposition (Eq. 6). Changing one vector field in the sequence impacts the subsequent vector fields because any distinct tensor field gives a unique divergence-free solution, up to the addition of harmonic scalar fields. Thus, the requirement that all scalar fields in the sequence have to be in accordance with a specific tensor field (Eq. 8) results in a divergence-free vector field sequence that is different from that Eq. 7 provides.

In the context of this work, the problem can be incrementally solved for each term of the sequence, avoiding finding the direct operators $f_{\mathbf{T}_i}(\cdot)$ of Eq. 8. The challenge is, for any element t, to conform all previous solutions $\{\delta\phi_0, \delta\phi_1, \cdots, \delta\phi_{t-1}\}$ and the t-th vector field $\mathbf{u}_t$ to the current tensor field $\mathbf{T}_t$. There is a reason to solve Eq. 8 with an incremental approach. The series calculation focuses on finding divergence-free vector fields $\mathbf{u}_t'$ by subtracting a $\mathbf{T}_t$-irrotational vector field $\nabla_{\mathbf{T}_t}\delta\phi_t$ from the arbitrary vector field $\mathbf{u}_t$. Thus, we only have to guarantee that the incremental addition:

$$\phi_t = g_{\mathbf{T}_{t-1}}(\phi_{t-1}) + \delta\phi_t, \tag{9}$$

provides a $\mathbf{T}_t$-irrotational vector field in the form $\nabla_{\mathbf{T}_t}\phi_t$. Of course, this scheme implies that the previous scalar field summation ϕ_{t-1} gives a $\mathbf{T}_{t-1}$-irrotational vector field in the form $\nabla_{\mathbf{T}_{t-1}}\phi_{t-1}$. The operator $g_{\mathbf{T}_{t-1}}(\cdot)$ is responsible for converting the accumulated scalar field ϕ_{t-1} into another one that is adjusted by the current tensor field $\mathbf{T}_t$. Equation 9 is easier to handle since it takes into account only two consecutive vector fields of the sequence. Nevertheless, the last term of the sequence $\mathbf{u}_n'$ is divergence-free with respect to the last tensor field $\mathbf{T}_n$ and the vector field $\nabla_{\mathbf{T}_n}\phi_n$ is $\mathbf{T}_n$-irrotational, satisfying both requirements from Eq. 8.

The solution is to modify the Poisson equation that projects the arbitrary vector field $\delta\mathbf{u}_t$ (Eq. 6). Our solution obtains the accumulated scalar field ϕ_t directly from the decomposition. Also, it conforms to the previous $\mathbf{T}_{t-1}$-irrotational vector field $\nabla_{\mathbf{T}_{t-1}}\phi_{t-1}$ to the new tensor field $\mathbf{T}_t$. One of the main contributions of this work is following anisotropic Helmholtz decomposition that directly deals with the accumulated scalar fields:

$$\nabla \cdot \nabla_{\mathbf{T}_t}\phi_t = \nabla \cdot \left[\delta\mathbf{u}_t + \nabla_{\mathbf{T}_{t-1}}\phi_{t-1}\right], \tag{10}$$

by adding the $\mathbf{T}_t$-irrotational part of the vector field $\nabla_{\mathbf{T}_{t-1}}\phi_{t-1}$ to the $\mathbf{T}_t$-irrotational decomposition of $\delta\mathbf{u}_t$. The resulting divergence-free vector field is then:

$$\mathbf{u}'_t = \mathbf{u}'_{t-1} + \left[\delta \mathbf{u}_t + \nabla_{\mathbf{T}_{t-1}} \phi_{t-1} - \nabla_{\mathbf{T}_t} \phi_t\right]. \tag{11}$$

Indeed, the vector field $\nabla_{\mathbf{T}_{t-1}} \phi_{t-1}$ is not necessarily $\mathbf{T}_t$-irrotational. Equation 10 provides the $\mathbf{T}_t$-irrotational vector field $\nabla_{\mathbf{T}_t} \phi_t$ which is the sum of the $\mathbf{T}_t$-irrotational parts of $\delta \mathbf{u}_t$ and $\nabla_{\mathbf{T}_{t-1}} \phi_{t-1}$ vector fields. Also, the resulting accumulation scalar field ϕ_t is the sum of $\delta \phi_t$, which corresponds to the decomposition of $\delta \mathbf{u}_t$, to the previous accumulation ϕ_{t-1} conformed to $\mathbf{T}_t$. Analogously, Eq. 11 provides the divergence-free vector field $\mathbf{u}'_t$ which is the sum of the solenoidal parts of both $\mathbf{u}_t$ and $\nabla_{\mathbf{T}_{t-1}} \phi_{t-1}$ vector fields. As a consequence, the effect of every arbitrary vector field $\delta \mathbf{u}_t$ added in the sequence is preserved either in the last divergence-free vector field $\mathbf{u}'_n$ or in the last $\mathbf{T}_n$-irrotational vector field $\nabla_{\mathbf{T}_n} \phi_n$.

Equations 10 and 11 can be adapted to solve the anisotropic pressure segregation step in the problem of fluid simulation, as shown in the next section.

3.3 Tensor X-IVAS: X-IVAS with Tensor-Based Pressure Segregation

In this section, we present our numerical model, beginning with our advection scheme. At this stage, the explicit information of particle position and velocity is integrated in time. The description of the semi-implicit advection model presented in [7,9] is as follows:

$$\begin{cases} \mathbf{x}^{n+t} = \mathbf{x}^n + \int_n^{n+t} \mathbf{U}^n (\mathbf{x}^\tau) \, d\tau, \\ \mathbf{U}_p^{n+t} = \mathbf{U}_p^n + \frac{1}{\rho} \int_n^{n+1} \mathbf{A}^n (\mathbf{x}^t) + \mathbf{F}^n (\mathbf{x}^t) \, dt. \end{cases} \tag{12}$$

We propose to expand the n-th acceleration field term $\mathbf{A}^n$ as:

$$\mathbf{A}^n (\mathbf{x}^t) = \mu \nabla \cdot \left[\mathbf{T}^n \nabla \mathbf{U}^n (\mathbf{x}^t)\right] + \delta \sigma (\mathbf{x}^t) - \mathbf{T}^n \nabla \mathrm{P}^n (\mathbf{x}^t) - \delta \mathrm{P} (\mathbf{x}^t),$$

where $\delta \sigma$ and $\delta \mathrm{P}$ are the implicit viscosity and pressure terms, respectively. Both of these terms require careful treatment to ensure a fully explicit model. The equations governing these terms are as follows:

$$\delta \sigma (\mathbf{x}^t) = \mu \nabla \cdot \mathbf{T}^t \nabla \left(\mathbf{U}^t (\mathbf{x}^t) - \mathbf{U}^n (\mathbf{x}^t)\right),$$

and

$$\delta \mathrm{P} (\mathbf{x}^t) = \mathbf{T}^t \nabla \mathrm{P}^t (\mathbf{x}^t) - \mathbf{T}^n \nabla \mathrm{P}^n (\mathbf{x}^t).$$

We plug the implicit terms out of the integration scheme and solve them separately. Once discretized, Eq. 12 is numerically integrated. In our work, we employ the explicit three-stage third-order Runge-Kutta time integration scheme. This scheme is denoted as:

$$\begin{cases} \mathbf{k}_1 = f (\mathbf{q}_n), \\ \mathbf{k}_2 = f \left(\mathbf{q}_n + \frac{1}{2} \Delta t \mathbf{q}_1\right), \\ \mathbf{k}_3 = f \left(\mathbf{q}_n + \frac{3}{4} \Delta t \mathbf{q}_2\right), \\ \mathbf{q}_{n+1} = \mathbf{q}_n + \frac{2}{9} (\Delta t \mathbf{k}_1) + \frac{3}{9} (\Delta t \mathbf{k}_2) + \frac{4}{9} (\Delta t \mathbf{k}_3). \end{cases} \tag{13}$$

where Δt is the simulation time-step. Here, $f(\mathbf{q})$ represents the derivative of $\mathbf{q}$ concerning time, and $\mathbf{q}$ denotes a vector term as position and velocity. The time integration of the implicit terms is described by the following equation:

$$\int_n^{n+1} \left[\delta\sigma\left(\mathbf{x}^t\right) - \delta P\left(\mathbf{x}^t\right)\right] dt \approx \frac{\Delta t}{\theta} \left[\delta\sigma\left(\mathbf{x}^{n+1}\right) - \delta P\left(\mathbf{x}^{n+1}\right)\right],$$

where θ is a scalar that defines the integration scheme that will be used. If $\theta = 1$, the integration scheme is Forward Euler. If $\theta = 2$, the integration is a Backward Euler. In this work, we use a first-order approximation, $\theta = 1$. Therefore, the implicit term delta will consider only the ending point of the integration streamline [1].

The implicit terms with the first-order integration scheme will be expressed by the following equations:

$$\delta\sigma\left(\mathbf{x}^{n+1}\right) = \mu\nabla \cdot \left[\mathbf{T}^{n+1}\nabla\mathbf{U}_p^{n+1} - \mathbf{T}^n\nabla\mathbf{U}^n\left(\mathbf{x}^{n+1}\right)\right],$$

and

$$\delta P\left(\mathbf{x}^{n+1}\right) = \mathbf{T}^{n+1}\nabla P_p^{n+1} - \mathbf{T}^n\nabla P^n\left(\mathbf{x}^{n+1}\right). \tag{14}$$

These terms are solved separately and will be referred to as separate terms. The new velocity integration model will be:

$$\mathbf{U}_p^{n+1} = \mathbf{U}^n\left(\mathbf{x}^{n+1}\right) + \hat{\hat{\mathbf{A}}}^n\left(\mathbf{x}^{n+1}\right) + \frac{1}{\rho}\int_n^{n+1} \hat{\mathbf{A}}^n\left(\mathbf{x}^{n+1}\right) dt, \tag{15}$$

where $\hat{\hat{\mathbf{A}}}$ and $\hat{\mathbf{A}}$ are the new terms for the implicit and explicit part of the acceleration, respectively. The acceleration implicit part is:

$$\hat{\hat{\mathbf{A}}}^n\left(\mathbf{x}^{n+1}\right) = \frac{\Delta t}{\rho}\left[\delta\sigma\left(\mathbf{x}^{n+1}\right) - \delta P\left(\mathbf{x}^{n+1}\right)\right],$$

and the explicit part is:

$$\hat{\mathbf{A}}^n\left(\mathbf{x}^{n+1}\right) = \mu\nabla \cdot \left[\mathbf{T}^n\nabla\mathbf{U}^n\left(\mathbf{x}^{n+1}\right)\right] - \mathbf{T}^n\nabla P^n\left(\mathbf{x}^{n+1}\right) + \mathbf{F}^n\left(\mathbf{x}^{n+1}\right). \tag{16}$$

The velocity integration of Eq. 15 is divided into three steps. This division is required to solve the implicit viscosity and pressure terms independently. The first step predicts velocity by integrating the explicit acceleration term. In this step, the Runge-Kutta time integration scheme described by Eq. 13 is used. This first velocity approximation is denoted as:

$$\hat{\mathbf{U}}_p^{n+1} = \mathbf{U}^n\left(\mathbf{x}^{n+1}\right) + \frac{1}{\rho}\int_n^{n+1} \hat{\mathbf{A}}^n\left(\mathbf{x}^{n+1}\right) dt, \tag{17}$$

where $\hat{\mathbf{U}}^{n+1}$ is the first velocity approximation term referred to as "advected velocity". The second step will account for the effects of viscosity over the first velocity approximation. At this step, we obtain a second velocity approximation as:

$$
\begin{cases}
\left[\rho - \frac{\Delta t}{\theta}\left(\nabla \cdot \mu \mathbf{T}^{n+1}\nabla\right)\right]\delta\sigma_p^{n+1} = \rho\left[\hat{\mathbf{U}}_p^{n+1} - \mathbf{U}^n\left(\mathbf{x}^{n+1}\right)\right], \\
\hat{\mathbf{U}}_p^{n+1} = \hat{\mathbf{U}}_p^{n+1} + \delta\sigma_p^{n+1},
\end{cases}
\tag{18}
$$

where $\hat{\mathbf{U}}$ is the viscosity-velocity prediction term.

Finally, the divergence-free velocity field will be obtained in the third step using the pressure correction method:

$$
\mathbf{U}_p^{n+1} = \hat{\mathbf{U}}_p^{n+1} - \frac{1}{\rho}\frac{\Delta t}{\theta}\delta\mathrm{P}\left(\mathbf{x}^{n+1}\right).
\tag{19}
$$

Applying the divergence operator at both sides of Eq. 19, and considering the divergence-free restriction. The following **T**-Poisson equation is obtained:

$$
\frac{\Delta t}{\theta}\frac{1}{\rho}\nabla \cdot \delta\mathrm{P}\left(\mathbf{x}^{n+1}\right) = \nabla \cdot \hat{\mathbf{U}}_p^{n+1}.
\tag{20}
$$

Expanding this **T**-Poisson equation with Eq. 14, we have:

$$
\nabla \cdot \left[\mathbf{T}^{n+1}\nabla\mathrm{P}_p^{n+1}\right] = \nabla \cdot \left[\frac{\theta\rho}{\Delta t}\hat{\mathbf{U}}_p^{n+1} + \mathbf{T}^n\nabla\mathrm{P}^n\left(\mathbf{x}^{n+1}\right)\right],
\tag{21}
$$

as proposed in Eq. 10. We were only able to achieve this using the contribution presented in Sect. 3.2. Finally, the divergence-free velocity field is obtained as:

$$
\begin{cases}
\mathbf{U}_p^{n+1} = \hat{\mathbf{U}}_p^{n+1} + \frac{1}{\rho}\frac{\Delta t}{\theta}\left[\mathbf{T}^n\nabla\mathrm{P}^n\left(\mathbf{x}^{n+1}\right) - \mathbf{T}^{n+1}\nabla\mathrm{P}_p^{n+1}\right], \\
\nabla \cdot \mathbf{U}^{n+1} = 0.
\end{cases}
\tag{22}
$$

as proposed in Eq. 11. The accumulation of pressure within the solution of the Poisson equation is an important aspect, as discussed in Sect. 3.2. Indeed, Eqs. 21 and 22 convert kinetic energy into kinetic pressure and vice versa. After each iteration: 1) the pressure gradient field $\mathbf{T}^{n+1}\nabla\mathrm{P}^{n+1}$ is always $\mathbf{T}^{n+1}$-irrotational; 2) the divergence-free velocity field $\mathbf{U}_p^{n+1}$ is **I**-solenoidal with the influence of $\mathbf{T}^{n+1}$ that modulated both the incremental velocity vector field $\hat{\mathbf{U}}_p^{n+1}$ and the previous accumulated pressure $\mathbf{T}^n\nabla\mathrm{P}^n\left(\mathbf{x}^{n+1}\right)$.

3.4   Boundary Conditions

In this work, special attention is given to two types of boundaries: the free-surface boundary and the solid wall boundary. The enforcement of boundary conditions is achieved within the framework of the MAC grid, similar to a fully Eulerian solver. In our case, the boundaries occur at the faces and edges of each grid cell. The boundary conditions are enforced following the advection step and before the projection step. This adjustment is applied to the RHS of Eq. 21. It affects the velocity divergence that is taken into account during the projection step, modifying the linear system to solve the **T**-Poisson equation.

Free-Surface Boundary: Since we are simulating a single-phase fluid, the treatment of the boundary is relatively straightforward. In this work, a Dirichlet boundary condition is employed at this interface, setting both the pressure and pressure gradient fields to zero.

Solid Phase Boundary: Following the approach outlined in [12], the solid phase boundary condition is applied when a cell is classified as fluid and has at least two neighboring cells that are solid. We use the no-slip condition [1], where the fluid velocity on the face or edge of the grid cell forming an interface is set to the solid velocity in the interface's normal direction.

In addition to the RHS of Eq. (21), the no-slip condition must also be enforced on the pressure gradient and acceleration fields. This reinforcement takes place after the projection step and has a direct impact on the particle advection step.

3.5   Implementation

In this section, we present the two core aspects to implement the solution for our proposed method: the particle velocity update scheme and the extended MAC Grid which is used to represent the domain.

Implementation on an Extended MAC Grid: Our Tensor X-IVAS method is discretized on an extended 3D staggered MAC grid, which was proposed by [12]. It provides a higher level of accuracy for solving the anisotropic $\mathbf{T}$-Poisson (Eq. 1) problem, coping well with tensors with eigensystem not aligned with the main axes. In this version, the vector quantities are stored in the faces and the edges of each voxel cell. The scalar and tensor quantities are stored at the cell centers. Tensor quantities are interpolated to the faces and edges in the extended gradient operator needed to solve the $\mathbf{T}$-Poisson problem (Eq. 1).

Particle Velocity Update: The particle velocity update scheme combines our Tensor X-IVAS method with the FLIP updating scheme as follows:

$$\mathbf{u}^{n+1} = \mathbf{u}_p^{n+1} + (1 - \alpha) \left(\hat{\mathbf{u}}^{n+1} - \tilde{\hat{\mathbf{u}}}_p^{n+1} \right), \tag{23}$$

where $\mathbf{u}_p^{n+1}$ is the interpolated divergence-free velocity obtained from the projection in step 9. The $\hat{\mathbf{u}}^{n+1}$ term is the first particle velocity approximation obtained from step 2. $\tilde{\hat{\mathbf{u}}}_p^{n+1}$ is the particle velocity approximation before the projection step, without no-slip condition. The α term is a scalar parameter that can assume a value in the interval of $\alpha \in [0, 1]$. The particle velocity update will change as α changes. If $\alpha = 1$, the velocity update will be a PIC update scheme. If $\alpha < 1$, the new update term increments the particle velocity. This results in an advection with even numerical diffusion.

4   Experiments with Time-Dependent Tensor Fields

In this section, we present qualitative experimental results generated by the proposed method. All tensor fields considered for the following experiments vary in time.

The fluid density ρ, the time step Δt, and the cell width Δx remained constant throughout all experiments. They were assigned values of $\rho = 1$ kg/m^3, $\Delta t = 1/60$ s, and $\Delta x = 1$ m, respectively. Gravity exerted a force with a magnitude of 10 m/s^2 in the negative z-axis direction, except in Sect. 4.2, where gravity was directed towards the center of the domain. Although our method is capable of modulating both viscosity and pressure terms, to evaluate the impact of pressure modulation on fluid flow, the viscosity was set to zero. This avoids the interference of non-null viscosity in the analysis of our method's ability to anisotropically modulate and deviate the fluid flow pressure terms.

Our domain space was discretized into a grid with a resolution of $60 \times 60 \times 60$ cells. An additional layer of cells, labeled as solids, surrounded the domain space. The no-slip condition was applied in all experiments, as discussed in Sect. 3.4. Without loss of generalization, stationary solid walls were considered throughout all simulations. More detailed descriptions and specific setups of each experiment are provided in the corresponding sections.

In our experiments, the range of colors shows the pressure magnitude and goes from the lowest values being represented as dark blue colors and the highest ones as bright red. These values range from -100 (Pa) to 100 (Pa) The values outside this interval are clamped and, consequently, dark blue and bright red particles may have values arbitrarily beyond it.

The experiments were performed on an Intel Xeon E5-4607 @ 2.20 GHz processor with 32 GB RAM DDR3.

4.1   Simulation with Axis-Aligned Planar Tensors

The purpose of this experiment is to illustrate the impact of abruptly modifying the tensor field configuration on pressure relief. This modification allows us to redirect the fluid flow in specific directions given by the tensor fields. All tensors eigenvectors are axis-aligned with $\mathbf{e}_1$ and $\mathbf{e}_2$ aligned with the xy-axis (planar tensor).

We provide two simulations with distinct values for the α term in Eq. 23. The first simulation sets the α term to 1, whereas the second simulation sets it to 0.15. We intend to highlight the influence of the proposed update velocity equation on the simulation of fluid flow and its numerical dissipation.

In each simulation, 12 planar tensor layers are positioned at the bottom of our domain ($k \in [1, 12]$). These layers restrict pressure exchange to the xy-plane. We set a λ_3 eigenvalue of 10^{-3} to the planar tensors, decreasing pressure exchange in the z direction by a factor of 10. Also, the planar tensor layers have "holes" filled with isotropic tensors. Throughout the simulation, we present three variations of the tensor field configuration, each occurring every 200 iterations. Initially, the planar layers have a single central hole, allowing the fluid to exchange pressure

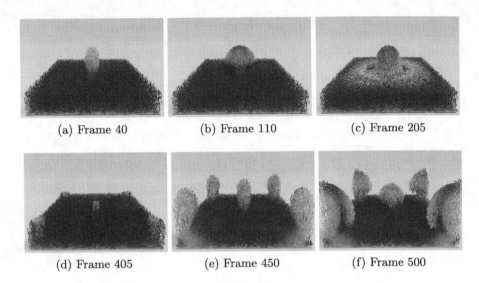

(a) Frame 40   (b) Frame 110   (c) Frame 205

(d) Frame 405   (e) Frame 450   (f) Frame 500

Fig. 1. Geyser simulation with $\alpha = 1$.

in the z-axis through it. After 200 iterations, the isotropic tensors on the central hole are changed to planar tensors, limiting again the pressure exchange to the xy-plane. Finally, in the last 200 iterations, the planar layers contain five holes: one at its center and four at each corner.

The experiment utilizes a quiescent pool of fluid located at the bottom of the domain ($k \in [1, 11]$). The entire bottom of the domain is occupied by this fluid pool, with an initial quantity of 20 particles per voxel. With the pool having dimensions of $60 \times 60 \times 11$ voxels, there is a total of $792,000$ particles.

In this experiment, we aim to observe the impact of the pressure relief scheme and particle velocity update variations on the velocity of fluid flow. Figures 1 and 2 depict arrows indicating the particle velocity vectors. These arrows are color-coded based on the magnitude of the velocity, ranging from 0 m/s to 30 m/s. Dark blue colors represent lower values, while bright reddish colors represent higher values.

When comparing Figs. 1 and 2, the geyser altitudes and arrow colors demonstrate the impact of the velocity update and the tensor field variation in time. The arrow colors of the fluid in Fig. 2 appear more reddish, indicating that the pressure relief in the experiment with 0.15 yields a higher acceleration compared to the $\alpha = 1$ simulation. Consequently, the simulation with $\alpha = 1$ (Fig. 1) reaches a significantly lower altitude compared to the $\alpha = 0.15$ simulation. This is evident by comparing both simulations on frames 110 and 500. Frames 205 and 405 show how the fluid behaves slightly after the tensor field variation. These frames showcase the rapid flow redirection towards the pressure relief points. An intriguing aspect of the $\alpha = 0.15$ simulation is that a single-hole geyser reaches a higher altitude than the one with five holes. With multiple holes, the fluid's

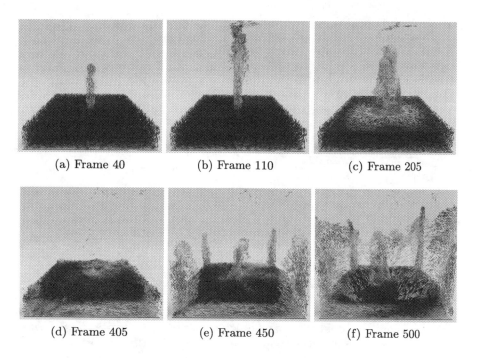

(a) Frame 40   (b) Frame 110   (c) Frame 205

(d) Frame 405   (e) Frame 450   (f) Frame 500

Fig. 2. Geyser simulation with $\alpha = 0.15$.

kinetic energy is distributed, limiting the height it can reach when compared to a geyser with a single hole. This is less evident with $\alpha = 1$ (Fig. 1).

The graphs in Fig. 3 display the integration of the Bernoulli equation throughout the simulation. They are only for visualization purposes since our method does not conserve mass and momentum. The Bernoulli equation states that the sum of the kinetic, potential, and pressure energy per unit mass must remain constant along a streamline for the system to conserve energy. In Fig. 3a, the pressure energy is three orders of magnitude higher than the other energies from iteration 400 when the central hole is closed. This is due to the $\lambda_3 = 10^{-3}$ eigenvalue which compresses the fluid in z direction. As expected, the kinetic energy (green curve in Fig. 3b) exhibits a substantial increase after adding holes in the domain (steps 0 and 800) due to pressure relief. It is followed by a decline and then a rise, when the ejected fluid gets back to the bottom. Furthermore, both gravitational potential and kinetic energy experience an uptick when five holes appear in the domain (step 800) because a greater volume of fluid is put in motion.

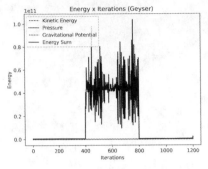
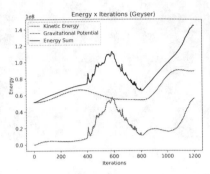

(a) Bernoulli equation integration   (b) Integration without pressure

Fig. 3. Bernoulli Equation Integration for the geyser simulation in Fig. 2. (Color figure online)

4.2   Simulation with the Strain-Rate Tensors

This subsection proposes a continuous adjustment to the tensor field across the entire fluid simulation. The primary objective is to demonstrate the utilization of the tensor field to influence the pressure of fluid flow throughout each step of the simulation. Our focus lies in ensuring that the fluid alleviates its pressure in the direction of deformation while limiting pressure exchange in other directions.

In this experiment, the strain-rate tensor is used to design the tensor field for this experiment. Our method, outlined in Sect. 3.2, mandates that our tensor must be positive-definite. This limitation can be resolved by integrating the strain-rate tensor in time, generating:

$$\mathbf{T} = \sum_{i=1}^{M} e^{\gamma(\Delta t \lambda_i)} \mathbf{e}_i \mathbf{e}_i^{\mathrm{T}}, \tag{24}$$

where λ_i and $\mathbf{e}_i$ are the i-th eigenvalues and eigenvectors of the strain-rate tensor, respectively. The scalar factor parameter, denoted as γ, is incorporated into the equation to control the tensor influence on each simulation. Analyzing the behavior of the aforementioned equation, a positive-definite tensor is consistently generated. If $\lambda_i < 0$, the resulting tensor indicates fluid compression along the corresponding axis. If $\lambda_i = 0$, the tensor will have no impact on the pressure exchange along the referenced axis. Conversely, if the i-th eigenvalue surpasses 1, the tensor will enhance pressure relief along the i-th axis.

We present two variations of the proposed experiment. The first simulation serves as a reference, where the standard X-IVAS method is employed. This first simulation is denoted over Fig. 4a. Subsequently, another simulation is conducted with a strain rate tensor with $\gamma = 5$ as we want to emphasize the tensor's impact on the fluid flow. This simulation is presented in Fig. 4b.

Frame 36   Frame 180   Frame 350

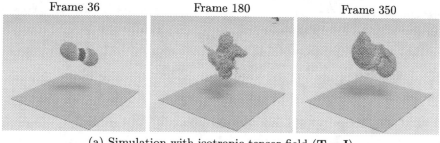

(a) Simulation with isotropic tensor field ($\mathbf{T} = \mathbf{I}$)

Frame 36   Frame 180   Frame 350

(b) Using anisotropic tensor fields from strain rate tensors with $\gamma = 5$ (Eq. 24)

Fig. 4. Simulating two colliding spheres with radial gravitational force.

The velocity update term, denoted as α, has a fixed value of 0.15. Additionally, the gravity force is directed towards the center of the simulation domain, with a magnitude of 10 m/s^2.

The experiment consists of two diagonally opposed spheres of fluid. Each sphere has a radius of 6 voxels, and an initial particle density of 100 particles per voxel. Thus, the total number of particles in this experiment is calculated as $2 \times (4\pi/3) \times 6^3 \times 100 = 180,956$ particles. Both spheres possess identical initial velocity vectors but in opposing directions, represented as $\mathbf{u}_0 = [5, 0, 5]$ and $\mathbf{u}_1 = [-5, 0, -5]$.

Upon comparing the frames of the reference simulation depicted in Fig. 4a with the experiment with $\gamma = 5$ depicted in Fig. 4b the influence of the strain-rate tensors is evident. Notable distinctions can be observed, such as the collision portrayed in frame 72 and the formation of a fluid sphere at the center of the domain. Additionally, the color of the fluid following the collision illustrates a lower-pressure configuration. As the fluid splashes, it generates a sparser layer of fluid, leading to a broader area of low pressure. This sparsity arises from the generation of high pressure during the sphere collision. The motion toward the opposing collision direction is accentuated by the strong influence of the tensor field ($\gamma = 5$), propelling the fluid flow in the direction of deformation. Furthermore, radial gravitational forces pull the fluid towards the domain's center, which is intensified by the tensor field that enhances the fluid pressure exchange in this

deforming direction. Consequently, a dense fluid sphere forms, distinguishing it
from the other two simulations.

Table 1. Summary of experiments setup and simulation times

Experiment	Parameter			Simulation	
	# particles	Tensor	α	Sec./frame	Total time
Geysers 1 (Fig. 1)	792,000	Varying aligned planar	1.0	20.40	06:47:55
Geysers 2 (Fig. 2)	792,000	Varying aligned planar	0.15	20.69	06:53:52
Colliding Spheres (Fig. 4a)	180,956	Strain	0.15	1.89	00:37:52
Colliding Spheres $\gamma = 5$ (Fig. 4b)	180,956	Strain	0.15	6.70	02:13:58

4.3   Discussion

The core parameters of our experiments are presented in Table 1. It includes
the computational time cost for each experiment. It increases significantly when
dealing with time-varying tensor fields. The main factor is the high-cost computation of the Laplacian mask proposed by [12]. Nevertheless, a constant tensor
field throughout the simulation keeps the time cost manageable.

Throughout all experiments, and despite introducing a whole new computational complexity on the computation of the tensor field, our method yields very
low average magnitude error around 10^{-11} for all divergence-free vector fields.
This is possible by the discretization proposed by [12] on an extended MAC grid.
For the sake of repeatability, our source code and all videos of experiments are
available in www.gcg.ufjf.br/files/tensor-xivas.

The proposed method yielded appealing results across our experiments.
While we maintained fixed grid resolution and time step, we observed that plausible results can be generated even with higher time steps and lower resolutions.
Although we presented specific tensor field configurations and showcased their
impact on fluid flow, this work does not encompass an exhaustive enumeration
of all potential applications and effects of the proposed method.

The utilization of planar tensors made a significant contribution to artifi-
cially increasing the pressure over the fluid volume, as depicted in Sect. 4.1. The
utilization of linear tensor fields is valuable when the pressure exchange needs
to occur in specific directions, as shown in Sect. 4.2. Linear tensors appear frequently in the strain tensor simulation with $\gamma = 5$, during the fluid collision. As
a consequence, the deformations appeared in specific directions thereafter.

Our method maintains stability over higher time steps, as suggested by the
default X-IVAS method presented in the work of [7]. As expected, when the
FLIP update is fully used with $\alpha \approx 0$, the simulation can present instabilities.
This is a well-known behavior, that happens when the velocity field does not
necessarily have divergence-free.

The tensor field modulation over the pressure and viscous terms in our model
does not preserve momentum, as is seen in Sect. 4.1. Thus, tensor fields can
increase and decrease local velocities and consequently can represent dynamic

medium attributes. A deeper analysis of the moment and mass conservation is a future work to improve our propositions.

5 Conclusion

We present a mathematical and computational model that deals with anisotropic incompressible fluid transport. The model is based on second-order positive-definite tensor fields that can change over time. We propose a new numerical method for anisotropic advection based on the X-IVAS method. This solution takes into account the influence of tensors on viscous forces and accumulated pressure gradient.

We also propose a novel computational method for tensor-based anisotropic decomposition (Eq. 21). It is designed to accumulate and adjust pressure as the tensor field evolves in time (Sect. 3.2). Unlike previous literature works [7–9,11], our model was discretized using the extended MAC grid proposed by [12]. However, our method can be implemented on various discretization schemes, such as PFEM. Furthermore, we devised a velocity update scheme that guarantees that it remains divergence-free as the tensor field varies in time (Eq. 22).

In Sect. 4, we explored different parameter and tensor field variations for comparison purposes. Our results show that our method succeeds in anisotropic modulation of the pressure term. In future works, we aim to incorporate tensor influence into our advection scheme, without compromising numerical accuracy and stability. Designing tensor fields to modulate and deviate fluid dynamics is still a challenge. Its inherent multivariate effect locally in space is not intuitive. Furthermore, in our work, we introduce one more degree of freedom by allowing the tensor field to change in time. Consequently, mathematical models are needed to design meaningful tensor fields, application-based tensor fields, and perhaps families of tensor fields with valuable differential properties.

As discussed in Sect. 4.3, our anisotropic pressure and viscous term modulation do not preserve momentum. Therefore, future works will delve deeper into the analysis of momentum and mass conservation. Also, flow simulations with isotropic methods will be included in future works for comparison purposes.

References

1. Bridson, R.: Fluid simulation for computer graphics. CRC press (2015)
2. Codina, R., Badia, S.: On some pressure segregation methods of fractional-step type for the finite element approximation of incompressible flow problems. Comput. Methods Appl. Mech. Eng. **195**(23), 2900–2918 (2006)
3. Codina, R., Soto, O.: Approximation of the incompressible Navier-stokes equations using orthogonal subscale stabilization and pressure segregation on anisotropic finite element meshes. Comput. Methods Appl. Mech. Eng. **193**(15), 1403–1419 (2004)
4. Dassios, G., Lindell, I.V.: Uniqueness and reconstruction for the anisotropic Helmholtz decomposition. J. Phys. A: Math. Gen. **35**(24), 5139 (2002)

5. Gao, H., Sun, L., Wang, J.X.: Phygeonet: physics-informed geometry-adaptive convolutional neural networks for solving parameterized steady-state pdes on irregular domain. J. Comput. Phys. **428**, 110079 (2021)
6. Gresho, P.M.: On the theory of semi-implicit projection methods for viscous incompressible flow and its implementation via a finite element method that also introduces a nearly consistent mass matrix. part 1: Theory. Int. J. Num. Methods Fluids **11**(5), 587–620 (1990)
7. Idelsohn, S., Nigro, N., Limache, A., Oñate, E.: Large time-step explicit integration method for solving problems with dominant convection. Comput. Methods Appl. Mech. Eng. **217**, 168–185 (2012)
8. Idelsohn, S.R., Marti, J., Becker, P., Oñate, E.: Analysis of multifluid flows with large time steps using the particle finite element method. Int. J. Numer. Meth. Fluids **75**(9), 621–644 (2014)
9. Idelsohn, S.R., Nigro, N.M., Gimenez, J.M., Rossi, R., Marti, J.M.: A fast and accurate method to solve the incompressible Navier-stokes equations. Engineering Computations (2013)
10. Marston, J., Tobias, S.: Recent developments in theories of inhomogeneous and anisotropic turbulence. Annu. Rev. Fluid Mech. **55**, 351–375 (2023)
11. Nadukandi, P., Servan-Camas, B., Becker, P.A., García-Espinosa, J.: Seakeeping with the semi-Lagrangian particle finite element method. Comput. Particle Mech. **4**, 321–329 (2017)
12. Parreiras, E.A.: Métodos Particle-in-Cell para Simulação de Fluidos Anisotrópico. Master's thesis, Universidade Federal de Juiz de Fora, Juiz de Fora, MG (fev 2022)
13. Parreiras, E.A., Vieira, M.B., Machado, A.G., Renhe, M.C., Giraldi, G.A.: A particle-in-cell method for anisotropic fluid simulation. Comput. Graph. **102**, 220–232 (2022)
14. Perot, J.B.: An analysis of the fractional step method. J. Comput. Phys. **108**(1), 51–58 (1993)
15. Raissi, M., Perdikaris, P., Karniadakis, G.E.: Physics-informed neural networks: a deep learning framework for solving forward and inverse problems involving nonlinear partial differential equations. J. Comput. Phys. **378**, 686–707 (2019)
16. Renhe, M.C., Vieira, M.B., Esperança, C.: A stable tensor-based method for controlled fluid simulations. Appl. Math. Comput. **343**, 195–213 (2019)
17. Spurk, J., Aksel, N.: Fluid mechanics. Springer Science and Business Media (2007)
18. Stam, J.: Stable fluids. In: Proceedings of the 26th Annual Conference on Computer Graphics and Interactive Techniques, pp. 121–128 (1999)
19. Vieira, M.B., Giraldi, G.A., Ribeiro, A.C.A., Renhe, M.C., Esperança, C.: Anisotropic Hdelmholtz decomposition for controlled fluid simulation. Appl. Math. Comput. **411**, 126501 (2021)

Wave Source Localization Among Multiple Knife-Edges

Mikhail S. Lytaev$^{(\boxtimes)}$ (iD)

St. Petersburg Federal Research Center of the Russian Academy of Sciences,
14-th Linia, V.I., No. 39, Saint Petersburg 199178, Russia
mikelytaev@gmail.com

Abstract. The problem of localizing a monochromatic source in a two-dimensional unbounded environment is considered. The environment contains arbitrarily positioned thin vertical obstacles (knife-edges), leading to diffraction effects and multiple reflections. The problem is formulated using the method of adjoint equations. Two most commonly used types of the matched field processing (MFP) method are analyzed: Bartlett and minimum variance (MV). Numerical experiments are conducted for various arrangements of obstacles and receivers. It is shown that the MFP method can be successfully used for localizing radiation sources under conditions of multiple reflections.

Keywords: inverse problem · knife-edge diffraction · matched field processing · wave propagation · ill-posed problem · adjoint equation

1 Introduction

The search and localization of radiation sources based on measurement data belong to the class of inverse problems [5]. From a mathematical point of view, their complexity lies in their ill-posedness (in the sense of Hadamard) [8]. Commonly, it manifests in insufficient measurement data for the unambiguous determination of the source's location - there may be multiple possible solutions. The most obvious way to improve accuracy is by increasing the number and spatial coverage of measurements, although this comes with equally obvious practical difficulties. A significant reduction in uncertainty and hence an increase in localization accuracy can be achieved by incorporating information about the signal propagation environment. This approach requires knowledge of propagation environment in each specific case, as well as complex mathematical models that simultaneously account for arbitrary environmental inhomogeneities and measurements.

Significant progress in this field has been achieved in computational hydroacoustics. Since the late 1980s, the matched field processing (MFP) method has been actively developed [2]. Typically, the MFP method is applied in shallow and deep water waveguides, considering the sound speed height and range profiles as well as the profile and physical properties of the seabed. The method imposes

O. Gervasi et al. (Eds.): ICCSA 2024, LNCS 14813, pp. 83–95, 2024.
https://doi.org/10.1007/978-3-031-64605-8_6

no restrictions on the relative placement of receivers, allowing it to be used for vertically and horizontally arranged arrays of hydrophones. There are extensions of this method for localizing multiple sources simultaneously [3,4]. The method can also be used for localizing moving sources [19]. Additionally, MFP has been successfully applied in seismology [14,18] and radar systems [7].

The aim of this study is to investigate the possibility of localization in conditions where diffraction and multiple reflections have a significant impact on the wave propagation. The study is based on a model environment with several vertically positioned thin impenetrable obstacles (so called knife-edges) [6,17]. This model is commonly used in radio physics to describe the radio wave propagation over complex terrain or in urban environments.

The paper is organized as follows. The next section presents the mathematical formulation of localizing a point source in a medium with multiple knife-edges. Section 3 proposes a general solution scheme based on the method of adjoint equations and demonstrates that the existing MFP-based localization methods are its consequence. Section 4 describes the solution scheme for the direct problem of computing the field from a known source, which is required for solving the inverse problem. Analysis of the results of numerical modeling is carried out in Sect. 5.

2   Problem Statement

The wave process is described by the two-dimensional Helmholtz equation, which we will write in operator form

$$A\psi = q,$$

where

$$A\psi = \frac{\partial^2 \psi}{\partial x^2} + \frac{\partial^2 \psi}{\partial z^2} + k^2 \left(1 + i\alpha\right)\psi,$$

α is a small parameter responsible for wave dissipation, k is the wavenumber, q is a point source of harmonic signals with an unknown amplitude Q at coordinates (x_s, z_s) that are need to be determined

$$q = Q\delta\left(x_s, z_s\right).$$

$\psi\left(x, z\right)$ is the spatial distribution of the complex field amplitude

$$\psi : \Omega \to \mathbb{C},$$

defined on half-plane

$$\Omega = \left\{(x, z) \,|\, x \in (-\infty, +\infty), z \in [0, +\infty)\right\}.$$

Dirichlet boundary condition is imposed at the lower boundary

$$\psi\left(x, 0\right) = 0, \ x \in (-\infty, +\infty).$$

There are M thin vertical impermeable obstacles, called "knife-edges". They are characterized by its distance x_i^e and height H_i^e. It is required that the Dirichlet boundary condition also be satisfied on the boundaries of the obstacles

$$\psi\left(x_i^e, z\right) = 0, \ z \in [0, H_i].$$

A set of N measurements is given: $\{x_i^m, z_i^m, v_i\}$, where $i = 1 \ldots N$. Here, x_i, z_i are the coordinates of the measurements, and $v_i \in \mathbb{C}$ represents the complex amplitude.

The schematic representation of the problem setup is shown in Fig. 1.

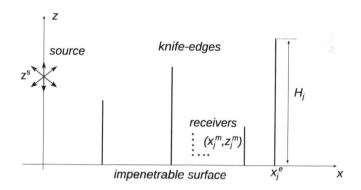

Fig. 1. Schematic description of the problem statement.

3 Matched Field Processing

For a mathematically rigorous derivation of the MFP method, we will utilize the method of adjoint equations [12], which is commonly employed in solving the inverse problems of various nature [13].

3.1 Adjoint Method Formulation

Consider a Hilbert space with a scalar product

$$(f, g) = \int_\Omega f\bar{g}$$

and adjoint operator [12] A^*, defined as follows

$$(Af, g) = (f, A^*g). \tag{1}$$

Suppose we have a measuring device that records a certain integral characteristic of the field, i.e.

$$J_p\left(\psi\right) = \int\limits_{\Omega} \psi\bar{p} = \left(\psi, p\right).$$

In the simplest case, $p = \delta\left(x_m, z_m\right)$, which corresponds to measuring the field with a point receiver at some point $\left(x_m, z_m\right)$.

Next we consider the following adjoint equation

$$A^*\varphi_p^* = p, \tag{2}$$

and substitute it into definition (1)

$$\left(A\psi, \varphi_p^*\right) = \left(\psi, A^*\varphi_p^*\right),$$

which gives us the following equalities

$$\left(q, \varphi_p^*\right) = \left(\psi, p\right) = J_p\left(\psi\right) = Q\bar{\varphi}_p^*\left(x^s, z^s\right). \tag{3}$$

By solving Eq. (3) with respect to $\left(x_s, z_s\right)$, one can estimate the location of the original source. In particular, for a point receiver, this equation takes the following form

$$J_p\left(\psi\right) = \psi\left(x_i^m, z_i^m\right) = v_i = Q\bar{\varphi}_p^*\left(x^s, z^s\right).$$

Naturally, for a single receiver, such an equation does not have a unique solution. Additionally, the amplitude of the source Q is usually unknown. Therefore, for a more reliable determination of the source location, several spatially separated point receivers are required. Furthermore, in a real situation, measurements contain noise and uncertainties.

The main difference between the various MFP methods lies in the way of comparing and matching the value of the conjugate field and measurements. Next, we will consider the two most commonly used MFP methods: Bartlett and minimum variance (MV) [2].

3.2   Bartlett MFP Processor

We first describe the simplest and most widely used method. Consider the following vectors, made up of the measurements and their corresponding solutions of the adjoint Eqs. (2)

$$\mathbf{v} = \left(v_1 \; v_2 \; ... \; v_N\right)^T,$$

$$\mathbf{g}\left(x, z\right) = \left(\bar{\varphi}^*_{\delta\left(x_1, z_1\right)}\left(x, z\right) \; \bar{\varphi}^*_{\delta\left(x_2, z_2\right)}\left(x, z\right) \; ... \; \bar{\varphi}^*_{\delta\left(x_N, z_N\right)}\left(x, z\right)\right)^T.$$

The problem of localizing the source is formalized as the least squares minimization

$$\arg \min_{(x,z)\in\Omega} \min_{Q\in\mathbb{C}} ||\mathbf{v} - Q\mathbf{g}||^2. \tag{4}$$

The minimization problem with respect to Q can be easily solved analytically [11]. Then, the problem (4) can be rewritten as follows

$$\arg \max_{(x,z)\in\Omega} \frac{|\mathbf{v}^H \mathbf{g}(x,z)|^2}{||\mathbf{g}(x,z)||^2}. \tag{5}$$

In such a formulation, the maximization problem is solved by simple enumeration of all possible variants. The complexity of its solution is $O(n_x n_z N)$, where n_x and n_z are the sizes of the computational grid along x and z respectively. If necessary, various optimization methods or dimensionality reduction techniques can be employed to accelerate this procedure [11].

For convenience, we rewrite (5) as follows

$$\arg \max_{(x,z)\in\Omega} B_{Bart}(x,z),$$

where function $B_{Bart}(x,z)$ is called "processor" or "ambiguity surface" and is defined as follows

$$B_{Bart}(x,z) = |\mathbf{v}^H \mathbf{w}(x,z)|^2 = \mathbf{w}^H(x,z) \mathbf{K}\mathbf{w}(x,z),$$

where

$$\mathbf{w}(x,z) = \frac{\mathbf{g}(x,z)}{||\mathbf{g}(x,z)||},$$

$$\mathbf{K} = \mathbf{v}\mathbf{v}^H.$$

3.3   Minimum Variance

The main idea of this modification is to minimize the value of the ambiguity surface at all points in space except where the source is actually located [9]. The result is the following processor

$$B_{MV}(x,z) = \left[\mathbf{w}^H(x,z) \mathbf{K}^{-1} \mathbf{w}(x,z)\right]^{-1},$$

for which it is also necessary to find the maximum to determine the source location.

4   Multiple Knife-Edge Diffraction

As we saw in the previous section, the solution to the inverse problem is based on solving the direct one. That is, to determine the radiation source location based on field measurements, a method is required to compute the field value for an arbitrary source at an arbitrary point in space.

For simplicity and without loss of generality, we assume that the point source is located at the coordinates $(0, z_m)$. Then, following [17], the solution can be expressed as follows

$$\psi(x,z) = \sqrt{\frac{2}{\pi}} \int\limits_0^{+\infty} \tilde{\psi}(x,p)\sin(pz)dz,$$

where

$$\tilde{\psi}(x,p) = -\frac{k^2}{\sqrt{2\pi}} \sum_{j=1}^{M} \tilde{G}(x,x_j,p)\varphi_j(p) + \sqrt{\frac{2}{\pi}}\sin(z_m p)\,\tilde{G}(x,0,p), \qquad (6)$$

$$\tilde{G}(x,x',p) = -\frac{1}{2\gamma(p)}e^{-\gamma(p)|x-x'|},$$

$$\gamma(p) = \sqrt{\frac{\sqrt{(p^2-k^2)^2+(k^2\alpha)^2}-(k^2-p^2)}{2}} - i\sqrt{\frac{\sqrt{(p^2-k^2)^2+(k^2\alpha)^2}+(k^2-p^2)}{2}}.$$

Functions $\varphi_j(p)$ satisfy the following system of integral equations

$$\begin{cases} \varphi_1(p) + \sum\limits_{j=1}^{M}\int\limits_{-\infty}^{+\infty} K_{1,j}(p,p')\varphi_j(p')dp' = g_1(p) \\ \varphi_2(p) + \sum\limits_{j=1}^{M}\int\limits_{-\infty}^{+\infty} K_{2,j}(p,p')\varphi_j(p')dp' = g_2(p) \\ \dots \\ \varphi_m(p) + \sum\limits_{j=1}^{M}\int\limits_{-\infty}^{+\infty} K_{m,j}(p,p')\varphi_j(p')dp' = g_m(p) \end{cases} \qquad (7)$$

with kernel

$$K_{i,j}(p,p') \approx -\frac{bhk^2}{2\pi}\frac{\sin\left((p-p')\,H_i^e\right)}{(p-p')\,\gamma(p')}e^{-\gamma(p')|x_i^e - x_j^e|},$$

and right-hand side

$$g_i(p) \approx -bh\frac{2}{\pi}\int\limits_{-\infty}^{+\infty}\frac{\sin\left((p-p')\,H_i^e\right)}{2\,(p-p')\,\gamma(p')}\sin(z_m p')\,e^{-\gamma(p')x_i^e}dp'.$$

b and h are parameters responsible for the permeability and thickness of the obstacles, respectively. Furthermore, we assume that $bh = 400$, choosing this value ensures the required level of impermeability and allows us to consider the obstacle as negligibly thin. It should be noted that this model does not allow b and h to approach infinity and zero, respectively, just as in nature there are no infinitely impermeable or infinitely thin obstacles.

In work [17], it is justified that the numerical solution of system (7) is the most efficient for the given problem. In fact, the essentially two-dimensional problem is reduced to a one-dimensional one. A rigorous justification of the correctness of such an approach and the derivation of system (7) are presented in works [15, 16].

The most closely related alternative is the two-way parabolic equation method [1]. It can account not only for knife-edges but also for other obstacles of arbitrary shape. However, there are issues with its theoretical justification and convergence speed [17]. Full-wave methods, such as the finite element method, require too much computational recourses even for very small integration domains. Ray methods cannot accurately account for diffraction and multiple reflections effects, which are significant in the considered problem.

5 Numerical Results and Discussion

This section presents the results of numerical modeling for various configurations of obstacles and receivers. The source in all examples is located at point $(0, 50)$ and emits a signal at a frequency of $300\,\mathrm{MHz}$ ($1\,\mathrm{m}$ wavelength). The modeling process for each example consists of the following steps:

1. Compute the two-dimensional field distribution from the source ψ using the method from the previous section. It is depicted on the left figure in each example.
2. Choose N space points (x_i^m, z_i^m) corresponding to the receiver locations. The field value at these points is used as the measurement $\psi(x_i^m, z_i^m) = v_i$, forming the vector $\mathbf{v}$.
3. Compute N two-dimensional fields $\bar{\varphi}^*{}_{\delta(x_i, z_i)}(x, z)$ using the method from the previous section and form the vector-valued function $\mathbf{g}(x, z)$.
4. Use $\mathbf{g}(x, z)$ and $\mathbf{v}$ to compute the ambiguity surface using the two methods: Bartlett (B_{Bart}) and MV (B_{MV}). Their two-dimensional distributions are respectively shown on the central and right figures.
5. Find the point at which the ambiguity surface takes the maximum value. It will be the source location.

In all examples below, white asterisks denote the source position, and black asterisks denote the receiver positions.

The modeling was performed using the PyWaveProp software library developed by the author [10].

5.1 Free Space

First, we consider the obstacle-free space. A vertical array of receivers is located at a distance of $900\,\mathrm{m}$ from the source. There are 25 point receivers, uniformly distributed at heights of 10–60 m with a 2-m interval. The results of the simulation are shown in Fig. 2. The ambiguity surface obtained by the Bartlett method provides a more "spread out" solution in space. However, the maximum coincides precisely with the location of the original source. The MV method provides a solution that practically eliminates uncertainty in determining the source, the maximum can only be seen with zoom. However, the determined maximum is 7 m away from the true position in distance and 0.4 m in height.

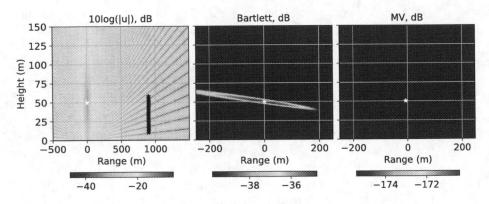

Fig. 2. Source localization in free space. Bartlett: (0, 50); MV: (-7, 50.4).

5.2   Source in Front of the Knife-Edge

Now we place a thin obstacle with a height of 70 m at a distance of 200 m behind the source. As seen in Fig. 3, the reflection from the obstacle did not hinder the determination of the source location. Moreover, the uncertainty in determining its location decreased for the Bartlett method. Both methods accurately determined the source location without errors. Apparently, it was facilitated by additional "information" contained in the reflected field.

5.3   Non Line of Sight

Now we move the obstacle in such a way that it ends up between the source and the array of receivers. So there is no direct line of sight between them. As seen in Fig. 4, the Bartlett method exhibits greater uncertainty in the area behind the obstacle. Nevertheless, it accurately determined the location of the source. However, the MV method, despite the absence of uncertainty, incorrectly detected the source location.

5.4   Two Knife-Edges

Next example is a scenario where the source and the receiver are located between two obstacles. Besides diffraction, the effects of multiple reflections between obstacles are significantly pronounced in this example. As seen in Fig. 5, even in these complex conditions, both methods generally correctly determine the position of the source.

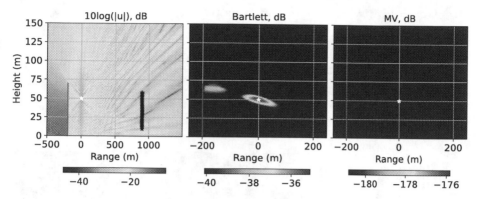

Fig. 3. Source localization in a presence of single knife-edge. Bartlett: (0, 50); MV: (0, 50).

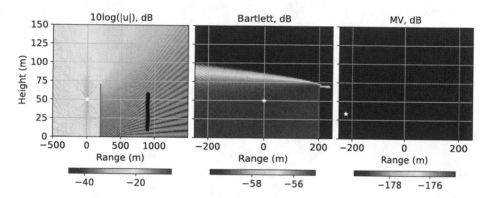

Fig. 4. Source localization in the absence of line of sight. Bartlett: (0, 50); MV: (−223, 33.2).

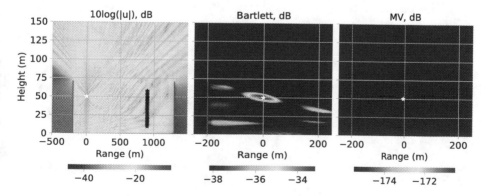

Fig. 5. Source localization between two knife-edges. Bartlett: (0, 50); MV: (−5, 50.4).

5.5   Horizontal Arrangement of Receivers

Next, we arrange the array of sources horizontally. 20 point receivers are positioned at distances ranging from 500 to 1000 m from the source at a height of 10 m. The results are shown in Fig. 6. The Bartlett method exhibits slightly greater uncertainty compared to the previous example. However, the position was detected correctly by both MFP processors.

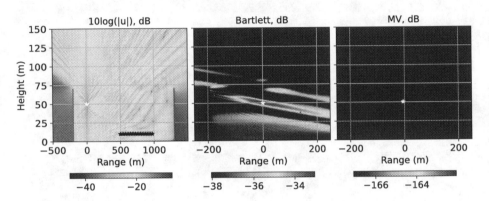

Fig. 6. Source localization using a horizontal array of receivers. Bartlett: (0, 50); MV: (−5, 50.6).

5.6   Multiple Knife-Edges

To demonstrate the capabilities of the method under consideration, we examine an environment with four obstacles. It is evident that the complexity of system (7) increases with the number of obstacles M. Nevertheless, the method easily allows for the consideration of 5–7 obstacles on a standard personal computer. If the size of the system exceeds the computer's memory capacity, its solving becomes practically impossible. The same problem arises within the finite element method, but for a significantly smaller number of obstacles and computational domain.

The results are shown in Fig. 7. As we can see, increasing the number of obstacles increases the uncertainty of the Bartlett method. However, the position was detected correctly. On the other hand, the error of the MV method amounted to 23 m in distance.

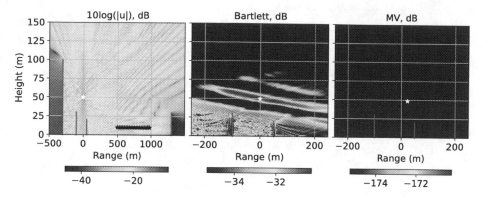

Fig. 7. Source localization among multiple obstacles. Bartlett: (0, 50); MV: (23, 48.6).

Summary results for all six examples are shown in Table 1. It is evident that the Bartlett method perfectly determined the source position in all cases. However, the MV method almost always yielded results with some degree of error.

Table 1. Summary table of the localization results.

Example	Number of obstacles	Line of sight	Bartlett	MV
1	0	yes	(0, 50)	(−7, 50.4)
2	1	yes	(0, 50)	(0, 50)
3	1	no	(0, 50)	(−223, 33.2)
4	2	yes	(0, 50)	(−5, 50.4)
5	2	yes	(0, 50)	(−5, 50.6)
6	4	yes	(0, 50)	(23, 48.6)

6   Conclusion

It is impossible to encompass all the variety of possible scenarios and configurations in one paper, but the software library PyWaveProp developed by the author [10] enables researchers to conduct computational experiments similar to those outlined above.

The main achievement of this work lies in demonstrating the capability of precise source localization simultaneously in conditions of interference, diffraction, and multiple reflections. These effects are encountered in signal propagation in densely built urban areas or complex underwater conditions. The most widely used Bartlett method demonstrated excellent results. The MV method obviously needs some improvements to be used in the multiple reflections scenarios.

This study focused only on a basic model scenario. The problem considered in this study for a monochromatic source can be easily generalized to the case of broadband sources. Further plans include addressing a more realistic scenario considering noise and other uncertainties in the environment. Additionally, the two-way parabolic equation is intended to be used for source detection among vertical inhomogeneities of arbitrary shape.

Acknowledgments. This study was supported by the Russian Science Foundation grant No. 23-71-01069.

References

1. Apaydin, G., Ozgun, O., Kuzuoglu, M., Sevgi, L.: A novel two-way finite-element parabolic equation groundwave propagation tool: tests with canonical structures and calibration. IEEE Trans. Geosci. Remote Sens. **49**(8), 2887–2899 (2011)
2. Baggeroer, A.B., Kuperman, W.A., Mikhalevsky, P.N.: An overview of matched field methods in ocean acoustics. IEEE J. Oceanic Eng. **18**(4), 401–424 (1993)
3. Collins, M.D., Fialkowski, L.T., Kuperman, W., Perkins, J.S.: The multivalued Bartlett processor and source tracking. J. Acoust. Soc. Am. **97**(1), 235–241 (1995)
4. Collins, M.D., Fialkowski, L.T., Lingevitch, J.F.: Localizing submerged acoustic sources under adverse conditions. J. Theor. Comput. Acoust. **30**(01), 2230001 (2022)
5. Colton, D., Kress, R.: Inverse Acoustic and Electromagnetic Scattering Theory. Springer, Cham (2012)
6. Deygout, J.: Multiple knife-edge diffraction of microwaves. IEEE Trans. Antennas Propag. **14**(4), 480–489 (1966)
7. Gingras, D.F., Gerstoft, P., Gerr, N.L., Mecklenbrauker, C.: Electromagnetic matched field processing for source localization. In: 1997 IEEE International Conference on Acoustics, Speech, and Signal Processing, vol. 1, pp. 479–482. IEEE (1997)
8. Goncharsky, A., Stepanov, V., Tikhonov, A., Yagola, A.: Numerical Methods for the Solution of ill-Posed Problems. Springer, Dordrecht (1995). https://doi.org/10.1007/978-94-015-8480-7
9. Jensen, F.B., Kuperman, W.A., Porter, M.B., Schmidt, H.: Computational Ocean Acoustics. Springer, Cham (2014)
10. Lytaev, M.S.: PyWaveProp (2024). https://github.com/mikelytaev/wave-propagation
11. Mantzel, W., Romberg, J., Sabra, K.: Compressive matched-field processing. J. Acoust. Soc. Am. **132**(1), 90–102 (2012)
12. Marchuk, G.I.: Adjoint Equations and Analysis of Complex Systems, vol. 295. Springer, Cham (2013)
13. Marchuk, G.I.: Mathematical Models in Environmental Problems. Elsevier (2011)
14. Schippkus, S., Hadziioannou, C.: Matched field processing accounting for complex earth structure: method and review. Geophys. J. Int. **231**(2), 1268–1282 (2022)
15. Vavilov, S.A., Lytaev, M.S.: Modelling equation of electromagnetic scattering on thin dielectric structures. J. Math. Sci. **238**(5), 621–670 (2019)
16. Vavilov, S., Lytaev, M.: Electromagnetic waves scattering on an array composed of thin dielectric objects. J. Math. Sci. **243**, 689–697 (2019)

17. Vavilov, S.A., Lytaev, M.S.: Modeling equation for multiple knife-edge diffraction. IEEE Trans. Antennas Propag. **68**(5), 3869–3877 (2020)
18. Walter, F., et al.: Distributed acoustic sensing of microseismic sources and wave propagation in glaciated terrain. Nat. Commun. **11**(1), 2436 (2020)
19. Zala, C.A., Ozard, J.M.: Matched-field processing for a moving source. J. Acoust. Soc. Am. **92**(1), 403–417 (1992)

Image Segmentation Applied to Multi-species Phenotyping in Fish Farming

Fabrício Martins Batista$^{(\boxtimes)}$ and José Remo F. Brega

Sao Paulo State University (UNESP), Bauru, Brazil
{fabricio.batista,remo.brega}@unesp.br
https://sgcd.fc.unesp.br/#!/liv

Abstract. Fish farming has been gaining prominence in recent years, almost doubling world production in a ten-year period. Fish farming products are an important source of protein in coastal or insular countries, as they are the most abundant natural resource in these regions and are part of the daily diet of their populations. Recent technological advances allow the evolution of the practice of fish farming through new tools such as Artificial Intelligence and Internet of Things. Among the tasks that stand out is the phenotyping of animals raised in captivity during various stages of growth to assess the interaction of the species with the environment or even the prevalence of certain characteristics after successive reproductive selections. Phenotyping is usually performed manually through a digital image taken by an expert and post-processed in specialized measurement software using an object of known size as a reference in the image. Based on this problem, this work proposes a Computer Vision System to automate the phenotyping of two common species in Brazilian fish farming: *Piaractus Mesopotamicus (Pacu)* and *Colossoma macropomum (Tambaqui)*. The results indicate a positive correlation between the measurements performed by humans and the proposed Computer Vision system, presenting itself as a viable alternative to accelerate the process of collecting information for reproductive selection in commercial fish farming.

Keywords: Precision Agriculture · Artificial Intelligence · Genetic Selection · Image Segmentation · Computer Vision

1 Introduction

World aquaculture production grew at an average rate of 5.3% per year in the period from 2001 to 2018, amounting to 82.1 million tonnes (US$ 250.1 billion) of aquatic animals in 2018. In Latin America, aquaculture significantly advanced in the global ranking [1].

The main group of native fish species produced in Brazil is composed of Serrasalmidae species (tambaqui *Colossoma macropomum*, pacu *Piaractus mesopotamicus*, pirapitinga *Piaractus brachypomys*, and their interspecific hybrids), corresponding to about 30% of the national production, estimated at 529.6 thousand tonnes in 2019 [2].

In addition to the applications of Internet of Things (IoT), Computer Vision, Image Processing, and Artificial Intelligence are also highlighted, with various applications such as disease detection [3], species classification [4], quality estimation [5], counting, and phenotyping (extraction of physical traits of animals) [6].

For the present work, data from the Pacu species (scientifically called *Piaractus mesopotamicus*) and Tambaqui (scientifically called *Colossoma macropomum*) were used, characterized by being a freshwater fish and belonging to the same family as the piranhas.

A partnership was made with the Laboratory of Genetics in Aquaculture and Conservation (LaGeAC) at Unesp Jaboticabal to initially carry out experiments related to data collection about the animals. Thus, for this study, imagetic data from the fish were used to build the automatic measurement system.

2   Theoretical Foundation

2.1   Phenotyping

Phenotyping can be defined as the process of extracting specific measurements from certain animals, such as weighing or measuring specific regions of interest like head size, total length, or height. These data are used by researchers or producers to assess the species' interaction with the environment or the prevalence of certain traits after successive reproductive selections [7].

This type of process is manual and quite costly, subject to biases from the researchers responsible for performing the measurements. As the number of animals can be quite large, carrying out this type of process manually becomes unfeasible in commercial applications.

2.2   Reproductive Selection

Reproductive selection, in turn, aims to identify and select individuals that have desirable traits such as disease resistance or total weight achieved after maturation. Through this process, it is possible to achieve genetic refinement with the individuals [8].

Reproductive selection for genetic improvement essentially focuses on choosing individuals that reach higher weights or have a high daily weight gain. However, in the context of commercial fish farming in Brazil, genetic improvement is not yet widely practiced due to the difficulties and intensive manual work required for carrying out such programs on a large scale. To solve this problem, it is necessary to find ways to eliminate some of the manual work involved in the process.

This work presents a method to achieve this goal and collect granular information on individuals of the species for incorporation into genetic improvement programs for *Piaractus Mesopotamicus (Pacu)* and *Colossoma macropomum (Tambaqui)*.

Among the measurements obtained by the constructed system are total height (th), total length (tl), standard length (sl), pelvic width (pl), head height (hh), head width (hl), as well as the area in pixels of each region obtained according to Fig. 1.

Fig. 1. Measurements to be obtained by the proposed system in this work.

2.3   Convolutional Neural Networks and the R-CNN Family of Methods

Convolutional Neural Networks (CNNs) present an important technique for object detection. Before their re-introduction in the early 2010's the dominant approaches consisted of two main techniques: HOG [9] and SIFT [10]. The techniques used a grid of gradients to highlight edges to act as feature extractors and then were combined with classifiers such as SVMs [11]. After the success of CNNs with AlexNet in 2012 scaling up the LeNet architecture [12] by using a GPGPU parallelized implementation of CNNs, a promising idea would be to apply the feature extraction capabilities of CNNs to the object detection problem. R-CNN [13] was one of the first movements in this direction.

2.4   R-CNN

R-CNN is a multi-step prediction method: selection, extraction, and classification. The name R-CNN comes from the division of images into regions, from the English "Region-based Convolutional Neural Networks".

The image division occurs through the selective search technique [14]. In the first step of the algorithm, about 2000 regions are extracted from the image.

Each of these regions is then resized to be compatible with the input dimensions of pre-trained CNNs on ImageNet. Specifically, the authors conducted two experiments, one using AlexNet [15] and VGG [16] as feature extractors.

After the feature extraction step using CNNs, the obtained feature maps were fed to multiple linear SVMs using the One-vs-All strategy, i.e., one linear SVM for each class of interest in the problem.

The detection of the object bounding box is modeled as a regression problem from the feature maps extracted from the initial regions. From the description of the architecture, it is not difficult to see that these are operations with extremely high computational cost. The architecture of the R-CNN is depicted in Fig. 2.

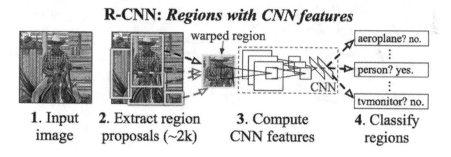

Fig. 2. R-CNN Architecture

After all, it is necessary to apply the convolution at least 2000 times, one for each region extracted by the CNN, without considering the cost of the SVM also applied to each of the regions.

In addition to that, a large part of the regions extracted in the first step overlap, which leads to redundant calculations.

Despite this, object detection observed a leap in performance with this approach. The issue of computational cost would be addressed in subsequent works.

2.5   Fast R-CNN

The main bottleneck of R-CNN was the amount of redundant calculations. To avoid this problem and speed up R-CNNs, SPPNet [17] performed the CNN application only once for the entire image and then performed region selection operations on the feature map, resulting in sub-regions of interest.

This way, it was possible to avoid redundant calculations. However, the approach of SPPNet, like R-CNN, was a multi-step prediction system: selection, extraction, and classification using SVMs.

This forces the freezing of the CNN, which only acts as a feature extractor, leading to lower performance in case of fine-tuning needs for problems that diverge greatly from the original data of the ImageNet dataset.

Based on these issues, the new iteration of R-CNN, Fast R-CNN [18], proposes an architecture with a single step, allowing end-to-end training of the model. Fast R-CNN introduced another element, the RoI (Region of Interest) Pooling layer. The general architecture of the Fast R-CNN is depicted in Fig. 3.

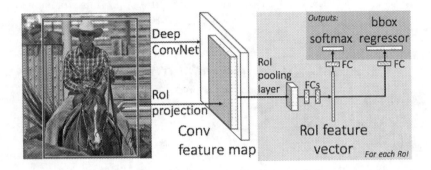

Fig. 3. Fast R-CNN Architecture

This layer is responsible for extracting a fixed-length vector from a region of the feature map, which is then fed to fully connected layers, generating a feature vector that is then sent to two prediction heads, a regressor for the bounding boxes and a softmax classifier. Thus, the training of the architecture now becomes feasible for end-to-end execution, allowing fine-tuning even of the early layers of the feature extractor. The cost function of this architecture is given by the sum of the cost functions of each distinct objective function for the regressor and classifier, thus configuring a multi-objective cost function for the architecture.

2.6   Faster R-CNN

Despite the advances achieved by Fast R-CNN, the operation of region selection through the Selective Search technique was still used. The implementations of this technique are generally based on CPUs, and therefore do not take advantage of the parallel computing power offered by modern GPUs. The average time spent on calculating regions using Selective Search is around 2 s per image, accounting for most of the time spent in the algorithm's application.

The authors of this new iteration of R-CNN, Faster R-CNN [19], argue that it would be possible to implement the Selective Search operations on GPUs. However, this would not properly leverage the improvements in shared calculations made previously. Instead, the authors proposed a new way of selecting important regions in the image through a Region Proposal Network (RPN).

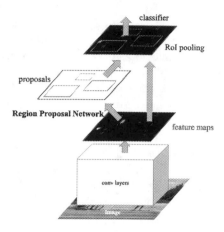

Fig. 4. Region Proposal Network

RPN is a Convolutional Neural Network that takes an image as input, calculates feature maps using the trunk of a pre-trained CNN on the ImageNet dataset, and outputs rectangular regions associated with an "objectness" score. This score represents the probability that the extracted rectangular region contains an object of interest or only the background of an object. The general architecture of an RPN is depicted in Fig. 4.

In this way, it is possible to take advantage of the feature maps that are extracted only once and reuse them for multiple purposes. RPNs produce multiple regions of interest, often redundant and overlapping regions.

To avoid this problem, the Non-Max Suppression technique is used to merge subregions into a single contiguous region when there is a significant overlap rate (greater than 0.7) calculated from the Intersection over Union (IoU) metric.

The calculation of the cost function for training the architecture is the sum of the 4 cost functions for each of the objectives: the regressors of the RPN's regions of interest, the objectness classifier of the region, the bounding box regressor of the Fast R-CNN, and the classifier of the object contained in the identified bounding box.

2.7   Mask R-CNN

Besides object detection and classification, another relevant problem in image processing is semantic segmentation. Semantic segmentation consists of classifying pixels into contiguous regions belonging to an object.

Mask R-CNN [20] extends the Faster R-CNN architecture by adding a new prediction head responsible for generating a mask for each detected object in parallel with the class and bounding box prediction heads.

This mask prediction head adds little computational cost to the Faster R-CNN, while maintaining the performance gain obtained in previous iterations of the architecture.

In addition to the prediction head, Mask R-CNN also introduced an intermediate layer called ROI Align. The idea of this intermediate layer is to align the spatial regions of the original image with the corresponding regions in the feature map.

As discussed earlier, extracting feature maps through CNNs reduces the spatial dimensions such as height and width of the image and increases the depth of the representation.

To align the region of the original image with a feature map with potentially smaller height and width, the authors used bilinear interpolation. Bilinear interpolation is an operation used in computer vision for image resizing.

The objective function optimized for the additional head of the architecture is a binary problem modeled through a sigmoid function. Thus, the output of this prediction head is a matrix with the spatial dimensions of the original image, and for each pixel, a sigmoid-applied output value between 0 and 1 is obtained.

If the value is greater than 0.5, the pixel is considered in the mask. For each detected object instance in the image, a binary mask is generated in the process.

Mask R-CNN has also shown relevance in another problem: pose estimation. Pose estimation involves classifying the position of a person's joints and identifying the position of each of the 14 key points in the human body.

The success of Mask R-CNN in these two tasks has established the R-CNN family as extremely important methods in the field of computer vision.

3   Development Methodology

The dataset used in this work consists of approximately 1802 animals of the Pacu species and 365 animals of the Tambaqui species. The number of animals is approximate because during handling, some animals end up dying in the process, and the number presented refers to the first collection made. Four regions of interest were annotated in the images: the head, the body, the fins, and the pelvic region.

Due to morphological differences at different growth stages, the images of both species were captured at two different moments, at 15 months and 28 months, in order to make the model invariant to the animals' development stage.

To extract the images, the animals were submerged in a benzocaine solution (0.1 mg/l), identified through an RFID tag, weighed, and placed on a polystyrene base with a ruler for later verification of the model results. After collection, for validation of the measurement system, the images from an independent set not used during training were individually calibrated. Calibration consists of mapping a distance of 1 cm on the ruler in the image to a pixel value using the ImageJ software.

The annotation process was carried out using the Labelbox software by a single annotator and reviewed by a second expert. Incorrectly annotated images were invalidated and corrected until all were correctly annotated.

Four regions of interest were annotated in the images: the head, the body, the fins, and the pelvic region, as shown in Fig. 5. The measurements are initially

Fig. 5. Mask annotated with regions of interest, left: *Colossoma macropomum*, right: *Piaractus mesopotamicus*

extracted in pixels and then mapped to a measurement in millimeters through scaling. A calibration process in pixels was manually performed on each image of the validation dataset to facilitate the validation of the measurement extraction. A ruler was positioned on a styrofoam platform for this calibration.

Specifically, the implementation of Mask R-CNN was adjusted to adhere to the field constraints related to computational cost. To minimize stress on the fish during the measurement process, the trained model needs to be compact and fast enough to run on an edge device as close as possible to the fish tanks.

4   Implementation

The original work of Mask R-CNN employs a 50-layer Convolutional Neural Network called ResNet-50 as the feature extractor.

However, a variant of the ResNet architecture with only 18 layers was used to reduce the computational cost. This effectively reduced the number of floating-point operations (FLOPs), required parameters, and training time to achieve similar results.

During training, data augmentation techniques were applied to the images. The images were vertically and horizontally flipped, rotated by 90° or 270°, and resized at scales of 0.10, 0.25, 0.5, and 0.75 with a probability of 0.5.

These transformations help make the model more tolerant to linear transformations of the input images.

The dataset was randomly divided, stratified to preserve the proportions of different species, into three subsets: training (80%), validation (20%), and 5% of the training set was used as the development set.

The development set was used to tune hyperparameters during experimentation, avoiding the direct use of the validation set and preventing potential overfitting.

The experiment was conducted using an NVIDIA RTX 2060 GPU with 8 GB of RAM, and an Intel i5 9600f CPU with 6 physical cores. The experiment ran for 350 epochs and took approximately 22 h.

The optimized metric was Intersection over Union (IoU). At the end of each epoch, the IoU was calculated for the development set. During the experiments, training was interrupted several times to optimize the learning rate, which was the hyperparameter with the greatest sensitivity in the model, using the performance on the development set as the decision parameter.

IoU was calculated using the area obtained by the model A and the expected (annotated) area B with the formula $A \cap B / A \cup B$. A IoU value of 1.0 indicates that the annotated area exactly overlaps with the area obtained as the output by the model.

Based on the outputs obtained by Mask R-CNN, the bounding box was used to calculate the morphometric measurements of the fish in pixels, and the segmented masks were used to calculate the area in pixels of the regions of interest.

For evaluating the measurement results obtained by the model, two metrics were assessed: Pearson Correlation and Mean Squared Error (MSE) between the measurements obtained by the model and the manual measurements performed by an expert.

5   Results

5.1   Model Training

The model was trained for 350 epochs, with a learning rate fixed at 10^{-5}. Table 1 shows the values of IoU for Precision and Recall on the test set calculated for the bounding boxes.

The indices are divided into intervals and different detection scales. IoU indices with a value of -1 in the table indicate that there were no object detections in the respective scale.

Table 2 shows the values of IoU for Precision and Recall on the test set calculated for segmentation.

The loss curves of the model are presented in Fig. 6. The total loss is given by the sum of all cost functions $L = L_{cls} + L_{box} + L_{mask} + L_{objectness}$, which corresponds to the multi-objective function optimized by Mask R-CNN. The optimization had significant variations until epoch 150. After this point, the model was further optimized for 200 epochs because the IoU metrics continued to improve with the optimization focused on finer details of the images.

Table 1. IoU Table for Bounding Boxes

Metric	IoU/Size	Value
Average Precision (AP)	0.50:0.95/all	0.941
Average Precision (AP)	0.50/all	0.995
Average Precision (AP)	0.75/all	0.995
Average Precision (AP)	0.50:0.95/small	−1.000
Average Precision (AP)	0.50:0.95/medium	0.869
Average Precision (AP)	0.50:0.95/large	0.953
Average Recall (AR)	0.50:0.95/all	0.960
Average Recall (AR)	0.50:0.95/small	−1.000
Average Recall (AR)	0.50:0.95/medium	0.906
Average Recall (AR)	0.50:0.95/large	0.964

Table 2. IoU Table for Segmentation

Metric	IoU/Size	Value
Average Precision (AP)	0.50:0.95/all	0.899
Average Precision (AP)	0.50/all	0.995
Average Precision (AP)	0.75/all	0.995
Average Precision (AP)	0.50:0.95/small	−1.000
Average Precision (AP)	0.50:0.95/medium	0.879
Average Precision (AP)	0.50:0.95/large	0.921
Average Recall (AR)	0.50:0.95/all	0.919
Average Recall (AR)	0.50:0.95/small	−1.000
Average Recall (AR)	0.50:0.95/medium	0.909
Average Recall (AR)	0.50:0.95/large	0.926

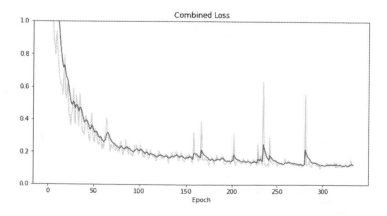

Fig. 6. Multi-objective Cost Function Loss of Mask R-CNN

5.2   Phenotyping *Piaractus mesopotamicus*

Due to the image collection process being carried out by different teams and at different stages of animal development, in order to ensure the quality of the results reported in this work, the images in the validation set used to evaluate the model were individually calibrated.

However, the calibration showed low variability in this set, where 1 cm varied from 46.68 to 51.67 pixels (mean of 49.49 pixels). The validation set of measurements for Pacu contained 1031 animals, of which only 979 had valid observed values.

Another important point to highlight is that the images were captured by two devices with different resolutions. Segmentation anomalies were detected in only 9 images of the set, which were excluded from the visualizations and metrics presented below. These images had anomalous values above the upper limit of $\mu + 3 * \sigma$ and below the lower limit $\mu - 3 * \sigma$ of the automatically obtained measurements.

For the measurement in this particular test set, the pelvic measurement was disregarded as the data for this metric had not yet been standardized. Therefore, the measurements of pelvic length (pl) and pelvic height (ph) were not considered in this particular analysis.

Figure 7 presents a scatter plot where the X-axis represents the value estimated by the system and the Y-axis represents the value annotated by a human.

The other measurements are standardized according to Fig. 1. Table 3 presents the metrics obtained from the comparison of automatic measurement with the one observed by human annotators.

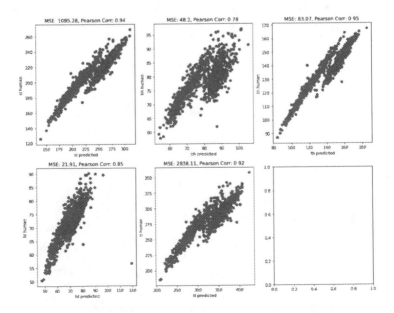

Fig. 7. Scatter Plot X = estimated, Y = observed

The color differentiation in Fig. 7 is due to the fact that the images were captured at different times by devices with different resolutions. Figure 8 shows box plots comparing the values obtained through automatic measurement and human measurement.

Table 3. MSE and Pearson's Coefficient Table

Measure	MSE (mm)	Pearson's Coefficient
tl (Total Length)	2720.83	0.92
th (Total Height)	81.27	0.95
hh (Head Height)	46.47	0.78
hl (Head Length)	22.87	0.85
sl (Standard Length)	1054.11	0.94

Since the calibration was performed individually and the values converted to the same scale, it is possible to observe them on the same graph. However, there is a small deviation in relation to the two groups, also observed in the following graph.

Despite the high correlation (greater than 0.70) in all measurements, the mean squared error for the length measurements tl and sl draws attention.

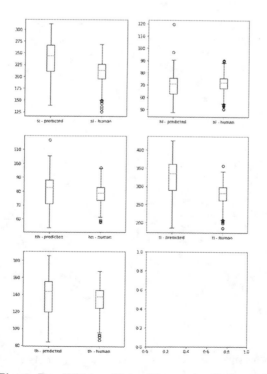

Fig. 8. Box-Whisker Plot - Observed x Estimated

Through Fig. 8, it is possible to observe that there is greater variability as well as a higher number of outliers in the two length measurements, tl and sl, manually collected by human annotators.

This phenomenon was attributed to differences in the manual measurement methodology. Therefore, the benefits obtained from the application of an automatic measurement system go beyond simply automating the process.

The measurement system eliminates the differences in methodology between different human annotators, bringing not only automation but also standardization of the results and greater reliability of the information produced in this type of operation.

5.3 *Colossoma macropomum* Phenotyping

Figure 9 presents a scatter plot where the X-axis represents the value estimated by the system and the Y-axis represents the value annotated by a human. The capture device used was standardized for a 12-megapixel digital camera integrated into the Motorola One Action smartphone, configured at maximum resolution and autofocus. During the collection of this sample, the distance between the camera and the styrofoam platform was standardized at 80 cm. Following the previous experiment, the other measurements are standardized according to Fig. 1. In order to ensure the quality of the results reported in this work, the images in the validation set were individually calibrated.

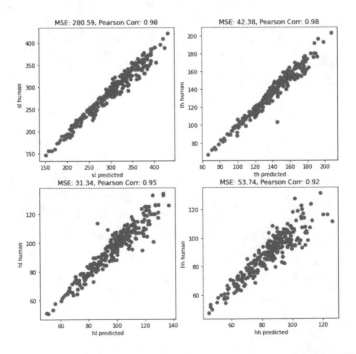

Fig. 9. Scatter Plot X = estimated, Y = observed

Table 4. MSE and Pearson's Coefficient Table

Measure	MSE (mm)	Pearson's Coefficient
th (Total Height)	42.38	0.98
sl (Standard Length)	280.59	0.98
hh (Head Height)	53.74	0.92
hl (Head Length)	31.34	0.95

Table 4 presents the metrics obtained from the comparison of automatic measurement with the one observed by human annotators.

Figure 10 compares the measurements made by a human with those estimated by the algorithm using a box-whisker plot. The calibration also showed low variability in this set, where 1 cm ranged from 45.5 to 51.0 pixels (average of 48.1 pixels). The validation set for Tambaqui measurements contained 303 animals, of which only 273 had valid observed values.

With the standardization of the collection methodology in this second experiment, it was not possible to observe the existence of outliers.

For the measurement in this particular test set, the pelvis measurement and total length were disregarded because the data for these metrics were not collected by human observers. Therefore, the measurements of pelvis length (pl),

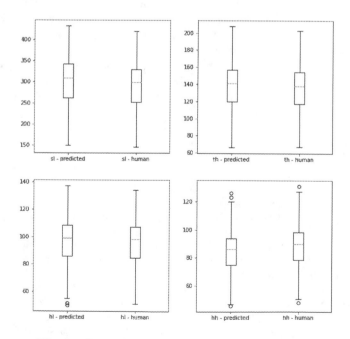

Fig. 10. Box-Whisker Plot - Observed x Estimated

pelvis height (ph), and total length (tl) were not considered in this particular analysis.

However, it is important to consider that in the experiment conducted with *Piaractus mesopotamicus*, the evaluated set is almost four times larger. The scarcity of outliers in this set can also be attributed to this fact.

6   Conclusion

Computer vision has shown great potential for automation of tasks in the context of Precision Fish Farming.

The application of Mask R-CNN in the context of live animal phenotyping, under natural lighting conditions, allows for a lower stress load on the animals in question, as it can be performed closer to their natural habitat, reducing mortality during the handling of such operations.

In addition to reducing the required time, the algorithm is able to standardize the operation, avoiding the variability of measurement methodologies and enabling large-scale phenotyping for genetic improvement programs in fish farming, both in commercial and research aspects.

Furthermore, the created measurement system can be used for the measurement of more than one species simultaneously, as demonstrated by the presented results.

For future work, it is intended to evaluate the possibility of using the obtained pixel area metrics for estimating other values of interest through regressions. Some values can only be obtained by sacrificing the animals, so it is interesting to evaluate the quality of the obtained estimates, avoiding the sacrifice of potential breeders who can generate increasingly genetically refined individuals with high commercial value.

References

1. FAO. The state of world fisheries and aquaculture 2020. Sustainability in action Rome (2020)
2. IBGE (2020). https://cidades.ibge.gov.br/brasil/pesquisa/18/0
3. Malik, S., Kumar, T., Sahoo, A.K.: Image processing techniques for identification of fish disease. In: 2017 IEEE 2nd International Conference on Signal and Image Processing (ICSIP), pp. 55–59 (2017)
4. Cao, Y., Lei, Q., Wei, T., Zhong, H.: A computer vision program that identifies and classifies fish species. In: 2021 International Conference on Electronic Information Engineering and Computer Science (EIECS), pp. 384–390 (2021)
5. Taheri-Garavand, A., Fatahi, S., Omid, M., Makino, Y.: Meat quality evaluation based on computer vision technique: a review. Meat Sci. **156**, 183–195 (2019)
6. Wang, G., Hwang, J.-N., Wallace, F., Rose, C.: Multi-scale fish segmentation refinement and missing shape recovery. IEEE Access **7**, 52836–52845 (2019)
7. Blay, C., et al.: Genetic parameters and genome-wide association studies of quality traits characterised using imaging technologies in Rainbow trout, Oncorhynchus mykiss. Front. Genetics **12** (2021)

8. Lhorente, J.P., Araneda, M., Neira, R., Yáñez, J.M.: Advances in genetic improvement for salmon and trout aquaculture: the Chilean situation and prospects. Rev. Aquac. **11**(2), 340–353 (2019)
9. Dalal, N., Triggs, B.: Histograms of oriented gradients for human detection. In: 2005 IEEE Computer Society Conference on Computer Vision and Pattern Recognition (CVPR 2005), vol. 1, pp. 886–893 (2005)
10. Lowe, D.G.: Object recognition from local scale-invariant features. In: Proceedings of the Seventh IEEE International Conference on Computer Vision, vol. 2, pp. 1150–1157. IEEE (1999)
11. Cortes, C., Vapnik, V.: Support-vector networks. Mach. Learn. **20**(3), 273–297 (1995)
12. LeCun, Y., et al.: Backpropagation applied to handwritten zip code recognition. Neural Comput. **1**(4), 541–551 (1989)
13. Girshick, R.B., Donahue, J., Darrell, T., Malik, J.: Rich feature hierarchies for accurate object detection and semantic segmentation. CoRR, vol. abs/1311.2524 (2013)
14. Uijlings, J.R.R., van de Sande, K.E.A., Gevers, T., Smeulders, A.W.M.: Selective search for object recognition. Int. J. Comput. Vis. **104**(2), 154–171 (2013)
15. Krizhevsky, A., Sutskever, I., Hinton, G.E.: ImageNet classification with deep convolutional neural networks. In: Proceedings of the 25th International Conference on Neural Information Processing Systems - Volume 1, NIPS 2012, (Red Hook, NY, USA), pp. 1097–1105. Curran Associates Inc. (2012)
16. Simonyan, K., Zisserman, A.: Very deep convolutional networks for large-scale image recognition (2014)
17. He, K., Zhang, X., Ren, S., Sun, J.: Spatial pyramid pooling in deep convolutional networks for visual recognition. CoRR, vol. abs/1406.4729 (2014)
18. Girshick, R.: Fast R-CNN. In: 2015 IEEE International Conference on Computer Vision (ICCV), pp. 1440–1448 (2015)
19. Ren, S., He, K., Girshick, R.B., Sun, J.: Faster R-CNN: towards real-time object detection with region proposal networks. CoRR, vol. abs/1506.01497 (2015)
20. He, K., Gkioxari, G., Dollár, P., Girshick, R.: Mask R-CNN (2017). arxiv:1703.06870Comment. Open source; appendix on more results

Solving the Convection-Diffusion Equations via a Multiscale and Discontinuous Galerkin Approach

Enéas Mendes de Jesus[1,2]([⊠]) [iD] and Isaac Pinheiro dos Santos[2,3] [iD]

[1] Federal Institute of Espírito Santo (IFES), 660 Augusto Costa de Oliveira St.,
Piúma, ES 29285-000, Brazil
eneas.jesus@ifes.edu.br
[2] Postgraduate Program in Computer Science (PPGI), Federal University of Espírito
Santo (UFES), Av. Fernando Ferrari, 514 - Goiabeiras, Vitória, ES 29075-910, Brazil
eneas.jesus@edu.ufes.br, isaac.santos@ufes.br
[3] Department of Applied Mathematics (DMA), Federal University of Espírito Santo
(UFES), BR-101, km 60 - Litorâneo, São Mateus, ES 29932-540, Brazil

Abstract. We present a multiscale and discontinuous Galerkin approach for solving the convection-dominated diffusion problems. The unresolved fine-scales are discretized element-wise using bubble functions. A discontinuous Galerkin discretization is employed in the resolved macro scales. To enhance stability to the numerical formulation, we add a nonlinear artificial diffusion operator inside of the elements, acting on both scales, and an extra stabilization on the interelement edges. Numerical tests demonstrate that the method is stable and accurate in solving transport problems with dominant convection.

Keywords: Convection-Diffusion equations · Convection-dominated · Discontinuous Galerkin · Artificial diffusion · Multiscale discontinuous Galerkin method

1 Introduction

Discontinuous Galerkin (DG) methods have been widely used in solving convection-dominated problems. These methods capture discontinuities well when solving purely hyperbolic problems and have good stability properties when solving convection-diffusion problems with dominant convection. However, DG solutions may suffer nonphysical oscillations in the vicinity of discontinuities and steep gradients. Thus, most DG methods need the addition of some appropriate stabilizing terms to obtain stable numerical solutions [1,3]. Many methods are proposed in the literature to combat the oscillations of DG solutions. Some of them are based on slope limiters [5], artificial diffusion [11,15]; nonlinear multiscale methods [2,3], and post-processing techniques [7,8].

Following the ideas of the NSGS method [12], in [2] a discontinuous and multiscale formulation is presented for solving convection-dominated problems,

© The Author(s), under exclusive license to Springer Nature Switzerland AG 2024
O. Gervasi et al. (Eds.): ICCSA 2024, LNCS 14813, pp. 112–124, 2024.
https://doi.org/10.1007/978-3-031-64605-8_8

where a residual-based nonlinear artificial diffusion operator is added to the fine scales. The amount of artificial diffusion is scaled by the resolved scale solution at the element level. Also, two nested meshes must be built: a mesh representing the macro space and a more refined mesh where the problem is solved. This results in a formulation with a higher computational cost than the classical DG methods. In [3], a modification of this method is presented by introducing the artificial diffusion on both scales. The method proposed in [3] was rewritten in the continuous Galerkin framework using bubble functions to discretize the micro scale [13,14], resulting in a method with good convergence and stability properties. Since this bubble-based method needs only a mesh, it has a computational cost of the same order as the standard continuous Galerkin formulation.

In this work we present a new formulation which rewrites the continuous method [13,14] using broken spaces. The discontinuous framework is applied only on the macro scale, while the fine scales are discretized element-wise using bubble functions. Thus, it requires only a mesh associated with the macro scale to solve the problem. To enhance stability to the numerical formulation, we add a nonlinear artificial diffusion operator inside the elements, acting on both scales, and an extra stabilization on the interelement edges. The new numerical scheme improves stability of the DG methods while being more economical than the discontinuous methods described in [2,3].

The outline of this paper is organized as follows. Section 2 presents the convection-diffusion equation, the concepts and notations used throughout the text, as well as the DG formulation. Section 3 describes the new numerical methodology. Numerical test are discussed in Sect. 4 and Sect. 5 concludes this paper.

2   Discontinuous Galerkin Formulation

Let $\Omega \in \mathbb{R}^2$ be a bounded open domain with Lipschitz boundary Γ. The convection-diffusion-reaction equation is given by

$$-\kappa\Delta u + \boldsymbol{\beta}\cdot\nabla u + \sigma u = f \text{ in } \Omega,$$
$$u = g \text{ on } \Gamma, \tag{1}$$

where $\kappa \in \mathbb{R}$, $\kappa > 0$, is the diffusion coefficient, $\boldsymbol{\beta}$ is the divergence-free velocity field, σ is the reaction coefficient, and f is the source term. We also define the inflow boundary

$$\Gamma_- = \{x \in \Gamma; \ \boldsymbol{\beta}(x)\cdot\mathbf{n}(x) < 0\}, \tag{2}$$

where $\mathbf{n}(x)$ denotes the unit outward normal vector to Γ at $x \in \Gamma$. Moreover, all assumptions for well-posedness, existence and uniqueness of the solution to the problem (1) are considered here, but, for simplicity, are omitted and can be consulted on [6].

Let $\mathcal{T}_h = \{K\}$ be a triangulation of the domain Ω. The area of a triangle $K \in \mathcal{T}_h$ is denoted by $|K|$, and the mesh parameter is $h = \max_{K \in \mathcal{T}_h}\{h_K\}$, where

$h_K = \sqrt{|K|}$. We denote by $\mathcal{E}_h$ the set of all edges in $\mathcal{T}_h$, defined by

$$\mathcal{E}_h = \bigcup_{K \in \mathcal{T}_h} \partial K. \tag{3}$$

The set of internals and boundaries edges are represented by $\mathcal{E}_h^0$ and $\mathcal{E}_h^\Gamma$, respectively. For the inflow edge on the domain boundary and on each element, the notations are $\mathcal{E}_h^{0-}$ and $\mathcal{E}_h^{\Gamma-}$, respectively. Since we use a discontinuous approach, we need to present the definition of typical tools such as averages and jumps on the edges for scalar and vector valued functions. An edge $e \in \mathcal{E}_h^0$ is shared by two elements K_1 and K_2. Let φ be a scalar piecewise smooth function on $\mathcal{T}_h$ with $\varphi^i = \varphi|_{K_i}$. We define the jump and average of φ, respectively, over e as

$$[\![\varphi]\!] = \varphi^1 \mathbf{n}^1 + \varphi^2 \mathbf{n}^2, \quad \{\varphi\} = \frac{1}{2}(\varphi^1 + \varphi^2), \tag{4}$$

where $\mathbf{n}^i$ is the outward unit normal vector of K_i on e. To a vector function $\boldsymbol{\tau}$, those definitions are give by

$$[\![\boldsymbol{\tau}]\!] = \boldsymbol{\tau}^1 \cdot \mathbf{n}^1 + \boldsymbol{\tau}^2 \cdot \mathbf{n}^2, \quad \{\boldsymbol{\tau}\} = \frac{1}{2}(\boldsymbol{\tau}^1 + \boldsymbol{\tau}^2). \tag{5}$$

For $e \in \mathcal{E}_h^\Gamma$ we set

$$[\![\varphi]\!] = \varphi \mathbf{n}, \quad \{\varphi\} = \varphi, \quad \{\boldsymbol{\tau}\} = \boldsymbol{\tau}. \tag{6}$$

Following the approach of [9], we shall introduce the variational formulation of (1). The standard notations and definitions of Lebesgue and Sobolev space and their norms will be used. The space of discontinuous piecewise linear functions on Ω is defined as

$$V_h = \{v \in L^2(\Omega) : v|_K \in P_1(K), \ \forall K \in \mathcal{T}_h\}, \tag{7}$$

where $P_1(K)$ denotes the space of linear polynomials on element K. The inner products are defined by

$$(u, v)_K = \int_K uv \, d\boldsymbol{x}, \quad \langle \hat{u}, \hat{v} \rangle_e = \int_e \hat{u}\hat{v} \, ds, \tag{8}$$

where $u, v \in L^2(K)$ and $\hat{u}, \hat{v} \in L^2(e)$. A discontinuous Galerkin formulation for solving (1) is given as follow: find $u_h \in V_h$ such that

$$B_{DG}(u_h, v_h) = F_{DG}(v_h), \quad \forall v_h \in V_h, \tag{9}$$

where

$$
\begin{aligned}
B_{DG}(u_h, v_h) = & \sum_{K \in \mathcal{T}_h} (\kappa \nabla u_h, \nabla v_h)_K + \sum_{K \in \mathcal{T}_h} (\boldsymbol{\beta} \cdot \nabla u_h + \sigma u_h, v_h)_K \\
& - \kappa \sum_{e \in \mathcal{E}_h^0} \langle \{\nabla u_h\}, [\![v_h]\!] \rangle_e + \kappa \sum_{e \in \mathcal{E}_h^0} \langle [\![u_h]\!], \{\nabla v_h\} \rangle_e \\
& + \eta \sum_{e \in \mathcal{E}_h^0} \langle [\![u_h]\!], [\![v_h]\!] \rangle_e - \sum_{e \in \mathcal{E}_h^{0-}} \langle \boldsymbol{\beta} \cdot [\![u_h]\!], v_h \rangle_e \\
& - \kappa \sum_{e \in \mathcal{E}_h^{\Gamma}} \langle \nabla u_h \cdot \mathbf{n}, v_h \rangle_e + \kappa \sum_{e \in \mathcal{E}_h^{\Gamma}} \langle u_h, \nabla v_h \cdot \mathbf{n} \rangle_e \\
& + \eta \sum_{e \in \mathcal{E}_h^{\Gamma}} \langle u_h, v_h \rangle_e - \sum_{e \in \mathcal{E}_h^{\Gamma-}} \langle (\boldsymbol{\beta} \cdot \mathbf{n}) u_h, v_h \rangle_e,
\end{aligned}
\tag{10}
$$

$$
\begin{aligned}
F_{DG}(v_h) = & \sum_{K \in \mathcal{T}_h} (f, v_h)_K + \kappa \sum_{e \in \mathcal{E}_h^{\Gamma}} \langle g, \nabla v_h \cdot \mathbf{n} \rangle_e \\
& + \eta \sum_{e \in \mathcal{E}_h^{\Gamma}} \langle g, v_h \rangle_e - \sum_{e \in \mathcal{E}_h^{\Gamma-}} \langle (\boldsymbol{\beta} \cdot \mathbf{n}) g, v_h \rangle_e,
\end{aligned}
\tag{11}
$$

where $\eta = \eta_0 \kappa / h$ is a stabilization parameter, and η_0 is a user-chosen parameter. Throughout this work, inspired by [3] and informed by comprehensive testing, we established $\eta_0 = 4$.

3 Multiscale Framework

In this section, we introduce a multiscale approach to reduce spurious oscillations that persist in certain convection-dominated convection-diffusion problems. To achieve this, we consider two scales of discretization. The DG formulation (9) is applied to the macro scale, while bubble functions are employed for the micro scale. Additionally, a nonlinear artificial diffusion operator is added to both discretization scales.

The coarse space, V_h, defined as in (7) is enriched with bubble functions space, defined by

$$
V_b = \{w \in H^1(\Omega) : \ w|_K \in H_0^1(K), \ \forall K \in \mathcal{T}_h\}.
\tag{12}
$$

Here, we use the simple cubic polynomial function $\varphi_b = 27 N_1^K N_2^K N_3^K$, where $N_j^K = N_j^K(x, y)$ are the basis function on the V_h space. The enriched space is represented as a direct sum of V_h and V_b, that is,

$$
V_E = V_h \oplus V_b.
\tag{13}
$$

Thus, if $w_E \in V_E$, we can write $w_E = w_h + w_b$ with $w_h \in V_h$ and $w_b \in V_b$.

The proposed method is established from the DG formulation (9) considering the multiscale framework and adding a nonlinear operator defined by

$$D(u_h; u_E, v_E) = \sum_{K \in \mathcal{T}_h} \int_K \xi(u_h) \boldsymbol{\nabla} u_E \cdot \boldsymbol{\nabla} v_E \, d\boldsymbol{x} + \sum_{e \in \mathcal{E}_h} \int_e \eta_1(u_h) [\![u_h]\!] \cdot [\![v_h]\!] ds, \quad (14)$$

where u_E, $v_E \in V_E$.

The first term on the right side of the Eq. (14), defined on the interior of the elements, introduces an artificial diffusion on all scales of discretization, given by

$$\xi(u_h) = \begin{cases} \dfrac{\hbar}{2} \dfrac{|R(u_h)|}{\|\boldsymbol{\nabla} u_h\|}, & \text{if} \quad \|\boldsymbol{\nabla} u_h\| > tol_\xi, \\ 0, & \text{otherwise,} \end{cases} \quad (15)$$

where $\hbar = c_0 \sqrt{|K|}$, $c_0 \in \mathbb{R}$, and tol_ξ is a positive number small enough to avoid division by zero. Throughout this work, we set $tol_\xi = 10^{-5}$. That artificial diffusion is computed dynamically in terms of the residual of the macro scale solution, $R(u_h) = -\kappa \Delta u_h + \boldsymbol{\beta} \cdot \boldsymbol{\nabla} u_h + \sigma u_h - f$, aiming to minimize the kinetic energy related to the unresolved scales [12].

The second term on the right side of the Eq. (14) introduces an extra stabilization term on the edges of the elements belonging to the macro scale mesh since the bubble functions vanish on the edges. A similar term is present in the bilinear form (10), but here, the stabilization parameter, η_1, is given by the average of the artificial diffusion, Eq. (15), calculated in the two elements sharing the edge, that is,

$$\eta_1(u_h) = \eta_0 \frac{\xi^1(u_h) + \xi^2(u_h)}{2h}, \quad (16)$$

where $\xi^i(u_h) = \xi(u_h)|_{K^i}$, $i = 1, 2$ and K^i are the elements sharing the edge.

The variational formulation of the new method is given as follow: find $u_E = u_h + u_b \in V_E$, with $u_h \in V_h$ and $u_b \in V_b$, such that

$$B_{DG}(u_E, v_E) + D(u_h; u_E, v_E) = F_{DG}(v_E), \quad \forall v_E \in V_E, \quad (17)$$

where $v_E = v_h + v_b$, with $v_h \in V_h$, $v_b \in V_b$, $B_{DG}(\cdot, \cdot)$ and $F_{DG}(\cdot)$ are the bilinear and linear operators, respectively, of the discontinuous Galerkin method defined in (10) and (11).

3.1 Nonlinear Process

Since the proposed method insert a nonlinear operator in the discontinuous formulation, an iterative procedure is employed: given u_h^n, we find u_h^{n+1} satisfying

$$B_{DG}(u_E^{n+1}, v_E) + D(u_h^n; u_E^{n+1}, v_E) = F_{DG}(v_E), \quad \forall v_E \in V_E. \quad (18)$$

It is well known that for the continuous approach the discrete nonlinear process has difficulties in converging, a characteristic observed in the majority of nonlinear stabilization schemes [10,14]. To improve the convergence of the iterative process we combine two strategies:

Relaxation scheme as defined in [12]:

$$\xi^* \longleftarrow \omega\xi(u_h^n) + (1 - \omega)\xi(u_h^{n-1}),$$
$$\xi(u_h^n) \longleftarrow \xi^*,$$

with $\omega = 0.5$;

Freezing of the artificial diffusion presented in [14]: *if* $|R(u^k)|$ *is close enough to* $|R(u^{k-1})|$ *we set* $\omega = 0$. In this work we utilize the criterion $|(|R(u^k)| - |R(u^{k-1})|)| < 0.001$ starting from the second iteration.

4   Numerical Experiments

In this section, four standard benchmark problems for convection-diffusion equations are considered to illustrate the behavior of the proposed methodology. Furthermore, the convergence rates of the proposed method in the $L^2(\Omega)$ and $H^1(\Omega)$ norms are evaluated using a problem with a smooth solution. The numerical results are compared with the DG method described in Eq. (9). Despite the numerical formulation considering the reaction term, for our purposes, $\sigma = 0$, and we adopt $c_0 = \sqrt{2}$, so that $\hbar = \sqrt{2|K|}$. In all examples the spatial domain is given by $\Omega = (0, 1) \times (0, 1)$ and we use a regular triangular mesh with 20 partitions in the x and y directions. All the approximate solutions are represented in a continuous way. To do that, we compute the average of discontinuous solution over each node of the mesh.

4.1   Example 1: Boundary Layers

This problem exhibits parabolic layers at $y = 0$ and $y = 1$ and an exponential layer at $x = 1$. The coefficients of the equation are $\kappa = 10^{-4}$, $\beta = (1, 0)^T$, and $f = 1$. Homogeneous Dirichlet boundary conditions are imposed on Γ. In Fig. 1 we represent the approximate solutions obtained by DG method and our method for that problem.

Visually, both the solutions presents overshoots next to the parabolic layer, but these oscillations are more pronounced for DG method. This can be better observed in Fig. 2, where we have represented the profiles of the solutions at $x = 0.8$ and $y = 0.5$. Once the Dirichlet boundary conditions are weakly imposed, oscillations not appear at the exponential layer.

4.2   Example 2: Boundary Layers

The next example consider a problem with non-homogeneous Dirichlet boundary conditions and exact solution. The data of the problem are $\kappa = 10^{-2}$, $\beta = (1, 1)^T$ and

$$f(x, y) = 2 + \frac{(1 - x)^2 - (1 - x) - (1 - y) + (1 - y)^2}{\kappa(1 - e^{-1/\kappa})e^{(1-x)(1-y)/\kappa}} - x - y. \tag{19}$$

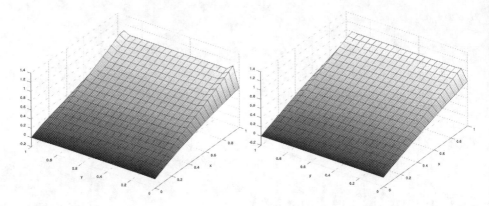

Fig. 1. Example 1. Approximate solutions obtained by DG method (left) and our method (right).

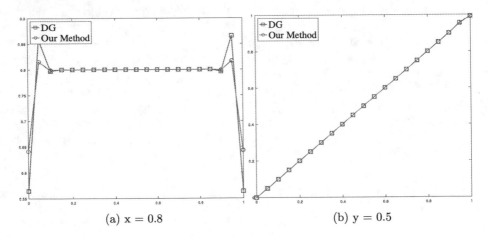

(a) x = 0.8   (b) y = 0.5

Fig. 2. Example 1. Profile of the approximate solutions at $x = 0.8$ and $y = 0.5$ obtained by DG method and our method.

With the following Dirichlet conditions

$$u(x,y) = \begin{cases} 0, & \text{if } x = 1, \text{ or } y = 1; \\ x - \dfrac{(1 - e^{x/\kappa})}{1 - e^{1/\kappa}}, & \text{if } y = 0; \\ y - \dfrac{(1 - e^{y/\kappa})}{1 - e^{1/\kappa}}, & \text{if } x = 0, \end{cases} \qquad (20)$$

the analytical solution is given by

$$u(x,y) = x + y(1 - x) + \frac{e^{-1/\kappa} - e^{-(1-x)(1-y)/\kappa}}{1 - e^{-1/\kappa}}, (x,y) \in \Omega. \qquad (21)$$

If $\kappa \ll 1$ the solution u has a boundary layer along $x = 1$ and $y = 1$. The exact solution and approximations obtained by DG method and our method are depicted in Fig. 3.

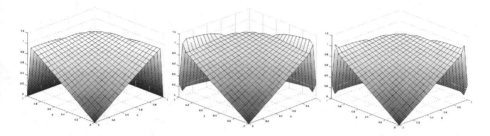

Fig. 3. Example 2. Exact solution (left) and approximate solutions obtained by DG method (center) and our method (right).

Observe that for the chosen data, the DG approximation exhibits oscillations at the boundary layers, whereas the solution obtained by our method is nearly free of oscillation. This can be better observed in Fig. 4, where we have represented the profiles of the solutions along of diagonal, $x = 0.1$ and $y = 0.1$. Notice that an oscillation remains on the inflow boundary next to the points $(0, 1)$ and $(1, 0)$, which can be eliminated using a post-processing, as the exact values of the solution are known on boundary.

4.3   Example 3. Internal Layer

This convection-dominated convective-diffusive problem presents a solution with an internal layer. The velocity field is given by $\boldsymbol{\beta} = (1, 1)^T$, the source term, $f = 0$, and the Dirichlet boundary conditions are defined by

$$u = \begin{cases} 1, & \text{if } x \in [0.3, \ 1], \ y = 0; \\ 0, & \text{otherwise.} \end{cases} \tag{22}$$

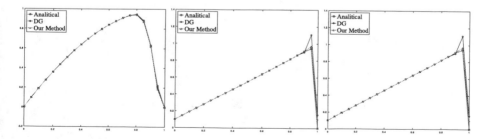

Fig. 4. Example 2. Profile of the exact and approximate solutions at $x = y$, $x = 0.1$, and $y = 0.1$ obtained by DG method and our method.

In the case of a highly convection-dominated problem, DG approximations behave as if the problem were purely hyperbolic [4]. No oscillations occur, since the discontinuity of the inflow boundary propagates to the interior of domain along the direction of convection. In this case, the internal layer is missed in the numerical solution. To represent minimally the internal layer, we adopt $\kappa = 10^{-4}$, considered a moderately convection-dominated problem [8]. In Fig. 5 we represent the approximate solutions where the convection is aligned with the mesh.

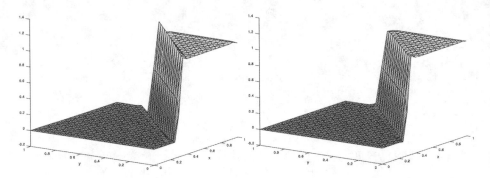

Fig. 5. Example 3. Approximate solutions obtained by DG method (left) and our method (right)

As in the previous examples, the DG approximation exhibits overshoots and undershoots along the internal layer. The current approach reduces the spurious oscillations, leaving only a small oscillation on the inflow boundary next to the discontinuity, which can be addressed with a post-processing technique. This behavior can be observed in Fig. 6.

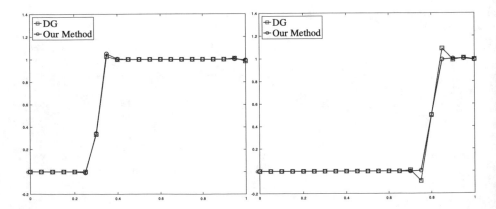

Fig. 6. Example 3. Profile of the approximate solutions at $y = 0$, and $y = 0.5$ obtained by DG method and our method.

4.4   Example 4. Internal Layer

This experiment is basically the same as the previous example, with the only change is the direction of the velocity field β. While in the previous example, $\beta = (1,1)^T$, aligned with the mesh, here $\beta = (cos(\pi/6), sin(\pi/6))^T$, not aligned with the mesh. Figures 7 and 8 represent the approximate solutions and some profiles, respectively. Once again, the solution obtained with the new numerical scheme is superior to that obtained by the DG method.

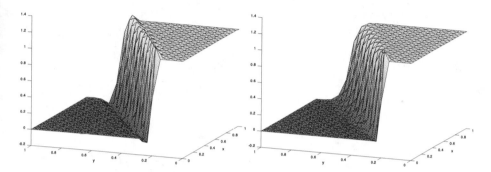

Fig. 7. Example 4. Approximate solutions obtained by DG method (left) and our method (right)

4.5   Convergence Rate

We conclude with a convection-diffusion problem with a smooth solution to evaluate the convergence rates of our method compared with DG method. The convection is given by $\beta = (1,0)^T$ and f such that $u(x,y) = \sin(\pi x)\sin(\pi y)$ is

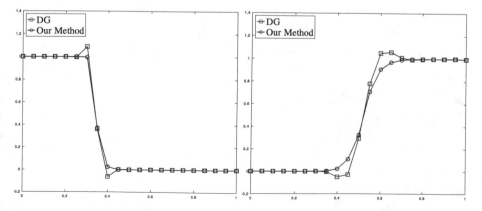

Fig. 8. Example 4. Profile of the approximate solutions at $x = 0.25$, and $y = 0.5$ obtained by DG method and our method.

the exact solution of the problem (1) with $\sigma = 0$ and homogeneous Dirichlet boundary conditions. The approximate solutions are computed for a sequence of five uniform meshes with 128, 242, 450, 800, and 1682 elements. Figure 9 plots the error in $L^2(\Omega)$ associated with the mesh size on a log-log scale. In Fig. 10, under the same conditions, we observe the rates in $H^1(\Omega)$ norm.

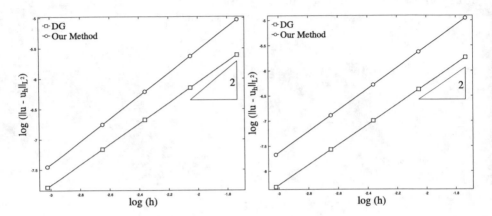

Fig. 9. Convergence rates in the $L^2(\Omega)$-norm considering $\kappa = 10^{-3}$ (left) and $\kappa = 10^{-9}$ (right).

One can note that when the regime is moderately convection-dominated, $\kappa = 10^{-3}$, the DG method exhibits a slight loss of convergence rate. For stronger convection-dominates problem, $\kappa = 10^{-9}$, optimal convergence rates are achieved for both methods. Moreover, the proposed method yields errors in the $L^2(\Omega)$ norm slightly larger than the errors obtained by the DG method.

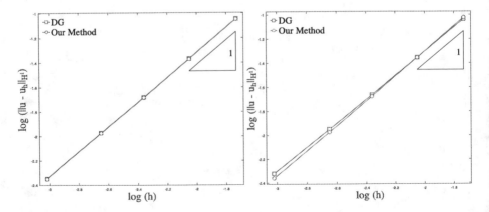

Fig. 10. Convergence rates in the $H^1(\Omega)$-norm considering $\kappa = 10^{-3}$ (left) and $\kappa = 10^{-9}$ (right).

5   Conclusion

This article introduces a multiscale discontinuous Galerkin method for convection-dominated convection-diffusion problems. The methodology involves a discontinuous formulation, which is then enhanced by enriching the resolved space (macro scale) with bubble functions (micro scale). Additionally, to improve the stability of the numerical formulation, we incorporate a nonlinear operator that adds artificial diffusion inside the elements, acting on both scales, along with extra stabilization at the interelement edges. The artificial diffusion is dynamically computed from the residual of the macro scale solution. The edge stabilization utilizes the average of the artificial diffusion of elements sharing each respective edge, making this new stabilization self-adaptive. Numerical experiments demonstrate that the proposed method reduces oscillations in both internal and external layers, with optimal convergence rates observed in the $L^2(\Omega)$ and $H^1(\Omega)$ norms.

Disclosure of Interests. The authors have no competing interests to declare that are relevant to the content of this article.

References

1. Antonietti, P.F., Brezzi, F., Marini, L.D.: Bubble stabilization of discontinuous Galerkin methods. Comput. Methods Appl. Mech. Eng. **198**(21), 1651–1659 (2009)
2. Arruda, N.C.B., Almeida, R.C., do Carmo, E.G.D.: Dynamic diffusion formulation for advection dominated transport problems. Mecanica computacional **XXIX**(20), 2011–2025 (2010)
3. Arruda, N.C., Almeida, R.C., Dutra do Carmo, E.G.: Discontinuous subgrid formulations for transport problems. Comput. Methods Appl. Mech. Eng. **199**(49), 3227–3236 (2010)
4. Ayuso, B., Marini, L.D.: Discontinuous Galerkin methods for advection-diffusion-reaction problems. SIAM J. Numer. Anal. **47**(2), 1391–1420 (2009)
5. Bernardo Cockburn, S.H., Shu, C.W.: The Runge-Kutta local projection discontinuous Galerkin finite element method for conservation laws. IV. The multidimensional case. Math. Comput. **54**(190), 545581 (1990)
6. Di Pietro, D.A., Ern, A.: Mathematical Aspects of Discontinuous Galerkin Methods, vol. 69. Springer, Cham (2011)
7. Frerichs, D., John, V.: On reducing spurious oscillations in discontinuous Galerkin (DG) methods for steady-state convection-diffusion equations. J. Comput. Appl. Math. **393**, 113487 (2021)
8. Frerichs, D., John, V.: On a technique for reducing spurious oscillations in DG solutions of convection-diffusion equations. Appl. Math. Lett. **129**, 107969 (2022)
9. Houston, P., Schwab, C., Süli, E.: Discontinuous HP-finite element methods for advection-diffusion-reaction problems. SIAM J. Numer. Anal. **39**(6), 2133–2163 (2002)
10. John, V., Knobloch, P.: On spurious oscillations at layers diminishing (SOLD) methods for convection-diffusion equations: Part II - Analysis for P1 and Q1 finite elements. Comput. Methods Appl. Mech. Eng. **197**(21–24), 1997–2014 (2008)

11. Persson, P.O., Peraire, J.: Sub-cell shock capturing for discontinuous Galerkin methods. In: 44th AIAA Aerospace Sciences Meeting and Exhibit, p. 112 (2006)
12. Santos, I.P., Almeida, R.C.: A nonlinear subgrid method for advection-diffusion problems. Comput. Methods Appl. Mech. Eng. **196**(45–48), 4771–4778 (2007)
13. Santos, I.P., Malta, S.M., Valli, A.M., Catabriga, L., Almeida, R.C.: Convergence analysis of a new dynamic diffusion method. Comput. Math. Appl. **98**, 1–9 (2021). https://doi.org/10.1016/j.camwa.2021.06.012
14. Valli, A.M., Almeida, R.C., Santos, I.P., Catabriga, L., Malta, S.M., Coutinho, A.L.: A parameter-free dynamic diffusion method for advection-diffusion-reaction problems. Comput. Math. Appl. **75**(1), 307–321 (2018)
15. Yücel, H., Stoll, M., Benner, P.: Discontinuous Galerkin finite element methods with shock-capturing for nonlinear convection dominated models. Comput. Chem. Eng. **58**, 278–287 (2013)

Iterated Local Search with Tabu Search for the Bandwidth Reduction Problem in Graphs

Alexandre Augusto Alberto Moreira de Abreu[1,2,3(✉)] ⬤ and
Sanderson L. Gonzaga de Oliveira[2] ⬤

[1] Instituto Federal de Educação, Ciência e Tecnologia de Santa Catarina, Canoinhas, SC, Brazil
[2] Universidade Federal de São Paulo, São José dos Campos, SP, Brazil
{alexandre.abreu,sanderson.oliveira}@unifesp.br
[3] Instituto Tecnológico de Aeronáutica, São José dos Campos, SP, Brazil

Abstract. This paper addresses the bandwidth reduction problem in graphs, which is relevant in several applications, such as reducing memory consumption and computational cost in solving systems of linear equations. This problem consists of renumbering the vertices of a graph so that the difference between the labels of adjacent vertices is as low as possible. This paper shows a novel hybrid method based on the Iterated Local Search and Tabu Search (ILSTS) metaheuristics. The paper conducted the experiments using several graphs from the SuiteSparse Matrix Collection and compared the results with the current state-of-the-art Dual Representation Simulated Annealing (DRSA). The obtained results highlight that, although ILSTS demonstrates promising outcomes in terms of bandwidth reduction while maintaining low computational cost, it does not achieve competitive results compared to the quality of the solution delivered by DRSA.

Keywords: Bandwidth reduction problem · Graph · Metaheuristics

1 Introduction

The bandwidth reduction problem is a well-known and relevant graph layout problem. Researchers originally applied this problem to accelerate sparse matrix computations. The bandwidth reduction problem is to label the n vertices of a graph with distinct integers ranging from 1 to n such that the new layout reduces the maximum absolute difference between the labels of adjacent vertices. One can also use symmetric matrices to determine the problem. A method reorders the rows and columns of the matrix such that non-null elements are as close as possible to the main diagonal [25]. Bandwidth reduction is relevant in several

Supported by Instituto Federal de Educação, Ciência e Tecnologia de Santa Catarina and Universidade Federal de São Paulo, Brazil.

applications, such as hypertext navigation, small-world networks, analysis of data sets using visual similarity matrices, entropy rate minimization in graphs, symbolic model checking, mesh layout optimization, and the seriation problem [18].

This paper proposes a hybrid heuristic that explores the characteristics of both Iterated Local Search [1,2] and Tabu Search [10] metaheuristics. The computational experiment compares the results of the new metaheuristic algorithm with the DRSA heuristic [41] in 82 sparse matrices taken from the SuiteSparse Matrix Collection [5].

We describe the bandwidth reduction problem and some basic definitions in Sect. 2. Section 3 reviews recent approaches to bandwidth reduction, including the state-of-the-art methods and the most commonly used method in practical applications. Section 4 describes the proposed hybrid metaheuristic. Section 5 describes the data used and the conducted experiments. Finally, we present the results, analysis, conclusions, and future work in Sects. 6 and 7.

2   Bandwidth Reduction

One can define the bandwidth of a matrix as the maximum distance of a non-zero element to the main diagonal. The bandwidth β of an $n \times n$ symmetric matrix $A = [a_{ij}]$ can be defined as $\beta = \beta(A) = \max_{1 \leq i \leq n}[\beta_i(A)]$, where $\beta_i(A) = i - \min_{1 \leq j \leq i, a_{ij} \neq 0}[j]$ represents the bandwidth of the i-th row of matrix A. Equivalently, one can directly determine the bandwidth for an undirected graph $G = (V, E)$, where V is a set of n vertices and E is a set of edges, corresponding to the symmetric matrix A, by considering a function $s : V \to \{1, 2, \ldots, n\}$ that labels the vertices, where $|V| = n$. Thus, a vertex labeling $S = \{s(v_1), s(v_2), \ldots, s(v_n)\}$ is defined as $\beta = \beta_S(G) = \max_{(u,v) \in E}[|s(u) - s(v)|]$.

In simple terms, the problem of bandwidth minimization in a matrix involves rearranging the non-zero coefficients of the matrix to be closer to the main diagonal. When considering the corresponding graph, the objective is to renumber the graph's vertices without altering the adjacencies, aiming to minimize $\beta(s)$. The goal is to swap the vertex labels to minimize the maximum difference between the new labels of adjacent vertices. For example, in Fig. 1, the label swapping in a graph G with $|V| = 6$ and $|E| = 7$ is presented, reducing the initial bandwidth $\beta = 5$ to $\beta = 2$. In the original graph, as shown in Fig. 1(a), $\beta(s) = \max[1, 2, 2, 3, 1, 5, 4] = 5$, considering the edges $\{3, 4\}, \{3, 5\}, \{1, 3\}, \{2, 5\}, \{5, 6\}, \{1, 6\}, \{2, 6\}$, respectively. After the new labeling, presented in Fig. 1(b), $\beta(s) = \max[1, 2, 1, 2, 1, 2, 1] = 2$, considering the edges $\{1, 2\}, \{2, 4\}, \{2, 3\}, \{4, 6\}, \{4, 5\}, \{3, 5\}, \{5, 6\}$, respectively.

With bandwidth reduction, it is possible to optimize memory storage [6]. Additionally, one can obtain solutions for linear systems of equations with lower computational costs [16]. Therefore, over the last decades, hundreds of heuristic methods [3,15] have been developed and applied to the bandwidth reduction problem, as the bandwidth reduction problem is known to be $\mathcal{NP}$-Hard [33]. For a graph $G = (V, E)$ with $|V| = n$, there are $n!$ possible labelings.

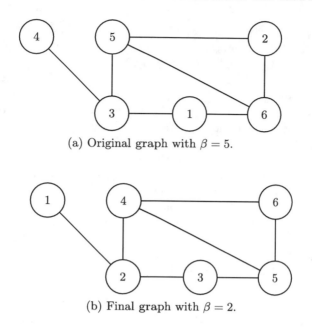

(a) Original graph with $\beta = 5$.

(b) Final graph with $\beta = 2$.

Fig. 1. Example of bandwidth reduction from $\beta = 5$ to $\beta = 2$.

3   Related Works

The development of metaheuristic algorithms for bandwidth reduction began in the 1990 s [3]. Researchers have designed heuristics with the most different metaheuristics, including GRASP-PR [36], genetic algorithm [4,27,37], simulated annealing [38,41], ant colony optimization [4,16,19,20,22,34,35], variable neighborhood search [32], genetic programming [26], charged system search algorithm [23], colliding bodies optimization [21], brain storm optimization [28,29], biased random-key genetic algorithm [39], and iterated local search [17].

Silva et al. [39] proposed an approach grounded on the metaheuristic called Biased Random-Key Genetic Algorithm (BRKGA) [11]. BRKGA uses a permutation vector and vectors of random real numbers called keys to represent possible solutions. A deterministic decoding algorithm associates a solution vector with a feasible solution, allowing the algorithm to calculate the fitness function for the problem. The method is biased because one of the parents in the genetic algorithm is always selected from the elite group and has a high probability of passing its genes on [39]. The authors compared the results obtained with BRKGA with the metaheuristics Dual Representation Simulated Annealing (DRSA) [41], GRASP, and RCM. The results indicated that BRKGA did not perform as well as DRSA for bandwidth reduction but was better than the GRASP and RCM [7] approaches. DRSA dominated the other methods.

A previous investigation [17] proposed a heuristic method based on the iterated local search metaheuristic. The authors referred to the algorithm as the ILS-band heuristic. Gonzaga de Oliveira et al. [12,17] proposed a method named FNCHC+ heuristic. The FNCHC+ heuristic dominated the VNS-band [32] (and, hence, DRSA), and ILS-band heuristics concerning the solution quality and running times when applied to large-scale matrices [17], i.e., with matrices with dimensions higher than one million. The FNCHC+ heuristic also surpassed the resulting heuristics from the ACHH approach [19] regarding the quality solution of large-scale matrices. Additionally, the FNCHC+ heuristic outperformed GPS [9] concerning the solution quality and running times when applied to large-scale matrices [12].

One of the most recent works published by Koohestani [25] presents a study on uninformed search methods, such as breadth-first search and depth-first search. The author also analyzed informed search methods such as Tabu Search and Simulated Annealing, in which information about the problem was used to find more promising solutions. Koohestani [25] conducted numerical experiments to compare his proposal in a Genetic Algorithm implementation, called GA-GBP, with the Biased Random-Key Genetic Algorithm (BRKGA) [39], Greedy Randomized Adaptive Search Procedure (GRASP) [36], and the classic Reverse Cuthill-Mackee (RCM) method [7]. Koohestani [25] obtained the results for BRKGA, GRASP, and RCM from Silva et al. [39]. The author concluded that his proposal provided better guidance in the search employed by GA-GBP.

One could consider the proposal of Rodriguez-Tello et al. [38] the state-of-the-art method until 2010 when Mladenovic et al. [32] proposed the Variable Neighborhood Search for bandwidth reduction (VNS-band), which became the new state of the art until 2015. Gonzaga de Oliveira et al. [13,14] used a one-dimensional self-organizing map for reducing bandwidth and profile in directed and undirected graphs. The publication included experimental comparisons between this proposed method and the VNS-band heuristic. The experimentation involved 113 matrices from the SuiteSparse Matrix Collection and two sets of instances comprising linear systems with sparse symmetric positive-definite matrices that were solved using the Jacobi-preconditioned Conjugate Gradient Method. The results indicated that the VNS-band heuristic outperformed the proposed heuristic.

The DRSA metaheuristic [41], from 2015, differs from the original Simulated Annealing proposed by Kirkpatrick et al. [24] by maintaining a dual internal representation for the current problem solution and implementing three perturbation operations that allow a balance between searching for unknown solutions and exploring known and promising solutions [41]. In its dual representation, DRSA uses a vector of positive integers $\pi = (\pi_1, \pi_2, \ldots, \pi_n)$, where π_i represents the new label of vertex i, and another vector of positive integers $\rho = (\rho_1, \rho_2, \cdots, \rho_n)$, where ρ_i represents the vertex to which label i is assigned. Torres-Jimenez et al. [41] defined three perturbation operations for each vector. Whenever a vector is modified, DRSA propagates the change to the other to maintain consistency between the two representations. The first and second operations are applied to the π vector and swap two positions i and j, randomly selected. In the second operation, the selected vertices must be adjacent. The third operation is a rotation applied to the ρ vector. It selects two positions, i

and j, with $i < j$. DRSA moves the element in position i to j and shifts to the left the elements between positions $i + 1$ and j. The authors conducted experiments with various parameter variations and compared their results with the metaheuristics GRASP [36], classic Simulated Annealing [38], and VNS-band [32]. After using the Wilcoxon test to evaluate their results, Torres-Jimenez et al. [41] presented a statistically significant difference in favor of DRSA, which has been considered the state-of-the-art method in very small matrices (with sizes up to approximately 1000) since then.

4   Iterated Local Search with Tabu Search

The proposed hybrid heuristic explores the characteristics of both Iterated Local Search [1,2] and Tabu Search [10] metaheuristics. The details of the heuristic, named here as Iterated Local Search with Tabu Search (ILSTS), are presented in Algorithm 1. In line 1, r_0 receives the initial labeling of vertices through a constructive method. The constructive method used is the Reverse Cuthill-Mackee method [7] starting with a pseudo-peripheral given by the George-Liu algorithm [8].

Algorithm 1: *Iterated Local Search with Tabu Search (ILSTS)*

---

    input : graph $G = (V, E)$, maximum number of iterations *iter_max*, and tabu list size k.
    output: bandwidth β
1 $r_0 \leftarrow G.initial\_labeling()$;
2 $tabu\_list.size \leftarrow k$;
3 $iter \leftarrow 0$;
4 $level \leftarrow 1$;
5 $r \leftarrow G.local\_search(r_0)$;
6 $\beta \leftarrow G.calculate\_bandwidth(r)$;
7 **while** $iter < iter\_max$ **do**
8     $r' \leftarrow G.perturbation(r, level, tabu\_list)$;
9     $r'' \leftarrow G.local\_search(r')$;
10   **if** $G.calculate\_bandwidth(r'') < G.calculate\_bandwidth(r)$ **then**
11       $r \leftarrow r''$;
12       $\beta \leftarrow G.calculate\_bandwidth(r'')$;
13       $iter \leftarrow 0$;
14       $level \leftarrow 1$;
15   **else**
16       $level \leftarrow level + 1$;
17   **end if**
18    $iter \leftarrow iter + 1$;
19 **end while**
20 **return** β;   // returns the bandwidth β

The method initializes the *tabu_list* with size k in line 2. The variables controlling the number of iterations and the perturbation level are set to their initial values in lines 3 and 4, respectively.

Line 5 obtains the labeling r from a local search on r_0, and β receives the bandwidth considering this labeling in line 6. The local search method used is the *hill climbing* strategy proposed by Martí et al. [30], which uses the concept of critical vertex set defined by $C(S) = \{v : \beta_S(v) = \beta_S(G)\}$, where $\beta_s(v) = \max_{\{v,u\}\in E} [\|s(v) - s(u)\|]$ is the bandwidth of vertex v, and s is the labeling function of the vertices in G. It means that a vertex is critical if its bandwidth is equal to the bandwidth of G. The local search consists of exchanging the label of each critical vertex with the labels of vertices $u \in N'(v)$ in ascending order of the value $|mid(v) - s(u)|$ until it finds a better solution. The set of candidates to be exchanged with vertex v is defined by $N'(v) = \{u : |mid(v) - s(u)| < |mid(v) - s(v)|\}$, where $mid(v) = \lfloor \frac{\max[v]+\min[v]}{2} \rfloor$, $\max[v] = \max_{\{v,u\}\in E} [s(u)]$, and $\min[v] = \min_{\{v,u\}\in E} [s(u)]$.

The ILSTS heuristic executes lines 7 to 19 a maximum of *iter_max* times. The perturbation presented in Algorithm 2 is invoked in line 8. Thus, the method obtains a new candidate solution r'. The algorithm then applies the previously mentioned local search again in line 9. The criterion of acceptance, in line 10, checks if there is a reduction in the bandwidth for the new labeling r'' compared to labeling r. If this is the case, r'' becomes the new incumbent solution, and the values of β, *iter*, and *level* are updated. If not, the method increases the perturbation level in line 16. Afterward, the algorithm updates the iteration counter *iter* in line 18. Finally, at the end of the algorithm, in line 20, the found bandwidth β is returned.

The local search method allows for the improvements' intensification in the incumbent solution. In contrast, the approach attains diversification of ILSTS through the perturbation method outlined in the Algorithm 2, employing a tabu list to prevent the re-exploration of previously visited solutions. Initially, r_0 receives the incumbent solution r, the variable *iter* is initialized, and the method assigns the critical vertices $C(r_0)$ to the vector *critical*, in lines 1, 2, and 3, respectively.

The method repeats lines 4 to 12 while *iter* $\leq$ *level*. Line 5 randomly chooses a critical vertex u. Another vertice v is randomly selected from vertices of G in line 7. The vertices u and v do not need to be adjacent, but $\{u, v\}$ cannot be in the tabu list. The method creates the tabu list with a HashMap data structure that allows insertion and access in $O(1)$.

The method exchanges labels of vertices u and v to generate a new candidate solution r' in line 9. In line 10, $\{u, v\}$ is appended to the *tabu_list*, and *iter* is incremented in line 11. Finally, in line 13, the candidate solution r' is returned.

Algorithm 2: *Perturbation method.*

---

input : labeling vector r, perturbation *level*, and *tabu_list*.
output: vector r' for labeling the vertices of G.

1 $r_0 \leftarrow r$;
2 $iter \leftarrow 1$;
3 $critical \leftarrow G.critical\_vertices(r_0)$;
4 **while** $iter \leq level$ **do**
5      $u \leftarrow random\_choice(critical)$;
6   **repeat**
7 | $v \leftarrow random\_choice(G.V \setminus \{u\})$;
8   **until** $\{u, v\} \notin tabu\_list$;
9      $r' \leftarrow G.swap\_labels(s(u), s(v))$;
10     $tabu\_list.Insert(\{u, v\})$;
11     $iter \leftarrow iter + 1$;
12 **end while**
13 **return** r'; // returns the labeling vector r'

---

5 Description of the Data and Tests

Publicly available matrix instances from the SuiteSparse Matrix Collection [5] were used in the computational experiments. Torres-Jimenez et al. [41] conducted tests with 33 matrices considered tiny and 82 matrices with dimensions ranging from 207 to 1104. In this paper, we used these 82 matrices extracted from the SuiteSparse Matrix Collection to evaluate the results yielded by the hybrid metaheuristic algorithm proposed in this study.

We implemented the ILSTS method in the Rust programming language [31] version 1.69.0 and utilized a memory representation scheme known as Compressed Sparse Row (CSR) [40] or Yale format. We conducted all computational experiments with ILSTS on an Acer Aspire 3 computer with an Intel® Core™ i3-8130U 2.200 GHz processor, 8 GiB of main memory DDR4 1600 MHz, and GNU/Linux Deepin operating system with the Kernel 5.15.77-amd64.

After empirical testing, we established the parameters $iter\_max = 200$ and $k = 50$ for ILSTS with all instances. The findings of DRSA reported by Torres-Jimenez et al. [41] were used to evaluate the results yielded by ILSTS.

6 Results and Analysis

Table 1 presents the results obtained by ILSTS and DRSA for the 82 instances used by Torres-Jimenez et al. [41]. Columns n and β_0 refer to the number of vertices and initial bandwidth of the instances. The table presents the execution times (t) of ILSTS in seconds.

Despite demanding reduced processing time compared to DRSA [41], ILSTS outperformed DRSA in only two instances (nos3 and gr_30_30) and achieved identical results in five matrices (nos1, saylr1, steam2, nos2, and sherman4). In

Table 1. Results for bandwidth reduction using DRSA and ILSTS.

Instance	n	β_0	DRSA	ILSTS	t	Instance	n	β_0	DRSA	ILSTS	t
impcol_a	207	167	32	130	0.13	pores_3	532	77	13	15	0.91
dwt_209	209	184	23	163	0.15	fs_541_1	541	540	70	537	0.57
gre_216a	216	36	21	36	0.17	dwt_592	592	259	29	189	0.47
dwt_221	221	187	13	150	0.17	steam2	600	331	63	**63**	18.86
impcol_e	225	92	42	92	0.28	west0655	655	564	157	562	0.73
dw_234	234	48	11	45	0.32	662_bus	662	335	39	334	0.41
nos1	237	4	3	**3**	0.38	shl_0	663	661	224	632	0.77
saylr1	238	14	14	**14**	0.40	shl_200	663	661	233	654	0.79
steam1	240	146	44	50	1.82	shl_400	663	662	229	613	1.56
dwt_245	245	115	21	114	0.16	nnc666	666	262	40	177	0.94
nnc261	261	64	24	36	0.51	nos6	675	30	16	30	0.32
bcspwr04	274	265	24	248	0.19	fs_680_1	680	600	17	600	0.35
ash292	292	24	19	24	0.22	685_bus	685	550	32	471	0.49
can_292	292	282	38	215	0.31	can_715	715	611	71	456	0.98
dwt_310	310	28	12	14	0.22	nos7	729	81	65	81	0.46
gre_343	343	49	28	49	0.30	fs_760_1	760	740	37	185	0.78
dwt_361	361	50	14	48	0.28	mcfe	765	187	126	187	17.79
plat362	362	249	34	248	1.01	bcsstk19	817	567	14	514	0.62
plskz362	362	248	18	247	0.27	bp_0	822	820	234	774	2.00
str_0	363	359	115	307	0.62	bp_1000	822	820	283	776	3.26
str_200	363	359	124	322	0.96	bp_1200	822	820	287	781	2.44
str_600	363	359	131	320	1.40	bp_1400	822	820	291	774	2.70
west0381	381	363	149	323	0.46	bp_1600	822	820	292	778	2.94
dwt_419	419	356	25	329	0.53	bp_200	822	820	257	783	6.07
bcsstk06	420	47	45	47	1.24	bp_400	822	820	267	787	3.08
bcsstm07	420	47	45	47	1.01	bp_600	822	820	272	777	2.51
impcol_d	425	406	39	213	0.35	bp_800	822	820	278	775	2.67
hor_131	434	421	54	72	1.99	can_838	838	837	86	624	1.19
bcspwr05	443	435	27	415	0.18	dwt_878	878	519	25	458	0.87
can_445	445	403	52	329	0.45	orsirr_2	886	554	85	113	1.79
nos5	468	178	63	178	0.59	gr_30_30	900	31	33	**31**	0.84
west0479	479	388	119	386	0.44	dwt_918	918	839	32	763	0.83
bcsstk20	485	20	13	20	0.28	jagmesh1	936	778	27	643	0.69
494_bus	494	428	28	403	0.22	nos2	957	4	3	**3**	0.42
mbeacxc	496	490	260	486	127.45	nos3	960	43	44	**43**	1.91
mbeaflw	496	490	260	485	123.47	west0989	989	855	207	855	0.83
mbeause	496	490	254	482	96.03	jpwh_991	991	197	88	175	2.29
west0497	497	416	85	363	0.41	dwt_992	992	513	35	513	3.14
dwt_503	503	452	41	358	0.90	saylr3	1000	100	46	54	1.30
lnsp_511	511	57	44	57	0.51	sherman1	1000	100	46	54	1.29
gre_512	512	64	36	64	0.55	sherman4	1104	368	27	**27**	1.48

2 matrices (bcsstk06, bcsstm07), ILSTS found results 10% close to the results obtained by DRSA. In five instances (steam1, dwt_310, pores_3, saylr3, and sherman1), the results found by ILSTS were worse than those found by DRSA by a margin smaller than 20%. DRSA was considerably better than ILSTS in reducing bandwidth in all other instances. Figure 2 shows that DRSA performed better in most instances, even though there is no relationship between the size of the matrices and the difference between the bandwidths found.

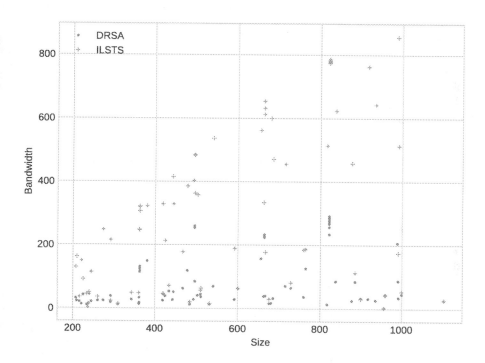

Fig. 2. Comparison of results for bandwidth reduction using DRSA and ILSTS.

7   Conclusions

This paper implemented a hybrid metaheuristic algorithm to leverage the characteristics of Iterated Local Search and Tabu Search (ILSTS). The paper compared the results yielded by the ILSTS with the Dual Representation Simulated Annealing (DRSA) [41], which is the current state-of-the-art metaheuristic algorithm for the bandwidth reduction problem in very small matrices. From the obtained results, we concluded that ILSTS demonstrates promising outcomes in terms of bandwidth reduction while maintaining low computational cost. However, ILSTS does not achieve competitive results when compared with DRSA when one only considers the bandwidth reduction and not the execution time.

Due to its reduced computational cost, ILSTS is a candidate for utilization in situations that require bandwidth reduction with low computational cost. In future work, we intend to evaluate the performance of ILSTS in conjunction with the conjugate gradient method to reduce the computational cost required to solve systems of linear equations. Furthermore, we intend to verify if the ILSTS presents competitive results when applied to large matrices. These future investigations are necessary to establish the potential of ILSTS as a viable alternative approach to bandwidth reduction since there is no record of the previous use of the metaheuristic Iterated Local Search with Tabu Search for this purpose.

Acknowledgment. The authors gratefully acknowledge the support of the FAPESP (Fundação de Amparo à Pesquisa do Estado de São Paulo) and IFSC (Instituto Federal de Educação, Ciência e Tecnologia de Santa Catarina).

References

1. Baum, E.B.: Iterated descent: a better algorithm for local search in combinatorial optimization problems. Technical report, Caltech, Pasadena, CA (1986)
2. Baxter, J.: Local optima avoidance in depot location. J. Oper. Res. Soc. **32**(9), 815 (1981)
3. Chagas, G.O., Gonzaga de Oliveira, S.L.: Metaheuristic-based heuristics for symmetric-matrix bandwidth reduction: a systematic review. Procedia Comput. Sci. (ICCS 2015 International Conference on Computational Science) **51**, 211–220 (2015)
4. Czibula, G., Crişan, G.C., Pintea, C.M., Czibula, I.G.: Soft computing approaches on the bandwidth problem. Informatica **24**(2), 169–180 (2013)
5. Davis, T., Hu, Y.: The university of florida sparse matrix collection. ACM Trans. Math. Softw. **38**, 1 (11 2011)
6. Freire, M., Marichal, R., Gonzaga de Oliveira, S.L., Dufrechou, E., Ezzatti, P.: Enhancing the sparse matrix storage using reordering techniques. In: Barrios H., C.J., Rizzi, S., Meneses, E., Mocskos, E., Monsalve Diaz, J.M., Montoya, J. (eds) High Performance Computing, CARLA 2023, CCIS, vol. 1887, pp. 66–76. Springer, Cham (2024). https://doi.org/10.1007/978-3-031-52186-7_5
7. George, A., Liu, J.: Computer Solution of Large Sparse Positive Definite Systems. Prentice-Hall, Englewood Cliffs, New Jersey, USA (1981)
8. George, A., Liu, J.W.H.: An implementation of a pseudoperipheral node finder. ACM Trans. Math. Softw. **5**(3), 284–295 (1979)
9. Gibbs, N.E., Poole, W.G., Stockmeyer, P.K.: An algorithm for reducing the bandwidth and profile of a sparse matrix. SIAM J. Numer. Anal. **13**(2), 236–250 (1976)
10. Glover, F.: Future paths for integer programming and links to artificial intelligence. Comput. Oper. Res. **13**(5), 533–549 (1986)
11. Gonçalves, J.F., Resende, M.G.C.: Biased random-key genetic algorithms for combinatorial optimization. J. Heuristics **17**(5), 487–525 (2011)
12. Gonzaga de Oliveira, S.L.: An evaluation of heuristic methods for the bandwidth reduction of large-scale graphs. Revista Pesquisa Operacional **43**(e268255), 1–22 (2023)
13. Gonzaga de Oliveira, S.L., de Abreu, A.A.A.M., Robaina, D., Kischinhevsky, M.: A new heuristic for bandwidth and profile reductions of matrices using a self-organizing map. In: Gervasi, O., et al. (eds.) ICCSA 2016. LNCS, vol. 9786, pp. 54–70. Springer, Cham (2016). https://doi.org/10.1007/978-3-319-42085-1_5

14. Gonzaga de Oliveira, S.L., Abreu, A.A.A.M., Robaina, D.T., Kischnhevsky, M.: An evaluation of four reordering algorithms to reduce the computational cost of the Jacobi-preconditioned conjugate gradient method using high-precision arithmetic. Int. J. Bus. Intell. Data Min. **12**(2), 190–209 (2017)

15. Gonzaga de Oliveira, S.L., Chagas, G.O.: A systematic review of heuristics for symmetric-matrix bandwidth reduction: methods not based on metaheuristics. In: Proceedings of the Brazilian Symposium on Operations Research (SBPO 2015), Sobrapo, Pernambuco, Brazil, August 2015

16. Gonzaga de Oliveira, S.L., Silva, L.M.: Evolving reordering algorithms using an ant colony hyperheuristic approach for accelerating the convergence of the ICCG method. Eng. Comput. **36**(4), 1857–1873 (2019)

17. Gonzaga de Oliveira, S.L., Carvalho, C.: Metaheuristic algorithms for the bandwidth reduction of large-scale matrices. J. Comb. Optim. **43**, 727–784 (2022)

18. Gonzaga de Oliveira, S.L., Silva, L.M.: Low-cost heuristics for matrix bandwidth reduction combined with a Hill-Climbing strategy. RAIRO-Oper. Res. **55**(4), 2247–2264 (2021)

19. Gonzaga de Oliveira, S., Silva, L.M.: An ant colony hyperheuristic approach for matrix bandwidth reduction. Appl. Soft Comput. **94**, 106434 (2020)

20. Guan, J., Lin, G., Feng, H.B.: Ant colony optimisation with local search for the bandwidth minimisation problem on graphs. Int. J. Intell. Inf. Database Syst. **12**(1–2), 65–78 (2019)

21. Kaveh, A., Bijari, S.: Bandwidth optimization using CBO and ECBO. Asian J. Civel Eng. **16**(4), 535–545 (2015)

22. Kaveh, A., Sharafi, P.: Nodal ordering for bandwidth reduction using ant system algorithm. Eng. Comput. **26**, 313–323 (2009)

23. Kaveh, A., Sharafi, P.: Ordering for bandwidth and profile minimization problems via charged system search algorithm. IJST Trans. Civil Eng. **36**, 39–52 (2012)

24. Kirkpatrick, S., Gelatt, C.D., Vecchi, M.P.: Optimization by simulated annealing. Science **220**(4598), 671–680 (1983)

25. Koohestani, B.: On the solution of the graph bandwidth problem by means of search methods. Appl. Intell. **53**(7), 7988–8004 (2022)

26. Koohestani, B., Poli, R.: A hyper-heuristic approach to evolving algorithms for bandwidth reduction based on genetic programming. In: Bramer, M., Petridis, M., Nolle, L. (eds.) Research and Development in Intelligent Systems XXVIII, SGAI 2011, pp. 93–106. Springer, London (2011). https://doi.org/10.1007/978-1-4471-2318-7_7

27. Lim, A., Rodrigues, B., Xiao, F.: Heuristics for matrix bandwidth reduction. Eur. J. Oper. Res. **174**(1), 69–91 (2006)

28. Mafteiu-Scai, L., Mafteiu, E., Mafteiu-Scai, R.: Brain storm optimization algorithms for solving equations systems. In: Cheng, S., Shi, Y. (eds.) Brain Storm Optimization Algorithms. Adaptation, Learning, and Optimization, vol. 23, pp. 189–220. Springer, Cham (2019). https://doi.org/10.1007/978-3-030-15070-9_8

29. Mafteiu-Scai, L.O., Mafteiu-Scai, E., Voina, T.: Bandwidths optimization on sparse matrices using brain storm optimization. In: 19th International Symposium on Symbolic and Numeric Algorithms for Scientific Computing (SYNASC), pp. 219–224. IEEE, Timisoara, Romania (2017)

30. Martí, R., Laguna, M., Glover, F., Campos, V.: Reducing the bandwidth of a sparse matrix with tabu search. Eur. J. Oper. Res. **135**(2), 450–459 (2001)

31. Matsakis, N.D., Klock, F.S.: The rust language. In: Proceedings of the 2014 ACM SIGAda Annual Conference on High Integrity Language Technology, HILT 2014, pp. 103–104. Association for Computing Machinery, New York, NY, USA (2014)

32. Mladenovic, N., Urosevic, D., Pérez-Brito, D., García-González, C.G.: Variable neighbourhood search for bandwidth reduction. Eur. J. Oper. Res. **200**(1), 14–27 (2010)
33. Papadimitriou, C.H.: The NP-completeness of the bandwidth minimization problem. Computing **16**(3), 263–270 (1976)
34. Pintea, C.-M., Crişan, G.-C., Chira, C.: A hybrid ACO Approach to the Matrix Bandwidth Minimization Problem. In: Graña Romay, M., Corchado, E., Garcia Sebastian, M.T. (eds.) HAIS 2010. LNCS (LNAI), vol. 6076, pp. 405–412. Springer, Heidelberg (2010). https://doi.org/10.1007/978-3-642-13769-3_49
35. Pintea, C.M., Crişan, G.C., Shira, C.: Hybrid ant models with a transition policy for solving a complex problem. Log. J. IGPL **20**(3), 560–569 (2012)
36. Piñana, E., Plana, I., Campos, V., Martí, R.: Grasp and path relinking for the matrix bandwidth minimization. Eur. J. Oper. Res. **153**(1), 200–210 (2004)
37. Pop, P., Matei, O., Comes, C.A.: Reducing the bandwidth of a sparse matrix with a genetic algorithm. Optim. A J. Math. Program. Oper. Res. **63**(12), 1851–1876 (2014)
38. Rodriguez-Tello, E., Hao, J.K., Torres-Jimenez, J.: An improved simulated annealing algorithm for bandwidth minimization. Eur. J. Oper. Res. **185**(3), 1319–1335 (2008)
39. Silva, P.H.G., Brandão, D.N., Morais, I.S., Gonzaga de Oliveira, S.L.: A biased random-key genetic algorithm for bandwidth reduction. In: Gervasi, O., et al. (eds.) ICCSA 2020. LNCS, vol. 12249, pp. 312–321. Springer, Cham (2020). https://doi.org/10.1007/978-3-030-58799-4_23
40. Tinney, W., Walker, J.: Direct solutions of sparse network equations by optimally ordered triangular factorization. Proc. IEEE **55**(11), 1801–1809 (1967)
41. Torres-Jimenez, J., Izquierdo-Marquez, I., Garcia-Robledo, A., Gonzalez-Gomez, A., Bernal, J., Kacker, R.N.: A dual representation simulated annealing algorithm for the bandwidth minimization problem on graphs. Inf. Sci. **303**, 33–49 (2015)

The Weighted Vector Finite Element Method for Vector Wave Equation with Singularity

Viktor A. Rukavishnikov$^{(\boxtimes)}$ [ID] and Elena I. Rukavishnikova [ID]

Computing Center, Far-Eastern Branch Russian Academy of Sciences, Khabarovsk, Russian Federation
vark0102@mail.ru

Abstract. Boundary value problems for wave vector equations with singularity are used in mathematical models of electromagnetism problems in domains with a boundary containing reentrant corners. The solutions to such problems do not belong to the Sobolev space W_2^1 and the approximate solution by the classical finite element method has a low rate of convergence to the exact solution.

We define an R_ν-generalized solution to the boundary value problem for a wave vector equation with corner singularity in a set of the weighted Sobolev-Monk space. A weighted vector finite element method (WVFEM) is constructed to find an approximate R_ν-generalized problem. The WVFEM basis functions contain weighting functions to a degree depending on the sizes of the reentrant corners at the domain boundary. This allows us to weaken the influence of the singularity on the accuracy of finding the solution. The method has a convergence rate of $O(h)$ in the norm of the weighted space $L_{2,\alpha}(\Omega)^2$. Numerical calculations of model problems confirmed the theoretical estimate of the convergence rate.

Keywords: Vector wave equations with a singularity · R_ν-generalized solution · Weighted vector finite element method

1 Introduction

Over the past few decades, various numerical methods have been developed for solving boundary value problems of mathematical physics. One such method is the vector finite element method which was first proposed by J.C. Nédélec [8,9] and was further developed in works [2,4–7,26,27].

Vector FEM is used to solve various problems of electrodynamics, elasticity theory and other problems of mathematical physics (see, for example, [10,11]).

The main difference between the vector finite element method and the nodal method is that the degrees of freedom are associated with the sides of the finite elements, and not with the nodes of the finite element mesh. This makes it possible to accurately fulfill the solinoidal condition of the solution and to easily

O. Gervasi et al. (Eds.): ICCSA 2024, LNCS 14813, pp. 137–147, 2024.
https://doi.org/10.1007/978-3-031-64605-8_10

take into account the boundary conditions and behavior of the solution at the interface between the media. However, the convergence rate of the vector finite element method when solving a problem in a domain containing a reentrant corner at the boundary is reduced (see, for example, [3,25]). This circumstance requires the construction of a special numerical method for solving problems with corner singularity.

We proposed to define the R_ν-generalized solution for boundary value problems with the singularity [12]. The existence and uniqueness, coercive and differential properties of the R_ν-generalized solution for various problems with singularity in weighted Sobolev spaces and sets were studied in [15,18,21,24]. The introduction of the R_ν-generalized solution made it possible to create numerical methods in which the singularity does not affect the accuracy of finding the solution. We have created a weighted nodal finite element method for elliptic problems, problems in the theory of elasticity and hydrodynamics [13,14,19,20,22]. The proposed approach does not lead to ill-conditioned systems of linear equations and makes it possible significantly reduce the computation time to achieve a given accuracy [17,23].

In this paper, we introduce a special weight set from the weighted Sobolev-Monk space $H(\text{rot}, \Omega)$. The R_ν-generalized solution of the boundary value problem for vector wave equation with corner singularity is defined in this set. The weighted vector finite element method is constructed to find an approximate R_ν-generalized solution to the problem under consideration. A special feature of this method is that a weight function is introduced into the definition of basis functions the degree of which depends on the asymptotic behavior of the singular component of the solution to the original boundary value problem. This makes it possible to better approximate solution near the singularity point and increase the rate of convergence of the approximate solution to the exact one in the norm of the weighted space $L_{2,\alpha}(\Omega)^2$. Numerical analysis of a series of model problems showed that the convergence rate of the constructed method is one and a half times higher than in the singular addition method and the regularization method.

2   Notations and Problem Setting

Let $\Omega = (-1, -1) \times (-1, -1) \setminus [-1, 0] \times [-1, 0]$ – L-shaped domain in $\mathbb{R}^2$, $\partial\Omega$ be a boundary of domain Ω and the point $O(0, 0)$ be the vertex of the reentrant corner $3\pi/2$.

We denote the vector-function by $\mathbf{u}(x) = (u_1(x), u_2(x))$ with $x = (x_1, x_2)$, $\mathbf{n}$ and τ are the unit outward normal and the tangent vector to point of the boundary $\partial\Omega$, $\{\mathbf{i}, \mathbf{j}\}$ is an orthonormal basis in $\mathbb{R}^2$.

We introduce the spaces $L_2(\Omega)$, $L_2(\Omega)^2$ and $H^1(\Omega)$, $H^1(\Omega)^2$ with norms

$$\|u\|_{L_2(\Omega)} = \sqrt{\int_\Omega u^2 dx}, \qquad \|\mathbf{u}\|_{L_2(\Omega)^2} = \sqrt{\|u_1\|_{L_2(\Omega)} + \|u_2\|_{L_2(\Omega)}},$$

$$\|u\|_{H^1(\Omega)} = \sqrt{\sum_{\|i\|\leq 1} \int_\Omega |D^i u|^2 dx}, \qquad \|\mathbf{u}\|_{H^1(\Omega)^2} = \sqrt{\|u_1\|_{H^1(\Omega)} + \|u_2\|_{H^1(\Omega)}},$$

where $D^i = \dfrac{\partial^{|i|}}{\partial x_1^{i_1} \partial x_2^{i_2}}$; $|i| = i_1 + i_2$, i_1, i_2 are nonnegative integer numbers.

For functions $u(x)$ and vector-functions $\mathbf{u}(x)$ we define differential operators:

$$\operatorname{div} \mathbf{u} = \frac{\partial u_1}{\partial x_1} + \frac{\partial u_2}{\partial x_2}, \qquad \mathbf{rot}\, u = \left(\frac{\partial u}{\partial x_2}, -\frac{\partial u}{\partial x_1} \right), \qquad \operatorname{rot} \mathbf{u} = \frac{\partial u_2}{\partial x_1} - \frac{\partial u_1}{\partial x_2}.$$

Let $H(\operatorname{rot}\Omega) = \{\mathbf{u} \in L_2(\Omega)^2, \operatorname{rot} \mathbf{u} \in L_2(\Omega)\}$ be the space of functions with norm

$$\|\mathbf{u}\|^2_{H(\operatorname{rot},\Omega)} = \int_\Omega \left(u_1^2 + u_2^2 + (\operatorname{rot} \mathbf{u})^2 \right) dx$$

and $\mathring{H}(\operatorname{rot},\Omega) = \{\mathbf{u} \in L_2(\Omega)^2, \operatorname{rot} \mathbf{u} \in H(\operatorname{rot},\Omega), \mathbf{u} \cdot \boldsymbol{\tau} = 0$ almost everywhere on $\partial\Omega\}$.

Denote by $\Omega' = \left\{ x \in \overline{\Omega} : (x_1^2 + x_2^2)^{\frac{1}{2}} \leq \delta \ll 1 \right\}$ the δ-neighborhood of the point O in Ω. Let us introduce a weight function $\rho(x)$ which satisfies the following conditions: $\rho(x) = (x_1^2 + x_2^2)^{\frac{1}{2}}$ for $x \in \overline{\Omega'}$, $\rho(x) = \delta$ for $x \in \overline{\Omega} \setminus \overline{\Omega'}$.

We define the weighted spaces $L_{2,\alpha}(\Omega)$, $L_{2,\alpha}(\Omega)^2$ and $H_\alpha(\operatorname{rot},\Omega)$ of functions with norms:

$$\|u\|_{L_{2,\alpha}(\Omega)} = \sqrt{\int_\Omega \rho^{2\alpha} u^2 dx}, \qquad \|\mathbf{u}\|_{L_{2,\alpha}(\Omega)^2} = \sqrt{\|u_1\|_{L_{2,\alpha}(\Omega)} + \|u_2\|_{L_{2,\alpha}(\Omega)}},$$

$$\|\mathbf{u}\|^2_{H_\alpha(\operatorname{rot},\Omega)} = \|\mathbf{u}\|^2_{L_{2,\alpha}(\Omega)} + \|\operatorname{rot} \mathbf{u}\|^2_{L_{2,\alpha}(\Omega)} = \int_\Omega \rho^{2\alpha} \left(u_1^2 + u_2^2 + (\operatorname{rot} \mathbf{u})^2 \right) dx. \quad (1)$$

Let $\mathring{H}_\alpha(\operatorname{rot},\Omega) = \{\mathbf{u} \in H_\alpha(\operatorname{rot},\Omega), \mathbf{u} \cdot \boldsymbol{\tau} = 0$ almost everywhere on $\partial\Omega\}$. Here α is real number.

By $H_\alpha(\operatorname{rot},\Omega,\delta)$ we denote a set of functions satisfying the following conditions:

(a) $|u_i(x)| \leq C_1 \rho^{-\alpha}(x)$ $(i = 1, 2)$, $|\operatorname{rot} \mathbf{u}| \leq C_1 \rho^{-\alpha-1}(x)$, $x \in \Omega'$, $C_1 > 0$;
(b) $\|\mathbf{u}\|_{L_{2,\alpha}(\Omega\setminus\Omega')^2} \geq C_2 > 0$

with norm (1).

We define the weighted sets
$\mathring{H}_\alpha(\operatorname{rot},\Omega,\delta) = \{\mathbf{u} \in H_\alpha(\operatorname{rot},\Omega,\delta), \mathbf{u} \cdot \boldsymbol{\tau} = 0$ almost everywhere on $\partial\Omega\}$,
$V(\Omega,\delta) = \{\mathbf{u} \in \mathring{H}_\alpha(\operatorname{rot},\Omega,\delta), \operatorname{div} \mathbf{u} = 0\}$.

Let us consider the boundary value problem for vector wave equation

$$\operatorname{rot} \operatorname{rot} \mathbf{E} - k^2 \mathbf{E} = \mathbf{f}, \qquad \text{in } \Omega, \qquad (2)$$

$$\operatorname{div} \mathbf{E} = 0, \qquad \text{in } \Omega, \qquad (3)$$

$$\mathbf{E} \cdot \boldsymbol{\tau} = 0, \qquad \text{on } \partial\Omega. \qquad (4)$$

Comment. The solution of the problem (2)–(4) belongs to the space $H(\text{rot}, \Omega)$ (see, for example, [1]) and does not belong to $H^1(\Omega)^2$. A solution from this space does not allow to construct a numerical method of high degree of accuracy on the basis of the principle of consistent estimates (see, for example, [3,25]). We will define an R_ν-generalized solution in the weighted set V to construct a weighted vector finite element method with a high rate of convergence of the approximate solution to the exact one.

Denote by

$$a(\mathbf{u}, \mathbf{v}) = (\text{rot } \mathbf{u}, \text{rot}(\rho^{2\nu}\mathbf{v})) - k^2(\mathbf{u}, \rho^{2\nu}\mathbf{v}) =$$

$$\int_\Omega \left(\frac{\partial u_2}{\partial x_1} - \frac{\partial u_1}{\partial x_2}\right)\left[\rho^{2\nu}\left(\frac{\partial v_2}{\partial x_1} - \frac{\partial v_1}{\partial x_2}\right) - \left(\frac{\partial \rho^{2\nu}}{\partial x_2}v_1 - \frac{\partial \rho^{2\nu}}{\partial x_1}v_2\right)\right]dx - k^2\int_\Omega \rho^{2\nu}\left(u_1v_1 + u_2v_2\right)dx,$$

$$b(\mathbf{v}) = (\mathbf{f}, \rho^{2\nu}\mathbf{v}) = \int_\Omega \rho^{2\nu}\left(f_1v_1 + f_2v_2\right)dx$$

the bilinear and linear forms, respectively.

Definition 1. A function $\mathbf{E}_\nu$ in the weighted set $V(\Omega, \delta)$ is called a R_ν-generalized solution of the boundary value problem (2)–(4) if for any $\mathbf{v} \in V(\Omega, \delta)$ the identity

$$a(\mathbf{E}_\nu, \mathbf{v}) = b(\mathbf{v}) \tag{5}$$

holds.

3   Construction of the Weighted Vector Finite Element Method

The scheme of the weighted vector finite element method for determination of an R_ν-generalized solution was constructed in [16]. Here we briefly describe construction of the WVFEM for the boundary value problem of vector wave Eq. (2)–(4).

We perform a quasi-uniform triangulation of the domain Ω. Let mesh step $h = \frac{2}{N}$, N is a positive even integer. We divide Ω by straight lines $x_1 = -1 + jh$, $x_2 = -1 + lh$, $j, l = 0, \dots, N$, into a set of finite elements $\{K\} = \{K_i\}_{i=1}^{N_h}$, $N_h = \frac{3N^2}{4}$. Let S_i be the side of the finite element. Let S be a subset of $\{K\}$:

$$S = \{S_i, i = 1, \dots, N_S, S_i \not\subset \partial\Omega, N_S = \frac{3N^2}{2} - 2N\}.$$

Let us introduce notation for a separate finite element K_i (Fig. 1): $S_j^{K_i}$ $(j = \overline{1,4})$ are its sides K_i, $M_j^{K_i}\left(m_{1j}^{K_i}, m_{2j}^{K_i}\right)$ are the centers of $S_j^{K_i}$, $O^{K_i}\left(o_1^{K_i}, o_2^{K_i}\right)$ is its center K_i. The rule for local numbering of sides K_i is shown in Fig. 1.

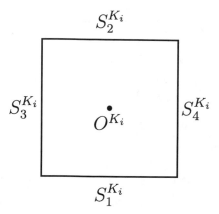

Fig. 1. [16] The rule for the local numeration $S_j^{K_i}$ $\left(j = \overline{1,4}\right)$ of the finite element K_i

For every finite element K_i we define form functions associated with its sides $S_j^{K_i}$ $\left(j = \overline{1,4}\right)$:

$$\psi_1^{K_i} = \frac{1}{h}\rho^{-\gamma}\left(m_{11}^{K_i}, x_2\right)\left(\frac{h}{2} + o_2^{K_i} - x_2\right)\mathbf{i}, \quad \psi_2^{K_i} = \frac{1}{h}\rho^{-\gamma}\left(m_{12}^{K_i}, x_2\right)\left(\frac{h}{2} - o_2^{K_i} + x_2\right)\mathbf{i},$$

$$\psi_3^{K_i} = \frac{1}{h}\rho^{-\gamma}\left(x_1, m_{23}^{K_i}\right)\left(\frac{h}{2} + o_1^{K_i} - x_1\right)\mathbf{j}, \quad \psi_4^{K_i} = \frac{1}{h}\rho^{-\gamma}\left(x_1, m_{24}^{K_i}\right)\left(\frac{h}{2} - o_1^{K_i} + x_1\right)\mathbf{j}.$$

Here γ is a real number.

Remark 1. The weight function is introduced into the form functions in such a way as to preserve the property of their solenoidality.

Now we define the basis functions ψ_i, $i = \overline{1, N_S}$. Let S_i be common side for elements K_m and K_n and $\psi_j^{K_m}, \psi_l^{K_n}$ be the form functions associated with S_i. For side S_i we assign the basis function

$$\psi_i = \begin{cases} \psi_j^{K_m}, & x \in K_m, \\ \psi_l^{K_n}, & x \in K_n, \\ 0, & x \in \overline{\Omega} \setminus (K_m \cup K_n). \end{cases}$$

Let us denote by $\tilde{V}^h$ the linear span $\{\psi_i\}_{i=1}^{N_S}$. Obviously, $\tilde{V}^h \in \mathring{H}_\nu\left(\text{rot}, \Omega\right)$. By virtue of the conditions of basis functions, we have div $\mathbf{v}_h = 0$ for any $\mathbf{v}_h \in \tilde{V}^h$. We define the weighted sets $V_\nu^h\left(\Omega, \delta\right) = \tilde{V}^h \cap H_\nu\left(\text{rot}, \Omega, \delta\right)$.

Definition 2. A function $\mathbf{E}_\nu^h \in V_\nu^h\left(\Omega, \delta\right)$ we call an approximate R_ν-generalized solution of problem (2)–(4) by weighted vector finite element method if for any $\mathbf{v}_h \in V_\nu^h\left(\Omega, \delta\right)$ the following integral identity

$$a\left(\mathbf{E}_\nu^h, \mathbf{v}_h\right) = b\left(\mathbf{v}_h\right)$$

holds.

An approximate solution $\mathbf{E}_\nu^h$ will be found in the form

$$\mathbf{E}_\nu^h = \sum_{i=1}^{N_S} d_i \psi_i,$$

where $d_i = \rho^\nu\left(M_i\right) q_i$, $q_i = \text{const}$.

The coefficients d_i are defined from the system of equations

$$a\left(\mathbf{E}_\nu^h, \psi_i\right) = b\left(\psi_i\right), \quad i = \overline{1, N_S}.$$

4   Numerical Results

We have carried out a set of numerical tests for boundary value problem (2)–(4) using a weighted vector FEM. The first problem contains only a singular component in the solution (problem A), and the second problem contains a singular component and a regular function from the space $H^2\left(\Omega\right)$ (problem B). Calculations were carried out on meshes with different numbers of partitions $N = 16, 32, 64, 128$. We have established the optimal parameters ν, δ, γ for the calculations (see [23]). For the found approximate R_ν-generalized solutions $\mathbf{E}_\nu^h$ we calculated the value of the relative error in the norm of the space $L_{2,\alpha}\left(\Omega\right)^2$: $\eta = \dfrac{\|\mathbf{E}_\nu - \mathbf{E}_\nu^h\|_{L_{2,\alpha}(\Omega)^2}}{\|\mathbf{E}_\nu\|_{L_{2,\alpha}(\Omega)^2}}$. The values of η for various numbers of partitions N in Tables 1 and 3 for problems (A) and (B) are presented. In addition, these tables show the ratios λ between error norms obtained on meshes with number of segments N increasing twice. Convergence rate graphs for problems (A) and (B) are presented in Figs. 2 and 4. At each point M_i the absolute error $\delta_{ij} = |E_{i\nu}\left(M_i\right) - E_{i\nu}^h\left(M_i\right)|$, $i = 1, 2$ was calculated. We also determined the number and coordinates of points M_i with an absolute error δ_{ij} less than the specified limit error $\overline{\Delta} = 10^{-3}$. The results of numerical experiments are shown in Tables 2, 4 and Figs. 3, 5.

Model Problem (A). We introduce an auxiliary function

$$\varphi = x_1 x_2 \sin\left(\pi x_1\right) \cos\left(0.5\pi x_1\right) \sin\left(\pi x_2\right) \cos\left(0.5\pi x_2\right) \left(\sqrt{x_1^2 + x_2^2}\right)^{-3.3}.$$

We define the solution to problem (A) as $\mathbf{E} = \mathbf{rot}\ \varphi$ and calculate the right side of Eq. (2) for two values of the coefficient $k_1 = 300$ and $k_2 = 220$ (frequency 14.314 and 10.497 GHz, respectively).

Table 1. Dependence of the relative errors η_ν for problem (A) from number of segments N. The parameters of weighted vector FEM are $\nu = 2.0$, $\delta = 0.063$ ($k = k_1$); $\nu = 1.9$, $\delta = 0.055$ ($k = k_2$)

N	16	λ	32	λ	64	λ	128
$\eta, k = k_1$	0.537303	1.84	0.291715	2.44	0.119754	2.24	0.053544
$\eta, k = k_2$	0.543997	1.77	0.307029	2.29	0.134271	2.08	0.064547

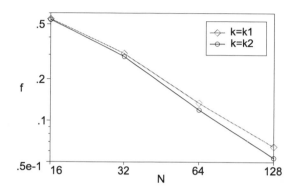

Fig. 2. Convergence rate of the relative error η_ν of the approximate R_ν-generalized solution of the problem (A) on the number of segments N.

Table 2. The percentage of points from the total number of points M_i in which the absolute error δ_{ij} is less than the specified limit error $\overline{\Delta} = 10^{-3}$

N	16	32	64	128
$\eta, k = k_1$	4.55%	13.59%	42.05%	73.56%
$\eta, k = k_2$	4.55%	13.18%	42.05%	73.58%

Remark 2. For the function φ the exponent was chosen equal to -3.3 so that the asymptotic of the solution **E** in the vicinity of the singularity point would be close to the theoretical $\rho^{-1/3}$.

Model Problem (B). For model problem (B) we introduce an auxiliary function

$$\varphi = x_1 x_2 \sin(\pi x_1) \cos(0.5\pi x_1) \sin(\pi x_2) \cos(0.5\pi x_2) \left(\left(\sqrt{x_1^2 + x_2^2} \right)^{-3.3} + 10 \right).$$

We present results for model problem (B).

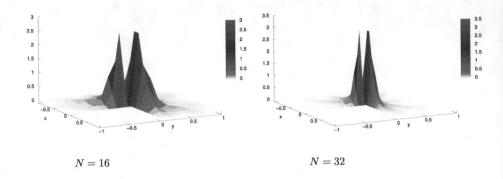

$$N = 16 \qquad\qquad N = 32$$

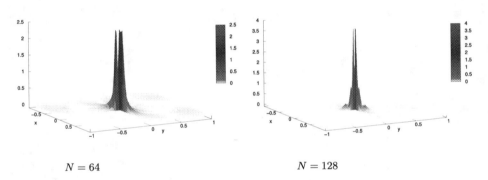

$$N = 64 \qquad\qquad N = 128$$

Fig. 3. Graph of the absolute error δ_{1j} for the component $E^h_{1\nu}$ of the approximate R_ν-generalized solution of the problem (A) using the weighted vector finite element method on meshes with the number of partition segments N.

Table 3. Dependence of the relative errors η_ν for the problem (B) from number of segments N. The parameters of weighted vector FEM are $\nu = 2.0$, $\delta = 0.063$ $(k = k_1)$; $\nu = 1.9$, $\delta = 0.055$ $(k = k_2)$

N	16	λ	32	λ	64	λ	128
$\eta, k = k_1$	0.310778	1.87	0.166349	2.41	0.069088	2.18	0.031701
$\eta, k = k_2$	0.308519	1.92	0.160973	2.41	0.066790	2.17	0.030406

Table 4. The percentage of points from the total number of points M_i in which the absolute error δ_{ij} is less than the specified limit error $\overline{\Delta} = 10^{-3}$

N	16	32	64	128
$\eta, k = k_1$	4.55%	12.17%	36.85%	69.03%
$\eta, k = k_2$	4.55%	12.78%	36.05%	68.18%

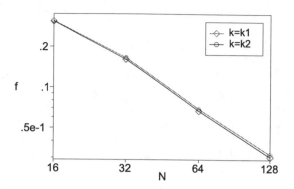

Fig. 4. Convergence rate of the relative error η_ν of the approximate R_ν-generalized solution of the problem (B) on the number of segments N.

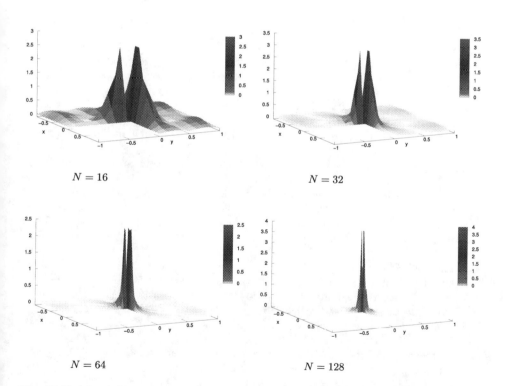

$N = 16$ $N = 32$

$N = 64$ $N = 128$

Fig. 5. Graph of the absolute error δ_{1j} for the $E_{1\nu}^h$ of the approximate R_ν-generalized solution of the problem (B) using the weighted vector finite element method on meshes with the number of partition segments N.

5   Conclusions

In this paper, a weighted vector finite element method for solving vector wave boundary value problems with singularity is constructed. We proposed to define the solution to the problem as an R_ν-generalized solution in a special weighted set $V(\Omega, \delta)$. The basis functions of the constructed method include a weight function to a degree depending on the asymptotic behavior of the solution near the singularity point.

Numerical experiments were carried out for model problems of two types: with a solution containing only a singular component, and with a solution containing both singular and regular components. The results of a series of calculations showed that when the mesh is refined, the approximate R_ν-generalized solution converges to the exact solution with a rate $O(h)$ in the $L_{2,\alpha}(\Omega)^2$ norm. This convergence rate is more than one and a half times higher in order of degree h than in the singular complement method and the regularization method. Also noteworthy is the algorithmic simplicity of WVFEM and the naturalness of the solution definition.

References

1. Assous, F., Ciarlet, P.J., Garcia, E.: Singular electromagnetic fields: inductive approach. C.R. Acad.Sci. Paris, Ser. I **341**(10), 605–610 (2005). https://doi.org/10.1016/j.crma.2005.09.034
2. Bossavit, A.: Computational Electromagnetism, 2nd edn. Academic Press, Boston (1998)
3. Ciarlet, P.G.: The Finite Element Method for Elliptic Problems. North-Holland, Amsterdam (1978)
4. Hiptmair, R.: Finite elements in computational electromagnetism. Acta Numer **11**, 237–339 (2002). https://doi.org/10.1017/S0962492902000041
5. Jin, J.M.: The Finite Element Method in Electromagnetics, 2nd edn. John Wiley & Sons Inc, New York (2002)
6. Monk, P.: A finite element method for approximating the time-harmonic Maxwell equations. Numer. Math. **63**, 243–261 (1992). https://doi.org/10.1007/BF01385860
7. Monk, P.: Finite Element Methods for Maxwell's Equations. Clarendon Press, Oxford (2003). https://doi.org/10.1093/acprof:oso/9780198508885.001.0001
8. Nédélec, J.C.: Mixed finite elements in R^3. Numer. Math. **35**, 315–341 (1980). https://doi.org/10.1007/BF01396415
9. Nédélec, J.C.: A new family of mixed finite elements in R^3. Numer. Math. **50**, 57–81 (1986). https://doi.org/10.1007/BF01389668
10. Pechstein, A., Schoberl, J.: Tangential-displacement and normal-normal-stress continuous mixed finite elements for elasticity. Math. Models Methods Appl. Sci. **21**, 1761–1782 (2011). https://doi.org/10.1142/S0218202511005568
11. Rossi, R., Larese, A., Dadvand, P., Oñate, E.: An efficient edge-based level set finite element method for free surface flow problems. Int. J. Numer. Meth. Fluids **71**, 687–716 (2013). https://doi.org/10.1002/fld.3680
12. Rukavishnikov, V.A.: On a weighted estimate of the rate of convergence of difference schemes. Sov. Math. Dokl. **288**, 1058–1062 (1986)

13. Rukavishnikov, V.A.: Weighted FEM for two-dimensional elasticity problem with corner singularity. Lect. Notes Comput. Sci. Eng. **112**, 411–419 (2016). https://doi.org/10.1007/978-3-319-39929-4_39

14. Rukavishnikov, V.A.: Body of optimal parameters in the weighted finite element method for the crack problem. J. Appl. Comput. Mech. **7**(4), 2159–2170 (2021). https://doi.org/10.22055/jacm.2021.38041.3142

15. Rukavishnikov, V.A., Kuznetsova, E.V.: The R_ν-generalized solution of a boundary value problem with a singularity belongs to the space $W^{k+2}_{2,\nu+\frac{\beta}{2}+k+1}(\Omega, \delta)$. Differ. Equ. **45**, 913–917 (2009). https://doi.org/10.1134/S0012266109060147

16. Rukavishnikov, V.A., Mosolapov, A.O.: New numerical method for solving time-harmonic Maxwell equations with strong singularity. J. Comput. Phys. **231**(6), 2438–2448 (2012). https://doi.org/10.1016/j.jcp.2011.11.031

17. Rukavishnikov, V.A., Mosolapov, A.O., Rukavishnikova, E.I.: Weighted finite element method for elasticity problem with a crack. Comput. Struct. **243**, 106400 (2021). https://doi.org/10.1016/j.compstruc.2020.106400

18. Rukavishnikov, V.A., Nikolaev, S.G.: On the R_ν-generalized solution of the Lamé system with corner singularity. Dokl. Math. **92**, 421–423 (2015). https://doi.org/10.1134/S1064562415040080

19. Rukavishnikov, V.A., Rukavishnikov, A.V.: New numerical method for the rotation form of the Oseen problem with corner singularity. Symmetry **11**(1), 54 (2019). https://doi.org/10.3390/sym11010054

20. Rukavishnikov, V.A., Rukavishnikov, A.V.: Theoretical analysis and construction of numerical method for solving the Navier-Stokes equations in rotation form with corner singularity. J. Comput. Appl. Math. **429**, 115218 (2023). https://doi.org/10.1016/j.cam.2023.115218

21. Rukavishnikov, V.A., Rukavishnikova, E.I.: Finite-element method for the 1st boundary-value problem with the coordinated degeneration of the initial data. Dokl. Akad. Nauk **338**, 731–733 (1994)

22. Rukavishnikov, V.A., Rukavishnikova, E.I.: Error estimate FEM for the Nikol'skij-Lizorkin problem with degeneracy. J. Comput. Appl. Math. **403**, 113841 (2022). https://doi.org/10.1016/j.cam.2021.113841

23. Rukavishnikov, V.A., Rukavishnikova, E.I.: Weighted finite element method and body of optimal parameters for elasticity problem with singularity. CAMWA **151**, 408–417 (2023). https://doi.org/10.1016/j.camwa.2023.10.021

24. Rukavishnikov, V.A., Rukavishnikova, H.I.: Existence and uniqueness of an R_ν-generalized solution of the Dirichlet problem for the Lamé system with a corner singularity. Differ. Equ. **55**, 832–840 (2019). https://doi.org/10.1134/S0012266119060107

25. Samarskii, A.A., Lazarov, R.D., Makarov, V.L.: Finite-difference schemes for differential equations with generalized solutions. Vysshaya Shkola, Moscow (1987)

26. Webb, J.P.: Edge elements and what they can do for you. Transaction on magnetics **29**(2), 4160–1465 (1993). https://doi.org/10.1109/20.250678

27. Webb, J.P.: Hierarchal Vector Basis Functions of Arbitrary Order for Triangular and Tetrahedral Finite Elements. Trans. on Antennas and Propagation **47**(8), 1244–1253 (1999). https://doi.org/10.1109/8.791939

Geometric Modeling, Graphics and Visualization

Enhancing Explainability in Oral Cancer Detection with Grad-CAM Visualizations

Arnaldo V. Barros da Silva[1]($\boxtimes$) , Cristina Saldivia-Siracusa[2] ,
Eduardo Santos Carlos de Souza[3] , Anna Luíza Damaceno Araújo[4] ,
Marcio Ajudarte Lopes[2] , Pablo Agustin Vargas[2] , Luiz Paulo Kowalski[4] ,
Alan Roger Santos-Silva[2] , André C. P. L. F. de Carvalho[3] ,
and Marcos G. Quiles[1]

[1] Institute of Science and Technology, Federal University of São Paulo (UNIFESP),
São José Dos Campos, SP, Brazil
{arnaldo.barros,quiles}@unifesp.br
[2] Oral Diagnosis Department, Piracicaba Dental School, University of Campinas
(FOP-UNICAMP), Piracicaba, SP, Brazil
c234721@dac.unicamp.br, malopes@fop.unicamp.br,
{pavargas,alan}@unicamp.com.br
[3] Institute of Mathematical and Computer Sciences, University of São Paulo
(ICMC-USP), São Carlos, SP, Brazil
{eduardo.santos.souza,andre}@usp.br
[4] Head and Neck Surgery Department, University of São Paulo Medical School,
Sao Paulo, SP, Brazil
lp_kowalski@uol.com.br

Abstract. Late diagnosis of oral cancer significantly compromises patient outcomes. A promising approach to speed up the diagnostic process involves the use of Deep Learning (DL) models for medical image analysis. However, a notable challenge with these models is their lack of interpretability. To address this, techniques like Gradient-weighted Class Activation Mapping (Grad-CAM) have been developed. Grad-CAM generates heatmaps that highlight image regions most influential for classification decisions. In our study, we evaluated the performance of two DL models renowned for their high accuracy in oral cancer classification. Our analysis extended beyond mere accuracy metrics; we employed Grad-CAM to provide visual explanations of the models' decisions. Furthermore, we investigated subclass accuracy rates and the distribution of prediction confidences to gain a deeper insight into the models' performance and robustness in oral cancer detection. This comprehensive evaluation approach offers a more nuanced understanding of the capabilities and limitations of DL methods in the context of oral cancer diagnosis.

Keywords: Oral cancer diagnosis · Deep Learning · Interpretability · Grad-CAM · Model evaluation

O. Gervasi et al. (Eds.): ICCSA 2024, LNCS 14813, pp. 151–164, 2024.
https://doi.org/10.1007/978-3-031-64605-8_11

1   Introduction

Oral cancer ranks among the most common types of cancer worldwide [21], characterized by late diagnoses and high mortality rates. The delay in diagnosis can be attributed to various factors, with scant public awareness and lack of knowledge among healthcare professionals cited as primary contributors to this scenario [28]. Developing effective strategies to promote early detection is crucial to improve treatment outcomes and survival prospects for patients affected by this condition.

Using Computer-Aided Diagnosis (CAD) [7] is a highly effective approach for reducing diagnosis time. By analyzing medical images from various sources such as Hyperspectral Imaging, Magnetic Resonance Imaging, Computed Tomography, among others [16], it can enhance lesion detection. A key example of the power of CAD is illustrated in the work conducted by [25]. They employed a Deep Learning model to classify oral cancer on a dataset of clinical oral photographs and achieved 99% precision and 100% recall. This provides clear evidence that CAD is an indispensable tool in the context of medical diagnosis.

Deep Learning methods have the capability to automatically learn complex features from images as they enhance classification accuracy without relying on direct intervention from human experts [11]. However, a significant limitation of these models is their "black-box" nature [3], where the internal decision-making process is not easily understood by humans. This lack of interpretability can be a critical obstacle, especially in sensitive applications such as the medical field. In response, methods like CAM [30], Grad-CAM, Grad-CAM++ [4,19], LIME [18] and SHAP [15] have been developed, enabling the visualization of specific regions in input images that most influenced predictions generated by Convolutional Neural Networks (CNNs) [1].

The study [29] investigated the effectiveness of CAM, Grad-CAM, and Grad-CAM++ techniques in interpreting CNNs used for classifying multiple sclerosis (MS) cases from brain magnetic resonance imaging scans. It found that integrating Grad-CAM with robust CNN models like VGG19 yielded superior results. The research underscored the importance of combining Grad-CAM with advanced CNN architectures and quantification methods to identify key brain regions affected by MS pathology. In study [2], researchers investigated the interpretability of models in detecting retinoblastoma in fundus images. They utilized InceptionV3 to train a neural network on a dataset consisting of 400 retinoblastoma images and 400 images without the condition. Subsequently, they employed LIME and SHAP to explain the model's predictions. The findings demonstrated that these techniques effectively identified critical features in the images for precise diagnosis. This study implies that such an approach holds promise for enhancing the detection and treatment of retinoblastoma.

The main objective of this study is to refine the evaluation pipeline for oral cancer classification models, focusing on two ConvNeXt-based models [14] trained on a proprietary dataset developed by the authors. This dataset, which remains undisclosed to the public, serves as a novel resource for testing the efficacy of these models. Through multiple experimentation, these models demonstrated superior efficacy with comparable performance, albeit employing different fine-tuning strategies during their development.

This paper is structured as follows: Sect. 2 reviews related literature, Sect. 3 details the experimental methodology, Sect. 4 discusses the findings, and Sect. 5 concludes the study, highlighting its contributions to the field of medical diagnostics and early cancer detection.

2   Related Works

In this section, studies applying Explainable Artificial Intelligence (XAI) methods in medical images will be presented, both to assess model accuracy and to provide additional tools to healthcare professionals. Additionally, works justifying the selection of Grad-CAM as an XAI method compared to other approaches will be discussed.

2.1   XAI for Medical Imaging

The work by Hauser et al. [10] sheds light on the increasing interest in Explainable Artificial Intelligenc (XAI) to address the black-box nature of Deep Neural Networks (DNNs) in skin cancer detection. The authors analyzed 37 articles published between January 2017 and October 2021 and found that while 19 studies applied existing XAI methods to interpret classifier decisions, 4 proposed new approaches or refined established techniques. Besides, only 3 studies evaluated the performance and confidence of healthcare professionals when using DNN-based decision support systems with XAI. These findings underscore the need for a more systematic and rigorous evaluation of the utility of XAI in this context.

In a similar vein, Warin et al. [26] evaluated the performance of CNN algorithms in classifying and detecting potentially malignant oral diseases and Oral Squamous Cell Carcinoma (OSCC) and Oral Potentially Malignant Disorders (OPMD) in photographic images. The researchers developed several image classification models, highlighting DenseNet-196 as the most effective, achieving AUCs of 1.00 and 0.98 for OSCC and OPMDs, respectively. Furthermore, object detection models were employed, with Faster R-CNN leading, achieving AUCs of 0.88 and 0.64 for OSCC and OPMDs, respectively. The researchers used Grad-CAM to illustrate the model's assertiveness. Similarly, the study of the DiCoMLP-Mixer model [17] combined dilated convolutions and a multilayer perceptron to assess oral connective tissue, capturing dense contextual representations at multiple scales. The backbone of DiCoMLP-Mixer also incorporates the attention mechanism of a transformer model. Once again, Grad-CAM was used to reinforce the assertiveness of the method.

In contrast, the work proposed by Figueroa et al. [9] developed a training method that makes the network's predictions more understandable, accurately directing its attention to cancerous regions of the image. The adopted strategy involves using Grad-CAM with the guided attention inference network

[12]. Results indicate that this approach enhances CNN interpretability, enabling more reliable lesion classification.

Finally, the study by Dorrich et al. [8] investigated the ability of CNNs to classify head and neck cancer histopathology, addressing the lack of interpretability with XAI techniques. The researchers trained a CNN to classify tumor and non-tumor tissue and another CNN for semantically segmenting four classes. The classification model's performance reached an accuracy of 89.9% on previously unseen data, while the segmentation model achieved a mean Intersection over Union of 0.690 and 0.782 specifically for tumor tissue. Explainable Artificial Intelligence methods evidenced that both networks base their decisions on features consistent with pathology experts' opinions.

2.2   Comparisons Between XAI Methods

In the work [5], a CNN was trained to classify images of LEGO pieces, and the LIME and Grad-CAM methods were applied to generate visual explanations. The results indicated that, overall, Grad-CAM outperformed LIME. According to 80% of the respondents, Grad-CAM produced more reliable heatmaps, providing more robust visual interpretations of the CNN's decisions.

In the study [23], a variety of models such as Vision Transformers, MobileNet, and ResNet were trained on a dataset of endoscopic images. Among the XAI techniques evaluated, propagation-based methods such as GradCAM, GradCAM++, and LayersCAM, as well as feature-based methods like SHAP and LIME, stood out. It was observed that among the propagation methods, Grad-CAM exhibited superior performance, especially in challenging classes such as the Ileocecal Valve. In overall comparison, it also outperformed SHAP and LIME, although it was noted that if the model does not employ backpropagation mechanisms, such as decision trees or k-nearest neighbors, the path to pursue would be SHAP or LIME. Another limitation of Grad-CAM was also identified: when trying to locate objects with multiple occurrences of the same class, most of the time it generated a failure.

Finally, the investigation [27] explored models for classifying lesions on fruit leaves, employing the methods GradCAM, SmoothGrad, and LIME for explainability. The results revealed that GradCAM offers more intuitive and understandable interpretations. SmoothGrad, despite highlighting the importance of pixels in lesion areas, lacks clarity in explaining leaf appearance. Similarly, the results of LIME were considered unsatisfactory, limited to describing leaf appearance without providing a robust explanation.

3   Experiments

3.1   Dataset

The dataset that has been analyzed in this study includes a total of 837 clinical photographs that were taken by professional cameras or mobile devices. These

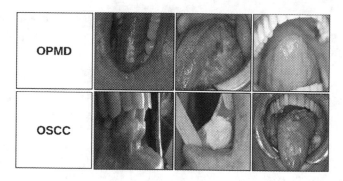

Fig. 1. Examples of images in the dataset. The first row depicts images of the OPMD class, while the second row displays images of the OSCC class.

photographs were obtained from three different institutions. The majority of the images, which corresponds to 758 patients, were collected from the *Faculdade de Odontologia de Piracicaba* (FOP) in Piracicaba, São Paulo, Brazil. In addition to this, the dataset also includes contributions from 11 patients from the *Universidade Federal de Minas Gerais* (UFMG) in Belo Horizonte, Minas Gerais, and 38 patients from the *Universidade Federal do Pará* (UFPA) in Belém, Pará, Brazil. To ensure that the patient labeling was accurate, a group of specialists conducted a histopathological analysis of the corresponding glass slides, aiming to review the diagnosis and eliminate any doubts.

The images were categorized into two main categories following the World Health Organization (WHO) guidelines from 2017 [20]. The first category was labeled as OPMDs, which included 351 cases ranging from no evidence to mild or moderate dysplasia. The second category as labeled as OSCC, which included 486 cases ranging from carcinoma in situ and micro-invasive to overtly invasive/conventional and verrucous forms. Some examples of images from each class can be seen in Fig. 1.

Our experimental evaluation was conducted using the test subset of the dataset, which represents 10% of the entire dataset. This subset comprises 33 examples of Oral Potentially Malignant Disorders (OPMDs) and 46 examples of Oral Squamous Cell Carcinoma (OSCC), totaling 79 unique cases. The distribution of these images, categorized by their collection location, is detailed in Table 1, providing a clear view of the dataset's composition.

It is important to note that the models utilized in this research were pretrained and directly applied to the test data without undergoing any further fine-tuning or hyperparameter adjustments. This approach was deliberately chosen because the primary focus of our investigation was to assess the performance and applicability of these already-trained models in the context of our specific dataset. Consequently, there was no need to employ the training or validation sets typically used in the model development phase.

Table 1. Distribution of clinical photographs by collection location and class for the test subset: FOP (Faculdade de Odontologia de Piracicaba), UFMG (Universidade Federal de Minas Gerais), UFPA (Universidade Federal do Pará).

Class	Images			
	FOP	UFMG	UFPA	Total
OPMD	30	1	2	33
OSCC	45	0	1	46

3.2 Models

Several models with distinct architectures have been trained based on the constructed dataset, with results indicating that the most promising architecture is ConvNeXt. Built upon a classical convolutional network such as ResNet [13], ConvNeXt incrementally evolves by incorporating distinctive features from transformers [24]. Among these features are the introduction of a "patchify" layer, deep and wide convolutions, the implementation of non-local self-attention, and the utilization of larger kernels.

The two best-performing ConvNeXt models were obtained using two different strategies. **Model A** involved fine-tuning a pre-trained model on the ImageNet dataset [6], while **Model B** followed the same approach with an additional fine-tuning step using the ISIC 2019 dataset [22]. The accuracy achieved by Model A was 78.48%, whereas Model B achieved higher accuracy of 79.75%. The chosen ConvNeXt architecture has a total of 49,456,226 trainable parameters with an input shape of $224 \times 244 \times 3$.

3.3 Grad-CAM

As previously mentioned, the selected XAI technique for the experiments was Grad-CAM. An advantage of this approach is its universal applicability to any CNN architecture, without requiring modifications to the network structure. This sets it apart from its predecessor, Class Activation Mapping (CAM), which necessitates the inclusion of specific additional layers like the Global Average Pooling (GAP) layer and softmax activation within the network architecture. By bypassing the need for these supplementary layers, Grad-CAM streamlines the interpretability process.

To explain its results, Grad-CAM calculates the gradient ($\frac{\partial y^c}{\partial A^k}$) of the score y^c for class c with respect to the activation of the feature map A^k from convolution k in the deepest convolutional layer. The gradients are then globally aggregated via max-pooling to determine the convolution's significance for the class, represented as α_c^k. This computation yields a localization map L^c, obtained through weighted summation followed by a Rectified Linear Unit (ReLU) activation function, which highlights only positive contributions.

4   Results

4.1   Accuracy by Class and Collection Location

In order to obtain a comprehensive understanding of the performance of the classification models, we have compiled two tables - Table 2 for model A and Table 3 for model B - which present the accuracy rates by class and collection location. These tables reinforce the notion that the selection of a model should not be solely based on overall accuracy values. For instance, Model A achieves a 10% higher accuracy rate in predicting the OPMD class for images collected at FOP, while Model B exhibits a 6.67% higher accuracy rate for the OSCC class. It is worth mentioning that only Model B presents an accurate prediction in the only OSCC example collected at UFPA.

Table 2. Model A accuracy separated by class and institution for each example in the test set.

Class	FOP	UFMG	UFPA
OPMD	**83,33%**	0%	50%
OSCC	77,77%	–	0%

Table 3. Model B accuracy separated by class and institution for each example in the test set.

Class	FOP	UFMG	UFPA
OPMD	73,33%	0%	50%
OSCC	**84.44%**	–	**100%**

4.2   Venn Diagram

The results obtained from the subclass and collection region accuracy indicate that even though the models have similar architecture and overall accuracy, they learned different image features to produce their predictions. To verify this, we can create a Venn diagram that represents shared correct predictions, distinct correct predictions, and common errors between the models. Figure 2 shows the diagram with the results for the two analyzed models. We noticed that there were images that one model classified correctly while the other did not. This suggests that the models may have learned some divergent features. Furthermore, the results emphasize that it is not as straightforward to claim that one model is better than another. For such a statement to hold, the model with higher accuracy must correctly classify all instances that the other model got right along with additional examples.

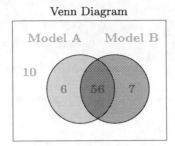

Fig. 2. A Venn Diagram illustrating the predictions of ConvNeXt with only ImageNet fine-tuning (Model A) and ConvNeXt utilizing both ImageNet and ISIC 2019 fine-tuning (Model B).

4.3   Confidence Distribution

In the domain of utilizing models in CAD systems, minimizing false positives is of vital importance, given that such erroneous predictions could gravely misdirect a patient towards incorrect treatment paths. To this end, analyzing classification confidences assumes significant importance as it facilitates the detection of misguided predictions, which are made with low confidence. Moreover, it may prove beneficial to establish a separate class for "undefined predictions," which could help in eliminating certain false positives.

In Figs. 3 and 4 we show the distributions of confidences for wrong and correct predictions for Model A and Model B respectively. Upon analyzing the figures, it is evident that creating a new class is not a simple task. Overall, the models, both in correct and incorrect predictions, tend to exhibit a high confidence value in their decisions.

4.4   Visual Explanations

In order to expand upon the analysis of model performance beyond just accuracy rates, we utilized Grad-CAM to generate visual explanations for all test images using both models. These visualizations were then presented side by side to better understand the differences between them.

The first observation is that in many cases, both models correctly predicted the OSCC class. However, when this happened, Model B generated a less scattered heatmap than Model A, as seen in Fig. 5. This characteristic suggests that Model B may have learned better to detect lesion regions.

Another observation is that when the models predicted the OPMD class, their heatmaps focused on regions that had little or no intersection with the lesions observed by specialists. This suggests that perhaps both models have learned to distinguish between "with lesion" and "without lesion" rather than OPMD and OSCC. Figure 6 shows this trend.

Finally, Fig. 7 shows examples where the models diverge from each other, indicating that even with similar architectures and similar training methods, both models learn different features.

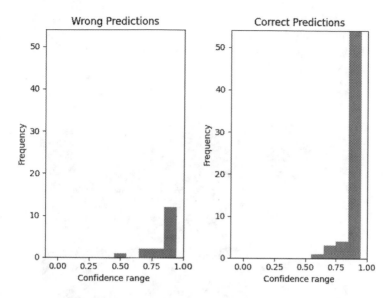

Fig. 3. Distribution of confidences for wrong predictions (red) and correct predictions (green) made by Model A in the test set. (Color figure online)

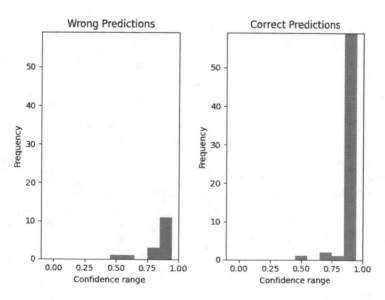

Fig. 4. Distribution of confidences for wrong predictions (red) and correct predictions (green) made by Model B in the test set. (Color figure online)

Delving deeper, according to medical experts, during a visual assessment, model B appeared more confident in its visual explanations. Approximately 56.96% of the maps generated for the test set by model B focused on the correct regions of the lesions, while only 40.51% of the maps from model A showed this level of accuracy.

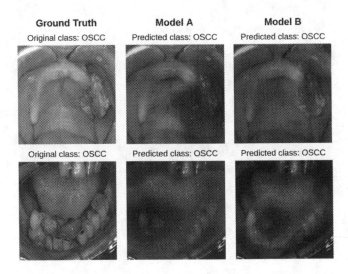

Fig. 5. Examples of visual explanations generated via Grad-CAM in images from the test set (first column) using Model A (second column) and Model B (third column) where Model B showed less spread out heatmaps.

4.5   Data Preprocessing

After noticing that the heatmap was focusing on areas of the image that were not related to the lesion, such as the teeth, we decided to crop the image to only include the lesion region based on segmentation annotations provided by specialists. We hoped that this would improve the accuracy of our classification without retraining the models. However, our results showed that this hypothesis was incorrect. The accuracy of the first model decreased from 78.48% to 75.95% after implementing the preprocessing step, and the accuracy of the second model decreased from 79.75% to 70.89%.

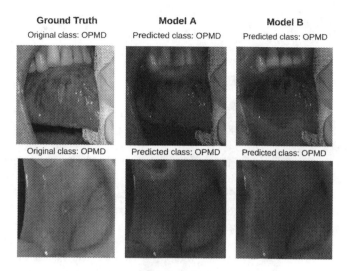

Fig. 6. Examples of visual explanations generated via Grad-CAM on images from the test set (first column) using Model A (second column) and Model B (third column) where both models showed heatmaps that did not intersect with lesions identified by experts.

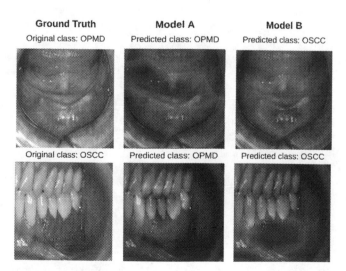

Fig. 7. Examples of visual explanations generated via Grad-CAM in images from the test set (first column) using Model A (second column) and Model B (third column) where the predictions generated by the models diverge.

5   Conclusion

This study aimed to provide a more robust pipeline for evaluating medical image classification models, given the cautious nature of tasks directly impacting people's health. To achieve this, two models based on the ConvNeXt architecture were analyzed, and trained on the same data but with different fine-tuning strategies.

Initially, when considering only overall accuracy, Model B seemed to be the optimal choice, showing a 0.9% improvement over Model A. However, when dividing the test set into subclasses, more significant differences emerged: Model A exhibited superiority in OPMD classification, while Model B excelled in OSCC classification.

Delving deeper into the investigation, a Venn Diagram was constructed to compare the predictions of each model. The results revealed that the models are not easily interchangeable, suggesting that they likely learned distinct features despite sharing similar architectures and being trained on the same data.

This distinction between models became even clearer when examining the regions each model focused on during predictions, using the Grad-CAM technique. Remarkably, while Model B excelled in identifying lesion regions in OSCC cases, both models did not demonstrate a focus on lesion regions in OPMD cases.

Using the explanations provided by Grad-CAM with the assistance of medical expertise, we found that model B was the most reliable overall. However, the overall confidence was still low, which likely hinders the use of this model in the real world despite its high accuracy.

Furthermore, other analyses were conducted, such as evaluating the distribution of model confidences and making data modifications to potentially improve results. In summary, this study provided a clear experimentation pipeline, indicating that the choice of the best model depends more on the specific context and objectives of the application than on the overall accuracy achieved.

Acknowledgements. The authors gratefully acknowledge support from FAPESP (São Paulo Research Foundation), projects No. $2020/09835 - 1$, $2022/13069 - 8$ and $2022/09285 - 7$, and the CNPq (National Council for Scientific and Technological Development), project No. $313680/2021 - 3$.

Disclosure of Interests. The authors declare no competing interests relevant to the content of this article.

References

1. Albawi, S., Mohammed, T.A., Al-Zawi, S.: Understanding of a convolutional neural network. In: 2017 International Conference on Engineering and Technology (ICET), pp. 1–6. IEEE (2017)
2. Aldughayfiq, B., Ashfaq, F., Jhanjhi, N., Humayun, M.: Explainable AI for retinoblastoma diagnosis: interpreting deep learning models with lime and shap. Diagnostics **13**(11), 1932 (2023)

3. Castelvecchi, D.: Can we open the black box of AI? Nat. News **538**(7623), 20 (2016)
4. Chattopadhay, A., Sarkar, A., Howlader, P., Balasubramanian, V.N.: Grad-cam++: Generalized gradient-based visual explanations for deep convolutional networks. In: 2018 IEEE Winter Conference on Applications of Computer Vision (WACV), pp. 839–847. IEEE (2018)
5. Cian, D., van Gemert, J., Lengyel, A.: Evaluating the performance of the lime and grad-cam explanation methods on a LEGO multi-label image classification task. arXiv preprint arXiv:2008.01584 (2020)
6. Deng, J., et al.: ImageNet: a large-scale hierarchical image database. In: 2009 IEEE Conference on Computer Vision and Pattern Recognition, pp. 248–255. IEEE (2009)
7. Doi, K.: Computer-aided diagnosis in medical imaging: historical review, current status and future potential. Comput. Med. Imaging Graph. **31**(4–5), 198–211 (2007)
8. Dörrich, M., et al.: Explainable convolutional neural networks for assessing head and neck cancer histopathology. Diagn. Pathol. **18**(1), 121 (2023)
9. Figueroa, K.C., et al.: Interpretable deep learning approach for oral cancer classification using guided attention inference network. J. Biomed. Opt. **27**(1), 015001–015001 (2022)
10. Hauser, K., et al.: Explainable artificial intelligence in skin cancer recognition: a systematic review. Eur. J. Cancer **167**, 54–69 (2022)
11. LeCun, Y., Bengio, Y., Hinton, G.: Deep learning. Nature **521**(7553), 436–444 (2015)
12. Li, K., Wu, Z., Peng, K.C., Ernst, J., Fu, Y.: Tell me where to look: guided attention inference network. In: Proceedings of the IEEE Conference on Computer Vision and Pattern Recognition, pp. 9215–9223 (2018)
13. Li, S., Jiao, J., Han, Y., Weissman, T.: Demystifying resnet. arXiv preprint arXiv:1611.01186 (2016)
14. Liu, Z., Mao, H., Wu, C.Y., Feichtenhofer, C., Darrell, T., Xie, S.: A convnet for the 2020s. In: Proceedings of the IEEE/CVF Conference on Computer Vision and Pattern Recognition, pp. 11976–11986 (2022)
15. Lundberg, S.M., Lee, S.I.: A unified approach to interpreting model predictions. In: Guyon, I., Luxburg, U.V., Bengio, S., Wallach, H., Fergus, R., Vishwanathan, S., Garnett, R. (eds.) Advances in Neural Information Processing Systems 30, pp. 4765–4774. Curran Associates, Inc. (2017). http://papers.nips.cc/paper/7062-a-unified-approach-to-interpreting-model-predictions.pdf
16. McAuliffe, M.J., Lalonde, F.M., McGarry, D., Gandler, W., Csaky, K., Trus, B.L.: Medical image processing, analysis and visualization in clinical research. In: Proceedings 14th IEEE Symposium on Computer-Based Medical Systems, CBMS 2001, pp. 381–386. IEEE (2001)
17. Pratiher, S., Chattoraj, S., Nawn, D., Pal, M., Paul, R.R., Konik, H., Chatterjee, J.: A multi-scale context aggregation enriched mlp-mixer model for oral cancer screening from oral sub-epithelial connective tissues. In: 2022 30th European Signal Processing Conference (EUSIPCO), pp. 1323–1327 (2022). https://doi.org/10.23919/EUSIPCO55093.2022.9909942
18. Ribeiro, M.T., Singh, S., Guestrin, C.: "why should I trust you?": Explaining the predictions of any classifier. In: Proceedings of the 22nd ACM SIGKDD International Conference on Knowledge Discovery and Data Mining, San Francisco, CA, USA, 13-17 August 2016, pp. 1135–1144 (2016)

19. Selvaraju, R.R., Cogswell, M., Das, A., Vedantam, R., Parikh, D., Batra, D.: Grad-cam: visual explanations from deep networks via gradient-based localization. In: Proceedings of the IEEE International Conference on Computer Vision, pp. 618–626 (2017)
20. Soluk-Tekkeşin, M., Wright, J.M.: The world health organization classification of odontogenic lesions: a summary of the changes of the 2017 (4th) edition. Turk Patoloji Derg **34**(1), 1–18 (2018)
21. Tranby, E.P., et al.: Oral cancer prevalence, mortality, and costs in medicaid and commercial insurance claims data. Cancer Epidemiol. Biomark. Reven. **31**(9), 1849–1857 (2022)
22. Tschandl, P., Rosendahl, C., Kittler, H.: The ham10000 dataset, a large collection of multi-source dermatoscopic images of common pigmented skin lesions. Sci. Data **5**(1), 1–9 (2018)
23. Varam, D., et al.: Wireless capsule endoscopy image classification: an explainable AI approach. IEEE Access **11**, 105262–105280 (2023)
24. Vaswani, A., et al.: Attention is all you need. In: Advances in Neural Information Processing Systems, vol. **30** (2017)
25. Warin, K., Limprasert, W., Suebnukarn, S., Jinaporntham, S., Jantana, P.: Automatic classification and detection of oral cancer in photographic images using deep learning algorithms. J. Oral Pathol. Med. **50**(9), 911–918 (2021)
26. Warin, K., Limprasert, W., Suebnukarn, S., Jinaporntham, S., Jantana, P., Vicharueang, S.: Ai-based analysis of oral lesions using novel deep convolutional neural networks for early detection of oral cancer. PLoS ONE **17**(8), e0273508 (2022)
27. Wei, K., Chen, B., Zhang, J., Fan, S., Wu, K., Liu, G., Chen, D.: Explainable deep learning study for leaf disease classification. Agronomy **12**(5), 1035 (2022)
28. Welikala, R.A., et al.: Automated detection and classification of oral lesions using deep learning for early detection of oral cancer. IEEE Access **8**, 132677–132693 (2020). https://doi.org/10.1109/ACCESS.2020.3010180
29. Zhang, Y., Hong, D., McClement, D., Oladosu, O., Pridham, G., Slaney, G.: Grad-cam helps interpret the deep learning models trained to classify multiple sclerosis types using clinical brain magnetic resonance imaging. J. Neurosci. Methods **353**, 109098 (2021)
30. Zhou, B., Khosla, A., Lapedriza, A., Oliva, A., Torralba, A.: Learning deep features for discriminative localization. In: Proceedings of the IEEE Conference on Computer Vision and Pattern Recognition, pp. 2921–2929 (2016)

Multi Modal Aware Transformer Network for Effective Daily Life Human Action Recognition

Hend Basly[1]([✉])[ID], Mohamed Amine Zayene[1,2], and Fatma Ezahra Sayadi[1]

[1] NOCCS-Lab.: Networked Objects Control and Communication Systems
Laboratory, University of Sousse, National Engineering School of Sousse (ENISO),
Tunisia National Engineering School of Sousse, University of Sousse, BP 264 Erriadh,
Sousse 4023, Sousse, Tunisia
{basly.hend,Fatmazahra.sayadi}@eniso.u-sousse.tn
[2] Faculty of Sciences, University of Monastir, Monastir, Tunisia
mohamedamine.zayene@fsm.rnu.tn

Abstract. Multimodal approaches for human action recognition leverage the complementary nature of different data modalities to improve system performance in healthcare, sports, smart homes, and surveillance. However, effectively fusing features from different modalities is challenging. Generally, action recognition involves extracting spatial and temporal information from video footage. To this end, 3D poses are fed into an STGCN to effectively capture spatial relationships between body parts and the temporal dependencies between consecutive frames. Self-attention was applied in the spatial dimension to focus on joint relationships dynamically in the same frame. External attention was used in the temporal dimension to capture relevant temporal dynamics between different joints over time. A 3D CNN was applied to extract spatial and temporal information from RGB data. Both were combined using the Intermodal Attention-based Fusion (IAF) component, which makes it possible to take into account the context information modalities by enabling the model to concentrate on the highly informative aspects of each modality during fusion. By learning attention weights, the model can selectively weight the contributions of different modalities based on their relevance to the action being recognized. Tested on the NTU-RGB+D dataset, the architecture outperformed existing approaches, showing promising effectiveness.

Keywords: Self-Attention Mechanism · External-Attention Mechanism · Daily Life Action Recognition

1 Introduction

In this paper, we delve into the domain of human activity recognition, a broad field that deals with videos sourced from diverse origins, including films, recordings,

---

Supported by organization x.

surveillance cameras, and web content. Recognizing actions in videos, particularly in the context of Daily Life Actions (DLAs), poses a set of challenges. DLA videos require a different approach as contextual information becomes less significant, making the task more complex. DLA videos exhibit distinct characteristics that increase their complexity. These challenges encompass the need to develop camera view-invariant representations, model temporal information effectively, handle variations among actions that exhibit resemblances (analogous actions), recognize actions presenting fine details (fine granularity actions), and manage substantial variability intraclass within one same activity category. Covering a diverse set of actions, particularly focusing on the context of DLA, demands more robust action recognition algorithms. One potential solution to these challenges involves employing 3D convolutional neural networks (3D ConvNets) for video analysis. However, it is crucial to question the effectiveness of these networks for DLA recognition. Existing networks like I3D [1], ResNet [2] and ResNeXt [3] were primarily predestined to handle generic video structures, not the specific spatiotemporal cubes encountered in DLAs. They lack the capacity to capture long-term temporal relationships, a vital aspect of tackling DLA challenges. While some recent works have highlighted the efficiency of 3D convolutional operations in modeling temporal information, the intricate nature of DLA recognition requires additional skills beyond fixed convolutional operations. To meet these challenges comprehensively, we introduce leveraging multiple modalities to harness the complementary nature of their features, thus obtaining the most discriminative information for each action. Utilizing 3D ConvNets allows us to capture short-term motion and appearance information without relying on optical flow, which is less relevant in DLAs that primarily involve subtle motions. However, combining 3D skeleton data with different stream networks can lead to overfitting due to the high parameter count in multimodal networks. To address these issues, we turn to Graph Convolutional Networks (GCNs), which effectively represent 3D skeleton data. Spatio-Temporal Graph-Convolutional-Networks (STGCNs) gather data pertaining to both spatial and temporal aspects by examining bone connections in 3D skeleton data. Yet, they have limitations related to their graph structure. In the past, Recurrent Neural Networks (RNNs) were commonly used for modeling temporal dependencies. However, RNNs have a limited window to reference from, which becomes problematic with longer videos. To address these limitations, we turn to transformers, basically developed for Natural Language Processing (NLP). Transformers, making use of their self attention mechanism, can effectively model long-term temporal dependencies and are well-suited for the hierarchical and sequential nature of skeletal sequences. While self-attention mechanisms are effective for capturing local relationships within data samples, they may fall short in fully capturing the inter-joint dynamics over a sequence of skeletal data. Therefore, we introduce the concept of external attention to address this limitation. Our proposed framework combines the strengths of these approaches by innovative approach combining 3D poses in a self attention mechanism unit in the spatial dimension and an external attention mechanism unit in the temporal dimension to influence RGB data through Intermodal Attention-based Fusion (IAF) module. Thus, we employ two separate spatial an temporal streams. The spatial stream focuses on the local relationships among skeleton joints in the context of every individual frame. Meanwhile, the temporal stream detects global temporal connections among joints across time, depicting action dynamics across the video sequence. We then enhance our proposal by fusing the significant spatial-temporal data of the 3D pose data with spatiotemporal visual information in the RGB data using the Intermodal Fusion (IAF) component. This fusion process extracts crucial spatial and temporal information from the 3D pose graph representation and the 3D visual feature representation from RGB clips, ultimately contributing to more effective DLA recognition in real-world scenarios. The remainder of this paper is structured as follows; in Sect. 2, we present the related work. In Sect. 3, we present our suggested Action Recognition methodology. In Sect. 4, we provide our experimental analysis conducted on the publicly accessible NTU-60 dataset and finally, we conclude in Sect. 5.

2   Related Work

Human action recognition has received greater attention in the field of computer vision and pattern recognition owing to its large variety of applications such as video monitoring, human-computer interaction and activity analysis.

This section reviews the existing literature and research contributions in this field, aiming to provide an overview of the latest techniques and advancements. We begin by discussing early works laid the foundation for progress in human action recognition, which has seen significant advancements in recent years, largely driven by deep learning. Convolutional neural networks (CNNs) have been a key tool, with notable studies introducing two-stream CNN architectures for capturing appearance and motion information [4,5]. However, these models are limited to 2D inputs and overlook motion patterns across multiple frames. For DLA recognition, Recurrent Neural Networks (RNNs), especially Long Short-Term Memory (LSTM) networks, have been used to model temporal relationships [6]. Combining CNNs and LSTMs has gained interest, effectively addressing spatial and temporal feature extraction [6]. However, they often rely on strong human motion videos, impacting their performance on DLA videos [7,8]. 3D CNNs have emerged as effective models for learning representations from volumetric data, extracting both appearance and motion information across contiguous frames [1]. However, they require pretraining on large datasets and only cover a small portion of video sequences, limiting their ability to capture long-range temporal dynamics. Graph Neural Networks (GNNs), specifically Graph Convolutional Networks (GCNs), have been employed to recognize actions from skeleton data, effectively capturing spatial and temporal dependencies between joints [9]. Several architectures, like DPRL [10] and DGNN [11], have leveraged GCNs for Human Activity Recognition. The ST-GCN model extends GCN to represent skeletal data and transform joints and bones into nodes and arcs, respectively [12]. While Both approaches relying on RGB data and those relying on 3D pose information have their merits, the latter excels in actions characterized by Notable human motion and resemblance in appearances.

The representation of temporal information has evolved, with RGB methods using spatio-temporal convolutions and 3D pose methods adopting spatio-temporal graph-based operations. Attention mechanisms have gained attention recently, improving action recognition accuracy by selectively focusing on important spatial or temporal regions within sequences [13–17]. These mechanisms have been employed in various ways, such as multilayer LSTM networks with spatio-temporal attention [13], attention clusters with shift operations [14], and global and local knowledge-aware attention networks [18]. In the following sections, we present our proposed methodology for human action recognition, taking inspiration from the advancements discussed in this "Related Work" section.

3   Proposed Architecture

In this section, we describe our proposed deep network DLA recognition. For a better video's analysis and understanding, we opted for the video action representation from multimodal data to reap the benefits of RGB data and skeleton, hence, acquire more distinct representations for intricate scenarios in Daily Life Actions (DLAs). To this end, we propose an innovative methodology based on Spatial Self Attention module-based transformer and Temporal External Attention module in conjunction with Highly effective 3D convolutional network. Extracted features are fused by an attention-based inter-modal fusion module, which enables the model to focus on the most informative parts of each modality during the fusion task. By learning attention weights, the model can selectively weight the contributions of different modalities based on their relevance to the activity being recognized. This allows for a more fine-grained fusion that takes into account the semantic relationships between modalities. The inputs of the proposed model are the RGB data frames of each video for the 3D CNN network and their corresponding 3D skeleton data modality for the spatial and temporal streams. We have applied data augmentation operations as center crops, random crops and horizontal and vertical random flips. A 4D feature map was extracted from the layer preceding the Global Average Pooling (GAP) layer of the RGB stream (I3D network) to represent spatial-temporal features. Both spatial and temporal streams are based on STGCN network for modeling spatio-temporal data. Its architecture is composed of nine layers, see [20] to have clear sight. In fact, STGCN combines two main components which are; Graph Convolutional Network (GCN) followed by Temporal Convolutional Network (TCN). GCN layers are typically used to capture the spatial relationships among different locations in the data and TCN layers are used to model the temporal aspects of the data, such as how the data evolves or changes over time. STGCN effectively captures both the spatial and temporal dependencies in spatio-temporal data. This makes it a powerful architecture for DLA recognition task.

In our architecture, from the 4th layer, we apply Spatial Self Attention Unit (SAU) instead of GCN for the spatial stream and we apply Temporal External Attention Unit (TEU) instead of TCN in the temporal stream. The results of spatial and temporal streams are respectively the spatial and temporal characteristics of the skeleton modality, taking into account spatial and temporal

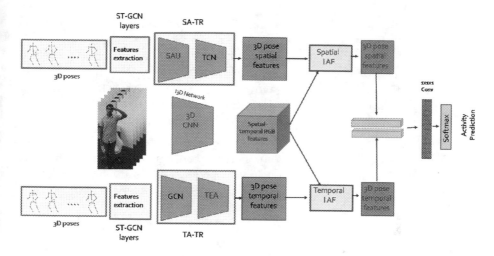

Fig. 1. End-to-End Spatial-Temporal Attention Network for Action Recognition

dependencies that have greater contribution to the realization of the performed action. The spatial extracted features from 3D poses and the spatio-temporal extracted features from RGB clips (see Fig. 1) are fused through the Intermodal Attention Fusion (IAF) module and produces new spatial features. This module allows the features extracted from skeleton data to re-calibrate features extracted from RGB data allowing the model to take into account contextual information to focus on the most informative parts of each modality during fusion. Similarly, The temporal attention features of the skeleton modality and the spatio-temporal features of the RGB modality (see Fig. 1) are fused through the Inter-modal Attention Fusion (IAF) module to produce new temporal features. New spatial and temporal resulting features are concatenated and passed by softmax activation function to predict actions.

3.1   Spatial Self Attention Unit (SAU)

The SAU unit is typically employed to spotlight local correlations between different spatial body joints within each frame of a video or spatiotemporal sequence. In SAU, each frame is treated as an independent entity, and the goal is to extract low-level features that encode the interconnections and dependencies between various body joints. This is achieved through the use of self attention mechanism a per-frame basis, operating between adjacent skeleton joints, enabling the model to assess the importance of relationships between each pair of skeleton joints. In fact, part of the transformer encoder, the SAU unit converts a fully connected body skeleton node graph into a weighted graph, with weights reflecting the importance of intra-frame joint connections. These weights are then employed to evaluate each node's impact on the performed action. Essentially, SAU is the outcome of multiple parallel attention heads, each utilizing self attention to capture correlations among input sequence embeddings.

Given a sequence of n nodes of the skeleton, denoted as $ns_i^f \in R^{C_{inp}}$ for $i = (1, ..., E_v)$ embeddings, where C_{inp} represents the channel input for each frame $f \in F = 1, ..., N$, and N represents the overall count of frames. For every graph's node ns_i^f, we calculate $q_i^f \in R^{dq}$, $q_i^f \in R^{dq}$ and $q_i^f \in R^{dq}$, representing the query matrix, the key matrix and the value matrix respectively, through linear transformations of the joint data. Subsequently, for every pair of nodes (nd_i^f, nd_j^f), we compute a score $\alpha_{ij} \in R$ which quantifies the importance of associations between the two body joints, expressed through $\alpha_{ij}^f = q_i^f k_j^{f^F}$ for all $f \in F$. The resulting score is then applied to to assign weights to each joint, then the score is multiplied by the value of the joint v_j^f. In order to assess the overarching node's importance ns_i within a sequence, as depicted in Fig. 2, we calculate the weighted node Z_i^t using the softmax activation function, expressed as follows:

$$Z_i^f = \sum_j softmax \left(\frac{\alpha_{ij}^f}{\sqrt{d_k}} \right) V_j^f \tag{1}$$

The spatial stream (SA-TR) employs the principle of transformer network on 3D pose data using SAU. The self attention mechanism is applied instead the sub-module GCN through SAU to extract spatial relevant features.

3.2   Temporal External Attention (TEA) Unit

The TEA unit focuses on studying how each body joint behaves independently across multiple frames in the sequence. It treats each joint as a distinct entity and explores how these joints evolve over time, considering the temporal dimension. Unlike traditional self-attention mechanisms, TEA introduces an external memory unit that stores information relevant to these body joints [19]. TEA allows the model to dynamically adapt and learn temporal dependencies and interactions between different joints across various time steps. For example, it can uncover how specific body joints in one frame correlate with the same joints in subsequent frames, enabling the capture of complex and discriminative features. This adaptability is particularly valuable when analyzing human body movements, as it can reveal intricate relationships and dynamics that may be challenging to capture with conventional convolutional approaches using fixed kernel sizes. The following equation is used to calculate the temporal attention scores (alpha) based on the interaction between temporal features ($\mathbf{F}_i$) at time i and the information stored in the external memory M_k at position j.

$$\alpha_{i,j} = \exp \left(\frac{\mathbf{F}_i \cdot \mathbf{M}_j^T}{\sum_k \exp(\mathbf{F}_i \cdot \mathbf{M}_k^T)} \right) \tag{2}$$

The softmax function is employed to normalize these scores, ensuring that they sum to 1.

$$\alpha'_{i,j} = \frac{\exp(\alpha_{i,j})}{\sum_k \exp(\alpha_{k,j})} \tag{3}$$

Additional normalization is performed to provide a meaningful interpretation of the scores.

$$\alpha_{i,j} = \frac{\alpha'_{i,j}}{\sum_k \alpha'_{k,j}} \qquad (4)$$

Temporal features are then weighted according to the attention scores $\alpha_{i,j}$ and the M_v matrix, emphasizing the most significant frames of the temporal sequence for activity classification. Just like the (SA-TR) stream, the (TA-TR) can be understood as the conventional graph convolution sub-module (GCN) [12] followed by the TEA unit instead of TCN. The spatial and temporal attention units (SAU and TEA) are integrated into the encoder module of the transformer network through the use of the multi-headed attention sub-module.

3.3   Intermodal Attention-Based Feature Fusion Module (IAF)

The Intermodal Attention-based Fusion (IAF) module depicted in Fig. 2 is designed to fuse information from the 3D poses' features extracted from the spatial and the temporal models into RGB's features extracted from the convolutional model. To take into account multimodal interactions between RGB and Skeleton data, we employ bilinear pooling operation. This specific application is particularly useful for fine-grained action classification.

$Feat_{rgb}$ and $Feat_{ske}$ are the characteristics Derived from the RGB stream and skeleton stream (in spatial domain or temporal domain), respectively. We apply the bilinear pooling operation, the resulting vector of feature combination is:

$$F_C = V_{AP}(Feat_{rgb} \otimes Feat_{ske}) \text{ where } F_C \in R^{M \times 1} \text{ and } M = Ch \times Ch \qquad (5)$$

where Ch indicates the feature channels' number, we use the average pooling vector denoted as V_{AP} to transform the input features into vectors, ensuring that they all share identical dimensions. The symbol $\otimes$ signifies the outer-product operation performed on resultant matrices. Subsequently, we apply l2 normalization to regularize the F_C vector, and this is achieved as follows:

$$F_C = \text{sign}(F_C) \cdot \sqrt{|F_C|} \text{ where } F_C \in R^{M \times 1} \qquad (6)$$

$$F_C = \frac{F_C}{\|F_C\|_2} \qquad (7)$$

Following this, F_C is propagated via a fully-connected layer and subsequently via the ReLU layer to introduce nonlinearity, enabling our model to learn additional features. This process results in the generation of a new combined feature, denoted as $F'_C \in R^{Ch \times 1}$, represented as:

$$F'_C = \text{ReLU}(W \cdot F_C) \text{ with } W \text{ representing the weight matrix.} \qquad (8)$$

The fusion process continues as follows; The resultant fusion feature undergoes a 1D convolution layer, followed by the application of the sigmoid activation function to generate new weights. This procedure enhances the importance of specific features, yielding the final fusion features for both the RGB and skeleton modalities, as described by the following equations:

$$Y_T = Feat_{rgb} * \sigma(\text{conv1D}(F_C'))\qquad(9)$$

The "*" operator represents the Hadamard product, while σ denotes the sigmoid activation function. The outcome is a representation of the scaled weights, reflecting features' importance. The weight values are then used to multiply the initial feature map, resulting in new weights denoted as Y_T. These updated weights signify the reconfiguration of the original features Gathering the underlying semantic insights pertaining to identical human actions expressed across diverse data modalities. The IAF is employed to explore possible semantic relationships among different modalities of data.

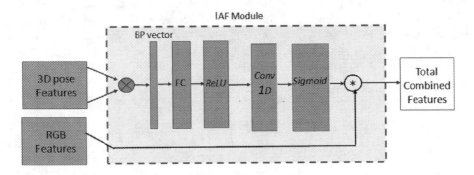

Fig. 2. IAF Module.

4 Model Evaluation Procedure

We conduct a series of experiments within our suggested framework to assess the effectiveness of the proposed architectural modules, particularly their impact on recognition performance. We evaluate our model's performance and compare it with several recent methods using the dataset [22], which is known for its complexity and extensive scope in the realm of DLA recognition. It's a large-scale resource capturing RGB, depth, skeleton, and infrared data from diverse action classes executed by 40 participants and recorded from 80 unique perspectives. This dataset complies with two suggested evaluation procedures, Cross-View and Cross-Subject, making it a robust platform for our evaluation.

4.1   Implementation Details

In our implementation, we carefully follow a series of steps to train our multimodal action recognition network. Here is a summary of the key implementation details, including the algorithm steps:

1. Initialization and Pretraining: We utilize the PyTorch deep learning framework for our experiments. The I3D network is pretrained on the ImageNet dataset, and its initial weights are set accordingly.
2. Data Augmentation and I3D Training: Data augmentation techniques are applied, and the I3D network is trained on consecutive human body segments extracted from RGB video frames. This procedure entails the random selection of an initial image from the first half of the sequence and then including subsequent frames at intervals of 2.
3. Fine-Tuning I3D Backbone: The network undergoes separate fine-tuning using the SGD optimizer on the NTU—60 benchmark dataset. Key hyperparameters include a learning-rate equal to 0.01, a weight-decay equal to 0.0001, and drop-out-rate of 0.5.
4. Feature Extraction: We extract RGB feature maps from the Mixed-5c-layer of our backbone, yielding features with dimensions of (1024 channels × 8 frames × 7 × 7 pixels).
5. Training Spatial and Temporal attention Models: Our Spatial and Temporal skeleton branches are trained using sequences of 3D pose sampled from video clips. The sequence length (L) is 300, the training involves 120 epochs with a batch size of 32. We use the SGD optimizer with an initial learning rate of 0.1, applying learning rate reduction by a factor of 10 at specified epochs.
6. Training Complete Network for Classification: For the classification task, we incorporate a Global Average Pooling (GAP)layer, apply a drop-out rate of 0.5, and include a Soft-Max layer towards the final stages of the network. Hyperparameters γ_1 and γ_2 are set to 10^{-5}. The complete training process spans thirty epochs and utilizes the SGD optimizer method. It commences with an initial-learning rate of 10^{-3}, employing learning-rate-decay every ten epochs. The batch size remains constant at 32 throughout the training.

Our implementation runs on 4 Titan RTX graphics processing units (GPU).

4.2   Comparison of Proposed Methodology and State of the Art Approaches on NTU— RGB+D Dataset

We evaluate our STA-IAF model against the most current and advanced techniques using the NTU dataset, presenting precision measurements for each of the NTU-Cross-Sub and the NTU-Cross-View evaluation protocols, as depicted in Table 1. Remarkably, STA-IAF surpasses the performance of existing approaches. In comparison to works like [20,21], which rely solely on 3D pose data as input, STA-IAF achieves a classification accuracy that closely matches theirs for the NTU-Cross-View protocol, alongside marginal differences of; 1% compared to [20] and 0.9% compared to [21]. This closeness in accuracy can be attributed

Table 1. Accuracy Comparison on NTU— RGB+D Dataset using NTU-Cross-Sub and NTU-Cross-View Evaluation Protocols. '+' indicates that the specified modality type was exclusively employed during the training stage. '*' designates that the checked work has employed the depth modality type.

Method	Modality		Attention		Protocol	
	RGB	3D pose	with	without	NTU-Cross-Sub	NTU-Cross-View
S, Yan et al. (2018) [12]	–	x	–	x	81.5%	88.3%
F, Baradel et al. (2017) [23]	x	x	x	–	82.5%	88.6%
F, Baradel et al. (2018) [24]	x	x	x	–	84.8%	90.6%
G, Liu et al. (2019) [25]	x	x	x	–	85.4%	91.6%
F, Baradel et al. (2018) [26]	x	+	x	–	86.6%	93.2%
L, Shi et al. (2018) [27]	–	x	x	–	88.5%	95.1%
F, Shi et al. (2021) [28]	–	x	x	–	83.4%	89.0%
Y, Tang et al.(2018) [10]	–	x	x	–	83.5%	89.8%
R.M.R, Guddeti et al[+] (2024) [37]	–	x	x	–	83.8%	89.75%
C, Li et al. (2018) [29]	–	x	–	x	86.5%	91.9%
M, Li et al. (2019) [30]	–	x	x	–	86.8%	94.2%
S, Cho et al. (2020) [31]	–	x	x	–	87.2%	92.7%
Y, Sun et al. (2021) [32]	–	x	x	–	88.4%	93.2%
C, Plizzari et al. (2020) [20]	–	x	x	–	89.9%	96.1%
Z, Zhang et al. (2020) [33]	–	x	x	–	89.3%	95.8%
L, Shi et al. (2019) [11]	–	x	–	x	89.9%	96.1%
HRV, Joze et al. (2020) [22]	x	x	x	–	91.9%	95.3%
S, Cho et al. (2020) [21]	–	x	–	x	91.5%	96.2%
T, Ahmad et al. (2023) [36]	–	x	x	–	91.5%	96.8%
M, Liu et al. (2018) [34]	x	x	x	–	91.7%	95.2%
S, Das et al. (2019) [35]	x	x	x	–	92.2%	94.6%
STA-IAF (ours)	x	x	x	–	**94.8%**	**97.1%**

to their robustness in handling view variations and capturing motion patterns. However, it's worth noting that these pose-only approaches struggle with distinguishing actions that have very similar visual appearances, leading to lower precision in the NTU-Cross-Sub protocol.

Furthermore, in comparison to other methods employing 3D poses and attention mechanisms for fusion, such as 2 s-AGCN [27], STAR [10, 20, 28, 30–32], our approach, which combines bilinear pooling and attention mechanism demonstrates superior performance, as showcased in Table 1. These results validate the potential and generalization capability of our proposed approach. Additionally, our STA-IAF proposed model is compared with previous approaches implementing 3D poses, RGB and attention mechanism such as [22–25, 34, 35], STA-IAF outperforms all these methods. The outstanding performance of STA-IAF highlights the efficacy of our suggested methodology, particularly in generating adaptable data representations for different views. By combining transformer concept into the STGCN and incorporating Intermodal fusion through the external attention module (IAF), our model excels in capturing long-term relationships from 3D poses data and effectively merges them with visual appearance information from the RGB data. In conclusion, our STA-IAF model, with the integration of the spatial self attention module, the temporal external attention module and the intermodal fusion strategy, excels in extracting significant and discriminative spatial-temporal features essential for actions of daily life (DLA) recognition.

4.3   Ablation Study

In this part, we make an ablation study on the proposed STA-IAF to justify the effectiveness of this framework with NTU— RGB+D dataset.

Effect of Associating or Dissociating Spatial and Temporal Attention Mechanisms. We test the robustness of the model first by dissociating the attention modules, each in a single one, (spatial (SA-TR) or temporal (TA-TR)) and second by associating them. Table 2 displays the performance comparison of all the implemented configurations. The first line shows results for the I3D base network without attention mechanism (without-TR); the second one shows the results of the combination of the I3D base network and the STGCN model through IAF model (STGCN-I3D-IAF). The third row shows the results of applying the spatial self attention (SA-TR) and then the temporal external attention (TA-TR) inside the STGCN network and combining the result with I3D by the IAF fusion module. The forth is intended only for the spatial self attention (SA-TR-I3D-IAF) which consists of combining the spatial self attention module by I3D and fuse them using IAF model,the next is for the temporal external attention solely (TA-TR-I3D-IAF) , which consists of combining the temporal self attention by I3D and their fusion using IAF model. The last line is our STA-IAF, which dissociates the two attention modules in two separate streams and then combines them with I3D by the IAF fusion module.

Table 2. Comparison of Accuracy (%): STA-IAF vs. Various Model Configurations. without-TR designates without attention.

Configuration Method	NTU-Cross-Sub	NTU-Cross-View
I3D (without-TR)	85.5	87.3
ST-GCN-I3D-IAF	90.8	92.5
ST-GCN-TR-I3D-IAF	92.6	94.3
SA-TR-I3D-IAF	92.9	95.9
TA-TR-I3D-IAF	93.3	95.3
Dissociated STA-I3D-IAF	**94.8**	**97.1**

As displayed in Table 2, our STA-IAF model outperforms all other configurations by a significant margin. Unlike in STGCN-TR-I3D-IAF, the association of the spatial and temporal attention modules in a single stream to guide RGB cues through 3D ConvNet decreases the classification performance (accuracy). This can be explained by the nature of the activities included in the NTU—RGB + D benchmark; In fact, it involves activities with significant motion variation (such as punching, slapping, kicking, etc.) that require the application of the temporal external attention module to help the model focus on specific temporal segments of the action sequence yielding to accurate action recognition. The dataset involves also human interactions with objects (such as playing with phone/tablet, put on a hat/cap, throw up cap/hat, etc.) that require the module of spatial self attention for the representation of the manipulated objects for the discrimination between actions. Therefore, the spatial self attention and the temporal external attention modules contribute in the improvement of the classification performance. As a consequence, we consider to dissociate the two attention modules instead of associating them in succession.

5   Conclusion

In this study, we introduced an innovative approach for human activity recognition, combining 3D skeletal data in spatial and temporal models based transformer network and RGB data as input to I3D network. Our approach surpasses the most advanced existing techniques when evaluated on the widely-used NTU—60 dataset. To establish an in-depth comprehension of semantics between multimodal characteristics, we incorporated the intermodal fusion module based attention (IAF). This module intelligently merges features using attention mechanisms, allowing us to capture the most discriminative features enabling to predict the action category. Our exhaustive experiments consistently demonstrate our superior performance compared to existing approaches. Our research addresses the challenges associated with disambiguating similar actions and recognizing actions presenting fine details (fine granularity actions) by introducing the attention mechanism in graphs networks. Additionally, we leverage the existing pretrained CNN backbone to improve the extraction of spatio-temporal characteristics in video sequences. However, it's worth noting that 3D CNN models, like I3D, are typically designed for short videos. Additional areas of focus for future work will involve expending our model's capabilities for handling long-term videos that involve complex actions, addressing the unique challenges posed by such scenarios.

Acknowledgments. This research work was supported by Abu Dhabi National Oil Company (ADNOC), Emirates NBD, Sharjah Electricity Water & Gas Authority (SEWA), Technology Innovation Institute (TII) and GSK as the sponsors of the 4th Forum for Women in Research (QUWA): Sustaining Women's Empowerment in Research & Innovation at University of Sharjah.

References

1. Carreira, J., Zisserman, A.: Quo vadis, action recognition? a new model and the kinetics dataset. In: Proceedings of the IEEE Conference on Computer Vision and Pattern Recognition, pp. 6299–6308 (2017)
2. He, K., Zhang, X., Ren, S., Sun, J.: Deep residual learning for image recognition. In: Proceedings of the IEEE Conference on Computer Vision and Pattern Recognition, pp. 770–778 (2016)
3. Xie, S., Girshick, R., Dollár, P., Tu, Z., He, K.: Aggregated residual transformations for deep neural networks. In: Proceedings of the IEEE Conference on Computer Vision and Pattern Recognition, pp. 1492–1500 (2017)
4. Simonyan, K., Zisserman, A.: Two-stream convolutional networks for action recognition in videos. Adv. Neural Inf. Process. Syst. **27** (2014)
5. Cheron, G., Laptev, I., Schmid, C.: P-CNN: pose-based CNN features for action recognition. In: Proceedings of the IEEE International Conference on Computer Vision, pp. 218–3226 (2017)
6. Ercolano, G., Riccio, D., Rossi, S.: Two deep approaches for ADL recognition: a multi-scale LSTM and a CNN-LSTM with a 3D matrix skeleton representation. In: 26th IEEE International Symposium on Robot and Human Interactive Communication (RO-MAN), pp. 877–882 (2017)
7. Abu-El-Haija, S., et al.: YouTube-8M: a large-scale video classification benchmark. arXiv preprint arXiv:1609.08675 (2016)
8. Das, S., Koperski, M., Bremond, F., Francesca, G.: Action recognition based on a mixture of RGB and depth-based skeletons In: 2017 14th IEEE International Conference on Advanced Video and Signal Based Surveillance (AVSS), pp. 1–6 IEEE (2017)
9. Kipf, T.N., Welling, M.: Semi-supervised classification with graph convolutional networks. arXiv:1609.02907
10. Tang, Y., Tian, Y., Lu, J., Li, P., Zhou, J.: Deep progressive reinforcement learning for skeleton-based action recognition. In: Proceedings of the IEEE Conference on Computer Vision and Pattern Recognition, pp. 5323–5332 (2018)
11. Shi, L., Zhang, Y., Cheng, J., Lu, H.: Skeleton-based action recognition with directed graph neural networks. In: Proceedings of the IEEE/CVF Conference on Computer Vision and Pattern Recognition, pp. 7912–7921 (2019)
12. Yan, S., Xiong, Y., Lin, D.: Spatial temporal graph convolutional networks for skeleton-based action recognition. In: Thirty-second AAAI Conference on Artificial Intelligence (2018)
13. Song, S., Lan, C., Xing, J., Zeng, W., Liu, J.: An End-to-End Spatio-temporal attention model for human action recognition from skeleton data. In: Proceedings of the AAAI Conference on Artificial Intelligence, vol. 31 (2017)
14. Sharma, S., Kiros, R., Salakhutdinov, R.: Action recognition using visual attention. arXiv:1511.04119 (2015)
15. Girdhar, R., Ramanan, D.: Attentional pooling for action recognition. Adv. Neural Inf. Process. Syst. **30** (2017)
16. Long, X., Gan, C., De Melo, G., Wu, J., Liu, X., Wen, S.: Attention clusters: Purely attention based local feature integration for video classification. In: Proceedings of the IEEE Conference on Computer Vision and Pattern Recognition, pp. 7834–7843 (2018)
17. Baradel, F., Wolf, C., Mille, J., Taylor, G.W.: Glimpse clouds: human activity recognition from unstructured feature points. In: Proceedings of the IEEE Conference on Computer Vision and Pattern Recognition, pp. 469–478 (2018)

18. Zheng, Z., An, G., Wu, D., Ruan, Q.: Global and local knowledge-aware attention network for action recognition. IEEE Trans. Neural Netw. Learn. Syst. **32**(1), 334–347 (2020)
19. Guo, M.H., Liu, Z.N., Mu, T.J., Hu, S.M.: Beyond self-attention: External attention using two linear layers for visual tasks. arXiv preprint arXiv:2105.02358 (2021)
20. Plizzari, C., Cannici, M., Matteucci, M.: Spatial-temporal transformer network for skeleton-based action recognition. In: Del Bimbo, A., et al. (eds.) ICPR 2021. LNCS, vol. 12663, pp. 694–701. Springer, Cham (2021). https://doi.org/10.1007/978-3-030-68796-0_50
21. Liu, Z., Zhang, H., Chen, Z., Wang, Z., Ouyang, W.: Disentangling and unifying graph convolutions for skeleton-based action recognition. In: Proceedings of the IEEE/CVF Conference on Computer Vision and Pattern Recognition, pp. 143–152 (2020)
22. Joze, H.R.V., Shaban, A., Iuzzolino, M.L., Koishida, K.: MMTM: multimodal transfer module for CNN fusion. In: Proceedings of the IEEE/CVF Conference on Computer Vision and Pattern Recognition, pp. 13289–13299 (2020)
23. Baradel, F., Wolf, C., Mille, J.: Human action recognition: pose based attention draws focus to hands. In: Proceedings of the IEEE International Conference on Computer Vision Workshops, pp. 604–613 (2017)
24. Baradel, F., Wolf, C., Mille, J.: Human activity recognition with pose-driven attention to RGB. In: BMVC 2018-29th British Machine Vision Conference, pp. 1–14 (2018)
25. Liu, G., Qian, J., Wen, F., Zhu, X., Ying, R., Liu, P.: Action recognition based on 3D skeleton and RGB frame fusion. In: 2019 IEEE/RSJ International Conference on Intelligent Robots and Systems (IROS), pp. 258–264, IEEE (2019)
26. Baradel, C., Wolf, F., Mille, J., Taylor, G.W.: Glimpse clouds: human activity recognition from unstructured feature points. In: Proceedings of the IEEE Conference on Computer Vision and Pattern Recognition, pp. 469–478 (2018)
27. Shi, L., Zhang, Y., Cheng, J., Lu, H.: Two-stream adaptive graph convolutional networks for skeleton-based action recognition. In: Proceedings of the IEEE/CVF Conference on Computer Vision and Pattern Recognition, pp. 12026–12035, IEEE (2019)
28. Shi, F., et al.: Star: sparse transformer-based action recognition. arXiv:2107.07089 (2021)
29. Li, C., Zhong, Q., Xie, D., Pu, S.: Co-occurrence feature learning from skeleton data for action recognition and detection with hierarchical aggregation. arXiv:1804.06055 (2018)
30. Li, M., Chen, S., Chen, X., Zhang, Y., Wang, Y., Tian, Q.: Actional structural graph convolutional networks for skeleton-based action recognition. In: Proceedings of the IEEE/CVF Conference on Computer Vision and Pattern Recognition, pp. 3595–3603, IEEE (2019)
31. Cho, S., Maqbool, M., Liu, F., Foroosh, H.: Self-attention network for skeleton-based human action recognition. In: Proceedings of the IEEE/CVF Winter Conference on Applications of Computer Vision, pp. 635–644, IEEE (2020)
32. Sun, Y., Shen, Y., Ma, L.: Msst-rt: multi-stream spatial-temporal relative transformer for skeleton-based action recognition. Sensors **21**(16), 5339 (2021)
33. Zhang, Z., Wang, Z., Zhuang, S., Huang, F.: Structure-feature fusion adaptive graph convolutional networks for skeleton-based action recognition. IEEE Access **8**, 228108–228117 (2020)

34. Liu, M., Yuan, J.: Recognizing human actions as the evolution of pose estimation maps. In: Proceedings of the IEEE Conference on Computer Vision and Pattern Recognition, pp. 1159–1168 (2018)
35. Das, S., et al.: Toyota smarthome: real-world activities of daily living. In: Proceedings of the IEEE/CVF International Conference on Computer Vision, pp. 833–842, IEEE (2019)
36. Ahmad, T., Rizvi, S.T.H., Kanwal, N.: Transforming spatio-temporal self-attention using action embedding for skeleton-based action recognition. J. Vis. Commun. Image Represent. **95**, 103892 (2023)
37. Guddeti, R.M.R.: Human action recognition using multi-stream attention-based deep networks with heterogeneous data from overlapping sub-actions. Neural Comput. Appl. 1–17 (2024). https://doi.org/10.1007/s00521-024-09630-0

Enhancing Image Registration Leveraging SURF with Alpha Trimmed Spatial Relation Correspondence

Paluck Arora[✉], Rajesh Mehta, and Rohit Ahuja

Computer Science and Engineering Department, Thapar Institute of Engineering and
Technology, Patiala, Punjab, India
`parora_phd20@thapar.edu`

Abstract. In medical image registration, traditional approaches such as Harris corner detector, Oriented FAST and Rotated Brief (ORB), and scale invariant feature transform (SIFT) encounters several challenges for achieving precise alignment. These challenges arise from their limited ability to adapt scale, rotation, and illumination variations. To confront these challenges, the proposed methodology leverages the speeded-up robust features (SURF) algorithm for feature point extraction. Additionally, it employs the alpha trimmed spatial relation correspondence (ATSRC) algorithm as an efficient alternative to the conventional random sample consensus (RANSAC) method to effectively eliminate mismatches. In the pre-processing phase, the reference image undergoes Gaussian filtering to remove noise, and subsequent normalization is applied. Furthermore, feature detection is performed on both the reference and target images using SURF. A brute force (BF) matcher is applied, followed by alpha trimmed spatial relation correspondence to remove outliers. The process continues with computing the homography matrix and generating the registered image. Numerous experiments are conducted on monomodal and multimodal medical images acquired from the Kaggle dataset. The proposed methodology outperforms existing technique by significantly improving mutual information (MI) from 2.53 to 3.654, 2.257 to 3.17389 and cross correlation (CC) from 0.9219 to 0.95475.

Keywords: Image registration · SURF feature extraction · Multimodal medical images

1 Introduction

Image registration (IR) is the process of aligning two medical images, whether monomodal or multimodal to depict the same scene [17]. In this case, one image serves as the reference (source) while the other acts as a target (template) image. The objective of IR is to achieve precise alignment between source and template image, which enables integration of information from both images to generate accurate and robust register image. Medical image registration approaches may be broadly classified into two

O. Gervasi et al. (Eds.): ICCSA 2024, LNCS 14813, pp. 180–191, 2024.
https://doi.org/10.1007/978-3-031-64605-8_13

categories: area-based and feature-based. The area-based method identifies the transformation model between two images without separating their features by utilizing an optimization algorithm. Medical imaging modalities can be broadly categorized into two types: functional images, such as single-photon emission computerized tomography (SPECT) and positron emission tomography (PET), which reveal soft tissues and their internal activities, and anatomical images, such as computed tomography (CT), magnetic resonance imaging (MR), and ultrasound (US), which display detailed structures of body organs. IR comprises of three essential components: rigid [25] transformation model, evaluation metrics, and feature extraction techniques. Rigid transformation model aims to find out the best transformation for image alignment by simulating geometric changes using rotation, scaling, and translation. Afterwards, alignment accuracy of the images is evaluated using several kinds of similarity metrics. Structural similarity index measure (SSIM), root mean square error (RMSE), and mutual information (MI) [4] are extensively utilized metrics. MI, peak signal to noise ratio (PSNR), cross correlation (CC), SSIM are maximized, while MSE is minimized, to achieve the successful registration. Finally, image registration employs a variety of feature extraction and matching algorithms, such as oriented FAST rotated BRIEF (ORB), SIFT, and SURF, brute force (BF) matcher. Monomodal and multimodal are two major categories that are used for image registration. Monomodal image registration refers to the alignment of images for same modality, such as MR-MR or CT-CT. In contrast, multimodal image registration involves categorizing images with a variety of modalities, like CT-MR scans. The integration of CT and MRI scans through registration methods improves the precision of patient data for a variety of applications including tracking tumour growth [14], confirming treatments [17] (such as surgery or radiotherapy), and facilitating clinical applications like tracking tumour growth and surgery planning. This paper introduces an innovative method that amalgamates SURF with Alpha trimmed spatial relation correspondence combined with affine transformation. This approach aims to speed up the feature detection process in images and enhance the registration speed of medical images by removing outliers. The proposed technique undergoes experimental testing on both monomodal and multimodal images. Finally, its performance is assessed based on evaluation metrics through experiments as compared to existing state-of-the-art methods [15, 27].

The key contributions of proposed methodology for the registration of multimodal/monomodal medical images are outlined as follows:

- A novel image registration method by hybridizing SURF feature extractor with alpha-trimmed spatial relation correspondence to effectively remove outliers.
- Extensive experiments are carried out to validate that SURF suits best for feature extraction as compared to ORB, SIFT as well as Harris corner detection algorithm. In addition, experiments state that ATSRC outperforms for removing outliers while RANSAC fails to generate register image.
- Efficacy of proposed methodology is experimentally proven by comparing with existing state-of-art approaches considering MI and cross- correlation as an evaluation metrics which explicitly states that the proposed approach outperforms.

The rest of the paper is structured as follows: literature review is discussed in Sect. 2, whereas the proposed methodology for medical image registration method is described in Sect. 3. The experimental and comparison results showcased in Sect. 4 whereas, conclusion and future directions is presented in Sect. 5.

2 Literature Survey

This section outlines the rigid medical image registration method proposed by many academics. Traditional techniques for image registration observed issues with speed, precision, and mismatched feature points, especially in medical, SAR, remote sensing, and histopathology slide images. Moreover, SIFT limits in efficient descriptor representation, preventing precise image alignment. The proposed approach further addresses these challenges by providing robust image alignment along with efficient feature extraction. Furthermore, it improves feature matching by using the best method for finding outliers, like alpha-trimmed spatial relation correspondence.

Engin et al. [10] had demonstrated the technique which leverages the combined SIFT and SURF descriptors, significantly improved alignment precision, especially with SIFT-based feature matching. Wu et al. [26] described the method which combines SURF and FREAK, leveraging robust feature extraction and strong regional description abilities, ensuring precise matching through rough matching and RANSAC-based filtering. Sreeja et al. [24] highlights modifications of SIFT and SURF for SAR image alignment, aiming to enhance registration accuracy and applicability across various SAR image processing applications [7]. Li et al. [18] presented the technique which combines SIFT with a feature point pair verification mechanism, leveraging affine transformation invariance and angle constraints for more accurate image registration. Darshana et al. [9] described their strengths and weakness of SIFT and SURF of each parameters like scale, rotation, blur, and speed. Sedaghat et al. [22]. Had outlined an improved SURF detector and AB-SIFT descriptor for robust feature extraction and correspondence establishment, followed by blunder detection using LGTM and accuracy enhancement using OLSM [6]. Ihmeida et al. [16] had recommended SIFT and SURF, renowned for their invariance and robustness, to improve SAR image alignment. Sabry et al. [21] had evaluated ORB as an alternative to address these limitations, assessing its performance against SIFT in various scenarios including multi-image feature extraction and real-to-sketch image matching [13]. Oad et al. [20] had studied ORB, SIFT, and SURF algorithms using a dataset of 170 CT Scan brain images in aiding medical diagnosis. Arora et al. [4] had demonstrated the combination of affine transformation as well as optimization technique for rigid medical image registration [3, 5]. Adhikari et al. [1] had focused on feature-based registration, evaluating ORB, KAZE coupled with RANSAC, GC-RANSAC, and MAGSAC + +. Hamzehei et al. [15] had integrated SIFT and ResNet50 for feature extraction and adaptive likelihood-based outlier detection using Maximum Likelihood Estimation Sample Consensus (MLESAC) for medical image registration [12]. Li et al. [19] had studied the Shi-Tomasi algorithm with SIFT to enhance efficiency, utilizing PROSAC for mismatch removal, significantly reducing matching time [2].

3 Proposed Methodology

Step 1. The source (reference) and target images undergo pre-processing using a Gaussian filter for noise reduction prior to normalization. Afterwards, normalization is conducted to standardize the image data consistently (Fig. 1).

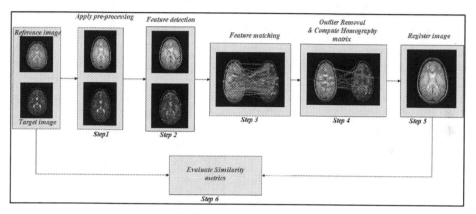

Fig. 1. Framework of proposed methodology

Step 2. Following pre-processing, identify distinctive features in the images using SIFT, SURF, and ORB. SIFT detects keypoints by scale and orientation, SURF finds blob-like structures using Haar wavelets, and ORB identifies corners using binary descriptors for efficiency.

Step 3. In this step, feature matching is carried out using brute force matcher and K-nearest neighbors (KNN) with an aim to align similar features across the entire dataset for subsequent analysis.

Step 4. After feature matching step, next step is to compute homography estimation and apply outlier removal techniques such as alpha trimmed spatial relation correspondence, RANSAC, spatial trimmed correspondence, PROSAC, and LORANSAC, aiming to eliminate inconsistent or erroneous feature correspondences.

Step 5. Compute the registered image, leveraging the transformations derived from the processed data to create a unified representation of the images.

Step 6. Evaluate the similarity metrics (SSIM, PSNR, MI, and cross-correlation) to quantify the resemblance between the reference and registered images to provide insights into their alignment and similarity.

4 Experimental and Comparison Results

This section exhibits the effectiveness of the proposed methodology using evaluation metrics (SSIM, MI, RMSE, PSNR and CC) to analyse monomodal and multimodal medical images. Furthermore, we determine the extracted features, number of matches and visual quality of reference and target image.

4.1 Experimental Results

All experiments are conducted on the PYTHON 3.9.4 platform, using a system equipped with 16.0 GB RAM and a 2.80 GHz Intel(R) Core TM I7-1165G7 CPU. In order to analyze both monomodal and multimodal medical images, the proposed methodology employs two distinct Kaggle datasets [11, 23] for validating the scheme. Furthermore, the experiments are performed on monomodal and multimodal medical images as shown in Fig. 2(a1–a8) and (a9–a16) respectively. These CT and MRI monomodal and Multimodal medical brain images with dimensions of (256 × 256) in (Fig. 2a1–a16) are the reference images that are taken into consideration for the analysis. Following, the reference and target images undergo pre-processing as shown in Fig. 2(a1–a16) and (b1–b16) respectively. Subsequently, key point extraction is performed on both the pre-processed reference and target image as depicted in Fig. 2(c1–c16) and (d1–d16) respectively. Following that, a brute force matcher is employed to identify matches, and alpha-trimmed spatial relation correspondence is employed to remove outliers as displayed in Fig. 2(e1–e16) and (f1–f16) respectively. This process ensures the detection of the most suitable matches, which eventually results in the generation of the registered image as depicted in Fig. 2(g1–g16).

As depicted in Table 1, the quantitative analysis of the proposed methodology (SURF-ATSRC) is compared to traditional approaches (Harris corner detection, ORB, SIFT).

Table 2 and Fig. 3 illustrate that across all monomodal and multimodal test images, the register image of proposed methodology performs better in terms of assessment metrics including MI, RMSE, SSIM, CC, and PSNR. Bold value in Table 2 states higher similarity metrics corresponding to the proposed methodology.

4.2 Comparative Results

A comparative analysis is conducted between proposed methodology and recently developed feature extraction technique [12] to assess its performance in monomodal medical image registration. In order to provide a fair comparison, the identical image with [12, 27] are analyzed. Monomodal and multimodal test image, namely MRI-T1 and CT, obtained from [15, 27] with dimensions of 256 × 256, as shown in Fig. 3. The results depicted in Tables 3 and 4 illustrates that the proposed methodology achieves an effective registered image with higher MI and CC value (Fig. 4).

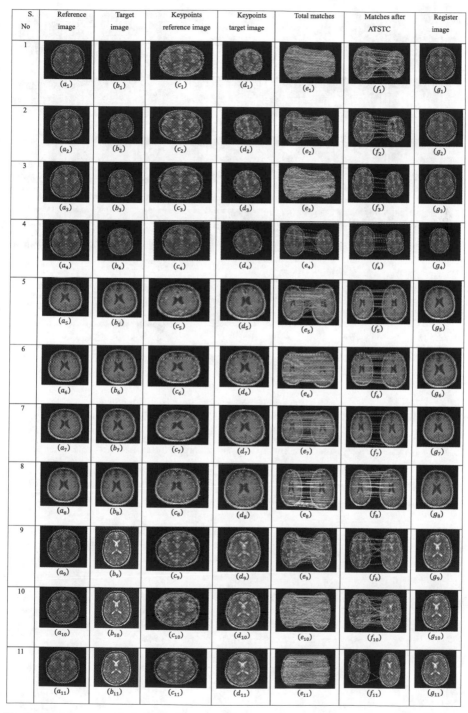

Fig. 2. Experiment conducted on various monomodal/multimodal medical images (a) Reference image (b) Target image (c) Keypoints of reference image (d) Keypoints of target image (e) Total matches (f) Matches after ATSRC (g) Register image

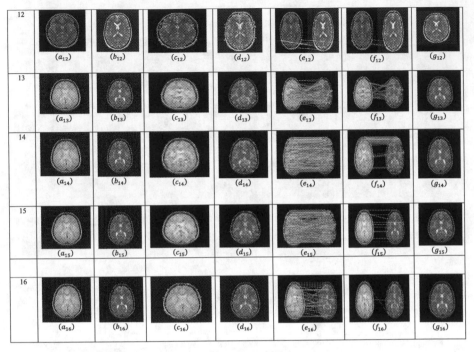

Fig. 2. (*continued*)

Table 1. Experimental outcomes on various monomodal/multimodal medical images taken from Kaggle dataset [11, 23]

S. No.	Images	Reference image keypoints	Target image keypoints	Total matches	Matches after ATSRC
1	MRI-Flair & MRI-Flair	467	423	350	68
2		372	396	126	25
3		158	130	630	5
4		53	48	17	12
5	MRI-T1 & MRI-T1	291	191	143	25
6		241	182	279	55
7		137	142	110	22
8		78	65	52	27
9	MRI- Flair & MRI-T2	372	394	131	22
10		467	334	366	69

(*continued*)

Table 1. (*continued*)

S. No.	Images	Reference image keypoints	Target image keypoints	Total matches	Matches after ATSRC
11		158	252	327	2
12		372	394	131	22
13	CT &	270	394	111	19
14	MRI-T2	239	229	245	48
15		131	160	230	10
16		104	74	10	2

Table 2. Computed evaluation metric for monomodal and multimodal medical images

S. No.	Algorithm	RMSE	MSE	SSIM	PSNR	Cross correlation	MI
1	Harris corner detection	25.4532	647.86539	0.83652	29.8765	0.87654	2.0987
2	ORB	21.4321	459.33491	0.85142	31.3245	0.89643	2.31432
3	SIFT	18.4322	339.745997	0.86754	33.4562	0.91342	2.5432
4	**Proposed Methodology**	**16.5643**	**274.376034**	**0.87654**	**35.6754**	**0.93452**	**2.76532**
5	Harris corner detection	21.3574	456.14130	0.83212	31.53923	0.93924	2.39973
6	ORB	20.3428	455.51745	0.85295	34.54575	0.939354	2.69345
7	SIFT	20.6343	385.50573	0.86143	37.42513	0.95143	3.024265
8	**Proposed Methodology**	**17.5432**	**307.763866**	**0.89765**	**40.32456**	**0.96543**	**3.23452**
9	Harris corner detection	58.3421	3403.80063	0.76543	22.4568	0.7689	1.1532
10	ORB	54.6325	2984.71006	0.786543	24.6754	0.78654	1.4998
11	SIFT	50.9843	2599.39885	0.819872	26.7843	0.79834	1.8321
12	**Proposed Methodology**	**44.6543**	**1994.00651**	**0.832465**	**28.9765**	**0.81987**	**1.9876**
13	Harris corner detection	38.5821	1488.57844	0.70253	26.60862	0.80753	1.4547

(*continued*)

Table 2. (*continued*)

S. No.	Algorithm	RMSE	MSE	SSIM	PSNR	Cross correlation	MI
14	ORB	36.8765	1359.87625	0.72431	27.89765	0.83245	1.5432
15	SIFT	35.4536	592.55730	0.75326	29.75321	0.85423	1.85231
16	**Proposed Methodology**	**33.5432**	**1125.14627**	**0.76549**	**30.8765**	**0.86573**	**1.98654**

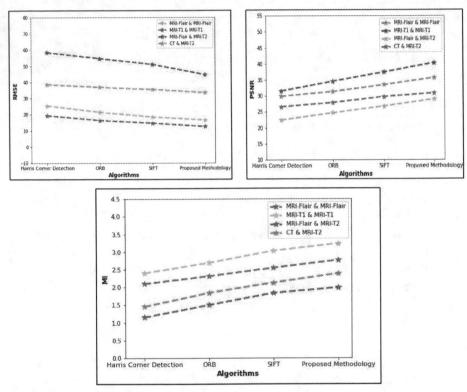

Fig. 3. Comparison of various similarity measures for medical images with proposed methodology

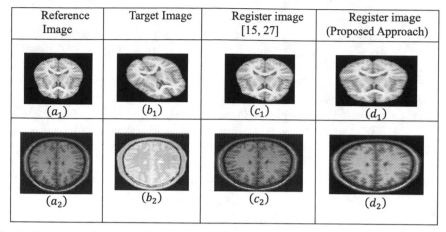

Reference Image	Target Image	Register image [15, 27]	Register image (Proposed Approach)
(a_1)	(b_1)	(c_1)	(d_1)
(a_2)	(b_2)	(c_2)	(d_2)

Fig. 4. Experimental comparison of [15, 27] and proposed approach for monomodal images from dataset [8]

Table 3. Comparison of MI for proposed methodology with existing scheme [15]

Transformation	Evaluation metric
	MI
MLESAC (Affine)	2.35
MLESAC (Rigid)	1.53
MLESAC (Rotated)	1.54
MLESAC (Translated) [15]	2.53
Proposed Approach	**3.654**

Table 4. Evaluation of proposed methodology with existing scheme [27] corresponding to MI and CC

Evaluation metric	MI	CC
P1-SURF [27]	2.2577	0.9219
Proposed Methodology	3.17389	0.95475

5   Conclusion and Future Work

Conventional medical image registration methods, including Harris corner detector, ORB, and SIFT fail to achieve precise alignment due to limitations in adapting to scale, rotation, and illumination variations. Moreover, in this paper introduces a novel image registration method that amalgamates SURF with the alpha trimmed spatial relation correspondence method to achieve robust register image. The analysis systematically evaluated four feature detection algorithms, namely Harris corner, ORB, SIFT and SURF, along with an outlier detection algorithm, alpha trimmed spatial relation correspondence. Through experimental evaluation, it can be observed that employing SURF for key point extraction, in combination with efficient alpha trimmed spatial relation correspondence algorithm, outperformed traditional methods for reducing mismatches. The experimental results highlight the effectiveness of the proposed methodology in enhancing key similarity metrics, including MI, RMSE, PSNR, and SSIM, leading to optimal image alignment. The proposed method can be extended to integrate deep learning with a feature extraction algorithm, offering the potential for further improvements in overall registration performance.

References

1. Adhikari, P., et al.: Experimental analysis of feature-based image registration methods in combination with different outlier rejection algorithms for histopathological images †. pp. 1–9 (2023)
2. Chowdhury, A.R., Ahuja, R., Manroy, A.: A Machine learning driven approach for forecasting Parkinson's Disease progression using temporal data. In: Devismes, S., Mandal, P.S., Saradhi, V.V., Prasad, B., Molla, A.R., Sharma, G. (eds.) Distributed Computing and Intelligent Technology. ICDCIT 2024. LNCS. vol. 14501. Springer, Cham (2024). https://doi.org/10.1007/978-3-031-50583-6_18
3. Arora, P., et al.: A novel image alignment technique leveraging teaching learning-based optimization for medical images. **785**, 317–328 (2024). https://doi.org/10.1007/978-981-99-6544-1_24
4. Arora, P., et al.: An adaptive medical image registration using hybridization of teaching learning-based optimization with affine and speeded up robust features with projective transformation. Cluster Comput. 3 (2023). https://doi.org/10.1007/s10586-023-03974-3
5. Arora, P., et al.: An integration of meta-heuristic approach utilizing kernel principal component analysis for multimodal medical image registration. Cluster Comput. 1 (2024). https://doi.org/10.1007/s10586-024-04281-1
6. Arora, S., et al.: An efficient approach for detecting anomalous events in real-time weather datasets. Concurr. Comput. Pract. Exp. **34**(5), 1–15 (2022). https://doi.org/10.1002/cpe.6707
7. Arora, S., et al.: SETL: a transfer learning based dynamic ensemble classifier for concept drift detection in streaming data. Clust. Comput. (2023). https://doi.org/10.1007/s10586-023-04149-w
8. Chakrabarty, N.: Brain MRI Images for Brain Tumor Detection (2023). https://www.kaggle.com/navoneel/brain-mri-images-for-brain-tumor-detection. Accessed Dec 2023
9. Darshana, M., Asim, B.: Comparison of feature detection and matching approaches: SIFT and SURF. GRD J. Global Res. Dev. J. Eng. 2, 4, 7 (2017)
10. Engin, M., et al.: An evaluation of image registration methods for chest radiographs. In: IntelliSys 2015 - Proceedings of 2015 SAI Intelligent Systems Conference, pp. 822–827 (2015). https://doi.org/10.1109/IntelliSys.2015.7361237
11. Fernando Feltrin: Brain Tumor MRI images 44 classes (2024). https://www.kaggle.com/datasets/fernando2rad/brain-tumor-mri-images-44c. Accessed Jan 2024
12. Garg, S., et al.: An effective deep learning architecture leveraging BIRCH clustering for resource usage prediction of heterogeneous machines in cloud data center. Cluster Comput. **6** (2024). https://doi.org/10.1007/s10586-023-04258-6

13. Garg, S., et al.: GMM-LSTM : a component driven resource utilization prediction model leveraging LSTM and Gaussian mixture model. Clust. Comput. **26**(6), 3547–3563 (2023). https://doi.org/10.1007/s10586-022-03747-4

14. Guan, S.-Y., et al.: A review of point feature based medical image registration. Chinese J. Mech. Eng. **31**(1), 76–92 (2018). https://doi.org/10.1186/s10033-018-0275-9

15. Hamzehei, S., et al.: 3D Biological/Biomedical image registration with enhanced feature extraction and outlier detection. In: ACM-BCB 2023 - 14th ACM Conference on Bioinformatics, Computational Biology, and Health Informatics (2023). https://doi.org/10.1145/3584371.3612965

16. Ihmeida, M., Wei, H.: Image registration techniques and applications: comparative study on remote sensing imagery. In: Proceedings - International Conference on Developments in eSystems Engineering, DeSE, pp. 142–148, December 2021. https://doi.org/10.1109/DESE54285.2021.9719538

17. Jiang, X., et al.: A review of multimodal image matching: methods and applications. Inform. Fusion. **73**(2020), 22–71 (2021). https://doi.org/10.1016/j.inffus.2021.02.012

18. Li, D., et al.: A novel image registration method based on SIFT and verification mechanism. In: 2017 2nd International Conference on Advanced Robotics and Mechatronics, ICARM 2017, pp. 462–467 (2017). January 2018. https://doi.org/10.1109/ICARM.2017.8273207

19. Li, X., Li, S.: Image registration algorithm based on improved SIFT. In: 2023 4th International Conference on Electronic Communication and Artificial Intelligence, ICECAI 2023, pp. 264–267 (2023). https://doi.org/10.1109/ICECAI58670.2023.10176776

20. Oad, A., et al.: Performance comparison of ORB, SURF and SIFT using Intracranial Haemorrhage CTScan Brain images. Int. J. Artif. Intell. Math. Sci. **1**(2), 26–34 (2023). https://doi.org/10.58921/ijaims.v1i2.41

21. Sabry, E.S., et al.: Evaluation of feature extraction methods for different types of images. J. Opt. (India) **52**(2), 716–741 (2023). https://doi.org/10.1007/s12596-022-01024-6

22. Sedaghat, A., Mohammadi, N.: High-resolution image registration based on improved SURF detector and localized GTM. Int. J. Remote Sens. **40**(7), 2576–2601 (2019). https://doi.org/10.1080/01431161.2018.1528402

23. Simeon, A.: Brain Tumor Images Dataset (2023). https://www.kaggle.com/datasets/simeondee/brain-tumor-images-dataset. Accessed Aug 2023

24. Sreeja, G., Saraniya, O.: A comparative study on image registration techniques for SAR images. In: 2019 5th International Conference on Advanced Computing and Communication Systems, ICACCS 2019, ICACCS, pp. 947–953 (2019). https://doi.org/10.1109/ICACCS.2019.8728390

25. Tareen, S.A.K., Saleem, Z.: A comparative analysis of SIFT, SURF, KAZE, AKAZE, ORB, and BRISK. In: International Conference on Computing, Mathematics and Engineering Technologies: Invent, Innovate and Integrate for Socioeconomic Development, iCoMET Proceedings, vol. 01, pp. 1–10 (2018). https://doi.org/10.1109/ICOMET.2018.8346440

26. Wu, Y., et al.: Image registration method based on SURF and FREAK. In: 2015 IEEE International Conference on Signal Processing, Communications and Computing, ICSPCC 2015, pp. 1–4 (2015). https://doi.org/10.1109/ICSPCC.2015.7338825

27. Zheng, Q., et al.: A medical image registration method based on progressive images. Comput. Math. Methods Medicine, Hindawi **2021**(7), 1 (2021). https://doi.org/10.1155/2021/4504306

Tomato Disease Detection from Tomato Leaf Images Using CNN-Based Feature Extraction, Feature Selection with Whale Optimization Algorithm, and SVM Classifier

Le Thi Thu Hong$^{(\boxtimes)}$ [ID], Nguyen Sinh Huy [ID], and Doan Quang Tu [ID]

Institute of Information Technology, AMST, Ha Noi, Viet Nam
lethithuhong1302@gmail.com

Abstract. Tomatoes, a popular crop, thrive on nearly any soil with good drainage. Identifying tomato diseases early on is crucial to maintaining quality and yield. This article proposes a hybrid model approach for early tomato disease detection from tomato leaf images. With the applied hybrid model approach, feature extraction was accomplished by employing a lightweight CNN model on images. These extracted features were then optimized by Whale optimization algorithm and utilized to train the SVM classifier for image classification. Validation of the test set utilizing Accuracy, Recall, Precision, and F1 score showed the proposed method achieved an accuracy score of 98.46%. Furthermore, the accuracy improvement obtained was 3.53% when using the proposed compared to the base CNN model. The findings validated that the proposed method outperforms state-of-the-art tomato disease detection methods with high accuracy and a lightweight model.

Keywords: Tomato Disease Detection · CNN-based Feature Extraction · Feature Optimization · SVM Classifier

1 Introduction

In agriculture, it is essential to detect plant diseases early to enhance productivity and the quality of agricultural products. Tomato plants stand out as renowned and vital crops due to their considerable market demand and nutritional benefits. However, insects and pests that prey on these plants and introduce various diseases hold the capacity to hinder the production of this popular commodity [5]. Diagnosing tomato plants at an early stage can save farmers from costly crop sprays and contribute to an increase in food production. Observing tomato plants closely for manual disease diagnosis is laborious and challenging. Farmers frequently encounter challenges in seeking advice from experts in distant areas and implementing preventive measures for uncommon diseases. Therefore, designing computer-aided systems for tomato crop disease recognition is critical.

© The Author(s), under exclusive license to Springer Nature Switzerland AG 2024
O. Gervasi et al. (Eds.): ICCSA 2024, LNCS 14813, pp. 192–205, 2024.
https://doi.org/10.1007/978-3-031-64605-8_14

(a) Bacterial spot   (b) Early blight   (c) Late blight

(d) Leaf mold   (e) Mosaic virus   (f) Septorial leaf spot

(g) Spider mite   (h) Target spot   (i) Yellow leaf curl virus

Fig. 1. Instances of tomato plant leaves affected by diseases

These systems can aid farmers in identifying diseased tomato plants, determining the specific diseases they are afflicted by, and utilizing that information to enhance the overall efficiency of the crop, minimizing losses.

The image classification models can be used to detect diseases in tomato plants from tomato leaf images by categorizing images of tomato leaves into healthy and diseased groups. The objective of this research is to detect and classify nine diseases commonly occurring in tomato plants, namely Early Blight, Late Blight, Septoria Leaf Spot, Yellow Leaf Curl Virus, Bacterial Spot, Mosaic virus, Target Spot, Spider Mite and Leaf Mold. Figure 1 is an example of tomato plant leaves affected by disease, taken from the PlantVillage dataset [19]. We proposes a hybrid model approach for tomato disease detection based on tomato leaf images. Firstly, features were extracted from the leaf images using a lightweight CNN; then, to select the optimal feature subset, we applied feature optimization using the Whale optimization algorithm [10]. Finally, an SVM (Support vector machines) [7] classifier automatically categorizes data into one of ten classes: healthy or diseases. The proposed model is lightweight with a small parameter count and minimal memory requirements. The main contribution of this study includes:

1) Implementing a lightweight CNN to extract features from tomato leaf images for classifying them into ten classes, including the healthy and nine diseases.
2) Performing feature selection using a Whale optimization algorithm to improve tomato disease detection accuracy.
3) Utilizing an SVM classifier for tomato leaf image classification.
4) Using public open-access PlanVillage dataset for training and testing the proposed model. The results on the testing set, separate from the training set, indicate that the model achieves high accuracy with 98.46%.

The remainder of this article consists of "Related Work", "Proposed Method", "Experiments and Results" "Discussions" and "Conclusions" sections. Some existing research related to the same topic is included in the "Related Work" section. The "Proposed Method" section explains feature extractors based on the CNN models, feature optimization using the Whale optimization algorithm, and SVM classifier in detail. The "Experiments and Results" section includes all calculation and classification results from the proposed method. Finally, conclusions are drawn in the "Conclusions" section.

2   Related Work

Many proposed methods for predicting crop diseases have been based on machine learning in recent years. The suggested methodologies can be categorized into two primary strategies: conventional machine learning methods employing manually engineered feature extraction techniques, and deep learning techniques that directly analyze images using CNNs to identify crop diseases. Traditional machine-learning techniques often rely on segmenting crop images and subsequently classifying diseases based on features extracted from the segmented images. Zhang, Shanwen, et al. [19] proposed using image segmentation, PHOG features, and classification rules to identify diseases in apple and cucumber plants. In [17] the authors focused on detecting plant diseases. Utilizing the KNN classifier, they achieved a commendable accuracy of 98.56% when predicting plant leaf diseases. Mohammed A. Hussein and Amel H. Abbas [6] proposed an automatic disease detection system for tomato plants, wheat, and cucumbers. They employ preprocessing methods like cropping, resizing, fuzzy histogram equalization, and extraction of color and texture features. Then, they utilize the results to train a support vector machine classifier to detect and diagnose plant leaf diseases. In [12], the image segmentation employed the GrabCut algorithm, and sample features were extracted using the LBP method. Subsequently, the SVM was trained on the extracted key points to classify leaf abnormalities. The proposed approach effectively identifies crop diseases, achieving an accuracy of 95%.

Recently, research based on CNN has been conducted in agriculture, and CNN analysis has demonstrated high performance in plant disease detection. In a study by Maeda-Gutiérrez, V. et al. [8], various deep learning-based models such as AlexNet, GoogleNet, Inception V3, ResNet-18, and ResNet-50 were assessed for categorizing tomato plant leaf samples into different classes. The GoogleNet model yielded the best results, attaining an accuracy of 99.39%. Zhao et al. [20] introduced a method for classifying various diseases in tomato plant leaves, employing a CNN with an integrated attention mechanism. This approach achieved an accuracy rate of 99.24%. Bhujel et al. [3] introduced a deep learning-based method, specifically employing the ResNet18 model with CBAM, for classifying diseases in tomato plant leaves. This approach achieved an impressive accuracy of 99.69%. Richey et al. [14] suggested a method for detecting maize crop diseases with an accuracy of 99%, employing the ResNet50 framework for feature computation and class determination. Although these methods yield very high results, they are not suitable for mobile device applications with limited resources due to high processing requirements.

This article proposes a hybrid model approach for tomato disease detection from tomato leaf images with feature extraction accomplished by employing a CNN model on images. These extracted features were then optimized and utilized to train the SVM classifier. The proposed method achieves high performance with a lightweight model. It can be a good choice for human expert-level crop disease diagnostics mobile systems.

3   Proposed Method

The objective of this study is to tackle the issue of classifying tomato leaf images by predicting the categories of tomato plant diseases (Healthy and nine specific diseases) based on their corresponding leaf images. We proposed a hybrid model approach, shown in Fig. 2, to achieve this objective. First, the tomato leaf images are collected from the PlantVillage database. Then, the images are resized and augmented before passing through the base CNN. Next, the feature from images is extracted using CNN. The features obtained from CNN extractors are optimized using the Feature Selection based on Whale Optimization Algorithm (FSWOA) to get a dominant feature vector, which is input to SVM classifier for final classification.

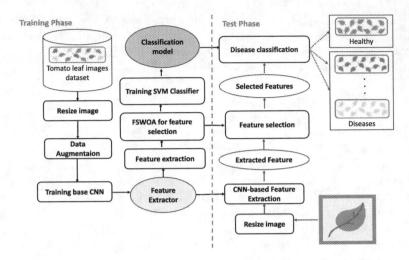

Fig. 2. The proposed method for Tomato disease detection

3.1   Dataset and Preprocessing

This study used tomato leaf images from PlanVillage, an open-access repository of plant leaf images for deploying plant disease detection models, to train and test the proposed model. The PlantVillage dataset comprises a total of 54,306 leaf images representing 14 types of plants. In this study, we only utilize images of tomato plant leaves from the PlantVillage dataset, belonging to 10 classes. Table 1 provides statistics on the number of tomato leaf images belonging to different categories, and Fig. 1 is an example of them from the PlantVillage dataset.

Table 1. The number of tomato leaf images in PlantVillage dataset.

No.	Category name	Total	No.	Category name	Total
1.	Healthy	1591	6.	Yellow Leaf	5357
2.	Bacterial spot	2127	7.	Septoria leaf spot	1771
3.	Early blight	1000	8.	Target spot	1404
4.	Late blight	1909	9.	Mosaic virus	373
5.	Two spotted spider mite	1676	10.	Leaf mold	952

The PlanVillage dataset includes RBG leaf image files with a dimension of $256 \times 256 \times 3$ pixels. Thus, it is necessary to resize images to match the input requirements of the CNN extractors. Using Open-CV, We resized the collected images to $224 \times 224 \times 3$ pixels. Furthermore, we have employed data augmentation to reduce the over-fitting problem in training models. The techniques employed for augmentation include flipping vertically and horizontally, rotating randomly within a range of –10 to 10 °C, scaling randomly between 0.5 and 1.5, shearing randomly within –5 to 5 °C, applying random Gaussian blur with a sigma of 3.0, normalizing contrast randomly by a factor of 1 to 1.5, adjusting brightness randomly within a range of 1 to 1.5, and performing random cropping and padding by 0–5% of both height and width.

3.2   The CNN-Based Feature Extractor

Feature extraction plays a vital role in enhancing the efficiency of the process and generating more meaningful datasets with larger and higher-quality images. In contrast to alternative feature extraction techniques, CNNs can directly capture the images' features within the input dataset. CNN architecture comprises convolutional layers (CLs), pooling layers (PLs), fully connected layers, and rectified linear units (ReLU). CLs specialize in learning convolutions and optimizing data categorization performance. Pooling layers PLs are vital in mitigating overfitting, ensuring stable transformation, and improving computational efficiency by reducing the convolution's structural output. The ReLU activation function enhances the network's non-linear characteristics [2]. When CNNs are utilized as feature extractors, the features are derived from the convolutional and fully connected layers of the CNNs, and these features encompass abstract visual attributes.

In this study, we implemented a simple CNN (called base CNN) for feature extraction to build a compact model suitable for mobile applications. Details of the base CNN layers are presented in Table 2. The base CNN is relatively small, with six pairs of Convolution and MaxPooling layers, and the total number

Table 2. Summary of the base CNN for Feature Extractor.

Layer	Output Shape	Param#
input (InputLayer)	[(224, 224, 3)]	0
conv2d-1(Conv2D-3x3 Kernel,Depth 32)	(222, 222, 32)	896
maxpooling2d-1 (MaxPooling2D-2x2)	(111, 111, 32)	0
conv2d-2 (Conv2D-3x3 Kernel, Depth 64)	(109, 109, 64)	18496
maxpooling2d2 (MaxPooling2D-2x2)	(54, 54, 64)	0
conv2d-3 (Conv2D- 3x3 Kernel, Depth 64)	(52, 52, 64)	36928
maxpooling2d-3 (MaxPooling2D- 2x2)	(26, 26, 64)	0
conv2d-4 (Conv2D- 3x3 Kernel, Depth 64)	(24, 24, 64)	36928
maxpooling2d-4 (MaxPooling2D- 2x2)	(12, 12, 64)	0
conv2d-5 (Conv2D- 3x3 Kernel, Depth 64)	(10, 10, 64)	36928
maxpooling2d-5 (MaxPooling2D- 2x2)	(5, 5, 64)	0
conv2d-6 (Conv2D-3x3 Kernel, Depth 64)	(3, 3, 64)	36928
max-pooling2d-6 (MaxPooling2D- 2x2)	(1, 1, 64)	0
flatten (Flatten)	(64)	0
dense (Dense with SoftMax activation)	(10)	650

Total params: 167,754

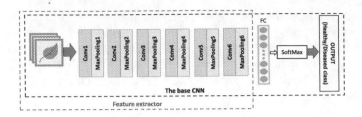

Fig. 3. The architecture of the Feature Extractor

of trainable parameters is only 167,754. Figure 3 illustrates the architecture of the Feature Extractor. First, the base CNN model was instantiated with layers presented in Table 2, and then it was trained from scratch using tomato leaf images from the PlantVillage dataset. Finally, the Feature extractor was obtained by removing the last layer (the Fully Connected layer with SoftMax activation).

3.3   Feature Selection with Whale Optimization Algorithm

In the proposed scheme, after CNN feature extractors, we receive feature vectors with a length of 64. Not all of these features are useful for fitting the classification models. Using unnecessary features diminishes the model's generalization ability and potentially lowers the classifier's accuracy. Furthermore, adding the number of features in a model elevates its overall complexity. Thus, it is necessary to have a feature selection procedure in the proposed scheme to avoid the over-fitting problem and improve the model's performance.

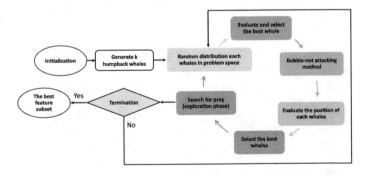

Fig. 4. Feature Selection based on Whale Optimization Algorithm

The conventional approaches for feature selection utilize a selected mathematical framework to decrease the feature vector, whereas heuristic algorithm-based (HA-based) feature optimization is commonly used to diminish the dimension of the feature vector. The Whale optimization algorithm, devised by Mirjalili and Lewis [9], is an effective heuristic algorithm that emulates humpback whales' foraging and hunting strategies. In this study, we use the FSWOA (Feature Selection based on Whale Optimization Algorithm), proposed by Zamani et al. [18] for feature selection. Figure 4 depicts the flowchart of FSWOA. The algorithm comprises three primary phases: initially, it generates k whales and disperses them randomly throughout the search space. Subsequently, each whale's position undergoes evaluation to identify the optimal whale; the remaining whales then adjust their positions relative to the best whale's position. In the second phase, whales engage in a bubble-net attack, akin to an exploitation stage, where each whale proposes a feature subset. These subsets are evaluated based on the classifier's accuracy on the testing set, with the highest accuracy determining the best whale. Finally, in the third phase, or the exploration stage, whales pursue prey randomly based on their respective positions.

3.4   The SVM Classifier

The last part of the proposed scheme is a classifier that automatically categorizes data into one of ten classes. In this work, the SVM classifier was implemented and evaluated for tomato leaf disease classification. Support Vector Machine (SVM) [7] is a class of supervised learning algorithms for classification and regression tasks. They are extensively utilized due to their capability in handling complex datasets, as they identify the optimal decision boundary, also known as a hyperplane, that maximizes the margin between distinct classes. The mathematics behind this process is described as follows:

$$W * x + b = 0 \tag{1}$$

SVMs can be primarily categorized into two types: linear SVM and non-linear SVM. In the case of linear SVM, the algorithm seeks to identify an optimal hyperplane that effectively separates two classes in a dataset exhibiting linear separability. The margin is calculated as the distance between the hyperplane and the closest data points from each class. However, it's important to note that numerous real-world datasets are not linearly separable. Non-linear SVM expands the algorithm's ability to address such datasets by mapping them into a higher-dimensional feature space. This transformation is accomplished using kernel functions like Polynomial, Radial Basis Function (RBF), and Sigmoid Function, which enables SVM to identify non-linear decision boundaries. In this work, we use a non-linear SVM classifier with RBF kernel.

4   Experiments and Results

4.1   Experimental Setting

We use a dataset consisting of 18,136 tomato leaf images belonging to 10 classes from the PlantVillage dataset for training and testing the model. The training set consists of 16,344 images, and the test set consists of 1,792 images. The data was divided into training and validation sets in the training phase, with 13075(80%) allocated to training and 3269(20%) to validation. We train the base CNN to classify 10 classes of tomato leaves from scratch. The entire network was updated via the Adam optimizer, and Adam's learning rate was set to 0.0001. The model produced during the epoch with the highest accuracy value on the validation set is our final model. All algorithms were developed and trained using the Keras framework with a Tensorflow backend and the Scikit learn library on a PC with a GeForce GTX 1080 Ti GPU.

In this study, to attain a thorough assessment of a model's performance in classification task, we employ well-known evaluation functions such as, Accuracy, Recall, Precision, and F1-score. These metrics are utilized to evaluate the congruence between the model's classification results and the assigned class labels for the tomato leaf images. The Recall, as depicted in Eq. (2), signifies the correct classification of samples within the positive classes. Precision, also known as Positive Predictive Value (PPV), is determined by Eq. (3). The F1 score amalgamates both precision and recall into a unified metric, calculated using Eq. (4). The proposed algorithm's cost function is defined by the classifier's accuracy, as illustrated in Eq. (5), where the sum of True Positives (TP) and False Positives (FP) represents the total number of subjects with positive tests, and the sum of False Negatives (FN) and True Negatives (TN) represents the total number of subjects with negative tests.

$$Recall = \frac{TP}{(TP + FN)} \tag{2}$$

$$Precision(PPV) = \frac{TP}{(TP + FP)} \tag{3}$$

$$F1 = 2 \times \left(\frac{precision \times recall}{(precision + recall)} \right) \tag{4}$$

$$Accuracy = \frac{TP + TN}{TP + TN + FP + FN} \tag{5}$$

4.2   Performance of the Base CNN for Tomato Disease Detection

In the initial step, we trained and tested the base CNN for tomato disease image classification. The network employ the Softmax classifier to perform the classification task. The Fig. 5 illustrates the accuracy and loss curves of the CNN throughout the training process. As described in Fig. 5, the training and validation sets' accuracy approximates each other and gradually increases towards 1. Meanwhile, the loss values on the training and validation sets exhibit a closely correlated relationship and tend to decrease towards the value of 0. This indicates that the classification task leads to convergence for the network.

Table 3 shows the accuracy results achieved by the base CNN on the test set. On average, across all classes, the CNN achieved an accuracy of 94.93%, with precision and recall values both equal to 95%. The highest accuracy was

attained in the 'Healthy' and 'Yellow Leaf Curl Virus' classes, reaching 100%.
Meanwhile, the 'Two-spotted spider mite' class had the lowest accuracy, reaching
only 86%. The average accuracy of the model is acceptable; however, there is
a significant disparity in accuracy across different classes. This motivates us to
continue improving the model to enhance accuracy and prediction balance across
various classes.

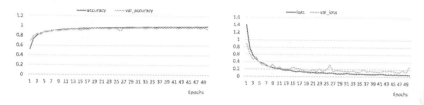

Fig. 5. The CNN base Training Process

Table 3. Accuracy of the base CNN on test set.

Category name	Samples#	Acc(%)	PPV(%)	Recall(%)	F1-score(%)
Bacterial spot	210	95.24	97	95	96
Early blight	110	89.09	92	89	90
Late blight	179	97.77	95	98	96
Leaf Mold	88	95.45	99	95	97
Septoria leaf spot	195	90.26	96	90	93
Two-spotted spider mite	167	86.23	94	86	90
Target Spot	122	90.16	85	90	87
Yellow Leaf Curl Virus	544	98.71	100	99	99
Tomato mosaic virus	39	97.44	100	97	99
Healthy	162	100.00	85	100	92
The average	*1816*	*94.93*	*95*	*95*	*95*

4.3   Tomato Disease Detection Performance of SVM Classifier with FSWOA

After training the base CNN, we use part of the CNN as feature extractors
to extract features of tomato leaf images. These extracted features were then
optimized using the FSWOA and utilized to train the SVM classifier. Finally,
we used the trained SVM classifier to classify the tomato leaf images in the
test set. Table 4 shows the accuracy results achieved by the proposed model.
The average accuracy of the proposed model across all classes is quite high,
reaching 98.53%. Absolute accuracy was achieved 100% in the 'Healthy' and

'Tomato mosaic virus' classes. Additionally, the accuracy in the remaining classes is consistently high, ranging from 97% to 99%. These results surpass the base CNN model significantly. Table 5 compares the accuracy between the proposed model and the base CNN model, while Fig. 6 compares the confusion matrices of the two models. Figure 6 shows that the number of correct predictions for each class in the proposed model has increased compared to the base CNN model. The proposed model shows an average accuracy improvement of 3.53% compared to the base CNN model. There is an improvement in accuracy across all classes, with the most considerable improvement observed in the 'Two-spotted spider mite' class at 10.69%. Furthermore, the accuracy across classes in the proposed model is more uniform compared to the base CNN model.

Table 4. Accuracy of SVM classifier with FSWOA on test set.

Category name	Samples#	Acc(%)	PPV(%)	Recall(%)	F1-score(%)
Bacterial spot	210	97.62	99	98	98
Early blight	110	97.27	91	97	94
Late blight	179	99.44	99	99	99
Leaf Mold	88	96.59	99	97	98
Septoria leaf spot	195	96.59	99	97	98
Two-spotted spider mite	167	96.92	97	100	98
Target Spot	122	96.72	96	97	96
Yellow Leaf Curl Virus	544	98.90	100	99	99
Tomato mosaic virus	39	100.00	100	100	100
Healthy	162	100.00	100	100	100
The average	*1816*	*98.46*	*98.46*	*98.46*	*98.46*

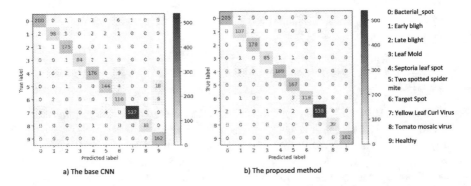

Fig. 6. Comparation confusion matrixes of the base CNN and proposed method

Table 5. Improvement of the proposed method compares to the base CNN.

Category name	Accuracy of base CNN	Accuracy of proposed method	Improvement
Bacterial spot	95.24	97.62	2.38
Early blight	89.09	97.27	8.18
Late blight	97.77	99.44	1.67
Leaf Mold	95.45	96.59	1.14
Septoria leaf spot	90.26	96.59	6.33
Two-spotted spider mite	86.23	96.92	10.69
Target Spot	90.16	96.72	6.56
Yellow Leaf Curl Virus	98.71	98.9	0.19
Tomato mosaic virus	397.44	100	2.56
Healthy	100	100	0
The average	*94.93*	*98.46*	*3.53*

4.4   Comparative Discussion

This section presents the tomato disease detection results from existing methods. We have chosen the studies that used the PlantVillage dataset the same way we did. Due to the absence of evaluation scenarios facilitating an equitable comparison between methods and the unavailability of code for the methods mentioned, the comparison was conducted based on the performance metrics documented in the literature. The results are presented in Table 6. From Table 6, it can be observed that the accuracy of tomato disease detection in current studies is quite high. Some studies achieved approximately 100% accuracy, such as [4,11]. Our proposed model also gains a relatively high accuracy, ranking second among the mentioned models. Meanwhile, the model's parameter count is the smallest, approximately only 0.8% of the highest accuracy model [11], and our model's storage space is also minimal. This makes our model more compact, requiring fewer computational resources and achieving faster execution times. These advantages are crucial in the context of mobile systems supporting tomato disease detection using tomato leaf images.

Table 6. Comparing methods for tomato disease detection

Papers	Model	Acc	Storage Space	Params#
Rangarajan et al.(2018) [13]	VGG19	97.49%	n/a	143.7M
Agarwal et al. (2019) [1]	CNN	91.2%	1,696KB	208,802
Trivedi et al. (2021) [16]	CNN	98.49%	22,565KB	1,422,542
Nawaz et al. (2022) [11]	ResNet-34	**99.97%**	n/a	21.5M
Sakkarvarthi et al. (2022) [15]	CNN	88.17%	n/a	1,060,138
Debnath et al. (2023) [4]	EfficientNetV2B2	99.80%	n/a	10.2M
Proposed method	CNN Hybrid	98.46%	**409 KB**	**167,754**

5   Conclusion

This work proposes a hybrid model approach for tomato disease detection using tomato leaf images. Firstly, features were extracted from the images using a simple CNN. Then, the extracted features were optimized using the FSWOA algorithm. Finally, an SVM classifier automatically categorizes data into one of ten classes: one healthy class and nine disease classes. The proposed model was trained and tested using the PlantVilliage dataset, a publicly available dataset of plant leaf images. The test results on an independent test set, separate from the training set, indicate that the model achieves a high accuracy of 98.46%. Furthermore, the proposed model is lightweight, with a small parameter count and minimal memory requirements. Therefore, the proposed method can be utilized for mobile systems. The main limitation of this study is that we tested the proposed method on only one publicly available dataset of tomato leaf images. Therefore, to affirm the generalizability of the proposed method, further testing will be conducted on different datasets, not limited to tomato leaf images but potentially including many other plant leaves.

References

1. Agarwal, M., Singh, A., Arjaria, S., Sinha, A., Gupta, S.: Toled: tomato leaf disease detection using convolution neural network. Procedia Comput. Sci. **167**, 293–301 (2020)
2. Albawi, S., Mohammed, T.A., Al-Zawi, S.: Understanding of a convolutional neural network. In: 2017 International Conference on Engineering and Technology (ICET), pp. 1–6. IEEE (2017)
3. Bhujel, A., Kim, N.E., Arulmozhi, E., Basak, J.K., Kim, H.T.: A lightweight attention-based convolutional neural networks for tomato leaf disease classification. Agriculture **12**(2), 228 (2022)
4. Debnath, A., et al.: A smartphone-based detection system for tomato leaf disease using efficientnetv2b2 and its explainability with artificial intelligence (ai). Sensors **23**(21), 8685 (2023)
5. Elnaggar, S., Mohamed, A.M., Bakeer, A., Osman, T.A.: Current status of bacterial wilt (ralstonia solanacearum) disease in major tomato (solanum lycopersicum l.) growing areas in egypt. Arch. Agric. Environ. Sci **3**(4), 399–406 (2018)
6. Hussein, M.A., Abbas, A.H.: Plant leaf disease detection using support vector machine. Al-Mustansiriyah J. Sci. **30**(1), 105–110 (2019)
7. Ma, Y., Guo, G. (eds.): Support Vector Machines Applications. Springer, Cham (2014). https://doi.org/10.1007/978-3-319-02300-7
8. Maeda-Gutiérrez, V., et al.: Comparison of convolutional neural network architectures for classification of tomato plant diseases. Appl. Sci. **10**(4), 1245 (2020)
9. Mirjalili, S., Lewis, A.: The whale optimization algorithm. Adv. Eng. Softw. **95**, 51–67 (2016)
10. Mirjalili, S., Mirjalili, S.M., Saremi, S., Mirjalili, S.: Whale optimization algorithm: theory, literature review, and application in designing photonic crystal filters. In: Mirjalili, S., Song Dong, J., Lewis, A. (eds.) Nature-Inspired Optimizers. SCI, vol. 811, pp. 219–238. Springer, Cham (2020). https://doi.org/10.1007/978-3-030-12127-3_13

11. Nawaz, M., et al.: A robust deep learning approach for tomato plant leaf disease localization and classification. Sci. Rep. **12**(1), 18568 (2022)
12. Pantazi, X.E., Moshou, D., Tamouridou, A.A.: Automated leaf disease detection in different crop species through image features analysis and one class classifiers. Comput. Electron. Agric. **156**, 96–104 (2019)
13. Rangarajan, A.K., Purushothaman, R., Ramesh, A.: Tomato crop disease classification using pre-trained deep learning algorithm. Procedia Comput. Sci. **133**, 1040–1047 (2018)
14. Richey, B., Majumder, S., Shirvaikar, M., Kehtarnavaz, N.: Real-time detection of maize crop disease via a deep learning-based smartphone app. In: Real-Time Image Processing and Deep Learning 2020, vol. 11401, pp. 23–29. SPIE (2020)
15. Sakkarvarthi, G., Sathianesan, G.W., Murugan, V.S., Reddy, A.J., Jayagopal, P., Elsisi, M.: Detection and classification of tomato crop disease using convolutional neural network. Electronics **11**(21), 3618 (2022)
16. Trivedi, N.K., et al.: Early detection and classification of tomato leaf disease using high-performance deep neural network. Sensors **21**(23), 7987 (2021)
17. Tulshan, A.S., Raul, N.: Plant leaf disease detection using machine learning. In: 2019 10th International Conference on Computing, Communication and Networking Technologies (ICCCNT), pp. 1–6. IEEE (2019)
18. Zamani, H., Nadimi-Shahraki, M.H.: Feature selection based on whale optimization algorithm for diseases diagnosis. Int. J. Comput. Sci. Inf. Secur. **14**(9), 1243 (2016)
19. Zhang, S., Wang, H., Huang, W., You, Z.: Plant diseased leaf segmentation and recognition by fusion of superpixel, k-means and phog. Optik **157**, 866–872 (2018)
20. Zhao, S., Peng, Y., Liu, J., Wu, S.: Tomato leaf disease diagnosis based on improved convolution neural network by attention module. Agriculture **11**(7), 651 (2021)

Advanced and Emerging Applications

Trajectories in Rutherford Dispersion According to Lagrangian Dynamics

Sara L. Chunga-Palomino$^{(\boxtimes)}$ ⓘ, Edwarth Maza-Cordova ⓘ,
and Robert Ipanaqué-Chero ⓘ

Universidad Nacional de Piura. Urb., Miraflores S/n, Castilla, Piura, Perú
{schungap,ripanaquec}@unp.edu.pe

Abstract. This study delves into the dynamics of physical systems using the Lagrangian formalism within polar coordinates, starting with the Lagrange function, $L = T - U$, where T denotes the kinetic energy and U is the potential energy. The kinetic term is reformulated regarding the radial distance and angular velocity by adapting Lagrange's equation to polar coordinates. In contrast, the possible term is inversely proportional to the square of the radial distance. By implementing the Euler-Lagrange equations, the Lagrange function is differentiated concerning the radial coordinate and its time derivative, leading to a differential equation regarding r and ϕ. A substitution to $u = 1/r$ simplifies and solves this equation, producing a solution correlating angular positions with time. Integrating the initial conditions identifies the constants of integration, culminating in a comprehensive description of the motion in polar terms, illustrating the relationship between inverse radial distance, angular position, and time, and providing a detailed understanding of the dynamic governed by an inversely quadratic central force. This approach reveals the dynamics of complex systems without direct analysis of forces, underscoring the usefulness of the Lagrangian perspective in fields such as celestial mechanics, particle physics, and field theory.

Keywords: Lagrangian Formalism · Polar Coordinates · Euler-Lagrange Equations

1 Introduction

This research explores the dynamics of physical systems by applying Lagrangian formalism in polar coordinates to deepen the understanding of phenomena beyond the scope of classical Newtonian mechanics, such as Rutherford dispersion. The limitation of Newton's inverse square law in the face of subatomic and nuclear phenomena highlights the need for more general theoretical tools to describe the complex interactions in these systems. The study transforms the equations of motion through Lagrangian formalism, revealing crucial symmetries and conservation laws and expanding the understanding of the fundamental forces at play. This approach opens the possibility of approaching particle

Supported by Universidad Nacional de Piura.

dynamics from a perspective that integrates classical and modern physics, thus providing a more holistic interpretation of physical processes at various scales. The objective is to provide a comprehensive analysis of motion in polar terms, using the Euler-Lagrange equations to derive a detailed description of the dynamics under an inversely quadratic central force, which has significant applications in fields such as celestial mechanics, the physics of particles, and field theory, and also facilitates the transition towards a Lagrangian understanding of quantum mechanics.

1.1   Rutherford's Dispersion Challenge: Beyond Newton's Law

Rutherford's scattering experimentation challenged Newtonian understanding, suggesting that forces operating at the subatomic level do not necessarily align with classical laws of motion. The approach of Goldstein et al. [9] clarifies that Newton's inverse square law, applicable in planetary motion and ballistics, found limitations in the face of nuclear dispersion, which better fit the quantitative descriptions provided by particle physics (See Fig. 1). This divergence pointed to an inherent complexity in atomic forces that could not be effectively addressed by classical mechanics alone. Furthermore, Landau and Lifshitz [14] expand this perspective by examining the implications of theoretical mechanics in microscopic systems, highlighting the insufficiency of Newton's law to explain the interaction between particles with an atomic nucleus, which was more adequately described by the Quantum theory.

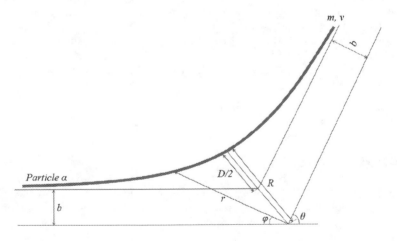

Fig. 1. Path of an Alpha particle scattered by a nucleus.

On the other hand, the formalization of a mathematical framework that overcomes these limits is manifested in the work of Arnold [2], who explains that Lagrangian and Hamiltonian mechanics provide the necessary tools to transcend the restrictions of Newtonian mechanics by using principles variations that are congruent with the phenomena observed in Rutherford dispersion. Likewise, José and Saletan [13] show that classical dynamics, from a contemporary approach, can be complemented with more modern interpretations that allow integration between classical and contemporary physics, thus contributing to a more holistic understanding of the physical processes in different scales.

1.2 Fundamentals and Objectives of Lagrangian Analysis in Particle Scattering

Lagrangian analysis provides a robust theoretical framework for studying particle scattering by allowing the characterization of complex systems by simplifying the equations of motion. According to Hand and Finch [11], the Lagrangian formalization is especially useful in particle scattering since it transforms second-order differential equations into first-order equations, facilitating the identification of the conserved quantities of the system. Applying this formalism reveals the underlying symmetries and conservation laws essential for predicting the trajectory of particles after a collision. This approach expands the understanding of fundamental interactions and provides a methodology for calculating the scattering cross-section, a key goal for understanding the nature of forces between elementary particles.

Additionally, Greenwood [10] argues that the Lagrangian is a central element of variational principles that allow an elegant and versatile formulation that can be applied even when forces cannot be easily derived from a potential, as in specific dispersion interactions. On the other hand, Sussman and Wisdom [21] point out that Lagrangian mechanics not only simplifies calculations in systems with numerous particles but is also essential for the transition to quantum mechanics, providing a coherent connection between theories. Classic and modern. Consequently, Lagrangian analysis constitutes a critical foundation for advancing the study of particle interactions at a fundamental level.

1.3 Principles of Lagrangian Dynamics

The principles of Lagrangian dynamics are rooted in the variational principle, which stipulates that the actual motion of a system between two states is dictated by the stationarity of the action, an integral quantity defined as the time critical of the Lagrangian. Ván and Kovács [22] discuss how variational principles, applied to systems outside of thermodynamic equilibrium, can be extended to include non-equilibrium conditions, opening new horizons in understanding complex dynamical systems.

This approach aligns with the interpretation that equations of motion can be derived from a principle of most minor action. This simplifies the analysis of physical systems by providing a single scalar equation instead of multiple force vector equations [19].

Furthermore, the elegance of Lagrangian principles lies in their ability to directly incorporate the constraints of a physical system into the formulation through Lagrange multipliers, thus allowing a more direct and general treatment of the constraints [15]. Rosenau [19] exposes how Lagrangian structures can be deployed even in systems of evolution equations that initially appear to have no variational structure. This demonstrates the versatility of the Lagrangian to describe a wide variety of physical phenomena, from classical mechanics to fluid dynamics and field theories.

The Lagrangian formulation provides a unified framework for mechanics that extends well beyond the conservative systems traditionally associated with classical mechanics, integrating the dissipative effects and driving forces that are fundamental in treating natural physical systems [20].

1.4   Historical Comparison: Newton's Law Versus Lagrange's Formalism

The historical comparison between Newton's law and Lagrange's formalism represents a fundamental transition in theoretical mechanics from the description of forces acting on particles to an energy-based approach. Newton's laws, formulated in the 17th century, constitute the basis of classical mechanics, providing a set of three equations that directly relate forces to the movement of a body. These equations are extremely powerful in predicting the motion of objects under the influence of conservative forces, and their application can be seen in contemporary studies of complex systems, such as flagellar synchronization in micro-swimmers [17].

In contrast, Lagrangian formalism, developed in the 18th century, offers a more generalized description of motion, not limiting itself to conservative systems. This formalism introduces the concept of Lagrangian, which is the difference between a system's kinetic and potential energy and the action, which must be extreme for the movement to be realizable [5].

Although the Lagrangian approach is traditionally considered more suitable for conservative systems, recent research has extended its application to non-conservative systems, providing methods for including dissipative forces within the Lagrangian formalism [4]. This progress allows using the Lagrangian formalism in a broader range of physical situations, including systems with friction or forces that do not derive from a potential, as in specific orbital dynamics and control problems.

Furthermore, significant interest has developed in the identification of non-linear dynamical systems using sparse data, where the Lagrangian formalism provides a systematic approach to modeling the equations of motion, even when forces are not directly accessible or when they are subject to geometric constraints [18]. In conclusion, while Newtonian mechanics provides a direct and concrete description of force interactions, Lagrangian mechanics offers a more abstract but robust framework for analyzing the dynamics of a system under a broader range of conditions [16].

2   Methodology

2.1   Elaboration of the Lagrangian Model for Rutherford Scattering

To model Rutherford scattering via Lagrangian dynamics, we consider an alpha particle approaching a stationary atomic nucleus. In this approach, the Lagrangian function, $L = T - U$, is constructed from the kinetic energy T and potential energy U of the system. The kinetic energy in polar coordinates is:

$$T = \frac{1}{2}m(\dot{r}^2 + r^2\dot{\theta}^2)$$

while the potential energy due to the electrostatic interaction is:

$$U = \frac{1}{4\pi\epsilon_0}\frac{zZe^2}{r}$$

where m is the mass of the alpha particle, z and Z are the charges of the particle and the nucleus, respectively, and ϵ_0 is the permittivity of the empty.

2.2   Differential Equations in Particle Dynamics

The equations of motion are derived by applying the Euler-Lagrange equations to the Lagrangian function. For the radial coordinate r, the equation of motion is obtained as:

The Euler-Lagrange equation is:

$$\frac{d}{dt}\left(\frac{\partial L}{\partial \dot{r}}\right) - \frac{\partial L}{\partial r} = 0$$

For our Lagrangian function, we have:

$$\frac{\partial L}{\partial \dot{r}} = m\dot{r}, \quad \frac{d}{dt}\frac{\partial L}{\partial \dot{r}} = m\ddot{r}, \quad \frac{\partial L}{\partial r} = mr\dot{\phi}^2 + \frac{zZe^2}{4\pi\epsilon_0 r^2}$$

Which leads to the following second order differential equation in r:

$$m\ddot{r} - mr\dot{\phi}^2 - \frac{zZe^2}{4\pi\epsilon_0 r^2} = 0$$

Or alternatively:

$$m\frac{d^2r}{dt^2} - mr\dot{\phi}^2 - \frac{zZe^2}{4\pi\epsilon_0 r^2} = 0$$

This is a second-order differential equation in r.

2.3   Analysis of Initial Conditions and Physical Variables Involved

The initial conditions of the alpha particle are considered, which define its position and speed at the beginning of dispersion, and the constants of movement are established, such as angular momentum:

$$M = mr^2\dot{\phi} = m \vee b = \text{constante}$$

where m is the mass of the alpha particle, r is the radial distance, $\dot{\phi}$ is the angular velocity, v is the linear velocity and b is the impact parameter.

2.4   Derivation of the Lagrangian Differential Equation

We begin the analysis with the inverse relationship between u and r, where $r = \frac{1}{u}$. This transformation facilitates the description of the trajectory in terms of the dependent variable u and the independent variable ϕ. By differentiating r with respect to ϕ, we obtain the following relations:

$$\frac{dr}{dt} = \frac{dr}{du}\frac{dr}{d\phi}\frac{d\phi}{dt} = -\frac{dr}{u^2}\frac{dr}{d\phi}\frac{M}{mr^2} = -\frac{du}{d\phi}\frac{M}{m}u^2 \tag{1}$$

$$\frac{dr}{dt} = -\frac{M}{m}\frac{du}{d\phi}$$

$$\frac{d^2r}{dt^2} = \frac{d}{d\phi}\left(\frac{dr}{dt}\right)\frac{d\phi}{dt} = \frac{d}{d\phi}\left(-\frac{M}{m}\frac{du}{d\phi}\right)\frac{M}{m}u^2$$

$$\frac{d^2r}{dt^2} = -\frac{M^2}{m^2}u^2\frac{d^2u}{d\phi^2} \tag{2}$$

By substituting these relationships into the differential equation of particle dynamics, we arrive at:

$$m\left(-\frac{M^2u^2}{m^2}\right) - \frac{M^2u^3}{m} - \frac{zZe^2u^2}{4\pi\varepsilon_0} = 0$$

$$-\frac{M^2}{m}\frac{d^2u}{d\phi^2} + u = \frac{zZe^2}{4\pi\varepsilon_0}$$

$$\frac{d^2u}{d\phi^2} + u = -\frac{mzZe^2}{4\pi\varepsilon_0 M^2}$$

With the relation $M = mvb$, the equation simplifies to:

$$\frac{d^2u}{d\phi^2} + u = -\frac{mzZe^2}{4\pi\varepsilon_0(m^2v^2b^2)} = \frac{zZe^2}{4\pi\varepsilon_0\frac{mv^2}{2}2b^2}$$

Defining the constant D as:

$$D = \frac{zZe^2}{4\pi\varepsilon_0\frac{mv^2}{2}}$$

we can rewrite the differential equation in its final form:

$$\frac{d^2u}{d\phi^2} + u = -\frac{D}{b^2}$$

This equation is identical to the equation obtained through Lagrange dynamics, without resorting to Newton's second law.

2.5   Transformations and Solutions of the Equation of Motion

The general solution of the differential equation for u is expressed as a combination of trigonometric functions and the constant derived from the initial conditions:

$$u = A\cos\phi + B\sin\phi - \frac{D}{2b^2}$$

Imposing the boundary conditions, where $\phi \to 0$ when $r \to \infty$ and that the radial velocity $\frac{dr}{dt} \to -v$ when $r \to \infty$, we determine that:

$$\frac{1}{r} = 0 = A\cos\theta + B\sin\theta - \frac{D}{2b^2}$$

$$A = \frac{D}{2b^2}$$

$$\frac{dr}{dt} = -\frac{M}{m}\frac{du}{dt} = -v = -\frac{M}{m}(-A\cos\theta + B\sin\theta)$$

$$B = \frac{mv}{M} = \frac{mv}{mvb} = \frac{1}{b}$$

These constants allow us to write the complete solution for u as:

$$u = -\frac{D}{2b^2}\cos\phi + \frac{1}{b}\sin\phi - \frac{D}{2b^2}$$

2.6   Physical Implications of the Lagrangian Solution

Finally, the relationship between u and ϕ translates into a description of the trajectory of the alpha particle in terms of the distance r and the angle ϕ:

$$\frac{1}{r} = \frac{1}{b}\sin\phi + \frac{D}{2b^2}(\cos\phi - 1)$$

This expression provides a framework to analyze how the alpha particle disperses when interacting with the nucleus, allowing to predict the qualitative and quantitative behavior of the Rutherford scattering phenomenon.

3   Results

3.1   Comparison of Trajectories: Newtonian Approach vs. Lagrangian

The differential equation obtained through Lagrange dynamics,

$$\frac{d^2u}{d\phi^2} + u = -\frac{D}{2b^2} \tag{3}$$

where $u = \frac{1}{r}$, is compared with the analogous equation derived from the Newtonian approach. Direct comparison reveals that both formulations are consistent and produce identical equations for the trajectory of the alpha particle in the electrostatic field of the nucleus. This validates the equivalence of the Lagrangian and Newtonian approaches for this specific scattering problem.

The solution to the differential equation provides a function $u(\phi)$ that describes how the inverse distance of the alpha particle from the nucleus varies with the polar angle ϕ. The calculated trajectory is consistent with the expected and previously known results of Rutherford scattering, demonstrating that the Lagrangian method is a viable tool to study this phenomenon.

3.2   Physical Interpretation of the Lagrangian Solution

The Lagrangian solution of the differential equation, expressed as

$$\frac{1}{r} = \frac{1}{b}\sin\phi + \frac{D}{2b^2}(\cos\phi - 1) \tag{4}$$

provides a deep physical interpretation of Rutherford scattering. The angle dependence ϕ reflects how the alpha particle is deflected from its original trajectory as it passes near the nucleus. The constant D, which incorporates the charge of the alpha particle and the nucleus, as well as the initial kinetic energy of the alpha particle, is essential in determining the magnitude of the scattering.

The term $\sin(\phi)$ dominates when ϕ is small, indicating minimal deflection, consistent with the small-angle scattering observed experimentally. As ϕ increases, the term proportional to $\cos(\phi)$ becomes more significant, reflecting greater deflection of the particle, which is consistent with scattering at larger angles.

This interpretation of the solution not only confirms the validity of the Lagrangian model but also reinforces our understanding of the physical process underlying Rutherford scattering. The results obtained are consistent with experimental observations and demonstrate the usefulness of the Lagrangian formalism in the description of systems governed by central forces.

4   Discussion

4.1   Critical Analysis of the Applicability of Lagrange Formalism in Dispersion

The use of the Lagrangian formalism to describe Rutherford scattering has proven to be a robust theoretical tool. According to Arnold et al. [3], the under-lying symplectic geometry provides a general framework for dynamical systems that is particularly suitable for studying conservation and symmetry properties. The application of this formalism to the specific problem of dispersion allows for elegant manipulation of the system variables and equations of motion. Adame-Carrillo et al. [1] highlight the importance of second-order approaches for k-presymplectic Lagrangian field theories, which could imply broader applications of Rutherford scattering in fields such as quantum gravity.

However, the applicability of Lagrangian formalism is not without criticism. Some studies, such as those by Frolov A. V. and Frolov V. P. [8], suggest that in systems with inequality constraints, conventional Lagrangian formulations may require modifications. Although Rutherford sparseness imposes no such restrictions, the possibility that Lagrange's formalism needs adaptations in more general contexts is a topic of continued research.

4.2   Advantages and Limitations of the Lagrangian Approach

The advantages of the Lagrangian approach are multiple. As Cortizo [6] high-lights, Lagrange's equations offer a more general description than Newton's second law, especially useful in systems where conservative forces are predominant. Additionally, the Lagrangian formulation often simplifies the analysis by work-ing with scalar quantities instead of vectors, which can simplify the calculation of the equations of motion.

However, there are limitations inherent to the Lagrangian formalism. Wagner and Guthrie [23] discuss how the Lagrangian formulation may be less intuitive than Newtonian methods for those with little experience in the subject. On the other hand, in systems where non-conservative forces play a significant role, or where non-holonomic constraints are prominent, the Lagrangian formulation may be less effective or require non-trivial adaptations, as discussed in the works of Jarab'ah [12] and Fan et al. [7].

Thus, while the Lagrangian approach offers a powerful alternative to Newto-nian methods, it is important to recognize its limitations and apply it carefully, especially in complex systems or under conditions that challenge its fundamental assumptions.

5   Conclusions and Recommendations

5.1   Synthesis of Findings and Contributions to the Field of Particle Physics

This study has demonstrated the validity of the Lagrangian formalism in the analysis of Rutherford dispersion. The differential equation obtained and its corresponding solution are consistent with the results that would be derived from Newtonian mechanics, confirming that Lagrangian mechanics is a powerful tool to address dispersion problems in particle physics. The congruence between the Lagrangian and Newtonian approaches strengthens the understanding of Rutherford scattering and offers a different perspective for addressing similar problems in physics. Furthermore, this work highlights the importance of symmetries and conservation laws in particle physics, and how the Lagrangian formalism naturally incorporates these features into its mathematical structure. These findings contribute to the field by providing an alternative framework that may be particularly useful in systems where forces are conservative and symmetries play a central role.

5.2 Recommendations for Future Research and Practical Applications

In light of the results obtained, it is recommended that future research explore the applicability of the Lagrangian formalism to more complex problems in particle physics, such as those involving non-central interactions or quantum mechanical effects. The adaptation of the formalism to systems with non-conservative forces or non-holonomic constraints also deserves special attention, which could open new paths in the simulation of particle systems and in the understanding of complex phenomena. Regarding practical applications, the use of the Lagrangian formulation is suggested in the design of dispersion experiments and in the development of simulation software that can benefit from its simplified structure and its focus on scalar quantities. Additionally, formalism can be a valuable resource in physics education, providing students with a deeper understanding of the underlying principles of classical and modern mechanics.

References

1. Adame-Carrillo, D., Gaset, J., Román-Roy, N.: The second-order problem for k-presymplectic Lagrangian field theories: application to the Einstein-Palatini model. Revista de la Real Academia de Ciencias Exactas, Físicas y Naturales. Serie A. Matemáticas **116**(1), 20 (2021). https://doi.org/10.1007/s13398-021-01136-x
2. Arnold, V.I.: Mathematical Methods of Classical Mechanics, Graduate Texts in Mathematics, vol. 60. Springer, New York, NY (1989). https://doi.org/10.1007/978-1-4757-2063-1
3. Arnol'd, V.I., Givental', A.B., Novikov, S.P.: Symplectic geometry. In: Arnold, V.I., Novikov, S.P. (eds.) Dynamical Systems IV: Symplectic Geometry and its Applications, pp. 1–138. Encyclopaedia of Mathematical Sciences, Springer, Berlin, Heidelberg (2001). https://doi.org/10.1007/978-3-662-06791-8_1
4. Bolatti, D.A., de Ruiter, A.H.J.: Inclusion of non-conservative forces in geometric integrators with application to orbit-attitude coupling. J. Guidance, Control Dyn. **44**(7), 1266–1279 (2021). https://doi.org/10.2514/1.G005510, publisher: American Institute of Aeronautics and Astronautics _eprint: https://doi.org/10.2514/1.G005510

5. Bucataru, I., Constantinescu, O.: Generalized helmholtz conditions for non-conservative lagrangian systems. Math. Phys. Anal. Geom. **18**(1), 25 (2015). https://doi.org/10.1007/s11040-015-9196-3
6. Cortizo, S.F.: Classical mechanics — on the deduction of Lagrange's equations. Rep. Math. Phys. **29**(1), 45–54 (1991). https://doi.org/10.1016/0034-4877(91)90011-B, https://www.sciencedirect.com/science/article/pii/003448779190011B
7. Fan, P., Qin, H., Xiao, J., Xiang, N.: General field theory and weak Euler-Lagrange equation for classical particle-field systems in plasma physics. Phys. Plasmas **26**(6) (2019). https://doi.org/10.1063/1.5092131, https://www.osti.gov/biblio/1526658, publisher: American Institute of Physics
8. Frolov, A.V., Frolov, V.P.: Classical mechanics with inequality constraints and gravity models with limiting curvature. Universe **9**(6), 284 (2023). https://doi.org/10.3390/universe9060284, https://www.mdpi.com/2218-1997/9/6/284, number: 6 Publisher: Multidisciplinary Digital Publishing Institute
9. Goldstein, H., Poole, C., Safko, J.: Classical Mechanics. Pearson, San Francisco Munich (2001)
10. Greenwood, D.T.: Classical Dynamics. Dover Publications Inc., Mineola, N.Y (1997)
11. Hand, L.N., Finch, J.D.: Analytical Mechanics. Cambridge University Press, Cambridge; New York (1998)
12. Jarab'ah, O.A.: Lagrangian formulation of fractional nonholonomic constrained damping systems. Adv. Pure Math. **13**(9), 552–558 (2023). https://doi.org/10.4236/apm.2023.139037, https://www.scirp.org/journal/paperinformation.aspx?paperid=127766, number: 9 Publisher: Scientific Research Publishing
13. José, J.V., Saletan, E.J.: Classical Dynamics: A Contemporary Approach. Cambridge University Press, Cambridge (1998)
14. Landau, L.D., Lifshitz, E.M.: Mechanics, vol. 1. Elsevier, Oxford New York (1976)
15. Meghea, I.: Solutions for some specific mathematical physics problems issued from modeling real phenomena: part 2. Axioms **12**(8), 726 (2023). https://doi.org/10.3390/axioms12080726, https://www.mdpi.com/2075-1680/12/8/726, number: 8 Publisher: Multidisciplinary Digital Publishing Institute
16. Mestdag, T., Sarlet, W., Crampin, M.: The inverse problem for Lagrangian systems with certain non-conservative forces. Diff. Geom. Appl. **29**(1), 55–72 (2011). https://doi.org/10.1016/j.difgeo.2010.11.002, https://www.sciencedirect.com/science/article/pii/S0926224510000719
17. Polotzek, K., Friedrich, B.M.: A three-sphere swimmer for flagellar synchronization. New J. Phys. **15**(4), 045005 (2013). https://doi.org/10.1088/1367-2630/15/4/045005, publisher: IOP Publishing
18. Purnomo, A., Hayashibe, M.: Sparse identification of Lagrangian for nonlinear dynamical systems via proximal gradient method. Sci. Rep. **13**(1), 7919 (2023). https://doi.org/10.1038/s41598-023-34931-0, https://www.nature.com/articles/s41598-023-34931-0, number: 1 Publisher: Nature Publishing Group
19. Rosenau, P.: Unfolding a hidden lagrangian structure of a class of evolution equations. Axioms **12**(1), 2 (2023). https://doi.org/10.3390/axioms12010002, https://www.mdpi.com/2075-1680/12/1/2, number: 1 Publisher: Multidisciplinary Digital Publishing Institute
20. Stark, S.: A systematic approach to standard dissipative continua. Axioms **12**(3), 267 (2023). https://doi.org/10.3390/axioms12030267, https://www.mdpi.com/2075-1680/12/3/267, number: 3 Publisher: Multidisciplinary Digital Publishing Institute

21. Sussman, G.J., Wisdom, J.: Structure and Interpretation of Classical Mechanics. MIT Press, Cambridge, Mass (2001)
22. Ván, P., Kovács, R.: Variational principles and nonequilibrium thermodynamics. Philos. Trans. Royal Soc. Math. Phys. Eng. Sci. **378**(2170), 20190178 (2020). https://doi.org/10.1098/rsta.2019.0178, https://royalsocietypublishing. org/doi/10.1098/rsta.2019.0178, publisher: Royal Society
23. Wagner, G., Guthrie, M.W.: Demystifying the lagrangian of classical mechanics, February 2022. https://doi.org/10.48550/arXiv.1907.07069, http://arxiv.org/abs/ 1907.07069, arXiv:1907.07069 [physics]

Is There a Space in Landslide Susceptibility Modelling: A Case Study of Valtellina Valley, Northern Italy

Khant Min Naing[✉] [iD], Victoria Grace Ann[iD], and Tin Seong Kam[iD]

Singapore Management University, 80 Stamford Road, Singapore 178902, Singapore
{mnkhant.2020,victoriaann.2021,tskam}@scis.smu.edu.sg

Abstract. Landslides pose significant and ever-threatening risks to human life and infrastructure worldwide. Landslide susceptibility modelling is an emerging field of research seeking to determine contributing factors of these events. Yet, previous studies rarely explored the spatial variation of different landslide factors. Hence, this study aims to demonstrate the potential contribution of spatial non-stationarity in landslide susceptibility modelling using Global Logistic Regression (GLR) and Geographically Weighted Logistic Regression (GWLR). The second objective of this study is to demonstrate the important role of data preparation, data sampling, variable sensing, and variable selections in landslide susceptibility modelling. Using Valtellina Valley in Northern Italy as the study area, our study shows that by incorporating spatial heterogeneity and modelling spatial relationships, the measures of Goodness-of-fit of GWLR outperform the traditional GLR. Furthermore, the model outputs of GWLR reveal statistically significant factors contributing to landslides and the spatial variation of these factors in the form of coefficient maps and a landslide susceptibility map.

Keywords: Landslide Susceptibility · Geographically Weighted Logistic Regression · Logistic Regression · Explanatory Modelling

1 Introduction

Landslides refer to the geomorphic phenomenon of slope failure and mass movement in mountainous regions due to eroding and depositing sediment. They are an ever-present threat to critical infrastructure and urban communities worldwide expanding costly damage and massive displacement hampering urban development [1, 2]. Within the past five decades landslide events have increased tenfold [3]. By and large, they are driven by many triggers and conditioning factors [4] including historical evolutions in topography or environment, changes in weather patterns, vegetation cover and river networks and other man-made stimuli.

Extensive engineering prevention works such as concrete surfacing, terracing [5] and slope modification [6] are typical and successful landslide risk mitigations for more gradually sloped areas. However, implementing these works on steeper terrains incurs greater costs due to the complexity of these modifications. Slope geometry alterations,

© The Author(s), under exclusive license to Springer Nature Switzerland AG 2024
O. Gervasi et al. (Eds.): ICCSA 2024, LNCS 14813, pp. 221–238, 2024.
https://doi.org/10.1007/978-3-031-64605-8_16

complex drainage systems installations and reinforcing internal structures for a single high-risk site easily cost millions [6]. Landslide susceptibility maps and assessments can serve as decision-support tools for urban planners and engineers by tiering areas based on their susceptibility levels. This information can then be used to identify highest-risk areas to be prioritised for formulation of preventive measures and site suitability assessments for new developments [7].

This paper aims to demonstrate the potential use of Geographically Weighted Logistic Regression (GWLR) to determine factors influencing landslide susceptibility. GWLR is an extension of Global Logistic Regression (GLR) and offers a significant advantage in binary classification over GLR by addressing spatial non-stationarity present in the global models. Landslide occurrences are closely linked to environmental characteristics and render spatial heterogeneity, thus explanatory variables are unlikely to have an equal contribution to landslide events [8]. Applying local techniques like GWLR to datasets with inherent spatial heterogeneity enables to capture local variations based on the location and proximity of the data samples. Such local variations tend to be lost or averaged out in the global parameter estimates. As a result, GWLR produced more spatially adaptive and accurate outcomes. This paper discusses how GWLR, compared to GLR, is more appropriate for analysing the contribution of each factor to landslides in different parts of the study area.

This paper consists of seven sections, namely literature review, study design, study area and data overview, results, discussion, and conclusion. The literature review presents an overview of existing landslide modelling techniques and factors used in landslide susceptibility modelling. The study design section explains the research questions, research methodology, and the models explored in the study. The study area and data overview sections account for Valtellina's geographical background and the preparation of its landslide inventory and susceptibility factors. The results section covers the experiment results and observations. Finally, the discussion and conclusion sections summarise the key research findings and interpretations, maps of landslide factor coefficient and landslide susceptibility and potential follow-ups on this research.

2   Literature Review

2.1   Landslide Susceptibility Modelling Approaches

Landslide susceptibility modelling is a rapidly evolving field of research given the urgency for landslide prediction and mitigation. Previous studies have investigated and established various methodology frameworks, each with different objectives and modelling techniques. Generally, these studies were focused on either explanatory landslide modelling or predictive landslide modelling, or both. Explanatory landslide studies seek to identify, illustrate, and explain critical factors contributing to landslide events within a study area and their level of influence on these events. Predictive modelling attempts to identify and predict potential landslide occurrences in the study area and to tier the study area into *high-risk* and *low-risk* zones for future preventive measures.

In terms of variation in modelling techniques, landslide susceptibility studies can be broadly classified into four groups: physically based, expert-based, statistical, and machine learning-based models. Physically based models are considered to have the highest utility [9] as historically accurate analytical outcomes and clear interpretation are extracted using physical and mechanical principles [9]. Models like the Shallow Landsliding Stability Model (SHALSTAB) use a deterministic approach to analyse slope failures under steady-state conditions relying on physical data such as rainfall, topography, local slope, and soil transmissivity [10]. However, physically based models are challenged with uncertainties mainly due to limited spatially differentiated geotechnical data that are not readily available [9, 11]. Consequently, these models are applied mostly to smaller-scale landslide risk assessments. Expert-based models are less data-intensive than physically based models mostly developed from expert knowledge of local interactions between landslide occurrences and their controlling factors [12]. Previous studies have used heuristic models by qualitative multicriteria analysis [13] and index methods [14]. These models have proven effective in geographical settings exhibiting high spatial variability. However, such expert models with a qualitative nature tend to be subjective and have limited reproducibility [9, 14, 15] and comparability [16] with other models or locations. Therefore, quantitative methods are more commonly used than qualitative approaches in scientific research.

Statistical landslide susceptibility modelling aims to estimate the relative spatial probability of spatial units with future landslide incidents such that the relationships between the dependent variable (landslides) and the independent variables (individual or combination of conditioning factors) can be identified and quantified. These models are widely adopted since less data input is required than physically based models and quantitative and objective results are provided which expert-based models lack [9, 17].

Machine learning (ML) models are emerging, suitable alternatives to statistical-driven models given their potential for high predictive accuracy [9]. They are favoured for solving non-linear associations between landslides and factors [8] and improving predictive performance across various classifiers. Recent studies have successfully applied machine learning techniques, such as random forest, convolutional neural network [2], deep learning and tree-based models [18] to identify landslide susceptibility with higher accuracy. Despite improved accuracies, many ML techniques suffer from limited interpretability and explainability due to model complexity [9] and hence are primarily used in predictive rather than explanatory modelling.

Overall, a literature review of previous studies has demonstrated that each model type has its unique strengths and limitations, and choosing an appropriate model depends largely on specific research objectives [9] or context of study area or datasets.

2.2 Factors Influencing Landslide Susceptibility

There are numerous causes and factors for landslides. While slope movement can be triggered by heavy rainfall, snowmelt events, earthquakes or volcanic activities, landslide susceptibility is usually attributed to several underlying conditions and factors [4] which weaken slope stability over time. A trigger event causes weakened slopes to undergo mass movements and landslides. Previous research has extensively explored factors including topographical, geological, hydrological, and environmental characteristics in landslide susceptibility modelling. However, many of these studies overlook anthropogenic, or human factors, creating a research gap in the role of human-environmental interaction factors in landslide susceptibility. Today's rapid urbanisation has expanded the spatial scope of human activities [19], often at the expense of ecosystems and the geological environment. Recent research also reveals a growing correlation between urbanisation and landslide risk [20], particularly concerning construction activities, mining and hill cutting [4]. The dynamic changes in land use land cover and infrastructure underscores the need for a more comprehensive approach that includes geo-environmental and anthropogenic factors in landslide susceptibility studies.

Furthermore, limited explanatory landslide susceptibility studies assess the significance of different susceptibility factors and their geomorphic impacts on model outcomes. Moreover, the growing interest in spatial properties, such as spatial heterogeneity and spatial non-stationarity, calls for more studies to explore, illustrate and explain how such spatial properties intercept with the influence of different landslide factors.

3   Study Design

3.1   Research Questions

Landslide susceptibility modelling using statistical techniques heavily relies on spatial input data, which exhibit inherent spatial characteristics. Given the First Law of Geography which states that *"everything is related to everything else, but near things are more related than distant things"* [21], traditional global models generalising study areas cannot capture the relationship among parameter attributes relative to geographical space. Fotheringham, Charlton and Brunson [22] highlighted how regression estimates can fluctuate across space and underscored the need for model calibration to accommodate spatial heterogeneity in spatial dataset.

Through a comparative analysis of GLR and GWLR models, this study examines whether calibrating global models into local derivatives accounts for spatial relationships and enhances model outcomes. The study also investigates the role of "space" in landslide susceptibility and the individual influence of landslide factors on susceptibility results. Three research questions guide this study – i) which landform properties and human-environment interaction factors affect landslide susceptibility; ii) whether the contribution of landslide factors varies across the study area and iii) whether landslide susceptibility is geospatially independent.

3.2   Research Methodology

The research methodology for this study is summarised in Fig. 1. First, the study will build and calibrate a GLR model. This model serves as a basis for understanding the general influence of geo-environmental and human factors on landslide occurrences. The study then builds and calibrates different GLR and GWLR models to analyse the local and spatially adaptive effect of different geo-environmental and human factors on landslide occurrences. Model calibrations are determined by a stepwise selection algorithm to improve model performance per iteration. By comparing the results from calibrated global and local models, the study attempts to develop a methodology framework for explanatory landslide susceptibility modelling.

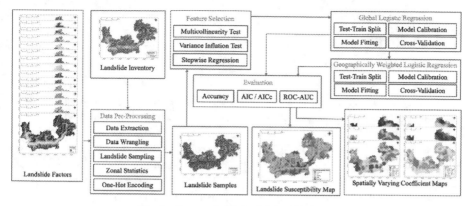

Fig. 1. Research Methodology Diagram.

3.3 Global Logistic Regression (GLR)

Global Logistic Regression (GLR) is a multivariate statistical method established as a common technique for binary classification. GLR is appropriate for landslide susceptibility modelling due to the binary nature of the response variable representing either the landslide presence (indicated as positive class or value of 1) or absence (indicated as negative class or value of 0). Moreover, the target variables can be either discrete or continuous and are not required to satisfy the normal distribution [23]. The GLR model first calculates the log-odds ratio of the event being a positive class by the probability of the event being a negative class. This is done by the linear combination of the independent variables [11, 24]. Next, this linear combination is transformed into a probability value by fitting a sigmoid function. The GLR model can be formulated as:

$$log\left(\frac{p}{1-p}\right) = \beta_0 + \beta_1 x_1 + \cdots + \beta_k x_k \tag{1}$$

$$p(y = 1|x) = \frac{e^{(\beta_0 + \beta_1 x_1 + \cdots + \beta_n x_n)}}{1 + e^{(\beta_0 + \beta_1 x_1 + \cdots + \beta_n x_n)}} \tag{2}$$

where x_1, x_2, ..., x_n are the independent variables. β_n is the coefficient estimate of the independent variable x_n. The coefficient estimates of the GLR model are calculated using *maximum likelihood estimation* [23, 24] which maximises the likelihood of observing the given target results by iteratively updating the previously fitted coefficients until the optimal coefficient values are obtained.

3.4 Geographically Weighted Logistic Regression (GWLR)

Geographically Weighted Logistic Regression (GWLR) is a local regression framework proposed by Fotheringham, Charlton and Brunson [22]. This model is suited for spatial analysis as it extends traditional and global regression frameworks such as Ordinary Least Squares (OLS) and GLR by integrating spatial weights and generating local-level model statistics [25]. GLR model can be calibrated to GWLR as follows:

$$p(u_i,v_i) = \frac{e^{(\beta_{0(u_i,v_i)}+\beta_{1(u_i,v_i)}x_{i1}+\cdots+\beta_{ik(u_i,v_i)}x_{ik})}}{1 + e^{(\beta_{0(u_i,v_i)}+\beta_{1(u_i,v_i)}x_{i1}+\cdots+\beta_{ik(u_i,v_i)}x_{ik})}} \tag{3}$$

where (u_i, v_i) denotes the coordinates of ith sample in space. $\beta_k(u_i, v_i)$ is a realisation of the continuous function $\beta_k(u, v)$ at i[th] sample point. In this way, the coefficient estimates of independent variables are calculated at different sample points. As a result, the GWLR equation does not assume the coefficients to be spatially constant or random but varies within the sample space [16, 22]. In GWLR, spatial weighting quantifies spatial dependencies between variables into an $n \times n$ weight matrix, $W(u_i, v_i)$. The assigned weights vary according to the proximity, with observations nearer to i are assigned higher weight compared to distant ones [22]. This geographic weighting allows nearby observations to exert more influence on the estimation of local regression coefficients.

There are three key elements in building a weight matrix: (i) The distance metric element calculates the distances between locations; (ii) The kernel function defines how weights decay with distance and captures spatially varying relationships; (iii) The bandwidth controls a location's neighbourhood influenced by a fixed distance or an adaptive distance determined by a fixed number of neighbours. The model is then calibrated by data points within the coverage of the bandwidth. GWLR generates location-specific realisations of model goodness-of-fit measures and parameter estimates. These local estimates of explanatory variables can be visualised as a surface to illustrate spatial variations in the relationship between landslide factors and susceptibility [25].

4   Study Area and Data Overview

4.1   Study Area

Located in the Central Alps of Northern Italy, Valtellina Valley extends between 515,000 m and 620,000 m in easting (9.24°E to 10.63°E in longitude), and between 5,050,000 m and 5,170,000 m in northing (46.00°N to 46.64°N in latitude) and covers about 3308 square kilometres. Its average mountain elevation ranges from 2,500 to 3,000 m with the bottom of the valley lying about 1000 to 1100 m above sea level. The East-West orientation of the valley is also attributed to the Periadriatic Line which imposes tectonic lineament upon the valley [26–28]. The region's susceptibility to disasters has been attributed to geological instability from tectonic and post-glacial conditions [28], soil type and moisture, and soil acclivity activating mass movements [29]. Tourism-related activities have indirectly remodified the landform's geomorphology and raised the susceptibility of landslides [28, 29] (Fig. 2).

4.2   Data Acquisition and Processing

The quality of landslide inventory plays a critical role in effectively assessing and predicting the likelihood of landslide occurrences [30]. Inventory of historic landslides can be constructed using traditional field surveys or remote sensing and satellite imageries.

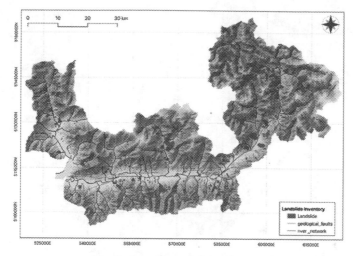

Fig. 2. Location map of study area.

Remote sensing images in particular can capture high-resolution surface data and allow for more precise detection and delineation of landslide areas.

For this study, a total of 10,483 instances of translational, rotational shallow land-slides and debris flows were gathered from the Inventory of Landslide Phenomena in Italy (IFFI). The inventory is maintained by The Italian Institute for Environmental Protection and Research (ISPRA) [31] through collaboration between regional and autonomous provinces building a comprehensive and quality national inventory corroborating the suitability for this study. The landslide inventory also include non-landslide samples developed by The Geomatics and Earth Observation laboratory (GIS-GEOLab @Politecnico di Milano) and complement landslide samples for training and testing sets of this study.

4.3 Landslide Data Sampling

High-quality input data is heavily emphasised for landslide susceptibility models, but it is challenging to sample precise landslide initiation points. Hussin et al. [32] mitigated this with sampling strategies like the mass center, body mass, crown and scarp method. Gaidzik & Ramírez-Herrera [9] highlighted sampling rupture zones and undisturbed close vicinity. However, these strategies lack consistency between non-landslide and landslide sampling methods. Gaidzik & Ramírez-Herrera [12] and Regmi et al. [7] found landslide mass sampling and scarp samples more effective than mass centre sampling. In contrast, Steger and Kofler [9] argued that one-cell sampling is superior given its reduced uncertainties in identifying landslide initiation zones and boundaries (Fig. 3).

In this study, five randomly distributed random points within landslide boundaries were sampled in this study to mitigate centroid-based sampling bias and the uncertainties of body mass sampling (see Fig. 4). Random point sampling counters the biasedness of randomly sampling absence data causing the underrepresentation or overrepresentation of landslide absences that may reinforce misleading modelling results [9].

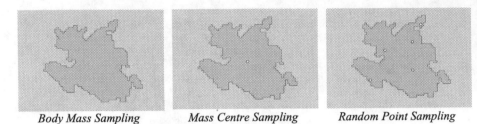

Body Mass Sampling   *Mass Centre Sampling*   *Random Point Sampling*

Fig. 3. Landslide sampling methods.

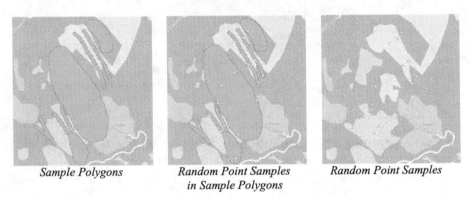

Sample Polygons   *Random Point Samples*   *Random Point Samples*
                              in Sample Polygons

Fig. 4. Random point sampling of landslide inventory.

4.4 Complete and Quasi-Complete Separation

Complete and quasi-complete separation are common conditions preventing the convergence for maximum likelihood estimates in logistic regression by perfectly or partially separating the target variable from predictors [33].

A quasi-complete separation is observed for slope angle values in Fig. 5. Most landslide samples are found in steep-sloping areas (angles > 20), while non-landslide samples predominantly occupy areas with gentler slopes (angles between 0 and 20). This data imbalance could bias predictions and any instance with a slope angle greater than 20 is classified as a landslide. The slope angle exhibits an IV value of 5.3575 significantly higher than the other features, whose IV values range from 0 to 0.5120, indicating that the slope angle feature has the greatest predictive capability.

To correct data imbalance and ensure the model is trained on a more representative sample, a slope angle threshold of up to 20 degrees is established to reduce the sample to areas with gentler slopes. The stratification ensures the relationship between slope angle and landslide occurrence is captured without the influence of the data balance in steeper slope areas, leading to a more reliable and robust model.

4.5 Landslide Susceptibility Factors Selection and Preparation

Careful consideration and acquisition of appropriate data for various landslide susceptibility factors is of equal significance to landslide inventory. To this end, Geoportale

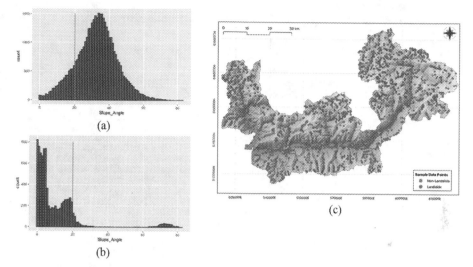

Fig. 5. Distribution of slope angle values in (a) landslide samples, (b) non-landslide samples and (c) slope-based stratified sample points for modelling GLR and GWLR.

della Lombardia has maintained a comprehensive collection of geospatial data tailored for the Lombardy Region [31]. Moreover, the digital lithology compiled by Bucci et al. [34] has furnished an extensive classification of geological formations in Italy at a scale of 1:100 000. A selection and preparation of 15 landslide susceptibility factors (See Table 1) have been undertaken for this study. These factors encompass a wide range of geological, topological, meteorological, hydrological, and human-related aspects.

4.6   Curse of Multicollinearity

Multicollinearity arises when two or more explanatory variables display moderate or high correlation, and it complicates the assessment of the importance and significance of each individual predictor. Nonetheless, multicollinearity can be detected constructing a correlation matrix of the explanatory variables. Pearson's correlation coefficient is commonly used to calculate and construct a correlation matrix. It quantifies the linear association between two variables, with its values ranging from -1 (indicating a completely negative correlation) to 1 (indicating a completely positive correlation). A value of 0 signifies no correlation. The maximum correlation coefficient is observed at 0.57 for *elevation* and *distance to settlement*, and *elevation* and *distance to road*. Other factors exhibit a range of low to moderate correlations. Overall, no factors among those selected for this study had a high positive correlation.

Subsequently, variance inflation factor (VIF) and tolerance (TOL) values are calculated to evaluate landslide variables. VIF is a statistical measure used in regression analysis to observe the increase in variance of the regression coefficient estimates due to multicollinearity. There are currently no established criteria for identifying the extent of VIF values that result in poorly estimated coefficients, but a frequent benchmark in

Table 1. Summary of landslide susceptibility factors used for modelling.

Factor	Source	Scale	Type
Topographic Factors			
(1) Elevation	Geoportale della Lombardia, Derived from DEM	15 × 15 m	Continuous
(2) Slope Angle		15 × 15 m	Continuous
(3) Aspect		15 × 15 m	Categorical
(4) Profile Curvature		15 × 15 m	Continuous
(5) Plan Curvature		15 × 15 m	Continuous
Geological Factors			
(6) Lithology	Bucci et al., 2021	1:100 000	Categorical
(7) Distance to Faults	Geoportale della Lombardia	15 × 15 m	Continuous
Meteorological Factors			
(8) Average Precipitation	ARPA Lombardia	15 × 15 m	Continuous
Hydrological Factors			
(9) Distance to Streams	Geoportale della Lombardia, Derived from DEM	15 × 15 m	Continuous
(10) Topographic Wetness Index		15 × 15 m	Continuous
(11) Steam Power Index		15 × 15 m	Continuous
(12) Sediment Transport Index		15 × 15 m	Continuous
Anthropogenic Factors			
(13) Distance to Settlements	OpenStreetMap	15 × 15 m	Continuous
(14) Distance to Road Networks	Geoportale della Lombardia	15 × 15 m	Continuous
(15) Land Use Land Cover		15 × 15 m	Categorial

numerous regression studies is $VIF \geq 5$ [35]. $VIF \geq 5$ indicates significant multicollinearity and may necessitate further investigation or actions [8]. Three lithological categories – metamorphic, sedimentary, and unconsolidated – show high VIF values (7.85, 5.98 and 9.42 respectively), indicating significant multicollinearity. To avoid potential issues in subsequent modelling results, the variable with the highest VIF value, lithology (unconsolidated) is removed from the dataset. Post-removal, all VIF values are less than 2.27 and TOL values are above 0.44, indicating no further multicollinearity issues.

4.7   Stepwise Selection of Significant Landslide Factors

When using multiple logistic regression to model landslide susceptibility, it is important to evaluate each variable's significance level to avoid overcomplexity. In this regards, stepwise regression can be employed to iteratively select variables by adding or removing them based on likelihood ratio and p-value [11]. Variables are included based on their statistical significance, i.e., $p < 0.05$ and are removed otherwise, thereby selecting only meaningful predictors. The selection continues until no variables meet the inclusion or exclusion criteria. AIC can indicate the optimal complexity where selecting the model with the lowest AIC score will optimise the performance solely based on the reliance on p-values. The final 8 landslide factors – slope angle, profile curvature, plan curvature, lithology (plutonic), lithology (metamorphic), distance to roads, landuse (vegetation) and average precipitation – were and used for subsequent model training.

5   Results

5.1   Model Evaluation and Validation

Different GLR and GWLR models were fitted and calibrated using *GWmodel* package in the R Environment [36]. A total of 8 landslide factors from stepwise selection are the selected independent variables. An adaptive bandwidth of 76 and Gaussian kernel were used in the GWLR model to calibrate the model. Upon completion, three Goodness-of-Fit measures, namely deviance, AICc and pseudo-R^2 were used to compare the performance of GLR and GWLR models. Deviance assesses how well the fitted model compares to the null model, indicating goodness of fit. A higher deviance indicates a poorer fit than the *"best case"*. Pseudo-R^2 serves as a versatile goodness-of-fit indicator for logistic regression models. AIC and corrected AIC (AICc). When the sample size is smaller, a higher penalty term is needed and corrected AIC (AICc) is a more reliable criterion. AIC and AICc can be used to rank models based on their model fit, and smaller values indicate a better model. Model diagnostic values of the GLR model are given in Table 2 and it reveals that GWLR outperforms GLR in all three measures of Goodness-of-Fit as there is an improvement in the indicators.

Table 2. Evaluation of GLR and GWLR Model.

Performance Measures	Models	
	GLR	GWLR
Pseudo-R^2	0.402259	0.532152
Deviance	2291	1793.14
AIC	2309	2103.232
AICc	2309.047	2121.513

The coefficient estimates results, and statistical significance measures derived from the GLR model have been reported in Tables 3 and 4. The coefficient for slope angle and landuse (vegetation) is estimated to have positive relationships with landslide events at 0.2455, and 0.7871 respectively. On the other hand, two curvature measures - profile and plan, two lithology classes – plutonic and metamorphic as well as the distance to roads and average precipitation show a negative relationship, implying that an increase in these variables leads to a decrease in the probability of landslide occurrence. All the coefficient estimates from the GLR model show statistical significance. On the other hand, GWLR produces a coefficient estimate for every sample location, rather than a single fixed value.

The minimum, maximum, and quantile values of the coefficient estimates are reported in Table 4.

Table 3. Coefficient Estimate Results of GLR Model.

Landslide Factors	Coefficient Estimates from GLR		
	Coefficients	z value	Pr(>|z|)
Slope Angle	0.2455	24.3025	0.0000
Profile Curvature	−879.6932	−15.3261	0.0000
Plan Curvature	−732.9813	−11.3090	0.0000
Lithology (Plutonic)	−1.3382	−4.2717	0.0000
Lithology (Metamorphic)	−0.3410	−2.8987	0.0037
Distance to Roads	−0.0077	−2.9310	0.0034
Landuse (Vegetation)	0.7871	7.003	0.0000
Average Precipitation	−2.5301	−2.1931	0.0283

Table 4. Coefficient Estimate Results of GWLR Model.

Landslide Factors	Coefficient Estimates from GWLR				
	Min	1st Quantile	Median	3rd Quantile	Max
Slope Angle	−0.096495	0.2094	0.25654	0.30969	0.4220
Profile Curvature	−1325.6	−1020.9	−882.82	−765.73	−316.9567
Plan Curvature	−1884.14	−1007.3	−664.35	−443.95	−329.3031
Lithology (Plutonic)	−10.819	−3.0798	−1.5746	−0.47993	1.8951
Lithology (Metamorphic)	−1.7751	−0.57195	−0.27482	−0.18384	2.1692
Distance to Roads	−0.054247	−0.0262	−0.013533	0.00157	0.0324
Landuse (Vegetation)	−0.22363	0.5102	0.8376	1.0731	3.7799
Average Precipitation	−29.477	−5.8893	2.9382	12.095	46.7696

6   Discussion

The study explored the influence and significance of space in landslide susceptibility modelling and detected spatial non-stationarity in the relationships between the landslide factors and the landslide locations. The GWLR model has the influence and significance of landslide explanatory factors that vary locally. Table 4 details such variations in numerical forms. Figure 6 provides a visual representation of the coefficient estimates for each variable on a planar surface, highlighting the spatially varying degrees of influence each variable exerts on the landslide susceptibility results.

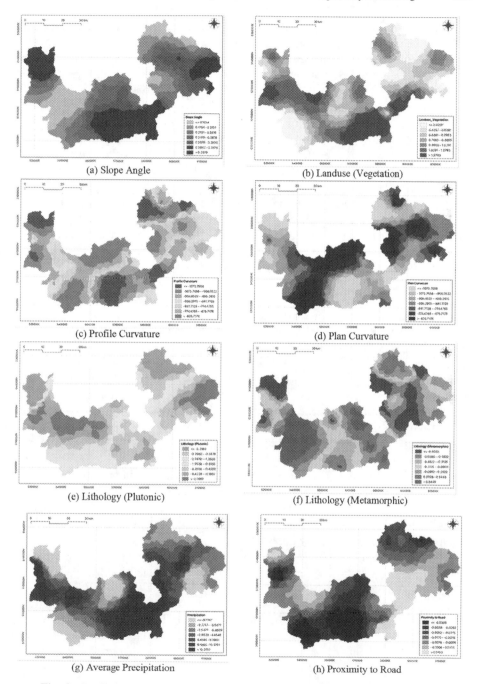

(a) Slope Angle

(b) Landuse (Vegetation)

(c) Profile Curvature

(d) Plan Curvature

(e) Lithology (Plutonic)

(f) Lithology (Metamorphic)

(g) Average Precipitation

(h) Proximity to Road

Fig. 6. Coefficient estimate maps of GWLR showing spatially-varying estimates.

The results from GWLR reveal spatial variations in the coefficient estimates of different variables. The slope angle has small variations ranging from –0.096 to 0.42 due to stratified sampling. Except for minimum coefficient estimates, other estimate ranges reflect a positive correlation with landslide, indicating that a unit degree increase in slope angle contributes to a relative increase in landslide risk in different scales for most of the study area. The coefficient estimates for profile and plan curvature are larger than other variables (coefficient range: –1325.6 to –317.0 for profile curvature and – 1884.1 to –329.3 for plan curvature). This may be attributed to the smaller scale of the values of these variables, and as a result, a slight change in the value leads to a significant change in landslide risk. Notably, the coefficient estimates remain negative across the study areas. It can be interpreted that upward convexness in profile curvature and sideward concaveness in plan curvature increase landslide risks.

Plutonic and metamorphic lithology variables exhibited variations ranging from negative to positive coefficient estimates with negative predominance across quantiles, indicating such lithology does not increase landslide risk in most areas. As for distance to roads, similar regions with positive and negative correlations are observed. The magnitude only ranges from –0.054 to 0.032, which may be attributed to smaller variations in proximity values of the sampled data. Nonetheless, relating the varying coefficient estimates to underlying geological structures or soil types could provide further insights into how these factors influence the changing relationships between predictors and landslide susceptibility across the study area.

Interestingly, landuse (vegetation) is positively correlated to landslide risk in most of the study area. Though this contradicts the initial hypothesis that urban and industrial landuse areas are more susceptible to landslides due to geomorphological modifications, a counterargument can be made that actual developments on the ground may largely differ from the planned landuse classification at a policy level, suggesting the need for alternative, empirical data quantifying landuse in future studies. Lastly, for average precipitation, except for the first quantile (coefficient of –0.22 and lower), a positive correlation is observed to landslide risk. On average, increases in precipitation slightly raised landslide risk (coefficient of 2.94), but there are also extreme cases observed in two ends – an increase in precipitation either increases (coefficient of –29.48) or decreases landslide risk (coefficient of 46.77) to a greater deal. The identical unit increase in precipitation thus leads to vastly different outcomes.

Figure 7 shows the landslide susceptibility map derived by using GWLR methods. Overall, there is variation in the susceptibility level estimated by the GWLR model across our study area. The distribution of susceptibility levels across the region is not uniform. A large proportion of *very high* susceptible areas are found in the southern part of the study area. The other areas observing *high* susceptibility include the northeastern edge of Valtellina Valley and the western peripheries. These are areas estimated to have a 0.8 probability likelihood of landslide events. Many areas with *high* risk are generally closely located to *very high-risk* areas, proving the existence of spatial autocorrelation. Expanding the GWLR model to surrounding regions can also enable the understanding of the changes in coefficient estimates and susceptibility patterns over larger land areas.

Specifically to this study area, it is worth further investigating how the northern region between Easting 585000 and 600000 coinciding with the area of highest coefficients of at least 0.0103 for proximity to roads in Fig. 6h has a *very low* risk of landslide which deviates from the general trend of the study area. However, given the lower coefficient values for proximity to roads compared to the other selected predictors, future research can focus on benchmarking the significance of such coefficient estimates.

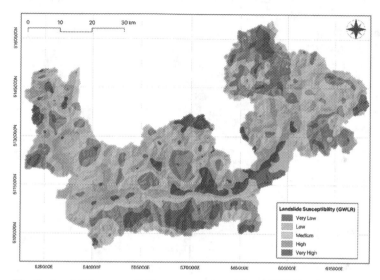

Fig. 7. Landslide susceptibility map produced from GWLR model results.

Overall, the comparison of results from GLR and GWLR models demonstrates the importance of considering spatial variability when developing landslide susceptibility models. By incorporating this spatial non-stationarity, more accurate, region-specific models can be created to better predict and mitigate landslide risks in different areas.

7   Conclusion

In conclusion, our study shows that the coefficient estimates from GLR model indicate that both landform properties (slope angle, curvature, and lithology) and human-environmental factors (distance to roads, landuse, precipitation) have statistically significant contributions to landslide susceptibility. Complementing this, the application of a geographically weighted regression model in this study reveals the presence of spatial heterogeneity as an inherent characteristic in landslide susceptibility mapping. The spatially varying relationships between landslide explanatory variables and landslide occurrence probability were visualized and interpreted through maps. The study discussed how the landslide events across different regions of the study area may be influenced by a distinct set of landslide explanatory variables, each contributing at varying levels of significance. The landslide susceptibility map produced by this study also indicate that landslide susceptibility is not geospatially independent. This is evidenced by the observation that nearby locations tend to exhibit similar levels of susceptibility, underscoring that landslide susceptibility is not a random process but a function of an underlying spatial process influenced by susceptibility factors. This finding underscores the importance of considering spatial dependencies when assessing landslide susceptibility.

This study has laid a methodology framework for landslide susceptibility modelling which is reproducible[1] and can be established as a baseline for further studies in other geographical areas. Landslide susceptibility map presented in Fig. 7 provides useful insights that can facilitate the surety in gazetting high landslide susceptibility areas and prevent urban development in such *high-risk* areas. Such measures will be helpful in the long term, especially with increasing demand for socio-economic infrastructure to support rural-urban migration demand. By referencing the landslide susceptibility maps produced using the methodological approach in this study, planners and decision-makers can make informed choices regarding land use planning and development to minimize landslide hazard risks and safeguard the communities living in susceptible areas.

Acknowledgments. We are grateful to Professor Chris Poskitt from Singapore Management University, School of Computing and Information Systems. We also thank anonymous peer-reviewers for their comments.

Disclosure of Interests. The authors have no competing interests to declare that are relevant to the content of this article.

References

1. Aleotti, P., Chowdhury, R.: Landslide hazard assessment: summary review and new perspectives. Bull. Eng. Geol. Environ. **58**, 21–44 (1999)
2. Wang, H., Zhang, L., Yin, K., Luo, H., Li, J.: Landslide identification using machine learning. Geosci. Front. **12**, 351–364 (2021)
3. Cendrero, A., Forte, L.M., Remondo, J., Cuesta-Albertos, J.A.: Anthropocene geomorphic change. Climate or human activities? Earth's Future **8** (2020)
4. Froude, M.J., Petley, D.N.: Global fatal landslide occurrence from 2004 to 2016. Nat. Hazards Earth Syst. Sci. **18**, 2161–2181 (2018)
5. Shrestha, A.B., Ezee, G.C., Adhikary, R.P., Rai, S.K.: Resource manual on flash flood risk management; module 3 - structural measures (2012)
6. Popescu, M.E., Sasahara, K.: Engineering measures for landslide disaster mitigation. In: Sassa, K., Canuti, P. (eds.) Landslides – Disaster Risk Reduction, pp. 609–631. Springer, Berlin, Heidelberg (2009). https://doi.org/10.1007/978-3-540-69970-5_32
7. Regmi, N.R., Giardino, J.R., McDonald, E.V., Vitek, J.D.: A comparison of logistic regression-based models of susceptibility to landslides in western Colorado, USA. Landslides **11**, 247–262 (2013)
8. Achu, A.L., et al.: Machine-learning based landslide susceptibility modelling with emphasis on uncertainty analysis. Geosci. Front. **14**, 101657 (2023)
9. Steger, S., Kofler, C.: Statistical modeling of landslides: landslide susceptibility and beyond. In: Pourghasemi, H.R. and Gokceoglu, C. (eds.) Spatial Modeling in GIS and R for Earth and Environmental Sciences, pp. 519–546. Elsevier, Amsterdam, Netherlands (2019)

---

[1] Researchers interested in further investigation can access the complete code and methodology framework employed in this study. Please direct requests to the corresponding author.

10. Moore, I.D., O'Loughlin, E.M., Burch, G.J.: A contour-based topographic model for hydrological and ecological applications. Earth Surf. Process. Landf. **13**(4), 305–320 (1988)
11. Kuriakose, S.L., van Beek, L.P., van Westen, C.J.: Parameterizing a physically based shallow landslide model in a data poor region. Earth. Surf. Proc. Land. **34**, 867–881 (2009)
12. Gaidzik, K., Ramírez-Herrera, M.T.: The importance of input data on landslide susceptibility mapping. Sci. Rep. **11** (2021)
13. Castellanos Abella, E.A., Van Westen, C.J.: Qualitative landslide susceptibility assessment by multicriteria analysis: a case study from San Antonio del Sur, Guantánamo, Cuba. Geomorphology **94**, 453–466 (2008)
14. Ruff, M., Czurda, K.: Landslide susceptibility analysis with a heuristic approach in the eastern alps (Vorarlberg, Austria). Geomorphology **94**, 314–324 (2008)
15. van Westen, C.J., Rengers, N., Soeters, R.: Use of geomorphological information in indirect landslide susceptibility assessment. Nat. Hazards **30**, 399–419 (2003)
16. Boussouf, S., Fernández, T., Hart, A.B.: Landslide susceptibility mapping using maximum entropy (Maxent) and geographically weighted logistic regression (GWLR) models in the Río Aguas catchment (Almería, SE Spain). Nat. Hazards **117**, 207–235 (2023)
17. Guzzetti, F., Carrara, A., Cardinali, M., Reichenbach, P.: Landslide hazard evaluation: a review of current techniques and their application in a multi-scale study, Central Italy. Geomorphology **31**, 181–216 (1999)
18. Saha, S., et al.: Comparison between deep learning and tree-based machine learning approaches for landslide susceptibility mapping. Water **13**, 2664 (2021)
19. Wu, W., Guo, S., Shao, Z.: Landslide risk evaluation and its causative factors in typical mountain environment of China: a case study of Yunfu City. Ecol. Indic. **154** (2023)
20. Ozturk, U., Bozzolan, E., Holcombe, E.A., Shukla, R., Pianosi, F., Wagener, T.: How climate change and unplanned urban sprawl bring more landslides (2022)
21. Tobler, W.R.: A computer movie simulating urban growth in the Detroit Region. Econ. Geogr. **46**, 234 (1970)
22. Fotheringham, A.S., Brunsdon, C., Charlton, M.: Geographically Weighted Regression the Analysis of Spatially Varying Relationships. Wiley, Hoboken (2010)
23. Sun, X., Chen, J., Bao, Y., Han, X., Zhan, J., Peng, W.: Landslide susceptibility mapping using logistic regression analysis along the Jinsha River and its tributaries close to Derong and Deqin County, southwestern China. ISPRS Int. J. Geo Inf. **7**, 438 (2018)
24. Matsche, D.T.: A Geographically Weighted Regression Approach to Landslide Susceptibility Modeling. Theses and Dissertations Collection, University of Idaho Library Digital Collections (2017)
25. Matthews, S.A., Yang, T.-C.: Mapping the results of local statistics: using geographically weighted regression. Demogr. Res. **26**, 151–166 (2012)
26. Azzoni, A., Chiesa, S., Frassoni, A., Govi, M.: The valpola landslide. Eng. Geol. **33**, 59–70 (1992)
27. Camera, C., Apuani, T., Masetti, M.: Modeling the stability of terraced slopes: an approach from Valtellina (Northern Italy). Environ. Earth Sci. **74**, 855–868 (2015)
28. Alexander, D.: Valtellina landslide and flood emergency, Northern Italy, 1987. Disasters **12**, 212–222 (1988)
29. Luino, F., et al.: The role of soil type in triggering shallow landslides in the Alps (Lombardy, northern Italy). Land. **11**, 1125 (2022)
30. Lu, J., et al.: Investigation of landslide susceptibility decision mechanisms in different ensemble-based machine learning models with various types of factor data. Sustainability. **15**, 13563 (2023)
31. Xu, Q., Yordanov, V., Brovelli, M.A.: Landslide Influencing Factors for Landslide Susceptibility Mapping in Lombardy, Italy. Zenodo (2023)

32. Hussin, H.Y., et al.: Different landslide sampling strategies in a grid-based bi-variate statistical susceptibility model. Geomorphology **253**, 508–523 (2016)
33. Heinze, G., Schemper, M.: A solution to the problem of separation in logistic regression. Stat. Med. **21**, 2409–2419 (2002)
34. Bucci, F., et al.: A new digital lithological map of Italy at the 1:100 000 scale for geomechanical modelling. Earth Syst. Sci. Data. **14**, 4129–4151 (2022)
35. Li, Y., Huang, S., Li, J., Huang, J., Wang, W.: Spatial non-stationarity-based landslide susceptibility assessment using PCAMGWR model. Water **14**, 881 (2022)
36. Gollini, I., Lu, B., Charlton, M., Brunsdon, C., Harris, P.: GWMode: an r package for exploring spatial heterogeneity using geographically weighted models. J. Stat. Softw. **63** (2015)

Study of Relationships Between Time Series by Co-spectral Analysis

Francesco Domenico d'Ovidio[1] and Najada Firza[1,2(✉)]

[1] Department of Economics and Finance, University of Bari "Aldo Moro", Largo Abbazia Santa Scolastica, Bari, Italy
najada.firza@uniba.it
[2] Catholic University Our Lady of Good Counsel, Tirana, Albania

Abstract. In the literature, cross correlation is often used to analyze the relationships between time series. When the objective of the study is to determine the antecedents and consequences between two or more data sets, cross-correlation analysis is a useful but not sufficient tool to provide information. This paper presents an exploratory technique for investigating relationships between time series. The chosen technique can provide information about priority or precedence within a series, which may establish dependency relationships that cross-correlation analysis cannot identify. The proposed solution is based on the transformation of the observed data into Fourier series and the joint analysis of two series by co-spectral analysis. An example is presented to demonstrate the application of time series analysis to the study of financial data. The article emphasizes the usefulness of these techniques for subsequent analysis.

Keywords: Time series · Cross correlations · Fourier transform · Spectrogram · Co-spectral analysis · Cross gain

1 Introduction

In time series analysis, it is common to evaluate the relationships between them using cross-correlation, which measures the similarity of two observed data series over time as a function of a time shift or translation applied to one of them.

However, if the goal of analysis is not the generic inter-relationship between two or more sets of data, but rather the determination of which among them might be antecedent and which might be consequent (implying concepts that are often preparatory to causality, though not necessarily implying it), the study of cross-correlations proves to be a necessary tool, but not sufficient to provide the required information directly or as an exploration of the different studied phenomena.

To address the issue of identifying antecedent and consequent time series for targeted analysis, we followed the recommendations of a 50-year-old study (Delvecchio 1974), paying attention for this purpose to co-spectral analysis. This technique is based on transforming observed data into Fourier series and analyzing them jointly with techniques that operate in the frequency domain instead of the temporal domain, where cross-correlation

O. Gervasi et al. (Eds.): ICCSA 2024, LNCS 14813, pp. 239–254, 2024.
https://doi.org/10.1007/978-3-031-64605-8_17

analysis is typically used. Fourier techniques are well-known in Signal Theory, but their exploratory value in the economic and social sciences may be underestimated.

This study first explains the mathematical and methodological foundations of spectral analysis (Sect. 2). Then, Sect. 3 delves into the specifics of co-spectrum analysis. Section 4 provides a detailed examination of the application of this technique to the study of financial series. Finally, Sect. 5 presents some concluding remarks.

2 Time Series Analysis and Fourier Series Transformation

To determine the statistical significance of cyclic variations in a stationary time series [1], the analysis of the correlogram can be used. The correlogram is the series of autocorrelation coefficients rh = C /Ch 0, where Ch (h = 0, 1, 2,..., m) are the lag autocovariances of the detrended series, which is assumed to be stationary. The eigenvariances for each lag h, in the case of stationary time series with zero mean can be best determined as described in Bendat and Piersol (1966, 2004):

$$C_h = \frac{1}{s-h} \sum_{t=1}^{s-h} (x_t - \overline{x})(x_{t+h} - \overline{x}) = \frac{1}{s-h} \sum_{t=1}^{s-h} x_t x_{t+h}$$

To achieve stationary data series, it is typically necessary to adjust the trend by taking the difference with respect to an analytic function or by using prime differences. The second technique is preferred because it allows for obtaining a self-stationary series in the mean without complex functional analysis and without altering the structure of polynomial-type evolutionary series 2 (see, e.g., Yaglom 1958);

2.1 Verification of Stationarity of Time Series

Various tests can be used to evaluate the stationarity of the observed series, which is a necessary condition for time domain analysis, and its opposite, integration. In this study, two tests were used in addition to graphical observation of the differentiated series. The most well-known test for this topic is the Augmented Dickey-Fuller (ADF) test, which was also the first test proposed on this topic (see, Dickey and Fuller 1979; Said and Dickey 1984). This test compares a stationary AR(p) to a stochastic process (random walk) after excluding deterministic components. To apply the Augmented Dickey-Fuller (ADF) test, an auxiliary regression is conducted using the T-statistic (at a prefixed α level of significance). The number of lags of the differenced variable must be predetermined and set as the limit of the summation of differenced terms in the regression function

$$\Delta y_t = \mu + \beta t + \varphi y_{t-1} + \sum_{j=1}^{k} \delta_j \Delta y_{t-j} + \varepsilon_t$$

where μ is a constant, β is the coefficient of a hypothetical residual trend, and φ is the coefficient of the unit root of the original series while the coefficients δj represent the

---

[1] A time series is considered "stationary in the strong sense" (or *narrow sense*) when its mean, variance and all moments of third order and higher are independent of time.

autoregression of the differentiated series. The number of lags k can be selected using Akaike's, Schwarz's, or Hannan-Quinn's information criterion: different models can be estimated, and the value of k that results in the minimum value of the chosen statistic should be chosen (Cottrell and Lucchetti 2016, 2017).

The ADF test is unidirectional with the basic hypothesis H0: $\varphi = 0$ and alternative hypothesis H1: $\varphi < 0$. When testing the null hypothesis, yt must be differentiated at least once to be considered stationary. However, under the alternative hypothesis, yt is already stationary and does not require further differentiation[2]: therefore, largely and significantly negative values of the DFτ test statistic (and thus p-values $< \alpha$) imply the rejection of the basic hypothesis. To compare with the critical values tabulated by Dickey and Fuller using simulation techniques, it is necessary to standardize the test statistic by dividing it by its s.e.: $DF_\tau = \hat{\varphi}/s.e.(\hat{\varphi})$.

This test is highly flexible because the shape of its distribution (and therefore the set of critical values for the test) depends on the constraints placed on some of the parameters of the auxiliary regression (Hamilton 1994).

The full model described in the previous equation is applicable when the time series is assumed to be nonstationary in mean and variance, meaning it has a trend with quite different cyclical or conjunctural variations. If nonstationarity in variance is assumed with a nonzero stationary mean, the β parameter should be set to zero. If the mean is instead zero and nonstationarity in variance is assumed, the μ parameter should also be zero. Note that by setting all parameters δj to zero (i.e., by setting k = 0, i.e., no lag), transforms the ADF test into the Dickey-Fuller test for 1st-order integration.

The KPSS test (Kwiatkowski et al. 1992), while less powerful than the ADF test, resolves some of its application uncertainties: ADF gives unreliable results if the time series is neither stationary nor integrated, meaning that the differentiated series is also nonstationary. This test, in fact, has as its basic assumption the stationarity of the studied series and not its integration: its rationale is that if the elements of the series are expressed as $y_t = \mu_y + u_t$, then the sample mean of y_t is a consistent estimator of μ_y if (and only if) u_t represents a stationary process with zero mean. Additionally, the long-run variance of u_t is a finite number.

In practice, after estimated the u_t with $e_t = y_t - \bar{y}$, one should calculate their empirical $\hat{c}$ autocovariances from order -m to order m: the bandwidth m must be large enough to allow short-term persistence of the et but not too large relative to the length T of the series: the authors of the GRETL recommend m values of k = INT[(4 × T/100)0,25] or not much larger (Cottrell and Lucchetti 2017).

In this work, m = 2 × k = 16 was chosen.

Starting from the autocovariances $\hat{c}$, we can estimate the long-run variance with

$$\overline{\sigma}^2 = \sum_{i=-m}^{m} \left(1 - \frac{|i|}{m+1}\right) \cdot \hat{c}_i.$$

---

[2] The *rationale* for the ADF test is that if the series is integrated, then the lagged level of the series $\{y_{t-1}\}$ will not provide relevant information to predict changes in y_t beyond that provided by the lagged differences $\{\Delta y_{t-j}\}$. In this case, therefore, $\varphi = 0$ may be posited, which is precisely the basic assumption H_0.

The KPSS test statistic is

$$\eta = \frac{\sum_{t=1}^{T} \left(\sum_{i=1}^{t} e_i \right)}{T^2 \bar{\sigma}^2}$$

and, under the basic hypothesis, its distribution is asymptotic and independent of disturbance parameters, as defined by the authors using simulation methods. The assumption of stationarity should be rejected if the empirical value of the test exceeds the tabulated asymptotic critical value for the predetermined significance level ($\eta_{0,10} = 0.347$; $\eta_{0,05} = 0.463$; $\eta_{0,025} = 0.574$; $\eta_{0,01} = 0.739$).

2.2 Correlograms and Spectrograms

In autocorrelation analysis, it is recommended to limit the maximum shift m to no more than $s/3$, where s is the number of terms in the time series (Malinvaud 1971). This ensures good accuracy, even though shifts equal to half the length of the series itself can be placed in series of conspicuous numerosity.

Empirical autocorrelation coefficients have a useful property: they are invariant, meaning they do not depend on the units of measurement or point of origin. In the case of incorrelation, they follow an approximately normal distribution law (Hannan 1960), allowing for the drawing of confidence intervals given by $\pm 2\,\hat{\sigma}$ or $\pm 3\,\sigma$) (see Kendall 1973; Kendall and Stuart 1976), within which these coefficients should be included when the residuals distribute randomly (e.g., a self-stationary series should have coefficients that are all nonsignificant, except possibly for the first one).

Correlogram analysis is helpful in analyzing cycles (Malinvaud 1971), but it may not provide precise indications. In the presence of time cycles of different frequencies, each autocorrelation coefficient is affected by all existing cycles, and partial autocorrelation function (PACF) analysis may not always be sufficient to solve this problem. The purpose of the partial autocorrelation function is to evaluate each autoregressive coefficient net of the effect of the previous ones: this reduces the possibility of considering significant components of 'spurious autoregression', which could be caused by the combination of two or more autoregressive components. For example, consider a series that has significant autoregressive components for lag 2, lag 5, and lag 10. The problem is to identify how much of the component with lag 10 is due to the 'beating' between the component with lag 2 and that with lag 5. Moreover, when dealing with series that have a small or large number of terms, the significance of the coefficients may be underestimated or overestimated, respectively. These flaws can make the results considerably less useful, or otherwise less clear. Therefore, the applicability of the method must be evaluated on a case-by-case basis.

However, there are statistical methodologies that provide more robust information, such as spectrogram analysis also known as spectral analysis (Malinvaud 1971; Hamilton 2020). These techniques are well-known in various fields of scientific research and can be easily applied to the phenomenon discussed in this note, as well as many others.

For instance, periodogram and spectrogram enable the estimation of the variance in series explained by different cycles of varying frequencies, which together generate the series itself. These are defined in the so-called 'frequency domain', which differs in properties and developments from the 'time domain' where source data and even autocorrelation functions are defined.

There is a clear relationship between these functions and the representation of the various spectral densities, as correlogram and spectrogram can provide similar information. However, spectral analysis is particularly useful when multiple cyclic or erratic components are present in the series and can be advantageously used in conjunction with autocorrelation analysis.

The robustness of the solutions identified by spectral analysis is not dependent on the amount of available data, since this technique is based on purely mathematical transformations and computations, rather than assumptions about the generating processes of the series, making it almost entirely nonparametric (IBM Corp. 2012). Furthermore, according to the assumptions of Fourier analysis, the correlation between the sine functions used is always zero: therefore, all individual terms of a periodogram are mathematically and statistically independent of each other. Additionally, it is always possible to reconstruct the original series from the spectral coefficients, which implies that this analysis is lossless.

Regarding the methodological references for spectral analysis, it is important to note that we define each kth term of the periodogram of a stationary stochastic process {Xt} (such as the residual series considered in this study) with the notation:

$$I_k = a_k^2 + b_k^2$$

The coefficients for Ik, as proposed by Malinvaud (1971), are given by:

$$a_k = \sqrt{\frac{2}{s}} \sum_{t=1}^{s} x_t \cos \frac{2\pi t}{s}, \, b_k = \sqrt{\frac{2}{s}} \sum_{t=1}^{s} x_t sen \frac{2\pi t}{s}$$

in this context, we will have:

$$a_0 = \frac{1}{\sqrt{s}} \sum_{t=1}^{s} x_t, \, a_p = 1/\sqrt{s} \cdot \sum_{t=1}^{s} (-1)^t x_t, \, b0 = bp = 0.$$

Ik also represents the contribution that the sinusoidal component of period s/k makes to the sum of squares of xt. Assuming that the observed series has a zero mean, we can develop this expression to obtain $I_k = 2 \sum_{h=-s}^{s} C_h \cos \frac{2\pi kh}{s}$, where Ch represents the shift autocovariances of the series. This equivalence does not apply to Io (which is null by assumption) nor, if the number of terms in the series is even, to the pth term of the periodogram: $I_p = \sum_{h=-s}^{s} C_h \cos(\pi h)$.

However, it is generally not appropriate to assign significance to every peak in the periodogram. To reduce variance and disturbance components, it is preferred to apply smoothing functions, known as 'windows'. These windows correspond, generally, to moving averages of three or more terms of the periodogram.

The *spectral density function* (Malinvaud 1971; Bendat and Piersol 1966, 2004) is the result of the periodogram transformation at point k, and its Cartesian representation is precisely the *spectrogram*. For interpretation purposes, it is important to consider only spectra of sufficient magnitude, which represent points of relative maxima in the spectrogram. This is because the spectral density is the result of a smoothing function of the kth term of the periodogram, which can be likened to a centered moving average.

The following text includes graphs that display spectra at the null frequency (although this frequency corresponds, mathematically, to a period of time that is unquantifiable but tends towards infinity). The purpose of displaying this information is to show the overall trend of the spectrogram and, more importantly, the actual contribution made by each individual component to the variability of the residual series. According to Stuart's theorem, the ordinate value of the spectrum measuring the contribution is expressed in terms of the deviance of the series:

$$\frac{f(0)}{2} + \sum_{k=1}^{m-1} f(\omega_k) + \frac{f(\omega_m)}{2} = DEV(X).$$

3 Cross-Correlation and Co-spectral Analysis

In probability and statistics, given two stochastic processes $X = \{X_t\}$ and $Y = \{Y_t\}$, *cross-covariance* is a function that returns the covariance of each process with the other at pairs of time points (t, s). This means that if $E(X_t) = \mu_{x(t)}$ and $E(Y_t) = \mu_{y(t)}$, the cross-covariance can be calculated as follows:

$\text{Cov}(X_t, Y_s) = C_{xy}(t, s) = E[(X_t - \mu_{x(t)})(Y_s - \mu_{y(s)})] = E(X_t Y_s) - \mu_{x(t)} \mu_{y(s)}.$

If X and Y are weakly stationary stochastic processes, it follows that:

$E(X_t) = \mu_x, E(Y_s) = \mu_y, \text{Cov}(X_t, X_s) = E(X_t X_s) - \mu^2_x, \text{Cov}(Y_t, Y_s) = E(Y_t Y_s) - \mu^2_y;$

However, to consider a *stationary* (second-order) *stochastic bivariate process*, it is necessary to confirm that the cross-moments $\text{Cov}(X_t, Y_s)$ also depend solely on (t-s). This condition is met when $\text{Cov}(X_t, Y_s) = E(X_t Y_s) - \mu_x \mu_y$, to prevent any distortion of the results (Harris 1995; Johansen 1995, 2000; Cottrell and Lucchetti 2017).

Keep in mind that the cross-covariance function is not an even function: generally, $\text{Cov}(X_t, Y_s) \neq \text{Cov}(X_s, Y_t)$. It is *not positive semidefinite* and, unlike autocovariance, does not exhibit a maximum for null lag (h = t-s = 0), but its maximum value can occur at any lag (Battaglia 2007). If one wishes to compare the relationships between different pairs of stationary stochastic processes, it is necessary to construct a standardized index with respect to the maximum, similar to the correlation coefficient. This index measures *cross-correlation*:

$$r_{xy}(h) = \frac{\text{Cov}(X_t, Y_{t+h})}{\sqrt{Var(X_t) \cdot Var(Y_{t+h})}} = \frac{C_{xy}(h)}{\sqrt{\sigma^2_x \cdot \sigma^2_y}}$$

Thus, cross-correlation is a measure of the similarity between two time series, and a function of the time between individual observations. It is important to note that the amplitude values of cross-correlation are not fully normalized[3], meaning that the maximum correlation (positive or negative) will be less than 1 in absolute value. Additionally, the cross-correlation function results only display half of the correlation coefficients to be studied (times t, t + 1, t + 2,..., t + h). To examine the other half, simply reverse the order of the series (cross-correlate B with A instead of A with B).

When cross-correlation is not applicable, such as when the cointegration test fails or when there are too few series to apply statistical tests with sufficient power, co-spectral analysis (also known as *cross-spectral analysis*) can still provide reliable additional information. This technique, like spectral analysis, operates in the frequentist domain and is a quasi-parametric method.

In fact, the (univariate) spectrograms of two processes $\{X_t\}$ and $\{Y_t\}$ describe each series as a combination of cyclic components (of frequency ω between 0 and π) that are uncorrelated with each other. It is shown that any linear relationships between $\{X_t\}$ and $\{Y_t\}$ only act between components of equal frequency (Battaglia 2007; Bendat and Piersol 1966); therefore the amplitudes of the harmonics of $\{X_t\}$ and $\{Y_t\}$ are mutually uncorrelated for all components of different frequencies.

The joint spectral density function of $\{X_t\}$ and $\{Y_t\}$ can be obtained by taking the Fourier transform of the cross-covariance. However, it is typically represented by separating the real and imaginary parts due to its complex values:

$$S_{xy}(\omega) = c(\omega) + iq(\omega).$$

The co-spectral density (real part of the previous expression) is the even function $c(\omega)$, meaning that $f(x) = f(-x)$, and measures the correlation of the in-phase frequency components of the two series. The quadrature spectrum[4] is the odd function $iq(\omega)$, meaning that $f(x) = -f(-x)$, and corresponds to the correlation of the out-of-phase components.

Co-spectral analysis provides further information about the relationships between the series in the frequentist domain.

- first, *coherence*, which is a normalized form of the cross-spectrum measuring the overall correspondence between the spectra of the two related series. In practice, this is referred to as the 'correlation between spectra':

$$K_{xy}(\Omega) = \frac{S_{xy}(\Omega)}{\sqrt{S_x(\Omega) \cdot S_y(\Omega)}}.$$

$K_{xy}(\omega) = 1$ indicates a high degree of similarity between the frequency component ω in both signals, with a perfect linear relationship if applicable for each ω. Conversely, $K_{xy}(\omega) = 0$ indicates no similarity at all, and if this is the case for each ω, the series

---

[3] The cross-correlation coefficients are proportional to the relative covariances. Therefore, their maximum functional is $|r_{xy}(h)| < 1$, as they are not even functions. Additionally, at the null lag, the cross-correlation will be exactly equal to the linear correlation coefficient between the two variables: $r_{xy}(0) = r_{xy}$.

[4] If the two series are mutually uncorrelated, i.e., $r_{xy}(h) = 0$ for each h, then $c(\omega) = iq(\omega) = 0$; on the other hand, if $Y = Xt$, then $S_{xy}(\omega) = S_x(\omega)$, and thus we fall into the univariate case, being $c(\omega) = S_x(\omega)$ and $iq(\omega) = 0$.

will be completely uncorrelated, resulting $r_{xy}(h) = 0$ for each h^5. Sometimes, the *square coherence* is calculated as the square of the ratio mentioned above. This can be interpreted similarly to the well-known *index of determination*, which is the square of the linear correlation coefficient. Consistency and squared coherence are insensitive to linear transformations of the processes $\{X_t\}$ and $\{Y_t\}$; therefore, the information they provide applies not only to the stationary series describing them but also to the non-stationary series of which the former are a linear transformation.

However, interpreting coherence values independently is inadvisable. For instance, when the spectral density estimates in both series are very small, large coherence values can be generated (due to a very small divisor in the calculation of coherence values), even if there are no strong cyclic components in both series in their respective frequencies.

- In the second instance, the *crossed amplitude* (also known as 'phase amplitude') should be considered:

$$A_{xy}(\omega) = \sqrt{c(\omega)^2 + {}_iq(\omega)^2}$$

This index measures the extent to which each frequency component of a given series is influenced by the components of the other series.

- The *spectral gain* of the series is a noteworthy measure, calculated by the cross-amplitude value related to the estimated spectral density for one of the two series in the analysis. Accordingly, it is necessary to calculate *two* distinct gain values: $A_{xy}(\omega)/S_x(\omega)$ and $A_{xy}(\omega)/S_y(\omega)$. These values can be interpreted as OLS regression coefficients of the respective frequencies of the series. They serve as *confirmation* (in the frequentist domain) of the cross-correlation coefficients in the time domain.
- Finally, the *phase shift* (or *phase spectrum*) estimates are calculated by taking the arctangent of the ratio between the estimated quadrature spectrum and the co-spectral density. These estimates are typically represented by the Greek letter φ: $\varphi(\omega) = \arctan[q(\omega)/c(\omega)]$. The *phase shift* indicates the time difference between each frequency component of one series and those of the other series.

Due to the considerations outlined in this section, it is reasonable to conclude that the results of the co-spectral analysis, specifically the *gain* and *shift* values of the studied series, have intrinsic value in terms of analysis in the frequentist domain. They are also excellent complements to cross-correlation analysis, which provides clear and immediately identifiable results in the temporal domain. Co-spectral analysis does not suffer from some of the methodological constraints of cross-correlation analysis, such as the necessary cointegration conditions and a *substantial number of terms* in the data series.

Additionally, similar to the correlogram, some lagged terms may appear statistically significant due to 'spurious autoregression.' Similarly, certain components among the cross-correlations may only be significant due to the interaction of components with smaller delays (*beat*), which can be difficult to identify without partial cross-correlation information.

---

[5] This means that the result of co-spectral analysis can be used as confirmatory information for cross-correlation, which may be unreliable due to a lack of cointegration or low series numerosity. Additionally, since $K_{xy}(\omega) = K_{yx}(\omega)$ it is generally preferable to omit the indices and write simply $K(\omega)$.

This analysis procedure can be applied to various types of time series, including economic, social, financial, or physical-technical data. For example, see the following section for its application to financial series.

4 Application of the Proposed Technique to Financial Series Case

To apply the proposed study technique to real data, non-recent financial data was chosen. This was done to comply with the rules of use stipulated by the data providers, which often require long periods of embargo for their free use in research and scientific dissemination operations. The data covers the time span from January 2008 to September 2014 and includes the opening, high, and low prices, as well as the daily closing prices within each working week (5 days) for the following assets:

- *Gold Future*, a popular instrument among traditional investors, which has recently experienced periods of significant upward interest alternating with periods of bearish crisis, even long ones;
- *Copper Spot*, which concerns the prices of copper, a consumer good rather than an investment good like the former, and is therefore closely linked to the performance of the real economy and the industrial sector;
- the *Thomson-Reuters-Jefferies CRB*, which is a commodity index that replaced the former CRBMET. The CRBMET became less and less representative, and therefore was adjusted from 2010 onward;
- the *U.S. 10-yrs Treasure Note*, which is an asset that represents the yield on the main U.S. medium- to long-term government bond with a 10-year maturity. It is a useful indicator of the health of the U.S. economy and is likely to influence the choices of large investors;
- the *Standard & Poor's 500 index*, that is the world's leading stock market index, but it only covers U.S. companies;
- The *S&P 500 volatility index with a 30-day expiration* (representing the average value of the "risk premium" investors are willing to pay for options on the S&P 500, offering a forecast of the variability of the stock market over the next 30 days.)
- The S&P 500 volatility index with 60- and 90-day expiration.

The described series provide comprehensive coverage for the period under consideration, with minimal midweek interruptions, usually only for holidays. In the U.S. market, there are fewer holidays than in Italy and other countries.

Any missing data occurring in sequences of no more than 2–3 days were estimated using rectilinear interpolation of contiguous values (Figs. 1, 2 and 3).

Fig. 1. Daily closures of Gold Future and Spot Copper.

Fig. 2. Daily closures of the Standard&Poor's 500 and Thomson-Reuters-Jefferies CRB indices.

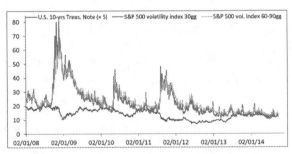

Fig. 3. Daily closures of U.S. 10-Year Treas. Note and S&P500 volatility index at 30 days and 60–90 days expiration.

The financial series exhibits various forms of trend, including both increasing and decreasing trends, as well as internal cycles of different cadence. This indicates non-stationarity on average, with significant differences in variance over time, particularly for Gold Future, Standard&Poor's 500, and the S&P 500 volatility index at both described time frames. It is important to note the non-stationarity in variance. To avoid spurious relationships between time-bound series, it is recommended to obtain stationary data series. This can be achieved by first applying a logarithmic transformation of the data (Box-Cox 1964) and then calculating their prime differences. The transformation used is as follows:

$$y_t = ln(xt) - ln(xt - 1) = ln[xt/(xt - 1)].$$

As a result of this operation, the transformed series is assimilated into stationary processes of the second order (see Fig. 4).

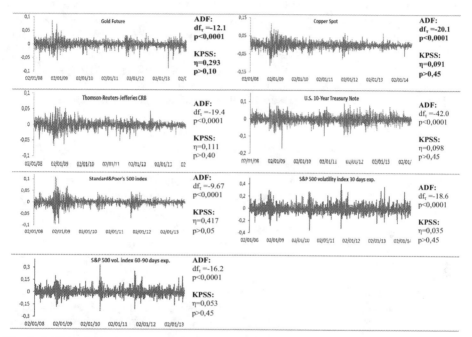

Fig. 4. Differential logarithmic series of daily asset closures. Statistical significance of ADF and KPSS tests for each asset.

This assumption was tested for each series by both ADF unit root test (with a significance level of $\alpha = 0.01$) and KPSS test with 16 lag periods (with a critical value $\eta_{0,025} = 0,574$). The significance level $\alpha = .025$ was chosen instead of the more critical $\alpha = .01$ due to the lower power of the test, which increases the risk of accepting a false baseline hypothesis if the significance level is too small. However, the redundancy of statistics is justified by the constraint that only weak stationarity of the series is necessary for proper use of the analysis in the frequentist domain, as discussed in Sect. 2, while the ADF test is also limited by series integration.

Pairwise cointegration analysis was conducted using both techniques available in GRETL, after verifying the stationarity of each individual series with comforting findings: just the empirical KPSS test value for the Standard&Poor's 500 index series approached $\alpha = 0.05$, but it was not significant enough to raise doubts, considering its lower power. For the combinations obtained by setting the Gold Future series as a fixed term, the results of the Engle-Granger test and those of the Johansen test generally coincide perfectly. The basic hypothesis (integration of the residuals of the linear combination the first, presence of nonzero eigenvalues the other) is rejected with p-values < 0.001. An exception to the rule is the relationship between Gold Future indices and Standard & Poor's indices. The Johansen trace test shows that $.010 < p < .015$, which means that, for a significance level $\alpha = .01$, we can accept the basic hypothesis that at least one linear combination of the two series is nonstationary.

The analysis is limited to investigating the potential effects of the various indices on the Gold Future related index (and viceversa). Since causal relationships cannot be hypothesized, only antecedence/consequence of the data is considered. To achieve this, co-spectral analysis is used, specifically examining the gain function of Gold Future index with respect to each of the other financial indicators, using a 5-term Tukey-Hamming window. When the gain function indicates an antecedent relationship, it is accompanied by an analysis of the corresponding cross-correlation function with a lag of up to 20 days.

Figure 5 displays the gain functions taken from the co-spectral (bivariate) analysis between the Gold Future index and each of the other financial indices described above. This analysis may indicate the antecedent and consequent relationships between the compared indices.

The co-spectral gain function in the first image shows the degree of dependence between Copper spot (trend marked by the green line) and Gold Future (trend marked by the blue line). The largest gain is evident when considering Copper spot prior to Gold Future. Almost all the phases observed in the graph are lower if Copper spot is assumed as consequent. Therefore, it is recommended to assume Gold future as consequent to Copper spot.

In this brief exploratory-methodological analysis, we can observe significant relationships between Gold Future and U.S. 10-year Treasury Note through the co-spectral gain function. Additionally, Gold Future has significant relationships with the S&P 500 volatility at 30-day and S&P 500 volatility T 60–90-day indices.

Instead, the gain functions produced by the correlation between Gold Future and S&P500, as well as between Gold Future and Thomson-Reuters-Jefferies CRB, are not relevant: therefore, no antecedence/consequence can be assumed. This corresponds to the statistical independence of the two financial series when transitioning from the frequency domain to the time domain.

At this stage, it is appropriate to consider cross-correlation functions that relate only to the relationships clearly identified through the gain function. This will help to define relational lags. In cases where the gain function is not relevant, the cross-correlation function cannot adequately identify the relationships between the variables under study, and therefore it is not useful to study it.

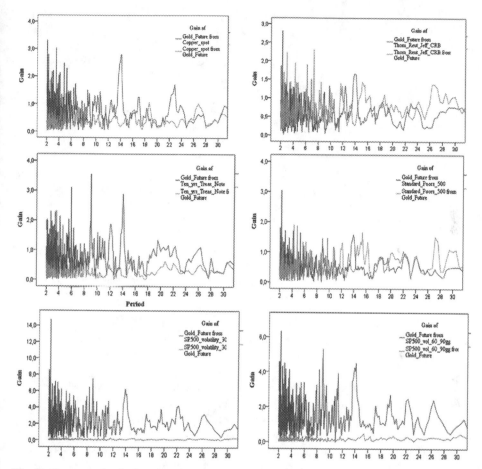

Fig. 5. Co-spectral gain functions between Gold Future and other financial indexes (linear scale period 1–30).

The graphs in Fig. 6 show the significance of a relationship with a kth lag. If the relationship is statistically significant, it indicates the influence of the identified series on the values of the Gold future k days later. This influence may be direct or inverse, depending on whether the lag is of positive or negative sign.

For instance, the cross-correlation between Copper spot and Gold Future indicates that the closing prices of the former asset have a direct influence on the day itself (at lag 0, a relationship that could still be spurious, i.e., both assets can be influenced by others), but also a slight but significant negative influence with lags 8 and 17. Borderline influences (positive, but almost insignificant) are also found at lags 6, 9, and 15.

The impact of the 10-year U.S. Treasury note asset on Gold Future is predominantly negative, albeit not very significant. This holds true for lag 0 (the same day) and even less so for lags 5, 8 and 19. However, there is a minor positive impact at lag 2 (i.e. 2 days later).

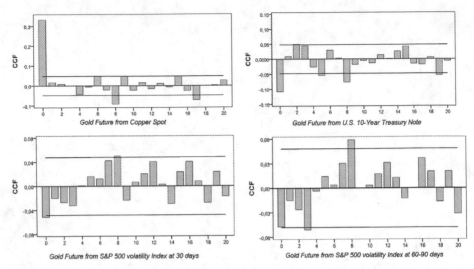

Fig. 6. Cross-correlation functions between Gold Future and its financial antecedent indices.

The influence of the 30-day S&P500 and 60–90-day S&P500 volatility indices on the Gold future is minimal and almost insensitive. However, there is a borderline negative influence with lag 0 (and in the second case, also with lag 2) and a positive influence with lag 8.

As argued and demonstrated here, it is difficult to interpret significant relationships when the gain function does not allow for the determination of antecedent and consequent series, as is the case with the Thomson-Reuters-Jefferies CRB and S&P500 indices. For instance, in the first graph of Fig. 7, we observe (without considering the correlation at lag 0) that, in addition to some relationships on the right side of the cross correlograms, there are significant relationships between the TRJ-CRB and Gold future with lags of 8 and 12, indicating a negative influence, and with lags of 1 and 15, indicating a slight positive influence.

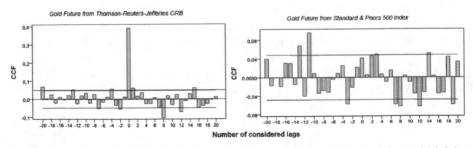

Fig. 7. Cross-correlation functions between Gold Future and financial indexes from which it has undetermined relationships.

The TRJ-CRB was also found to be minimally influenced by the Gold future, with negative influences at lags of –2 and –7, and a positive influence at lags of –4, –13, and –20.

Even more confusing turns out to be the relationship between the Gold Future and the S&P500, which not surprisingly is the most problematic pair of assets in the Johansen test.

5 Concluding Remarks

The work carried out has demonstrated the validity of the frequency approach in time series analysis. This has allowed for exploration of the different relationships that exist among highly relevant financial variables in the U.S. market. The empirical analysis has identified some interesting elements (years 2008–2014). The Gold Future is typically an affected asset rather than an influencer of changes in other financial market indices, even after making the series stationary. It is important to maintain objectivity and avoid biased language when discussing financial market indices.

A statistically significant relationship, albeit of slight magnitude, exists between the closing values of various indices and the Gold Future closing price 8 (working) days later.

In the next work we will focus on the frequency domain analysis which lacks inference characters and thus well-defined probabilities of replication of results with different time data sets.

Therefore, observation of more recent financial series could lead to different conclusions. However, early explorations of the 2015–2022 data confirm the observations treated by earlier data. These explorations are not still publishable and therefore cannot be used in this study.

References

1. Battaglia, F.: Statistical Forecasting Methods. Springer, Milan (2007)
2. Bendat, J.S., Piersol, A.G.: Measurement and Analysis of Random Data. J. Wiley, New York (1966)
3. Bendat, J.S., Piersol, A.G.: Random Data Analysis and Measurement Procedures, Wiley Series in Probability and Statistics (3rd Edition) (2004)
4. Box, G.E.P., Cox, C.: An Analysis of transformations. J. Am. Stat. Assoc. **65** (1964)
5. Cottrell, A., Lucchetti, R.: Gretl - Gnu Regression, Econometrics and Time-series Library, Samurai Media Limited (2016). ISBN: 978-9888406272
6. Cottrell, A., Lucchetti, R.: Gretl User's Guide, gretl documentation (2017). http://sourceforge.net/projects/gretl/files/manual/gretl-guide-a4.pdf/download
7. Delvecchio, F.: Structural changes in the marriage curve in Italy. J. Econ. Annals Econ. Year XXXVI (new series), no. 3–4, March–April 1974
8. Dickey, D.A., Fuller, W.A.: Distribution of the estimators for autoregressive time series with a unit root. J. Am. Stat. Assoc. **74**(366), 427–431 (1979). https://doi.org/10.2307/2286348
9. Engle, R.F., Granger, C.W.J.: Co-integration and error correction: representation, estimation, and testing. Econometrica **55**, 251–276 (1987)

10. Granger, C.W.J., Newbold, P.: Spurious regressions in econometrics. J. Econ. **2**(2), 111–120 (1974). https://doi.org/10.1016/0304-4076(74)90034-7
11. Hamilton, J.D.: Time Series Analysis. Princeton University Press, Princeton (1994)
12. Hannan, E.J.: Time Series Analysis. Methuen, London (1960)
13. Harris, R.: Using Cointegration Analysis in Econometric Modelling. Prentice-Hall (1995)
14. IBM Corporation: IBM SPSS Forecasting 21 (2012). ftp://public.dhe.ibm.com/software/analytics/spss/documentation/statistics/21.0/en/client/Manuals/IBM_SPSS_Forecasting.pdf
15. Kendall, M.G.: Time-Series, Charles Griffin & Co. Ltd., London & High Wycombe (1973)
16. Kendall, M.G., Stuart, A.: The Advanced Theory of Statistics - Volume 3 - Design and Analysis, and Time-Series, Charles Griffin & Co. Ltd., London & High Wycombe (1976)
17. Kwiatkowski, D., Phillips, P.C.B., Schmidt, P., Shin, Y.: Testing the null of stationarity against the alternative of a unit root: how sure are we that economic time series have a unit root? J. Econ. **54**, 159–178 (1992)
18. Johansen, S.: Likelihood-Based Inference in Cointegrated Vector Autoregressive Models. Oxford University Press, Oxford (1995)
19. Johansen, S.: Modelling of cointegration in the vector autoregressive model. Econ. Model. **17**, 359–373 (2000)
20. Malinvaud, E.: Statistical methods of econometrics. UTET, Turin (1971)
21. Oppenheim, A., Verghese, G.C.: Signals, Systems, and Inference, MIT OpenCourseWare (2010). https://ocw.mit.edu/courses/electrical-engineering-and-computer-science/6-011-introduction-to-communication-control-and-signal-processing-spring-2010/readings/MIT6_011S10_notes.pdf
22. Said, S.E., Dickey, D.A.: Testing for unit roots in autoregressive-moving average models of unknown order. Biometrika **71**(3), 599–607 (1984). https://doi.org/10.1093/biomet/71.3.599
23. Stuart, J.S.: Fourier Analysis. Methuen & Co, London (1961)
24. Trantner, C.T.: Integral Transforms in Mathematical Physics. Methuen London (1951)
25. Hamilton, J.D.: Time Series Analysis. Princeton University Press (2020)
26. Yaglom, A.M.: Correlation Theory of processes with random stationary n^{th} increments, Trans. Am. Math. Soc. Series 2, **8**, 87–141, Original (1955) (1958). Корреляционная теория процессов со случайными стационарными *n-ми* приращениями, Математический сборник, 37(79), 1: 141–196. https://gretl.sourceforge.net/index.html

Asymptotic Full Wave-Form Inversion in the Image Domain

Maxim Protasov$^{(\boxtimes)}$ (iD)

Institute of Petroleum Geology and Geophysics, Koptyug st. 3, Novosibirsk 630090, Russia
protasovmi@ipgg.sbras.ru

Abstract. This study considers the Full Waveform Inversion (FWI) method in the image domain based on the asymptotic solution of the Helmholtz equation. The paper provides ray tracing and beam migration to get the images used to compute the tomographic part of the asymptotic FWI gradient. The comparison of asymptotic FWI and Common Image Point (CIP) tomography show that the computational time for both methods is similar while they provide reconstruction of different model parts. A series of numerical experiments show that CIP tomography is effective in reconstructing the low frequency model, while asymptotic FWI provides recovery of the details of complex velocity structure.

Keywords: full wave-form inversion · asymptotic solution · image domain · tomography

1 Introduction

Exploration and production of new oilfields is one of the most important and toughest challenges that geosciences have ever faced. In recent years, the most accessible and well-studied areas of oilfield production are coming to their end. Exploration of new resources has to be carried in regions with severe environments and complex geological conditions. In such areas, there is a strong demand for new methods of acquisition and processing of seismic data, which should allow to record and retrieve as much as possible reliable information about the structure of the subsurface. One of the potential approach for improving depth-velocity models in areas with complex geology is a full wave-form inversion technique, which seeks the solution of seismic inverse problem by minimizing the least-squares misfit between the observed and the simulated data [1, 2].

The full wave-form inversion approach has got successful applications in several studies using computationally expensive finite difference methods [3, 4] and finite element methods [5]. Modern implementations of FWI attempt to recover a sufficiently broad spatial spectrum of the model. Examples of wide azimuth data illustrate the possibility of recovering all spatial spectrums of the medium [6]. Some of the recent researches have investigated multi-parameter FWI [7], and FWI solutions in complex models, for example, containing high contrast salt bodies [8]. Another important direction for providing new solutions is based on the application of accurate forward modeling techniques [9].

O. Gervasi et al. (Eds.): ICCSA 2024, LNCS 14813, pp. 255–267, 2024.
https://doi.org/10.1007/978-3-031-64605-8_18

However, FWI has essential limitations in practical application, and the motivation of the presented paper is to provide solutions that allow overcoming these limitations. There are two main reasons for these limitations: the computational cost and the quality of seismic data. The main computation cost of FWI is a direct result of the numerical modeling of seismic wave-fields. Therefore, the development of methods for numerical modeling of seismic wave-fields and the acceleration of algorithms for such modeling is an extremely urgent task. Asymptotic methods are much faster than finite difference or finite element methods, which are used in most of the developed inversion algorithms. Therefore, in the previous work [10], the authors demonstrate the practical computational benefits and possibilities of the asymptotic FWI in the data frequency domain, and show that it can be practically useful. However, the success of the full wave-from inversion is very sensitive to the quality of the registered data, and it is almost impossible to satisfy the requirements of this approach, for example, in areas with complex near-surface conditions. It comes from the standard implementation of FWI in the data domain, while the potential solution can be the inversion of seismic wave-fields in the image domain [11] where the signal-to-noise ratio is much higher.

Therefore, in this paper, we propose to perform the inversion of seismic wave-fields in the image domain, contrary to the classical full wave-form inversion, which is done in data domain. The key point which we use for wave-form inversion is a wave-field modeling and imaging scheme based on asymptotic wave-equation solutions constructed using Gaussian beams summation. This allows achieving very high signal-to-noise ratio because of the massive directional summation of data for each imaging point. Also, the proposed asymptotic modeling scheme should work much faster and efficiently than the classically used methods for full-waveform inversion based on finite differences or finite elements solutions. Together, the combination of such modeling and migration procedure and inversion in the image domain should provide a robust method for imaging and inversion of seismic wave fields in areas with complex geology. In order to investigate the proposed inversion scheme and to understand its benefits and drawbacks in details we provide the realization of the proposed approach and its numerical investigation on a realistic Marmousi model.

2 Asymptotic Full Wave-Form Inversion: Theory

2.1 Full Wave-Form Inversion in the Image Domain

The acoustic media is considered, and the wave field in the frequency domain $u(x, z; \omega)$ satisfies the Helmholtz equation:

$$\left(\Delta + \omega^2 m\right)u = -f(\omega)\delta(x - x_s)\delta(z - z_s), \tag{1}$$

here $m = c^{-2}(x, z)$ is the square of slowness, and $c(x, z)$ is the wave propagation velocity, $f(\omega)$ is the wavelet at the source in the frequency domain, ω is the frequency, (x_s, z_s) is the source coordinate.

Then, introduce an operator that computes the wave field from a single point source for a fixed frequency at points corresponding to the receiver locations. Thus, the following forward modeling operator is obtained:

$$F : M \rightarrow D, \tag{2}$$

where D is the data space, M is the model space. In these notations, the inverse dynamic problem of constructing a velocity model from seismic data reduces to solving a nonlinear operator equation:

$$d^{obs} = F(m_{true}), \tag{3}$$

here d^{obs} is the observed data, m_{true} is the true velocity model.

Full-wave inversion in the image domain minimizes the functional built in the image domain:

$$m_* = arg\left(\min_{m \in M} \|M < F(m) - d > \|_I^2 \right). \tag{4}$$

Here, M is the migration operator, which transfers the data to the image domain I, where the minimization takes place. To do this, we use migration on Gaussian beams [12]:

$$M < d > (y, p) = \sum_{x_s, x_r, \omega} T_{gbs}^m(x_s; y, p; \omega) \cdot T_{gbr}^m(x_r; y, p; \omega) \cdot d(x_s, x_r, \omega). \tag{5}$$

Here $T_{gbs}^m(x_s; y, p; \omega)$, $T_{gbr}^m(x_r; y, p; \omega)$ are the summation weights of the migration operator M [12].

When using local optimization methods, the key step is also the calculation of the gradient, which in this case has the following representation:

$$\nabla_k(x) = Re\left\{ \sum_{y, p} \delta Image_k(y, p) \cdot \left(\frac{\partial \delta Image_k(y, p)}{\partial m_\kappa(x)}\right)^* \right\}. \tag{6}$$

Here $\delta Image_k(y, p) = Image_k(y, p) - Image_{dk}(y, p)$ is the residual in the image domain, where $Image_{dk}(y, p) = M_k < d > (y, p)$ and $Image_k(y, p) = M_k < F(m_\kappa) > (y, p)$:

$$Image_k(y, p) = \sum_{x_s, x_r, \omega} T_{gbs}^{m_k}(x_s; y, p; \omega) \cdot T_{gbr}^{m_k}(x_r; y, p; \omega) \cdot F(m_\kappa)(x_s, x_r, \omega). \tag{7}$$

The derivative of the image misfit function has the following form:

$$\frac{\partial \delta Image_k(y, p)}{\partial m_\kappa(x)} = \sum_{s, r, \omega} \{ T_{gbs}^{m_k}(x_s; y, p; \omega) \cdot T_{gbr}^{m_k}(x_r; y, p; \omega) \cdot \frac{\partial F(m_\kappa)(x_s, x_r, \omega)}{\partial m_k(x)} +$$
$$+ [\frac{\partial T_{gbs}^{m_k}(x_s; y, p; \omega)}{\partial m_k(x)} \cdot T_{gbr}^{m_k}(x_r; y, p; \omega) + \frac{\partial T_{gbr}^{m_k}(x_r; y, p; \omega)}{\partial m_k(x)} \cdot T_{gbs}^{m_k}(x_s; y, p; \omega)] \cdot F(m_\kappa) \}. \tag{8}$$

It turns out that the gradient in the image domain is the sum of two components: an analogue of the gradient in the data domain and the part associated with the dependence of the migration operator on the model. Therefore, on the one hand, the FWI in the image domain should be more informative. On the other hand, it is more stable, since images have a better signal-to-noise ratio than seismic data.

2.2 Tomographic Part of Asymptotic Full Wave-Form Inversion in the Image Domain vs Common Image Point Tomography

Next, in the gradient (9) the data domain analogue is omitted, and the expression for the derivative of the image misfit function (11) is transformed, and the gradient gets the following asymptotic approximation:

$$\nabla_k(x) = \text{Re}\left\{ \sum_{y,p} \delta Image_k(y, p) \cdot Image_k^{i\omega}(y, p) \left[\frac{\partial \tau_s(y, p)}{\partial m_k(x)} + \frac{\partial \tau_r(y, p)}{\partial m_k(x)} \right]^* \right\}. \tag{9}$$

Here $\tau_s(y, p)$, $\tau_r(y, p)$ are travel times to sources and receivers, computed in the model m_k, from the point y, and $Image_k^{i\omega}$ has the following expression:

$$Image_k^{i\omega}(y, p) = \sum_{x_s, x_r, \omega} -i\omega \cdot T_{gbs}^{m_k}(x_s; y, p; \omega) \cdot T_{gbr}^{m_k}(x_r; y, p; \omega) \cdot F(m_k). \tag{10}$$

The gradient (12) is similar to the gradient of the tomography operator because there are the travel time derivatives with respect to model parameters. Therefore, this part of the gradient is called a tomographic part of asymptotic full wave-form inversion in the image domain.

From another point of view, when considering the linear step of the full wave-form, one can come to the following asymptotic representation of the image misfit function containing only the tomographic part:

$$\delta Image_k(y, p) \approx \sum_x [\frac{\partial \tau_s(y, p)}{\partial m_k(x)} + \frac{\partial \tau_r(y, p)}{\partial m_k(x)}] Image_k^{i\omega}(y, p) \langle \delta m_k(x) \rangle. \tag{11}$$

The linear step of the reflection tomography problem provides the following expression:

$$\delta T(y, p) \approx \sum_x [\frac{\partial \tau_s(y, p)}{\partial m_k(x)} + \frac{\partial \tau_r(y, p)}{\partial m_k(x)}] \langle \delta m_k(x) \rangle. \tag{12}$$

Here $\delta T(y, p)$ is the travel time residuals between observed reflected travel times and the computed in the model $m_k(x)$ travel times, which is the sum of $\tau_s(y, p)$, $\tau_r(y, p)$. One can observe the similarity of the expressions (11) and (12). For the tomography case, it has a tomographic operator in right-hand side and travel time residuals in left - hand side. For the asymptotic FWI case, the expression consists of the weighted tomographic operator in the right-hand side and image misfit in the left-hand side. This means the expression (11) is the dynamic analogue of the kinematic problem (12).

3 Numerical Experiments

3.1 Description of the Synthetic Marmousi Model and Data

Today, the standard has become the need to test any developed algorithm on synthetic models and data. To date, a fairly large number of synthetic data for realistic models. One of the most well-known datasets is the freely available Marmousi2 P-wave velocity model [13], one can observe the model on the Fig. 1a. The acoustic modeling using the finite difference scheme for the wave equation provides seismic data. The dataset simulates a 2D line seismic survey, in which observations consist of 320 sources, and the distance between sources equals to 50 m. Each source provides a signal recorded by 81 receivers, the distance between the receivers equals to 25 m, and therefore the maximum source-receiver offset equals 4000 m. The modeling utilizes the Ricker impulse, the dominant frequency is 15 Hz. Figure 1b provides the example of the seismogram, the source position is at x = 500 m.

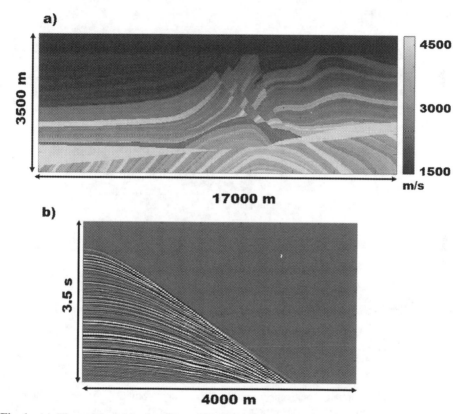

Fig. 1. (a) The original Marmousi2 model: P-wave velocity. (b) Seismogram got via finite-difference acoustic modeling in Marmousi2 model for the source position at x = 500 m.

3.2 Inversion Scenarios

For the investigation of the possibilities of proposed asymptotic FWI in the image domain, the inversion process uses different initial models. The investigation provides three essentially different scenarios.

In the first one, the initial model come from a reasonable 1D depth trend of the model and finally it represents a laterally homogeneous model (see Fig. 2a). This model has a big difference with the true model. In that model, the beam migration result shows the highly defocused events and the essentially incorrect positions of the reflection interfaces, especially below the depth of 2500 m (see Fig. 2b).

For the second scenario, the initial model contains the lateral variations that come from the true model. The initial model is a strong smoothing of the true Marmousi model (see Fig. 3a). Here, the initial model has a smaller difference with the true Marmousi model in comparison with the initial model from the first scenario. However, the difference is still essential. The beam migration results in this case provide better focused events and more correct positions of the reflectors while they are still mis-positioned significantly (see Fig. 3b).

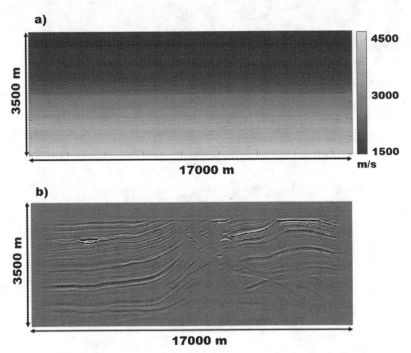

Fig. 2. (a) The initial laterally homogeneous model for the asymptotic FWI in the image domain: it has a big difference with the true Marmousi model. (b) The corresponding seismic image got via beam migration.

For the last scenario, the initial model is an average smoothing of the true Marmousi model (see Fig. 4a). Here, the initial model has no big difference with the true Marmousi model. But it does not contain the high-frequency component of the true model and it provides a sensible difference of the kinematic properties in comparison with the true model. The beam migration result in this model provides an image with reflectors positions that are close the true ones. However, there is slight difference in most of the model, and it becomes essential in the central most complex part of the model (see Fig. 4b).

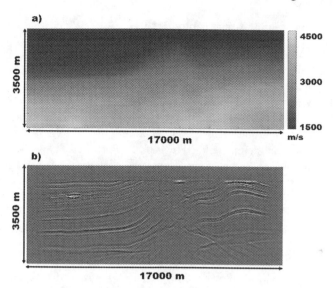

Fig. 3. (a) The initial highly smoothed Marmousi model for the asymptotic FWI in the image domain: it has an essential difference with the true Marmousi model. (b) The corresponding seismic image got via beam migration.

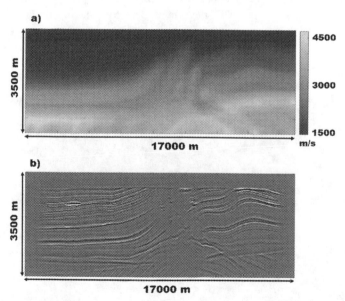

Fig. 4. (a) The initial averagely smoothed Marmousi model for the asymptotic FWI in the image domain: it has a reasonable difference with the true Marmousi model. (b) The corresponding seismic image got via beam migration.

3.3 Common Image Point Tomography Results

The first series of experiments provides the results of CIP tomography [14] application for the described above inversion scenarios. Such decision is logical because the liner step of CIP tomography has a similar statement of the Problem (Formula (15)) as the linear step of asymptotic FWI in the image domain (Formula (14)). Also, the input data (before picking the kinematic events in CIP tomography technology) are the same, and this data are the common image point seismograms i.e. migrated images for the different angle/offset parameters (defined by p in the Formulas (14) and (15)). It means that CIP tomography uses the kinematic properties of the migrated images, while the asymptotic FWI in the image domain uses dynamic properties of the same migrated images. Moreover, CIP tomography is a standard practical tool for the depth model reconstruction. Therefore, it is interesting to understand what can provide the proposed asymptotic FWI in the image domain in comparison with its kinematic analogue, i.e. CIP tomography.

Figures 5, 6 and 7 show the results of the linear step application of CIP tomography for the three described above correspondent scenarios. In those figures, the upper ones provide the inverted velocity model, while the bottom ones show the corresponding velocity update. One can observe that, for all three cases, the tomography provides the inverted model that becomes closer to the true model in comparison with the initial one. The most impressive result one can observe in the Fig. 5 for the first scenario when the initial model has a big difference with the true model. Here, the inverted model is similar to the smoothed Marmousi model shown in the Fig. 3a. However, for all 3 cases, the model update gives a rather smooth solution. This is an important observation, especially

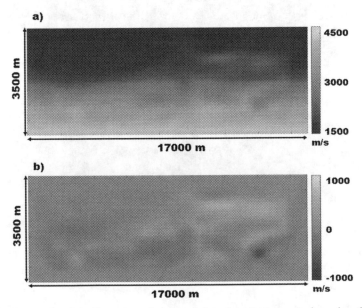

Fig. 5. (a) The result of the liner step of common image point tomography using the laterally homogeneous initial model. (b) The corresponding velocity update.

for the third scenario, when the migration model is close to the ideal. However, in this case, the tomography does not provide an update of fine structure, but still it gives the residual smooth part of the model.

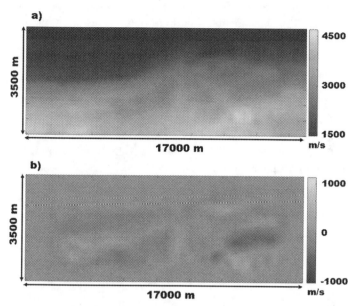

Fig. 6. (a) The result of the liner step of common image point tomography using the highly smoothed Marmousi initial model. (b) The corresponding velocity update.

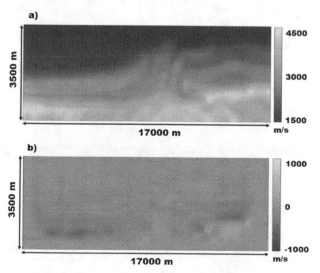

Fig. 7. (a) The result of the liner step of common image point tomography using the averagely smoothed Marmousi initial model. (b) The corresponding velocity update.

3.4   Results of Tomographic Part of Asymptotic FWI in the Image Domain

Finally, the proposed asymptotic FWI in the image domain is tested. Figures 8, 9 and 10 show the results of the linear step application of asymptotic FWI in the image for the three described above correspondent scenarios. On those figures, the upper ones provide the inverted velocity model, while the bottom ones show the corresponding velocity update. The computational time for all experiments is almost the same, and it equals to the computational time for CIP tomography experiments. It means that proposed asymptotic FWI in the image domain provides the computational speed up comparing to the standard FWI because it is well-known fact that CIP tomography is much faster than standard FWI approach. For example, computational cost of CIP tomography applied to real seismic data from the area around 1000 km^2 is estimated by days using rather powerful computational cluster, while computation cost of standard FWI based on finite-difference modelling is estimated by months on the same data and using the same computational cluster.

The results of the proposed asymptotic FWI in the image domain are different completely from the results of CIP tomography. One can observe that, for the first two scenarios, when the initial model has an essential difference with the true model the proposed FWI does not give the satisfactory inverted model result (Figs. 8 and 9). The explanation of such results consequence from the investigations for the time domain FWI, where the so-called cycle-skipping problem arises [15]. Because traces in the image domain are analogue to the traces in the time done, therefore image domain inherits this cycle-skipping problem.

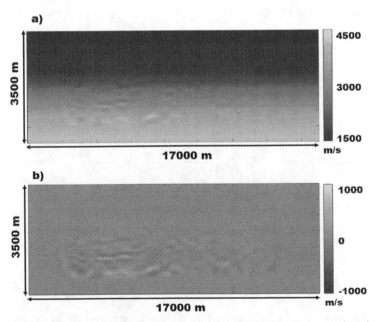

Fig. 8. (a) The result of liner step of the proposed asymptotic FWI in the image domain using the laterally homogeneous initial model. (b) The corresponding velocity update.

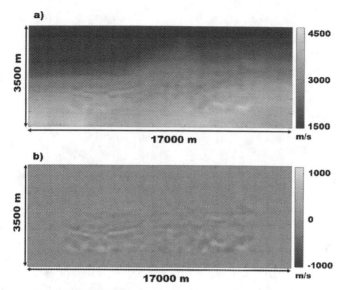

Fig. 9. (a) The result of liner step of the proposed asymptotic FWI in the image domain using the highly smoothed Marmousi initial model. (b) The corresponding velocity update.

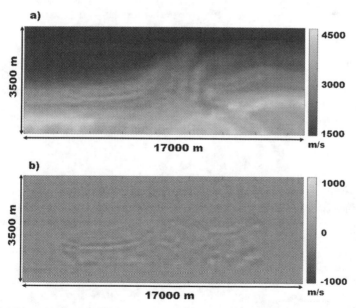

Fig. 10. (a) The result of the liner step of the proposed asymptotic FWI in the image domain using the averagely smoothed initial Marmousi model. (b) The corresponding velocity update.

The results of the proposed asymptotic FWI in the image domain for the third scenario show the model improvement (see Fig. 10). Here, the initial model is not very different from the true model therefore, there is no influence of cycle-skipping problem. The reconstructed model is closer to the true model in comparison to the initial model used for the inversion. Here the model update (see Fig. 10b) contains higher frequency components comparing with the model update got by CIP tomography (see Fig. 7b). Here, asymptotic FWI in the image domain provides a more detailed model in comparison with the initial model and the recovered model by CIP tomography.

4 Conclusions

This work provides the new asymptotic full-wave inversion method in the image domain and its investigation. The classical FWI solution uses a computationally expensive procedure for the finite difference solution of the wave equation. The asymptotic approach uses ray tracing to solve wave equation, and migration on Gaussian beams to go to the image domain, which makes it possible to speed up the gradient construction procedure in comparison with the standard FWI. The comparison of asymptotic FWI and Common Image Point (CIP) tomography shows that the speed of calculations for both methods is similar, while CIP tomography is much faster than standard FWI approach. Also, the comparison shows that proposed asymptotic FWI and CIP tomography provide reconstruction of different model parts. A series of numerical experiments for a rather complex Marmousi model show that CIP tomography is effective in reconstructing low frequency model while asymptotic FWI provides recovery of the details of complex velocity structure.

Acknowledgements. The presented research is supported and done within the scope of investigations of RSF grant 21-71-20002. We use the computational resources of Peter the Great Saint-Petersburg Polytechnic University Supercomputing Center (scc.spbstu.ru) to provide the numerical experiments and to obtain the numerical results.

References

1. Lailly, P.: The seismic inverse problem as a sequence of before stack migrations. In: Conference on Inverse Scattering Theory and Application, pp. 206–220 (1983)
2. Tarantola, A.: Inversion of seismic reflection data in the acoustic approximation. Geophysics **49**, 1140–1395 (1984)
3. Pica, A., Diet, J., Tarantola, A.: Nonlinear inversion of seismic reflection data in laterally invariant medium. Geophysics **55**, 284–292 (1990)
4. Djikp'ess'e, H., Tarantola, A.: Multiparameter 1-norm waveform fitting: interpretation of Gulf of Mexico reflection seismograms. Geophysics **64**, 1023–1035 (1999)
5. Choi, Y., Min, D.-J., Shin, C.: Two-dimensional waveform inversion of multi-component data in acoustic-elastic coupled media. Geophys. Prospect. **56**, 863–881 (2008)
6. Pratt, R.G.: Seismic waveform inversion in the frequency domain, part 1: theory and verification in a physical scale model. Geophysics **64**, 888–901 (1999)
7. Luo, J., Wu, R.S., Chen, G.: Angle domain direct envelope inversion method for strong scattering velocity and density estimation. IEEE Geosci. Remote Sens. Lett. **17**, 1508–1512 (2020)

8. Chen, G., Yang, W.C., Liu, Y.N., Wang, H., Huang, X.: Salt structure elastic full waveform inversion based on the multi-scale signed envelope. IEEE Trans. Geosci. Remote Sens. **60**, 1–12 (2022)
9. Aghamiry, H.S., Gholami, A., Aghazade, K., Sonbolestan, M., Operto, S.: Large-scale highly-accurate extended full waveform inversion using convergent Born series. arXiv:2202.08558 (2022)
10. Protasov, M., Gadylshin, K., Neklyudov, D., Klimes, L.: Full waveform inversion based on an asymptotic solution of Helmholtz equation. Geosciences **13**, 1–13 (2023)
11. Zhang, S., Schuster, G.: Image-domain full waveform inversion: field data example. In: SEG Technical Program Expanded Abstracts, pp. 966–970 (2014)
12. Protasov, M., Tcheverda, V.: True amplitude imaging by inverse generalized Radon transform based on Gaussian beam decomposition of the acoustic Green's function. Geophys. Prospect. **59**, 197–209 (2011)
13. Martin, G.S., Wiley, R., Marfurt, K.J.: Marmousi2: an elastic upgrade for Marmousi. Lead. EdgeEdge **25**, 156–166 (2006)
14. Woodward, M., Nichols, D., Zdraveva, O., Whitfield, P., Johns, T.: A decade of tomography. Geophysics **73**, VE5–VE11 (2008)
15. Yang, J., Li, Y., Liu, Y., Wei, Y., Fu, H.: Mitigating the cycle-skipping of full-waveform inversion by random gradient sampling. Geophysics **85**, R493–R507 (2020)

Frequency Dependent Rays of qP-Waves in 3D Weak Tilted Transversely Isotropic (TTI) Media

Dmitry Neklyudov$^{(\boxtimes)}$ [iD] and Maxim Protasov [iD]

Institute of Petroleum Geology and Geophysics SB RAS, Prospect Acad. Koptuga 3,
630090 Novosibirsk, Russia
neklyudovda@ipgg.sbras.ru

Abstract. The paper provides a simple and numerically effective method to calculate frequency dependent rays of qP-wave in three-dimensional TTI media. Our
method involves propagating a locally plane fragment of the wave front, which is
sensitive to the distribution of the model parameters in some sub volume of the
medium near a ray. The wavelength in each point on the ray determines the width of
the sensitivity area. For numerical realization we apply approximate expressions
for phase and group velocities which are valid for weak TTI media. Numerical
experiments demonstrate the effectiveness of the proposed approach.

Keywords: Frequency dependent rays · anisotropy · TTI

1 Introduction

The ray method [1, 2] plays an important role in seismic data processing. The implementation of key seismic data processing procedures, such as seismic travel-time tomography
and Kirchhoff migration are based on the ray tracing. First, the ray method is used to
calculate ray trajectories and the first arrival travel-times of seismic waves. The classical formulation of the ray method relies on high-frequency approximations to obtain
solutions to the system of equations in the dynamic theory of elasticity. The use of
such approximation neglects the fact that real seismic signals are broad-band and have
limited spectra. Because of such approximation, rays exhibit "unphysical" behavior in
models with significant inhomogeneities and sharp interfaces [3, 4]. The rays in these
circumstances become unpredictable and differ significantly from the expected propagation path. Shadow zones, which are areas where rays cannot pass, are present in
the computational domain. Firstly, this behavior clearly contradicts the physics of real
seismic wave propagation processes. In complex geological environments, ray based
seismic data processing procedures such as tomography may produce inaccurate results
[5]. It is necessary to overcome the limitations of the standard ray method in practice.
It is known that the distribution of physical parameters influences the propagation of a
signal with a limited band-width inside a specific volume located in the vicinity of a
ray [6, 7]. This volume is referred to as the "Fresnel volume". The dominant frequency
of the signal determines its width. Quite some time ago, researchers realized that they

needed to consider this fact and reduce the limitations of the ray method associated with high-frequency approximation. Several approaches have been proposed [8–13] to solve this problem, with varying degrees of effectiveness. All of these approaches have their advantages and disadvantages. The most significant drawback is the computational complexity, which becomes particularly apparent when considering the three-dimensional case. The paper [9] presented a promising approach that approximates the propagation of broadband seismic signals through frequency dependent ray tracing. The key finding is that the velocity used for ray tracing is determined by smoothing actual velocity along a locally flat element of the wave front. The aperture of such smoothing is chosen proportional to the wavelength. A predefined parameter, which has a frequency dimension controls the wavelength. Compared to the standard ray method, the differential equations that describe ray propagation are almost unchanged, except for substituting interval velocities with velocities smoothed along the wave front. In [14], an adaptation of this idea without solving a system of differential equations was proposed. The method is designed for the calculation of frequency-dependent rays in 3D acoustic media. The ray tracing procedure involves moving a locally flat fragment of a wave front whose orientation depends on the velocity distribution inside a certain frequency-dependent aperture. The parameters of the medium affect the ray within a certain volume around it. We refer to it as a "fat" ray because of this reason. The suggested approach has proven to be robust and easy to implement. Numerical experiments demonstrate that "fat" rays are more stable in complex situations than standard rays, and may provide reliable traveltimes and trajectories when the standard ray method fails.

The industry widely acknowledges the need to consider seismic anisotropy in data processing practices. This paper discusses an algorithm that can be used to compute frequency-dependent rays of qP-waves (quasi-primary waves) in a three-dimensional tilted transversely isotropic (TTI) medium with arbitrary oriented symmetry axis. It is an extension of the approach proposed in [14] for anisotropy. Numerical experiments prove that "fat" rays can be quite successfully used for rays and travel-times calculation in complex three-dimensional TTI media.

2 Approximate Expressions for Phase and Group Velocities of qP-Waves in Weak TTI Media

The following section presents approximate expressions for the phase and group velocities of qP-waves that we used to calculate frequency dependent rays in weak TTI media.

In most realistic cases, the assumption of weak anisotropy is fulfilled [15]. By making this assumption, the expressions for phase and group velocities can be greatly simplified, which significantly increases the computational efficiency of ray tracing in anisotropic media [16, 17]. The weak anisotropy assumption means that the stiffness tensor of anisotropic medium c_{ijkl} can be decomposed into two components $c_{ijkl} = c_{ijkl}^{ISO} + \delta c_{ijkl}$, where c_{ijkl}^{ISO} is the reference isotropic component of the model, δc_{ijkl} is anisotropic component which is small compared to reference isotropic term. Practical experience demonstrates that the weak anisotropy assumption is valid if the anisotropic term is no more than 10% of the isotropic reference value.

Consider Christoffel matrix whose elements depend on the direction vector $\vec{p}$, $\Gamma_{jk} = p_i p_l a_{ijkl}$, where $a_{ijkl} = c_{ijkl}/\rho$ are density normalized stiffness tensor elements, p_j are components of the slowness vector $\vec{p}$ which is related to the phase velocity V in the normal direction to the wave front, $\vec{p} = \vec{n}/V(\vec{n})$. Vector $\vec{n}$ is a unit normal vector to the front. Three types of waves can exist in an arbitrary anisotropic medium: qP, qSV, qSH. Each wave mode corresponds to one of the three eigenvalues of the Christoffel matrix. qP-wave corresponds to the largest eigenvalue. Its wave polarization vector coincides with the first eigenvector. The phase velocity is determined by the eigenvalue of the Christoffel matrix $G(\vec{n})$ as:

$$V^2(\vec{n}) = G(\vec{n}) \tag{1}$$

The group velocity components are given by the expression:

$$v_j = \frac{1}{2}\frac{\partial G(\vec{p})}{\partial p_j} \tag{2}$$

In seismic exploration, the propagation of qP-waves is mostly interesting. A set of parameters that has become standard for most practical applications is used to parametrize the anisotropic medium, when only qP-waves are taken into account [18]: V_p is the phase velocity of qP-waves along the symmetry axis, two angles characterizing orientation of symmetry axis in each point, θ_{AZ} (azimuth) and θ_{DIP} (dip angle regarding to vertical axis) and two anisotropy parameters, ε, δ (so called Thomsen parameters), [15]. The Thomsen parameters are expressed through the density-normalized stiffness tensor coefficients in the following manner: $\varepsilon = \frac{a_{11}-a_{33}}{2a_{33}}$, $\delta = \frac{a_{13}-a_{33}+2a_{44}}{a_{33}}$. [19] presented a simplified way to calculate the qP-wave eigenvalue in vertical transversely isotropic (VTI) media (vertical symmetry axis), under the assumption of weak anisotropy. In the paper [20], a generalization of this expression is provided for a tilted transversely isotropic medium with an arbitrary orientation of the symmetry axis.

Let $\vec{e}$ be a unit vector that defines the orientation of the symmetry axis. $\vec{e}$ is parallel to the axis of symmetry. Its components are expressed via angles θ_{AZ}, θ_{DIP} as $\vec{e} = (sin\theta_{DIP}\cdot cos\theta_{AZ}, sin\theta_{DIP}\cdot sin\theta_{AZ}, cos\theta_{DIP})$. We make use of the following notations below: $P = |\vec{p}|^2$ is the square of the norm of the slowness vector, $D = \vec{e}\cdot\vec{p}$ is the dot product of the vectors $\vec{e}$ and $\vec{p}$, $D_N = \vec{e}\cdot\vec{n}$ is the dot product of the unit normal $\vec{n}$ and the vector $\vec{e}$. Using these notations, it is possible to write an approximate expression for the first eigenvalue of the Christoffel matrix [20]:

$$G(\vec{x}, \vec{p}) = V_P^2\{P(1 + 2\varepsilon) + 2(\delta - 2\varepsilon)D^2 - 2(\delta - \varepsilon)\frac{D^4}{P}\}. \tag{3}$$

Phase velocity of qP-wave in the direction normal to the front is defined by the expressions (1) and (3):

$$V^2(\vec{x}, \vec{n}) = V_P^2\{1 + 2\varepsilon + 2(\delta - 2\varepsilon)D_N^2 - 2(\delta - \varepsilon)D_N^4\}, \tag{4}$$

Regarding the formula (2), by calculating derivatives of the eigenvalue $G(\vec{x}, \vec{p})$ with respect to the components of the slowness vector $\vec{p}$, the approximate expression for the components of the group (ray) velocity $\vec{v}$ is found:

$$v_j = \frac{1}{2}V_P^2\left\{\left[2(1+2\varepsilon) + 4(\delta - \varepsilon)\frac{D^4}{P^2}\right]p_j + \left[2(\delta - 2\varepsilon)D - 8(\delta - \varepsilon)\frac{D^3}{P}\right]e_j\right\}, \quad (5)$$

where p_j and e_j are components of the vectors $\vec{p}$ и $\vec{e}$ respectively. The value of the group velocity is given as $v = |\vec{v}|$.

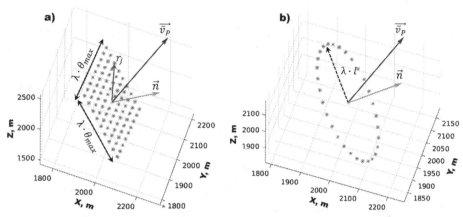

Fig. 1. a) Rectangular area cut along a locally flat wave front. The blue asterisks represent the points in the regular grid where phase velocity values are calculated for smoothing along the wave front. The central point is shown as a red star. Vector $\vec{n}$ denote current normal to the front. Green arrow shows group velocity vector (ray propagation direction). b) The control points are situated around the central point on the ray in the plane of the wave front. They are employed to determine the normal to the front during the next step along the ray. (Color figure online)

3 "Fat" Ray in 3D TTI Media

In [14], we proposed an algorithm for the calculation of frequency dependent rays ("fat" rays) in three-dimensional acoustic media. Below, we describe the adaptation of this method to weak TTI media. The basic idea inherent in "fat" rays is to take into account the distribution of physical parameters of the medium in the vicinity of a ray. The predetermined parameter, which has a frequency dimension, controls the width of this area. By decreasing the frequency (i.e. by increasing the wavelength), a "fat" ray can be made "wider", i.e. more sensitive to the parameters of the model or vice versa, to obtain "fat" rays that are similar to the ones provided by the classical ray method. A fragment of a locally flat wave front is propagated when tracing the "fat" ray. For each moment of time, "fat" ray tracing procedure consists of two stages. In the first stage, the ray moves from the known position towards a known direction that is determined by the current orientation of the unit wave front normal (in the isotropic case, direction of ray movement coincides with the normal to the front). Smoothed model parameters are used to make an elementary step along the ray. Smoothing is performed along a locally flat wave front element centered on the ray. As a result of this stage, the ray position is determined at the next moment of time. The second stage involves determining the orientation of the locally flat wave front at the new point on the ray. The movement of a set of 'control' points that are specifically chosen near the ray in the plane of the wave front is used for this purpose. The wavelength at the point on the ray determines how far the control points are located from the ray. The wavelength governs the sensitivity of the ray. Next, we describe how these steps are performed with the TTI media.

As an input to the procedure, two take-off angles φ_{AZ}, φ_{Dip} are given which define initial orientation of the wave front normal, where φ_{AZ} is azimuthal angle (an angle between initial normal direction and lateral X-axis in XY plane), φ_{Dip} is dip angle (an angle between initial normal and vertical (Z) coordinate axis). Also we define auxiliary parameter υ measured in Hz, which is called "frequency" of the ray.

1) Let $\overrightarrow{x}_p = (x_p, y_p, z_p)$ is a current point on the ray (we will call it the central point further). A unit vector $\overrightarrow{n} = (n_X, n_Y, n_Z)$ is given at this point that defines a normal to the front. To begin with, let's explain how the model parameters are smoothed in the vicinity of the ray along the flat wave front element. We construct a plane passes through the point $\overrightarrow{x}_p$ and orthogonal to the vector $\overrightarrow{n}$. A rectangle is cut with the center at point $\overrightarrow{x}_p$ in this plane, which has sizes that are dependent on the wavelength $\lambda = \frac{V(\overrightarrow{x}_p, \overrightarrow{n})}{\upsilon}$ as it is shown in Fig. 1a, where $V(\overrightarrow{x}_p, \overrightarrow{n})$ is the phase velocity in the point $\overrightarrow{x}_p$, υ is the frequency. A regular grid is defined on the selected wave front fragment. In Fig. 1a, blue asterisks represent these grid points. The phase velocity values $V(\overrightarrow{x}_j, \overrightarrow{n})$ at every point of the grid are determined by formula (4) using the same normal to the front $\overrightarrow{n}$. At the central point, the weighted sum of all phase velocities is used to calculate the value of the smoothed phase velocity along the flat wave front element:

$$V_{sm}\left(\overrightarrow{x}_p, \overrightarrow{n}, v\right) = \frac{\sum_{j=-N}^{N} w_j \cdot V(\overrightarrow{x}_j, \overrightarrow{n})}{\sum_{j=-N}^{N} w_j} \tag{6}$$

where w_j are the smoothing weights, N is a total number of grid points. 2D Gaussian function is used as a smoother. Here, the weights are given as:

$$w_j = \exp\left\{-\left(\frac{r_j}{\lambda \cdot \theta_{max} \cdot \alpha}\right)^2\right\} \tag{7}$$

where r_j is a distance between the central point and the point $\overrightarrow{x}_j$ in the wave front rectangular element. The input parameter θ_{max} defines which part of the wavelength is taken into account when choosing the smoothing aperture. Parameter α is responsible for the shape of Gaussian smoother [14]. When the parameter α is reduced, the smoothing function becomes narrower, concentrating near the center point. When increasing the parameter α, the Gaussian smoothing is reduced to simple averaging in the rectangular area.

Let dt be the time step along the ray. To move along the ray, the following scheme is applied (see Fig. 2). At the center point $\overrightarrow{x}_p$, the value of the smoothed phase velocity $\overline{V}_p = V_{sm}(\overrightarrow{x}_p, \overrightarrow{n}, v)$ is calculated as described above. Using the phase velocity $\overline{V}_p$ and the normal to the front $\overrightarrow{n}$, the corresponding group velocity vector $\overrightarrow{v}_P(\overrightarrow{n}) = (v_x, v_y, v_z)$ are calculated using the expression (5). During the time interval dt, the central point $\overrightarrow{x}_p$ moves to the certain new point $\overrightarrow{x}_p + d\overrightarrow{x}_p$ along the group velocity vector, where $d\overrightarrow{x}_p = (dx_p, dy_p, dz_p)$:

$$dx_p = dt \cdot v_x, dy_p = dt \cdot v_y, dz_p = dt \cdot v_z \tag{8}$$

It gives us a position of a next point on the ray. Now we need to determine wave front orientation at this point.

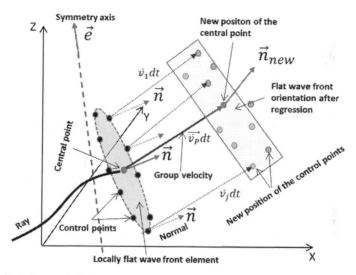

Fig. 2. Scheme of "fat" ray tracing in TTI medium (see the text for more details).

2) We do the following to establish the orientation of the wave front at the new point on the ray. Consider a circle lying within the plane of the wave front. The radius of the circle also depends on the local wavelength, $R = \lambda \cdot l$, where the parameter l has the same meaning as the parameter θ_{max}, controls the smoothing aperture width, but it is not necessary to have the same value. We pick a set of points on the circle that have constant angles increment (see Fig. 1b). Further, these points are referred to as "control" points. For each control point located on a circle centered on the ray, a group velocity vector $\overrightarrow{v}_j(\overrightarrow{x}_j, \overrightarrow{n}) = (v_x^j, v_y^j, v_z^j)$ is calculated using the given normal to the wave front $\overrightarrow{n}$ by expression (5). For the same time interval, dt, the control points will travel different distances because group velocity values may differ: $dx_j = dt \cdot v_x^j, dy_j = dt \cdot v_y^j,$ $dz_j = dt \cdot v_z^j$. It's highly probable that the new control points locations $\overrightarrow{x}_j + d\overrightarrow{x}_j$ won't be on the same plane. In order to determine the new orientation of the locally flat wave front, we calculate the plane that is closest to all points $\overrightarrow{x}_j + d\overrightarrow{x}_j$ in the least-squares sense. As a result, the classical linear regression problem arises. The numerical solution of the problem allows us to determine a new normal vector to the front, $\overrightarrow{n}_{new}$. We attach $\overrightarrow{n}_{new}$ to the new central point position $\overrightarrow{x}_p + d\overrightarrow{x}_p$ and repeat the process. Thus, there is a step-by-step movement along the ray. When the scheme is implemented, a locally flat fragment of the wave front moves. The physical parameters of the model in a particular vicinity of the ray affect its orientation at each moment of time.

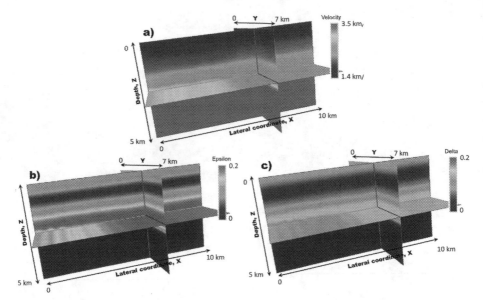

Fig. 3. Realistic 2.5D VTI model. a) Phase velocity along the vertical symmetry axis, b) Dimensionless Thomsen parameter ε distribution (its variations are within the interval [0 - 0.2]), c) Dimensionless Thomsen parameter δ distribution (its variations are within the interval [0 - 0.14]).

4 Numerical Examples

4.1 Numerical Verification: Comparison of "Fat" Rays with Standard Rays in a Smooth VTI Model

We verify the effectiveness of the proposed approach by comparing the frequency dependent rays constructed according to the proposed scheme with the standard rays in the smooth model. We choose the smooth model to prevent problems during the calculation of standard rays, as they exhibit unpredictable behavior when there are sharp inhomogeneities within the model. As the theory predicts, if the "ray frequency" parameter υ increases, the "fat" rays tend to be closer to the standard rays [9, 14]. Fat rays and standard rays become identical when the parameter υ reaches a certain value (as it was demonstrated by numerical experiments for the acoustic case, $\upsilon > 30$ Hz). The numerical validation of the proposed scheme will be based on this fact.

The numerical experiments presented below are based on a realistic model obtained during real seismic data processing. Dataset was acquired in some oil production area in Eastern Siberia. Anisotropic reflection travel-time tomography was utilized to recover

model parameters [21]. The model depicted in Fig. 3 is only dependent on two coordinates (X and Z). In order to obtain a three-dimensional model, two-dimensional sections
of phase velocity distribution and Thomsen parameters ε, δ, recovered along one profile,
were "replicated" in the cross-line direction (along lateral Y axis). Symmetry axis is
vertical at each point of the model (VTI model).

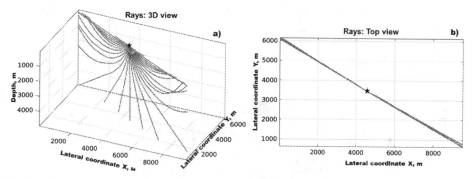

Fig. 4. Comparison of rays calculated in the VTI model from Fig. 3 for one source location
(marked as asterisk) and one fixed azimuth $\varphi_{AZ} = -30°$: a) 3D view of rays, b) rays projection
at XY plane (top view). "Fat" rays calculated for frequency parameter $\upsilon = 30$ Hz are shown in
blue, standard rays are shown in red. (Color figure online)

The phase velocities of the qP-waves along the vertical axis of symmetry vary
between 1400 and 3500 m/s. The dimensionless Thomsen parameters ε and δ lie within
ranges of [0–0.2] and [0–0.14] respectively. The model is provided on a regular grid with
the same spatial step in all directions, $dx = dy = dz = 10$ m, number of grid points are
$N_X = 951, N_Y = 701, N_Z = 501$. Total spatial size of the model is 9500 x 7000 x 5000 m
(two lateral directions and depth respectively). For "fat" ray construction the following
parameters have been used: "ray frequency" $\upsilon = 30$ Hz, $l = 0.25$, $\theta_{max} = 0.25$, $\alpha = 1$,
$dt = 0.002$ s. Number of control points was equal to 30. A point source is located in the
center of the model, $X_S = 4500$ m, $Y_S = 3500$ m, $Z_S = 100$ m.

Here, we want to exploit the high-frequency asymptotic properties of "fat" rays. In
that case, we must achieve the best match between "fat" rays and standard rays, as we
mentioned above. A software implementation of anisotropic ray tracing from the well-
known package Madagaskar is used to calculate standard rays [22]. Figure 4a shows a
3D view of 50 rays calculated for a fixed azimuth angle $\varphi_{AZ} = -30deg$. and uniform
dip angle increment of the wave front normal. In Fig. 4b projections of the rays on XY
plane are demonstrated (top view). It can be seen that "fat" rays correspond closely with
standard rays. Maximum deviations for ray trajectories for more than 5 km travel-paths
do not exceed a few meters.

We have compared the so-called "travel-times" tables of the first arrivals of qP-waves calculated using "fat" and standard rays. To produce the tables, a set of 400×400 rays is constructed (the number of rays that have varying azimuth and dip angles) with takeoff angles lying in the intervals $\varphi_{AZ} = [0, 360^0]$, $\varphi_{Dip} = [0, 360^0]$. Next, the first arrivals travel times computed along each ray are interpolated to the regular grid using the approach described in [14]. As can be seen, the table is completely filled, which means there are no shadow areas (see Fig. 5a). The travel-time residuals between "fat" rays and standard rays do not exceed 3 ms. (Fig. 5b).

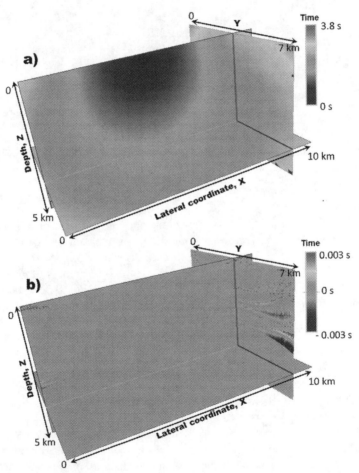

Fig. 5. a) First arrival travel-time table of the qP-wave calculated using the three-dimensional VTI model presented in Fig. 3 and "fat" rays with $\upsilon = 30$ Hz; b) First arrival travel-time residuals of the qP-wave calculated using "fat" rays with $\upsilon = 30$ Hz and standard rays (Madagaskar package).

We emphasize once again that the primary objective of the numerical experiment discussed above is to validate the correctness of both the concept of "fat" ray calculation in TTI media and its numerical implementation. For this reason, the appropriate value of the parameter υ has been chosen and the best match between the results obtained by the algorithm presented here and the standard procedure was required.

It is anticipated that "fat" rays will be utilized in media that are more sophisticated than the model presented above. When dealing with complex models with sharp interfaces, classical rays may struggle to calculate adequate ray trajectories and first arrival times. As previously demonstrated in [14], "fat" rays, with properly selected parameters, can handle this task quite effectively. Hence, it is necessary to choose the parameter υ optimally. The following considerations must be taken into account when selecting the "ray frequency". To ensure reliable passage of rays through sharp inhomogeneities (such as salt bodies), it is necessary to decrease the value of υ. It's crucial that "fat" rays don't differ too much from standard rays, and in simple parts of the model they should be similar to them. To fulfill this requirement, it is necessary to increase the value of υ. The choice of parameter υ for each particular case is a compromise between these two requirements and should be done empirically.

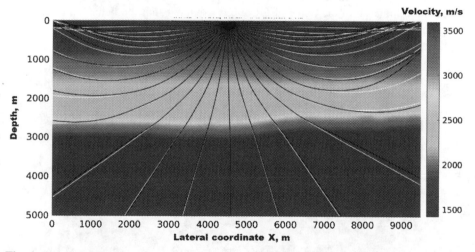

Fig. 6. Comparison of "fat" rays calculated for different frequencies. Rays for $\upsilon = 30$ Hz are shown in white (coincide with the standard rays), rays for $\upsilon = 5$ Hz are shown in black. Rays are calculated for a fixed azimuth $\varphi_{AZ} = 0$ and overlaid on 2D section of the phase velocity distribution.

Calculating "fat" rays takes much more computational time than standard rays for a given density of rays. One reason is that at each time step along the "fat" ray, multiple accesses to the velocity model are required to estimate the average phase velocity along the current front position. One more reason is that the number of control points chosen for ray tracing increases the computation time almost linearly. The number of control points should be sufficient to take into account the 3D velocity variation around a ray. If the number of control points is insufficient, it may cause instability of the ray. An excessive number of control points leads to a significant increase in computational time without any noticeable improvement in the final result.

4.2 "Fat" Rays for Different Frequencies

Let's demonstrate numerically how frequency affects the behavior of "fat" rays. Figure 6 displays the calculated rays for two cases: $\upsilon = 30$ Hz and $\upsilon = 5$ Hz. The most significant difference can be seen in rays that have a propagation direction that is close to horizontal, particularly in the upper right part of the model. The obvious reason is that the model from Fig. 3 has the greatest variability in the vertical direction. In these conditions, 5 Hz "fat" rays are most sensitive to changes in the model parameters along the vertical axis.

4.3 Impact of Weak Anisotropy

It's interesting to assess the impact of weak anisotropy on the behavior of rays in the proposed model. The comparison of fat" rays at $\upsilon = 30$ Hz in isotropic and anisotropic cases can be seen in Fig. 7. To create an isotropic model from the VTI model from Fig. 3, we simply set the anisotropy parameters ε, δ to zero. The rays were derived for zero azimuth, that is, in the plane of (X, Z). It's evident that the behavior of the rays is significantly different. Once again, it confirms that even weak anisotropy can have a significant impact on the seismic data processing results.

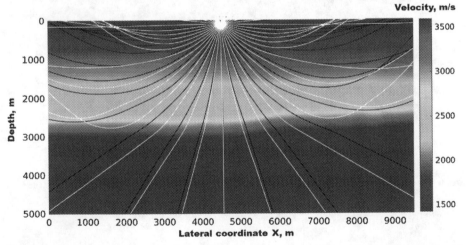

Fig. 7. Comparison of "fat" rays for $\upsilon = 30$ Hz in VTI model from Fig. 3 (shown in black) with the same rays in corresponding isotropic model ($\varepsilon = 0$, $\delta = 0$) (shown in white). Rays are calculated for a fixed azimuth $\varphi_{AZ} = 0$ and overlaid on 2D section of the phase velocity distribution.

In the general case of a TTI model with an arbitrary oriented symmetry axis, two additional arrays of parameters are required as input data. It is necessary to provide two volumes that provide symmetry axis orientation at every point in a model: a dip angle regarding the vertical axis, and azimuth.

4.4 qP-Waves Green's Function Calculation Using the Frequency Dependent Rays

In this chapter, we present numerical frequency domain elastic qP-wavefield simulation using the "fat" rays. The qP ray-based asymptotic Green's function in a weak anisotropic medium calculated at point R with the source at point S is defined as [20, 23, 24]:

$$G_{ij}(R, S) = \frac{g_j(S)g_i(R)}{4\pi \sqrt{\rho(S)\rho(R)V(S)V(R)}J(S, R)} \exp\{i\omega\tau(S, R)\} \tag{9}$$

where $g_j(S)$, $g_i(R)$ are components of polarization vector in the source and receiver points, V is phase velocity, ρ means density, $\tau(S, R)$ is traveltime between two points S and R. The symbol $J(S, R)$ means relative geometrical spreading along a ray. The geometrical spreading given by the expression:

$$J = \frac{dS}{d\Omega} \tag{10}$$

where dS is the elementary oriented surface of an orthogonal ray tube section at R and $d\Omega$ is the elementary solid angle associated with the ray tube at source. The finite-difference (FD) approximation of the geometrical spreading factor is calculated based on the theory provided in [2]. To utilize the FD approximation of geometrical spreading, one needs to consider a ray tube formed by three adjacent rays with small increments in take-off angles. In this case, it is important to have enough ray coverage in the target area. The amplitudes calculated along the ray tubes are interpolated into a regular grid. For ray-based wavefield simulation, we used a set of 500 x 500 rays. The parameters of ray tracing were as follows: $\upsilon = 5$ Hz, $l = 0.5$, $\theta_{max} = 0.5$, $\alpha = 1$. Density distribution was estimated using well known empirical Gardner equation [25]. In Fig. 10 we present three components of the frequency domain wavefield for frequency 5 Hz (real parts) calculated in the whole model. Vertical force was employed as the source at point S with coordinates $X_S = 4500$ m, $Y_S = 3500$ m, $Z_S = 100$ m. The solution error provided by "fat" rays in comparison with "exact" solution provided by exact 3D FD modelling does not exceed 9%.

All calculations presented above are done on a personal desktop computer with Intel Core i7-3770K 3.50 GHz CPU (4 core) and 32 Gb RAM. The "fat ray"-based Green function calculation for one source takes ~ 3.2 min of total computation time using all 4 CPU core. The most time-consuming part is ray tracing. It takes almost 80% of total time (Fig. 8).

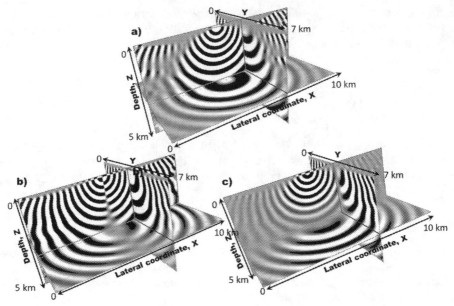

Fig. 8. qP-wave Green's function for frequency 5 Hz (real part) provided by the "fat" rays. a) Vertical (Z) component, b) Horizontal (X) component, c) Horizontal (Y) component. Vertical point force source was used.

5   Conclusions

In this work, an algorithm for constructing qP frequency-dependent rays ("fat" rays) in three-dimensional tilted transversely isotropic media with an arbitrary oriented axis of symmetry is developed, implemented and tested. The propagation of broadband seismic signals in real environments can be approximated using "fat" rays. The proposed scheme for calculating qP-"fat" rays consists of two stages. 1) Movement of the ray along the corresponding group velocity vector, which depends on the phase velocity smoothed along the flat element of the wave front and the current normal to the front. 2) Determination of the local orientation of the front at the ray point found in the first stage. The simultaneous movement of many control points, initially located on a fragment of a flat wave front in the vicinity of the ray, is used to find it. The motion of a locally flat fragment of the wave front is approximated in this manner. The distribution of model parameters in a specific volume of the medium concentrated around the ray is what determines the properties of "fat" rays. At each point, the wavelength determines the width of the sensitivity zone. To determine wavelength, a predefined parameter with frequency dimension is used, which is called the "ray frequency". In order to enhance numerical efficiency, approximate expressions for phase and group velocities for weak TTI media are employed. In most practical situations that arise in seismic exploration, this assumption is well-justified. To prove that the proposed concept is correct, a comparison was made between "fat" rays in the limiting case and standard rays using a smooth realistic model. In theory, both approaches should yield similar results in this situation. The accuracy of the proposed algorithm is confirmed by numerical results. Numerical experiments demonstrate that "fat" rays can be quite successfully used to solve direct and inverse seismic problems in complex three-dimensional tilted transversely isotropic media.

Acknowledgments. The work is supported by RSF grant 21–71-20002. The numerical results of the work were obtained using computational resources of Peter the Great Saint-Petersburg Polytechnic University Supercomputing Centre (scc.spbstu.ru).

Disclosure of Interests. The authors have no competing interests to declare that are relevant to the content of this article.

References

1. Babich, V.M., Buldyrev, V.S.: Asymptotic Methods in Short-Wavelength Diffraction Theory. Alpha Science (2009)
2. Cerveny, V.: Seismic Ray Theory. Cambridge University Press, Cambridge (2001)
3. Kravtsov, Y.A., Orlov, Y.I.: Geometrical Optics of Inhomogeneous Media. Springer-Verlag, Heidelberg (1990)
4. Ben-Menahem, A., Beydoun, W.B.: Range of validity of seismic ray and beam methods in general inhomogeneous media – I. General theory. Geophys. J. Int. **82**, 207–234 (1985)
5. Williamson, P.: A guide to the limits of resolution imposed by scattering in ray tomography. Geophysics **56**, 202–207 (1991)
6. Marquering, H., Dahlen, F.A., Nolet, G.: Three-dimensional sensitivity kernels for finite-frequency traveltimes: the banana-doughnut paradox. Geophys. J. Int. **137**, 805–815 (1999)
7. Birch, A., Kosovichev, A.: Travel time sensitivity kernels. Solar Phys. **192**, 192–201 (2000)
8. Cerveny, V., Soares, J.E.P.: Fresnel volume ray tracing. Geophysics **57**, 902–915 (1992)
9. Lomax, A.: The wavelength-smoothing method for approximating broad-band wave propagation through complicated velocity structures. Geophys. J. Int. **117**, 313–334 (1994)
10. Vasco, D.W., Peterson, J.E., Majer, E.L.: Beyond ray tomography: wavepaths and Fresnel volumes. Geophysics **60**, 1790–1804 (1995)
11. Bube, K.P., Washbourne, J.K.: Wave tracing: ray tracing for the propagation of band-limited signals: part 1 – theory. Geophysics **73**, VE377–VE384 (2008)
12. Yarman, C.E., Cheng, X., Osypov, K., Nichols, D., Protasov, M.: Band-limited ray tracing. Geophys. Prosp. **61**, 1194–1205 (2013)
13. Vasco, D.W., Nihei, K.: Broad-band trajectory mechanics. Geophys. J. Int. **216**, 745–759 (2019)
14. Neklyudov, D., Protasov, M.: "Fat" rays in three dimensional media to approximate a broadband signal propagation. In: Gervasi, O., et al. Computational Science and Its Applications – ICCSA 2023. LNCS, vol. 13957. Springer, Cham (2023). https://doi.org/10.1007/978-3-031-36808-0_8
15. Thomsen, L.: Weak elastic anisotropy. Geophysics **51**, 1954–1966 (1986)
16. Fowler, P.: Practical VTI approximations: a systematic anatomy. J. Appl. Geophys. **54**(3–4), 347–367 (2003)
17. Farra, V., Pšenčík, I.: Weak-anisotropy approximations of P-wave phase and ray velocities for anisotropy of arbitrary symmetry. Stud. Geophys. Geod. **60**, 403–418 (2016)
18. Grechka, V.: Applications of Seismic Anisotropy in the Oil and Gas Industry. EAGE (2009)

19. Farra, V.: High order expressions of the phase velocity and polarization of qP and qS waves in anisotropic media. Geophys. J. Int. **147**, 93–105 (2001)
20. Dehghan, K., Farra, V., Nicolétis, L.: Approximate ray tracing for qP-waves in inhomogeneous layered media with weak structural anisotropy. Geophysics **72**, SM47–SM60 (2007)
21. Woodward, V., Nichols, D., Zdraveva, O., Whitfield, P., Johns, T.: A decade of tomography. Geophysics **73**, VE5–VE11 (2008)
22. Madagaskar homepage. https://www.reproducibility.org/RSF/
23. Pšenčík, I.: Green's functions for inhomogeneous weakly anisotropic media. Geophys. J. Int. **135**, 279–288 (1998)
24. Pšenčík, I., Farra, V.: First-order P-wave ray synthetic seismograms in inhomogeneous weakly anisotropic media. Geophys. J. Int. **170**(3), 1243–1252 (2007)
25. Gardner, G., Gardner, L., Gregory, A.: Formation velocity and density – the diagnostic basics for stratigraphic traps. Geophysics **39**, 770–780 (1974)

Urban and Regional Planning

Implementation of Mutually Exclusive Pedestrian Accessibility Zones of the Metro on the Example of a Megalopolis

Valentin Markovskiy[1]($\boxtimes$) ⓘD, Tatiana Churiakova[1] ⓘD, Mikhail Kosovan[2] ⓘD, Irina Savina[1] ⓘD, and Sergey Mityagin[1] ⓘD

[1] ITMO University, 197101 Saint-Petersburg, Russian Federation
strong.markovskiy@niuitmo.ru
[2] Moscow Institute of Physics and Technology, 141701 Moscow, Russian Federation

Abstract. The article presents a novel method for assessing pedestrian accessibility zones around metro stations through the integration of isochrones and Voronoi polygons. The proposed method unfolds in four main stages: constructing isochrones, creating Voronoi polygons, adjusting isochrones to fit within Voronoi boundaries, and merging trimmed and remaining isochrones. Conducted experimental research utilizing the Moscow metro system as a case study validates the method's effectiveness. It outperforms traditional buffer zone approaches by offering improved explanatory capability and reduced prediction errors. The paper also explores how this method can be further improved by tailoring it to the unique characteristics of various metro stations. Implementing this advanced method for determining the influence zones of metro stations promises to significantly improve urban planning and transport management accuracy.

Keywords: Transit attraction zones · Isochrones and Voronoi polygons · Metro planning

1 Introduction

Forecasting metro passenger flow is a crucial aspect of planning and developing the urban infrastructure of major cities. It facilitates the optimization of metro operations, including scheduling train movements, allocating necessary resources such as trains and personnel at each station, and implementing strategies to maintain comfort in crowded stations. Such measures help to prevent overcrowding and service shortages that could disrupt the operation of a complex transportation system.

Traditional time series forecasting methods fail to account for the interaction between spatial and temporal dynamics, limiting their effectiveness primarily to short-term traffic flow predictions under typical conditions. These methods falter under anomalous circumstances [1]. For example, the development of new residential areas or the opening of the new metro stations can abruptly change passenger volumes. Consequently, long-term forecasting requires the use of techniques that incorporate spatial variations.

O. Gervasi et al. (Eds.): ICCSA 2024, LNCS 14813, pp. 285–297, 2024.
https://doi.org/10.1007/978-3-031-64605-8_20

Furthermore, this analysis aids in forecasting the necessity for future network expansion. Accurate predictions of potential passenger numbers are essential for deciding where new stations should be constructed. By estimating the prospective number of passengers, it's possible to identify areas that could benefit from new transportation infrastructure. Most often, analysis in forecasting is based on identifying factors influencing passenger flow. Typically, the most important factors are the population residing near metro stations and land use. Transit attraction zones are fundamental in assessing these factors, as several potential factors related to usage are usually measured based on the size of the station's catchment area [2, 3].

For instance, transit attraction zones define areas where potential passengers might reside or work and use the metro for transportation. Analysis of these zones helps to predict transit service demand and estimate passenger flow volumes at specific stations [4].

Transit attraction zones can be categorized into different types depending on the mode of access to transit stations. Specifically, access modes can be pedestrian, bicycle, bus, and automobile. The pedestrian access mode is often considered the most prevalent for various transit systems, such as urban metros. Therefore, there is a general agreement among researchers that the size of transit attraction zones should be determined considering pedestrian access (referred to as pedestrian catchment zones) [5, 6].

The rapid development of megacity transportation systems results in an expanding sphere of influence, characterized by a growing number of metro stations and an increased availability of stations withing the walking distance for passengers.

Therefore, people generally tend to use only the nearest station, even when multiple options exist within the catchment areas [7]. This leads to an increasing overlap of station catchment areas. Hence, developing methods for accurately determining catchment zones where the population concentrates is of critical importance. This article presents a new method for generating pedestrian catchment zones around metro stations. Government officials involved in urban management can apply this method both for forecasting—as the population increases in areas with high-density metro stations, the method can help determine which station is expected to experience a higher passenger flow—and for designing metro entrances that can regulate passenger flow at stations by more precisely defining their accessibility. It is also possible to determine the optimal distance between construction sites of stations to minimize overlapping zones. By applying this method, we are able to demonstrate how zones differ depending on the destination and how they change after the construction of new stations, opening of new exits, or the development of road networks.

2 Literature Review

The concept of a pedestrian influence zone is based on the assumption that there is a certain maximum time that most people are willing to spend to reach metro station entrances [8]. In contemporary studies of passenger flows, two main methods of zone delineation are commonly used: buffer based [9, 10] and Voronoi (or Thiessen) polygon construction [11]. However, both approaches have their drawbacks. For example, when using buffers, potential zone overlap is not considered. On the other hand, Voronoi polygons may create zones where the distance to the nearest point is too large, which does not accurately reflect pedestrian accessibility.

To overcome these issues, a modification method has been developed based on constructing buffers using trimmed Voronoi polygons. This method has been actively employed in many studies [12, 13]. It has helped avoid the problem of zone overlap, but it has not completely resolved the issue of accounting for pedestrian accessibility levels. The Euclidean method, based on using buffers, typically overestimates the size of real influence zones because it does not account for road networks and natural barriers (such as rivers) and allows for straight-line distances.

To avoid fixed boundaries for influence zones, Mengyang Liu, Yuxuan Liu, and Yu Ye proposed a method, which relies on data from public bicycle usage [14]. This method involves analyzing trip information provided by bike-sharing services. This data enables the identification of the starting and ending points of users' routes for each station, thereby determining the influence zone around it. However, this method may not be suitable for determining influence zones in winter period when bicycle usage decreases and may be inapplicable in car-oriented cities lacking developed cycling infrastructure. Another attempt to avoid using buffers was the construction of isochrones in the work of Diao Lin, Ruoxin Zhu, Jian Yang and Liqiu Meng. However, as the authors themselves claim in the conclusions, the created zones may overlap with each other [15]. This means that the selected parameters (such as population and land use type) can be accounted for in both the first and second station attraction zones. As a result, we cannot accurately determine how many people will use each station, which also affects multicollinearity between variables when attempting to forecast passenger flow.

Additionally, in most studies, station centroids are utilized [9, 10, 12, 13]. Using station centroids as focal points for assessing influence zones introduces additional complexities. Centroids fail to accurately represent the actual access points for pedestrians, who mainly enter and exit stations through designated entrances and exits. This discrepancy becomes particularly evident in large, complex metro stations featuring multiple access points over wide areas. Consequently, relying on centroids may therefore misrepresent the true catchment area, resulting in a misinterpretation of pedestrian accessibility and, by extension, the station's effective service area.

The main goal of this research is to develop a method for determining pedestrian accessibility zones around metro stations that will address the shortcomings of previous approaches. This method will take into account: 1) the location of station entrances and their role as transfer hubs (in cases where multiple stations share common entrances); 2) pedestrian access influenced by the street-road network and natural obstacles; 3) the exclusion of overlapping zones.

3   Method

3.1   Method Description

Exclusion zones in pedestrian accessibility for metro stations denote areas where the nearby stations' service coverage competes without overlapping due to their deliberate division. Particularly in areas with high station density, these zones are delineated to ensure that each station exclusively serves its designated territory, avoiding overlap with neighboring stations. The proposed method for determining zones is based on generating isochrones and Voronoi polygons. The method's scheme is presented in Fig. 1.

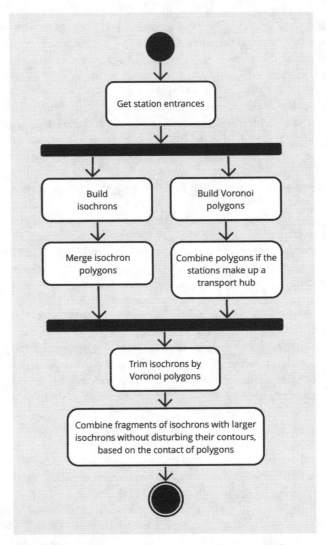

Fig. 1. Block diagram of the generation of zones of influence.

The generation method consists of four main parts: isochrone construction, Voronoi polygon construction, clipping isochrones to Voronoi polygons, and adding small sections of the original isochrones that were trimmed by Voronoi polygons. Figure 2 illustrates an example of the main stages of the method in action.

In the initial stage, isochrone generation takes place. Isochrones represent lines of equal travel time and are constructed for each entrance of the metro station. If generation is being done for the exits of a future metro station where infrastructure is not yet developed and road networks are not established, it is advisable to construct a single buffer at 0.7 of the selected distance from the centroid of the station. This area, on average, corresponds to the area of an isochrone.

In the second stage, Voronoi polygons are constructed for each metro station entrance. These polygons define geometric areas where any point within a polygon is closer to its respective station entrance than to any other station entrance, effectively delineating the local influence zone of each entrance. The entrance polygons of metro stations belonging to the same transport interchange hub are merged into a single polygon. This decision is justified by the common scenario, when one station can be accessed from several entrances belonging to other stations, facilitating transfers.

In the third stage, the original isochrone zones are trimmed according to the boundaries of Voronoi polygons. Segments that do not intersect with the trimmed zones are transferred to a separate geolayer. This is crucial for preserving potential small areas where populations reside within walking distance of metro stations.

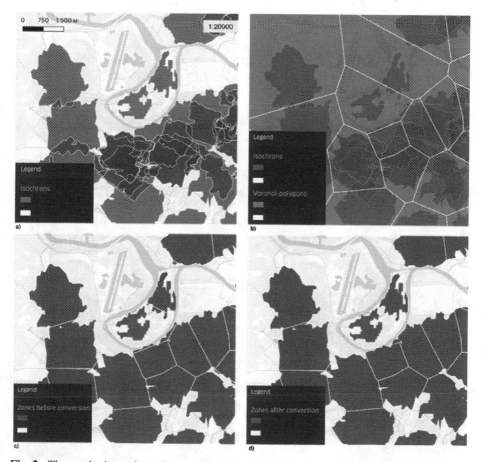

Fig. 2. The method consists of several stages: (a) isochrone generation, (b) Voronoi polygon construction, (c) clipping based on Voronoi polygons, and (d) joining clipped isochrones.

At the final stage, these zones are merged with the remaining isochrones. More details about the process are described in Sect. 3.2.

3.2 Restoration of Parts of the Original Isochrons Cut Off by Voronoi Polygons

During the trimming process based on Voronoi diagrams, a problem with mismatches between isochrones and polygon volumes emerged. This is particularly noticeable outside central areas due to lower station densities. Consequently, there are pieces of isochrones that end up inside polygons of other stations, even though they shouldn't belong to them (see Fig. 3a). To address this issue, it was decided to split the multipolygon layer into individual polygons. Two types of zones emerged: those touching entrance points and those not touching. The latter, accounting for approximately 2 to 5% of the population, introduced significant inaccuracies into the modeling results when misallocated. Therefore, in the proposed method, these fragments are merged with zones they connect with. If polygons have multiple touch points, the maximum distance from the selected ones is determined before merging (see Fig. 3b–d). This is explained by the peculiarities of isochrone construction observed at most stations with a similar situation. A larger touch size typically indicates that small fragments previously belonged to the influence zones of one transport interchange hub before trimming according to Voronoi

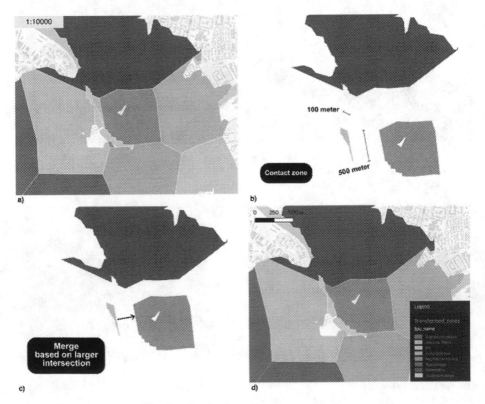

Fig. 3. Merging by polygon contact zone.

polygons. Additionally, the distance to station entrances for such fragments is usually shorter for polygons with a larger touch boundary.

This approach allows even small areas on the map that might have been missed or overlooked to be considered. This is helpful in determining station influence zones, which is crucial for accurate accessibility analysis and urban development planning.

4 Experimental Research of the Method

4.1 Study Area

The method was investigated in Moscow, Russia. Geodata was obtained for metro stations, the Moscow Central Circle (MCC), Moscow Central Diameters (MCD), railway stations (anticipated to integrate into new MCD lines) within the Moscow Ring Road (MKAD). Voronoi polygon boundaries were determined for construction purposes. Population data for Moscow covering both residents and employees were gathered for polygonal objects, specifically buildings, to support the analysis.

4.2 Data for Research

The initial dataset comprised point geodata of station entrances, obtained from the 2GIS platform. An online service designed for map creation, Mapbox, was employed to construct isochrones. Additionally, data regarding the annual passenger flow of stations and population density were acquired from the Moscow Department of Transport.

4.3 Building Accessibility Zones for Metro Stations

Pedestrian isochrones, covering areas within a 15-min (approximately equivalent to 1200 m) walk, were created for 1685 entrances of 351 metro stations. The selection of the threshold value is based on regional urban planning standards in the city of Moscow [16] and studies that determine the walking distance within a 15-min timeframe [17]. After trimming these zones in line with Voronoi polygons and merging polygons based on identifiers for status of transport interchange hubs, the number of zones was reduced from 1685 to 219 (see Fig. 4).

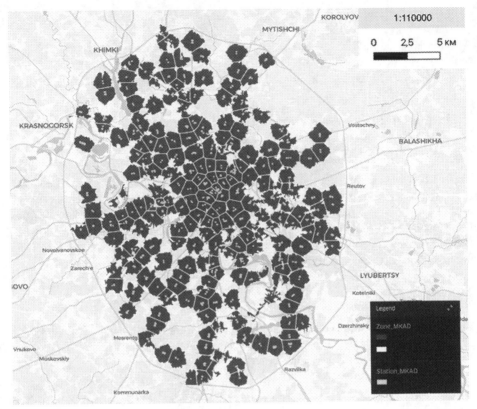

Fig. 4. Building accessibility zones for metro stations for the city of Moscow, Russia (blue – influence zones, yellow – station entrances). (Color figure online)

4.4   Evaluation of the Method

To avoid counting the population multiple times within each zone, buildings from which stations could not be accessed within the buffer zone were excluded. Consequently, the total number of people residing within a 15-min accessibility zone was reduced by 1.457.158 individuals, from 9.850.119 to 8.392.961. An illustrative case is the recently opened "Terekhovo" metro station, which is located in a former village and was until recently an uninhabited area of Moscow (see Fig. 5).

To evaluate the methodology, a passenger flow prediction was undertaken for metro stations along the Kalininskaya line within the Moscow Ring Road (MKAD), identifying a total of 7 such stations. The catchment areas of 6 stations were combined with those of other metro, MCC (Moscow Central Circle), and MCD (Moscow Central Diameters) stations to form unified transport interchange hub polygons. An Ordinary Least Squares (OLS) multiple regression model was employed, with the dependent variable being the 2023 passenger flow at the metro stations and transport interchange hubs. The choice of this model is motivated by its wide application for passenger flow forecasting [9, 10, 18]. Prior studies indicated that metro passenger flow is impacted by population density [19, 20] and land use structure [21]. Accordingly, independent variables in the analysis

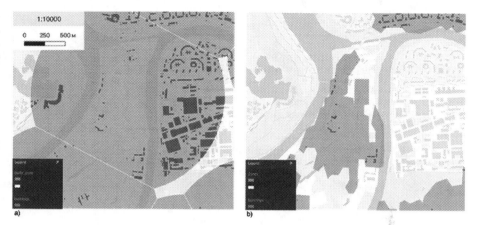

Fig. 5. The influence zone of the "Terekhovo" metro station (a – conventional method using buffers, b – proposed method).

included land use types and population density in the specified zones (see Fig. 6, input data for modeling: a, b, c – buffer method, d, e, f – proposed method). Initially, land use types such as commercial, green areas, industrial, railway, and residential zones considered.

However, in both cases, the variables "commercial," "grass," "industrial," and "residential" zones were found to be statistically insignificant, failing to meet the 0.05 significance threshold. Additionally, "commercial," "industrial," and "residential" zones exhibited high Variance Inflation Factor (VIF) values (exceeding 10), indicating high multicollinearity. It is assumed that this is related to the discrepancy between the designated land use types and their actual conditions. Currently, there are renovation zones where panel buildings are being demolished (which has been a practice in Moscow since 2017), however, these zones are classified as "residential". Additionally, there are residential complexes that have already been put into operation, and their residents were taken into account when determining population density, yet they are not classified as "residential". The same issue applies to lands classified as "industrial" - some of them have been adapted for public spaces, yet they are still marked as industrial sites. Some studies employ a different approach to land use determination – through point extraction and classification [13]. Additionally, incorporating new categories for specific uses such as administrative buildings, schools, or offices might refine land use assessments and could be explored in future studies.

The model characteristics using the proposed method are presented in Table 1. The model characteristics using the conventional method through buffers are presented in Table 2.

From Table 1 it is evident that the model based on the proposed method demonstrates a higher coefficient of determination (R-squared) of 0.929, in contrast to 0.838 achieved by the model using the conventional method (Table 2). This indicates that the proposed method better explains the variation in metro station passenger flow data. Furthermore, the Mean Absolute Error (MAE) and Mean Absolute Percentage Error (MAPE) for the proposed method are also lower, suggesting more accurate passenger

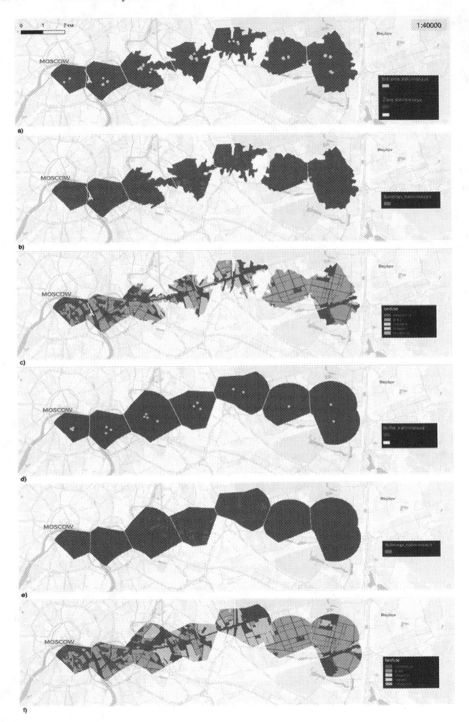

Fig. 6. Areas of influence of the Kalinskaya metro line.

Table 1. Characteristics of the model based on the proposed method of generating zones of influence of stations.

	coef	std err	t	P > ltl	[0.025	0.975]	VIF
const	0.533	0.543	0.982	0.382	-0.974	2.040	9.478
railway	0.327	0.045	7.217	0.002	0.201	0.453	1.111
populations	72.722	25.405	2.862	0.046	2.185	143.259	1.111
R-squared:	0.929	Adj. R-squared:	0.894	F-statistic	26.23	Prob (F-statistic)	0.005
MAE:	0.266			MAPE:	0.107		

Table 2. Characteristics of the model based on the generally accepted method through buffers.

	coef	std err	t	P > ltl	[0.025	0.975]	VIF
const	0.713	0.814	0.876	0.431	-1.548	2.974	9.325
railway	0.473	0.104	4.547	0.010	0.184	0.761	1.276
populations	83.106	40.223	2.066	0.108	-28.570	194.782	1.276
R-squared:	0.838	Adj. R-squared:	0.757	F-statistic	10.34	Prob (F-statistic)	0.026
MAE:	0.453			MAPE:	0.169		

flow predictions compared to the conventional method. Notably, in the model using the conventional method, the population density indicator has a p-value of 0.108 and is statistically insignificant at a significance level of 0.05.

Therefore, given the data presented, it is concluded that the proposed method of generating metro station influence zones suppresses the conventional method through buffers.

The methodology holds potential for future development, taking into account the unique significance and locations of different stations. A logical step forward would be to use Voronoi diagrams based on polygons. Station points can be replaced with polygons, the size of which would be regulated by centrality indicators or station type [22].

5 Conclusion

In conclusion, it is important to emphasize that the proposed method for determining the influence zones of the metro based on isochrones and Voronoi polygons offers a systematic and effective strategy. By utilizing these spatial analysis techniques, it is possible to accurately delineate the influence zones specific to each station entrance, thereby enhancing urban planning and transport management efforts.

By minimizing population duplication and prioritizing accessibility within walking reach, the proposed method optimizes zone delineation, leading to more accurate passenger flow forecasts. The effectiveness of this method was evaluated through experimental research conducted on the Moscow metro (Russia). Statistical analysis confirms the superiority of the proposed method, exhibiting higher explanatory power and lower forecasting errors compared to conventional buffer-based methods.

There are opportunities for further refinement and adaptation of the methodology, especially when considering the specific characteristics and requirements of various stations. Implementing centrality indicators or station types may offer additional insights and optimizations, thereby enhancing the effectiveness of metro station influence zone determination.

Disclosure of Interests. The authors have no competing interests to declare that are relevant to the content of this article.

References

1. Ni, M., He, Q., Gao, J.: Forecasting the subway passenger flow under event occurrences with social media. IEEE Trans. Intell. Transp. Syst. **18**, 1623–1632 (2017). https://doi.org/10.1109/TITS.2016.2611644
2. Ding, C., Chen, P., Jiao, J.: Non-linear effects of the built environment on automobile-involved pedestrian crash frequency: a machine learning approach. Accid. Anal. Prev. **112**, 116–126 (2018). https://doi.org/10.1016/J.AAP.2017.12.026
3. Langford, M., Fry, R., Higgs, G.: Measuring transit system accessibility using a modified two-step floating catchment technique. Int. J. Geogr. Inf. Sci. **26**, 193–214 (2012). https://doi.org/10.1080/13658816.2011.574140
4. Lee, S., Yi, C., Hong, S.P.: Urban structural hierarchy and the relationship between the ridership of the Seoul Metropolitan Subway and the land-use pattern of the station areas. Cities **35**, 69–77 (2013). https://doi.org/10.1016/J.CITIES.2013.06.010
5. Hsiao, S., Lu, J., Sterling, J., Weatherford, M.: Use of geographic information system for analysis of transit pedestrian access. Transp. Res. Rec., 50–59 (1997). https://doi.org/10.3141/1604-07
6. Zhao, J., Deng, W.: Relationship of walk access distance to rapid rail transit stations with personal characteristics and station context. J. Urban Plann. Dev. **139**, 311–321 (2013). https://doi.org/10.1061/(ASCE)UP.1943-5444.0000155
7. Upchurch, C., Kuby, M., Zoldak, M., Barranda, A.: Using GIS to generate mutually exclusive service areas linking travel on and off a network. J. Transp. Geogr. **12**, 23–33 (2004). https://doi.org/10.1016/J.JTRANGEO.2003.10.001
8. Macias, K.: Alternative methods for the calculation of pedestrian catchment areas for public transit. **2540**, 138–144 (2016). https://doi.org/10.3141/2540-15
9. Gan, Z., Feng, T., Yang, M., Timmermans, H., Luo, J.: Analysis of metro station ridership considering spatial heterogeneity. Chin. Geogr. Sci. **29**, 1065–1077 (2019). https://doi.org/10.1007/S11769-019-1065-8/METRICS
10. Zhao, J., Deng, W., Song, Y., Zhu, Y.: Analysis of Metro ridership at station level and station-to-station level in Nanjing: an approach based on direct demand models. Transp. (Amst.) **41**, 133–155 (2014). https://doi.org/10.1007/S11116-013-9492-3/TABLES/3

11. Sun, L.S., Wang, S.W., Yao, L.Y., Rong, J., Ma, J.M.: Estimation of transit ridership based on spatial analysis and precise land use data. Transp. Lett. **8**, 140–147 (2016). https://doi.org/10.1179/1942787515Y.0000000017

12. Pang, L., et al.: Research of metro stations with varying patterns of ridership and their relationship with built environment, on the example of Tianjin, China. Sustain. (Switz.) **15**, 9533 (2023). https://doi.org/10.3390/SU15129533/S1

13. Li, S., et al.: The varying pat-terns of rail transit ridership and their relationships with fine-scale built environment factors: big data analytics from Guangzhou. Cities **99**, 102580 (2020). https://doi.org/10.1016/J.CITIES.2019.102580

14. Liu, M., Liu, Y., Ye, Y.: Nonlinear effects of built environment features on metro ridership: an integrated exploration with machine learning considering spatial heterogeneity. Sustain. Cities Soc. **95**, 104613 (2023). https://doi.org/10.1016/J.SCS.2023.104613

15. Lin, D., Zhu, R., Yang, J., Meng, L.: An open-source framework of generating network-based transit catchment areas by walking. ISPRS Int. J. Geo-Inf. **9**, 467 (2020). https://doi.org/10.3390/IJGI9080467

16. Krestmain, M.G., et al.: A methodological approach to forecasting passenger flows in urban planning design of high-speed off-street transport. https://genplanmos.ru/project/algoritm-rascheta-passazhiropotokov-na-relsovom-transporte-moskvy/. Accessed 27 Mar 2024

17. Hongpeng, F., Zhifang, W., Hua, J., Lu, W.: Emotional characteristics and influencing factors of urban park users: a case study of south china botanical garden and Yuexiu park. Acta Scientiarum Naturalium Universitatis Pekinensis **57**, 1108–1120 (2021)

18. He, Y., Zhao, Y., Tsui, K.L.: Modeling and analyzing modeling and analyzing impact factors of metro station ridership: an approach based on a general estimating equation factors influencing metro station ridership: an approach based on general estimating equation. IEEE Intell. Transp. Syst. Mag. **12**, 195–207 (2020). https://doi.org/10.1109/MITS.2020.3014438

19. Cervero, R., Kockelman, K.: Travel demand and the 3Ds: density, diversity, and design. Transp. Res. D Transp. Environ. **2**, 199–219 (1997). https://doi.org/10.1016/S1361-9209(97)00009-6

20. Sohn, K., Shim, H.: Factors generating boardings at metro stations in the Seoul metropolitan area. Cities **27**, 358–368 (2010). https://doi.org/10.1016/J.CITIES.2010.05.001

21. Lin, C., Wang, K., Wu, D., Gong, B.: Passenger flow prediction based on land use around metro stations: a case study. Sustainability **12**, 6844 (2020). https://doi.org/10.3390/SU12176844

22. Liu, X., Yu, M.: Zenodo, 26 July 2020. longavailable/voronoi-diagram-for-polygons. https://doi.org/10.5281/ZENODO.3960407

Form-Based Semantic Caching on Time Series

Trung-Dung Le[1]([✉])[iD], Verena Kantere[2][iD], and Laurent d'Orazio[3][iD]

[1] Thuyloi University, Hanoi, Vietnam
dung_lt@tlu.edu.vn
[2] University of Ottawa, 75 Laurier Ave E, Ottawa, ON K1N 6N5, Canada
vkantere@uottawa.ca
[3] Univ Rennes, 2 rue du Thabor - CS 46510, 35065 Rennes Cedex, France
laurent.dorazio@univ-rennes1.fr

Abstract. Time Series Databases Management System (TSMS) has been overcoming the Database Management Systems (DBMS) in storing vast amounts of data [33]. Nevertheless, TSMS only supports simple aggregate functions to analyze Time Series Data (TSD). Besides, to accelerate and save data transferring between clients and servers in the DBMS, semantic caching can be used. However, the semantic caching approach is not efficient because of not fully supporting aggregate functions in TSMS. Furthermore, the query result of TSD in the semantic caching technique could be huge for the in-memory database where the semantic caching technique is running on. A model-based compression can be used to compress data, reducing the data space in the in-memory database. In this paper, we present Form-based semantic caching for TSD system. The approach reduces both query result storing based on semantic caching technique and the data transfer between clients and servers. In particular, the approach accelerates up to 122 and 1.82 times the execution speed, comparing to the without cache and basic semantic caching approaches, respectively. On the public Reference Energy Disaggregation Data Set, the compression model ratio in the approach can be reached to 526.8:1.

Keywords: Semantic Caching · Time Series Data · Linear Regression

1 Introduction

Smart cities applications face increasing pressure on the number of Internet of Things (IoT) connected devices and their data. In order to organize Time Series Data (TSD), which is generated by IoT devices, the Database Management System (DBMS) technology is used to represent, store, and query sensor data. It can be standard relational systems, key-value stores, document databases, or time series stores. Some systems are designed to provide fast ingestion rates and fast selection on time ranges, such as InfluxDB [5], GridDB [4], and Warp 10™ [9], called Time Series Management System (TSMS).

O. Gervasi et al. (Eds.): ICCSA 2024, LNCS 14813, pp. 298–315, 2024.
https://doi.org/10.1007/978-3-031-64605-8_21

The standard relational DBMS can process complex Online analytical processing (OLAP) queries, and semantic caching is often used to speed up the standard relational DBMS. However, it is hard to speed up these queries in a TSMS. The previous work, Think-Cities® [15], improves query processing by Form-based semantic caching technique in a specific TSMS, Warp 10^{TM}. However, Form-based semantic caching needs to improve experiments in TSMS.

Semantic caching is an approach which stores the answer of a query instead of just the raw data. It allows exploiting resources in the cache and knowledge contained in the queries themselves [19]. Form-based semantic caching technique is used to accelerate the complex OLAP queries in TSMS [15]. However, the sensor data can be stored in the in-memory database is huge. It leverages to reduce TSD semantic cache size to store more data in the same in-memory database memory. Besides, ModelarDB [34] uses models to store sensor data with lossy and lossless compression. This approach has not been applied to the semantic caching technique. Hence, the sensor data and semantic cache in TSMS can be compressed using *model-based* compression.

In this context of queries in a time series database system, the problem is how to improve time series processing in TMSM by the semantic caching technique and reducing the cache size in the in-memory database.

Semantic caching approaches [10, 18, 19, 26, 30, 32] have been studies to reduce network traffic and improve response time. These methods can be used in the standard relational DBMS. In addition, Form-based query makes it possible to optimize queries submitted via HTML forms [28, 29]. However, the existing works [10, 18, 19, 26, 28–30, 32] were built for Structured Query Language (SQL) query and the backend DBMS to execute, not TSMS.

Moreover, InfluxDB [5], GridDB [4], and ModelarDB [34–36] provide fast ingestion rates, good compression, and quick selection on time ranges. However, they fail to support complicated OLAP queries [24]. Hence, Form-based semantic caching [15] is proposed as a novel to solve the limitations above based on many aggregated functions in Warp. 10^{TM} [9], a specific time series system. Nevertheless, Warp 10^{TM} does not support Structured Query Language directly. Any query should be converted into a script written in WarpScript^{TM} language. It is not easy to translate an OLAP query into the form of WarpScript^{TM}.

Furthermore, the sensors are sampled at regular intervals, and it is currently impossible to store the huge amounts of data points in in-memory databases. The comparison of common storage solutions in ModarDB [34] showed that the compression solution can reduce 782.87 GiB of data storing in PostgreSQL to 2.41 GiB of data in ModarDB. This solution has not been used in semantic caching techniques.

To the best of our knowledge, none of these efforts fully address the issues of Form-based semantic caching of time series data systems.

This paper expands Form-based semantic caching in the previous work [15] for a specific time series data system. The approach aims to improve the performance of query processing in TSMS. In particular, the implementation shows that the approach accelerates up to 122 times the execution speed, comparing to the without cache approach. Comparing to the basic semantic caching technique, the proposed semantic caching can speed up to 1.82 times the execution speed, as can be shown in Sect. 4.

We also integrate the *model-based* compression to reduce the time series data storage in the semantic caching system. The *model-based* compression is also reused to restore all the data points and answer the incoming queries. In particular, the compress model ratio can be reached to 526.8:1 with the public Reference Energy Disaggregation Data Set [17], as can be shown in Sect. 4.

This paper is organized as follows. Section 2 defines the context and the motivation. Section 3 presents the detail of Form-based semantic caching approach. The implementations are described in Sect. 4. Section 5 describes the related works. The conclusion is presented in Sect. 6.

2   Preliminaries

First of all, the preliminaries of this paper show the background of techniques we use to propose Form-based semantic caching approach.

2.1   Time Series Data

Time Series Data Model can be as a relations *T(st, v)* with two attributes: st(time stamp) and v(value). For example, the time series of ocean tides heights are Time Series Data. Data in a smart city are from various sensors, such as rainwater, carbon footprint sensors, etc.

Methods for time series analysis [14, 16] may be divided into two classes: frequency-domain methods and time-domain methods. The former includes spectral analysis and wavelet analysis; the latter includes auto-correlation and cross-correlation analysis. In the time domain, correlation and analysis can be made in a filter-like manner using scaled correlation, thereby mitigating the need to operate in the frequency domain. Time series analysis can be divided into linear and non-linear, and univariate and multivariate [22, 25].

2.2   Linear Regression

The *model-based* compression [34] is used to compress a group of time series data by Linear Regression model:

$$y_i = \beta_0 + \beta_1 t_i + \epsilon, \tag{1}$$

where β_0, β_1 are parameter of the model; $t_i, i = 1, ..., N$, are time stamp values; $y_i, i = 1, ..., N$, are the time series data value, and ϵ is random error following normal distribution $\mathcal{N}(0, \sigma^2)$ with zero mean and variance σ^2.

The **fitted equation** is defined by:

$$\hat{y} = \hat{\beta}_0 + \hat{\beta}_1 t. \tag{2}$$

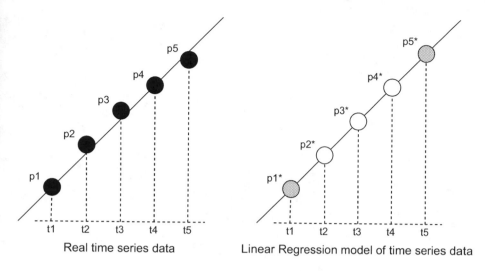

Fig. 1. Linear Regression Model.

Instead of storing all the data points, the *model-based* compression method stores the model's information, such as the size of the observation window, the min and max value of time series data. Figure 1 shows the *model-based* compression of time series data. For example, by storing $T_1(t_1, p_1^*)$ and $T_2(t_5, p_5^*)$, we can restore other data points by Linear Regression model with the user-defined error bound.

2.3 Semantic Caching

Semantic caching [10,32] allows us to exploit resources in the cache and knowledge contained in the previous queries. Consequently, it enables effective reasoning, delegating part of the computation process to the cache, reducing data transfers and the load on servers.

When a query is submitted, it is divided into two disjoint pieces: (1) a probe query, Q_{probe}, which retrieves the portion of the result available in the local cache, and (2) a remainder query, Q_{remain}, which retrieves any missing tuples in the answer from the server. If the remainder query exists, it is sent to the server for processing.

2.4 Motivation

Form-based semantic caching technique makes us possible to optimize, accelerate query processing in the environment of time series data and a specific TSMS. Moreover, we can use the *model-based* compression to store the value of data points in TSMS with the user-defined error bound or the data points in the gap time where there is no real data in the in-memory database. Using the *model-based* compression reduces TSD semantic cache size to store more data in the

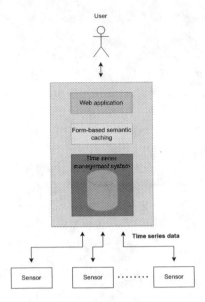

Fig. 2. The architecture.

same in-memory database memory. Also, processing a query with the *model-based* compression can reduce the volumes of data transferred between the client and server when the time data series is requested many times. Using the *model-based* compression also reduces TSD semantic cache size to store more data in the same in-memory database memory.

In conclusion, this paper introduces the novel and implementation of Form-based semantic caching on time series data to reproduce query result storing based on the semantic caching and the *model-based* compression techniques.

3   Form-Based Semantic Caching

The Form-based semantic caching architecture is shown in Fig. 2. A TSMS is used to organize TSD and Form-based semantic caching to accelerate query processing and reduce query results storing by semantic caching technique.

3.1   Form-Based Query

Example 1. The form of queries is:

```
SELECT sen.time, MIN(sen.value)
FROM SENSOR sen
WHERE T1 < sen.time < T2
```

We start with a Form-based query example. The query as shown in *Example* 1 is a function of calculating the min value of *sen.value* in a period of time from T1 to T2. When a user submits the update function in our project, a request

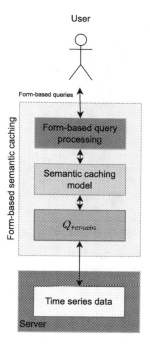

Fig. 3. Form-based semantic caching.

containing the parameters is sent to the server running a time series database engine.

Semantic caching is used to exploit resources in the cache and knowledge contained in the previous queries. Semantic caching approach is considered. When a query is submitted, only Q_{remain} is sent to the server to retrieve any missing tuples. A responding SQL query from the example template is given in *Example 1*. In particular, any aggregate function can be used in the Form-based query.

3.2 Cache Management

Memcached [6], Redis [8] are in-memory databases that are key-value stores. They are designed to simplify memory management [12]. Form-based query approach analyses, optimizes queries, and communicates through a simple set of APIs: Set, Add, Replace to store semantic data, Get or Remove to retrieve or remove semantic data. The data structure is simplified, and the access time is kept in specific period times. We use the Least Recently Used (LRU) policy for eviction of the data. Form-based semantic caching uses Memcached as the query result cache store. Furthermore, we use Linear Regression compression to reduce the data points and store these time series data on the key-value stores. By uncompressing data using model-based compression, Linear Regression model, in key-value stores, we can restore all data points of time series data with the user-defined error bound which is defined before the model is built.

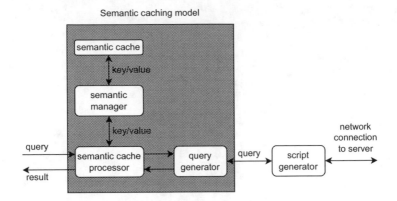

Fig. 4. The model.

3.3   Form-Based Semantic Caching Architecture

Form-based semantic caching architecture is shown in Fig. 3. It is built based on Form-based query and semantic caching approach. Form-based semantic caching allows us to exploit resources in the cache and knowledge contained in the queries themselves. Consequently, it enables effective reasoning, delegating part of the computation process to the cache, reducing both data transferring and the load on servers. The semantic caching model is built in a client in the client/server model where a time series data database engine is installed on servers to manage and simplify time series data processing.

Figure 3 presents an overview of our Form-based semantic caching approach. It relies on 3 phases: (1) Form-based querying, (2) semantic processing, and (3) time series optimization. A specific in-memory database is used to manage the *semantic cache*. When the client receives a query, as shown in Fig. 4, the *semantic cache processor* will check the previous query results via *semantic manager*. The necessary queries are generated by *query generator*. After that, Q_{remain} is translated into a script by *script generator*. Finally, the scripts are sent to servers to get the results. In particular, Form-based query processing enables users to access data via template queries. The obtained parameterized queries can then be decomposed into probe queries and remainder queries. The remainder queries will then be grouped into a query and translated into the instruction of time series database language, such as WarpScript™ in Warp 10™. After that, the script is sent to the specific time series database engine to get the results. As shown in Fig. 4 and Sect. 2, the semantic caching model can be deployed with an in-memory database. The semantic caching model and time series database engine can be implemented in the separate or same servers.

Example 2. Figure 5 shows an example of Form-based query and Form-based semantic caching. The form of queries is shown in *Example* 1, where the cache has the results of queries

– From 01-02-2020 to 05-02-2020,

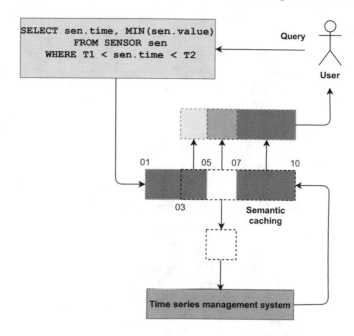

Fig. 5. An example of form-based semantic caching

- From 07-02-2020 to 10-02-2020.

The incoming query requires results from 03-02-2020 to 10-02-2020. Then, it is decomposed into Q_{probe} and Q_{remain}. Q_{probe} is optimized in the semantic caching to get results:

- From 03-02-2020 to 05-02-2020,
- From 07-02-2020 to 10-02-2020.

Q_{remain} is optimized and translated into a script. After that the script is sent and get results from Warp 10^{TM} server:

- From 05-02-2020 to 07-02-2020,

Finally, the results are integrated from 2 parts in caches and a part from distance server. They are shown as follows:

- Semantic caching: From 03-02-2020 to 05-02-2020,
- Warp 10^{TM} server: From 05-02-2020 to 07-02-2020,
- Semantic caching: From 07-02-2020 to 10-02-2020.

4 Validation

Our experiments use Memcached [6] to organize the cache on a client built-in Open JDK Java 1.8. All experiments are run on a machine with following parameters: Intel(R) Core(TM) i7-6600U CPU @ 2.60 GHz × 4, 16 GB RAM. The operating system is Linux Ubuntu 16.04.6 Long Term Support distribution based on kernel 4.15.0-106-generic.

4.1   Think-Cities®and Warp 10™

In this experiment, the servers organize time series data in Think-Cities® by Warp 10™ platform, as shown in Fig. 6. So, the remainder query should be translated into WarpScript™ scripts to process time series data.

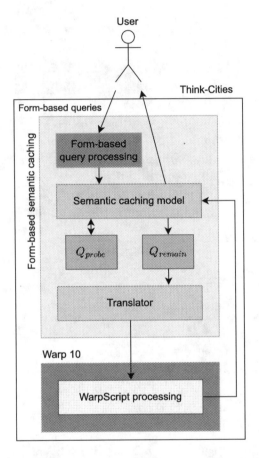

Fig. 6. Form-based semantic caching and Warp10 in Think-Cities®

Context. To analyze the efficiency in terms of time, we assume that time series data is organized in servers. A query often requires to get data in the form of an aggregate function of sensor values, such as the scoring metric of CO_2 in an area should be taken by the average function in a minute or an hour. The aggregate function of values should be calculated in the form of database engine languages, such as WarpScript™ in Warp 10™.

The results of 10 queries have already been stored in the cache, as shown in Table 1. The queries are formed in the uniform of Query X in Area *A* From *T1* to

T2. In this form, Query X means: Select TimeStamp, AggregateFunction(x), and area A means that the values of x are taken from all the sensors in geographic A. From $T1$ to $T2$ means that time series data are taken in a period of time from $T1$ to $T2$. The data of TimeStamp and the mean value of sensors around TimeStamp can be reused in the application. For example, the metric score of CO_2 in an area in the 1st quarter of 2020 can be calculated via the results of Q_1: Query X in Area A From 2020-01-01 to 2020-03-01 and Q_2: Query X in Area A From 2020-03-01 to 2020-03-31.

Results. The experiment focuses on comparing the execution time among Without Caching (WC), Basic semantic Caching (BC), and Form-Based Semantic Caching (FBSC) approaches. In BC and FBSC experiments, all the query results, as shown in Table 1, have already been stored in the semantic cache. Different workloads in various tests, as shown in Table 2, are used to compare the execution time in three methods. In the query processing, the data is transferred from servers to the client cache when queries miss hit (M) the previous results in the cache. In the basic semantic caching approach, the entire result that has already been stored in caches is returned from caches to answer the respective query, which are Hits (H) cases. In FBSC method, a part of the previous queries can be reused to return the request, which calls Partial hits (P). In particular, the approach reads all the keys in the cache and finds exactly where the answers are stored. Only the miss information in caches should be sent from servers to client caches in Form-based semantic caching. The ratios of Hits (H), Miss hits (M), or Partial hits (P) in tests are showed in Table 3.

Each test runs 100 times. Their average execution time is illustrated in Fig. 7. We have 4 experiments with different sizes of caches. Figure 7a, 7b, 7c, and 7d show the experiments of 597071, 479870, 359582, and 239231 bytes in the semantic cache, respectively. As shown in Fig. 7, the response time of query processing using FBSC is shorter than using WC and BC in most cases.

Table 1. Queries are stored in the cache.

	Query	Days
Q1	Query X Area A From 2020-02-01 To 2020-02-11	10
Q2	Query X Area A From 2020-02-11 To 2020-02-21	
Q3	Query X Area A From 2020-02-21 To 2020-03-02	
Q4	Query X Area A From 2020-03-02 To 2020-03-12	
Q5	Query X Area A From 2020-03-12 To 2020-03-22	
Q6	Query X Area A From 2020-03-22 To 2020-04-01	
Q7	Query X Area A From 2020-04-01 To 2020-04-11	
Q8	Query X Area A From 2020-04-11 To 2020-04-21	
Q9	Query X Area A From 2020-04-21 To 2020-05-01	
Q10	Query X Area A From 2020-05-01 To 2020-05-11	

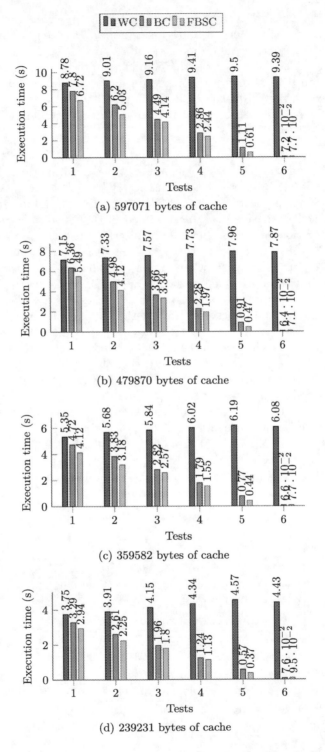

Fig. 7. Execution time in second of WC, BC and FBSC.

Table 2. Workload in tests

Test	Workload					
	Part1		Part2 (Q11)			
		Days	From	To	Days
1	Q1	10	2020-03-27	2020-06-25	90
2	Q1–Q3	30	2020-04-06	2020-06-15	70
3	Q1–Q5	50	2020-04-16	2020-06-05	30
4	Q1–Q7	70	2020-04-26	2020-05-26	30
5	Q1–Q9	90	2020-05-06	2020-05-16	10
6	Q1–Q10	100	Non	Non	0

Table 3. Percentage of hits in tests using to measure the execution time

Test	WC	BC	FBSC
1	100%M	10%H 90%M	10%H 45%P 45%M
2		30%H, 70%M	30%H, 35%P, 35%M
3		50%H, 50%M	50%H, 25%P, 25%M
4		70%H, 30%M	70%H, 15%P, 15%M
5		90%H, 10%M	90%H, 5%P, 5%M
6		100%H	100%H

4.2 Model-Based Compression

In this section, we show the semantic caching technique with and without the *model-based* compression. The data sets we used is The public Reference Energy Disaggregation Data Set (REDD) [17]. REDD includes data sets of energy consumption from six houses collected over two months. The Form-based semantic caching query has a form as shown below:

```
SELECT timestamp, value
FROM house1
WHERE sensor_id = sensor_x
AND timestamp > timeStamp1
AND timestamp < timeStamp2
```

Figure 8 and Fig. 9 shows the data of House1 and House2 of REDD [17] in four cases of storing, respectively. It compares the real data points and the data stored by Form-based semantic caching. As shown in Fig. 8, and Fig. 9, the Linear Regression model's compress ratio varies from 1.1:1 to 526:1 (number of data points/number of data points in Linear Regression models on the memory, Fig. 8b).

5   Related Work

This section presents some of the main works related to big data technologies (see Subsect. 5.1), semantic caching and Form-based query (see Subsect. 5.2).

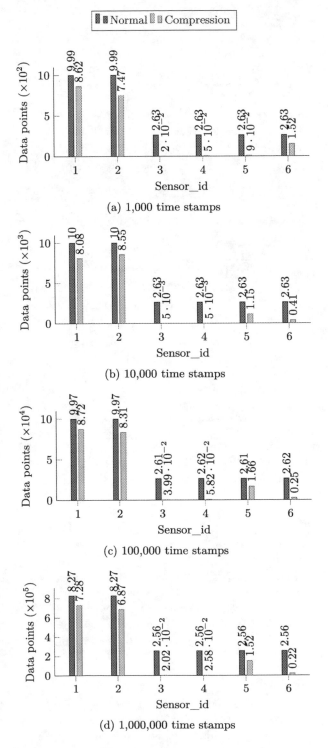

Fig. 8. Data point of time series data of house 1 of REDD.

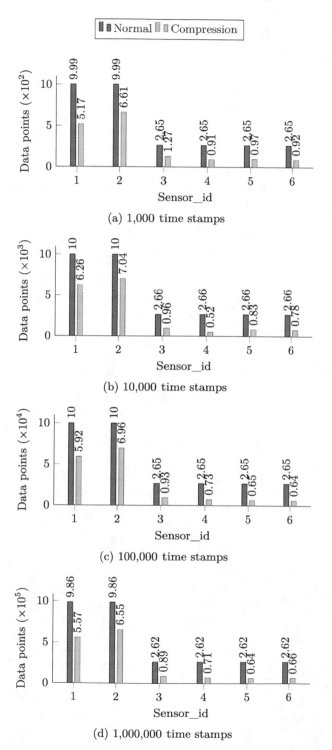

(a) 1,000 time stamps

(b) 10,000 time stamps

(c) 100,000 time stamps

(d) 1,000,000 time stamps

Fig. 9. Data point of time series data of house 2 of REDD.

5.1   Big Data Technologies

Hive [11], SparkSQL [20] provide cluster computing frameworks to manage big data. They provide the way to process complex OLAP queries on large amounts of data on multiple machines. However, they do not work well on data ingestion, simple selections, and real-time queries [24].

The stream processing systems, such as Apache Kafka [1], Storm [2], Flink [23], support fast response times on window-based continuous and real-time queries. However, they do not work well on historical data queries.

Moreover, there are various document store engines, such as MongoDB [7], Couchbase [3], and AsterixDB [31], which are used to store heterogeneous data. They support the time-applicable logical data model. However, they do not focus on time series data.

Furthermore, specialized time series database systems, such as GridDB [4], InfluxDB [5], and ModelarDB [34], are specialized time series database systems. They provide fast ingestion rates and fast selection on time ranges. However, the complex OLAP queries are not supported in these systems [24]. Although Warp 10^{TM} [9] supports many aggregated functions, the scripts should be written in WarpScript^{TM} language. It is not easy to translate an OLAP query into the form of WarpScript^{TM}.

5.2   Semantic Caching and Form-Based Query

As defined in [21], semantic caching is a technique that includes three key features. First, a description of the data stored is maintained in the cache in the form of brief specifications. Second, the policies of replacement policies are flexible in different semantic regions. Third, a semantic description of the data is maintained using sophisticated value functions that incorporate semantic notions locality.

A query cache using a semantic caching approach allows reducing data transfer between clients and servers [10,18,19,26,30,32]. While [32] studied the semantic data caching and replacement approach for a client-server model, Qun Ren et al. [30] focuses on select-project queries in the general application. A mobile environment of semantic caching is also studied in [18]. Besides, a mobile dual cache and a proxy dual cache are presented in [19]. Furthermore, to prepare the relevance cache, the semantic caching for rewriting aggregate queries is considered in [13,26,27]. They use functional dependencies to rewrite an aggregate query to optimize the storage required for materialized views.

Moreover, Form-based query via HTML forms [28,29] is used to optimize queries. They parameterize the query in a form. However, semantic caching is not considered in these methods. Hence, they can be integrated with the semantic caching approach in parameterizing the query.

Furthermore, the compress method in [34] has been integrated into Spark and Cassandra to manage time series data. This solution has not been applied in the semantic caching technique.

5.3   Limitations

In conclusion, TSMS has not supported the semantic caching, and complex OLAP queries as the standard DBMSs have done. The existing Form-based query methods do not fully address semantic caching issues for complex OLAP queries and time series data. Furthermore, Think-Cities® project [15] proposed Form-based semantic caching as a novel to improve query processing in a specific TSMS, Warp 10™. However, the novel needs to have experimented and extended to organize TSD in many TSMSs. Moreover, the *model-based* compression has not been applied in semantic caching technique as ModelarDB has done with Spark and Cassandra. To the best of our knowledge, none of the existing approach efforts fully address complex OLAP query processing issues in TSMS, and reducing TSD semantic cache size.

6   Conclusion

This paper introduces a Form-based semantic caching approach for time series database systems. Besides, we compress time series data and store it in the key-value store by the *model-based* compression, which helps us restore all the data points of time series data with the user-defined error bound.

We are currently implementing and validating these contributions and integrating both synthetic and real data. Future work includes more heterogeneous caches management. Besides, we will study traditional and specific policies for traditional and semantic caching.

Acknowledgment. The authors would like to thank members of SHAMAN team at Univ Rennes, CNRS, IRISA; School of Electrical and Computer Engineering, National Technical University of Athens; and Faculty of Electrical & Electronics Engineering, Thuyloi University for insightful comments.

References

1. The Apache Kafka, Stream Processing Engine. https://kafka.apache.org
2. The Apache Storm, Stream Processing Engine. https://storm.apache.org
3. The Couchbase, NoSQL Database. https://www.couchbase.com
4. The GridDB, NoSQL Database System For IoT. https://griddb.net/en
5. The InfluxDB, Time Series Database System. https://www.influxdata.com
6. The Memcache. https://memcached.org
7. The MongoDB. https://www.mongodb.com
8. The Redis. https://redis.io
9. The Warp10. https://www.warp10.io
10. Keller, A.M., Basu, J.: A predicate-based caching scheme for client-server database architectures. VLDB J. **5**(1), 35–47 (1996)
11. Thusoo, A., et al.: Hive: a warehousing solution over a map-reduce framework. PVLDB **2**(2), 1626–1629 (2009)

12. Wiggins, A., Langston, J.: Enhancing the Scalability of Memcached. In Intel document (2012). http://software.intel.com/en-us/articles/enhancing-the-scalability-of-memcached
13. Laurent, D., Spyratos, N.: Rewriting aggregate queries using functional dependencies. In: MEDES 2011, pp. 40–47 (2011)
14. Keogh, E.J., Ratanamahatana, C.A.: Exact indexing of dynamic time warping. Knowl. Inf. Syst. **7**(3), 358–386 (2005)
15. Carfantan, G., et al.: Think Cities: the accelerator for sustainable planning. In: ICDE Workshops 2020, pp. 64–70 (2020)
16. Lin, J., Keogh, E., Lonardi, S., Chiu, B.: A symbolic representation of time series, with implications for streaming algorithms. In: DMKD 2003, pp. 2–11 (2011)
17. Kolter, J.Z., Johnson, M.J.: REDD: a public data set for energy disaggregation research. Artif. Intell. **25** (2011)
18. Ken, C.K., Lee, H.V., Leong, A.: SI: semantic query caching in a mobile environment. ACM SIGMOBILE Mob. Comput. Commun. Rev. **3**(2), 28–36 (1999)
19. d'Orazio, L., Traoré, M.K.: Semantic caching for pervasive grids. In: IDEAS 2009, pp. 227–233 (2009)
20. Armbrust, M., et al.: Spark SQL: relational data processing in spark. In: SIGMOD Conference 2015, pp. 1383–1394 (2015)
21. Maghzaoui, M., d'Orazio, L., Lallet, J.: Toward FPGA-based semantic caching for accelerating data analysis with spark and HDFS. In: ISIP 2018, pp. 104–115 (2018)
22. Taniguchi, M., Matsunaka, R., Nakamichi, K.: A time-series analysis of the relationship between urban layout and automobile reliance: have cities shifted to integration of land use and transport? 415–424 (2008). https://doi.org/10.2495/UT080411
23. Carbone, P., Katsifodimos, A., Ewen, S., Markl, V., Haridi, S., Tzoumas, K.: Apache Flink^{TM}: stream and batch processing in a single engine. IEEE Data Eng. Bull. **38**(4), 28–38 (2015)
24. Gupta, P., Carey, M.J., Mehrotra, S., Yus, R.: SmartBench: a benchmark for data management in smart spaces. Proc. VLDB Endow. **13**(11), 1807–1820 (2020)
25. Vijai, P., Sivakumar, P.B.: Design of IoT systems and analytics in the context of smart city initiatives in India. Procedia Comput. Sci. **92**, 583–588 (2016). ISSN 1877-0509
26. Perriot, R., d'Orazio, L., Laurent, D., Spyratos, N.: A semantic matrix for aggregate query rewriting. In: ISIP 2015, pp. 46–66 (2015)
27. Perriot, R., d'Orazio, L., Laurent, D., Spyratos, N.: Rewriting aggregate queries using functional dependencies within the cloud. In: ISIP 2013, pp. 31–42 (2013)
28. Luo, Q., Naughton, J.F.: Form-based proxy caching for database-backed web sites. In: VLDB 2001, pp. 191–200 (2001)
29. Luo, Q., Naughton, J.F., Xue, W.: Form-based proxy caching for database-backed web sites: keywords and functions. VLDB J. **17**(3), 489–513 (2008)
30. Ren, Q., Dunham, M.H., Kumar, V.: Semantic caching and query processing. IEEE Trans. Knowl. Data Eng. **15**(1), 192–210 (2003)
31. Alsubaiee, S., et al.: AsterixDB: a scalable, open source BDMS. Proc. VLDB Endow. **7**(14), 1905–1916 (2014)
32. Dar, S., Franklin, M.J., Þór Jónsson, B., Srivastava, D., Tan, M.: Semantic data caching and replacement. In: VLDB 1996, pp. 330–341 (1996)
33. Jensen, S.K., Pedersen, T.B., Thomsen, C.: Time series management systems: a survey. IEEE Trans. Knowl. Data Eng. **29**(11), 2581–2600 (2017). https://doi.org/10.1109/TKDE.2017.2740932

34. Jensen, S.K., Pedersen, T.B., Thomsen, C.: ModelarDB: modular model-based time series management with spark and Cassandra. Proc. VLDB Endow. **11**(11), 1688–1701 (2018)
35. Jensen, S.K., Pedersen, T.B., Thomsen, C.: Scalable model-based management of correlated dimensional time series in ModelarDB+. In: IEEE 37th ICDE, pp. 1380–1391 (2021)
36. Jensen, S.K., Thomsen, C., Pedersen, T.B.: ModelarDB: integrated model-based management of time series from edge to cloud. In: Hameurlain, A., Tjoa, A.M. (eds.) Transactions on Large-Scale Data- and Knowledge-Centered Systems LIII. LNCS, vol. 13840, pp. 1–33. Springer, Heidelberg (2023). https://doi.org/10.1007/978-3-662-66863-4_1

Vehicle Navigation with Hexagonal Hierarchical Spatial Index

Ivan Ostroumov[✉] [iD]

National Aviation University, Liubomyra Huzara Avenue, 1, Kyiv 03058, Ukraine
ostroumov@ukr.net

Abstract. Spatial index of geoinformation theory proposes a new possibility for development of navigation methods with global coverage and rich hierarchical addressing with different precision levels. Hexagonal Hierarchical Spatial Index (H3) and Open Location Codes (OLC) are the most frequently used spatial indexes. Global spatial indexes use indexes instead of geodetic coordinates of latitude and longitude to address any point or data associated with this place. Spatial indexes may use different shapes of cells and different projections could be applied for data transformation from WGS84 to cell space. In this paper, basic methods of vehicle navigation Time of Arrival and Angle of Arrival have been adopted for use in the global spatial index. We use a hexagonal hierarchical spatial index due to multiple advantages of cell shape for support navigation. Vehicle position is identified as a cell address based on available indexes of reference points and measured ranges between vehicle and reference points. Navigation in spatial index is grounded on set theory and logical operations only which makes positioning system cheap for computation in comparison to classical positioning methods. In numerical calculation we consider airplane positioning with Time of Arrival method in H3.

Keywords: Spatial Index · Hexagon · H3 · Air Navigation · Positioning · Vehicle · Coordinates

1 Introduction

1.1 Introduction to the Problem

Vehicle navigation is an important process of successful transportation. Modern transportation networks set a strong requirement for performance and efficiency of vehicle trajectory selection logic and precision of approved trajectory maintaining.

Navigation is a process of movement from one point to another in a defined space. Navigation includes two processes positioning and guidance. Positioning identifies vehicle current position and guidance chooses the way of application forces to move vehicle in the desired direction. There are four basic positioning methods commonly used in different applications: Time of Arrival (ToA) [1, 2], Angle or Arrival (AoA), AoA/ToA [3, 4], and hyperbolic [5, 6]. ToA method uses measured distances from vehicle position to navigational aids with known coordinates. AoA grounds on available angle data to

O. Gervasi et al. (Eds.): ICCSA 2024, LNCS 14813, pp. 316–330, 2024.
https://doi.org/10.1007/978-3-031-64605-8_22

navigational aids. Positioning in 2D with AoA or ToA requires at least two measured parameters. In the case of navigational aid supports both distance and angle measurement an AoA/ToA method could be used for positioning by only one navigational aid [7]. Hyperbolic method is grounded on the primary property of hyperbola: range difference between any point of hyperbola and its focuses is constant. Hyperbolic positioning system counts the time difference between two synchronized signals received at the point of vehicle position [8]. This difference is proportional to the distance difference and specifies a hyperboloidal curve of vehicle position.

Each positioning method could be used with different parameters which is a function of angle, distance, or difference in distances. Based on applied volume navigation could be local or global. Also, there are many methods of vehicle localization which is opposite to positioning and detecting vehicle coordinates by ground facility.

Accuracy of positioning methods is grounded on performance of data measured by a particular sensor type [9, 10]. In most cases, distance measuring methods are much more precise in comparison to angle measuring. It makes ToA more accurate than other types.

Spatial indexing systems have been developed rapidly for the last decade [11]. Hierarchical spatial indexes provide a global addressing system with multiple precision levels. Spatial index divides the surface of Earth's ellipsoidal model WGS84 at a set of indexed cells. Each cell has a particular code or index which is hierarchal structured to support a different level of precision. A cell of different shapes could be used to solve particular tasks. Commonly used spatial indexes include Open Location Codes (OLC), Hexagonal Hierarchical Spatial Index (H3), and Hierarchical Triangular Mesh [12]. OLC uses a square or rectangular cell. H3 operates with hexagons and pentagons. Unique address of each cell in spatial indexes makes it possible to easily access data associated with a particular place globally [13, 14]. Spatial indexing system provides efficient data storage [15, 16] and interrogation with database [17, 18].

1.2 Motivation

Global addresses of spatial indexing system could be used to replace geographic coordinates of latitude and longitude in a variety of navigation applications. A spatial indexing system creates a set of cells in which navigation methods (AoA and ToA) can be applied.

Practical implementation of positioning methods puts some additional requirements for computation performance of equipment to support "real-time" operation or guarantee adequate feedback from automatic control system. Thus, one of the important ways of navigation theory development is finding ways of increasing performance of computation methods used in navigation systems. This problem is critical for low-weight automatic vehicles, which are limited by size and cannot support a speedy computation process. As a solution, an external computational cluster could be used, however, its practical implementation meets perils of bandwidth of wireless communication data link.

1.3 Contribution

In this paper, we study the application of general positioning methods in the theory of global spatial indexing systems. The paper contributes with a theoretical background of implementation positioning methods in the set of addresses of global spatial indexing. The aim of paper is to implement AoA and ToA positioning methods to use with Hexagonal Hierarchical Spatial Index. Proposed methods are grounded on logical operations only that are computationally more efficient than solution of navigation equations with trigonometric functions.

1.4   Organization of the Paper

The paper consists of six sections. The first section includes introduction to the problem with a detailed literature review, motivation, and contribution. The second section describes the basics of Hexagonal Hierarchical Spatial Index. The third section considers application of ToA positioning method in a hexagonal hierarchical spatial indexing system. The fourth section gives a theoretical statement of AoA positioning method application in spatial indexing systems. The fifth section provides a numerical demonstration of proposed positioning method for airplane navigation based on trajectory data of DLH 1010 flight.

2   Hexagonal Hierarchical Spatial Index

Global spatial index uses a set of cells to be associated with a particular map projection. Which represents a surface of reference ellipsoid with a set of cells. Hierarchic structure makes unique addressing for each cell of different precision levels.

There are four basic types of cells used in global spatial indexes: triangular, rectangular, pentagon, and hexagon (see Fig. 1). The cell shape with sides of equal length is more useful, due to simple recalculation of distances and computational cheap cell identification.

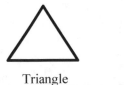

Triangle   Rectangle   Pentagon   Hexagon

Fig. 1. Geometrical shapes of cells used in spatial index.

The number of neighbor cells and length of connection border with other cells depend on the shape configuration that is critical for navigation purposes. Thus, a triangular shape has 12 neighbor cells, rectangular – 8, hexagonal – 6, pentagonal – 5. Another important criterion for navigation is the equality of ranges between centers of neighbor cells and reference cell. Unfortunately, triangular and rectangular shapes do not meet this requirement. Complementary area of cell at a circle could be used to choose an efficient shape for cell identification. Hexagon gives the smallest complementary area for the circles of identical radius which is important for algorithms of nearest neighbors search.

All of these advantages make hexagonal cells more useful for developing navigation applications based on spatial index.

Regular hexagon are formed by regular triangles with sides equal to circumcircle radius. Hexagon of regular shape has six rotations and lines of symmetry. Also, all internal angles are equal to 120°. Let's the side length of regular hexagon H be equal to a. Then the radius of inscribed circle could be calculated as follows:

$$r = \frac{\sqrt{3}}{2}a. \tag{1}$$

Geometry of hexagonal shape of the cell is presented in Fig. 2.

Representation of spherical coordinates with spatial index is performed with the help of map projections. Map projection transforms spherical data to 2D cartesian plane. Orientation of hexagonal cell in the spatial index could be different based on general system configuration [19]. If we use a cartesian reference frame with an X-axis directed to the North and a Y-axis pointed to the East, then coordinates of vertexes in the hexagon could be calculated as follows:

$$V_{xi} = \left[x_i + \frac{\sqrt{3}}{2}a; \, x_i; \, x_i - \frac{\sqrt{3}}{2}a; \quad x_i - \frac{\sqrt{3}}{2}a; \, x_i; \, x_i + \frac{\sqrt{3}}{2}a \right], \tag{2}$$

$$V_{yi} = \left[y_i + \frac{a}{2}; \, y_i + a; \, y_i + \frac{a}{2}; \quad y_i - \frac{a}{2}; \, y_i - a; \, y_i - \frac{a}{2} \right], \tag{3}$$

where x_i, y_i is coordinate of hexagon center; a is regular hexagon side length; V_x, V_y are matrixes of vertexes coordinates in NE reference frame.

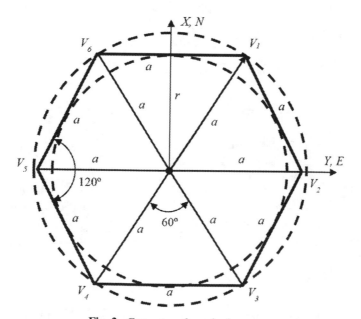

Fig. 2. Geometry of regular hexagon.

Regular hexagon configuration of the cell gives a possibility for easy operations with neighbor cells. Centers of all neighbor cells are located in vertexes of another bigger hexagon rotated at 30° (see Fig. 3).

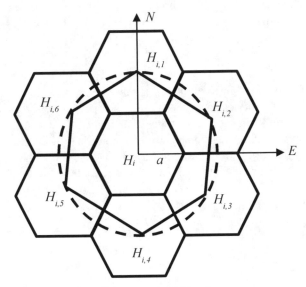

Fig. 3. Geometry of neighbor hexagons.

A set of neighbor hexagons $H_i = \{H_{i,1}, H_{i,2}, H_{i,3}, H_{i,4}, H_{i,5}, H_{i,6}\}$ could be calculated by hexagon centers:

$$n_{xi} = \left[x_i + \sqrt{3}a; \, x_i + \frac{\sqrt{3}}{2}a; \, x_i - \frac{\sqrt{3}}{2}a; \, x_i - \sqrt{3}a; \, x_i - \frac{\sqrt{3}}{2}a; \, x_i + \frac{\sqrt{3}}{2}a \right], \quad (4)$$

$$n_{yi} = \left[y_i; \, y_i + \frac{3a}{2}; \, y_i + \frac{3a}{2}; \, y_i; \, y_i - \frac{3a}{2}; \, y_i - \frac{3a}{2} \right]. \quad (5)$$

Based on centers of neighbor hexagons to the reference one, coordinates of vertexes of each neighbor hexagon could be obtained by (2) and (3).

Hexagonal symmetry helps to identify hexagons placed on the next level of grid distance. If we denote k as ordered number of hexagonal rings around a particular reference hexagon, then each side of hexagonal ring will include k + 1hexagons (see Fig. 4). Coordinates of hexagons center on a particular side are obtained after division of side length into lines of 2r width. The side length of the hexagonal circle could be calculated as follows:

$$L(k) = 2kr = ka\sqrt{3}. \quad (6)$$

Cells located in hexagonal circles are very important for navigation purposes. Each hexagonal circle includes 6 × k hexagons.

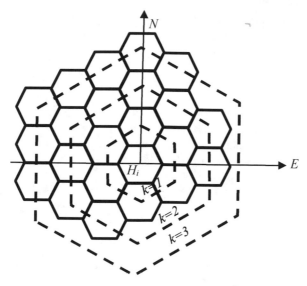

Fig. 4. Configuration of hexagons in k^{th} ring.

Indexing of hexagons could be organized differently. As an example, H3 uses a specific planar grid system with three axes of coordinates i-j-k applied at 120°. Coordinates of each hexagon in i-j-k integer frame are used to generate the address of each cell in the spatial index.

3 Time of Arrival Method

ToA is the most useful positioning method in navigation. ToA grounds on measuring distances from vehicle location to at least two navigational aids with given coordinates. Navigational aid is a specific reference point usually equipped with navigation equipment to perform measurements of distances to them [20, 21]. Navigation equation of ToA is based on equation of distances between two points in the local cartesian frame which could be applied for any number of measured distances to reference points. Navigation equation for the case of 2D positioning is the following:

$$D^2 = (x - X)^2 + (y - Y)^2,$$
$$D = [D_1, D_2, D_3, \dots, D_m], \ X = [X_1, X_2, X_3, \dots, X_m], \ Y = [Y_1, Y_2, Y_3, \dots, Y_m],$$

$$(7)$$

where D is a matrix of measured distances; X and Y are matrixes of navigational aids coordinates; m is a number of available distances; x and y are coordinates of vehicle position.

If there are only two navigational aids ($m = 2$) solution of (7) is analytical for 2D. In the case of $m > 2$ solution of (7) could be obtained as an iterative process of non-linear equation solution.

Let's consider application of ToA in the space of spatial indexes. Navigational aids or reference points could be associated with particular cells and specified as a set of indexes at the same level of precision:

$$NAV = \{nav_1, nav_2, nav_3, \ldots nav_m\}, \tag{8}$$

where m is the number of navigational aids used.

Vehicle is equipped with a distance measuring sensor which measures distances D to navigational aids NAV. Each distance D_i forms a circle of hexagons with a radius of k. Values D could be easily transformed to the metric of k:

$$K = \frac{D}{2r} = \frac{D}{\sqrt{3}a},$$
$$K = [k_1, k_2, k_3, \ldots, k_m], \tag{9}$$

where K is a matrix of transformed distances to k space.

A set of hexagon identification codes H_k which are located at the circle of a particular level k_i could be obtained as follows:

$$H_k = \{h_1, h_2, \ldots, h_j\}. \tag{10}$$

where h is a hexagon placed on a circular line; j is the number of hexagons placed on a hexagonal line.

The power of the set for each hexagonal circle is different based on k:

$$j_k = 6k. \tag{11}$$

Sets of identification codes (10) are subsets of a navigation set:

$$H_{NAV} = \{H_1, H_2, H_3, \ldots, H_m\}. \tag{12}$$

Result of navigation set (12) solution gives a unique hexagon index which is present in each subset of H_{NAV}. Hexagonal lines of vehicle position for the case of $m = 3$ are presented in Fig. 5.

Hexagon index which includes vehicle position could be obtained with logical operation of intersection of subsets in H_{NAV}:

$$POS = \cap_{i=1}^{m} H_i, \tag{13}$$

where POS is an identification code of a hexagon.

Identification code of hexagon obtained by (13) is a solution of navigation set (12). Address POS could be associated with vehicle position. Hexagonal shape of vehicle position line may give multiple solutions for the case of $m = 2$. Thus, all hexagons at the circular hexagon side could be marked a solution. This problem could be solved by using bigger values of m. Also, as a simplification for the case if a method returns more than one solution the closest cell could be selected.

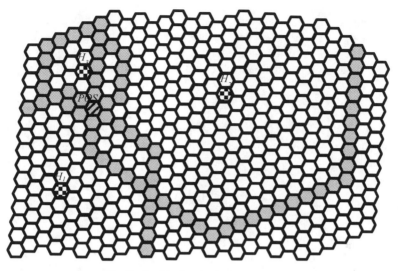

Fig. 5. Positioning by hexagonal rings.

4 Angle of Arrival Method

Method AoA uses angles as input data for positioning. AoA could use different reference directions to count angles [22, 23]. Angle of direction to navigational aid could be counted from some axis of body reference frame associated with vehicle construction (for example longitudinal axis could be used) or azimuth angle counted clockwise from vehicle center to the North. Also, angles counted from navigational aids to vehicle could be used [24]. As an example, an angle in navigational aid position from North to the vehicle is widely used in aviation for air navigation purposes. Navigation equation for AoA is based on trigonometric relations:

$$AP = B,$$
$$A = [tg(\alpha), -1]; \ P = [x, y]^T; \ B = [Xtg(\alpha) - Y], \tag{14}$$

where α is a matrix of measured angles from navigational aids; P is a matrix of vehicle position; X and Y are matrixes of navigational aid coordinates.

In the case of two navigational aids, a solution of (14) could be obtained analytically. For more numbers of input data, a Least Squares Method is helpful:

$$P = \left(\left(A^T A \right)^{-1} A^T B \right)^T. \tag{15}$$

In the space of spatial indexes, AoA could be realized based on an identified set of hexagons which are placed on a line by the given angle. If α is the angle counted from navigational aid to vehicle in the North direction clockwise then hexagons placed on line:

$$f(z) = tg(\alpha)z. \tag{16}$$

where z coincides with x axis of North-East plane; $f(z)$ corresponds to y.

Also, constraints to the geometrical quarter are used with reference to navigational aid location. Finally a set of hexagon identification codes H_k which placed on the line of particular angle from navigational aid could be obtained as follows:

$$S_i = \{h_1, h_2, \ldots, h_l\}. \tag{17}$$

Size l of set H_k is selected based on AoA maximum operational performance. A hexagon associated with vehicle position could be identified as an intersection of sets H identical to (13):

$$POS = \bigcap_{i=1}^{m} S_i, \tag{18}$$

where POS is an identification code of hexagon.

Geometrical representation of hexagons for the case of $m = 3$ is presented in Fig. 6.

Method AoA in hexagons is heavier than ToA based on computation time due to identification of sets by (16). Also, AoA is required to set up a size l. Bigger values l require more computation time for (18), lower l may lead to missing vehicle position point. Thus, the best l could be selected based on sensor capability level.

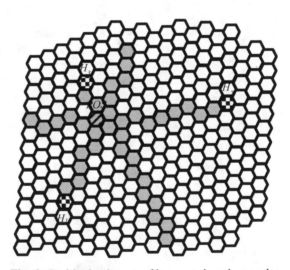

Fig. 6. Positioning by sets of hexagons based on angles.

5   Numerical Study

In the numerical study, we use application of ToA in hexagonal space for the case of civil airplane positioning. We use airplane trajectory data obtained with Automatic Dependent Surveilance-Broadcust (ADS-B) technology. ADS-B data are measured onboard of airplane and then transmitted omnidirectionally in the open data-transferring protocol.

Ground network of software-defined receivers receive transmitted ADS-B messages, decode and process them with a global network facility. Processed coordinates of airplane are saved with particular identification code separately by each flight. Nowadays, many databases provide easy access to the ADS-B database of flights, which could be used to study different transportation tasks.

We use trajectory data of DLH 1010 flight on December 16, 2023 for connection between Frankfurt am Main (EDDF) and Brussels (EBBR) airport. Flight time was 38 min. Total trajectory length is 216 NM. Trajectory data of DLH 1010 flight include only 87 points of not synchronized timestamps. Coordinates of data points are provided in angles of geodetic latitude and longitude. We use interpolation of data for 1Hz with linear regression separately for each parameter. Results of interpolation give 2280 data points.

To work with hexagonal spatial index a JavaScript library H3 was used. Transformed airplane flight path along a trajectory to the hexagonal space with 6th level of resolution is presented in Fig. 7.

The main idea of using hexagonal global spatial index is to use indexes instead of geographic coordinates. Also, measured data by on-board senor has a particular area of uncertainty that could be associated with hexagonal cell of particular resolution. This uncertainty area is represented as an ellipse or circle based on 95% confidence band.

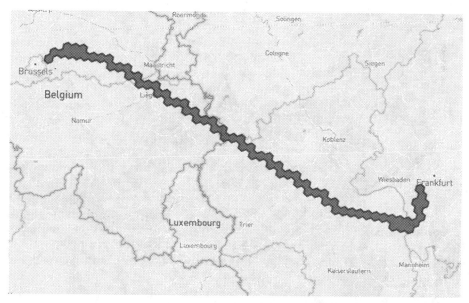

Fig. 7. Flight path of DLH 1010 in hexagons.

To simulate positioning by ToA let's consider airplane positioning by a network of navigational aids. Civil aviation uses Distance Measuring Equipment (DME) to measure ranges from airplane to ground network of DME navigational aids. Positioning by pair of two DME/DME is used as a stand-by positioning algorithm for hard back-up in case of primary positioning sensor lock. We consider particular cases of usage DME DIK (Diekirch, 49.5168° N, 6.0778°E) and DME FFM (Frankfurt, 50.0322°N, 8.3823°E).

At each cell of flight path, grid distances are calculated to DMEs. These distances have been used to model measurements in the space of cells from vehicle side. Simulated grid distances to both DMEs have been used for positioning by proposed ToA method in hexagons. Configuration of hexagons for vehicle position in 100th data point of trajectory at 8th level of resolution is presented in Fig. 8. A hexagonal distance from vehicle position to DME FFM is 51 hexagons. Hexagonal ring for FFM includes a set of 306 hexagons. Hexagonal ring of DIK is much bigger (171 hexagons range and includes 1026 hexagons) than FFM for 100th data point. Also, a configuration of both hexagons for this point is not optimal due to one leg of FFM hexagonal ring coincides with a leg of DIK. Thus solution of (13) for this case gives 51 hexagons of possible vehicle position. The exact position could be identified as the closest hexagon to the previously detected position from the set of possible solutions obtained by (13). A case of only two solutions is shown in Fig. 9 for the 300th trajectory point of 8th level of resolution. A case for 12th level of precision for 400th data point is shown in Fig. 10.

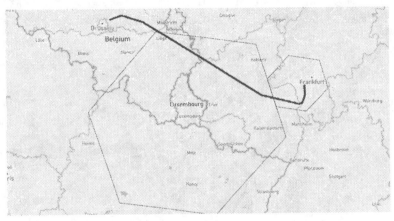

Fig. 8. Positioning by ToA for 100th point of airplane trajectory.

Solution of navigation set (13) at 12th level of resolution works with hexagons of 10.8 m side length. Navigation ring from FFM includes 10104 (with k = 1684) and from FFM includes 74748 (with k = 10774). Technically positioning in hexagons for a case of m = 2 grounds on a simple comparison of two sets of hexagons on rings to search identical indexes. In most cases, we get two or a set of identical indexes. Exact index is chosen based on the closest distance from previous positioning step.

Results of positioning at particular data points for different levels of resolutions are presented in Table 1.

Results in Table 1 show that by increasing the grid distance the number of hexagons at the hexagonal ring is increased. Results of number of hexagons calculation for different grid distances are shown in Fig. 11. An identification of hexagon side could be applied to minimize length of set of possible positions based on vehicle velocity vector. Only

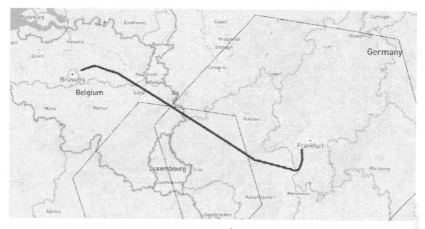

Fig. 9. Positioning by ToA for 300th point of airplane trajectory.

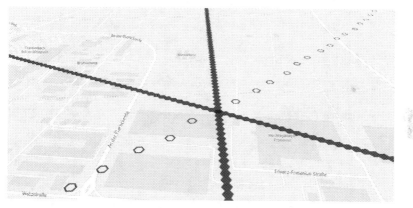

Fig. 10. Positioning by ToA for 400th point of airplane trajectory at 12th level of resolution.

hexagons on one side of hexagonal ring could participate in navigation process. It could reduce the set size by six times. Also, a geometrical configuration of both navigational aids is important due to possible cases of hexagonal rings touching one side of each other.

Positioning process in hexagonal space does not consider accuracy, because a set of global hexagons with defined size are used. It means that we operate with cells and the solution of navigation task is a cell (or group of cells) too. If we set up a level of resolution that corresponds with a particular parameter precision level then obtained cell could be associated with the uncertainty level of positioning process. Thus, level of resolution for solving navigation task should be selected based on standard deviation errors of data measuring device.

Table 1. Results of positioning by ToA in hexagons for selected data points

Point of trajectory	level of resolution	Grid distance to DME DIK	Grid distance to DME FFM	Index of airplane position
100	8	171 (1026)	51 (306)	881faecc83fffff
170	8	108(648)	114 (684)	881fa3b0ddfffff
300	8	143(858)	210(1260)	881fa03113fffff
400	8	191(1146)	306 (1836)	881fa09ae5fffff
400	9	1399(8394)	263(1578)	8a1fae08d91ffff
400	10	3610(21660)	715(4290)	8b1fae0c83a5fff
400	12	10774(74748)	1684(10104)	8c1fae0c8304bff

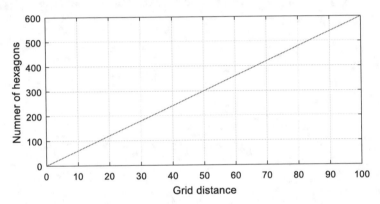

Fig. 11. Number of hexagons for different grid distances.

6   Conclusions and Future Works

Global spatial indexing system is a useful tool for geodata processing and visualization. Results of the study show the perspective of positioning methods usage in the theory of global spatial indexing. Paper presents a theoretical background of vehicle positioning based on indexes (addresses) instead of usage latitude and longitude during solution of navigation problems. The main advantage of proposed positioning methods (AoA and ToA) for spatial indexing system is a replacement of classical navigation equations (Eq. (7) for ToA and Eq. (15) for AoA) with equations based on logical operations only (Eq. (13) for ToA and Eq. (18) for AoA). In practical realization, these methods request a comparison of vehicle location sets to search identical addresses. Search in addresses is computationally more efficient than usage of numerical methods of navigation equations solution for both positioning methods. Therefore proposed methods could be useful for application in a variety of vehicle types with strong requirements for size of computation equipment used to support navigation and automatic vehicle control.

Performance of positioning methods in spatial indexing system is associated with a cell size of a particular level of resolution. Also, regular hexagonal shape of cell in spatial indexing system gives many advantages for practical implementation in navigation. Regular hexagon gives elementary equations for cell geometry calculation. Grid distance in a hexagonal spatial indexing system is useful to identify a hexagonal line of vehicle position based on particular level of resolution. Also, grid distance parameter makes it easy to get a set of cell indexes in which vehicle could be located.

A numerical study with real airplane trajectory for flight "DLH 1010" on Dec 16, 2023, shows the potential of H3 software library for airplane positioning. Airplane trajectory data could be coded by hexagon addresses of particular resolution levels. Position of airplane could be identified by ToA method based on measured grid distance to the reference points (a pair of DMEs DIK and FFM have been used as reference points).

Performance of positioning methods in hexagons could be a perspective for future study as well as application of hyperbolic positioning method in the spatial indexing system. Also, practical implementation of proposed positioning method based on global spatial indexing is at the development stage for light unmanned aerial vehicles.

References

1. Hsiao, Y.S., Yang, M., Kim, H.S.: Super-resolution time-of-arrival estimation using neural networks. In: Proceedings of the 28th European Signal Processing Conference (EUSIPCO), pp. 1692–1696. IEEE (2021)
2. Mosleh, M.F., Zaiter, M.J., Hashim, A.H.: Position estimation using trilateration based on TOA/RSS and AOA measurement. J. Phys. Conf. Ser. **1773**, 012002 (2021)
3. Yuan, P., Zhang, T., Yang, N., Xu, H., Zhang, Q.: Energy efficient network localisation using hybrid TOA/AOA measurements. IET Commun. **13**(8), 963–971 (2019)
4. Le, A.T., Huang, X., Ritz, C., Dutkiewicz, E., Bouzerdoum, A., Franklin, D.: Hybrid TOA/AOA localization with 1D angle estimation in UAV-assisted WSN. In: Proceedings of the 2020 14th International Conference on Signal Processing and Communication Systems (ICSPCS), pp. 1–6. IEEE (2020)
5. Xiong, H., Chen, Z., Yang, B., Ni, R.: TDOA localization algorithm with compensation of clock offset for wireless sensor networks. China Commun. **12**(10), 193–201 (2015). https://doi.org/10.1109/CC.2015.7315070
6. Offermans, G., et al.: eLoran initial operational capability in the United Kingdom–first results. In: Proceedings of the 2015 International Technical Meeting of the Institute of Navigation, pp. 27–39 (2015)
7. Wu, M., Hao, C.: Super-resolution TOA and AOA estimation for OFDM radar systems based on compressed sensing. IEEE Trans. Aerosp. Electron. Syst. **58**(6), 5730–5740 (2022)
8. Fengxun, G., Xiaoyun, J., Yanqiu, M.: Position performance analysis of airport surface multilateration. In: Proceedings of the IEEE/AIAA 42nd Digital Avionics Systems Conference (DASC), pp. 1–6. IEEE, Barcelona (2023). https://doi.org/10.1109/DASC58513.2023.10311294
9. Kuzmenko, N.S., Ostroumov, I.V.: Performance analysis of positioning system by navigational aids in three dimensional space. In: Proceedings of the 2018 IEEE First International Conference on System Analysis and Intelligent Computing (SAIC), pp. 1–4. IEEE, Kyiv (2018). https://doi.org/10.1109/SAIC.2018.8516790
10. Dergachov, K., Havrylenko, O., Pavlikov, V., Zhyla, S., Tserne, E., Volosyuk, V.: GPS usage analysis for angular orientation practical tasks solving. In: Proceedings of the 9th International Conference on Problems of Infocommunications, Science and Technology (PIC S&T), pp. 187–192. IEEE, Kharkiv (2022)

11. Azri, S., Ujang, U., Anton, F., Mioc, D., Rahman, A.A.: Review of spatial indexing techniques for large urban data management. In: International Symposium and Exhibition on Geoinformation (ISG), pp. 24–25 (2013)
12. Lv, Z., et al.: Spatial indexing of global geographical data with HTM. In: Proceedings of the 18th International Conference on Geoinformatics, pp. 1–6. IEEE (2010)
13. Uher, V., Gajdos, P., Snasel, V., Lai, Y.C., Radecky, M.: Hierarchical hexagonal clustering and indexing. Symmetry **11**(6), 731 (2019)
14. Lei, Y., et al.: Global multi-scale grid integer coding and spatial indexing: a novel approach for big earth observation data. ISPRS J. Photogramm. Remote Sens. **163**, 202–213 (2020)
15. Hjaltason, G.R., Samet, H.: Speeding up construction of PMR quadtree-based spatial indexes. VLDB J. **11**, 109–137 (2002)
16. Myllymaki, J., Kaufman, J.: High-performance spatial indexing for location-based services. In: Proceedings of the 12th international conference on World Wide Web, pp. 112–117 (2003)
17. Hussain, S., Mahaboob, M.H., Prasad, M., Kumar, P.: Performance evaluation of spatial indexing techniques. Int. J. Adv. Res. Comput. Sci. **2**(5), 59–64 (2011)
18. Iwuchukwu, T., DeWitt, D.J., Doan, A., Naughton, J.F.: K-anonymization as spatial indexing: toward scalable and incremental anonymization. In: Proceedings of the 23rd International Conference on Data Engineering, pp. 1414–1416. IEEE (2006)
19. Hexagonal hierarchical geospatial indexing system specification. https://h3geo.org. Accessed 8 Dec 2023
20. Ostroumov, I.V., Marais, K., Kuzmenko, N.S.: Aircraft positioning using multiple distance measurements and spline prediction. Aviation **26**(1), 1 (2022). https://doi.org/10.3846/aviation.2022.16589
21. Kuzmenko, N.S., Ostroumov, I.V., Marais, K.: An accuracy and availability estimation of aircraft positioning by navigational aids. In: Proceedings of the 5th International Conference on Methods and Systems of Navigation and Motion Control (MSNMC), pp. 36–40. IEEE, Kiev (2018). https://doi.org/10.1109/MSNMC.2018.8576276
22. Ostroumov, I.V., Kuzmenko, N.S.: Accuracy improvement of VOR/VOR navigation with angle extrapolation by linear regression. Telecommun. Radio Eng. **78**(15), 1399–1412 (2019)
23. Ostroumov, I.V., Kuzmenko, N.S.: Accuracy estimation of alternative positioning in navigation. In: Proceedings of the 4th International Conference of Methods and Systems of Navigation and Motion Control (MSNMC), pp. 291–294. IEEE, Kyiv (2016)
24. Ostroumov, I.V., Kuzmenko, N.S., Marais, K.: Optimal pair of navigational aids selection. In: Proceedings of the 5th International Conference on Methods and Systems of Navigation and Motion Control (MSNMC), pp. 32–35. IEEE, Kiev (2018). https://doi.org/10.1109/MSNMC.2018.8576293

Towards a Daily Agent-Based Transport System Model for Microscopic Simulation, Based on Peak Hour O-D Matrices

Ngoc-An Nguyen[1]([✉]) [iD], Cristian Poliziani[2] [iD], Joerg Schweizer[1] [iD],
Federico Rupi[1] [iD], and Virginia Vivaldo[1] [iD]

[1] Department of Civil, Chemical, Environmental and Materials Engineering, University of
Bologna, 40126 Bologna, Italy
ngocan.nguyen2@unibo.it
[2] Lawrence Berkeley National Laboratory, 1 Cyclotron Rd, Berkeley, CA 94720, USA

Abstract. This paper presents the development of a daily, large scale, agent-based microscopic transport simulation integrating diverse data-structures and including the following transport modes: car, bus, bicycle, motorcycle, and pedestrian. The daily simulation is built upon an already calibrated model for the morning peak hour of the city of Bologna, Italy. The transport supply integrates diverse open-source data such as OpenStreetMap (OSM), traffic light schemes and General Transit Feed Specification (GTFS). On the other hand, the transport demand is based on peak-hour Origin-Destination Matrices (ODMs) and uses traffic flow data extracted from detectors throughout the city to scale rush-hour trips accordingly and disperse their departing times over 24 h. The plan choice model is calibrated based on a simple utility function approach allowing to predict the latest city transport mode split. The model successfully distributes departure times of internal and external trips, compatible with absolute daily traffic flow profile from the detectors. A microscopic traffic simulation is executed at a 10% population demand. The validation process is then conducted by comparing the simulated and observed traffic flows at traffic counts by hour. Finally, total daily travel times by mode of individuals are interpreted and compared. The simulation outputs indicate significant differences in total daily travel time by mode. In particular, bus users have the longest travel time followed by cyclists, car drivers, motorcyclists and pedestrians. Therefore, the developed model is able to evaluate impacts of hypothetical scenarios over a day.

Keywords: daily agent-based model · activity-based model · microscopic simulation · multimodal simulation

1 Introduction

Travel demand estimation is a multifaceted challenge in transport planning. This requires accurate data on population, individuals and household demographic information, daily travel patterns, land-use characteristics, employment distribution, and a well-defined

© The Author(s), under exclusive license to Springer Nature Switzerland AG 2024
O. Gervasi et al. (Eds.): ICCSA 2024, LNCS 14813, pp. 331–345, 2024.
https://doi.org/10.1007/978-3-031-64605-8_23

transport network to build reliable travel demand models and forecasts. Since the 1950s, traditional four-step travel demand models (FSMs) have been a cornerstone of transportation planning. These trip-based models focus on estimation of travel demand between traffic analysis zones (TAZs) based on Origin-Destination Matrices (ODMs) and comprise four steps: trip generation, trip distribution, modal split, and route assignment. The shortcomings of the FSMs have been identified and discussed in different studies [1, 2]. A key limitation of FSM is its inability to capture individual 24 h trip patterns and trip chaining. Furthermore, new on-demand transport modes and traffic management systems cannot be modeled adequately, which severely limits the ability to predict the respective user behavior.

Activity-based models (ABMs) emerged in the 1970s to address the limitations of trip-based models. ABMs offer significant advancements, including the ability to model the location and timeline of trips made by a synthetic population throughout the day. ABMs can capture the sequential linkages of trips and are also highly sensitive to the changes of other factors that impact the daily travel behavior [3]. ABMs work at a disaggregate person-level rather than at an aggregate zone-level, like most trip-based models do [4]. Major challenges to move from a trip-based model to an activity-based model include the longer model runtimes (as each person needs to be simulated), more sophisticated hardware requirements, more and more detailed data requirements, larger efforts to calibrate, lack of experience with activity-based models, and lack of established software packages [3].

Thanks to the development of advanced computer-hardware and the availability of big-data resources, ABM models have been integrated into various traffic simulation packages as reported in [5]. The most popular modeling platforms are designed for microscopic traffic simulation such as SUMO and AIMSUN, while others are designed for mesoscopic simulation such as TRANSIMS, SimMobiity, BEAM CORE and MAT-Sim. These simulation platforms can estimate significant changes of individual activities and trips, in correspondence to changes of the transport supply, such as the introduction of new transport modes.

In our prior work, a large-scale, activity-based, micro-simulation model has been developed, improved and calibrated for the city of Bologna [6–8]. This peak hour model has been built by using the SUMOPy software, which is an advanced simulation suite for SUMO. The demand model is generated by disaggregating the morning peak hour O-D matrix for a wide variety of transport modes including car, bus, bicycle, motorcycle, and pedestrian. The supply model integrates data from diverse open sources and census data such as OpenStreetMap (OSM), General Transit Feed Specification (GTFS), GPS traces, traffic flow detectors, and traffic surveys.

This study aims at developing a large-scale, daily activity-based model for the city of Bologna. The demand generation leverages the existing peak hour ODMs and incorporates traffic flow data extracted from detectors throughout the city. Microscopic traffic simulation will be implemented using SUMOPy to analyze and validate the generated demand patterns and traffic profile. This model is expected to describe increasingly diversified and complex mobility patterns of every single person. Furthermore, it enables the evaluation of different implemented transport policies and the introduction of new transport modes.

The remaining parts of this paper are structured as follows: Sect. 2 reviews relevant existing research; Sect. 3 details the approach and methodology in developing the daily, activity-based microscopic model for the case of Bologna city; Sect. 4 and Sect. 5 present the simulation results and discussion; and Sect. 6 summarizes the conclusions and suggests and future work.

2 Related Work

The temporal dimension of transportation systems plays a crucial role in shaping travel behavior and traffic flow patterns. Traditional transportation models often overlooked the daily cycle, focusing instead on peak periods or average daily patterns. In this context, simulating a daily cycle becomes imperative for a comprehensive understanding of transportation dynamics.

The emergence of large-scale simulation tools and big data has spurred research efforts to refine the modeling of daily activity-based travel demand. These efforts leverage various simulation methodologies, ranging from macroscopic to microscopic scales, implemented by various simulation platforms.

Recent advancements have led to the development of daily activity-based models for entire countries like Switzerland [9] or the Greater Boston Area in the United States [10]. These models leverage mesoscopic agent-based modeling software including Sim-Mobility and MATSim or BEAM CORE to simulate multimodal trips. This capability enables a comprehensive analysis encompassing not only vehicular traffic, but also sustainable transport modes including public transit, cycling, and pedestrian. However, the main limitation of such mesoscopic simulations is the absence of direct vehicle to vehicle interaction in the form of vehicle following algorithms or interactions between pedestrians and vehicles.

The development of large-scale, daily microscopic simulation models remains limited in the scientific literature [11, 12]. It is noteworthy that none of these models incorporate a multimodal approach. The paper of Argota Sánchez-Vaquerizo et al. presents a daily microscopic simulation model of Barcelona but focusing solely on car traffic. Sánchez-Vaquerizo's study shares a similar methodology with the present work, in particular the reconstruction of the daily scenario from a disaggregated peak-hour ODMs uses a similar approach. The difference is that the present study utilizes traffic flow data acquired from induction loops, while the Barcelona scenario uses mobile-phone data to measure traffic intensity over the day.

3 Approach and Methodology

Figure 1 illustrates the methodological framework for developing the daily activity-based model employed in this study, which comprises transport models, key input data, analysis and outputs.

The Bologna metropolitan area, the capital of Emilia-Romagna, a region in northern Italy, is used as a case study. The city covers 3,703 km^2 with 1.02 million inhabitants, whereas the municipality itself covers 141 km^2 with 390,000 inhabitants and 2,769 inhabitants/km^2 in 2022 [13]. The core simulation area in the study is the city of Bologna and its surrounding towns with a total area of 50 km^2. The road network of the city of Bologna consists predominantly of motorways, major federal roads, provincial roads as well as urban roads, with a higher road density inside the outer ring road.

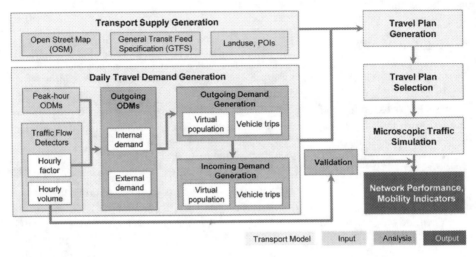

Fig. 1. Framework of developing daily activity-based model

Explanations of the study approach are presented in detail in the corresponding sections.

3.1 Transport Supply Generation

The daily supply model is developed based on the existing peak hour activity-based model [8], which is generated from various open sources and census data. The supply model consists of the road network (i.e. road links, nodes, lanes and associated attributes), the transit network (i.e. routes, stops and timetables) and the land use facilities (i.e. type, location, shape, size).

The road network was imported from OSM [14] - an open-source project that contains most of the transport network attributes, then converted to a SUMO-compatible XML format by means of the SUMO "netconvert" tool [15]. The SUMO-XML file provides a comprehensive geospatial dataset of the road network, including details on road links/edges, lane configuration, speed limits, access rights for various transport modes, lane connectivity, nodes/junctions, traffic lights and on-street parking. The network was then further refined with SUMO's "netedit" tool [16] based on satellite imagery, street-level view from Google Maps and on-site survey to capture the most up-to-date road network configurations. The road network of Bologna incorporates a detailed road network with 32,409 links, 14,724 intersections (including 530 signalized junctions) and 292,900 on-street parking spaces (see Fig. 2). In the micro-simulation network, each vehicle and person's location are uniquely identified by its road link/edge ID and its position along that edge.

The public transport model was developed based on the GTFS database, a common format used to represent all network and service information of a public transport system including routes, stops and stop-level timetables. The GTFS database was imported to SUMOPy by identifying bus stops ID and names on the corresponding edges. SUMOPy's map-matching procedure then identifies bus routes as sequences of these links and service frequency has been associated. Leveraging GTFS data from the open data of Trasporto Passeggeri Emilia Romagna (Tper) [17], the daily Bologna bus services was created. This resulted in a supply model with 234 urban bus lines, all with service times below 20 min.

Land-use facilities were also imported from the XML file, which was initially extracted from OSM, providing detailed information of land use attributes including type, shape and size. In addition, there are geo-referenced information extracted from the OSM data, which specify buildings or amenities, called "Points of interest" (POI). The POI associated with land-use facilities permits the association between the people's activities and facilities in the simulation area.

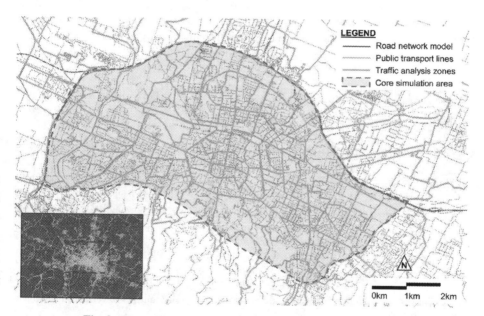

Fig. 2. Map of Bologna road network model and simulation area

3.2 Daily Travel Demand Generation

This section describes how daily travel demand is estimated based on peak hour data. Two key inputs are considered: peak hour ODMs and hourly traffic flows from road-side detectors. In particular, the daily commuting travel demand from 6:00 a.m. to 8:00 p.m. has been generated by disaggregating an updated morning peak hour ODMs (from 7:00 a.m. to 8:00 a.m.) and distributing based on the sum of hourly traffic flows.

The study utilized ODMs for the morning peak hour, obtained from the 14th population census of the city of Bologna [19]. Subsequent updates and disaggregation of these ODMs have been reported in [7, 8]. However, for computational reasons, the entire demand has been scaled down to 10%. In brief, the overall transport demand is composed of external trips (entering, leaving or crossing the study area) and internal travel demand originating and ending within the Bologna core area. The external demand is modeled by vehicular trips while internal demand is represented for active population within the study area.

Daily traffic volume profiles and hourly traffic volume factors within the study area were estimated based on 712 traffic flow detectors from traffic lights distributed across the city [18], as shown in Fig. 3a. The flow detectors measured daily traffic volumes by hour of cars, buses and trucks. The demand profile from traffic counts is computed by simply summing up the traffic counts of all detectors for each hour. Figure 3b shows the daily profile as the accumulated hourly traffic volumes measured by 712 traffic flow detectors on the working days in October 2022. The accumulated daily traffic vehicles passing through all the identified detectors are around 5.76 million vehicles per 24 h. In which, traffic volumes in morning (8:00 a.m. to 9:00 a.m.) and afternoon (5:00 p.m. to 6:00 p.m.) peak hours occupied 7.70% and 7.46%, respectively. The detector flows were further used in the validation process (see Sect. 4).

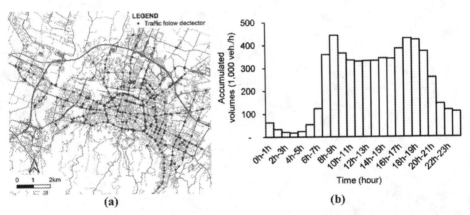

Fig. 3. The distribution of 712 flow measurement detectors in Bologna (a) and accumulated traffic volumes profile (b)

The 10% ODMs have been scaled by a factor equal to 6.37 – the hourly volume factor obtained from the daily traffic profile as shown in Fig. 3b, to generate the outgoing commuting demand during morning hours (i.e. home-to-work trips), matching the absolute traffic flow measured from traffic detectors up to 1:00 p.m. From each destination, an equivalent number of return trips has then been generated as evening incoming demand (i.e. work-to-home trips). This resulted in a replication of daily travel itineraries characterized by the home-work-home sequence as indicated in Fig. 4.

Successively, the outgoing and incoming trips departure times have been adjusted to reproduce the hourly demand profile extracted by the sum of traffic counts. In particular, we distributed departure times of the outgoing trips in the morning hours and incoming trips in the evening hours over the two respective, intersecting time intervals: the interval for the outgoing traffic has been fixed between 6:00 a.m. and 1:00 p.m., while the interval for the incoming traffic has been set between 10:00 a.m. and 8:00 p.m. The distribution of the number of trips departing during each hour for both intervals has been to match the distribution of the sum of detector flows.

In this way, the observed hourly flow profile is used to define the departure times to outgoing and incoming trips, for both, the trips linked to the internal and external transport demand.

Finally, to account for travel time of vehicles from origins to the traffic detectors, an estimated delay factor of 20 min for internal trips and 30 min for external trips was subtracted from all departure times to approximate the time vehicles required to reach the detectors which are predominantly located in central parts of the city.

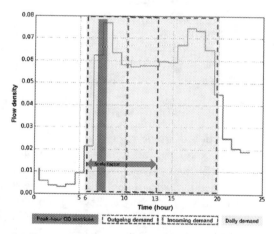

Fig. 4. Distribution of daily travel demand based on peak-hour OD matrix and detected traffic flow profile.

3.3 Travel Plan Generation

Once the departure times have been fixed, travel plans are generated for the internal synthetic population for different transport mode alternatives, based on vehicle availability. A plan is a sequence of elementary movements (e.g. walking, riding) to perform a door-to-door transfer between the location of two successive activities. The transport mode originally specified by the ODMs is initially kept as a "preferred" mode. During a plan choice calibration (see Sect. 3.4) agents can eventually change mode if a different mode will result in shorter (simulated) trips times or higher utilities with respect to the initial mode choice.

As a result of this initial demand generation, the down-scaled internal demand consists of 79,382 persons, which represents 10% of the active city population. In which, 205,500 plans were generated for 79,382 people, consisting of 18.52% car plans, 25.31%

bus plans, 11.53% bicycle plans, 6.01% motorbike plans and 38.63% walking plans. Note that plans are door-to-door and might involve multi-modality; for example, a bus or car user may also walk to a public transport stop or access a parked car before riding it. However, each plan has a dominant mode, so that plan choice and mode choice are interchangeable in the present context.

The down-scaled external demand is generated including 15,373 car and 1,075 motor-cycle trips between the urban and extra-urban areas, as well as between extra-urban areas passing through the core city area. These trips are modeled by a simple disaggregation of the relevant mode's OD matrix, with the distribution of edges within the zone of origin and destination determined by their length.

3.4 Travel Plan Selection

The mode choice model employed in this study seeks to accurately estimate mode shares as door-to-door timeframes become known as simulation result. The model assumes that a person's activity locations remain constant for the present calibration, except for travel times, which change depending on the mode choice. A maximum utility model has been used, with each mode's utility consisting of a mode-specific attribute and a time-dependent component, as summarized below:

$$U_{s,i} = \alpha_s - \beta T_{s,i} \qquad (1)$$

where: $U_{s,i}$ is the utility function of mode s for single person i; α_s is utility constant using mode s; $T_{s,i}$ is the door-to-door travel time using mode s of person i; and β is a value of time (VoT) for all people and modes.

The plan choice model is calibrated to reflect the latest mode share statistics of the city as reported in [13]. The calibration approach developed in [8] is utilized. In short, the calibration process involves two steps. In the first step, the travel times for all feasible mobility strategies for each individual are determined (either estimated free-flow travel times or executed travel times). This allows individuals to select feasible plans based on the utility function. In the second step, the model is iteratively calibrated to maintain the observed mode shares by swapping the selection of feasible mobility plans for each person. The utility parameters are then determined to minimize the difference between modeled and observed mode shares. Consequently, the utility function parameters are determined as presented in Table 1. The β value of 0.002 €/second has been used, based on relevant studies in Italy [20, 21].

Table 1. Parameters of the utility function to calibrate mode share model.

No	Mode	Car	Bicycle	Bus	Walking	Motorcycle
1	Utility constants α_s	0	−0.2604	1.855	2.016	−0.0761
2	Observed mode shares	35.60%	6.90%	25.60%	21.30%	10.60%
3	Calibrated mode shares	36.81%	6.70%	25.59%	20.41%	10.49%

3.5 Microscopic Traffic Simulation

The study uses the microscopic simulation suite SUMOPy/SUMO, basically the ones described in [8], which is able to track movements and interactions of every individual vehicle and person from origin to destination in desired time steps. The microscopic simulation models vehicle movements by considering factors like the vehicle speed, distance to the leader and desired speed to determine acceleration or deceleration as well as how vehicles interact with pedestrians at designated crossing points or shared areas. Given the low demand in the 10% population micro-simulation scenario, the shortest time routing approach was used to determine vehicle routes for all modes except buses, which have their fixed routes. In specific, the route of each vehicle and person is stochastically pre-determined before simulation by assigning shortest travel time with some randomness in the free-flow edge travel times.

4 Simulation Results

In this study, due to computational reasons, only 10% of the total demand has been simulated with an internal demand of 79,382 people and 6,448 external vehicles. During one microsimulation run in the relevant period from 6:00 a.m. to 8:00 p.m, the entire daily plan of each individual is simulated. One simulation run took approximately 12 h on a single core Intel i7 processor.

Figure 5 illustrates the successful distribution of departure times prior to simulation execution for the external trips and internal trips as modeled by virtual population compared to the accumulated traffic flow data collected from 712 actual detectors across the city. The values were normalized to constitute a consistent probability distribution. Travel demand exhibited a bimodal distribution, with peaks concentrated during the morning commute (7:00 a.m. to 10:00 a.m.) and the afternoon commute (4:00 p.m. to 8:00 p.m). These peak periods accounted for approximately 6% to 8% of the total daily demand. In contrast, the afternoon off-peak hours (10:00 a.m. to 4:00 p.m.) experienced a lower demand, ranging from 5% to 6% of the daily demand. Travel demand was lowest before the morning commute (prior to 7:00 a.m.) and after the evening commute (after 8:00 p.m.), constituting less than 5% of the total daily demand.

The validation procedure is carried out by comparing the simulated and observed hourly traffic flows across 712 network edges, in correspondence with the physical flow-detector locations. A linear regression is performed for hourly time intervals throughout

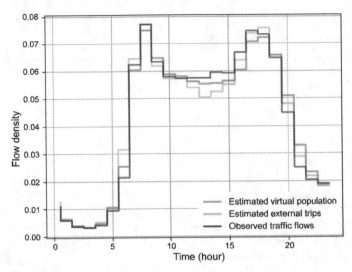

Fig. 5. Distribution of estimated external trips and virtual population departure time in comparison with detected flows over time.

the day. Table 2 illustrates the results of the regression analysis, while Fig. 6 shows the linear regression diagrams of different periods in a day. The results indicated that the slope (m) ranges from 0.082 to 0.129 and the intercept has relatively low values varying between 19 and 33 vehicles per hour. The variance between simulated and detected flows is relatively large, with typical values of R^2 between 0.28 and 0.35. An exception is the transition intervals at the beginning and end of the simulation period, with R^2 values below 0.2.

Table 2. Linear regression indicators of the simulated and observed traffic flows by hour.

No.	Time	Slope	Intercept	R^2
1	6:00–7:00	0.0904	23.788	0.1950
2	7:00–8:00	0.1165	32.471	0.3236
3	8:00–9:00	0.1268	30.073	0.3378
4	9:00–10:00	0.1283	26.265	0.3344
5	10:00–11:00	0.1260	25.607	0.3347
6	11:00–12:00	0.1169	26.233	0.3128
7	12:00–13:00	0.0940	19.161	0.3526
8	13:00–14:00	0.1022	22.602	0.3085
9	14:00–15:00	0.1116	25.380	0.3051
10	15:00–16:00	0.1297	25.839	0.2937
11	16:00–17:00	0.1105	23.927	0.2879
12	17:00–18:00	0.0901	24.419	0.3350
13	18:00–19:00	0.0959	23.324	0.2803
14	19:00–20:00	0.0822	21.607	0.3280

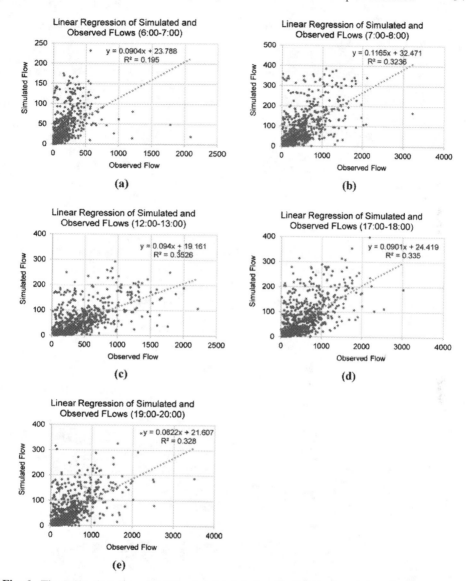

Fig. 6. The regression diagrams show the simulated traffic flow compared to the observed flow (vehicle/h) in early morning (a), morning peak (b), afternoon off-peak (c), afternoon peak (d) and early evening (e)

The door-to-door travel times of individuals in the simulated area were then compared. Table 3 presents the total finished trips associated with the mean, median and standard deviation of daily travel time of individuals by mode, while Fig. 7 shows the distribution of total travel times in interquartile ranges (IQRs). A total of 47,972 population trips were completed within the micro-simulation timeframe, representing a completion rate of 60% among the simulated population of 79,382 individuals.

Table 3. Number of simulated trips and total daily travel time by modes of individual in the daily simulation model

No.	Mode	Simulated trips (trip)	Mean (min/trip)	Median (min/trip)	Std. Deviation
1	Bus	7,342	70.4	67.5	27.7
2	Bicycle	3,295	51.5	44.5	27.6
3	Car	21,234	35.1	31.6	18.8
4	Motorcycle	5,254	20.5	19.5	8.2
5	Walking	10,847	12.9	4.9	16.6

It is noteworthy that the differences in total daily travel time of individuals by transport mode were significant. The simulation results showed that bus users have the longest travel time (mean: 70.4, IQR: 49.6–87.6 min/trip), followed by cyclists (mean: 51.5, IQR: 30.8–64.5 min/trip), car drivers (mean: 35.1, IQR: 24.1–40.9 min/trip), motorcyclists (mean: 20.5, IQR: 14.6–25.3 min/trip) and pedestrians (mean: 12.9, IQR: 2.5–17.9 min/trip).

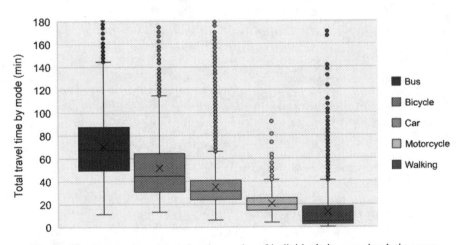

Fig. 7. The door-to-door travel time by modes of individuals in core simulation area

5   Discussion

The rich database leveraged from OSM and GTFS enables the generation of digital twins of the transport supply models. This is the foundation for building activity-based, agent-based transportation models. In particular, the combination of peak-hour ODMs and traffic flows from detectors has been used to determine the departure times over one day for both external trips and internal trips (e.g. the virtual population). This approach ensures that the distribution of departure times align with the city's daily traffic-flow profile. A plan choice model has been calibrated, which successfully reproduces the latest city modal split of the city of Bologna [13], thus providing a baseline for further analysis.

The model has been built and validated with only 10% of the city population demand. Literature suggests acceptable slope (m) values between 0.9 and 1.1 for a 100% demand scenario [22], which would translate into a range from 0.09 to 0.11 for a 10% demand. With these considerations, the found range shows plausible results, even though not entirely in the suggested interval.

The values of R^2 are expected to be low, as there is a systematic difference between the 100% demand and the 10% simulated demand, which increases the squared residuals in the R^2 function. Furthermore, the simulated network is almost uncongested, meaning that the vehicle's route choices correspond typically to the fastest route – which is in stark contrast with the real, congested network where edge travel times are increased and traffic flows are closer to a state of a user-equilibrium, especially during rush hours.

It is expected that the R^2 will improve considerably as the simulated demand approaches 100%. However, the simulation times for such a full-scale scenario are currently unacceptably long. Moreover, simulation time increases disproportionately when congestion occurs more frequently and the vehicle following algorithm needs to be executed more often for an increased number of vehicle-to-vehicle interactions.

SUMO is currently limited to a single core and several threats can be configured. However, in this case, the simulation has been unstable until recently. In any case, the computation time of the microsimulation should improve by an order of magnitude in order to be able to simulate daily multi-modal scenarios of large-scale urban areas. One possibility is the parallelization of the simulation kernel while using Graphical Processor Units (GPU), as demonstrated in [23].

The developed microscopic traffic simulation offers a significant advantage over classical, macroscopic traffic assignment methods because it outputs door-to-door travel times for various transportation modes, encompassing active mobility. This capability of accurately simulating daily door-to-door travel times facilitates the evaluation of the impacts of diverse transportation policy scenarios as well as the feasibility for individuals to make use of new, hypothetical transport modes.

6   Conclusion and Future Work

The present research addresses the current research gap in developing a daily, agent-based microscopic transport simulation for multiple transport modes including car, bus, bicycle, motorcycle and pedestrian. The daily macroscopic traffic simulation has been built upon an already calibrated model for the morning peak hour of the city of Bologna, Italy.

The model, based on the open-source micro simulator SUMO, incorporates transport supply, which has been created from various open-source data. OSM has been used to build the initial attribute-rich road network including traffic light schemes. The public transit services, including stops and timetables, have been built from the open access GTFS data of the local bus operator.

The daily transport demand has been generated based on peak hour ODMs and traffic flow data extracted from detectors located throughout the city to scale up and disperse their departing times. The disaggregated ODMs are used to generate a synthetic population and to determine the origins and destination of external trips. The daily trips are classified as outgoing trips (i.e. home-to-work as represented by the peak ODMs) and incoming trips (i.e. work-to-home as represented by the transposed ODMs) to represent the chained daily commuting patterns as home-work-home sequence. An estimated delay factor, subtracted from all departure times, for both internal and external trips has been applied to account for travel time of vehicles from origins to the traffic detectors. The model successfully distributed departure times of the synthetic population and external trips, compatible with absolute daily traffic flow profile from the detectors.

Travel plans for the internal synthetic population have been generated based on vehicle availability. The plan choice model has been calibrated based on a simple utility function approach, able to predict the latest city transport mode split. A microscopic traffic simulation has been executed at a 10% demand level. The validation process has been carried out by comparing the simulated and observed traffic flows from traffic counters on an hourly basis. The slope of the respective linear regression is between 0.082 to 0.129, which has been found reasonable for a 10% demand level. The R^2 values are generally low (between 0.28 and 0.35) because of the lower demand level and the absence of congestion effect of the simulated scenario. A simulation model of 100% travel demand expects to significantly improve these indicators. However, the simulation times for such a full-scale scenario are relatively high.

In order to use the microsimulation model also for congestion-sensitive applications, it is necessary to attempt to approach 100% demand levels. But at high demand levels, the computation time would become very high, even though multithreading will be possible with SUMO to a certain extent. However, another interesting development would be a complete parallelization, using hundreds or thousands of processors on a graphical processing unit.

Finally, the outputs of the model enabled to measure the door-to-door travel times for various transportation modes including active mobility. Total daily travel times of individuals are interpreted and compared for each transport mode. The simulation outputs indicate significant differences in total daily travel time by mode. In particular, bus users have the longest travel time followed by cyclists, car drivers, motorcyclists and pedestrians.

Acknowledgments. This research has been funded by the Italian PNRR program.

Disclosure of Interests. The authors have no competing interests to declare that are relevant to the content of this article.

References

1. Mladenovic, M., Trifunovic, A.: The shortcomings of the conventional four step travel demand forecasting process. J. Road Traffic Eng., January 2014

2. Chang, J., Jung, D., Kim, J., Kang, T.: Comparative analysis of trip generation models: results using home-based work trips in the Seoul metropolitan area. Transp. Lett. Int. J. Transp. Res. (2014). https://doi.org/10.1179/1942787514Y.0000000011

3. Moeckel, R., Kuehnel, N., Llorca, C., Moreno, A.T., Rayaprolu, H.: Agent-based simulation to improve policy sensitivity of trip-based models. J. Adv. Transp. (2020). https://doi.org/10.1155/2020/1902162

4. Delhoum, Y., et al.: Activity-based demand modeling for a future urban district. Sustainability 12(14) (2020). https://doi.org/10.3390/su12145821.hal-03364354

5. Bastarianto, F.F., Hancock, T.O., Choudhury, C.F., Manley, E.: Agent-based models in urban transportation: review, challenges, and opportunities. Eur. Transp. Res. Rev. 15(1) (2023). https://doi.org/10.1186/s12544-023-00590-5

6. Rupi, F., Bernardi, S., Schweizer, J.: Map-matching algorithm applied to bicycle global positioning system traces in Bologna. IET Intell. Transp. Syst. 10 (2016). https://doi.org/10.1049/iet-its.2015.0135

7. Schweizer, J., Rupi, F., Filippi, F., Poliziani, C.: Generating activity based, multi-modal travel demand for SUMO, pp. 118–101 (2018). https://doi.org/10.29007/794z

8. Schweizer, J., Poliziani, C., Rupi, F., Morgano, D., Magi, M.: Building a large-scale micro-simulation transport scenario using big data. ISPRS Int. J. Geo-Information 10(3) (2021). https://doi.org/10.3390/ijgi10030165

9. Scherr, W., Manser, P., Bützberger, P.: Simba Mobi: Microscopic mobility simulation for corporate planning. Transp. Res. Procedia 49(2019), 30–43 (2020). https://doi.org/10.1016/j.trpro.2020.09.004

10. Fournier, N., et al.: Integrated simulation of activity-based demand and multi-modal dynamic supply for energy assessment. In: IEEE Conf. Intell. Transp. Syst. Proceedings, ITSC, vol. 2018-Novem, pp. 2277–2282 (2018). https://doi.org/10.1109/ITSC.2018.8569541

11. Codeca, L., Frank, R., Engel, T.: Luxembourg SUMO Traffic (LuST) Scenario: 24 Hours of Mobility for Vehicular Networking Research. Ieee Vnc (2015)

12. Sánchez-Vaquerizo, J.A.: Getting real: the challenge of building and validating a large-scale digital twin of barcelona's traffic with empirical data. ISPRS Int. J. Geo-Information 11(1) (2022). https://doi.org/10.3390/ijgi11010024

13. Osservatorio PUMS. www.osservatoriopums.it/bologna

14. Open Street Map (OSM). www.openstreetmap.org

15. Eclipse, "SUMO netconvert," (2023). https://sumo.dlr.de/docs/netconvert.html

16. Eclipse, "SUMO netedit," (2023). https://sumo.dlr.de/docs/Netedit/index.html

17. Tper, "Bologna Bus Service GTFS," (2023)

18. Comune di Bologna, "Rilevazione Flusso Veicoli Tramite Spire - Anno 2022," (2022)

19. "Censimento Popolazione e Abitazioni" (2001). https://www.istat.it/it/archivio/3847

20. Wardman, M., Chintakayala, V.P.K., de Jong, G.: Values of travel time in Europe: review and meta-analysis. Transp. Res. Part A Policy Pract. 94, 93–111 (2016). https://doi.org/10.1016/j.tra.2016.08.019

21. Fezzi, C., Bateman, I.J., Ferrini, S.: Using revealed preferences to estimate the value of travel time to recreation sites. J. Environ. Econ. Manage. 67(1), 58–70 (2014). https://doi.org/10.1016/j.jeem.2013.10.003

22. Cascetta, E.: Transportation Systems Engineering: Theory and Methods (2001)

23. Yedavalli, P., Kumar, K., Waddell, P.: Microsimulation analysis for network traffic assignment (MANTA) at metropolitan-scale for agile transportation planning. Transp. A Transp. Sci. 18(3), 1278–1299 (2022). https://doi.org/10.1080/23249935.2021.1936281

Reinforcement Learning Applied to the Dynamic Capacitated Profitable Tour Problem with Stochastic Requests

Marvin Caspar[(⊠)] [iD] and Oliver Wendt[iD]

Business Information Systems and Operations Research (BISOR),
University of Kaiserslautern-Landau, Postfach 3049, 67653 Kaiserslautern, Germany
{marvin.caspar,wendt}@wiwi.uni-kl.de
https://wiwi.rptu.de/fgs/bisor

Abstract. This paper investigates the *Dynamic Capacitated Profitable Tour Problem with Stochastic Requests* (DCPTPSR), a variant of the *Traveling Salesman Problem* (TSP) with profits. In the DCPTPSR, online decisions must be made for accepting and scheduling requests over a finite number of periods. Requests follow a discrete-time stochastic process, and each request is characterized by a location, demand, and prize. Accepted requests must be served on a TSP tour such that the collected prize minus the transportation costs becomes maximal. The DCPTPSR has practical applications in food delivery and less-than-truckload transportation, where requests arrive in an online fashion and immediate decisions about acceptance and scheduling must be made. We model the DCPTPSR by a *Markov Decision Process* (MDP) and propose a *Stochastic Dynamic Programming* (SDP) algorithm for solving the problem to optimality. Addressing the computational challenges involved in SDP, we present a framework that integrates *Reinforcement Learning* (RL) as an alternative solution method. We perform an extensive numerical study where instances with up to incoming 25 requests can be solved by SDP while our RL approach can be used to adequately solve instances with even up to 100 incoming requests. Particularly, the performance of the RL approach is very close to the optimal policy by SDP and outperforms both the first come first serve heuristic and the first accept traveling salesman algorithm. The latter algorithm accepts requests if the available capacity enables it and fulfills these demands in an optimal TSP tour afterward. Especially instances with scarce capacity show considerable potential for savings in request acceptance and transportation scheduling decisions if both decisions are made simultaneously.

Keywords: Online Optimization · Profitable Tour Problem · Temporal Difference Learning · Stochastic Dynamic Programming

1 Introduction

Selecting from a sequential stream of requests those that maximize the expected total profit contribution is the main focus of revenue management (see [21]). The

O. Gervasi et al. (Eds.): ICCSA 2024, LNCS 14813, pp. 346–363, 2024.
https://doi.org/10.1007/978-3-031-64605-8_24

TSP with profits extends the well-known TSP by introducing a decision-making component for selecting requests and scheduling a tour to maximize profit [11]. However, in practical applications, e.g., less-than-truckload transportation (see [26]) or the scheduling of airline operations (see [35]), or in food delivery (see [39]) requests may not be known a priori and arrive in an online fashion. In such dynamic problems with stochastic incoming requests, the decision maker must immediately decide which requests to accept while anticipating the optimization problem (e.g., a TSP) that results from accepted requests. RL with the integration of neural networks enables the processing of huge amounts of information and can provide a generic and flexible framework for such request acceptance decision-making under uncertainty (see [7]).

In this paper, we address the research topic of online optimization in the capacitated profitable tour problem and make the following contributions. We provide a formulation of the DCPTPSR by an MDP and determine different request acceptance policies to maximize the expected profit over a time horizon. Since SDP cannot determine an optimal policy for all possible DCPTPSR instances in a reasonable time due to finite computation resources, inspired by related works and their success (as exemplified by [7,10]), we propose an approach that leverages reinforcement learning to outperform different straightforward greedy approaches. For managerial insights, we perform a sensitivity analysis on the DCPTPSR concerning the number of incoming requests and available capacity to determine the benefit of simultaneous compared to subsequent request acceptance and tour scheduling decisions.

The remainder of this paper is organized as follows. In Sect. 2, we provide a brief overview of results in the areas of revenue management, tour scheduling, and reinforcement learning. Furthermore, we state relevant literature that addresses request acceptance decisions under uncertainty in the background of tour problems. Section 3 shows a precise problem description and provides a Markov decision process formulation for the DCPTPSR and discusses the huge complexity of such a stochastic dynamic decision problem. In Sect. 4, we see how SDP and our RL approach can be used to maximize the expected profit in the DCPTPSR over a time horizon. Section 5 presents detailed results of our computational experiments where both solution methods are benchmarked with a first come first serve heuristic and a first accept traveling salesman algorithm. Finally, a conclusion and open questions are discussed in Sect. 6.

2   State of the Art: Related Research Fields

2.1   Revenue Management and Routing Problems with Profits

Revenue management is the process of allocating capacity to the right kind of customer at the right price to maximize sales or revenue [18]. Products that successively lose their ability to provide utility over time or decay entirely, called perishable products (see [32]) should be considered separately to maximize profit.

Especially airlines and hotels need to decide about request acceptance or rejection and how to allocate this potential demand in case of request acceptance to fixed capacity to maximize profit (see [21]).

Request acceptance decisions about continuous and independent arrival processes can be modeled as a *Markov Decision Process* (MDP) and solved to optimality by *Stochastic Dynamic Programming* (SDP) via a complete or implicit enumeration of the solution space [1]. Such dynamic decision problems under uncertainty can be represented by a tree structure where the edges represent the decisions, called actions $(a_1, a_2, ..., a_{|T|} \in A)$, and the nodes denote the system states $(s_1, s_2, ..., s_{|T|} \in S)$ called state space over a finite time horizon T with $|T| \in \mathbb{N}_{>0}$ discrete periods. For optimizing decisions, we define the reward $(R_1, R_2, ..., R_{|T|} \in R)$ that values a decision taken at a specific state over T. Furthermore, let us assume that there is no uncertainty about the number of requests that will be received over a given time horizon T and each request gets a backward-counting index $t \in T$ stating that after the request in period t, another $t - 1$ requests over $t - 1$ periods will arrive.

In the following example, let us consider six discrete capacity units, which will provide a service at a future point in time. Capacity units can be sold individually or bundled, i.e., the remaining capacity always takes one of the seven values of the state space $S := \{0, 1, 2, 3, 4, 5, 6\}$. Exactly one of three different types of requests $i \in 1, 2, 3$ can arrive in a period $t \in T$, which are specified by an (arriving probability, requested quantity d_i, revenue r_i) with $F_1 = (0.5, 1, 1), F_2 = (0.3, 2, 4)$, and $F_3 = (0.2, 3, 9)$. Now the task is to either accept or reject the stochastic incoming request in a period $t \in T$ to maximize the reward over T.

To find an optimal decision, not only the type of requests and the remaining available capacity are relevant at each period t. In case of rejecting the request at period t, the value $V_{t-1}(cap)$ of the remaining capacity cap available for the $t-1$ remaining requests, and the value $V_{t-1}(cap - d_i)$ of cap reduced by the capacity requirement d_i of the current request type i in period t in case of acceptance becomes essential. A request in period t should be accepted if:

$$R_t + V_{t-1}(cap - d_i) \geq V_{t-1}(cap)$$

and is otherwise rejected. Accordingly, in each period t, given a remaining capacity cap such a decision must be made. The optimal decision for the period $t = 1$ and thus $V_1(cap)$ can be calculated since no further requests are received and requests smaller than or equal to the remaining capacity cap are accepted. Based on this, it is also possible to determine an optimal decision for period $t = 2$. Now in period $t = 2$, the question of saving capacity at period $t = 1$ arises for the first time. Let $Pr(cap, a, cap')$ represent the transition probability from remaining capacity cap to a remaining capacity cap' under an action a (accept or reject). The expected reward at period $t = 2$ depends on the expected generated revenue $r_2(cap, a)$ at this period (either 0 or the revenue of the currently accepted request) and the value of the residual capacity $V_1(cap')$ resulting from period $t = 1$, with cap' indicating the new residual capacity for the next period:

$$V_2(cap) := \max_a \{ r_2(cap, a) + \sum_{cap'} Pr(cap, a, cap') V_1(cap')] \}$$

Consequently, for each possible state $cap \in S$, we need to find an optimal action a to maximize the reward, respectively the overall revenue.

Assuming that such requests come from different locations, it becomes necessary to simultaneously plan a tour to satisfy the demand of these accepted requests. The *Traveling Salesman Problem* (TSP) is the NP-hard problem of finding the shortest or cost-optimal Hamiltonian cycle in a graph, that starts at the depot, travels through all accepted requests, and ends at the depot.

In the class *Traveling Salesman Problem with Profits* (TSPPs) (refer to [11]) as in the *Vehicle Routing Problem with Profits* (VRPPs) (refer to [30]), we need to decide which customers to serve and how to sequence these accepted visits in an optimal tour under various possible objectives. The *Orienteering Problem* (OP) is about maximizing profit under an upper bound of given tour costs. Acceptance and rejection decisions also occur in the *Prize-Collecting TSP* (PCTSP), where we collect a prize for visiting a location and pay a penalty for unvisited locations under the objective of maximizing profit minus travel costs under a minimum total collected profit. Maximizing a weighted objective function of distance by subtracting traveling costs from the total collected profit is pursued in the *Profitable Tour Problem* (PTP) which constitutes the basis for our DCPTPSR. The authors in [30] stated, that most existing literature treats the single-vehicle case for the PTP, whereby a current overview of PTP works can be found in [9]. A recent and comprehensive survey of literature that integrates revenue and demand management with tour scheduling decisions is available in [12].

2.2 Reinforcement Learning

Problems in revenue management and tour scheduling problems under uncertainty with large instances usually cannot be solved efficiently by classical optimization as stochastic dynamic programming due to their complexity and resulting computational effort [28]. Reinforcement learning endeavors to maximize the cumulative generated reward $R_{ss'}^a = \mathbb{E}\{R_{t+1} | a_t = a, s_t = s, s_{t+1} = s'\}$ based on each period t as a result of selecting the action a_t which maximizes the expected reward at time t, given state s_t. With probability $Pr_{ss'}^a = Pr\{s_{t+1} = s' | s_t = s, a_t = a\}$ under the assumption of an MDP, the system transitions from state s to state s'. The transition probabilities only depend on the current state and action, not on process history. To determine optimal actions, a complete enumeration of the state space or a heuristic that allows the exclusion of suboptimal regions becomes necessary. Let $\gamma \in [0, 1]$ be the discount rate and an admissible way to find optimal results in this context is the Bellman equation (see [5]):

$$V^\pi(s) = \mathbb{E}_\pi\{R_t | s_t = s\} = \mathbb{E}_\pi \left\{ \sum_{k=0}^{\infty} \gamma^k \ R_{t+k+1} | s_t = s \right\} \tag{1}$$

A decision policy π defines a probability distribution over all possible actions in a state s. The state value $V^\pi(s)$ is defined as the expected sum value of the possible discounted state value $V^\pi(s')$ of the next state s' and the immediate expected reward in period $t+1$ following policy π. Unlike the state value $V^\pi(s)$, the action value $Q^\pi(s,a)$ of a policy π is directly related to the action a chosen in s:

$$Q^\pi(s,a) = \mathbb{E}_\pi \left\{ \sum_{k=0}^\infty \gamma^k \ R_{t+k+1} | s_t = s, a_t = a \right\}$$

The unchosen paths according to the policy π are not included in calculating $Q^\pi(s,a)$. However, at each following decision level, the Eq. (1) is used to determine the state value for the next state s'. To find a policy that maximizes $V^\pi(s)$, we define optimal state and action values:

$$V^{\pi^*}(s) = \max_a \{r(s,a) + \gamma \ V^{\pi^*}(s')\}$$

$$Q^{\pi^*}(s,a) = \mathbb{E}\{R_{t+1} + \gamma \ V^{\pi^*}(s_t+1) | s_t = s, a_t = a\}$$

A specific decision policy π, that is followed until the end of the episode, usually does not lead to an optimal solution. Varying this policy π to π' in state s can result in an improvement of $V^\pi(s)$, which also holds for applying the new policy π' in all further decision situations. The so-called policy improvement theorem (see [28]) proves that an iterative improvement of policy π to π' is possible if the value function $V^\pi(s)$ of policy π in node s is known and, a selection of the optimal policy for the next node in each visited state s is possible:

$$\pi'(s) = \max_a Q^\pi(s,a) = \max_a \sum_{s'} Pr_{ss'}^a (R_{ss'}^a + \gamma \ V^\pi(s'))$$

$$V^{\pi'}(s) = \sum_{s'} Pr_{ss'}^a (R_{ss'}^a + \gamma \ V^\pi(s'))$$

Once a policy π is improved to π' using $V^\pi(s)$, a new value function $V^{\pi'}(s)$ can be determined, which may be used later to improve π' to π'' and so on. This constant alternation of evaluation and improvement can approximate the optimal policy π^* (see [28]).

To learn an appropriate policy for revenue management and tour scheduling problems, there are numerous different reinforcement learning algorithms with a recent review in the field of transportation in [10].

In this work, we focus on *Temporal Difference* (TD) learning (see [28]) that learns value functions $V^\pi(s)$ of states gradually from current estimations and adjusts predictions not only when the reward is received, but after each action. TD learning has already been applied to revenue management for the dynamic pricing of information services (see [27]) and the VRP with time windows and stochastic customers (see [17]) or the multiple depot VRP (see [4]). Recently the authors in [20] have employed TD learning to address the online vehicle dispatching problem to serve stochastic on-demand customers efficiently.

2.3   Related Literature: Uncertainty in Tour Problems with Request Acceptance Decisions

This paper addresses the dynamic capacitated profitable tour problem with stochastic requests wherein the challenge is to simultaneously decide to accept or reject stochastic arriving requests with unknown location, demand, and revenue and how to schedule them in an optimal tour in case of acceptance over a finite number of periods. Deciding about request acceptance under uncertainty in the background of tour problems has already been addressed several times in literature.

Within the domain of TSPPs and VRPPs, stochastic variants are relatively limited, primarily centered around the OP. The authors in [29] are the first ones that integrate stochastic service times in the OP. Other contributions consider stochastic travel times in the OP (e.g., [8,31]). The authors in [15] formulate an OP with stochastic profits, where the objective function becomes to maximize the probability that the collected profit over all accepted customers exceeds a predefined target. The work [36] addresses a PCTSP with stochastic customers, where customer presence is uncertain but their locations are a priori known. The paper [37] treats a probabilistic PTP, where each customer requests a service with a given probability. Recently [2] introduced a probabilistic PTP where customers show up with a known probability after the tour is planned, while the objective becomes to maximize the expected net profit.

The online TSP with rejection options was treated by [16], where rejecting requests leads to a penalty. The authors regard a basic online version where requests can be accepted at any time after arrival and a real-time version where a decision about incoming requests must be made immediately. In [38] the authors extend this TSP with rejection options by time windows and build a framework to solve the problem by combining reinforcement learning with a greedy heuristic to outperform a tabu search heuristic. Recently [19] modeled the integrated demand-management and online tour scheduling problem as an MDP. Here the provider decides on a subset to offer in response to an incoming customer request and also selects a price for each delivery option with a delivery deadline by a fleet of vehicles.

The TSP can be reformulated as a single machine scheduling problem when interpreting distances as sequence-dependent setup times (see [13]). In *Order Acceptance and Scheduling* (OAS) problems, there is a trade-off between gaining revenue and diverting capacity from other orders by simultaneously scheduling them on machines. Uncertainty in OAS literature is usually not modeled as a sequential stochastic decision process but rather as a combinatorial or *Mixed-Integer Linear Programming* (MILP) optimization problem over a given set of orders with uncertainty relating to their attributes (see [23]). The authors in [23] consider uncertainty in processing and service durations in a stochastic OAS where a set of resources must process a set of orders. Each order with a due date is processed on one resource with a fixed cost, while tardy delivery of orders causes penalties. On the one hand, the authors formulate a deterministic version as a MILP model and also give a formulation with constraint programming. On the other hand, they regard a two-stage stochastic model, a robust model, a polyhedral-interval robust model, and a box robust model. As a notable exception [34] does present a model aggregating uncertainty about future requests that follow a Poisson distribution and present an MDP formulation. However, several differences still prohibit direct comparison with our model. Most notably their use of fixed product classes with fixed revenue and orders that have due dates and setup times do not reduce the profit by incurring any cost.

Concerning this state of research, we formulate to the best of our knowledge for the first time (inspired by the work in [33]) the *Dynamic Capacitated Profitable Tour Problem with Stochastic Requests* (DCPTPSR), where stochastic incoming requests must be accepted or rejected and an optimal tour through the locations of these accepted requests must be scheduled.

3   The Dynamic Capacitated Profitable Tour Problem with Stochastic Requests (DCPTPSR) Formulation

3.1   Problem Description

There is a depot location (l_0) hosting a vehicle with a maximum capacity of $C \in \mathbb{N}$ units over a finite time horizon $T = \{0, ..., T_d\} \subset \mathbb{N}$. Let $T_d \in \mathbb{N}_{>0}$ be the number of decision periods. In every decision period $t \in T \setminus \{0\}$ exactly one random request $[p, d, l]_i \in N$ with $i \in \{1, ..., |N|\}$ out of a request pool N arrives that demands a discrete positive quantity $d_i \in \{1, ..., C\}$ of the capacity C and yield a positive prize p_i (called revenue in the area revenue management) in case of acceptance. The same requests can occur several times in different periods and represent a discrete-time stochastic process. For each of these T_d stochastic incoming requests, we must dynamically decide whether to accept or reject the specific request and must plan a tour for the vehicle that visits all accepted request locations starting and ending at the depot. After rejecting or accepting such a request, there is no further possibility to alter the decision. Thus, the state space of the previous revenue management problem from Sect. 2.1 extends by a ($|N| + 1$)-dimensional bit vector of the depot location l_0 and the request locations $l_i (i \in \{1, ..., |N|\})$. A cost-optimal tour through all these accepted requested locations (1 bits in vector *loc*) under consideration of the residual capacity must be determined to achieve a maximum contribution margin (refer to the traveling salesman problem in [13]). This contribution margin is the sum of all accepted requests' prizes minus the costs incurred by the tour that starts and ends at the depot l_0 depending on the distance between the locations.

Let us extend and visualize the example from Sect. 2.1 to the DCPTPSR by adding a depot (l_0) and eight potential locations for customer requests ($|N| = 8$), which are arranged as shown in Fig. 1.

Accepting request type F_2 from location l_5 would result in a negative contribution margin since the new optimal tour would become $\{l_0, l_2, l_5, l_0\}$ and increase transportation costs by $\sqrt{18} \approx 4.24$, which would not be compensated by the additional prize of $p_5 = 4$ from accepting this request from location l_5.

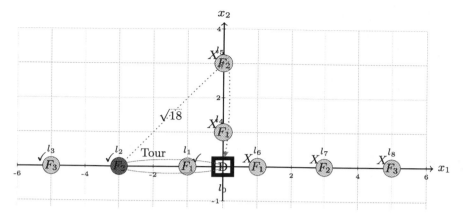

Fig. 1. State after acceptance of request type F_2 at l_2 with a remaining capacity of three capacity units. The current optimal tour is $\{l_0, l_2, l_0\}$.

Similarly, requests from locations in other directions than the already accepted location l_2 would also result in negative contribution margins (see X in Fig. 1). Here it is obvious that if the number of future requests yet to arrive is sufficiently high and the residual capacity is larger than three, the optimal strategy waits for a request type F_3 from the same cardinal direction. Only requests from the same direction can reduce the additional transportation costs to zero and maximize the total contribution margin.

3.2   Problem Formulation

In the following, we formulate the DCPTPSR as a MDP.
States: We denote cap as the residual capacity and loc as a binary vector with length $|N| + 1$ stating if a location must be visited or not over any period $t \in T$. The state space becomes the combination of all possible residual capacities cap and location vectors loc by $s_t = (cap, loc)$, with

- $t \in \{T_d, ..., 1\}$ is the down-counting index of periods that indicates the number of remaining requests, respectively, decision periods.
- cap states the current available residual capacity.
- loc is a binary vector with length $|N| + 1$. An entry of 1 at position i in loc shows that the location of request i must be visited in the tour. The first entry of loc is always 1 ($loc[0] = 1$) since it states the depot location where the tour must start and end

There is the initial state $s_{T_d} = (C, [1, 0, ...0])$ with start capacity C and where the first request will arrive. A terminal state where no more request arrives is given by s_0.
Actions: At each decision period $t \in \{1, ..., T_d\}$, a random request $[p, d, l]_i \in N$ arrives in the current state s_t and determines the actual action space A_s. This set A_s contains the request acceptance action $a_p \in \{0, 1\}$:

- A0: Requests can always be rejected. In case of rejection ($a_p = 0$), the residual capacity and accepted request locations for the next state s_{t-1} remain unchanged, without receiving any prize ($s_{t-1} = s_t$).
- A1: The incoming request $[p, d, l]_i \in N$ in decision period t can only be accepted ($a_p = 1$), if the residual capacity in the next state s_{t-1} holds $cap = cap - d_i \geq 0$ for this period $t - 1$.

Transitions: Between two states s_t and s_{t-1} with $t \in T \setminus \{0\}$ a transition occurs. If a request $[p, d, l]_i \in N$ arrives in period t, a decision a_p becomes necessary. The state transition principle for the DCPTPSR becomes:

- $1 \leq t \leq T_d$: If the current random request $[p, d, l]_i \in N$ with $i \in \{1, ..., |N|\}$ is accepted ($a_p = 1$) in s_t, the next state becomes $s_{t-1} = (cap - d_i, loc)$ with $loc[i] = 1$ since this accepted request location l_i must be part of the tour.
- $1 \leq t \leq T_d$: If the current random request $[p, d, l]_i \in N$ is rejected ($a_p = 0$) in state s_t, the next state stays the same with $s_{t-1} = s_t$.
- $t = 0$: No further requests will arrive and s_0 is the terminal state.

Rewards: The action-dependent rewards accrue to request acceptance decisions in every decision period $t \in T \setminus \{0\}$:

- $R_t^{A0}(s_t, a_p) = 0 \quad \forall a_p = 0, t \in T \setminus \{0\}$: the current request $[p, d, l]_i \in N$ in period t is rejected and no immediate reward follows with the same residual capacity and accepted request locations as in the period before.
- $R_t^{A1}(s_t, a_p) = p_i - \Delta_{TC}(loc, loc|\{loc[i] = 1\}) \quad \forall a_p = 1, t \in T \setminus \{0\}$: the current request $[p, d, l]_i \in N$ in period t is accepted and an immediate reward by the actual request prize p_i minus the additional transportation cost $\Delta_{TC}(loc, loc|\{loc[i] = 1\})$ due to this additional request location follows.

Policy: A policy $\pi(s_t) : S \longrightarrow A_s$ is a function that maps each state to an action. In the DCPTPSR the objective is to find the best action in each state to maximize the cumulative reward over the time horizon T.

Objective Function: Thus the objective function of the DCPTPSR becomes:

$$\max_{\pi(s_t)} \mathbb{E} \left\{ \sum_{t \in T \setminus \{0\}} R_t(s_t, \pi(s_t)) \right\}$$

and an appropriate policy must be found.

Value Function: To evaluate individual states a value function $V_t(cap, loc)$ represents the objective function value that can be expected at each decision period t. Let $Pr([p, d, l]_i)$ represent the probability that request $[p, d, l]_i \in N$ arrives in period t, the calculation of $V_t(cap, loc)$ can be expressed by:

$$V_t(cap, loc) = \begin{cases} -\infty & \forall cap \notin (\mathbb{R}_0^+), t \in T, \\ 0 & \forall cap \in (\mathbb{R}_0^+), t = 0, \\ \sum\limits_{[p,d,l]_i \in N} Pr([p, d, l]_i) \max\limits_{a_p \in \{0,1\}} \{a_p \cdot p_i - \Delta_{TC}(loc, loc|\{loc[i] = 1\}) \\ \qquad\qquad + V_{t-1}(cap - a_p \cdot d_i, loc|\{loc[i] = 1\})\} & \text{else} \end{cases}$$

with $\Delta_{TC}(loc, loc|\{loc[i] = 1\})$ determining the non-negative value difference between an optimal tour through loc and loc with $loc[i] = 1$.

Thus an exact computation of $V_t(cap, loc)$ requires the best acceptance decision in each decision period under the assumption that the optimal tour is determined through all accepted request locations. In each decision period t, the number of possible states is a function of the number $|N|$ of requests in the request pool and all possible tours through the accepted requests. Since one of the $|N|$ different requests can arrive and must be accepted or rejected in every decision period and these accepted request locations can be arranged in up to $T_d!$ possibilities within a tour, there are up to $(|N| \cdot 2 \cdot T_d!)^{T_d}$ possible states until a terminal state after the last decision period is reached. The astronomical complexity of such a dynamic stochastic decision problem becomes apparent since already a request pool of $|N| = 10$ and 10 decision periods ($T_d = 10$) leads up to $(10 \cdot 2 \cdot 10!)^{10} \approx 4.05 \cdot 10^{78}$ possible states until a terminal state. To solve such a complex problem as the DCPTPSR, we will show an optimal and two approximate solution methods in the following section.

4   Solution Methods for the DCPTPSR

In order to solve the DCPTPSR, we propose a stochastic dynamic programming algorithm and a temporal difference learning algorithm.

4.1   Stochastic Dynamic Programming

As already discussed in Sect. 2.1, dynamic and stochastic decision problems usually can be modeled by an MDP and solved to optimality by SDP. One concrete technique to solve such a value equation $V_t(cap, loc)$ of the DCPTPSR is an iterative algorithm known as SDP value iteration. Value iteration solves the value function $V_t(\cdot)$ by setting up a recurrence relation for which the Bellman equation (1) is a fixed point, while this iteration converges to the optimal value function $V_t^\star(\cdot)$ for arbitrary start values $V_0(\cdot)$ (see [6]). The value iteration iterates over all periods t, and all possible requests in N that can arrive in each period t. For all possible states and all possible arriving requests in a decision period t, we must check if the corresponding request can be accepted. If the acceptance is possible, the value $V_t(cap, loc)$ must be updated according to the higher value increase between accepting and rejecting the current request i. Let $\Delta_{TC}(loc', loc)$ be a function that returns the additional cost of the optimal TSP tour with location vector loc' (including the location of this new request location) compared to the optimal TSP tour with location vector loc. Acceptance of the request i leads to a value increase of $Pr(loc, a_p, loc')(p_i + V_{t-1}(cap', loc') - \Delta_{TC}(loc', loc))$ with new residual capacity cap' and new location vector loc'. In the case of rejection, $V_t(cap, loc)$ is increased by $Pr(loc, a_p, loc)V_{t-1}(cap, loc)$, since cap and loc remain unchanged. Algorithm 1 provides a generic description of how to solve the value equation $V_t(cap, loc)$ by such an SDP value iteration.

Algorithm 1: A Stochastic Dynamic Programming Algorithm as value iteration for the DCPTPSR

---

1 **Function** iterative_sdp($T, S_{|T|+1}, N$):
2   Initialize $V_t(cap, loc)$ arbitrarily for every period $t \in T$ and state (cap, loc)
   for *each period $t \in T$* **do**
3   **for** *each possible request $[p, d, l]_i \in N$* **do**
4   **for** *each possible state (cap, loc)* **do**
5   **if** $cap - q \geq 0$ **then**
6   Update loc' according to l_i
7                $V_t(cap, loc)+ = max\{V_{t-1}(cap, loc), p_i + V_{t-1}(cap -$
               $d_i, loc') - \Delta_{TC}(loc', loc)\}Pr(loc, a_p, loc')$
8   **else**
9                $V_t(cap, loc)+ = V_{t-1}(cap, loc)Pr(loc, a_p, loc)$

10   **return** $V_t^\star(cap, loc)$

Such problems as the DCPTPSR usually cannot be solved efficiently by SDP (see Algorithm 1) due to their complexity and resulting computational effort. For this reason, approximate solution methods for the DCPTPSR become inevitable.

4.2   Temporal Difference Learning for the DCPTPSR

As part of reinforcement learning, TD learning can learn directly without a model of the environment by updating an existing estimate in every time step without waiting for a final outcome (see [28]). Unlike the state value $V^\pi(s)$, the state action value $Q^\pi(s, a)$ of a policy π is directly related to the action a chosen in state s and a simple one step TD learning (called TD(0)) makes the update using the estimate $Q(s_{t+1}, a_{t+1})$, receiving reward R_{t+1} and learning rate α:

$$Q^\pi(s_t, a_t) = Q(s_t, a_t) + \alpha \left(R_{t+1} + \gamma Q(s_{t+1}, a_{t+1}) - Q(s_t, a_t)\right) \qquad (2)$$

Algorithm 2: Temporal Difference Algorithm TD(0) (see [28])

---

1 Initialize $Q(s, a)$ arbitrarily
2 **for** *each episode* **do**
3   Initialize s
4   Choose a from s using policy derived from Q (e.g., ϵ-greedy)
5   **for** *each step (period) of this episode* **do**
6   Take action a, observe reward R, and next state s'
7   Choose $a' \in A(s')$ using a policy derived from Q (e.g., ϵ-greedy)
8       $Q(s, a) = Q(s, a) + \alpha(R + \gamma Q(s', a') - Q(s, a))$
9       $s = s', a = a'$
10   **until** s is the terminal state

11 **return** Q

With probability $\epsilon \in (0, 1]$, we explore by selecting a random action from the action space, and with probability $1 - \epsilon$ we select a greedy action every time a request arrives. The corresponding policy iteration algorithm for the *Temporal Difference* TD(0) procedure estimating Q is stated in Algorithm 2:

For our DCPTPSR model, we set the discount rate to $\gamma = 1$ and after each incoming request, we must take an action, while in case of acceptance, we need to calculate the cost of integrating this request at an optimal position in the TSP tour. After observing the reward and the new state, we update the state action function according to the TD(0) rule (2) and iterate forward until the terminal state is reached.

For higher numbers of requests and capacity, several obstacles e.g., memory limits or residual value function information compression prohibit the explicit representation of the residual value function. In this context, reinforcement learning in connection with neural networks is worth highlighting and can lead to human-level performance and even beyond [22,28]. Thus, we investigate how the TD approach (Algorithm 2) performs in the DCPTPSR when we use an *Artificial Neural Network* (ANN), respectively a multi-layer perception (see [24]) with three layers. Hereby, input neurons represent the current available residual capacity *cap* and the location vector *loc* and there is a time neuron specifying the remaining number of requests. A single output neuron represents the remaining value determined by the values of the input neurons and the corresponding neurons in the hidden layer. Each time a request arrives, the ANN determines the residual value for two different (cap, loc) combinations, one for acceptance and one for rejection. The difference between these outputs determines the acceptance or rejection decision for this request, considering its immediate reward.

5   Computational Experiments and Results

This section compares the performance of the TD algorithm with SDP and two algorithms in several different experimental environments.

5.1   Experimental Setup

All experiments were performed on an Intel(R) Core(TM) i7-10750H CPU with 2.60GHz and access to 4 cores and 16 GB of RAM. The TD and SDP algorithm implementation was done in Java 16. We implemented the other two algorithms for benchmarking in Python 3.9 and used the branch-and-cut solver Gurobi Optimizer 10.0 [14] with a time limit of 6 h using 4 threads. Furthermore, the highly optimized Google OR-tools v9.7 [25] for finding optimal TSP tours is used.

Since the DCPTPSR is to the best of our knowledge addressed for the first time and there are no suitable benchmark test instances, we extend and test instances from the Capacitated Vehicle Routing Problem Library (CVR-PLIB) available at http://vrp.galgos.inf.puc-rio.br/index.php/en/. The chosen instances are taken from different sets and include up to 100 requests varying in request location, demand, and prize while arriving requests are independent and uniformly distributed. The procedure for generating the prize p_i of request i is similar to [3] with $p_i = h \cdot d_i$, where h is an integer random number uniformly generated in the interval $[1, 10]$.

We use four different algorithms to solve these DCPTPSR test instances:

- A first come first serve heuristic accepts over the T_d decision periods every stochastic incoming request if the available capacity enables it and schedules a tour according to the sequence of these accepted requests.
- The first accept traveling salesman algorithm accepts every stochastic incoming request if the capacity enables it and determines an optimal TSP tour through all these accepted request locations.
- Stochastic dynamic programming can solve some instances to optimality in an appropriate computation time (see Algorithm 1).
- A temporal difference learning algorithm with a 3-layer ANN is trained to mimic the value function (see Algorithm 2).

Preliminary experiments with the TD learning algorithm have shown that 128 neurons in the hidden layer of the neural network and a learning rate α of 0.05 with an $\epsilon = 0.1$ greedy strategy lead to promising results for our test instances. Each instance undergoes 5,000,000 training episodes and subsequent validation in 1,000,000 episodes.

5.2   Results of the Experiments

Within the first experimental part, we consider different test scenarios with up to 25 stochastic incoming requests, where it is possible to benchmark the reinforcement learning approach with the optimal solution by SDP given our computational resources. The first column states the instance with the pool size of requests and the capacity of the vehicle. Column two states the first come first serve heuristic solution and the third column gives the first accept traveling salesman algorithm solution. In column four we see the SDP solution Z^*, while the fifth column displays the needed computation time with Algorithm 1 in seconds. The sixth and seventh columns show the solution Z_{TD} of the TD Algorithm (see Algorithm 2) and the needed computation time. In the last column (Perf.) we see the ratio of the reinforcement learning solution Z_{TD} and the SDP solution Z^*.

Table 1 shows that our TD learning approach (see Algorithm 2) strongly outperforms the FCFS heuristic and the FATS algorithm and reaches on average around 98 % of the optimal solution obtained by SDP in only around 4 % of this SDP computation time. The FATS algorithm shows an average improvement of around 26 % compared to the FCFS heuristic in these instances, which underlines the importance of a subsequent tour optimization after accepting random incoming requests. Especially instances with smaller capacity ($C = 50$) show that a significant increase in profit is possible if acceptance and transportation scheduling decisions are made simultaneously (Z^*) compared to sequentially

Table 1. Numerical results for the DCPTPSR with varying T_d.

Id	Instance ($|N|, C$)	FCFS	FATS	SDP		TD		
		Z_{FCFS}	Z_{FATS}	Z^*	t	Z_{TD}	t	Perf.(%)
	$T_d = 5$							
1	A-n32-k5 (16,50)	15.74	48.39	118.65	7298 s	117.38	71 s	98.9
2	A-n32-k5 (16,100)	100.08	176.58	245.67	16993 s	239.88	142 s	97.6
3	E-n51-k5 (14,50)	35.33	40.48	96.43	762 s	95.14	47 s	98.9
4	E-n51-k5 (14,100)	104.96	126.43	152.46	1975 s	151.13	94 s	99.1
5	M-n101-k10 (10,50)	72.37	73.69	127.12	764 s	126.08	90 s	99.2
6	M-n101-k10 (10,100)	171.76	176.61	213.26	1827 s	209.96	207 s	98.5
7	P-n101-k4 (14,50)	98.88	116.92	231.71	1340 s	229.14	80 s	98.9
8	P-n101-k4 (14,100)	204.15	243.25	369.73	3144 s	364.65	152 s	98.6
	$T_d = 10$							
9	E-n51-k5 (14,50)	37.70	44.64	130.63	1548 s	128.87	87 s	98.6
10	E-n51-k5 (14,100)	127.39	159.16	265.99	4039 s	260.57	173 s	98.0
11	M-n101-k10 (10,50)	74.02	75.30	159.41	1519 s	157.88	167 s	99.0
12	M-n101-k10 (10,100)	213.31	219.81	311.39	3683 s	308.32	403 s	99.0
13	P-n101-k4 (14,50)	85.29	124.92	292.36	2707 s	282.57	155 s	96.7
14	P-n101-k4 (14,100)	265.88	352.37	573.85	6391 s	559.62	279 s	97.5
	$T_d = 25$							
15	E-n51-k5 (14,50)	38.25	46.12	165.80	3860 s	159.85	152 s	96.4
16	E-n51-k5 (14,100)	126.59	162.25	397.23	9329 s	376.95	297 s	94.9
17	P-n101-k4 (14,50)	102.20	130.99	361.16	6644 s	349.62	231 s	96.8
18	P-n101-k4 (14,100)	257.08	363.92	759.43	15782 s	718.82	502 s	94.7
Avg.	-		118.39	148.99	276.24	4978 s	268.69	185 s	97.9

(Z_{FATS}). Overall, the TD algorithm shows on average an 80 % profit increase compared to the FATS algorithm over the instances in Table 1.

To demonstrate the superiority of our TD algorithm in the DCPTPSR, we further extend the previous instances to up to 100 stochastic incoming requests and benchmark the results with the FCFS heuristic and the FATS algorithm. In analogy to the previous experiments, the last column (Imp.) of Table 2 shows the improvement in percentage between Z_{TD} from the fifth column and the solution of the FATS algorithm in column three.

Table 2 also clarifies for these instances, that our TD learning approach dramatically outperforms the FCFS heuristic and the FATS algorithm. In particular, the TD learning approach shows a significantly greater improvement over the FATS algorithm for instances with 100 stochastic incoming requests than for instances with 25 stochastic incoming requests. For these instances, the Z_{TD} solution is around 33 % better on average compared to Z_{FATS}.

Table 2. Numerical results for the DCPTPSR with varying T_d.

Id	Instance ($|N|, C$)	FCFS	FATS	SDP		TD		
		Z_{FCFS}	Z_{FATS}	Z^* t	Z_{TD}	t	Imp.(%)
				$T_d = 25$				
19	A-n32-k5 (16,100)	176.12	325.26	-	-	376.79	325 s	15.8
20	A-n32-k5 (16,300)	1027.54	1471.47	-	-	1522.91	956 s	3.5
21	M-n101-k10 (10,100)	212.69	219.45	-	-	393.42	621 s	79.2
22	M-n101-k10 (10,200)	499.79	513.48	-	-	713.26	3213 s	38.9
23	E-n51-k5 (14,300)	557.46	681.25	-	-	703.45	756 s	3.3
24	P-n101-k4 (14,300)	1418.08	1580.49	-	-	1647.24	2668 s	4.2
				$T_d = 100$				
25	A-n32-k5 (16,100)	179.11	330.97	-	-	546.71	612 s	65.2
26	A-n32-k5 (16,300)	1046.89	1491.04	-	-	1975.67	1878 s	32.5
27	M-n101-k10 (10,100)	211.81	218.40	-	-	401.27	1527 s	83.7
28	M-n101-k10 (10,200)	503.88	517.86	-	-	757.75	12782 s	46.3
29	E-n51-k5 (14,100)	216.75	223.25	-	-	412.80	78 s	84.9
30	E-n51-k5 (14,300)	562.17	684.47	-	-	1306.78	1748 s	90.9
31	P-n101-k4 (14,100)	395.40	452.08	-	-	748.61	775 s	65.6
32	P-n101-k4 (14,300)	1443.72	1606.93	-	-	2201.54	4859 s	37.0
Avg.	-	570.09	736.89	-	-	979.16	2343 s	46.5

To highlight the effective optimization process of our reinforcement learning algorithm we investigate learning curves of the TD algorithm (see Algorithm 2). Figure 2 shows the training process over 5,000,000 episodes for instance with Id 16 with $T_d = 10$ and instance Id 31 with $T_d = 100$ stochastic incoming requests, by analyzing the average objective value after each 10,000 independent episodes during the training process. A local regression for each 500 points is performed in Fig. 2 to clarify the graphical illustration.

Figure 2 shows that, at the beginning of the training process, the TD algorithm is unable to perform well, as actions are chosen randomly and the neural network is initialized with random weights. However, in the left diagram of Fig. 2(a) a performance of almost 96% is already achieved after 2,000,000 training episodes, which only increases marginally with the remaining 3,000,000 training episodes. By contrast, we see in the right diagram of Fig. 2(b) where 100 stochastic requests arrive that after 5,000,000 training episodes no clear convergence behavior can be observed and further training could probably still improve the performance.

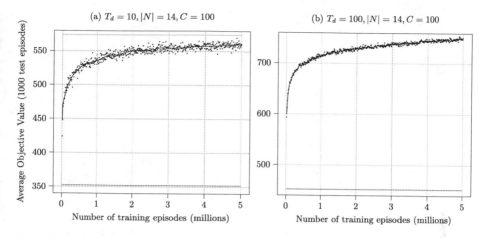

Fig. 2. Training evaluation of instance 16 (a) and 31 (b). On the x-axis, is the number of training episodes, and on the y-axis, is the average objective value over 1000 test episodes. The black dots indicate the average objective value for the TD algorithm, while the black line shows a local regression and the red line indicates the SDP solution (if found within the computational resource limit). (Color figure online)

6   Conclusion and Future Research

In this paper, we investigated the *Dynamic Capacitated Profitable Tour Problem with Stochastic Requests* (DCPTPSR) where requests characterized by a location, demand, and prize follow a discrete-time stochastic process and online decisions must be made for accepting and scheduling requests over a finite time horizon. In Sect. 2, we examined the decision-making process for accepting stochastic incoming requests within the context of revenue management and clarified the connection between tour problems with profits. Additionally, we briefly discussed reinforcement learning as a potential solution method for such problems. In Sect. 3, we described the DCPTPSR, emphasizing its objective of finding an optimal tour through all locations of the accepted requests, and contributed a Markov decision process formulation for the problem. Section 4 described how *Stochastic Dynamic Programming* (SDP) can solve the DCPTPSR to optimality. Given the inherent complexity of the problem and the computational demands associated with SDP, we proposed *Temporal Difference* (TD) learning in combination with a neural network as a solution method for the DCPTPSR. Our computational experiments in Sect. 5 demonstrated that our TD learning approach for the DCPTPSR heavily outperforms a first come first serve heuristic and the first accept traveling salesman algorithm even after relatively few training episodes. Thus we conclude that request acceptance and transportation scheduling decisions should be made simultaneously to achieve an appropriate solution quality in such a dynamic problem with stochastic incoming requests.

Building on the obtained results in the DCPTPSR, ongoing work should study the corresponding extended problem version with multiple vehicles. Furthermore regarding the promising performance of TD learning in the DCPTPSR it is worthwhile to analyze if such a solution method is also useful for other similar dynamic and stochastic problems in the area of revenue management or tour scheduling problems.

References

1. Alstrup, J., Boas, S., Madsen, O.B., Vidal, R.V.: Booking policy for flights with two types of passengers. Eur. J. Oper. Res. **27**(3), 274–288 (1986)
2. Angelelli, E., Mansini, R., Rizzi, R.: The probabilistic profitable tour problem under a specific graph structure. arXiv (2022)
3. Archetti, C., Feillet, D., Hertz, A., Speranza, M.G.: The capacitated team orienteering and profitable tour problems. J. Oper. Res. Soc. **60**, 831–842 (2009)
4. Bdeir, A., Boeder, S., Dernedde, T., Tkachuk, K., Falkner, J.K., Schmidt-Thieme, L.: RP-DQN: an application of Q-learning to vehicle routing problems. In: Edelkamp, S., Möller, R., Rueckert, E. (eds.) KI 2021. LNCS (LNAI), vol. 12873, pp. 3–16. Springer, Cham (2021). https://doi.org/10.1007/978-3-030-87626-5_1
5. Bellman, R.: Dynamic programming. Science **153**(3731), 34–37 (1966)
6. Bertsekas, D.: Dynamic programming and optimal control: Volume I, vol. 4. Athena scientific (2012)
7. Bondoux, N., Nguyen, A.Q., Fiig, T., Acuna-Agost, R.: Reinforcement learning applied to airline revenue management. J. Revenue Pricing Manag. **19**(5), 332–348 (2020)
8. Campbell, A.M., Gendreau, M., Thomas, B.W.: The orienteering problem with stochastic travel and service times. Ann. Oper. Res. **186**(1), 61–81 (2011)
9. Caspar, M., Schermer, D., Wendt, O.: Formulations for the split delivery capacitated profitable tour problem. In: International Conference on Computational Science and Its Applications, pp. 82–98. Springer, Cham (2023). https://doi.org/10.1007/978-3-031-36805-9_6
10. Farazi, N.P., Zou, B., Ahamed, T., Barua, L.: Deep reinforcement learning in transportation research: a review. Transp. Res. Interdisciplinary Perspectives **11**, 100425 (2021)
11. Feillet, D., Dejax, P., Gendreau, M.: Traveling salesman problems with profits. Transp. Sci. **39**(2), 188–205 (2005)
12. Fleckenstein, D., Klein, R., Steinhardt, C.: Recent advances in integrating demand management and vehicle routing: a methodological review. Eur. J. Oper. Res. **306**(2), 499–518 (2023)
13. Gilmore, P.C., Gomory, R.E.: Sequencing a one state-variable machine: a solvable case of the traveling salesman problem. Oper. Res. **12**(5), 655–679 (1964)
14. Gurobi Optimization, LLC: Gurobi Optimizer Reference Manual (2023)
15. Ilhan, T., Iravani, S.M., Daskin, M.S.: The orienteering problem with stochastic profits. IIE Trans. **40**(4), 406–421 (2008)
16. Jaillet, P., Lu, X.: Online traveling salesman problems with rejection options. Networks **64**(2), 84–95 (2014)
17. Joe, W., Lau, H.C.: Deep reinforcement learning approach to solve dynamic vehicle routing problem with stochastic customers. In: Proceedings of the International Conference on Automated Planning and Scheduling, vol. 30, pp. 394–402 (2020)
18. Kimes, S.E.: Yield management: a tool for capacity-considered service firms. J. Oper. Manag. **8**(4), 348–363 (1989)

19. Klein, V., Steinhardt, C.: Dynamic demand management and online tour planning for same-day delivery. Eur. J. Oper. Res. **307**(2), 860–886 (2023)
20. Liang, E., Wen, K., Lam, W.H., Sumalee, A., Zhong, R.: An integrated reinforcement learning and centralized programming approach for online taxi dispatching. IEEE Trans. Neural Networks Learn. Syst. (2021)
21. McGill, J.I., Van Ryzin, G.J.: Revenue management: research overview and prospects. Transp. Sci. **33**(2), 233–256 (1999)
22. Mnih, V., et al.: Human-level control through deep reinforcement learning. Nature **518**(7540), 529–533 (2015)
23. Naderi, B., Begen, M.A., Zhang, G.: Integrated order acceptance and resource decisions under uncertainty: Robust and stochastic approaches. SSRN (2022)
24. Pal, S.K., Mitra, S.: Multilayer perceptron, fuzzy sets, classifiaction. IEEE Trans. Neural Networks (1992)
25. Perron, L., Furnon, V.: Or-tools. google. OR-Tools v9.7 (2023)
26. Sawadsitang, S., Kaewpuang, R., Jiang, S., Niyato, D., Wang, P.: Optimal stochastic delivery planning in full-truckload and less-than-truckload delivery. In: 2017 IEEE 85th Vehicular Technology Conference (VTC Spring), pp. 1–5. IEEE (2017)
27. Schwind, M., Wendt, O.: Dynamic pricing of information products based on reinforcement learning: a yield-management approach. In: Jarke, M., Lakemeyer, G., Koehler, J. (eds.) KI 2002. LNCS (LNAI), vol. 2479, pp. 51–66. Springer, Heidelberg (2002). https://doi.org/10.1007/3-540-45751-8_4
28. Sutton, R.S., Barto, A.G.: Reinforcement Learning: An Introduction. MIT Press (2018)
29. Tang, H., Miller-Hooks, E.: Algorithms for a stochastic selective travelling salesperson problem. J. Oper. Res. Soc. **56**(4), 439–452 (2005)
30. Toth, P., Vigo, D.: Vehicle routing: problems, methods, and applications. SIAM (2014)
31. Verbeeck, C., Vansteenwegen, P., Aghezzaf, E.H.: Solving the stochastic time-dependent orienteering problem with time windows. Eur. J. Oper. Res. **255**(3), 699–718 (2016)
32. Weatherford, L.R., Bodily, S.E.: A taxonomy and research overview of perishable-asset revenue management: yield management, overbooking, and pricing. Oper. Res. **40**(5), 831–844 (1992)
33. Wendt, O., Goeke, D.: Revenue Management für tourenplanungsprobleme. In: Gössinger, R., Zäpfel, G. (eds.) Management integrativer Leistungserstellung, Festschrift für H. Corsten., vol. 168, pp. 455–486. Duncker-Humblot GmbH (2014)
34. Xu, L., Wang, Q., Huang, S.: Dynamic order acceptance and scheduling problem with sequence-dependent setup time. Int. J. Prod. Res. **53**(19), 5797–5808 (2015)
35. Yan, S., Tang, C.H., Fu, T.C.: An airline scheduling model and solution algorithms under stochastic demands. Eur. J. Oper. Res. **190**(1), 22–39 (2008)
36. Zhang, M., Qin, J., Yu, Y., Liang, L.: Traveling salesman problems with profits and stochastic customers. Int. Trans. Oper. Res. **25**(4), 1297–1313 (2018)
37. Zhang, M., Wang, J., Liu, H.: The probabilistic profitable tour problem. Int. J. Enterprise Inf. Syst. (IJEIS) **13**(3), 51–64 (2017)
38. Zhang, R., Prokhorchuk, A., Dauwels, J.: Deep reinforcement learning for traveling salesman problem with time windows and rejections. In: 2020 International Joint Conference on Neural Networks (IJCNN), pp. 1–8. IEEE (2020)
39. Zheng, J., et al.: Modeling stochastic service time for complex on-demand food delivery. Complex Intell. Syst. **8**(6), 4939–4953 (2022)

Generative Methods for Planning Public Transportation Systems

Aleksandr Morozov$^{(\boxtimes)}$, Polina Krupenina , Roman Bashirov ,
Valentina Soloveva , Vasilii Starikov , and Sergey Mityagin

ITMO University, Birzhevaya line, 14, Saint Petersburg, Russia
asmorozov@itmo.ru

Abstract. This paper considers a method for generating new bus routes
to optimize the transport connectivity of an area and the average travel
time, based on the use of a genetic algorithm on the intermodal graph of
public transport. This method is intended to identify the potential of the
transport system and routes for development by assessing and optimizing
the integral accessibility and connectivity of the area. For this purpose,
data on city blocks are collected and assembled into a network model.
The calculation of public transport travel time between blocks is done
using an intermodal graph. The result of the work is a new network of
optimal bus routes proposed by the algorithm. The proposed method
makes it possible to model on available open data the changes of the
public transport system for further development with change assessment.

Keywords: Public transport · Network model · Transport
connectivity · Generative approach · Genetic algorithm

1 Introduction

One of the key components of a city is transport system, which can be defined as a
complex network of interconnected elements designed to facilitate the movement
of people and goods. In assessing the quality of life in cities, it is important to
consider the presence of efficient and well-planned public transport networks,
which play an important role in ensuring sustainable urban development and
addressing the challenges of urbanization.

Important indicators for assessing the performance of transport in a city
can be the transport accessibility and connectivity of territories. Transportation
accessibility affects several aspects of citizens' lives. For example, increased supply affects the active lifestyles of citizens, as low-income groups or those who use
private transportation may be more likely to walk to bus stops [1]. Also, better
provision of transportation increases employment in certain neighborhoods. In
addition, lack of mobility can cause social exclusion, whereby people are excluded
from participating in the economic, political and social life of the community
[2,3]. To improve these indicators, optimization of the public transport system
is necessary.

O. Gervasi et al. (Eds.): ICCSA 2024, LNCS 14813, pp. 364–378, 2024.
https://doi.org/10.1007/978-3-031-64605-8_25

Addressing the optimization of public transport system is not just important; it is a pressing necessity in the current urban landscape. With the ongoing challenges of population growth and increased urbanization, the strain on existing public transport networks continues to escalate. Overcoming the reluctance of individuals to utilize public transport is crucial for the sustainable development of urban areas. The issues of overcrowded vehicles, inconvenient schedules, and slow speeds contribute to this reluctance, highlighting the immediate need for a solution [4]. Delays in resolving these challenges can exacerbate environmental issues, such as air pollution and traffic congestion, further impacting the overall quality of urban life.

Optimizing public transport systems can motivate people to switch from private cars to public transport, minimizing environmental damage from air pollution and reducing traffic. Existing methods of optimization and planning of public transport routes usually consider total costs, which include time costs. However, such modeling is resource-intensive both in terms of computational power and availability of the necessary data.

Urban planners also rely on transportation connectivity and average travel time to analyze transportation infrastructure, when making decisions about urban spatial development [5]. Depending on the objectives, the transport connectivity of urban areas can be defined differently. In this paper, connectivity is inseparable from accessibility, it reflects how different parts of a city or area are connected through the time cost of travel.

The purpose of this study is to develop a generative method for planning and optimizing public transportation systems by generating new transportation routes based on existing ones using a genetic algorithm. The optimality criterion is the average travel time, which is calculated from the connectivity matrix of a given area. The proposed method is designed to determine the potential of the public transport system and routes for development. Since full-scale transport modeling is long and expensive, and sometimes it is not clear whether it is time and whether it is worth doing. Therefore, a method is needed to assess whether it makes sense to invest in large-scale transformations or not.

2   Related Works

2.1   Optimization of Transport Systems

In the main problems of transport assessment in cities, the object under consideration is the transport system or transport model. The city transport model is a mathematical and computational representation of the system of transportation and traffic in the city [6]. It is intended for analysis, forecasting and optimization of transport infrastructure and traffic in the city.

The goal of transport system optimization is to enhance the overall functionality and effectiveness of transportation services. The resulting transport system should achieve several key objectives [7]:

– efficient resource utilization;

- minimized travel time;
- adaptability to passenger demand;
- enhanced accessibility;
- costs reduction;
- improved connectivity;
- enhanced customer experience;
- equitable distribution of services.

There are many approaches to describe transportation systems, including flow modeling to find optimal states. According to the level of detail, they can be divided into several groups: macroscopic, microscopic and mesoscopic [8]. Macroscopic methods include those that treat the flow of vehicles as an indivisible unit. These include peer models, the system dynamics model and traditional four-step transportation models [9]. Among the disadvantages of this type of models are their relative inaccuracy and static results with high calculation speed and low requirements for computational resources.

Microscopic models describe the behavior of individual flow participants and their interactions. Microscopic methods include agent-based modeling [6] known as multi-agent simulations for transportation networks [10]. Methods of this type require extensive input data and large computing power, but the results obtained are characterized by high accuracy. Mesoscopic methods combine the above approaches describing the behavior of individual agents and considering their behavior at the macroscopic level. An example of such a method is the gravity model and entropy model [11]. This type of model is often used in public transportation route planning problems. Despite their comparative compactness, mesoscopic models have disadvantages in the form of a small number of parameters for tuning and limited application.

Transportation demand modeling is an important component of transportation models. It can be done by several methods, including real-time traffic demand modeling and the use of mobile data [12–14].

A logical extension of the transportation demand modeling task is the problem of planning and optimization of public transport routes, commonly known as the transportation routing problem. Representing a variation of the traveling salesman problem, it is an NP-hard problem whose solution can be approximated using combinatorial optimization algorithms.

To solve this problem the method of branches and bounds can be used, but only with a small number of vertices it is effective if a transportation network is represented as a graph. Approximate metaheuristic approaches were used to solve the transportation routing problem [15]. Also, the papers mention the use of graphical methods and nomograms that demonstrate less efficiency [16]. Passenger flow density, total time spent by passengers, number of transfers, costs of transport organizations can be chosen as an optimality criterion.

2.2 Public Transport Routes Planning

The organization of an urban public transport system is based on the following input parameters: public demand, geographical characteristics, available transport quantity [17]. The objective is to create a set of routes and associated schedules and to allocate transportation units to these routes.

A more detailed route planning problem is to design a network of public transport stops and lines covering the maximum area, prioritizing direct trips with the shortest distances and minimizing the number of routes and their total length [18]. The solution to the problem is based on the processing of data on the existing road network, potential bus stop locations and transfer zones, the location of parking lots and public transportation service areas [19].

To identify the network of routes that best satisfy public demand, origin-destination (OD) matrices are used to describe the relationship between passengers' origin and destination points and reflect various parameters, such as the travel time spent between these points or the value of demand for such a route obtained through surveys or big data technologies [13,20].

There are several approaches to solve the transportation network design problem, detailed in survey papers [17,21,22]. The mathematical approach aims to find the best solution based on certain criteria such as minimizing travel time, route length [23], number of stops [24] and operating costs, maximizing coverage area. Since mathematical methods aim at finding the best solution, they require high time and computational resources.

Heuristic methods solve this problem by offering not the best but a "near-optimal" solution. They can be used to sequentially remove routes of a fully connected network, or to sequentially add them to an initially empty network [25].

According to the researches [26–28] traditional methods were replaced by generative metaheuristic methods (GA, SA, ASO). This shift is explained by the complexity of the problem, which can be described as NP-hard.

Generative approaches use automated processes to create numerous designs to address a specific problem, continuing until predefined conditions are met. The generative design offers significant advantages over traditional workflows, with a diversity of outputs being a standout feature [29]. It excels, especially in tackling complex, high-dimensional solution spaces that are often encountered in multi-objective and multi-criteria design problems. By incorporating objectives and constraints into the alternative generation or evaluation processes, the generative design enables the effective resolution of multifaceted problems with reasonable computational efforts and results.

Genetic algorithm is used as one the base of the scaled-down transport system [30]. The instance dataset is created by scaling down the street network as well as transforming pre-existing routes to fit it. This methodology is applied to Nottingham, UK, to create a benchmark dataset for bus route optimization. The paper employs a genetic algorithm tailored for restricted route start and end points. The optimization results are compared with actual bus routes in Nottingham, demonstrating the potential of this network design method for improving public transport systems. When a non-dominated sorted genetic algorithm is used, the initial population is randomly generated, focusing on demand satisfaction with the lowest transfer rate possible [31]. Genetic algorithms are widely used to optimize public transport route networks in agent-based models [32,33].

3 Method for Generating Public Transportation Routes

The objective of this paper is to develop a method for generating new public transport routes to optimize the transport connectivity of an area and the average travel time using open data. The optimization model is represented by the formula 1. This approach, despite its importance, has not been widely adopted in the existing literature.

$$\mathbf{mean}(C) = \frac{1}{n^2} \sum_{i=1}^{n} \sum_{j=1}^{n} c_{ij} \to \min \tag{1}$$

where

- C - connectivity matrix;
- n - number of zones in the selected territory;
- c_{ij} - travel time between zones of origin i and destination j.

The planning of potential public transport routes involves complex transport modeling that requires a large amount of data and computational power to assess the effects of potential transformations on the territory. The proposed method allows generating a new route and/or modify an existing one and see how it affects the accessibility of an area, using open available data.

Transport connectivity refers to the mutual transport accessibility of urban areas. Optimizing connectivity between city blocks holds paramount importance for several reasons. Firstly, efficient inter-blocks connectivity is instrumental in fostering economic growth and development by facilitating the seamless movement of goods, services, and human resources. A well-optimized network ensures that various city districts are interconnected, promoting accessibility and reducing transportation barriers. Secondly, optimizing connectivity enhances overall urban mobility, providing residents with reliable and convenient transportation options. This, in turn, contributes to improved quality of life, reduced travel times, and increased accessibility to essential services and amenities across different areas.

All computations are performed on a block-network model of the city [34], a simplified representation of the city to speed up the calculation of various indicators. The model is assembled using the BlocksNet library [35] and represents a set of city blocks in a given area, which are connected by paths calculated using an intermodal graph of public transport [36]. The method was tested on the territory of Vasilievsky Island, St. Petersburg, Russia's second most populous city.

3.1   Data

To model a given area and its public transportation, open data from Open-StreetMap are used [37], which are automatically collected using modules in the BlocksNet library. Using the urban blocks generation method, a geo-layer with blocks, the minimum spatial unit for urban environment evaluation, is obtained. The result is presented in Fig. 1a.

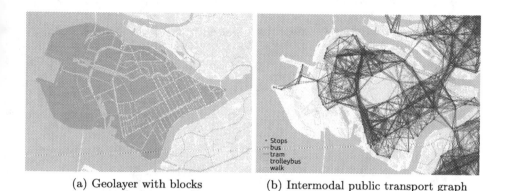

(a) Geolayer with blocks   (b) Intermodal public transport graph

Fig. 1. Input data

An intermodal graph is collected for transportation assessment. The edges of this graph are the pedestrian ways, and public transport routes are the nodes are the points of connection between the pedestrian sections and public transport stops (Fig. 1b). The graph contains the routes of buses, trams and trolleybuses. Travel delays due to traffic congestion are not considered in the graph. Each mode of public transport in the intermodal graph along the edge without taking into account traffic jams with a fixed averaged speed, which was taken from the estimation of the developers of this graph [36].

As an optimality criterion, we propose a value of the average block connectivity of a city or given area [5], obtained using the BlocksNet library and representing the average travel time between all possible pairs of city blocks using all available travel modes. Bus routes were taken for optimization. To evaluate the performance of the bus route system, we developed a fitness function that calculates the average blocks connectivity by combining a modified bus route with an unchanged part of the original intermodal graph containing information about other types of transportation and unchanged bus routes.

3.2   Description of the Optimization Method

Bus network modification consists of sequential route optimization, which involves removal and addition of new direct routes (edges) between pairs of existing stops (nodes) during the genetic algorithm, which will be described below.

The modified routes are later combined into a common new intermodal graph (Fig. 2).

The graph of the street-road network is used to obtain travel time information on the new edges. The transport speed for new edges to the optimized graph is taken to be the same as in the initial intermodal graph described above. If a pair of stops is not directly connected by an edge, the vertices of the street-road network graph that are closest to the ones under consideration are found, and the shortest travel time is found using Dijkstra's algorithm and summing the weights of the found edges. Figure 3 shows the mutual layout of bus stops and nodes of the street-road network graph used to create new edges. To make the genetic algorithm work quickly, the fully connected graph of all possible connections between bus stops can be calculated in advance if the area under consideration is small.

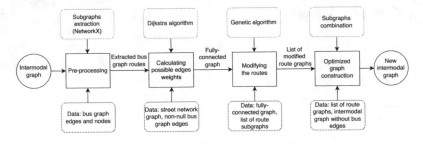

Fig. 2. Optimization algorithm block diagram

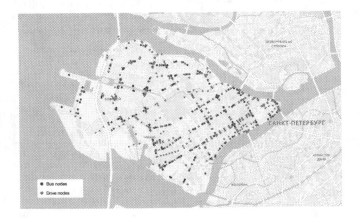

Fig. 3. Mutual location of bus stops and nodes of the street-road network graph

A genetic algorithm (GA) was chosen as a generative method, obtaining an optimal solution from the initial one over several iterations. Possible solutions (instances of the modified bus route graph) are represented as individuals subject to iterations (eras) of evolution. As the initial population for the algorithm, N modifications of the existing bus route are generated, obtained by replacing a random edge with a pair of edges, containing a new bus stop.

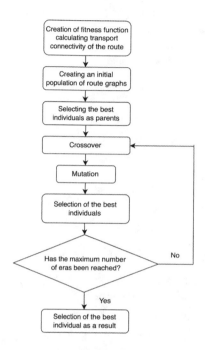

Fig. 4. Genetic algorithm block diagram

For each individual, the value of the fitness function is calculated, and 50% of individuals are selected as parents to create offspring using a tournament selection algorithm. Each pair of parents is formed from the best individuals from two random subsets of the initial population of a given size T.

After selecting pairs of parent individuals, the crossover is carried out between them: a list of edges of a parent is created, after which a random separator index is selected, according to which both lists are divided into two parts, which form a new pair of individuals after recombination.

With probability p, mutation is applied to each individual: random removal and addition of new edges, as described above. The routes obtained are combined with the initial population, and among them, the fittest ones are selected based on the value of the fitness function. If the condition for stopping the algorithm (a given number of iterations k) is not reached, a new era of choosing pairs of parents, crossing and mutation is started. The result of applying the algorithm is an individual with the best value of the fitness function (Fig. 4).

4   Experiments

4.1   Single Route Optimization

To test the method, the genetic algorithm was applied to a single bus route №220 in a given area (Fig. 5a). In different experiments, the route modification options may vary due to the stochastic nature of the generation algorithm. Figure 5b shows the modified route. As can be seen, the new route makes two "duplications" - it drives to stops that are close to other stops on its route.

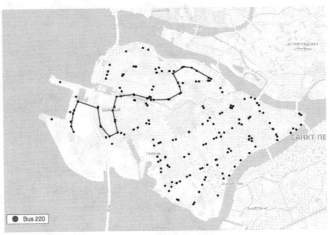

(a) Initial bus route 220

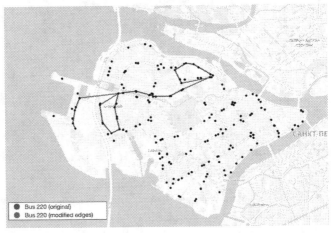

(b) Modified bus route 220

Fig. 5. Single bus route before and after GA application

(a) Before   (b) After

Fig. 6. Transport connectivity before and after GA application on the single route

Figure 6 shows the transport connectivity of the experiment area before and after the application of the genetic algorithm for one route. Connectivity shows the mutual transport accessibility of blocks in a given area. Each block has an average travel time (in minutes) to all other blocks. The longer the time, the worse the connectivity of one block with the others. The black outline of blocks in Fig. 6b shows the blocks where the connectivity values have changed: −1.92 min and −0.6 min, respectively.

4.2   Bus Routes Network Optimization

The existing routes are presented in Fig. 7a together with the current transport connectivity of the selected area (Fig. 7b). The average travel time for the entire given area is 23.3 min. Number of routes - 19. In this experiment, the number of bus stops does not change. However, there are stops in Fig. 7a that are not utilized by routes in the area. Such stops are part of routes that run in another territory but have one stop in the experiment territory. Such stops were subsequently used by the GA to modify the routes.

The transport connectivity metric shows how urban areas can be related to each other in terms of travel time when they are physically close or distant from each other. This approach allows us to integrally assess the quality of transportation service through time costs and to see which parts of the city are "cut off" from the rest through the public transportation network.

The result of the method - generated bus routes that optimized transport connectivity is shown in Fig. 8a. The number of routes has not changed. Improvement in terms of average travel time of about 1 min - 22.5 min (after optimiza-

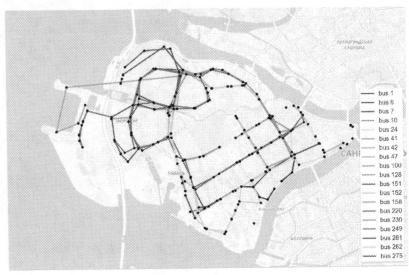

(a) Existing bus routes

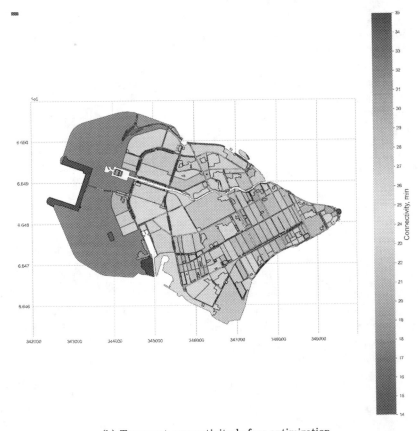

(b) Transport connectivity before optimization

Fig. 7. Existing bus routes and current transport connectivity in a given area

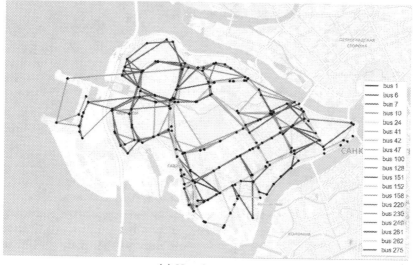

(a) New bus routes

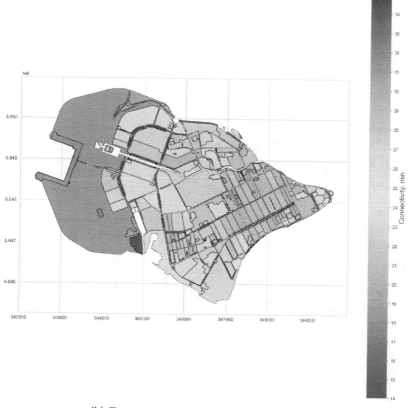

(b) Transport connectivity after optimization

Fig. 8. New bus routes and optimized transport connectivity in a given area

tion). The increase is insignificant, but in the context of connectivity (Fig. 8b) it can be seen that some remote areas have become better connected to the rest.

5   Discussion

The proposed route generation method has the potential for development. The main disadvantages of the proposed approach are the lack of consideration of important data on transportation demand, speed of transportation at different times of the day, frequency of transfers, etc. At the same time, this is also an advantage compared to modeling, if such data are not available. Traffic delays due to congestion on the road network are not taken into account. If there are such delays and public transport does not run on segregated tracks, then in future works, it is necessary to take the loaded graph of the street-road network and take into account the actual speed of traffic. Future developments of the method may include the addition of transport demand data so that route generation is responsive to the need for transport services in urban areas.

6   Conclusion

The aim of this study was to develop a generative method for planning and optimizing public transport systems by generating new transport routes based on existing ones using open data. A genetic algorithm (GA) was selected as the generative method to obtain an optimal solution for the bus route network. The GA approach optimizes the bus route network by iteratively evolving a population of candidate solutions. Starting from an initial set of modified bus route configurations, the algorithm applies principles of natural selection - evaluation, selection, variation, and replacement - to gradually improve the solutions over multiple generations, ultimately converging on an optimal or near-optimal bus route design. This method is intended to determine the potential of the transport system and routes for development in non-optimized public transport systems or in areas that are just developing, where data on the future street and road network are available. Since transportation modeling is time-consuming and expensive, this method can provide an estimate based on available data.

Acknowledgments. This research is financially supported by the Foundation for National Technology Initiative's Projects Support as a part of the roadmap implementation for the development of the high-tech field of Artificial Intelligence for the period up to 2030 (agreement 70-2021-00187).

References

1. Yang, R., Liu, Y., Liu, Y., Liu, H., Gan, W.: Comprehensive public transport service accessibility index–a new approach based on degree centrality and gravity model. Sustainability **11**, 5634 11, 5634 (2019). https://www.mdpi.com/2071-1050/11/20/5634/htm. https://www.mdpi.com/2071-1050/11/20/5634

2. Kurlov, A.V., Materuhin, A.V., Dresvyanin, A.V., Gvozdev, O.G.: Geoinformational approach to assessing the accessibility for urban areas. In: 2022 International Siberian Conference on Control and Communications, SIBCON 2022 - Proceedings (2022)
3. Pellicelli, G., Caselli, B., Garau, C., Torrisi, V., Rossetti, S.: Sustainable mobility and accessibility to essential services. an assessment of the san benedetto neighbourhood in Cagliari (Italy). LNCS, vol. 13382, pp. 423–438 (2022). https://doi.org/10.1007/978-3-031-10592-0_31
4. Kujala, R., Weckström, C., Mladenović, M.N., Saramäki, J.: Travel times and transfers in public transport: Comprehensive accessibility analysis based on pareto-optimal journeys. Comput. Environ Urban Syst. **67**, 41–54 (2018)
5. Morozov, A.S., et al.: Assessing the transport connectivity of urban territories, based on intermodal transport accessibility. Front. Built Environ. **9**, 1148708 (2023)
6. García-Cerrud, C.A., Mota, I.F.D.L.: Simulation models for public transportation: a state-of-the-art review. Procedia Comput. Sci. **217**, 562–569 (2023)
7. Georgiadis, G., Politis, I., Papaioannou, P.: Measuring and improving the efficiency and effectiveness of bus public transport systems. Res. Transp. Econ. **48**, 84–91 (2014)
8. Medina-Salgado, B., Sánchez-DelaCruz, E., Pozos-Parra, P., Sierra, J.E.: Urban traffic flow prediction techniques: a review. Sustainable Comput. Inform. Syst. **35**, 100739 (2022)
9. McNally, M.: The four step model. institute of transportation studies. Center for Activity 529 (2000)
10. Nagel, K., Marchal, F.: Computational methods for multi-agent simulations of travel behavior. In: Proceedings of International Association for Travel Behavior Research (IATBR), Lucerne, Switzerland (2003)
11. Wang, Z., Chen, Y.: Exploring spatial patterns of interurban passenger flows using dual gravity models. Entropy **24**, 1792 (2022). https://www.mdpi.com/1099-4300/24/12/1792/htm. https://www.mdpi.com/1099-4300/24/12/1792
12. Kung, K.S., Greco, K., Sobolevsky, S., Ratti, C.: Exploring universal patterns in human home-work commuting from mobile phone data. PLOS ONE **9**, e96180 (2014). https://doi.org/10.1371/journal.pone.0096180
13. Sobolevsky, S., Sitko, I., Combes, R.T.D., Hawelka, B., Arias, J.M., Ratti, C.: Cities through the prism of people's spending behavior. PLOS ONE **11**, e0146291 (2016). https://doi.org/10.1371/journal.pone.0146291
14. Khulbe, D., Belyi, A., Mikeš, O., Sobolevsky, S.: Mobility networks as a predictor of socioeconomic status in urban systems. Lecture Notes in Computer Science (including subseries Lecture Notes in Artificial Intelligence and Lecture Notes in Bioinformatics), vol. 13957. LNCS, pp. 453–461 (2023). https://doi.org/10.1007/978-3-031-36808-0_32
15. Afandizadeh, S., Khaksar, H., Kalantari, N.: Bus fleet optimization using genetic algorithm a case study of mashhad. Int. J. Civil Eng. **11**(1), 43–52 (2013)
16. Koryagin, M.E.: Balance models of urban passenger transportation system under conflict of interest conditions (in Russian). Novosibirsk department of "Nauka" publishing house (2011)
17. Guihaire, V., Hao, J.K.: Transit network design and scheduling: a global review. Transp. Res. Part A Policy Practice **42**, 1251–1273 (2008)
18. Farahani, R.Z., Miandoabchi, E., Szeto, W.Y., Rashidi, H.: A review of urban transportation network design problems. Europ. J. Oper. Res. **229**, 281–302 (2013)

19. Yakimov, M.R.: The use of various input data in the design of public transport route networks. In: 2020 Systems of Signals Generating and Processing in the Field of on Board Communications, March 2020

20. Welch, T.F., Widita, A.: Big data in public transportation: a review of sources and methods. Transp. Rev. **39**, 795–818 (2019). https://doi.org/10.1080/01441647.2019.1616849

21. Ibarra-Rojas, O.J., Delgado, F., Giesen, R., Muñoz, J.C.: Planning, operation, and control of bus transport systems: a literature review. Transp. Res. Part B: Methodol. **77**, 38–75 (2015)

22. Manser, P., Becker, H., Hörl, S., Axhausen, K.W.: Designing a large-scale public transport network using agent-based microsimulation. Transp. Res. Part A: Policy Practice **137**, 1–15 (2020)

23. Guan, J.F., Yang, H., Wirasinghe, S.C.: Simultaneous optimization of transit line configuration and passenger line assignment. Transp. Res. Part B: Methodol. **40**, 885–902 (2006)

24. Murray, A.T.: A coverage model for improving public transit system accessibility and expanding access. Ann. Oper. Res. **123**, 143–156 (2003). https://doi.org/10.1023/A:1026123329433

25. Mandl, C.E.: Evaluation and optimization of urban public transportation networks. Europ. J. Oper. Res. **5**, 396–404 (1980)

26. Kepaptsoglou, K., Karlaftis, M.: Transit route network design problem. J. Transp. Eng. **135**(8), 491–505 (2009)

27. Gkiotsalitis, K.: Public Transport Optimization. Springer Nature (2023)

28. de Dios Ortúzar, J., Willumsen, L.G.: Modelling transport. John wiley & sons (2024)

29. Wong, K.C.: Developing a Generative Design Framework for Optimising Public Transit Network Planning. Ph.D. thesis, University of Toronto (Canada) (2022)

30. Heyken Soares, P., Mumford, C.L., Amponsah, K., Mao, Y.: An adaptive scaled network for public transport route optimisation. Public Transport **11**(2), 379–412 (2019)

31. Jing, D., Yao, E., Chen, R., Sun, X.: Optimal design method of public transit network considering transfer efficiency. IET Intelligent Transport Systems (2023)

32. W Axhausen, K., Horni, A., Nagel, K.: The multi-agent transport simulation MATSim. Ubiquity Press (2016)

33. Manser, P., Becker, H., Hörl, S., Axhausen, K.W.: Evolutionary modeling of large-scale public transport networks. In: 2018 TRB Annual Meeting Online, pp. 18–02851. Transportation Research Board (2018)

34. Churiakova, T., Starikov, V., Sudakova, V., Morozov, A., Mityagin, S.: Digital master plan as a tool for generating territory development requirements. In: International Conference on Advanced Research in Technologies, Information, Innovation and Sustainability, pp. 45–57. Springer (2023). https://doi.org/10.1007/978-3-031-48855-9_4

35. Blocksnet - open library with tools for generation the city model and optimal requirements for future development with specified target parameters. https://github.com/aimclub/blocksnet

36. Mishina, M., Khrulkov, A., Solovieva, V., Tupikina, L., Mityagin, S.: Method of intermodal accessibility graph construction. Procedia Comput. Sci. **212**, 42–50 (2022)

37. Openstreetmap. https://www.openstreetmap.org

Addressing the Global Energy Crisis: Development of a Renewable Energy Model for Sustainable Cities—A Case Study in Yogyakarta Province

Dessy Rachmawatie[1]([✉]) [iD] and Akhmad Fauzi[2] [iD]

[1] Department of Economics, Faculty of Economics and Business, Universitas Muhammadiyah Yogyakarta, Kasihan, Indonesia
d.rachmawatie@umy.ac.id

[2] Department of Resource and Environmental Economics, Faculty of Economics and Management, Bogor Agricultural University, Bogor, Indonesia

Abstract. Energy is one prominent issue today. The current global energy crisis will affect domestic energy security. Yogyakarta Province is one of Indonesia's provinces with no reserves or potential for non-renewable primary energy resources. Meanwhile, although Yogyakarta Province has renewable energy sources, such as biogas, micro-hydro, solar energy, wind, and waste to energy, these have not utilized optimally on a large scale. The purpose of this research is to find, design, and analyze the key variables in the sustainability model of renewable energy in Yogyakarta Province. The method analysis uses the Cross Impact Matrix Multiplication Applied to Classification (MICMAC). The result showed that variables are influence variables, including economic indicators comprising scare energy supply, affordable energy prices, and rising global energy prices. Then, regulatory indicators encompassed laws and regulations supporting renewable energy from central and regional governments. The urgency of this research is that EBT-based power plant projects in Yogyakarta and several regions in Indonesia, in general, face intermittency and variability that is still not optimal. Intermittency here is a situation where electricity generated from renewable energy cannot always be generated. At the same time, the variability in question is the instability of the energy produced. So the sustainability aspect in the development of renewable energy-based power plants is essential. In addition, the constraints on NRE-based power plants are the high investment and operational costs, as well as institutional governance at the central and regional levels. Therefore, developing renewable energy-based power plants requires the collaboration of all parties, especially the community, central and regional governments, and the private sector.

Keywords: Energy Security · Key Variable · Sustainability Model · Renewable Energy

O. Gervasi et al. (Eds.): ICCSA 2024, LNCS 14813, pp. 379–394, 2024.
https://doi.org/10.1007/978-3-031-64605-8_26

1   Introduction

Energy is the source of life, and if energy runs out, it means life will be destroyed; along with the increase in a country's population, the need for energy will also increase [1]. In the context of global energy, several parts of the world (Europe, in particular the UK, and China) are experiencing an energy crisis marked by soaring gas and coal prices, followed by an increase in oil prices.

This global energy crisis will eventually affect all countries, including Indonesia, due to their import dependence. In the case of Indonesia, it will impact fuel and Liquid Petroleum Gas/LPG prices, the costs of which will increase sharply. Indonesia is a net exporter for coal and Liquid Natural Gas/LNG, so it principally benefits from the trade balance side. In addition, compared to other countries, primary energy consumption in Indonesia shows that Indonesia is the 3rd largest country in the world that consumes fossil energy after China and India.

Consequently, soaring energy prices will influence the rising prices of other commodities and services, thereby threatening an increase in inflation that exceeds the target. Therefore, Indonesia's condition is vulnerable to increases in primary energy prices, especially petroleum (including fuel oil and Liquid Petroleum Gas/LPG), due to its high dependence on imports, significantly since the government partly subsidizes it for the fuel price and LPG products (Fig. 1).

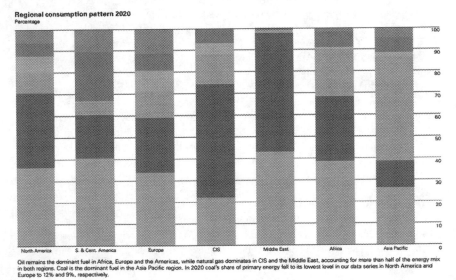

Fig. 1. Comparison of Regional Consumption Pattern 2020 in North America, South and Central America, Europe, CIS, Middle East, Africa and Asia Pacific. Source: [2].

For this reason, the urgencies of this research are as follows: First, the Special Region of Yogyakarta (DIY) Province is one of the provinces in Indonesia that does not have reserves or potential for non-renewable primary energy resources. So far, non-renewable energy needs, such as oil and natural gas, have been met from outside DIY. DIY is also in the Java-Madura-Bali (JAMALI) interconnection system and still needs a large-scale generating system. Meanwhile, DIY has renewable energy sources like biogas, water, sun, wind, waves, and biomass. This renewable energy source is alternative energy, although until now, it has yet to be used optimally. Hence, the absence of reserves of energy resources, which results in dependence on energy supply in DIY from other regions, must receive special attention from the DIY government. In meeting energy needs, it is indispensable to develop energy resources. Considering that the development of energy sources takes a long time and costs a lot, in planning for the future national energy transition, it is necessary to carry out good planning supported by policies in the region's energy sector.

Second, the energy transition policy that only looks at short-term needs (shortsighted) can fundamentally encourage under-investment in the face of growing demand for clean energy and fossil energy (which is still growing). Improper application of transitional energy can also make Indonesia vulnerable when supply disruptions occur domestically and in a global/regional context.

Third, energy needs not accompanied by increased energy production will cause the country to experience an energy crisis [3]. Modern technologies can produce energy from renewable and non-renewable sources, including nuclear, hydrogen, coal, methane gas, liquid coal, and carbon dioxide. Renewable energy is a source produced from sustainable energy resources if appropriately managed.

Therefore, it is necessary to study NRE planning, especially in assessing how sustainable NRE is in each region, so that each area can optimize the potential of NRE in its respective regions. Thus, in the future, an energy transition can be encouraged that sees the needs and opportunities not only in the short term but also in the long term.

The urgency of this research is that renewable energy-based power plant projects in Yogyakarta and several regions in Indonesia in general face intermittency and variability that is still not optimal [4]. Intermittency disini yaitu keadaan dimana listrik yang dihasilkan dari renewable energy tidak bisa dihasilkan sepanjang waktu. Sedangkan variability yang dimaksud yaitu ketidakstabilan energi yang dihasilkn. Sehingga aspek keberlanjutan (sustainability) pada pengembangan pembangkit listrik berbasis renewable energy sangat penting. Disamping itu kendala pada pembangkit listrik berbasis EBT adalah mahalnya biaya investasi maupun operasional, dan tata kelola kelembagaan di pusat maupun daerah. Oleh sebab itu pada pengembangan pembangkit listrik berbasis renewable energy diperlukan kolaborasi semua pihak, terutama masyarakat, pemerintah pusat dan daerah, serta swasta. Based on the research background and urgencies, the research objectives is to designing the key variable indicators (internal and external environment) in the sustainability of renewable energy development in the DIY Province.

1.1 Energy Resources

Energy is a source of life; if energy runs out, it means that life will increase the population of a country, then the need for energy will also increase [5]. Energy needs not accompanied by an increase in energy production will cause the country to experience an energy crisis. Energy sources that can be produced by new technologies, both from renewable energy sources and non-renewable energy sources, include nuclear, hydrogen, coal methane gas, liquefied coal, and carbon dioxide Fields [6]. Renewable energy is an energy source that is produced from sustainable energy resources if appropriately managed, including geothermal energy, wind, bioenergy, sunlight, currents, and waterfalls, as well as the movement and temperature differences of the sea layers [7].

Energy planning is essential to do to find out the potential use of energy needed by the community [8]. Indonesia's energy sources have fossil energy reserves such as oil, gas, and coal, as well as non-fossil energy reserves such as geothermal, water, wind, and solar power Fields [9]. The use of fossil fuels damages the environment, and its reserves continue to run out, so dependence on fossil energy must be reduced by replacing it with renewable energy with abundant reserves, including geothermal energi Fields [3].

1.2 Renewable Energy Sustainability

To overcome the energy supply crisis and avoid environmental damage due to global warming, new, renewable and more environmentally friendly alternative energy sources are needed [10]. The use and development of renewable energy is becoming increasingly important given the increasingly limited sources of fossil or renewable energy [11]. Energy sources available in an area, this must be done by studying the physical and chemical characteristics of the geothermal reserves [12].

Sources with large energy reserves can be developed into power plants, while resources with relatively small energy reserves can be used for other purposes, such as direct use for fisheries, agriculture and geotourism [13]. The potential that can be exploited is mainly in the fisheries, agriculture and geotourism sectors, for example in the Parangwedang area, Parangtritis Village, Bantul Regency [12].

1.3 Biogas Development

Technological developments show that almost all household appliances, offices, hotels and other equipment use electricity, all of which rely on fuel oil [14]. At the same time, energy conversion technologies have been discovered for power plants of various scales and capabilities, such as hydropower energy (PLTA), nuclear energy (PLTN), geothermal energy (geothermal), biodiesel energy, and others. Dependence on the use of petroleum cannot be tolerated, because energy needs continue to increase along with population growth, industrialization, and current technological developments [15].

Biogas is a fuel produced by the decomposition of organic matter under anaerobic conditions. The development of biogas technology in Indonesia has been widely recognized since the 1970s. The technology of using biogas equipment to process livestock manure has developed in rural areas, but now biogas technology has begun to be used in urban areas. In 1981, the development of waste processing technology in Indonesia through biogas installations was funded by the Food and Agriculture Organization (FAO), such as biogas installations in several provinces [16]. In the 2000s a household biogas reactor was developed with a simple structure, the material is made of plastic and can be installed at a relatively affordable price. The use of biogas to generate electricity is not a new technology. However, the application of household scale electricity generation from biogas fuel is still limited.

Biogas is a fuel produced from the decomposition of organic matter that occurs under anaerobic conditions. Animal waste processing techniques using biogas installations have developed in rural areas, but now biogas technology has begun to be used in urban areas. In 1981, the development of waste treatment technology with biogas installations in Indonesia was developed through financial support from the Food and Agriculture Organization (FAO) such as biogas installations in several provinces. In the 2000s a household-scale biogas reactor was developed with a simple construction, with materials made of plastic which were ready to be installed at relatively affordable prices. Utilization of biogas for electricity is not a new technology. However, the application of household-scale power plants using biogas fuel is still limited [1].

1.4 New and Renewable Energy in Rural Areas

Biogas is a renewable energy source because it is produced from biomass. Substrates for the biogas process can be grown locally at low cost, such as cow dung, agricultural waste or energy crops. Biogas will increase the energy supply of an area and also make an important contribution to natural resource conservation and environmental protection [12]. The development and implementation of a biogas power generation system based on local resource potential will increase regional energy supply and energy security, thereby reducing dependence on fuel [17].

The government's efforts to develop alternative energy sources have encouraged efforts to develop renewable energy from livestock, cattle farming is one of the industries that has great potential for alternative energy development. The use of alternative energy sources from livestock waste provides many advantages, namely high quality and odor-less fuels and products, therefore the use of alternative energy sources that are renewable and environmentally friendly, such as livestock manure is an option [18]. Indonesia has the potential to develop three alternative energy sources (renewable resources), namely nyamplung biofuel, geothermal, solar and biogas. One thing that can be done is to process livestock manure into an alternative energy source to replace fuel oil (BBM), namely biogas [19].

The prospects for developing biogas technology are very large, especially in rural areas where the majority of the population is engaged in animal husbandry and agriculture [20]. Converting cow manure into an alternative energy source for biogas is a very profitable way because you can take advantage of nature without destroying it, thus maintaining the ecological cycle [21]. Biomass with a high moisture content, such as animal manure and food processing waste, is very suitable as a raw material for biogas production. Biogas development faces enormous opportunities. Biogas energy can be obtained from household wastewater, livestock wastewater, market organic waste, and the food industry [22].

1.5 New and Renewable Energy in Cities

Development of new and renewable energy (EBT) as energy that can be renewed quickly through natural processes, such as geothermal energy, biomass, water, solar and wind [23]. The development of new and renewable energy (EBT) in global discourse continues to increase as a form of future energy integration and as part of sustainable development. Many countries in the world, especially developed countries, have used this energy, while in third world countries, including Indonesia, there are still many obstacles in developing EBT [24]. One of the reasons is energy policies that do not favor alternative energy. Developing countries still believe that fossil fuels are still used as a cheap source of energy and this fuel must continue to be obtained in large part by providing subsidies from the state budget, which in turn hinders the development of EBT [25].

In order to increase energy production while reducing the use of fossil fuels, the government has identified the greatest potential for new and renewable energy, which is one of the most effective ways to reduce greenhouse gas emissions, including hydroelectric power [26]. PLTA/PLTH itself is actually divided into two, namely mini hydro power plants and micro hydro power plants, this shows that there are many large rivers and several waterfalls with flowing water which are very suitable for hydroelectric power plants. This method is part of Indonesia's efforts to reduce greenhouse gas emissions [27].

1.6 Sustainable Cities

Sustainable cities utilize renewable resources lower than their generation rate, and use nonrenewable resources lower than the rate of developing renewable alternatives while reducing their impact on the environment [28] In the future, one of the main challenges for society is the transformation of cities into sustainable settlements [29] Diaman The city itself is a center of energy consumption, but has great potential for renewable energy integration due to the infrastructure and resources that exist in the city [30] The feasibility of a particular renewable source varies from place to place. However, prioritizing certain renewable energy resources is itself an important topic that must be considered in sustainable urban development [31].

According [32] a sustainable city is a knowledge-based city, hence every aspect of the city must demonstrate efficiency; energy efficiency is an important sustainability principle that must be enshrined in sustainable cities to prevent unnecessary energy wastage. Energy efficiency is defined as using less energy by increasing the system's efficiency to produce the same product output. For example, from light bulbs to HVAC units, the energy expended should be less than inefficient alternatives but with the same or much better output. This concept allows us to improve existing systems to achieve technical and economic performance while addressing environmental issues.

Sustainable urban development is increasingly recognized as essential to achieving collectively agreed sustainability goals at local, regional, and global scales and, more broadly, to ensure the well-being of people around the world [33]. Issues of management and sustainable use of urban landscapes require some theoretical framework to set goals and evaluate results. Resilience theory is arguably one of the most suitable in urban environments because it allows the integration of ecosystem function with the social dynamics [34].

2   Methods

This research was designed with mixed methods based on theoretical concepts and secondary and primary data. Explorative qualitative research in this study encompassed an in-depth understanding of the research subject and object, mapping the problems, directly observing the field, conducting in-depth interviews with core and supporting sources, and collecting primary and secondary data.

The secondary data used came from literature studies, and quantitative data came from the Ministry of Energy and Mineral Resources of the Republic of Indonesia and the DIY Provincial Public Works Office of Housing and Mineral Resources Energy. While the primary data used a research questionnaire covering economic, social, environmental, regulatory, and institutional governance dimensions, with a total of 20 variables (appendix 1. Long Theme Variable Used).

Based on the research background and urgencies, this research aims to determine what variables are the critical (internal and external environment) in the sustainable development model of renewable energy in Yogyakarta Province, using *the Cross-Impact Matrix Multiplication Applied to Classification (MICMAC)* (Fig. 2).

The stages of the cross-impact matrix multiplication applied to the classification (MICMAC) analysis method are as follows:

1. MICMAC analysis uses data with a non-parametric scale, i.e., ordinal, with 0 for no relationship, 1 for a weak relationship, 2 for a moderate relationship, and 3 for a strong relationship.
2. MICMAC uses expert assistance in obtaining data. The experts in this study comprised academics and NGOs engaged in empowerment activities in the new renewable energy sector in Yogyakarta Province, as well as local governments and industry.
3. Data were collected using a questionnaire with structured questions. Each expert filled out the questionnaire through a Focus Group Discussion (FGD), where they were asked to discuss and agree on each variable item by filling in questions for each indicator by dividing the group and asking them to answer the questionnaire; one group was for one answer.
4. The FGD or questionnaire to the experts was conducted twice. At the first meeting, the question focused on identifying all the system or program variables to be evaluated and their operational definitions. The operational definition agreement helps the experts have a collective understanding and perception. After collecting the variables, the experts were asked to fill in the relationship between each variable with a non-parametric value according to point 1.
5. The FGD results were then entered into the MICMAC module and discussed in the second FGD. The participants of the first and second FGDs were the same people. This second FGD aimed to confirm the results of the system under study, enrich information, determine the understanding of the system, and identify key drivers in the system.

Based on the identification results, 20 main variables were obtained with the potential for sustainability of waste to energy, influencing (influential), and influenced (dependent), as seen in Appendix 1.

Figure 3 presents the results of filling out the Matrix of Direct Influences (MDI). MDI revealed the relationship between variables and each other. The filling of the MDI was based on the Forum Group Discussion carried out with stakeholders, both from the government and the private sector.

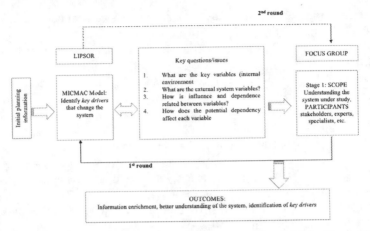

Fig. 2. Kerangka Kerja MICMAC (Modified from Stratigea, 2013 by Fauzi, 2019)

Influences ranged from 0 to 3, with the possibility to identify potential influences:

0: No influence
1: Weak
2: Moderate influence
3: Strong influence
P: Potential influences

Fig. 3. Matrix of Direct Influences of Key Variable Indicators in Sustainability Development Model of Renewable Energy in Yogyakarta Province

3   Result and Discussion

3.1   Direct and Indirect Key Variable's Indicator

The results of the MDI table analysis with MICMAC software produced a mapping as depicted in Fig. 4 Variables that fell into first quadrant, or called influences variables, include three economic indicator variables, consisting of scarcity of energy supply (PEL), cheap and affordable energy prices (HBT), and rising global energy prices (KHE). Also, two regulatory indicator variables emerged, i.e., laws and regulations supporting EBT, both from the Central and Regional Governments (UUPP & UUPD).

In this case, the influence or determining variable has the strongest influence compared to variables in other quadrants, with little dependence on other variables. Therefore, this variable can serve as a key factor in urban development of sustainability.

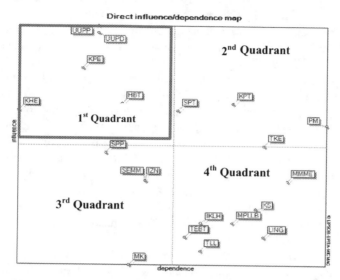

Fig. 4. Map of Sustainability Variables by Effect and Dependence

In this case, Yogyakarta Province is one of the provinces in Indonesia that does not have a network of power generation systems, so the energy supply is completely dependent on the JAMALI (Java-Madura-Bali) power system. Therefore, if there is a shortage of energy supply from the JAMALI power generation system, it will impact the sustainability of energy needs in the DIY Province and other areas with a network of power generation systems. Likewise, if there is an increase in the price of electrical energy, it will also impact sustainability and energy dependence in DIY. Hence, it is predicted that social unrest will occur if it happens. Then, the DIY government will face a critical situation because Yogyakarta does not have a network of power generation systems. Thus, the DIY government really must be able to condition that the variables influenced, consisting of cheap and affordable electrical energy prices, energy supply, as well as central and local government laws and regulations, support the development of sustainable cities, one of which is developing EBT in DIY. In this regard, DIY Regional Regulation No.15 of 2018 concerning New Renewable Energy and DIY Regional Regulation No.6 of 2020 concerning DIY Regional Energy General Plan 2020–2050 have been issued.

In addition, three of the four variables in the governance indicators are included in the relay variables (2nd quadrant). Relay variables illustrate that the variables in this quadrant are unstable in achieving sustainable EBT development since all interventions on this variable will impact the system. Among them are a controlled EBT management system (SPT), inter-stakeholder cooperation (KPT), transparent and equitable management of fossil energy (TKE), and community participation (PM), which fell under social indicators. For this reason, it is particularly important for the DIY Provincial Energy and Mineral Resources Office to cooperate with multi-stakeholders to accelerate the development of EBT, for example, by opening opportunities for collaboration with private investors who will develop NRE in Yogyakarta Province, universities in Yogyakarta, and its surroundings. Especially in the context of developing NRE in each university, the example is developing solar panel energy at each university for the domestic needs of the university. This is an effort to achieve sustainable urban development by utilizing energy resources.

In addition, one of the efforts made by local governments in carrying out sustainable urban development is inviting industry and households to develop EBT in their respective sectors jointly. For example, industries and households are equipped with RE technology, which is simple and can be implemented quickly. Thus, they can harvest electrical energy from their places to meet their energy needs. As in Africa, people are invited to use solar panel energy at home with simple solar panel technology, and then the technology is sold to residents using a community installment system. The Indonesian government has used solar panel energy as regulated in ESDM Minister Regulation No. 26 of 2021. It governs the use of solar panels and the electricity sale and purchase agreement between PLN and the community. However, in practice, the regulation is still widespread or has yet to be achieved by all levels of society.

Furthermore, environmental indicators are included in the dependent variable quadrant (3rd quadrant). Dependent variables cannot stand alone (highly dependent on other variables), so they have an insignificant effect. These variables include two variables in social indicators, including the realization of an energy-independent society (MMME) and the occurrence of social conflicts due to rising energy prices and the scarcity of energy supply (KS), and one regulatory indicator, i.e., a consistently applied NRE energy transition policy (TEBT).

MMME variables can be realized if other supporting variables exist, such as central and regional government policies to develop energy-independent communities through NRE development programs in the regions. Likewise, the KS variable needs to stand alone because this variable depends on other variables, such as the security of the NRE energy supply and the low and affordable price of NRE that needs to be pursued. The TEBT variable is also a dependent variable because it is very dependent on other variables, such as regulatory encouragement in the form of laws in the Central and Regional Governments so that DIY renewable energy transition policies can be sustainable for urban development.

Next, in quadrant 4, autonomous or excluded variables have little influence and dependence on other variables, so they will not stop the operation of a system. This quadrant consists of standardization of NRE supporting facilities (SPP), which is an indicator of governance; NRE energy subsidies for low-income communities (SEMM), which is an economic indicator; easy EBT investment licensing (IZN), which includes regulatory indicators and reducing poverty (MK) which is included in the social indicators. In this case, EBT energy subsidies have an insignificant effect as the demand for NRE in DIY is still low compared to the market for fossil energy circulating in the community. The investment level in DIY Province still needs to be higher, causing investment licensing to be in quadrant four or have little influence and dependence.

Likewise, the development of EBT in DIY has been insignificant, so it has not impacted poverty reduction.

The results of the MDI table analysis with MICMAC software produced a mapping, as depicted in Fig. 5. Variables that fell into quadrant one, or called influences variables, include three economic indicator variables, consisting of scarcity of energy supply (PEL), cheap and affordable energy prices (HBT), and rising global energy prices (KHE). Also, two regulatory indicator variables emerged, i.e., laws and regulations supporting EBT, both from the Central and Regional Governments (UUPP & UUPD).

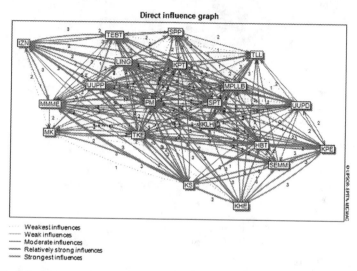

Fig. 5. Direct Influence Relationship Between Sustainability Variables (Color figure online)

Figure 5 is a graph of the direct influence of variables. The image describes the line where the dotted line indicates the strength is fragile, while the straight black line implies weak strength.

Likewise, a thin blue line signifies medium strength, and a thick blue line denotes muscular strength. Finally, a thick red line represents powerful strength. Also, Fig. 6 depicts that each variable was dominated by a powerful relationship, indicated by the dominance of the thick red graph [35].

Figure 6 is a graphic visualization of the indirect effect. The graph displays the relationship between each variable, showing that all NRE indicators have a relatively moderate and robust influence on each other. In addition, the most substantial impact in the indirect influence graph is indicated by the variables UUPD (local government law), UUPP (central government law), PM (community participation), TKE (transparent and equitable management of fossil energy), and MPLLB (reducing environmental pollution and hazardous waste). It indicates that the five variables have the most substantial influence on the development of EBT in Yogyakarta.

Figure 7 shows the shift in the order of several variables. For example, the cheap and affordable energy prices (HBT) variable in the MDI matrix is ranked 4th as an

Indirect influence graph

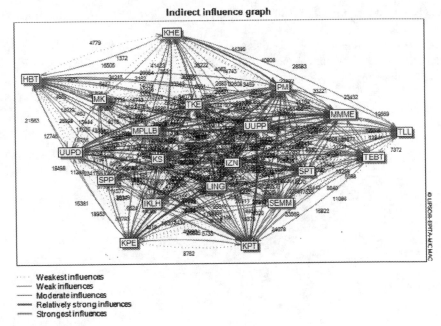

····· Weakest influences
───── Weak influences
───── Moderate influences
━━━━━ Relatively strong influences
▰▰▰▰▰ Strongest influences

Fig. 6. Indirect Influence Relationship Between Sustainability Variables

influential variable. Still, after iterations were carried out by considering the indirect influence factor, this variable is ranked 6th. Likewise, the energy governance variable, originally in the 9th place, becomes the 10th order. On the other hand, some variables have an increasing order, such as the increase in local energy prices, from 6th to 4th place.

Viewed from the dependence aspect, the three main variables (community participation, creating an energy-independent society, and creating a sustainable environment for future generations) are consistently in three significant orders as dependence variables. On the other hand, several variables have decreased by one level after the MDII iteration, i.e., energy governance, social conflicts due to rising energy prices and scarcity of energy supply, and environmental pollution and hazardous waste. Meanwhile, the variable of cooperation between related parties rose in rank from 7th to 4th after considering indirect effects. The shift in these variables due to the indirect impacts can be seen in Fig. 7.

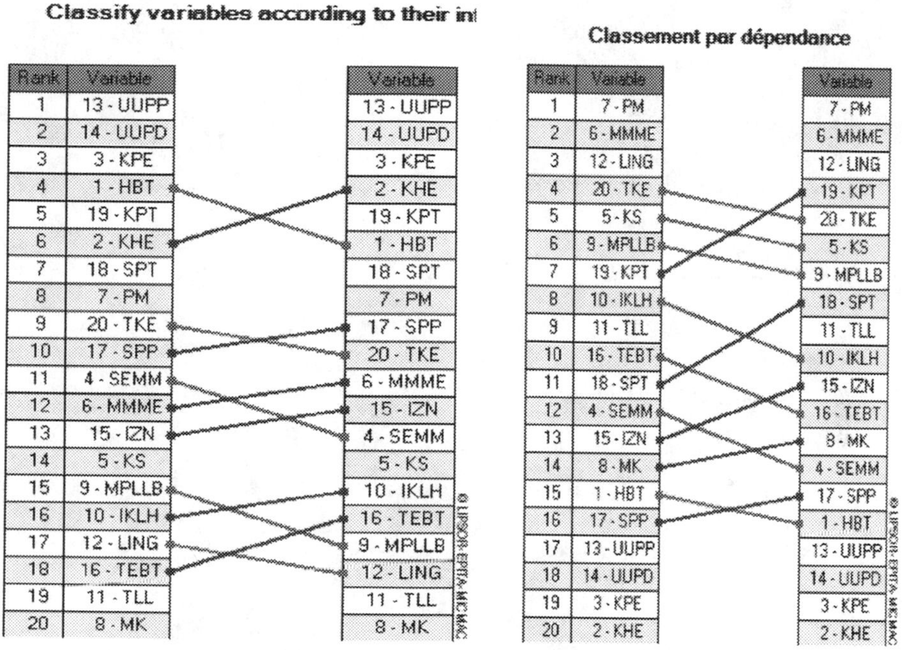

Classify variables according to their in[fluence]   **Classement par dépendance**

Rank	Variable	Variable
1	13 - UUPP	13 - UUPP
2	14 - UUPD	14 - UUPD
3	3 - KPE	3 - KPE
4	1 - HBT	2 - KHE
5	19 - KPT	19 - KPT
6	2 - KHE	1 - HBT
7	18 - SPT	18 - SPT
8	7 - PM	7 - PM
9	20 - TKE	17 - SPP
10	17 - SPP	20 - TKE
11	4 - SEMM	6 - MMME
12	6 - MMME	15 - IZN
13	15 - IZN	4 - SEMM
14	5 - KS	5 - KS
15	9 - MPLLB	10 - IKLH
16	10 - IKLH	16 - TEBT
17	12 - LING	9 - MPLLB
18	16 - TEBT	12 - LING
19	11 - TLL	11 - TLL
20	8 - MK	8 - MK

Rank	Variable	Variable
1	7 - PM	7 - PM
2	6 - MMME	6 - MMME
3	12 - LING	12 - LING
4	20 - TKE	19 - KPT
5	5 - KS	20 - TKE
6	9 - MPLLB	5 - KS
7	19 - KPT	9 - MPLLB
8	10 - IKLH	18 - SPT
9	11 - TLL	11 - TLL
10	16 - TEBT	10 - IKLH
11	18 - SPT	15 - IZN
12	4 - SEMM	16 - TEBT
13	15 - IZN	8 - MK
14	8 - MK	4 - SEMM
15	1 - HBT	17 - SPP
16	17 - SPP	1 - HBT
17	13 - UUPP	13 - UUPP
18	14 - UUPD	14 - UUPD
19	3 - KPE	3 - KPE
20	2 - KHE	2 - KHE

Fig. 7. Variable Ranking by Effect and Dependence.

4   Conclusion

This article highlights the importance of renewable energy planning and development in Yogyakarta Special Region (DIY) Province in the context of the global energy crisis and Indonesia's dependence on energy imports. This study identifies key variables that influence the sustainability of renewable energy development in DIY using the MICMAC method. The results showed that variables such as scarcity of energy supply, cheap and affordable energy prices, and rising global energy prices have a major influence on the sustainability of renewable energy in DIY. In addition, policies and regulations from central and local governments also play an important role in supporting the development of renewable energy.

This research is original because it focuses on identifying key variables in renewable energy development in provinces that do not have non-renewable energy reserves, and offers solutions based on multi-stakeholder collaboration to address these challenges. This research also provides insight into the importance of the role of communities and cooperation among stakeholders in accelerating the development of renewable energy.

The implications of this research for the future include the importance of long-term planning and policy development that supports the renewable energy transition. DIY local governments need to increase cooperation with various parties, including the private sector and academia, to optimize the potential of renewable energy in the region. In addition, this study emphasizes the need for simple and affordable renewable energy technologies for the community to increase energy independence and reduce dependence on fossil energy. Thus, this research makes an important contribution to efforts to achieve sustainable urban development through renewable energy resources.

Acknowledgments. Thank you to the Research and Innovation Institute, Universitas Muhammadiyah Yogyakarta, which has funded this research activity through the Internal Research Grant of Universitas Muhammadiyah Yogyakarta in 2021–2022.

Lampiran 1. Variable Used for Each Indicators

No	Long label	Short label	Theme
1	Cheap and affordable energy prices	HBT	Economy
2	Rise in global energy prices	KHE	Economy
3	Scarcity of energy supply	KPE	Economy
4	Energy subsidies for low-income people	SEMM	Economy
5	The occurrence of social conflicts as a result of rising energy prices and the scarcity of energy supply	KS	Social
6	Creating an energy independent society	MMME	Social
7	Increase community participation	PM	Social
8	Reduce poverty	MK	Social
9	Reduce environmental pollution and hazardous waste	MPLLB	Environment
10	Increasing the value of the Environmental Quality Index	IKLH	Environment
11	Creating a sustainable environment	TLL	Environment
12	Creating a sustainable environment for future generations	LING	Environment
13	Laws/Perpres/Presidential Decrees that support EBT from the Central Government	UUPP	Regulation
14	Laws/regulations of governors/regulations of regents/mayors that support EBT from local governments	UUPD	Regulation
15	Easy EBT investment licensing	IZN	Regulation
16	Consistently implemented NRE energy transition policy	TEBT	Regulation
17	Standardization of NRE supporting facilities	SPP	Governance
18	Controlled NRE management system	SPT	Governance
19	Cooperation between related parties	KPT	Governance
20	Fossil Energy Governance that is transparent and has the principle of Justice	TKE	Governance

References

1. Herdiansyah, H., Aisah, I.U.: Strategi pemberdayaan masyarakat dalam pelaksanaan program desa mandiri energi 1. SHARE Soc. Work J.**9**(2), 130–141 (2015). https://doi.org/10.24198/share.v9i2.21015

2. BP Statistical Review of World Energy: Statistical Review of World Energy globally consistent data on world energy markets and authoritative publications in the field of energy (2021)
3. F. Badal, "Open Access A survey on control issues in renewable energy integration and microgrid," vol. 8, 2019
4. Pratama, Y., Putra, N.E., Wibowo, A.Y.: Analisa Kuota Maksimum EBT Intermitten Pada Tahun 2025 Untuk Menjaga Kestabilan Frekuensi Di Sistem Sumatera. J. Energi dan Ketenagalistrikan 1(1), 30–36 (2023)
5. Gielen, D., Boshell, F., Saygin, D., Bazilian, M.D., Wagner, N., Gorini, R.: The role of renewable energy in the global energy transformation. Energy Strateg. Rev. 24, 38–50 (2019)
6. Setyaningsih, W.: C sehingga daerah Panasbumi Gedongsongo mempunyai potensi untuk digunakan untuk tenaga listrik dan kegiatan perekonomian lainnya. pada masa mendatang potensi tersebut dapat dimanfaatkan sebagai sumber energi alternatif yang mampu memenuhi kebutuhan masyar. J. Geogr. 8(1), 11–14 (2011)
7. Pickl, M.J.: The renewable energy strategies of oil majors – From oil to energy? Energy Strateg. Rev. 26, 100370 (2019)
8. Seetharaman, Moorthy, K., Patwa, N., Gupta, Y.: Breaking barriers in deployment of renewable energy. Heliyon 5, 1–23 (2019). https://doi.org/10.1016/j.heliyon.2019.e01166
9. Nurwahyudin, D.S., Harmoko, U.: Pemanfaatan dan Arah Kebijakan Perencanaan Energi Panas Bumi di Indonesia Sebagai Keberlanjutan Maksimalisasi Energi Baru Terbarukan 1(3), 111–123 (2020). https://doi.org/10.14710/jebt.2020.10032
10. Li, Q., et al.: Exploring the relationship between renewable energy sources and economic growth. The case of SAARC countries. Energies 14, 1–14 (2021)
11. Oakleaf, J.R., et al.: Mapping global development potential for renewable energy, fossil fuels, mining and agriculture sectors. Sci. Data 6, 1–17 (2019)
12. Sari, R.J.: Potensi Panasbumi Parangwedang Sebagai Sumber Energi Alternatif Dan Penunjang Perekonomian Daerah Kabupaten Bantul, vol. 2018, pp. 268–276, November 2018
13. Zhukovskiy, Y.L., Batueva, D.E., Buldysko, A.D., Gil, B., Starshaia, V.V.: Fossil energy in the framework of sustainable development: analysis of prospects and development of forecast scenarios (2021)
14. Pagliaro, M.: Renewable energy in Russia: a critical perspective, 950–957, September 2021. https://doi.org/10.1002/ese3.820
15. Kholiq, I.: Pemanfaatan energi alternatif sebagai energi terbarukan untuk mendukung subtitusi bbm. J. IPTEK 19(2), 75–91 (2015)
16. Djalante, R., et al.: Progress in disaster science review and analysis of current responses to COVID-19 in Indonesia: period of January to March 2020 6 (2020). https://doi.org/10.1016/j.pdisas.2020.100091
17. Lisowyj, M., Wright, M.M.: A review of biogas and an assessment of its economic impact and future role as a renewable energy source. 36(3), 401–421 (2020)
18. Siniscalchi-minna, S., Bianchi, F.D., De-prada-gil, M., Ocampo-martinez, C.: A wind farm control strategy for power reserve maximization. Renew. Energy 131, 37–44 (2019)
19. Ully, D.N., Mesin, J.T., Kupang, N., Ully, D.N.: TRADISIONAL (2019)
20. Putri, A., Purwanto, Purnaweni, H.: Perception of the community on the use of biogas as alternative energy (case study: Jetak Village, Getasan sub district). IOP Conf. Ser. Earth Environ. Sci., 1–10 (2020). https://doi.org/10.1088/1755-1315/481/1/012045
21. Mago, O.Y.T., Nirmalasari, M.A.Y., Kuki, A.D., Bunga, Y.N., Misa, A.: Pengaruh Jenis Limbah Organik dan Waktu Retensi terhadap Produksi Biogas dari Kotoran Sapi effect of the type of organic waste and retention time on biogas production from cow dung Pendahuluan Metode Penelitian. 5, 155–162 (2020). https://doi.org/10.24002/biota.v5i3.3682
22. Prifti, H., Floqi, T., Mico, M.: Potential energy production from biogas economically and environmental profitable. Case study: establishing a batch digester in ' Fogi ' farm. 6(5), 70–72 (2021)

23. Heryadi, M.D., Hartono, D.: Energy efficiency, utilization of renewable energies, and carbon dioxide emission: case study of G20 countries. **16**, 143–152 (2016)
24. Ramdani, D.F., Febriasari, A.: Model Kebijakan Pengembangan Energi Baru dan. J. Adm. Publik **8**(2), 192–202 (2018). https://doi.org/10.31289/jap.v8i2.1900
25. Souvannasouk, V., Shen, M., Trejo, M., Bhuyar, P.: Biogas production from napier grass and cattle slurry using a green energy technology. **4**(3), 174–180 (2021). https://doi.org/10.53894/ijirss.v4i3.74
26. Shea, R.O., Lin, R., Wall, D.M., Browne, J.D., Murphy, J.D.: Using biogas to reduce natural gas consumption and greenhouse gas emissions at a large distillery. Appl. Energy **279**, 115812 (2020). https://doi.org/10.1016/j.apenergy.2020.115812
27. Usman, Hasan, Kaharm, M.A., dan Elihami: Maspul J. Community Empower. **1**(1), 13–20 (2020). Universitas muhammadiyah enrekang
28. Goldman, T., Gorham, R.: Sustainable urban transport: four innovative directions. Technol. Soc. **28**(1–2), 261–273 (2006)
29. Petersen, J.-P.: Energy concepts for self-supplying communities based on local and renewable energy sources: a case study from northern Germany. Sustain. Cities Soc. **26**, 1–8 (2016)
30. Byrne, J., Taminiau, J., Kurdgelashvili, L., Kim, K.N.: A review of the solar city concept and methods to assess rooftop solar electric potential, with an illustrative application to the city of Seoul. Renew. Sustain. Energy Rev. **41**, 830–844 (2015)
31. Ribeiro, A.E.D., Arouca, M.C., Coelho, D.M.: Electric energy generation from small-scale solar and wind power in Brazil: the influence of location, area and shape. Renew. Energy **85**, 554–563 (2016)
32. Sodiq, A., et al.: Towards modern sustainable cities: review of sustainability principles and trends. J. Clean. Prod. **227**, 972–1001 (2019)
33. Bai, X., et al.: Sains Langsung Mendefinisikan dan memajukan pendekatan sistem untuk kota berkelanjutan Machine Translated by Google, pp. 69–78 (2016)
34. Andersson, E.: Urban landscapes and sustainable cities. Ecol. Soc. **11**(1) (2006). https://doi.org/10.5751/ES-01639-110134
35. Fauzi, A.: Teknik Analisis Keberlanjutan, 1st edn. PT Gramedia Pustaka Utama, Jakarta (2019)

Enhancing Urban Planning Through Improved Connectivity: A Genetic Algorithm Approach for Optimal Service Placement

Georgii Kontsevik(✉) ⓘ, Valeria Tikhevich ⓘ, and Sergey Mityagin ⓘ

ITMO University, Birzhevaya line, 14, Saint Petersburg, Russia
kontsevik@niuitmo.ru

Abstract. In this paper, a review of existing methods for optimal service placement to meet demand has been conducted. A problematic issue was identified in the form of insufficient flexibility of existing solutions for urban planning and development tasks in terms of optimal coverage location problem. The hypothesis that small improvements in connectivity between neighborhoods can significantly reduce the number of optimally placed services was confirmed. A sub-optimal solution was obtained using a genetic algorithm. As a result, recommendations were proposed to improve the transport connectivity between specific neighborhoods for the calculated time interval, which will reduce needed amount of additional facilities to fulfill the demand. The main contribution of this paper is to apply connectivity optimization and optimal service location algorithms together, resulting in a reduction in the number of services required.

Keywords: Heuristic optimization · Location coverage problem · Spatial inequality · Spatial analysis

1 Introduction

In modern society, characterized by the rapid pace of urban development and the growth of industrial enterprises, the issue of improving the quality of life of industrial workers becomes more than relevant. Given the continuous variability of the city's infrastructure, the constant need to provide city dwellers with basic services, as well as the desire to improve the overall level of well-being, the development of a method for optimal placement of urban services is of particular importance.

The concept of well-being is an important aspect of assessing the quality of life of an individual and society as a whole. It includes many factors that together determine the level of comfort and satisfaction with life [1]. The concept of well-being has been studying for decades, but there is still no consensus on its definition or how it should be measured [2]. Thus, the article [3] reveals the concept of well-being through a person's social behavior, his interaction with other people and his interpersonal relationships; article [4] refers to other

O. Gervasi et al. (Eds.): ICCSA 2024, LNCS 14813, pp. 395–407, 2024.
https://doi.org/10.1007/978-3-031-64605-8_27

main characteristics of well-being reflecting its understanding through spatial dimensions. Such components include:

1) all types of security (financial, physical, environmental and others);
2) participation and involvement in nearby social activities;
3) economic affordability of housing for all segments of the population with different income levels;
4) spatial accessibility to all services necessary for living;
5) a sense of identity with the human environment.

A high level of employee well-being is a key resource for increasing productivity and competitiveness of the country's economy as a whole. In the context of the modern world, where technological progress and automation are of great importance, ensuring the most comfortable working conditions and improving the well-being of employees in industrial industries is a strategic step towards sustainable development and prosperity of the country.

Satisfied and motivated employees demonstrate higher quality of labor, which leads to increased quantitative performance of the entire enterprise. Such employees may face special working conditions, safety requirements and specific professional skills. A distinctive feature of industrial workers is their close connection to production activities, which are often located outside the central city districts, where the density of urban services is higher than on the outskirts. This can create additional challenges for these employees as they have to commute to work from other neighborhoods. A solution to this problem may lie in providing better public transportation infrastructure or affordable housing near businesses. Therefore, the pursuit of employee well-being in enterprises requires a holistic approach that includes not only a comfortable working environment, but also accessibility to housing, transportation and a variety of services.

Spatial inequality manifests itself in the uneven distribution of resources and opportunities in different neighborhoods. For example, according to [5], the spatial mismatch between housing and work depends on the level of wages and prices for rent / purchase of housing. Thus, articles [6,7] shows that middle-class residents pays more than comfortable amount of money for rent half of the time.

According to [8] the factors influencing the use of urban services are proximity to residence, affordability and usability. In addressing spatial inequality, at least one of these aspects can be improved, which in turn will lead to an increase in overall well-being.

It can be seen that there are three main factors that affect spatial inequality: affordable housing, quality of transit options and connectivity to certain facilities.

The main contribution of this paper is to combine changes in both connectivity and additional services placement, since they used to be considered separately.

The following paper structures as follows: Sect. 2 presents related work on optimal location coverage algorithms, Sect. 3 presents the developed method in detail, Sect. 4 presents the application of developed method on specific urban area.

2   Related Works

The problem of optimal service placement usually lies in the notion of business and emergency facility locations. The problem is well studied and includes variety of algorithms for many specific tasks. However, in recent years it gained more attention since new technologies appeared in the field. The main trend in this sphere is to solve the problem of optimal service placement, including more scenarios, variables, agents and constraints.

In [9], the p-median problem is considered in detail, which is to choose the optimal location of facilities in the number of p units to serve the demand or cover the area with minimum cost. This problem is also considered in [10], which developed a location model for medical centers after analyzing their location, demand for medical services and road network in Jeddah city, Saudi Arabia. The study under review aims to optimize the network of medical services and provide location recommendations to maximize service coverage. The study [11] considers the p-median problem. However, in it, the object can serve any number of demand points, i.e., the problem is "uncapacitated P-Median".

The study [12] considers a problem, "the maximum coverage location problem" (MCLP), which is also one of the classical problems in resource allocation and facility location decision making. In contrast to the p-median problem, the MCLP considers a situation where a certain number of locations must be selected in order to maximize the total coverage of an area that is characterized by a set of customers or facilities. To solve that problem, a metaheuristic algorithm, AILS-PR, was proposed in [13]. Initially, there was an iterative local search (ILS). In ILS, the initial benchmark solution is iteratively refined by a local search followed by a perturbation phase. The perturbation phase aims to identify solutions that are "close" to the reference solution, but with a better local optimum within its neighborhood.

Optimal placement of various health care facilities is important for providing effective and timely medical care to the population. Therefore, it is their placement that is most often encountered in scientific articles. Thus, in [14] the above mentioned MCLP problem is considered to find the optimal placement of special health care facilities. For its solution, the proposed modified Particle Swarm Optimization (PSO) algorithm is used, which was compared with the results of the GAMS algorithm, where the former showed better results. PSO is a population-based stochastic optimization methodology (search algorithm). It simulates the social behavior of a flock of birds, where each particle represents a potential solution to the problem, i.e., a set of object locations.

However, not only the location of medical facilities is considered in scientific papers. For example, paper [15] presents a three-stage strategy to solve the cab stand location problem (TSLP). First, points with high cab demand are extracted from massive GPS cab data using a GIS platform, and the optimal area for cab parking locations is determined in the next steps. Then, the spatial interaction between cab demand and cab parking lots is investigated. Next, a cab stand location model (TSLM) is developed to minimize the total cost, which includes passenger access cost and construction cost of cab stands. A program based on genetic algorithm is written to optimize the TSLM.

The application of the genetic algorithm for solving the MCLP problem is also discussed in the source [16]. However, in this paper, in addition to this algorithm, the implementation of a heuristic algorithm is presented, as well as a comparison of these methods with the software package "CPLEX". The proposed algorithms showed results both in terms of time and quality better than the considered solver. In turn, the heuristic method has superiority over the genetic method.

In [17], another problem is considered, namely the capacitated location-routing problem (CLRP), which is a combination of a facility location problem and a transportation routing problem. The problem consists of determining the location of warehouses, assigning each customer to one of the warehouses and determining the routes. The approach proposed by the authors consists of 3 phases. In the first phase, customers are clustered near warehouses based on distance and demand using the developed two-level CSOM teacherless learning method. In the second phase, the transportation routing problem for each cluster is solved by the Clarke and Wright algorithm. In the third phase, the routes are improved by exchanging clients between different routes using the "Or-Opt" method. The computational results show better performance of the proposed approach and demonstrate its effectiveness in solving large size problems.

Another example of a problem combining facility location and transportation assignment/routing issues is [18], which deals with an optimization approach in firefighting. They present a robust optimization problem formulation, the so-called Facility Location and Equipment Emplacement Technique with Expected Coverage (FLEET-EXC) model, which maximizes the demand with respect to vehicle utilization. The approach proposed by the authors iteratively improves the solution of the fire station location and transportation assignment problem. Testing was performed on a dataset provided by the national association of firefighters of Chile. The results show that the considered method gave a more accurate representation of the accident process than those commonly used in the literature.

The article [19] questions the concept of urban development where all necessary services for living are within walking distance. Such a development vector has an increased attention due to its advantages in health, economy and environmental sustainability. A mixed integer linear programming (MILP) model, a constraint programming (CP) model, and a greedy algorithm were used for optimization. The authors tested their solutions on data describing disadvantaged neighborhoods in the city of Toronto, Canada. As a result, MILP finds the best solutions in most scenarios, but scales poorly with network size. The greedy algorithm scales well and finds near-optimal solutions.

Despite the fact that there are many studies on the optimal location of facilities, the distance between the facilities that provide the service and those facilities that provide the demand for the service is considered to be constant. However, in the context of urban management, public transport routes and roads are changing due to urban development and transportation reforms.

The contribution of this paper is to apply heuristic optimization to improve the transport accessibility time between blocks to enhance the solution of the location coverage problem. The results of the algorithm is a recommendation for service placements in city blocks. If there are conditions in a block that do not allow the placement of the service, such blocks could be remove from the location allocation process.

3   Method

3.1   Hypothesis

The following hypothesis was investigated in this paper: improving connectivity between neighborhoods by no more than 40% can reduce the minimum number of optimally placed new polyclinics.

3.2   Location Coverage Problem Setting

In this paper, the quality of life of a person will be considered as an average assessment relative to the assessments of provision with various services and the assessment of spatial mismatch between housing and work. For experimental purposes, we will consider the service "Polyclinic", the location of which we will optimize. As it was shown in the part with the review of existing solutions, the MCLP algorithm provides solutions to maximize the demand coverage (provision of all people living in a given area). In this paper we will use an improved version of the MCLP algorithm - "CLSCP-SO" (Capacitated Location Set Covering Problem-System Optimal), which takes into account the demand and capacity of services. However, this algorithm works with the cost matrix as a constant. In this case, the cost matrix is the availability matrix between the selected neighborhoods, which will be optimized in this solution with respect to the number of located clinics.

3.3   Genetic Algorithm Adoptation

This paper considers changing the cost matrix values (availability time between selected blocks) in order to reduce the required number of services to cover the unsatisfied demand. The flexibility of the developed method lies in the ability to customize the limit to improve services availability, and to account for any distribution of demand quantities across blocks.

As an example, the Polyclinic service was considered as one of the vital services directly affecting the quality of life of residents. There are accessibility standards for different services that provide basic services. In this case, for the polyclinic service this standard is 15 min. Consequently, if a service does not fall within the accessibility zone of a residential building, its residents are considered unserved.

In order to improve the provision of the necessary service to the residents, it is necessary to make it accessible: improve accessibility to existing services and / or add new services. Since this paper considers accessibility to service by public transportation (which city managers can improve through reforms), it is proposed to slightly improve transportation accessibility between the selected neighborhoods.

Since the norm for the selected Polyclinic service is 15 min and the selected limit for improving accessibility is up to 40 %, it is necessary to consider those connections between neighborhoods that are greater than the established norm (> 15 mins), but with improved connectivity could fall within the specified norm. Thus, it is necessary to consider connections between neighborhoods whose value does not exceed more than 25 min. ($25 * 0.6 = 15$)

Sample of cost matrix:
Colored cells indicate considered values to be optimized.

block id	0	1	2	3	4	5	6	7	8	9
0	0.0	11.3	21.0	25.0	27.6	26.5	34.6	32.4	26.1	25.0
1	11.3	0.0	24.5	27.3	29.9	28.8	36.9	34.7	28.4	27.3
2	17.3	20.4	0.0	13.8	22.8	21.8	29.9	27.7	21.3	20.2
3	25.9	29.0	13.8	0.0	17.2	29.0	37.3	35.1	20.3	19.2
4	26.3	29.4	26.6	18.6	0.0	21.2	35.6	33.4	25.8	24.4

In this case, the genetic algorithm is its standard implementation. It works by simulating the process of natural selection to optimize solutions to complex problems [20]. At its core, a genetic algorithm starts with a set of potential solutions presented as an initial population. These solutions are then evaluated based on their fitness function, which determines how well they do the task. Through the process of selection, crossover and mutation, the algorithm iteratively develops the population, contributing to the reproduction of individuals with higher fitness [21]. For several generations, the population has been striving for optimal or almost optimal solutions, which makes genetic algorithms especially effective in solving optimization problems in various fields, including urban studies. Figure 1 shows the block diagram of the algorithm.

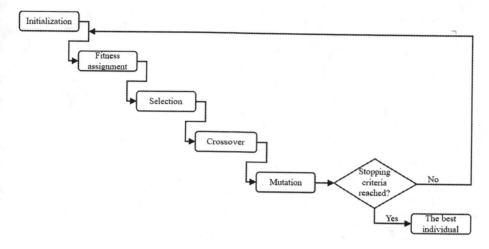

Fig. 1. The block diagram of the genetic algorithm

However, it is important to note how exactly the initial population and fitness function are specified.

Population initialization:
Matrices with modified considering values will be chosen as the initial population.

$$M_i \in \mathbb{R}^{n \times n} \quad \text{for } i = 1, 2, \ldots, \text{population\_size}$$

$$M_{i,ij} = \text{random\_uniform}(0.6, 1) \times \text{cost\_matrix}_{ij}, \text{if } (i, j) \in \text{selected cells}$$

Fitness function:
In this case, the result of the optimal service placement algorithm (number of services placed) will be used as a fitness function.

$$F(M) = \text{count}(\text{clscpso.fac2cli}[M])$$

As a result, the algorithm selects the best solution that contains a minimum of new services to be placed.

The scheme representation of implemented genetic algorithm optimization is shown in Fig. 2.

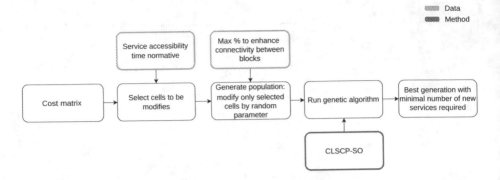

Fig. 2. Scheme of Genetic Algorithm implementation

4   Experiments

4.1   Study Area

This paper considers the scenario of new industrial enterprise location in the city within the development of priority industrial sectors according to the socio-economic development strategy of the city. This paper considers the location of an industrial enterprise in the port-industrial district of St. Petersburg. The placed enterprise and selected city blocks are presented in Fig. 3.

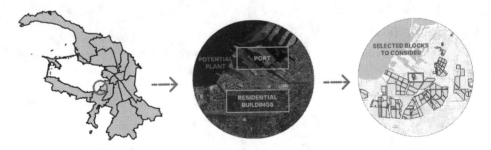

Fig. 3. Selected territory

The neighborhoods to be considered were chosen as follows: according to the hypothesis of jobs-housing mismatch, a balance between employee salary, potential average rent, and distance from work is needed. The wages of potential employees were taken as the average for skilled industrial workers in the city.

4.2 Data

All necessary data for services location, public transport networks, and residential building parameters (to calculate estimated population) were gathered from OpenStreetMap. The data on service capacity and demand were calculated according to the paper [22]. The implemented algorithm relies on gravitational model, limited number of residents and limited service capacities.

4.3 Method Implementation

The current estimation of availability "at the considered moment of time" was made with the help of the BlocksNet library [23]. The intermodal graph for the selected territory is presented in Fig. 4a. Estimation of availability of residents of the selected neighborhoods for the service "Polyclinic" is presented in Fig. 4b. Each service has its own standard of availability according to GOST (National Standard). For polyclinic the normative of accessibility is 15 min.

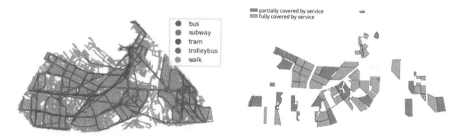

(a) Geolayer with intermodal graph of public transport

(b) Covered and not covered blocks by the service

Fig. 4. Input data

In this paper, all new polyclinics have a fixed (average) capacity of 400 people. It should be noted that a necessary but insufficient condition to consider a neighborhood as service-enabled is that it must fall within the service accessibility zone. The accessibility was calculated between neighborhoods on an intermodal graph built on OpenStreetMap public data.

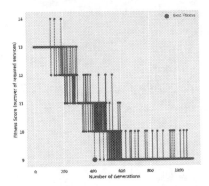
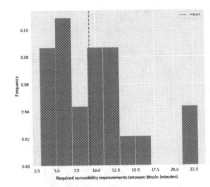

(a) Fitness progression in genetic algorithm (b) Distribution of required accessibility improvements (in minutes)

Fig. 5. Results of genetic algorithm

Since the number of possible combinations in this case is large, a genetic algorithm was chosen as a tool to select a sub-optimal solution. The genetic algorithm receives a connectivity matrix as input and changes the values only in the specified cells (i.e., neighborhoods that do not fit the condition for optimization do not change the connectivity among themselves). As a result, the CLSCP-SO algorithm calculates the optimal number of new clinics needed to meet demand. The results of the algorithm are presented in Fig. 5a and 5b.

Figure 5a shows that by optimizing the accessibility time between blocks, the required number of new services was reduced from 13 to 9. The results of the distribution of the delta of connectivity change between quarters are shown in Fig. 5a. Figure 5b shows that the average time to improve transportation connectivity is 10 min.

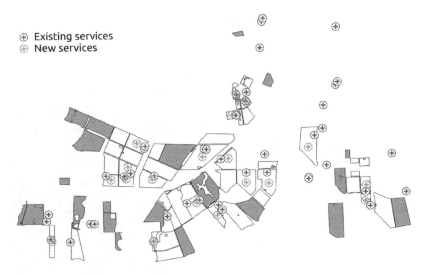

Fig. 6. The location of existing and additional services (Color figure online)

Figure 6 shows the blocks in which the service should be placed (the service is represented by a green marker), the blocks in which the service has already been previously (marked with red marker), and the uncovered blocks before optimization and placement of additional services (marked in red). Figure 7 shows reduce of travel time between blocks (lines, with gradient coloring depending on the required value of change).

It can be noted that in some cases the new service is placed in neighborhoods where the service already exists. This indicates that there is a need to expand or optimize the existing service. It can also be observed that due to the nature of the routes and road network, in some cases. Only a slight improvement in connectivity between distant neighborhoods is needed (2 to 4 min) and conversely, between spatially close neighborhoods a reduction in accessibility time may be required (10 to 13 min).

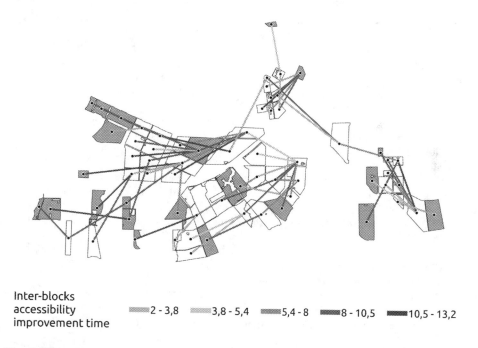

Inter-blocks accessibility improvement time   2 - 3,8   3,8 - 5,4   5,4 - 8   8 - 10,5   10,5 - 13,2

Fig. 7. Distribution of change in transportation connectivity between neighborhoods in a given area

5   Conclusion

Through the application of heuristic optimization, it was found that by improving transportation connectivity between blocks by applying optimal service placement algorithms, it is possible to reduce the required number of services. However, it should be noted that in order to fully solve the task, it is necessary to tackle the problem considering the entire city's data. In this case, the loads on services, including new ones, will be redistributed between all the neighborhoods both in case of adding new services and in case of changing the connectivity only on a given territory and on the whole city area. The flexibility of the developed method lies in the ability to customize the limit to improve availability, and to account for any distribution of demand quantities across quarters. Since any of the services, be it a kindergarten, school, polyclinic or multifunctional center, can be described through such criteria as demand and capacity, the developed algorithm is applicable to any type of urban service. The further work in this direction may include multi-criteria optimization of transportation and landuse types of urban blocks to consider changes in the scale of the whole city.

References

1. Mouratidis, K.: Urban planning and quality of life: a review of pathways linking the built environment to subjective well-being. Cities **115**, 103229 (2021)
2. Park, C.L., et al.: Emotional well-being: what it is and why it matters. Affect. Sci. **4**(1), 10–20 (2023)
3. Regan, A., Radoić, N., Lyubomirsky, S.: Experimental effects of social behavior on well-being. Trends Cogn. Sci. **26**, 987–998 (2022). https://api.semanticscholar.org/CorpusID:252188192
4. Shekhar, H., Schmidt, A.J., Wehling, H.W.: Exploring wellbeing in human settlements-a spatial planning perspective. Habitat Int. **87**, 66–74 (2019)
5. Blumenberg, E., Siddiq, F.: Commute distance and jobs-housing fit. Transportation **50**(3), 869–891 (2023)
6. Xiao, W., Wei, Y.D., Li, H.: Spatial inequality of job accessibility in shanghai: a geographical skills mismatch perspective. Habitat Int. **115**, 102401 (2021)
7. Zhang, L., Zhang, X., Huang, H., Zhang, L., Li, H.: Spatial accessibility of multiple facilities for affordable housing neighborhoods in Harbin, china. Land **11**(11), 1940 (2022)
8. Tuhkanen, H., et al.: Health and wellbeing in cities-cultural contributions from urban form in the global south context. Wellbeing Space Soc. **3**, 100071 (2022)
9. Bernábe-Loranca, M.B., González-Velázquez, R., Granillo-Martinez, E., Romero-Montoya, M., Barrera-Cámara, R.A.: P-median problem: a real case application. In: Abraham, A., Siarry, P., Ma, K., Kaklauskas, A. (eds.) ISDA 2019. AISC, vol. 1181, pp. 182–192. Springer, Cham (2021). https://doi.org/10.1007/978-3-030-49342-4_18
10. Murad, A., Faruque, F., Naji, A., Tiwari, A.: Using the location-allocation p-median model for optimising locations for health care centres in the city of Jeddah city, Saudi Arabia. Geospatial Health **16**(2) (2021)
11. Wang, C., Han, C., Guo, T., Ding, M.: Solving uncapacitated P-median problem with reinforcement learning assisted by graph attention networks. Appl. Intell. **53**(2), 2010–2025 (2023)
12. Yu, M., Fu, Y., Liu, W.: An optimization method for equalizing the spatial accessibility of medical services in Guangzhou. ISPRS Int. J. Geo Inf. **12**(7) (2023). https://www.mdpi.com/2220-9964/12/7/292
13. Máximo, V.R., Cordeau, J.F., Nascimento, M.C.: A hybrid adaptive iterated local search heuristic for the maximal covering location problem. Int. Trans. Oper. Res. (2023)

14. ElKady, S.K., Abdelsalam, H.M.: A modified particle swarm optimization algorithm for solving capacitated maximal covering location problem in healthcare systems. In: Hassanien, A.-E., Grosan, C., Fahmy Tolba, M. (eds.) Applications of Intelligent Optimization in Biology and Medicine. ISRL, vol. 96, pp. 117–133. Springer, Cham (2016). https://doi.org/10.1007/978-3-319-21212-8_5

15. Qu, Z., Wang, X., Song, X., Pan, Z., Li, H.: Location optimization for urban taxi stands based on taxi GPS trajectory big data. IEEE Access **7**, 62273–62283 (2019)

16. Gazani, M., Niaki, S.: The capacitated maximal covering location problem with heterogeneous facilities and vehicles and different setup costs: An effective heuristic approach. Int. J. Ind. Eng. Comput. **12**(1), 79–90 (2021)

17. Oudouar, F., Lazaar, M., El Miloud, Z.: A novel approach based on heuristics and a neural network to solve a capacitated location routing problem. Simul. Model. Pract. Theory **100**, 102064 (2020)

18. Rodriguez, S.A., Rodrigo, A., Aguayo, M.M.: A simulation-optimization approach for the facility location and vehicle assignment problem for firefighters using a loosely coupled spatio-temporal arrival process. Comput. Ind. Eng. **157**, 107242 (2021)

19. Huang, W., Khalil, E.B.: Walkability optimization: formulations, algorithms, and a case study of Toronto. In: Proceedings of the AAAI Conference on Artificial Intelligence, vol. 37, pp. 14249–14258 (2023)

20. Lambora, A., Gupta, K., Chopra, K.: Genetic algorithm-a literature review. In: 2019 international conference on machine learning, big data, cloud and parallel computing (COMITCon), pp. 380–384. IEEE (2019)

21. Mirjalili, S.: Evolutionary Algorithms and Neural Networks. SCI, vol. 780. Springer, Cham (2019). https://doi.org/10.1007/978-3-319-93025-1

22. Khrulkov, A., Mishina, M.E., Sobolevsky, S.L.: City services provision assessment algorithm. Procedia Comput. Sci. **212**, 93–103 (2022)

23. Blocksnet – open library with tools for generation the city model and optimal requirements for future development with specified target parameters. https://github.com/aimclub/blocksnet

Automated Identification of Existing and Potential Urban Central Places Based on Open Data and Public Interest

Anna Pavlova(✉) , Aleksandr Katynsus , Maksim Natykin ,
and Sergey Mityagin

ITMO University, Birzhevaya line, 14, Saint Petersburg, Russia
370012@niuitmo.ru

Abstract. Urban central places are scarcely identified and utilized in modern research. There are many interpretations of this concept and not so many methods for identifying, categorising and classifying such places. Previous works and studies are based on Christaller's Central Place Theory (CPT), which was introduced many years ago. All works are based on the concepts of CPT and they only extend or clarify these concepts, some works add new criteria and indexes for more accurate identification. This study presents a novel approach for automated identification of existing and potential urban central places based on open data and public interest, offering a data-driven and comprehensive perspective on centrality patterns that extends and complements the classical Central Place Theory (CPT) formulated by Christaller. In this paper, we describe the main types of central places to work with, and using data ingestion tasks, we analyse, scrape and extract centres from open data. We enrich service data from other sources such as social media networks and cartographic services. Points of interest, potential and existing services are defined and extracted using modern technologies such as Docker, Selenium, Airflow, Jupyter and Postgres DB. Our findings explain what central places are and how they can be found in modern cities. We also discovered potential and quasi-centres based on public interest and transport accessibility. The identification of central places is done through six different profiles - gastronomic, cultural, retail, multi-profile, potential central places and public interest hotspots - allowing a comprehensive understanding of centrality patterns driven by different urban functions and amenities that cater to the diverse needs and interests of residents and visitors. These results can be used in future exploratory city analyses.

Keywords: Open Data · Transport Accessibility · Centrality of urban blocks · Urban environment modeling · NLP · Data Engineering · Points of Interest · Central Places

1 Introduction

Every city is a complex mechanism consisting of a variety of interconnected parts. One of the most important parts of a city is its central places, which result from

O. Gervasi et al. (Eds.): ICCSA 2024, LNCS 14813, pp. 408–421, 2024.
https://doi.org/10.1007/978-3-031-64605-8_28

variations in natural resources, spatial inequality, different transport accessibility, collocation of urban services and citizen activities [1]. Neglecting such an important part of the city can lead to spontaneous migration, reduced quality of public places, limited access to services and a blurred urban environment [2].

This paper focuses on developing a new approach to identifying central places of cities, which takes into account modern technologies, open data, public interest and best practices in urban studies. Central places are underdeveloped and there are many interpretations and meanings of this concept, therefore there is a lack of methodological approaches that use all the data generated by people every day. A central place is understood as a territorial unit that attracts people who want to satisfy different needs, for example gastronomic, cultural or shopping. It is characterised by a wide range of urban services to satisfy needs, recognition and well-developed transport accessibility. Based on CPT [3] we decided to define the main types of central places to existing and potential. Existing centres can be divided into gastronomic, cultural, market or multi-profile, i.e. having several equally expressed profiles. Potential: based on accessibility and points of interest (POIs) and quasi based on POIs only. The developed methodology will provide opportunities for future insights, increased accuracy of urban research and effective urban planning for sustainable development.

The article is divided into the following parts: related works with the reviews of existing approaches, method description with a brief summary of each stage, results, experimental studies with results, and finally a discussion part with the conclusion.

2   Related Works

All methods of identification of urban central places refer to the main theory - Central Place Theory by Christaller [4] and similar one by Lösch. Christaller introduced the main concept of a central place and types of such places. Moreover, he defined some laws according to which urban central places are formed, identified a range of their functions, their hierarchy and location patterns. The main difference between Christaller's and Lösch's theories was that Christaller defined the hierarchy and then applied functions to each level, whereas Lösch started with the basic single economic activity. The production of goods, services and markets were the logical sequence in Lösch's theory. Numerous studies have been based on these theories, applied to many cities and generalised, extended and modernised. The main drawback of the two methods described above is the amount of data analysed, due to the time in which they were defined. Big data and modern technologies can improve and develop these methods, making them more accurate for use in the modern world.

In the research 'Investigating the central place theory using trajectory big data' [5] by Pengjun Zhao, Haoyu Hu and Zhao Yu, a new method of central place identification has been proposed. Their study aims to apply CPT combined with mobile phone trajectory big data in rural China. They investigated the benefits and insights of this hypothesis and created a new methodology. Using trajectory big data, the researchers revealed the dynamic connection between settlements, which reflects the main functions of services described by Christaller. To describe and identify city centres, the authors used spatial autocorrelation and geographically weighted regression. A major problem is that trajectory data is not open data and this method cannot be automated and reproduced. Furthermore, mobile phone data cannot describe emotions and intentions.

The next article 'Rethinking the Identification of Urban Centres from the Perspective of Function Distribution: A Framework Based on Point-of-Interest Data' [6] is based on the extraction of points of interest with their future classification and clustering. In this research, the authors proposed to identify urban centres using only POIs. They defined a model with three main steps: data classification, data computation and data visualisation. In the first step, all points ingested from social media networks and electronic maps were classified according to their contribution to urban functions. In the second step, the researchers used the DBSCAN algorithm and the CVNN method for clustering and validation. Finally, the last step was to visualise the distribution of these points and to reveal the implications. Based on the number of points, their quality and distribution, the students identified urban centres. Like the previous methods, this one was not automated and it had no characteristics of the points and centres included.

Another relevant work related to this study is 'Identifying city centre using human travel flows generated from location-based social networking data' [7] by Yeran Sun, Hongchao Fan, Ming Li and Alexander Zipf. The researchers proposed to use location-based social networking (LBSN) data to extract the main centres of cities. LBSN is represented as location-tagged data in social media networks and services such as Foursquare. This data was extracted and analysed, and then the main clusters were detected using the local Getis-Ord statistical method, which includes hotspots of travel flow detection and the clustering itself. The next steps were to apply DBSCAN and the Grivan-Newman (GN) algorithm to the extracted data. The last step was to determine the city centres by the rate defined in the work and to delineate them. The final result was areas represented by Voronoi polygons with precise boundaries. This work does not identify emotions and characteristics, so there are only central places and we can't really say why it is a centre and what emotions people feel there.

One of the approaches to identifying central places is described in the paper 'Urban Centrality: A Simple Index' [8]. The authors define a new centrality index that can be applied to urban areas. This index is based on variables such as employment and population density or trip generation rates. This new index was tested on the following metropolitan areas: Pittsburgh, Los Angeles, São Paulo, Brazil and Paris. The results were compared with other indices such as global and local Moran's I and density gradient estimates. This research has a major drawback - the data used is not open data, so the approach cannot be reproduced and automated.

3   Method

To test the developed method it was decided to choose the city of Saint Petersburg in Russia with a population of about 4.5 million people. The city was divided into districts and for each district all the central urban places were extracted. The Moscow district of St Petersburg was used for demonstration purposes. The Moscow district of St Petersburg was chosen for a number of reasons. Firstly, it is a well-established and densely populated area within the city. It represents a typical urban environment with a wide range of services and amenities. Secondly, it is known for its significant cultural and historical landmarks as well as a vibrant gastronomic and commercial scene. Thus, the study of this district allows for a comprehensive analysis of central places with different profiles. In addition, this district is industrially developed and accounts for 40% of the production of industrial products. By focusing on an area within a large city such as Saint Petersburg, the results and findings of the study can have direct relevance and applicability to real urban contexts.

It is implemented in a dedicated environment with all the necessary Python libraries and services such as Selenium, Airflow, Postgres DB and Jupyter Server. The business process modelling diagram of the method is shown in Fig. 1.

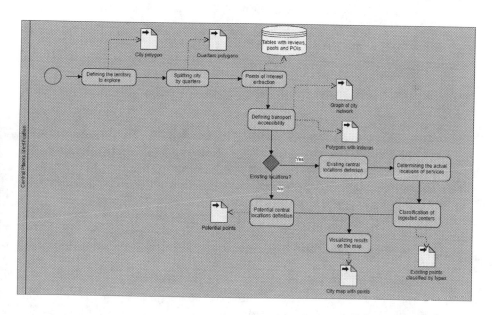

Fig. 1. Method Diagram

The new method developed in this article consists of six main stages:

1. Identification of the boundaries of the study area and dividing it into blocks;
2. Points of Interest extraction. On this stage we used data engineering techniques with natural language processing methods and models;

3. Transport accessibility definition. This stage uses a city network graph and quarters splitting to apply to every quarter an index;
4. Identification of existing urban central places via services and points of interest;
5. Identification of potential urban central places via transport accessibility and public interest;
6. Result visualisation on the map

3.1   Identification of Boundaries and Blocks of the Study Area

At the beginning of the method, the study area should be defined. Once the area has been selected, its boundaries are extracted from open sources such as OpenStreetMap. As the method takes transport accessibility into account, it is recommended to select an area of no more than 150 square kilometres. For larger cities, such as St. Petersburg or Moscow, the study is carried out within a single district.

Once the boundaries of the area have been determined, it is necessary to divide it into the smallest elements of the city - blocks. The division into blocks helps to evaluate each section of the territory in terms of points of public interest, transport accessibility and concentration of city services. In order to identify neighbourhoods, the researcher must divide the territory by roads, reservoirs and railway lines.

The result of this stage is a document containing information on the location of each block in the study area.

3.2   Points of Interest Extraction

The second step of the proposed method is to identify POIs in a city. POIs are objects on the map that contain information about important public places connected to the social infrastructure. They have various characteristics such as coordinates, names, degrees of public interest and purposes. The concept of POIs is accompanied by another one - the infrastructure of society, which can be understood as industries, sub-sectors indirectly related to the production process in the sense of ensuring the conditions of work and social activity of the population, activities in the field of culture, everyday life, social and interpersonal communication.

It is proposed to add the public interest for the identification of existing and potential centres due to the amount of data generated by people. This phase is based on open data, social media parsing, data engineering and natural language processing (NLP) [9]. The idea of POI extraction is to ingest data from cartographic services, social media networks and geoinformation services, enrich this data with context and process it using NLP methods and models to extract named entities associated with POIs. This type of data is open and easily ingested. It also represents many people who use the Internet and have an active civic position. There are many neighbourhood groups where people post problems and ideas on how to develop areas. We can easily find and use this data. The only limitation is that not all categories of citizens are represented by this data. This limitation cannot be solved by the idea of open data. We can't use data from surveys or questionnaires. More and more people use social media and leave reviews on maps, so very soon this will not be a problem.

The whole method works in a predefined environment with Airflow, PostGis, Selenium and Jupyter Server deployed in a docker container. This stage of the method is split into two parts: Data Ingestion and Data Processing.

The first part is an Airflow DAG (directed acyclic graph) with the following tasks:

1. Getting the polygon of the processed territory. It can be a city, a district or even a street;
2. Social media network parsing (VK). Receiving all the posts, photos and group posts where the territory was mentioned [10];
3. Buildings ingestion from the open data;
4. Reverse geocoding. On this stage all the buildings' polygons are converted to points, then the reverse geocoding is applied to every building without address;
5. Scrapping reviews from the cartographic service by the addresses.

The method has a stage where all the buildings of the city are ingested from open street map (OSM). It is a well-known fact that this service can have not accurate and not actual data. This problem is solved via using maps with reviews. All the buildins on the map are processed and connected to the buildings from OSM. While scrapping the data from maps all the posts are preprocessed to remove graphic information for the better results on the next stage.

All the scrapped and parsed data is saved into two Postgres tables: Reviews and Posts. Reviews table contain the name of the service in the building and the date when the reviews was made. Posts table contains group name, post itself, and date in UNIX timestamp. To ingest all the data it was decided to use Python programming language and special libraries such as vk (to parse data from VK social media network), selenium and web driver to scrape data from cartographic services, ArcGis to get existing points of interest, airflow to build DAG, and sqlalchemy to work with database.

When all the data is stored in tables, comes the second part - data processing. It is the second DAG with three main tasks:

1. NLP models initialization. Here main models for sentiment analysis, named entity recognition, and keywords extraction are defined. Stanza, RuBert, and KeyBert were chosen for this task. Stanza is used to extract named entities, RuBert is for emotions predictions, KeyBert is for keywords extraction;
2. Posts and reviews ingested before are processed with the three models to extract locations and organisations, emotions and keywords;
3. All the extracted locations are geocoded to receive points on the map;
4. Data analysis.

There are some limitations in the use of NLP models for sentiment analysis. Sometimes emotions are not well defined in texts, and models can't identify if the post contains positive or negative emotion. This can be fixed by transfer learning on the ingested data all the time we get new data.

Fig. 2. Points of Interest

The extracted data is saved in a new table with the name Processed posts. Then with the help of aggregate functions all the points are split in popular and not popular. The emotion degree of a point is an average of all the emotions (0 - Neutral, 1 - Positive, 2 - Negative). The second stage result of the defined method is represented as a map with the polygon of the explored territory and points of interest. To show the results it was decided to use Moscow district, Saint Petersburg, Russia, Fig. 2.

In the picture shown below a map of a district can be seen. Extracted points are colored according to their labels: Neutral - white, Negative - red, Positive - green. Radius of each point is a number of mentions of the point in social media network and map services.

As a result of this stage, each block is assigned a mention score (1 - frequently mentioned place, 2 - averagely mentioned place, 3 - rarely mentioned place), which means the concentration of mentions for the block.

3.3   Transport Accessibility Definition

In the third step of the method, the transport accessibility of each identified block is assessed. This is done by loading a road network from open sources. It contains information on pedestrian routes, public transport routes and cycle routes. In this study, we deliberately excluded the road network for cars, as the travel time by car depends on various situational factors that are difficult to access in open sources. Such factors may include traffic congestion during rush hours, traffic restrictions during holidays, and others.

Transport accessibility is calculated for each block based on the time it takes to travel from one block to all others. Finally, a block with the best transport accessibility and one with the worst accessibility are identified.

The result of this stage is a transport accessibility score for each block (1 - good transport accessibility, 0 - poor transport accessibility), which corresponds to the travel time required to get from each block to all others by walking, cycling or public transport.

3.4   Identification of Existing Urban Central Places

At this stage, the location of urban services is downloaded from open sources. Urban service refers to a service provided within the urban environment, aimed at meeting the needs of residents and visitors of the city. Data is uploaded across three profiles, corresponding to the highlighted profiles of existing central places:

- The gastronomic profile includes cafes, restaurants, pubs, canteens, snack bars and other catering establishments;
- The cultural profile consists of museums, exhibitions, art galleries, attractions and libraries;
- The trade profile includes shopping centers.

Table 1. Tags of city services by profiles of existing central places

Profile	Service Tags
Cultural	amenity = theatre, tourism = museum, tourism = gallery, amenity = library, amenity = arts_centre, tourism = attraction
Gastronomic	amenity = pub, amenity = bar, amenity = hookah_lounge, shop = bakery, amenity = cafe, amenity = restaurant, amenity = fast_food
Retail	amenity = marketplace, shop = supermarket, shop = mall

To retrieve the actual locations of urban services by profiles, the tags presented in Table 1 are used. The output consists of three files with point geometries.

After all services for three profiles have been unloaded, the concentration of its services for each quarter is determined separately for each profile.

That is, the result of this process will be three assessments for each quarter (1 - the most concentrated, 2 - moderately concentrated and 3 - not concentrated) for gastronomic, cultural and trade profiles.

This method also identifies other types of central places:

- The dominant central place profile is one in which a particular neighborhood scores higher than others. If the scores of several profiles are equal, the place is considered to be multi-profile.
- Further, places that have high public interest and good transport accessibility, but absolutely no developed services of any of the profiles, are considered potential.

Then the researcher needs to collect the data into a single table, which will contain the following data:

- Polygons. Information reflecting the border of the quarter in coordinate format;
- Mention score. Information reflecting the number of points of public interest;
- Transport accessibility. Information reflecting the extent to which the block is connected to other blocks by pedestrian and transport paths;
- Gastronomic concentration. Information reflecting the number of services related to the gastronomic profile;
- Cultural concentration. Information reflecting the number of services related to the cultural profile;
- Trade concentration. Information reflecting the number of services related to the trading profile;
- Centrality Score. A summary assessment of all indicators, allowing to assess existing central places and the influence of the central place on the studied area;
- Central place profile. Highlighting the dominant profile of an existing central location.

The degree of centrality (1 - the highest degree of centrality, 2 - a high degree of centrality, 3 - an average degree of centrality, 4 - a weak degree of centrality, 5 - a very weak degree of centrality) is determined by estimates of mentions, good transport accessibility and concentration of services. Neighborhoods with poor transport accessibility are not assessed because they do not belong to existing central locations.

- If both the mention score and the score of one of the profiles are equal to 1, then the researcher is facing a central place with the highest degree of centrality.
- If one of the scores is 1 and the other is 2, then the researcher is facing a central place with a high degree of centrality.
- If both the mention score and the score of one of the profiles are equal to 2, then the researcher is facing a central place with a medium degree of centrality.
- If one of the scores is 2 and the other is 3, the researcher is facing a central place with a low degree of centrality.
- If both values are equal to 3, then the researcher is facing a central place with a very weak degree of centrality, which does not stand out as an existing central place.
- Furthermore, places that have one score of 1 and another score of 3 are not considered central. This is because it is assumed that either the place is crowded with services that are not of interest to the population, or that the population is interested in a central place that has not yet been established in terms of services.

Based only on the assessment of the number of points of public interest per block, quasi-places are also identified, representing information about the popularity of the place among the population.

4   Results

As it was described in the previous sections, this method is focused on identifying urban central places by 5 categories. Each category is dependent of the city's infrastructure and should be extracted separately to receive more accurate results. Hence, the following central places in different profiles were identified:

1. Gastronomic centers shown on the Fig. 3(a).
2. Cultural centers shown on the Fig. 3(b).
3. Commercial center shown on the Fig. 3(c).
4. Multi-profile centers what can consist of the previously described types shown on the Fig. 4(a).
5. Potential central places presented in Fig. 4(b).

Figures 3 and 4 discover a real picture of services in the area. As it can be seen, almost all the services are concentrated on the north of the selected district. Such results can be explained with the closeness to the city's center, where all the goods are mostly placed.

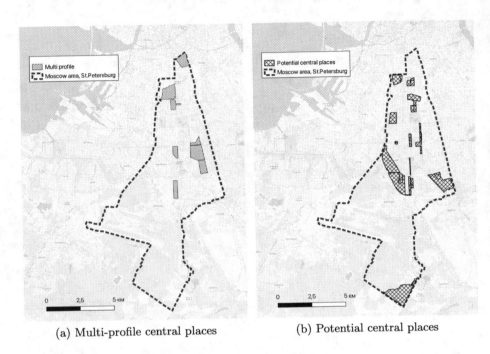

(a) Multi-profile central places   (b) Potential central places

Fig. 3. Other types of central places

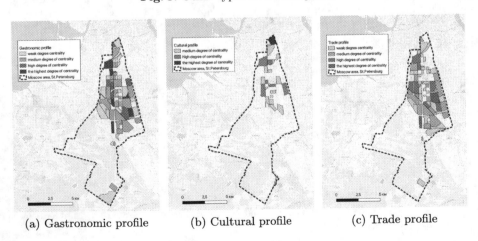

(a) Gastronomic profile   (b) Cultural profile   (c) Trade profile

Fig. 4. Central places of different profiles

The summary map, including existing central places of all degree of centrality and all profiles, as well as potential and quasi places are shown on the Fig. 5. These visual representations provide a comprehensive view of the central places in different profiles and highlight their respective degrees of centrality. The results contribute to a better understanding of the urban dynamics and support decision-making processes for urban planning and development in the Moscow District of Saint Petersburg.

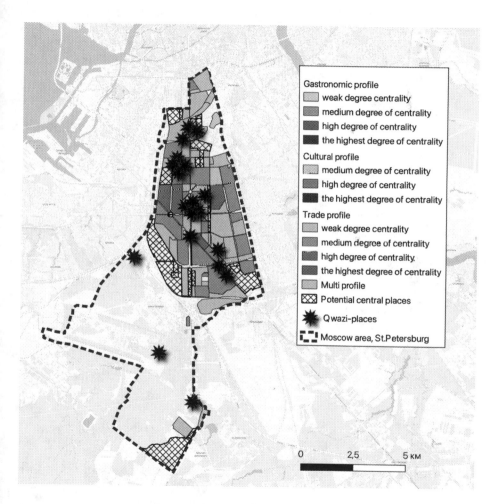

Fig. 5. Summary map

5   Discussion

In this study, an experimental investigation of the method for automatic identification of central places in a city was carried out, with the ability to identify existing central places and to determine places with the potential to become central.

Based on the results of this research, it can be concluded that this method is a valuable tool for both companies and city administrations in the planning and optimisation of urban areas. The data obtained through this method can be used to make decisions regarding the development of urban infrastructure, the identification of centres of attraction for residents and visitors, and the improvement of the urban environment and quality of life.

The identification of new central places helps to reduce the concentration of population and traffic in existing central zones, contributing to a more balanced development of urban spaces and an increased level of comfort for city dwellers. In addition, the identification of new central places can act as a stimulus for attracting investment and promoting tourism, which in turn can contribute to the economic development of the city and increase employment opportunities.

6   Conclusion

In conclusion, this study has demonstrated the applicability and effectiveness of the method for automatic identification of central places, confirming its significance for practical use in various areas of urban planning and development. The proposed method for automatic identification of central places based on open data and public interest is not limited to the case study of St. Petersburg, but can be easily extended and applied to cities in different countries and continents, providing a versatile and transferable approach to unravel centrality patterns in different urban contexts. The method provides valuable insights for stakeholders involved in urban development, enabling them to make informed decisions and optimise the growth and liveability of cities. Further research and refinement of the method can further enhance its utility and contribute to the sustainable development of urban environments.

References

1. Wong, Z., Li, R., Zhang, Y., Kong, Q., Cai, M.: Financial services, spatial agglomeration, and the quality of urban economic growth-based on an empirical analysis of 268 cities in China. Financ. Res. Lett. **43**, 101993 (2021)
2. Khan, M.F., Aftab, S., et al.: Quality of urban environment: a critical review of approaches and methodologies. Curr. Urban Stud. **3**(04), 368 (2015)
3. Christaller, W., Baskin, C.W.: Central places in Southern Germany. Prentice Hall, Englewood Cliffs, NJ, English translation of the German original: Christaller, Walter (1933). Die Zentralen Orte in Suddeutscland, Fischer, Jena (1966)
4. King, L.J.: Central place theory (2020)
5. Zhao, P., Hu, H., Yu, Z.: Investigating the central place theory using trajectory big data. Fundam. Res. (2023)
6. Yu, L., Yu, T., Wu, Y., Wu, G.: Rethinking the identification of urban centers from the perspective of function distribution: a framework based on point-of-interest data. Sustainability **12**(4), 1543 (2020)

7. Sun, Y., Fan, H., Li, M., Zipf, A.: Identifying the city center using human travel flows generated from location-based social networking data. Environ. Plan. **43**(3), 480–498 (2016)
8. Pereira, R.H.M., Nadalin, V., Monasterio, L., Albuquerque, P.H.: Urban centrality: a simple index. Geogr. Anal. **45**(1), 77–89 (2013)
9. Cai, M.: Natural language processing for urban research: a systematic review. Heliyon **7**(3) (2021)
10. Chen, N.C., Zhang, Y., Stephens, M., Nagakura, T., Larson, K.: Urban data mining with natural language processing: social media as complementary tool for urban decision making. In: The 17th International Conference on Computer Aided Architectural Design Futures, pp. 101–109 (2017)

The Aerial Transport in Urban Areas: Towards the Era of Manned VTOL-AV

Dimos N. Pantazis[1]([✉]), Vassilios Moussas[1,2], Anna Christina Daverona[1], and Panagiotis Argyrakis[1]

[1] SOCRATES LAB (Society for Organizations Cartography Remote Sensing/Road Design and Applications Using Technology/Transport Engineering on Earth and Space), Department of Surveying and Geoinformatics Engineering, University of West Attica (UniWA), Egaleo, Athens, Greece
dnpantazis@uniwa.gr
[2] Department of Civil Engineering, University of West Attica, Egaleo, Athens, Greece

Abstract. The use of manned drones as an urban transport mean is related with many parameters. Those parameters must create a functional multilevel system in order to a such "manned drone use" to be considered as a key factor for the urban air mobility. Such parameters could be (but not limited to): technological, infrastructure for landing and take-off in cities, legal framework, safety issues, personal data, navigation methods, privacy problems, etc. This article analyzes those key factors, after a short "historical" presentation of "the manned drones" idea. A literature review of the models created until now is also included. In addition, an innovative and original idea for the realization of a such vehicle is also presented in our work together with a short analysis of possible impacts of the manned drones on the urban transport in a smart city.

Keywords: Urban Aerial Transport · Manned VTOL (drones) · MVTOL-AV · Urban Verti-Port

1 Introduction

Drones, named also with the acronym UAV (Unmanned Aerial Vehicles) are in use our days in many scientific and professional areas having multiple roles and applications. Agriculture, cartography, research and rescue missions, environmental protection, infrastructure inspection is just a few of the thematic areas in which are used. Last years a new aerial vehicle (AV) category appeared, the so-called Manned Vertical Take off and Landing Aerial Vehicle (MVTOL-AV). Several other names also exist for this category of AV. The MVTOL-AV make possible the transportation of passengers like a helicopter or a small plane. A few proposals of such models exist already as prototypes while a few are in commercial production. MVTOL-AV could be a solution of the aerial mobility for the traffic problems in mega cities. The research goals are presenting in the following paragraphs.

In paragraph two we present the initial ideas in which are based such vehicles and an analytical list of the most important existed models of MVTOL-AV. Paragraph three summarizes the frame of the project SAV^2 (Socrates Aerial Vtol Vehicle) [1]. Paragraph four analyzes the parameters related with the MVTOL-AV and their fly in the cities, such as legal framework, privacy, necessary infrastructure, noise, safety matters etc. Paragraph five presents our conclusions.

2 Manned VTOL Aerial Vehicle (MVTOL-AV): Initial Ideas and Actual Efforts

European Commission claims that drones used for the transport of people and goods will be particularly oriented to the achievement of publicly accessible services, thus creating benefits for citizens and local communities [2]. Nevertheless, initial ideas for manned drones started in films and comics (Spirou and Fantasio, Metropolis, Oblivion, Elysium, Avatar, Edge of Tomorrow etc.) (see Fig. 1).

Our days different car/airplanes and other companies are creating and testing new prototypes MVTOL-AV. Taxi companies are installing drone stations (vertiports) or buy building rooftops for them. A number of construction companies are specialized on the Vertiport installation.

At its second annual summit in Los Angeles in 2018, Uber presented the six Uber Skyports prototypes and its latest aircraft designs while choosing Melbourne as the first non-U.S. location for its aerial ridesharing service and commercial operations in the next years [3]. Built near music halls and stadiums, the ports are near crowd-attracting city spots. Each port can handle over 4.000 passengers per hour in a three-acre footprint and meet noise, environmental, and eVTOL charging station regulations [4].

Fig. 1. A: Comic SPIROU AND FANTASIO (1935 Belgium) [5], B: Movie METROPOLIS 1927 Fritz Lang [6]

The European Commission (EC), in its smart and sustainable mobility strategy, which was adopted in December 2020, underlined its support for the deployment of drones.

The use of drones in urban areas was also highlighted in the Commission's new urban mobility framework, which was adopted in December 2021. Although the EC mobility strategy does not specifically refer to the MVTOL-AV, such aerial vehicles could be integrated in the same strategically frame. On 29 November 2022, the European Commission has subsequently adopted its Drone Strategy 2.0 for a smart and sustainable unmanned aircraft eco-system in Europe.

The MVTOL-AV for passengers and cargo transportation may be soon a central fundamental urban transport mean. In the near future the rapid development of megapolis (megacities) will make the MVTOL-AV the key factor of the urban air mobility, as it will be the only sustainable alternative solution in the traffic conjunction problem and the urban transport problem in general.

Concerning the infrastructures for UAV and MVTOL-AV in March 2022 EASA presents the Prototype Technical Design Specifications for Vertiports (places for take-off and landing of UAV). The Prototype Technical Design Specifications for Vertiports offers guidance to urban planners and local decision-makers as well as industry to enable the safe design of vertiports that will serve these new types of vertical take-off and landing (VTOL) aircraft/and MVTOL, which are already at an advanced stage of development [7] (see Fig. 2A, 2B).

In the EASA site is noted that *"…One of EASA's innovation is the concept of a funnel-shaped area above the vertiport, designated as an "obstacle free volume". This concept is tailored to the operational capabilities of the new VTOL aircraft, which can perform landing and take-off with a significant vertical segment. Depending on the urban environment and on the performance of certain VTOL-capable aircraft, omnidi-rectional trajectories to vertiports will be also possible. [Author's note: new proposals for private vertiports in urban buildings is presented in paragraph 4]. Such approaches can more easily take account of environmental and noise restrictions and are more suitable for an urban environment than conventional heliport operations, which are constrained in the approaches that can be safely applied"*. [7] All this kind of regula-tions can be used for the MVTOL-AV legislation framework. Such frameworks are under preparation in several countries.

Fig. 2. A: Vertiports EASA Prototype Technical Specifications March 2022 [7], B: Photo from Skyports company Vertipot depot [8]

Unlike conventional helicopters, MVTOL-AV are electrically powered and use multiple rotors to lift off the ground and maintain flight. They can operate autonomously or be remotely piloted, and their small size and the user friendly and safe flight process make them ideal for use in urban environments.

Recent studies underlined the economic and environmental gains of the use of MVTOL-AV [9, 10]. Other MVTOL-AV parameters under investigation concern: secure take-off and landing in urban environment, collision danger, cabin environment (it should alleviate vertigo and claustrophobia), aviation system (it should minimize human flight control and allow autonomous operation, since the MVTOL-AV should also fly autonomously). Last but not least, MVTOL-AV designers must create a cost-effective and commercially viable product concerning its cost. [11, 12].

Volocopter, EHang, Joby Aviation, and Airbus are developing manned passenger drones. These firms manufacture safe, reliable, and efficient aircraft that meet flight's standards of international aviation services (see Table 1). German company Volocopter has completed many successful manned test flights of different MVTOL-AV prototypes. The last VoloCity prototype (see Fig. 3A), can carry two people, into a maximum 35 km distance range. It has 18 vertical lift rotors and a 110 km/h top speed. Public flying demos of this MVTOL-AV have been realised in Singapore and Dubai [13, 14]. Chinese startup EHang has also present MVTOL-AV prototypes: one with two and another with four passengers EHang 216 and 216L respectively versions. EHang has also passed test flights and received regulatory certification in China and Norway [13] (see Fig. 3C). California-based Joby Aviation created the five-seater Joby S4 (see Fig. 3D) with a 240 km range. Six rotors provide vertical lift and 320 km/h cruising speed. Joby Aviation has attracted investment from Toyota and JetBlue, demonstrating significant interest for the MVTOL-AV technology from car manufactures. With Vahana, Airbus has joined the manned passenger drone market, demonstrating the same interest from airplanes manufactures. Vahana Alpha One is a single-passenger aircraft for short urban transport. Eight rotors of this MVTOL-AV provide vertical lift and a 120 km/h peak speed. The four-passenger CityAirbus is one of the latest MVTOL-AV Airbus's project (see Fig. 3B) [15].

Fig. 3. A: Volocity [16], B: City Airbus Passenger Drone [17], C: Ehang 216 [18], D: Joby S4 [19]

Table 1. General Characteristics of MVTOL-AV Prototypes

Model	Volocity	City Airbus Passenger Drone Nextgen	EHang 216	Joby S4
Weight	900 kg MTOM (maximum take-off mass)	2.200 kg	599 kg Max take-off	907 kg
Passengers Number (pilots included)	2	4 passenger / 1pilot (optional)	2	5
Dimensions	-	-	18′ 4″ wingspan, 5′ 9″ length	35 ft wingspan, 24 ft length
Width	-	8 m Wingspan	-	-
Flight time	-	15 min	25 min	77 min
Propeller (Nb)	18	8 vertical electric ducted fans	8 dual rotors	6 propellers
Battery	9 battery packs Li-Ion (exchangable)	-	-	-
Powerplant	-	8 × vertical electric ducted fan, 100 kW (130 hp) each specially designed Siemens SP200D direct-drive, 4 × 140 kW (190 hp) battery output	All-Electric	-
Speed	110 km/h	120 km/h	128 km/h	321 km/h
Range	35 km	-	70 km	241 km

3 SAV^2 Manned VTOL-AV Project

The "DOMINATE" school (DrOne MissIon desigN And daTa process)/ (https://dom inate.uniwa.gr/) – University of West Attica – Center for Long-term Education (https:// kedivim.uniwa.gr/en/), offers drone education programs for the European drone licenses A1/A3, A2 and specialization on drones applications in cartography, search and rescue, infrastructure inspection, and more. In conjunction with the National Service for Civil Aviation, we developed drone education programs in accordance with EASA Mobility requirements. The DOMINATE school immediately became a hub for new research and project development. The DOMINATE educators staff includes university academics from many areas: Computer Science, Geoinformatics, Civil Engineering etc. The SAV^2

project idea started six years ago. After testing many drone models, we opted to design and propose our MVTOL-AV based on the DJI Mavic Air 2 model (see Fig. 4A). The DJI Mavic Air 2 model's stability in heavy winds and user-friendly navigation functions were the main factors for this pick. The prototype's initial design was for carbon fiber bucket seats for passengers and pilots and aluminum for the remainder. Figure 4B is presented a 3D design of first SAV^2 prototype. Figure 4C and D present the model equipped with sensors to prevent collision (see Fig. 4C) and parachutes (see Fig. 4D) in case of total failure of all rotors [1].

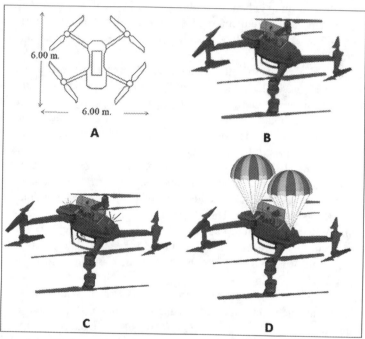

Fig. 4. A. SAV^2 dimensions. B. First basic model mainframe. C. First basic model mainframe with sensors. D. First basic model mainframe with parachutes

Our manned SAV^2 prototype is easy to fly, pilot training is similar to a car training license. Additionally, automated and pre-scheduled flights simplify things for the passengers. On this is based the idea of aerial autonomous taxi. Such MVTOL-AV, along with low-cost infrastructure and an appropriate legal framework, will be an important part of the solution of the city and megacity urban transport problems in the near future. Previous successful attempts confirm project feasibility (see Table 1). All aspects of the proposed SAV^2 design and construction use existing know-how. The cost is exceptionally low. The implementation of our theoretical design will follow a sequential order of flying tests using: 80 kg human dummy model, 80 kg passenger/pilot, two passengers with baggage (300 kg), four passengers with 320 kg maximum weight, ten passengers weighing up to 1000 kg.

4 Urban Air Mobility with MVTOL-AV: A Future that is Already Here?

4.1 Infrastructure for Urban Air Mobility

Today's major smart city projects give grate importance at Sustainable Urban Mobility (SUM) and consider it as a top-ranked topic. Apart of the new mobility services, electric cars and cars/bus without drivers, SUM includes initiatives for Urban Air Mobility (UAM) [20]. A Smart City and its basic component, the smart home, will be significantly transformed by the emerging Urban Air Mobility (UAM) and its associated technologies. New structural components, architectural designs, specialized infrastructure and new IT infrastructure, will emerge and will be installed or required in buildings that are planned to support UAM.

There are several projects that, focus on the development of the required infrastructure for UAM [21]. These plans and ideas will impose a significant change in classic building design in the near future. Let's not forget how, through the centuries, urban mobility and its corresponding means of transportation, imposed the various designs, requirements, restrictions, or additions in the domain of building manufacturing [23]. When mobility used horses, the stable was a major part of the building and in coastal areas the dock became also an integral part of the building. Today, the car parking place or box is always included in a home or building plan. Tomorrow's Architects and Civil engineers will naturally include a kind of docking platform in every building they design to serve the UAM needs (see film "The fifth element").

The challenge for Smart-City/Smart-Building designers today, is to incorporate as early as possible in their projects, the future needs for UAM. The addition of Vertical Take-off/Landing infrastructure (Verti-Ports) to every new architectural design will soon become a necessity.

This design extensions will cause various changes in building infrastructure, the strength of roof/pavement, the allowed height in the area, the distance from other obstacles, buildings or electrical wires, etc. They must also be rapidly deployable, cost-effective, and "compatible", i.e., vehicle-agnostic, ensuring access for all vehicle operators (see also previous reference EASA Vertiports Specifications [7].

On the other hand, existing buildings will also need 'struggle' to find a place to install their Urban-Verti-Port by making roof upgrades, reinforcements, and required additions to accommodate UAV docking stations. Larger buildings with big flat roofs may easily use their infrastructure for Verti-Ports. Already in London, companies such as Skyports are investing in roofs of large buildings or into new constructions for Verti-Ports [22].

4.2 Characteristics and Requirements for a Versatile Verti-Box Docking Station

As presented in [23], Verti-Box is a smart Docking Station and it is proposed as an alternative to other more complex installations (Verti-ports, Drone-dromes, Skyports, etc.). Verti-Box also serves as the transportation container and housing box of the proposed SAV^2 (SOCRATES Aerial Vtol Vehicle). The basic characteristics of this Docking Station are described below:

Basic Verti-Box Properties: Easy Transportation, Easy Installation-Deployment, All Weather Protection, All required Instrumentation by the SAV^2.

Basic Functional Requirements: All-weather Functionality (–50... +50 °C), Automatic Open/Close for takeoff/landing and protection, Automatic Battery Recharging/Replacing, Unique Station Identification, Stable and Secure Network connections. Uninterruptible and Sufficient Power, Compatibility with all Networks, Weather and Proximity Sensors, as well as, advanced Scheduling capabilities for Arrival/Departure and recharging of multiple UAVs.

As also presented in [23] Verti-Box is an easy to transfer and deploy docking station, that will provide the necessary support for SAV^2's take-off and landing, recharging, servicing, as well as, housing, transfer and delivery. After installation, the upper half of the box opens automatically to double the landing area and allow the deployment of SAV^2.

It is based on existing models of Container Boxes, standardized for road, rail or ship transportation. Using a crane, Verti-Box can be placed everywhere, from a building roof or terrace, to any suitable open area. In order to install, there is a number of requirements that need to be fulfilled, depending on where the Verti-Box will be placed:

Installation requirements on a building Roof/Terrace:
When installed on a building, at least the following requirements should be met or provided:

Roof/Terrace dimensions should provide a rectangular free space of at least 50 m^2, in order to permit to a 20 ft/6 m Shipping Container to unfold and offer a landing diameter of about 7,00 m.

Roof/Terrace should have weight support capabilities of at least 4 t or 80 kg/m2 for the Container and Equipment (2500 kg) and the SAV2 (700 kg net + 300 kg payload). Typical capabilities of 1–1.5 t/m^2, found in contemporary buildings, will suffice but every case should be checked as there are significant differences between buildings depending on the design and the use of the top floor.

Wind/Weather Shields (folding transparent panels for SAV^2 protection) especially for tall buildings should be a requirement.

Electricity connections (a combination of Mains and Solar panels for uninterruptible supply) for Battery Charging and support of all Electric/Electronic equipment.

Network Connections (above 1GB) supporting all types of communication for all subsystems/components, and, using: Cable (UTP), Wi-Fi, 5G, and IoT technologies.

Storage Facilities for Auxiliary Batteries, Oil, Water and Consumables, Replacement Parts (motors, blades, wheels), fire protection, etc.

Roof/building Access Facilities should be provided such as: Elevator to the roof, Parking space, as well as connections to other transportation means.

Open Area HUB Deployment requirements:
Using a number of Verti-boxes and their supporting facilities (easily transferred also in container boxes), one can create a quickly deployed airfield/Hub for specific uses, especially when far from any existing Verti-port or DroneDrome, e.g., Special Points-Of-Interest, Emergency Cases, Auxiliary Connections to other Hubs, etc.

The supporting facilities for open area deployment include all required infrastructure (also coming in easily deployed container boxes) that aims to provide access to the required electrical power and network connectivity (see Fig. 5) [24]. They may also come in container box with:

An Electricity Part: for the Electricity Generators, Solar Panels, Power Converters, Cabling and Connectors.

A Networking Part: for Network Antennas, Satellite dish, Mobile and Wi-Fi connections, as well as, a small Tethered UAV/repeater for areas with reception difficulties.

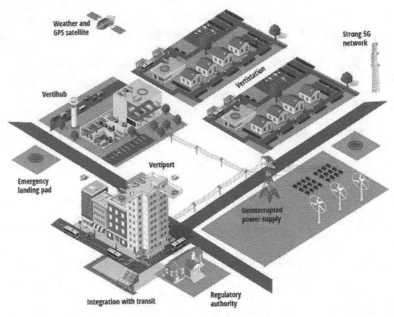

Fig. 5. According to Deloitte analysis, Urban Air Mobility (UAM) would require a robust city infrastructure [19].

4.3   How the Manned and Unmanned Drones Will Fly in the Urban Environment?

If large numbers of drones are ever to provide delivery services in urban areas, MVTOL-AV traffic legal frame, rules and relative legislation need to be created to safely manage the flow. The American Institute of Aeronautics and Astronautics' 2017 (AIAA) SciTech Forum in Grapevine, Texas, (https://www.aiaa.org/) provides some of the concepts that NASA's Ames Research Center developed for UAS traffic management in urban areas.

Three basic concepts [25] had been proposed (see Fig. 6): Sky-lanes: Vehicles must follow the centerline of each lane, and fly in one direction. / Sky-tubes: Vehicles move inside each tube, and fly only in one direction. / Sky-corridors: Vehicles can fly in any direction, but the vehicles themselves must maintain safe separation (probably the implementation of a such concept will be at a higher altitude than the first two concepts).

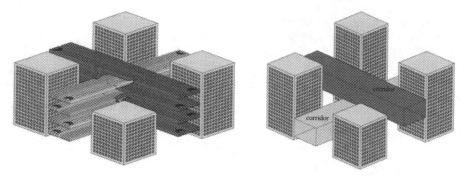

Fig. 6. UAS Traffic Management (UTM) concepts [26]

It is clear that in the near future the design development and implementation of an European Unmanned Traffic Management (UTM) System it is absolutely necessary in order to guarantee the integration of the remotely piloted aircraft systems (RPAS) - (including the MVTOL-AV) - into national and European airspace. The question that also arise is if such a system must be included in the general air traffic. [27].

5 Conclusions/Further Development

In our planet exist more than 34 mega cities. The first eight megacities are: Tokyo, Delhi, Shanghai, São Paulo, Mexico City, Dhaka, Cairo, Beijing. All confront big traffic problems making hard the life of their citizens. In addition, traffic problems don't concern only cities of such a size. Cities of a much smaller size also confront enormous traffic problems. The only solution seems to be the use of the third spatial dimension for mobility, the aerial mobility.

Although the technology of manned drones presents exciting opportunities in urban air mobility, a number of problems in their use have not found yet their solution. Overcoming these obstacles means: creation of legal regulations, solutions in different safety technical issues, infrastructure construction for take-off and landing, design of aerial corridors for safe navigation, aerial traffic MVTOL-AV flight rules ensuring safety in MVTOL-AV flights and many more.

As a consequence, a number of questions arise: How difficult is the construction of low-cost MVTOL-AV? Which are the difficulties of MVTOL-AV flights in an urban environment? Which are the necessary modifications in the existing legal frame? (e.g. in some countries the property of a house also extents above the house.) Where will be the places of take-off and landing? Exist urban planning studies concerning the urban air mobility and the impact to urban environment? Are ready the car manufacture companies to thing about a possible shift to the MVTOL-AV?

This paper gives a general frame of the aerial urban mobility based on the literature review, the SAV^2 project, and research efforts of Drones pilot School DOMINATE in UNIWA.

Acknowledgments. Authors would like to give thanks to all the people from the UNIWA administration for the support to our research and to DOMINATE school – UNIWA for continuing education and lifelong learning. Many thanks also go to all remote pilots involved in the design of SAV^2 for their valuable comments.

Disclosure of Interests. The authors have no competing interests.

References

1. Pantazis, D.N., et al.: Smart transport for smart cities: a futuristic scenario and a realistic project. ISPRS Ann. Photogrammetry Remote Sens. Spat. Inf. Sci. **X**-4/W3–2022, 213–220 (2022a). https://doi.org/10.5194/isprs-annals-x-4-w3-2022-213-2022
2. IRUD6PDUWDQG6XVWDLQDQDEOH8QPDQQHG$LUFUDIW (Fr communication from the .... https://transport.ec.europa.eu/system/files/2022-11/COM_2022_652_drone_strategy_2.0.pdf. Accessed 31 Jan 2024
3. Qatar Tribune: Qatar to build world's largest 'blue' ammonia plant worth over $1 billion, Qatar Tribune (2022). https://www.qatar-tribune.com/article/17445/latest-news/qatar-to-build-worlds-largest-blue-ammonia-plant-worth-over-1-billion. Accessed 31 Jan 2024
4. Gibson, E.: Uber reveals "Skyport" proposals for flying taxi services. Dezeen (2022). https://www.dezeen.com/2018/05/11/uber-air-elevate-skyports-flying-taxi-service/. Accessed 11 May 2022
5. De Blieck, A., Bacta, A., Lebourdais, J.C., Saincantin, J., Cockerham, Z., De Blieck Jr., A.: . Spirou and Fantasio V13: "Z is for Zorglub." PIPELINE COMICS, 14 February 2021. https://www.pipelinecomics.com/spirou-and-fantasio-v13-z-is-for-zorglub/
6. Metropolis. [film] Directed by F. Lang. Universum Film (UFA), Germany (1927)
7. EASA—European Union Aviation Safety Agency. https://www.easa.europa.eu/en/downloads/136259/en. Accessed 31 Jan 2024
8. Mullan, M.: Skyports andamp; Hanwha Systems Partnership: OUR VISION FOR THE FUTURE, Skyports Infrastructure (2022). https://skyports.net/skyports-hanwha-systems-partnership-our-vision-for-the-future. Accessed 31 Jan 2024
9. Kellermann, R., Biehle, T., Fischer, L.: Drones for parcel and passenger transportation: a literature review. Transp. Res. Interdiscip. Perspect. **4**, 100088 (2020)
10. Müller, S., Rudolph, C., Janke, C.: Drones for last mile logistics: baloney or part of the solution? Transp. Res. Procedia **41**, 73–87 (2019)
11. Khosravi, M., Enayati, S., Saeedi, H., Pishro-Nik, H.: Multi-purpose drones for coverage and transport applications. IEEE Trans. Wireless Commun. **20**(6), 3974–3987 (2021)
12. Rautray, P., Mathew, D., Eisenbart, B.: Users' survey for development of passenger drones. Proc. Des. Soc. Des. Conf. **1**, 1637–1646 (2020)
13. Volocopter (2022). https://www.volocopter.com/. Accessed 15 Jan 2024
14. Ehang.com: eHANG 216 autonomous aerial vehicle. http://www.ehang.com/ehangaav/. Accessed 05 Jan 2024
15. Airbus.com: CityAirbus NextGen (2022). https://www.airbus.com/en/innovation/zero-emission/urban-air-mobility/cityairbus-nextgen>. Accessed 18 Jan 2024
16. Volocity: Volocopter (2022). https://www.volocopter.com/solutions/volocity. Accessed 18 Dec 2023

17. Airbus.com. https://www.airbus.com/en/innovation/zero-emission/urban-air-mobility/cityairbus-nextgen. Accessed 13 Nov 2023

18. UAM - passenger autonomous aerial vehicle (AAV). EHang. https://www.ehang.com/ehangaav/. Accessed 03 Dec 2023

19. Joby Aviation: Joby. https://www.jobyaviation.com/. Accessed 31 Mar 2023

20. Smart-cities-marketplace.ec.europa.eu: Urban Air Mobility (UAM)—Smart Cities Marketplace (2022). https://smart-cities-marketplace.ec.europa.eu/action-clusters-and-initiatives/action-clusters/sustainable-urban-mobility/urban-air-mobility-uam. Accessed 07 Dec 2023

21. NASA: Advanced Air Mobility (AAM) (2022). https://www.nasa.gov/aam. Accessed 02 Dec 2023

22. Marcus, F.: London rooftops snapped up for "vertiports" as drone travel moves closer. Dezeen Magazine (2018). https://www.dezeen.com/2018/08/23/skyports-barr-gazetas-london-rooftops-vertiports-drones-technology/. Accessed 07 Dec 2023

23. Pantazis, D.N., et al.: Smart transport for smart cities: a futuristic scenario and a realistic project. ISPRS Ann. Photogrammetry Remote Sens. Spat. Inf. Sci. **X**-4/W3-2022, 213–220 (2022). https://doi.org/10.5194/isprs-annals-X-4-W3-2022-213-2022

24. Lineberger, R., Hussain, A., Metcalfe, M., Rutgers, V.: Infrastructure barriers to the elevated future of mobility, Deloitte Insights (part of a deloitte series on the future of mobility™). Deloitte Touche Tohmatsu Ltd. (2019)

25. Deciding rules of the road for urban UAS. Aviation Week Network (2017). https://aviationweek.com/aerospace/aircraft-propulsion/deciding-rules-road-urban-uas. Accessed 02 Dec 2023

26. AIAA. www. (n.d.). https://www.aiaa.org/. Accessed 03 Feb 2024

27. EASA: EASA issues world's first design specifications for vertiports—EASA (2022). https://www.easa.europa.eu/newsroom-and-events/press-releases/easa-issues-worlds-first-design-specifications-vertiports. Accessed 02 Dec 2023

Forecasting Cascading Effects in Network Models as Applied to Urban Services Provision Assessment

Vasilii Starikov[✉] , Ruslan Kozlyak , Polina Opletina ,
and Sergey Mityagin

ITMO University, Birzhevaya line, 14, Saint Petersburg, Russia
vastarikov@itmo.ru

Abstract. This paper proposes a method for evaluating the urban services provision based on a block-network city model in the context of cascade effects forecasting. Cascade effects are effects that arise in the urban environment as a result of the local territory development. Such effects can affect unknown quantity of city residents, which must be forecasted. The proposed method combines two approaches to assessing provision: predicting the number of interactions and evaluating provision according to regulatory requirements, as well as assessing the diversity of non-standardized urban services. The approach based on reducing the predicting of interactions to the knapsack problem using the Graph-Sage graph neural network architecture showed the best performance in evaluating provision with standardized services. Meanwhile, for assessing diversity, an approach based on block-by-block evaluation of the Shannon entropy index was used, followed by the use of weighting coefficients depending on the distance between city blocks.

Keywords: Network modeling · city network model · graph neural networks · spatial analysis · urban service provision · provision assessment · diversity of urban services · diversity assessment · cascade effects · urban development management

1 Introduction

The ongoing process of urbanization creates new challenges for cities in the context of urban development management. Urban services (also known as urban amenities) are one of the key entities of a city as a complex dynamic system, as they define the essence of the urban economy, can stimulate demand for services, and determine the quality of life in the city [1]. Thus, assessing the provision of such services is one way to evaluate the quality of the urban environment and life in the city as a whole. Such assessment is an important step in the development of territory transformation projects in the context of selecting areas for transformation [2] or establishing requirements for the territory [3]. This also raises the question of equitable access to urban services in the context of spatial inequality [4].

The implemented projects for urban environment transformation do not take into account the impact on the quality of life for residents in other areas of the city in the context of access to urban services. This can lead, among other things, to the overload of existing socially significant facilities. Such negative consequences may accumulate at a distance from the transformed area, causing an accumulating cascade effect. These effects may affect an unknown number of city residents, which nevertheless needs to be forecasted.

There is a need for urban models that allow evaluating the effects of urban environment transformation at the level of the entire urban system as a whole, as well as in the assessment method of city services provision in the context of cascade effects. The block-network model of the city can be applied as such a model.

2   Related Works

The theme is mainly reflected in the literature in an attempt to address the problem of insufficient accessibility of urban services. It can be formulated as the problem of the inability to uniformly provide services to all city residents. Related issues are considered, such as the inequality of access to medical facilities [5], the mismatch between the demand created and the capabilities of services [6], and spatial inequality in access to urban services [7].

There are types of services for which requirements for the level of provision are stipulated in regulatory documents [8,9]. Such services include general education schools, kindergartens, clinics, etc. In particular, the requirements for provision include:

Accessibility radius (in some cases, accessibility time) defines the area within a certain distance from the service that this type of service must normatively provide. The proportion of "those in need" (per thousand population), which directly generates demand for this type of service. The capacity level of the service for a specific area - the level of the number of those in need that the service provides for a given area. In this case, the task of evaluating the provision of urban services to an area may be reduced to the task of distributing the population among urban services of a certain capacity and subsequently calculating the ratio 1:

$$P = \frac{d_{within}}{d_{total}} \tag{1}$$

where d_{within} is the number of people provided for in the accessibility zone, and d_{total} is the total number of those in need. This ratio shows the proportion of people in need of a particular type of service who are provided for within the accessibility zone.

Various approaches are considered for the task of finding the number of interactions, including basic iterative methods [2], gravity models, linear optimization methods [10]. Gravity models can be too sensitive to the parameters of the city network model [11]. Graph neural networks are also gaining application in this context [10,12].

It is also assumed that the task of distributing people between services can be described as a task of many backpacks, by analogy with the article [13]. Based on this approach, one of the proposed methods for assessing regulatory provision was created. Since the city model is a graph, graph neural networks may be suitable for solving the topic problem. GNN generalizes data on the vertices and edges of the graph well and may be able to determine the hidden dependencies of provision on the demand of people and the capacity of services. GNN can be used to optimize the backpacks cost function.

The approach to assessing provision through the search for the number of interactions is particularly relevant for standardized types of services. However, to assess the provision of an area with non-standardized services, another approach based on diversity or heterogeneity assessment is required. Measures of homogeneity or biodiversity assessment [14] can be applied to such evaluation methods: Shannon entropy, Simpson index, etc.

Currently, there are about 40 biodiversity assessment indices. At the same time, each index either emphasizes the species richness or the degree of dominance of one species over others [15]. These indices can be divided into several groups, one of which is a group of indexes based on the relative abundance of species. To comply with this framework, it is advisable to pay attention to those that show not the degree of dominance of one species over another, but those that emphasize the species diversity in a particular territory. Such indices include the Shannon index and the Brillouin index.

The Shannon index is a measure of biodiversity based on the number of different species present in a particular area and the territory in which they are located. The index is calculated according to the formula 2:

$$H = -\sum_{i=0}^{N} p_i * log_2 p_i \tag{2}$$

where

- H - the Shannon index;
- p_i - the proportion of objects of the i-th type;
- N - total number of objects.

Compared to the Shannon index, the Brillouin index is rarely used to assess the diversity of objects, as it is difficult to calculate. The Brillouin index is used when the full composition of the community is known in advance and the sample itself is not random or small. The calculation takes place according to the formula 3:

$$HB_{max} = \frac{lnN! - \sum_{i=0}^{N} ln * n_i!}{N} \tag{3}$$

where

– HB_{max} - The Brillouin index;
– n_i - the number of objects of the i-th type;
– N - total number of objects.

Predicting cascade effects involves assessing changes in urban service provision indicators that occur in the city due to the transformation of the urban environment in a local area. Unfortunately, such effects are not tracked in existing provision assessment methods. There is a need for the creation of a method for assessing urban service provision that allows tracking the cascading effects of changes.

3   Method

To forecast cascade effects in the context of urban service provision, a comprehensive provision assessment method has been developed, aimed at evaluating potential changes in urban areas. The method is presented in Fig. 1. The result of the method consists of spatial data layer, describing the change in block-network city model provision. Negative assessment values indicate a decrease in the provision value, while positive values indicate an increase. Thus, the conclusion can be made on the impact of the development scenario.

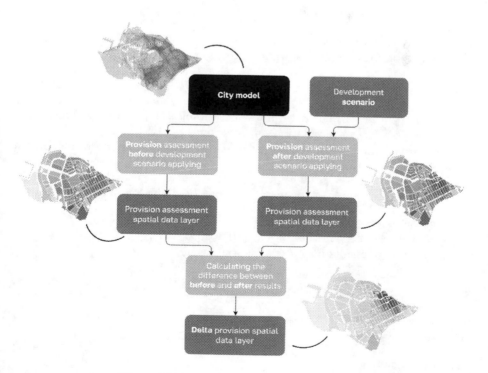

Fig. 1. Method for evaluating cascade effects

The method for evaluating cascade effects mostly relies on the urban service provision assessment method presented in Fig. 2.

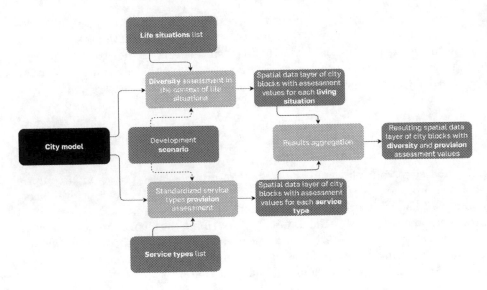

Fig. 2. Urban service provision assessment method

The method utilizes the following input data:

– A city model represented by the block-network model from the BlocksNet library [16].
– A territory transformation scenario describing changes in the local area, including services or population numbers.
– A life situation represented by a list of services relevant to city residents at a specific point in time.

Thus, the provision assessment method can be divided into several stages:

– Provision assessment for standard types of services;
– Diversity assessment in the context of life situations;
– Aggregation of results into a final spatial layer.

3.1   Block-Network City Model

Block-network city model is used to perform cascade evaluation. The model is presented by a complete graph, where:

– nodes – city blocks;
– edges – paths between city blocks on an intermodal graph, where edge weights present travel time.

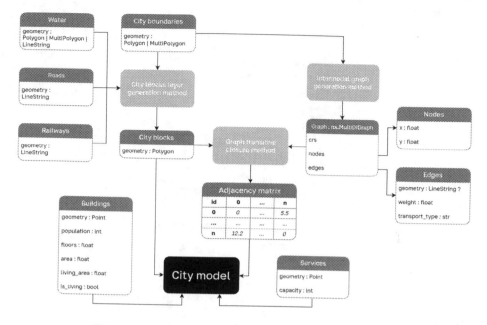

Fig. 3. Block-network city model initialization pipeline

City model initialization pipeline in BlocksNet Python library [16] is presented in Fig. 3. Data available for the provision assessment is described in "Buildings" and "Services" parts.

By default the BlocksNet city model consists of various service types, (such as schools and kindergartens) and its standardized parameters (accessibility time and demand value per 1000 population). These service types describe kinds of services, that can be added to the model.

3.2   Standardized Service Types Provision Assessment

The task of distributing people among services for provision assessment can be described as a multi-knapsack problem. Such a problem can be solved using a graph neural network [13]. The following are analogies of terms related to the provision task:

- Knapsack: A block-service aggregating services with a specified capacity.
- Weight: Demand generated by the population of a residential block for the block-service.
- Cost: Travel time between a residential block and a service block.

Figure 4 shows a diagram of a two-dimensional matrix, the values of which have to be found when solving the population distribution problem.

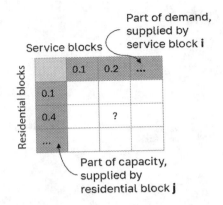

Fig. 4. Urban service provision assessment method

The minimized loss function is presented as follows:

$$\text{final\_loss} = \text{prices\_loss} + \text{space\_violation} - \text{used\_space} \tag{4}$$

where:

- prices_loss $= \sum_i^n pred_{ij} \cdot dist_i$ – a parameter penalizing the model for selecting too distant blocks during distribution.
- used_space $= \sum_j^m pred_{ij} \cdot demand_j$ – a parameter indicating the amount of satisfied demand.
- space_violation $= \sum_i^n Relu(usedspace_i - capacities_i)$ – a parameter preventing the network from predicting values exceeding block capacity.
- $pred$ is the prediction $n \times m$ matrix (n residential blocks, m service blocks) of the model.
- $dist$ is the vector of distances from the i-th residential block to each of the service blocks.
- $demand$ is the demand vector for each residential block.
- $capacities$ is the vector of capacity values for each service block.

The final loss function can be interpreted as follows: it is necessary to maximize provision with limited service capacities and taking into account the choice of the nearest service as the preferred one.

As a result of the method's execution, based on the obtained values in the two-dimensional demand matrix, an assessment of provision for the selected service type can be reconstructed before and after the application of the territory development scenario. The difference in provision values reflects the cascade effect of the specified development scenario.

3.3 Service Types Diversity Assessment in the Context of Life Situations

The diversity assessment is conducted in the context of life situations that may be relevant to city residents at different periods in time. For each such life situation, a list of supporting types of urban services (including non-standardized) can be determined. Assessing the provision of such service types involves evaluating the diversity of these service types in the selected block, calculated as follows:

$$D = -\sum_{i}^{n} \frac{H_i}{r} \tag{5}$$

where:

- $H_i = -\sum_{j}^{S} \frac{n_j}{N} \log_2 \frac{n_j}{N}$
- n_j – the number of services of the j-th type.
- r – the distance (travel time) between the selected block and the i-th block (in case it is the same block, the distance is taken as 1).
- S – the number of evaluated service types.
- N – the total number of services in the given block.

The result of the method is a spatial layer of city blocks with the obtained diversity assessment for each block. The difference in the diversity assessment resulting from the application of the territory development scenario and the obtained diversity assessment reflects the cascade effect of the specified development scenario.

4   Results

4.1   Input Data

As sources of input data, the OpenStreetMap service and the "Digital Urbanism Platform" of ITMO University were utilized. The data were adapted to the specifications of the block-network model in the BlocksNet library [16], on which the method investigation was based. The initial research area selected was the territory of Vasilievsky Island, St. Petersburg. The resulting model is presented in Fig. 5. Service types are also described in Table 1.

Table 1. Service types defined in the block-network city model

Service type	Kindergartens	Schools	Hospitals	Pharmacies	Polyclinics
Demand (per 1000 population)	61	120	9	50	27
Accessibility (min)	10	15	60	10	15

(a) Visualization of the model in terms of services and buildings

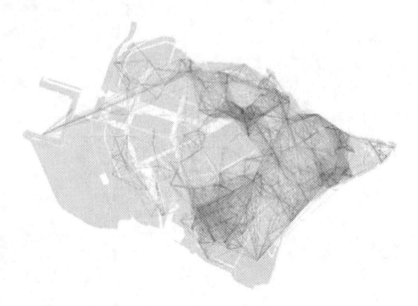

(b) Visualization of the model in the context of a graph

Fig. 5. Block-network city model

4.2   Provision Assessment

The provision assessment was conducted for the school service type. The Graph Neural Network architecture Unet was utilized, enabling the prediction of targets for provision assessment results obtained through solving a linear optimization problem. Due to excessive smoothing, this approach produces overly smoothed values and fails to capture the dependency of provision on the population count. The results of the architecture are presented in Fig. 6.

Since city residents do not always go to the nearest service, an architecture was chosen to more realistically model this behavior. The architecture based on random walks was selected for this purpose. The network shows results different from U-Net, but they are challenging to interpret due to the randomness of the walking process. The provision assessment result is presented in Fig. 7.

The provision assessment based on solving the knapsack problem showed the best results. The graph neural network was trained based on the GraphSage architecture, allowing it to handle large graphs. It was decided to use coefficients

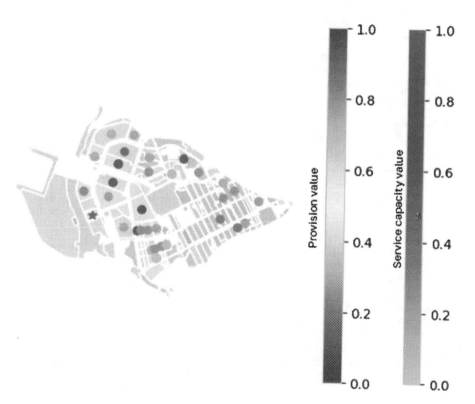

Fig. 6. Provision assessment based on U-Net architecture

that increase the penalty cost for choosing blocks outside the accessibility zone of the selected service type. However, the model performed best without modifying the coefficients both in terms of provision assessment and cascade effects. Figure 8 demonstrates the results of changes in the schools provision assessment. A negative delta value indicates a deterioration in the provision assessment, corresponding to the assumption that the provision level decreases with an increase in the population of the block, creating a burden on other blocks.

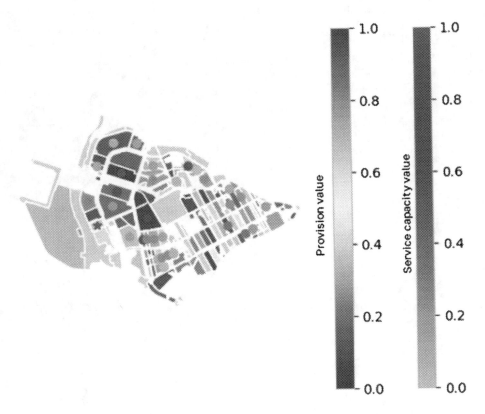

Fig. 7. Provision assessment based on random walk

The advantages of this approach include unsupervised learning and flexible adjustment of training rules. However, problems may arise when dealing with a large number of city blocks, particularly concerning the manipulation of small float values.

4.3   Diversity Assessment

The diversity assessment was conducted for the life situation 'Feeling unwell' which includes the following city service types:

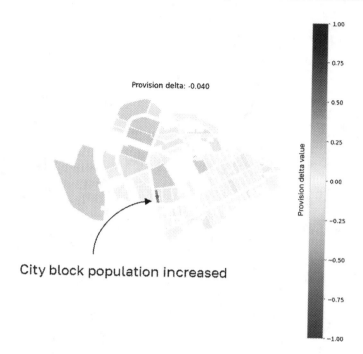

Fig. 8. Provision assessment delta based on GraphSage architecture and minimized loss function

- hospitals;
- polyclinics;
- pharmacies.

The initial diversity assessment based on the Shannon entropy index yields non-zero values only for areas containing services related to the life situation. The diversity assessment result is presented in Fig. 9. Cascade effects are not observed since the assessment is conducted independently of other city blocks.

There was a hypothesis that, for diversity assessment, it is necessary to consider not only the services within the city block itself but also those within a certain accessibility radius from it. Diversity assessments were made for accessibility zones of 5, 10, and 15 min from the city block. The results are presented in Fig. 10.

The diversity assessment as a weighted average of the Shannon entropy index on connected city blocks allows considering the accessibility of other services at a distance. A cascade effect is observed, opposite to the effect observed in the case of provision assessment with standardized service types. The result is presented in Fig. 11. With the addition of new services, diversity assessment improves most for nearby blocks and weakens at a distance.

Fig. 9. Diversity assessment based on Shannon index

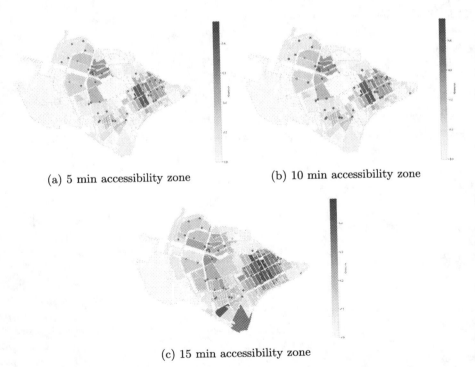

(a) 5 min accessibility zone

(b) 10 min accessibility zone

(c) 15 min accessibility zone

Fig. 10. Diversity assessment based on Shannon index and extended accessibility zone

(a) Diversity assessment delta

Fig. 11. Diversity assessment

5   Discussion

The approach to assessing standardized provision through solving the backpack problem exhibits several advantages, including the ability to operate independently of a teacher, the flexibility to configure learning rules, and the potential to manifest cascading effects. However, certain drawbacks are associated with this approach, such as limitations imposed by the number of blocks in the model. Challenges may arise when dealing with a substantial quantity of services, as the network may need to output very small values.

The limit to the number of blocks can be solved by changing the architecture of the model. Perhaps there are approaches that allows teaching a network with an arbitrary number of outputs. The method reflects cascade effects, but perhaps the result can be stabilized by applying special layers of the neural network that are specifically suitable for the task of assessing security. For example, it would be possible to develop a special aggregation function for convolutional layers or combine two data parameters, capacity and demand, into one parameter using a change reduction algorithm such as PCA or t-SNE.

It is also worth noting the peculiarities in the behavior of the standardized provision function itself. Thus, the function may nonlinearly respond to linear input. Primarily, this can be manifested in an increase in the provision assessment with an increase in the population in the city block, as presented in Fig. 8.

Such counterintuitive behavior of the function is primarily associated with the fact that existing urban services in the city block or its vicinity can supply the increased load, thereby increasing the value of the provision ratio 1. In practical terms, if we consider the neighborhood outside the urban context, this may mean that the neighborhood can accommodate an additional number of residents considering the existing urban services.

The difference in diversity assessment from standardized provision assessment lies in more evident response to local changes in the urban environment. As seen in Fig. 11, the emerging cascade effects attenuate as one moves away from the transformed city block. However, such attenuation will be heterogeneous, with some city blocks reacting more acutely to the transformation than others. However, it is difficult to quantify the effect on the life of residents.

The diversity assessment method, meanwhile, relies mostly on life situation concept, thus making it impossible to assess specific service type diversity of a city block. Further services categorization may be needed in the context of a certain service type.

6   Conclusion

As a result of the research, a provision assessment method has been developed, allowing for forecasting the impact of potential changes in the territory in the context of the entire city. The method can be applied to evaluate proposed urban environment transformation projects in the context of urban service provision. This assessment can be conducted during the master planning requirements generation step. Additionally, one of the potential applications could be the use of the method in optimization tasks as an objective function. Thus, the method can be useful in tasks related to optimal urban service placement or generating optimal urban development scenarios.

Two approaches to assessing provision with types of services have been considered: through diversity using the Shannon entropy index and through the search for the number of interactions between services and housing. Further development of the method may involve the use of graph neural networks to assess diversity based on the spatial distance between services and their parameters.

Acknowledgments. This research is financially supported by the Foundation for National Technology Initiative's Projects Support as a part of the roadmap implementation for the development of the high-tech field of Artificial Intelligence for the period up to 2030 (agreement 70-2021-00187).

References

1. Cai, Z., Kwak, Y., Cvetkovic, V., Deal, B., Mörtberg, U.: Urban spatial dynamic modeling based on urban amenity data to inform smart city planning. Anthropocene **42**, 100387 (2023). https://www.sciencedirect.com/science/article/pii/S2213305423000206

2. Khrulkov, A., Mishina, M.E., Sobolevsky, S.L.: City services provision assessment algorithm. Procedia Comput. Sci. **212**, 93–103 (2022)
3. Churiakova, T., Starikov, V., Sudakova, V., Morozov, A., Mityagin, S.: Digital master plan as a tool for generating territory development requirements. In: Guarda, T., Portela, F., Diaz-Nafria, J.M. (eds.) Advanced Research in Technologies, Information, Innovation and Sustainability. ARTIIS 2023. CCIS, vol. 1936, pp. 45–57. Springer, Cham (2023). https://doi.org/10.1007/978-3-031-48855-9_4
4. Ashik, F.R., Islam, M.S., Alam, M.S., Tabassum, N.J., Manaugh, K.: Dynamic equity in urban amenities distribution: an accessibility-driven assessment. Appl. Geogr. **164**, 103199 (2024). https://www.sciencedirect.com/science/article/pii/S0143622824000043
5. Duan, M., Tan, T., Zhang, B., Zhou, X.: A prediction of the paths to equalization of basic public health services based on gragh neural network (GNN) (2022)
6. Dadashpoor, H., Rostami, F., Alizadeh, B.: Is inequality in the distribution of urban facilities inequitable? Exploring a method for identifying spatial inequity in an Iranian city. Cities **52**, 159–172 (2016)
7. Morozov, A., Shmeleva, I.A., Zakharenko, N., Budenny, S., Mityagin, S.: Assessment of spatial inequality through the accessibility of urban services. In: Gervasi, O., et al. (eds.) Computational Science and Its Applications – ICCSA 2023. ICCSA 2023. LNCS, vol. 13957, pp. 270–286. Springer, Cham (2023). https://doi.org/10.1007/978-3-031-36808-0_18
8. Urban planning standards of St. Petersburg. https://docs.cntd.ru/document/456056520
9. Sp 42.13330.2016. urban planning. planning and development of cities and rural settlements. https://docs.cntd.ru/document/456054209
10. Mishina, M., et al.: Prediction of urban population-facilities interactions with graph neural network. In: Gervasi, O., et al. (eds.) Computational Science and Its Applications – ICCSA 2023. ICCSA 2023. LNCS, vol. 13956, pp. 334–348. Springer, Cham (2023). https://doi.org/10.1007/978-3-031-36805-9_23
11. Griffith, D.A., Fischer, M.M.: Constrained variants of the gravity model and spatial dependence: model specification and estimation issues. In: Patuelli, R., Arbia, G. (eds.) Spatial Econometric Interaction Modelling. ASS, pp. 37–66. Springer, Cham (2016). https://doi.org/10.1007/978-3-319-30196-9_3
12. Simini, F., Barlacchi, G., Luca, M., Pappalardo, L.: A deep gravity model for mobility flows generation. Nat. Commun. **12**(1), 6576 (2021)
13. Ghazanfari, M., Noujavan, M.: Using neural network and genetic algorithms to solve a multiple attributes knapsack problem (2002)
14. Chave, J., Thebaud, C.: Models of biodiversity. Math. Model. Vol. III **2**, 77 (2009)
15. Grishanov, G., Grishanova, Y.: Methods of studying and assessing biological diversity (2010). (in Russian)
16. aimclub/blocksnet: Open library with tools for generation the city model and optimal requirements for future development with specified target parameters. https://github.com/aimclub/blocksnet

Architectural Features of Museums Formation During the XX–XXI Century

Aoun Valentina[✉] and Solovyeva Anna

Department of Architecture, RUDN University, Moscow, Russia
information@rudn.ru

Abstract. This article provides an architectural analysis of renowned museums worldwide and a review of museum classification. Since the typology of museums is essential in museology, the purpose of this study is to demonstrate the wide range of museum types, structures and ideas, as they have evolved.

The first part will reveal the different types of museums classification, while the subsequent part will explore the museum architecture features, including their functionality and design concepts. This will involve the categorical method, systematic approach, and structural analysis to establish different typologies of museums and illustrate the evolutionary philosophy of museum development. The findings indicate that architects strive to diffuse their creations with a high level of expressiveness, sharing some distinctive features, and drawing on a holistic understanding of museums as an architectural piece of art.

Keywords: Museums Architecture · Museums Features · Museums Evolution

1 Introduction

Modern museum buildings are places where commerce, creativity, and culture converge, with architects being tasked to craft iconic structures that serve as symbols of the cities they inhabit. Further, museum architecture frequently acts as a striking visual centerpiece for the urban landscape, offering architects an ideal platform to showcase bold and innovative designs. According to the ICOM definition, a museum is a permanent, non-profit institution that aims to benefit society and contribute to its development. It is open to the general public and focuses on acquiring, researching, popularizing, and exhibiting material evidence related to individuals and their environments for educational and spiritual purposes [3]. Thus, the museum is a multifunctional social institution whose functions tend to grow.

Nowadays, many countries around the world are undergoing a significant construction boom of museums, primarily driven by advancements in science and technology, where museums are now in various forms, have different typologies and serve different purposes, ranging from art museums and history museums to science centers and cultural heritage institutions. By other means, "the typology of museums can be compared to the typology of books: (a) there are scientific books that present the results of a special

O. Gervasi et al. (Eds.): ICCSA 2024, LNCS 14813, pp. 450–464, 2024.
https://doi.org/10.1007/978-3-031-64605-8_31

research work of one scientist for other scientists; (b) educational ones intended for students; (c) popular ones designed for a wide range of readers[1]". Ergo, to gain insights into the diverse functions, structures, and missions of different types of museums, a study of museums classification and typology should be carried out.

Thus, the aim of this study is to identify the different components and features of museum's architecture, and to understand the underlying principles driving the museums evolution, by answering whether modern museums have common traits or not. To achieve this goal, the first part presents various museum classifications, followed by an examination of 8 renowned museums, encompassing architecture, functionality and design principles. This entail utilizing categorical methods, systematic approaches, analyses and comparison.

2 Materials and Methods

2.1 Museums Classification

The museum classification arose in the 1960s – 1980s in connection with the development of a network of museum ensembles and museum reserves. The typology of museums for public purposes was adopted in Soviet museology and is associated with the main category of visitors with whom the museum works: specialists, a wide range of tourists, students, children [7]. One of the most important categories of classification is the profile of the museum, that is, its specialization because museums are one of the main types of multifunctional buildings. And according to the Oxford English Dictionary, typology is defined as "the study of classes with common characteristics; classification, especially of human products, behavior, characteristics, etc., according to type; the comparative analysis of structural or other characteristics; a classification or analysis of this kind" [9].

Museum typology is essential for the development of the museum system and for the implementation of museum activities. The classification includes: historical museums [1, 4–6]; art museums [2–5]; literary museums [2, 4, 5]; Natural science museums [2–4, 7]; technical museums or science and technology museums [2, 4, 7]; scientific-educational museums [1]; branch museums [2, 4]; complex museums [2, 4, 7]; research and educational museums [7]; children's museums [7]; architectural museums [4]; musical and theatrical museums [5]; etc. Besides, while there are various types of museums, the most popular museums globally are art, history, science, and general museums, suggesting that all subjects can be equally popular [6]. Below, is a short description of some museum's classification provided with examples:

- The first famous type is the historical museum. Its primary goal is to chronicle and document a series of events or a complex representing a specific moment undergoing change [1]. For example, the State Historical Museum in Moscow and the Acropolis Museum in Athens. Moreover, by saying historical museum, it also groups the military historical (such as, the Central Museum of the Great Patriotic War of 1941–1945

---

[1] Schmit F. I. Museum business (in Russian). Questions of the exposition. L.: Academia, 1929. p. 245.

in Moscow), ethnographic, archaeological (like the archaeological museum reserve "Tanais"), religious history, historical personal, historical monograph (event), the history of individual enterprises [2], the Museum of political history (like the Museum of Political History in St. Petersburg) [3].

- Another famous type is art museums. Art museums include museums of fine arts, decorative and applied arts, folk art, palace, decorative and park art, personal art, and monographic art museums [2–5]. The group of art history museums consists of museums of theatrical art, musical art and musical instruments, photography and cinema, personal art criticism, and monographic art criticism [2, 4]. Hense, these museums focus on art, sometimes of a particular style, region, era, or a specific theme. For example: Guggenheim Museum (1959); The Neue Nationalgalerie (1968); Centre Georges Pompidou (1977); The High Museum of Art (1983); Guggenheim Bilbao (1997); Kunsthaus Bregenz (1997); Museu Oscar Niemeyer (2002); Louvre Abu Dhabi (2007); etc.
- Natural science museums cover geographical museums, biological (botanical, zoo-logical, museums of living objects), geological (paleontological, mineralogical), soil science museums, anthropological, and medical [2]. They might also be called muse-ums of a complex profile [3, 7], e.g.: The Central Museum of Soil Science named after V. V. Dokuchaev in St. Petersburg (1904) and the V. R. Williams Soil and Agronomy Museum in Moscow (1934).
- The science museum conveys the scientific spirit and mindset in three dimensions, to stimulate a natural desire for knowledge, and to provide information about research and development. This type includes museums of natural sciences, museums of applied sciences and museums of technology (polytechnic) [1, 7], such as the Central Museum of Physical Culture and Sports, founded in 1988.
- Branch museums are represented by agricultural, pedagogical, health, sports, branch personal, branch monographic museums [2, 4] like mining, shoe industry, and it can even be related to theater, music, cinema, etc.
- Complex museums include museums of local lore, architecture and history, architec-ture and ethnography, historical and artistic, literature and art, medicine and healthcare [2, 4].

2.2 Exploration of Art Museum

After outlining the characteristics of museum classification, in line with the research objective, we examine the architecture of 8 various Art museums as examples, to iden-tify any commonalities among this type of museum This exploration is motivated by the evolving role of museums since the mid-twentieth century, where museums have been acting not only as a repository, research, exhibition and cultural and educational center, but also as a tool for socio-cultural transformations. Therefore, the museums' analysis from the point of view of a systematic approach is associated with the consider-ation of its institutional nature, socio-cultural functions and the development of museum classification schemes.

Guggenheim Museum (1959)—Frank Lloyd Wright. A renowned art museum and one of the most considerable architectural icons of the XX century designed as an artistic, vast and organic sculpture, in an urban center in New York [8]. Wright stressed the need for significant change and envisioned both architecture and social reform as an ongoing process rather than a pursuit for some static absolute ideal; by this he expressed a vision for the role of architecture in reshaping American society [10].

Solomon R. The Guggenheim Museum had been on Wright's drawing boards for years before construction began, and was opened to the public shortly after Wright's death in 1959. The Guggenheim Museum was the first building design in which Wright destroyed everything square and rectangular. It was a peculiar-looking building, with an inverted cone [12]. Like many previous Wright works, this structure featured a vast interior space. A quarter-mile ramp ascended gradually in a spiral to a height of seventy-two feet, culminating in a high skylight dome to allow ample natural light and space. Visitors take an elevator to the top and amble down a gentle spiraling ramp viewing artworks in the process. The floor is supported and braced from the enclosing wall, with one floor seamlessly transitioning into the next, instead of the usual superimposition of the stratified layers cutting and butting into each other by post and beam construction. Finally, the building material is reinforced concrete.

Given that the Guggenheim Museum demonstrates a sculptural expressiveness, the extremely "free" boundaries of the object are clearly defined (and calculated on the computer) in their ultimate state - the feeling of peak tension is brought by the architect to the grotesque. The iconicity of the artistic image allowed the architectural structure to become a recognizable landmark. As a result, the transitional type from a separate volume to a developed complex represents the dynamic boundary of the museum's form, creating a sense of movement and openness within the space. This technique is common in the works of Richard Meier, Kisho Kurokawa, Christian de Portzamparc. Upon its completion in 1959, the museum's design was notably modern, featuring distinctive elements such as the use of poured concrete, its open atrium, its dramatic walkway [10]. These design choices reflected Wright's core principles of decentralization, human scale, inside-out and outside-in planning, space in motion, character, materials and ornament [11]. For Wright, "what we did yesterday, we won't do today. And what we don't do tomorrow will not be what we'll be doing the day after". Nevertheless, Mies van der Rohe's philosophy was just the opposite: "You don't start a new style each Monday[2]" - he argued.

However, the approach to museum architecture shifted in the era of contemporary design. Prior to the 1950s, museums were primarily seen as a beautiful shell to house collections, often resembling temples or palaces. Nevertheless, in the 1960s, Miss Van der Rohe, based in Berlin, introduced the new concept of the temple-museum.

The Neue Nationalgalerie (1968)—Mies van der rohe. Mies van der Rohe and Le Corbusier embraced a design approach that rejected traditional styles, the use of theories and principles derived from the industrial world and the belief in the ethical and social role of architecture and urbanism. Their iconic Modernist works are integral to architectural history, not just due to their chronological placement, but because they exemplify innovation in design and construction methods, while symbolizing the values of a city, society, and historical era [13]. If dissolution is found in Le Corbusier's aspect, then

---

[2] Tafel's discussion of Mies and his visit to Taliesin can be found in Edgar Tafel, Years with Frank Lloyd Wright; Apprentice to Genius. McGraw-Hill, 1979, p68–80, the quote is found on p70.

Mies van der Rohe expanded the universal space in his design and shaped his personal vision of space and architecture through an imposing steel and glass temple of modern, reinterpreting the classic style starting from its rules, laws and forms, and with the technique of his time in an innovative way, expressing a geometry based on a rigorous measurement and careful proportioning. This created metaphysical spatial properties. Indeed, every component of the museum structure is meticulously planned based on a fundamental 1.20x1.20-m module. This includes the granite slabs of the podium, the coffered steel cover, the structural grid of the lower floor, the length of side of the roof and that of the main hall, the height of the steel and glass facade, the height of the main hall, which influences the division of the space below according to the golden ratio of 5:8:5 [14]. Hence, every architectural aspect in this museum is pushed to its limits: the construction techniques, the structural constraints, the size of the columns, the wideness and emptiness of the space. The structural system, featuring a steel frame with large glass panels, creating a simple square layout, allows for an open and transparent facade, blurring the boundaries between the interior and exterior spaces. On the other side, inside the gallery, Mies van der Rohe's signature minimalist aesthetic is evident, with simple, clean lines and an emphasis on spatial purity. The interior spaces are designed to be flexible and adaptable for showcasing a variety of artworks. As a result, the emergence of the concept of universal space proposed by Ludwig Mies Van der Rohe, in many ways, influenced the development of a new type of exhibition space, which became one of the most commonly used in modern museums. Mies van der Rohe said "I try to make buildings a neutral frame in which people and works of art can live their own lives. This requires modesty [...] This is the only way to create free space" [13, p.60].

Thus, the Neue Nationalgalerie stands as a testament to Mies van der Rohe's mastery of modernist principles, showcasing a timeless elegance and a focus on structural clarity and spatial openness. It is a place of artistic enjoyment, not a place of isolation of works of art. Accordingly, the museum is considered an icon of the twentieth century and part of the legacy of the architect and is described as the ideal embodiment of the ideas of a "flexible container" [15].

Centre Georges Pompidou (1977)—Renzo Piano. Piano's architectural designs place a strong emphasis on functionality, sustainability, and spaces that prioritize the well-being of those who inhabit them. His commitment to creating buildings that inspire and elevate is evident in his focus on structures that not only serve their intended purpose but also have a positive impact on their surroundings and the people who interact with them. Natural light, ventilation, and green spaces are integrated into his designs, fostering a seamless connection between the built environment and nature. This is best shown in the Centre Georges Pompidou, also known as the Pompidou Center – a cultural complex in Paris, celebrated for its innovative and unconventional architectural design and is classified as structural expressionism, also as high-tech or late modernism [9]. It's one of R. Piano's most iconic creations because it exemplifies his innovative and unconventional design approach. Its unique exterior, featuring exposed steel framework and colorful pipes, defies traditional architectural aesthetics. Piano aimed to establish a structure that promotes transparency and openness, where people could engage with art and culture. Thus, this museum serves as a testament to Piano's dedication to pushing design boundaries and creating dynamic, interactive spaces [16].

The most distinctive feature of the Pompidou Center is its "inside-out" design, where structural components such as escalators, elevators, and mechanical systems are positioned on the building's exterior. This atypical arrangement creates open and versatile interior spaces, enabling unobstructed exhibition areas that can easily adapt to a range of cultural and artistic activities. By eliminating structural columns, the design provides uninterrupted exhibition spaces and facilitates the showcasing of large-scale artworks. During the day, the interior space is transparent and open to the outside eye, and in the evening, it seems like a light sculpture with recognizable architectural structures [17].

Summarizing, the Centre Georges Pompidou's radical architectural design has made it an iconic symbol of modern architecture and a major landmark in Paris. Its innovative approach to form, function, and urban integration continues to inspire architects and visitors from around the world. Consequently, the architecture of the R. Piano is characterized by the universal language of pure geometry - light, space, volume.

The High Museum of Art (1983)—Richard Meier. One of Richard Meier's distinctive architectural features is the integration of natural surroundings into his designs. This is evident in the Museum Angewandte Kunst in Frankfurt (museum of applied art - 1985), where the building incorporates green patios and square "windows" that visually connect the interior with the natural environment. Meier's work also includes various typological models of museums at different urban planning scales, with new structures harmonizing with their surroundings, as seen in the Getty Center in Los Angeles (1997). Additionally, Meier is known for creating separate sculptural volumes based on the concept of a "modernist box," as seen in the Barcelona Museum of Contemporary Art (1995) and the Athenaeum in the USA (USA, 1979). Meier is perhaps the best known of the group for his use of white in his designs, which enhances the qualities of light in space, since he believes that whiteness helps distinguish between opacity and transparency, solid and void, and structure and surface in his designs [18].

The High Museum of Art is a major public building and art repository that responds to the typological and contextual aspects of the museum's program. R. Meier embodies the modernist utopia (Corbusier dream of a "white world"), making it an equal member of interaction in the urban context. The composition of the structure is formed on the basis of the identification and analysis of urban planning lattices and attention to the context [12]. The museum refers to the typological aspect of a museum's program because it is created by a series of interconnected and distinct gallery spaces that are designed to showcase a variety of art forms. Meier's design incorporates large, open galleries with natural light, as well as more intimate and enclosed spaces, providing a range of environments suitable for different types of art. Additionally, the museum's layout and circulation paths are carefully considered to guide visitors through the various collections and exhibitions in a logical and engaging way. The floor plan is divided into four quadrants, with one quadrant carved out to create a distinctive monumental atrium, serving as the museum's lobby and ceremonial center. An extended ramp symbolically reaches out to the street and city, contrasting with the interior ramp, which serves as the building's primary formal and circulatory element. At the end of the ramp is the main entry and reception area, leading into the four-story atrium. This light-filled space is inspired by and provides commentary on the central space of the Guggenheim Museum. Unlike the Guggenheim, where the ramp also functions as a gallery, in Atlanta, the separation of circulation and gallery space allows the central space to dictate movement. This separation also allows the atrium walls to have windows, bringing in natural light and offering framed views of the city.

The tendency of volumes contrasting in geometric characteristics and in the facades, arrangement can be interpreted as a continuation of the tradition of modernism. Therefore, the figurative structure of R. Meier's museums and the "white architecture" has become his trademark. An untouched white sheet, an assumption of inspiration, and an illusion of an encompassing emptiness became metaphors for the museum of creativity. The method of geometric proportioning based on orthogonal lattice is used in all stages: from the organization of the scheme of the volumetric-spatial composition to the arrangement of the exterior shape of the building [12]. In a generalized form, the geometric concept of the proportion portrays some particular approaches:

- The use of a universal language of pure geometry;
- "White architecture" as the embodiment of the synthesis of the figurative metaphors;
- Museums as a creative laboratory of style;
- The use of an ideal and complete circular form of museums, which determines the dominant role of the structure in urban planning, architectural, artistic and social aspects: building-center and building-landmark.

However, Meier not only embraced modern architecture and pure form, reminiscent of Le Corbusier's work in the 1920s and 30s, but also shared a similar aesthetic with Peter Eisenman, Charles Gwathmey, Michael Graves, and John Hejduk, who were commonly called "the Whites".

Guggenheim Bilbao (1997)—Frank Gehry. One of the most iconic instances of architecture catalyzing urban revitalization is the creation of the Guggenheim Museum in Bilbao, Spain, which was designed by the Canadian-American architect Frank O. Gehry and opened in 1997. The resulting "Bilbao Effect" gained widespread recognition after transforming the industrial port city of Bilbao into a must-see tourist destination [8]. For that reason, the Guggenheim Bilbao would ultimately become the seminal example of how museums, or cultural institutions in general, can be utilized to regenerate post-industrial cities and bring new investment and life into the city. The unusual form is open to many associations: the expression of modern art, as well as metaphors for a ship, mountains, etc. The composition of shiny metal sheets at first glance is devoid of any order, starting to spiral and getting lost in a pile of metal. In fact, the structure acquires memorable and very different silhouettes when moving around, characterized by paradoxical integrity. The use of the reflective properties of titanium made it possible to transform the appearance of the museum during the day: at sunrise it looks silver-plated, during the day it is lost in a dazzling shine, and at sunset it acquires a golden tint. Lighting effects are also absorbed in the interior space: the refractions of the upper light from the central atrium contrast with the diffused dim light of the exhibition halls. The possibility of such an interpretation of the form is largely due to the introduction of high-tech glazing systems. Further, it has revealed extensive possibilities in both conceptual and artistic realms, transforming glass from a mere material into a convergence of technology and imagery. The trend towards "transparency" aligns with broader social and cultural movements in modern society, where "transparent architecture" has been widely adopted in museum design, enabling spatial synthesis and emphasizing on the contemporary conceptual art, which encourages viewer participation. This typology of museums reflects a social openness, in contrast to the traditional: "palaces of arts". In brief, it can be assumed that the use of glass in museum architecture best reflected the concept of "modern", including paradox, variability, and "transparency" as integral characteristics. The architecture of glass deliberately hides its formal-constructive nature, shifting the emphasis to the relationship of the object with the environment and its information filling [12].

The grotesque and at times aggressive visual impact, accentuated by the interplay of volumes and rugged finishes, imparted a sense of self-containment and autonomy to the multifunctional building, effectively distinguishing it within the urban landscape. As a result, the geometric design, layered volumes, and spatial composition are prominently showcased, highlighting the building's distinctive architectural character.

Kunsthaus Bregenz (1997)—Peter Zumthor. The architecture of the Museum Kunsthaus Bregenz is characterized by its striking, minimalist design and its seamless integration with its natural surroundings. Designed by the Swiss architect Peter Zumthor and completed in 1997, the museum is recognized for its innovative and thoughtful approach to exhibition spaces and architectural form. The museum's design and layout are tailored to provide an immersive and contemplative experience for visitors, allowing them to engage with the art in a thoughtfully curated environment. It's true that Zumthor's design for the Kunsthaus Bregenz features a minimalist and monolithic exterior, expressed with the clean lines and simple form, but this museum has key architectural elements, such as:

- Glass and Concrete Structure: The museum's exterior is primarily composed of glass and concrete, creating a clean, geometric form that allows natural light to flood the interior spaces. The use of glass also enables visitors to enjoy unobstructed views of Lake Constance and the surrounding landscape.
- Floating Exhibition Spaces: The museum's interior consists of a series of floating platforms that house the exhibition galleries. These platforms are suspended within the building, creating a sense of weightlessness and flexibility in the display of artwork.
- Integration with Nature: The museum is harmonized with its natural setting. The reflective glass facade mirrors the water and sky, blurring the boundary between the building and its environment. This adds its visual impact and makes it a landmark.
- Minimalist Interior: Inside, the museum features a minimalist, open-plan interior with clean lines and unobtrusive detailing. This design approach allows the focus to remain on the art, creating an immersive and contemplative environment for visitors. Thus, the internal has no connection with the external.

In result, the combination of these architectural features not only provides a dynamic space for art but also functions as a work of art in its own right. The museum's architecture mirrors Zumthor's commitment to creating an environment that enriches the experience of contemporary art while interacting with the natural and cultural context of its setting. It serves as a crucial component of the overall adventure experience. In summary, the

Museum Kunsthaus Bregenz's identity as a contemporary art museum is shaped by its innovative architecture, commitment to presenting modern art forms, and its harmonious integration with its surroundings [19].

Museu Oscar Niemeyer (2002)—Oscar Niemeyer. The Museum of Modern Art project in Caracas (1955) by O. Niemeyer was seen as a departure from modernist aesthetics in favor of a more expressive approach: "*a new stage, a stage in the search for purity and conciseness of forms*" [20, p. 62].

The Museu Oscar Niemeyer, also known as the "Eye Museum" due to its distinctive eye-shaped design, is a prominent architectural landmark in Brazil. The structure was conceived as a sculptural interpretation based on visual contrast. O. Niemeyer designed the museum in the shape of a tetrahedral pyramid situated atop and open to the sky's light - creating a striking contrast between the simplicity and seclusion of its external appearance and the openness and adaptability of the internal space, filled with light and air. In its relationship with the landscape, the desire to synthesize contrasting principles is also evident: attempting to blend into the surrounding landscape, which calls for compact monumental forms that sharply stand out from it [20, p. 64]. The Museu Oscar Niemeyer is distinguished by its exterior, predominantly constructed with concrete and glass, materials closely associated with Niemeyer's architectural style. The interplay of these elements creates an impression of weightlessness and transparency, enabling natural light to suffuse the interior spaces. The unexpected three-dimensional design dictated the layout of the internal areas. In the lower section, distanced from natural light sources, Niemeyer positioned the lobby, auditorium, and service rooms, while in the well-lit upper levels, he placed expansive exhibition halls, freeing them from supporting columns. The roof, intended to serve as both a protective covering and a means of connecting the inclined walls, also functioned as a large light diffuser and sunshade. Additionally, it featured platforms for displaying sculptures. The symbolic complexity of the form was conceived in multiple layers, aiming to embody the creative spirit of contemporary art and the development of Venezuela [20]. Simultaneously, the entire inverted pyramid structure of the museum stands in stark contrast to Le Corbusier's "growing museum" pyramid. The design, with its enclosed exterior and illuminated interior, evokes parallels with the spiraling form of Frank Lloyd Wright's Guggenheim Museum in New York. Moreover, within the museum, visitors are greeted by expansive and fluid exhibition spaces that embody Niemeyer's dedication to crafting dynamic and welcoming settings for art and cultural engagement.

The Museum was the culmination of the architect's concept of expressive symbolism of form and stands as a testament to Oscar Niemeyer's visionary approach to architecture, showcasing his ability to create structures that are both aesthetically captivating and functionally innovative [12].

Louvre Abu Dhabi (2007)—Jean Nouvel. One of Jean Nouvel's latest works, is the Louvre Abu Dhabi - an architectural masterpiece opened in 2007. Nouvel's design for the museum features a stunning dome structure that appears to float above the museum, creating a unique and visually striking appearance. The dome, 180 m in diameter, is made up of eight layers of perforated steel and aluminum, allowing sunlight to filter through and create a "rain of light" effect within the museum. The streams of light flowing through the openings give the architecture additional dynamics and expressiveness. The translucent ceiling is designed to reproduce the effect of light rays passing through the palm leaves. It is symbolic that its architecture resembles a desert.

The structure is based on the priority of rigid rectangular geometry and related principles of proportionality, where the architecture of the Louvre Abu Dhabi also incorporates elements of traditional Arabic design, such as the use of geometric patterns and intricate latticework, while also incorporating modern, minimalist elements. The result is a testament to Jean Nouvel's skill as an architect, creating a space that is both visually stunning and culturally where it also honors its cultural surroundings and stands as a symbol of contemporary architectural innovation. We can mention that this museum has several distinctive structural features making it a remarkable architectural marvel. Some of these features include: Reflecting Pools, Open Spaces and Natural Light. The museum is surrounded by a series of reflecting pools, which not only provide a visually stunning backdrop but also serve as a cooling mechanism for the building, helping to regulate the temperature within the museum. Additionally, The Louvre Abu Dhabi is designed to seamlessly blend indoor and outdoor spaces, with open plazas and courtyards that connect different parts of the museum. This design creates a sense of fluidity and openness throughout the complex. And finally, the design of the museum emphasizes the use of natural light, with strategically placed skylights and windows that allow sunlight to filter into the galleries and public spaces, creating a unique ambiance [21].

Describing the structure of his work, Nouvel uses sublime metaphors: the material of architecture is light, and language is glass. Transparency, light, abstraction, and concept are the key properties of Nouvel's architectural characteristics. It is quite fair to call the concept of J. Nouvel in museum architecture: the notion of intellectual dematerialization. As stated by Nouvel, the essence of architecture is a shell, a boundary at a given point in time, an event. According to the principle of dematerialization, the architecture of glass dissolves the form and fills it with unexpected illusions and mirages in reflections, glare, in layers of transparent volumes. At the same time, the formation of the volumetric-spatial composition of the structure is carried out on the basis of the priority of rigid rectangular geometry and the proportionality principles associated with it. The rational organization of the illusory world creates the impression of a second reality with a special, complex, order - the virtual space of architecture and art [12]. These features come together to create a museum that is not only architecturally stunning but also provides an immersive and culturally rich experience for visitors.

In closing and by all means, there are other architects expressing their concepts and ideologies in the museum foundation, like Tadao Ando and Arata Isozaki, where they used a sparse language of pure and minimalistic geometry as a symbolic signification in view of the fact that geometry interacts with natural factors including the sunlight and the water. Furthermore, in the aspect of the syntheticism of the museum's architectural environment, other architects raise the theme of intermediate, "empty" space and the use of its integrating potential while taking into consideration the intentional blending of various architectural styles, materials, and design elements to create a cohesive and harmonious space that enhances the overall museum experience.

3 Results

The museum's architecture analyses showcased the diverse array of museum categories, structures, and concepts as they have developed over time. It was found common traits of museums' architecture between the XX and XXI centuries, such as: (a) a decrease in interest of copying what was before, even if some architects attempt to create an architecture close to traditional museums; (b) an increase in the influence of evolution and technology by featuring innovative materials, striking forms, and cutting-edge technology to attract visitors and enhance the museum's cultural significance.; (c) an increase in the artistic and symbolic expressiveness of architectural solutions. Moreover, the analysis of museum architecture typology made it possible to cover a significant and informative volume of geometric and figurative characteristics of museum construction in the studied periods. This showed that the evolution of the typology of museum architecture of the XX-XXI centuries is characterized by new patterns and more freedom in the shapes, forms and concepts. These characteristics continue to shape the design of museums around the world, creating diverse and inspiring spaces for art, culture, and heritage. However, despite the endless variety of typologies and architectural solutions of museum, the layout of exposition spaces remains quite conservative, even in the most expressive forms, akin to the Guggenheim Museum in Bilbao which hides the most typical exposition plans.

The idea of museum formation is associated with the development of synthesizing symbolism of the artistic image, including: the concepts of signification of form formation (e.g. T. Ando); expressive symbolism (e.g. F. Gehry); abstract symbolism (e.g. J. Nouvel); and the metaphorical symbolism (e.g. O. Niemeyer). Finally, the variety of modern museum architecture style demonstrated various features in the structural construction; in the aspect of the formation of the concept of "development" in the functional and typological models; in the technological approaches to architecture; and in identifying the key pattern of museum's architecture growth according to the architect's concept. Table 1 gives a summary of modern museums features.

Table 1. The components and features of modern museums architecture.

Modern museum components	Features
The types of structural construction	• linear (in horizontal and vertical directions); • planar (regular and free organization); • volumetric (according to the sum of development vectors)

(*continued*)

Table 1. (*continued*)

Modern museum components	Features
The functional and typological models	• the growing Museum inspired by Le Corbusier, which involves an unlimited expansion of the building; • universal museum, much like Mies van der Rohe with the obligatory possibility of transforming the internal space; • spiral museum, including Frank Lloyd Wright's, which sets the schedule of the visitor's movement
The constructive and technological approaches to architectures	• technical: transformation, dynamism, mobility; • informative: social openness, intellectual game, mediation; • ecological: adaptive architecture, "green architecture", symbiotic architecture; • figurative and symbolic: technical and technological metaphors, symbols, signs
The key patterns of museum architecture growth according to the architect's concept	• the significance of the formation and symbolism of the museum's artistic image as a unique building (F. Gehry); • dematerialization of the boundaries of form as a conceptual contextuality (J. Nouvel) • "transparent" architecture (Mies van der Rohe);

Overall, the evolution of museum architecture typology in the XX-XXI centuries reflects a dynamic interplay between tradition and innovation, functionality and aesthetics, sustainability and technological advancement, and inclusivity and cultural identity.

4 Discussion and Conclusion

Today, museums are in continuous evolution, where museums configurations are in fact an important aspect. In the transition between the nineteenth and the twentieth century, the rise of the architects (such as Frank O. Gehry, Mies van Der Rohe, and Frank Lloyd Wright) resulted in the architecture overpowering the art inside. The result of this tendency revealed that the role of the architect is not limited to high-quality spatial design or to only attracting potential visitors' attention, but also concerns the definition of the public image and its identity, such as the Centre Pompidou - designed by Renzo Piano and Richard Rogers - encouraging the evolution of the museum as a container, but by also embracing eclectic styles, historical references, and playful design elements. Thus, following the XX century, architects explored various modern design approaches, ranging from the classical geometric style of Mies van der Rohe's Altes Museum in Berlin to the innovative curvilinear designs seen in the Guggenheim Museums by Frank Lloyd Wright in New York City and Frank Gehry in Bilbao. The symbolic representation of the artistic image in museums, which evolved throughout the XX century, is still developing in the XXI century.

Nevertheless, certain museums share common features related to their structure, symbolism, technological approaches or other aspects (e.g. the use of glass and steel, creating a sense of transparency and openness). Although, the most recognized properties of museum architecture are informativeness, attractiveness, and expressiveness, where the proportional-geometric, universal and organic approaches, form the basis of modern concepts of museums growth. These aspects encompass a wide range of design considerations that create a successful and functional museum space, while also enhancing the visitor's experience.

To conclude, museum architecture is a dynamic field that constantly evolves to incorporate new technologies, materials, and design trends. By studying different typologies of museums, researchers and professionals can explore innovative approaches to architectural design and gain a deeper understanding of the diversity, complexity, and significance of museums. As well, to identify the museums' relationship with various scientific disciplines and cultural phenomena, aesthetic concepts and social characteristic of a particular era.

Acknowledgments. I would like to thank my supervisor Anna Victorovna Solovieva who made this work possible. Her support and advice accompanied me in all the stages of writing this research paper.

Disclosure of Interests. The authors have no competing interests to declare that are relevant to the content of this article.

References

1. Rasa, A.R.: Museums through the time: an essay on art museums [internet]. Eur. J. Agric. Rural Educ. (EJARE) **2**(6). (2021). https://scholarzest.com/index.php/ejare/article/view/991/842
2. Sapanzha, O.S.: Classification of museums and morphology of museology: structure and dynamics (in Russian). Mus. Mod. Cult. **1**(5) (2012). https://cyberleninka.ru/article/n/klassifikatsiya-muzeev-i-morfologiya-muzeynosti-struktura-i-dinamika/viewer
3. Ekinil, G.E.: Museology (in Russian). Rostov-on-Don (2017). https://de.donstu.ru/CDOCourses/structure/_new_/508192/4195/3492.pdf
4. Enottt: Modern typology and classification of museums (in Russian). iskusstvoed.ru (2018). https://iskusstvoed.ru/2018/08/19/sovremennaja-tipologija-i-klassifikac/print/
5. Kalonova, Y.M.: Types and classification of museums (in Russian). Cent. Asian J. Arts Des. **4** (2023). ISSN: 2660-6844. https://cajad.centralasianstudies.org/index.php/CAJAD/article/view/200/194
6. Hoffschwelle, S.: 8 types of museums. Travel2next (2023). https://travel2next.com/author/sarahhoffw-pp/

7. Myagtina, N.V.: Profile groups of museums: a textbook for students studying in the field of study 072300 - Museology and protection of cultural and natural heritage objects (in Russian). Ministry of Education and Science of the Russian Federation, Federal State Budgetary Educational Institution of Higher Education. "Vladimir State University named after Alexander Grigoryevich and Nikolai Grigoryevich Stoletov." - Vladimir (2011). ISBN 978-5-9984-0184-8. https://gi.vlsu.ru/fileadmin/departments/muzeol ogiya/Monografii/Metod_PGM_MZ_2011.pdf

8. Delphine, A.: Reshaping Museum Spaces: Architecture, design, exhibition. Macleod, S. (ed.). Politecnico di Milano, Faculty of Architecture and Society (2004). https://www.academia.edu/ 10571260/Reshaping_Museum_Spaces_Architecture_Design_Exhibitions

9. Kildyusheva, A.A.: Typology of museums and systematization of museum functions based on the categorical method "a number of information criteria" (in Russian). CyberLeninka (2023). https://doi.org/10.24147/1812-3996.2023.28(2).53-64. https://cyberleninka.ru/art icle/n/tipologiya-muzeev-i-sistematizatsiya-muzeynyh-funktsiy-na-osnove-kategorialnogo-metoda-ryad-informatsionnyh-kriteriev/viewer

10. Boulton, A.O., Wright, F.L.: Architect of an age. William & Mary. Dissertations, Theses, and Masters Projects. Paper 1539625790 (1993). https://doi.org/10.21220/s2-ehyt-6x16. https:// scholarworks.wm.edu/cgi/viewcontent.cgi?article=5259&context=etd

11. Hong, M.H.: An analysis of Frank Lloyd Wright's architectural principles and techniques with emphasis on applications in his works. Graduate research thesis and dissertations. Northern Illinois University. Huskie commons. University libraries (1963). https://huskiecommons.lib. niu.edu/allgraduate-thesesdissertations/1100/

12. Dutsev, M.V.: The concept of architecture of a modern art center. Dissertation for the degree of Candidate of Architecture. Nizhny Novgorod State University of Architecture and Civil Engineering. Nizhny Novgorod (2005). [Text: direct]

13. Surikova, K.V.: The evolution of the museum image: from the museum to the white cube (in Russian). Questions of museology. CyberLeninka (2012). https://cyberleninka.ru/article/ n/evolyutsiya-muzeynogo-obraza-ot-museyona-k-belomu-kubu/viewer

14. Pavia, L.: Icons of the modern between past and future: drawing, design and restoration in the Neue Nationalgalerie in Berlin. X Congresso UID. Patrimoni e siti UNESCO. Memoria, misura e armonia. Academia.edu (2013). https://www.academia.edu/11985519/Icons_of_ the_Modern_between_past_and_future_drawing_design_and_restoration_in_the_Neue_N ationalgalerie_in_Berlin

15. Canziani, A., Di Resta, S.: The Neue Nationalgalerie by Mies van der Rohe between preservation and minimal improvement. J. Civ. Eng. Archit. **14** (2020). https://doi.org/10.17265/ 1934-7359/2020.04.006. https://core.ac.uk/reader/323190810

16. Elif, A.F.: Unveiling the Design Secrets of Renzo Piano. Illustrarch (2023). https://ill ustrarch.com/articles/16635-unveiling-the-design-secrets-of-renzo-piano.html#:~:text=Pia no's%20use%20of%20natural%20light,cultural%20expression%20and%20human%20inte raction

17. Renzo Piano Building Workshop Piece by Piece. Biennale Internazionale Di Architettura Barbara Cappochin. Padua, Palazzo della Ragione (2014). https://architettura.unige.it/inf/ 2014/03/piano/eng.pdf

18. Allen, K.: Spotlight: Richard Meier. Archdaily (2019). https://www.archdaily.com/437459/ happy-birthday-richard-meier#:~:text=Meier%20is%20perhaps%20the%20best,and%20s urface%2C%22%20he%20explains

19. Rist-Stadelmann, C.: Ephemeral art in the museum field of tension between art and architecture: using the example of the Kunsthaus Bregenz. Dissertation, Vienna University of Technology (2015). https://doi.org/10.34726/hss.2015.34326

20. Hite, V.L.: Oscar Niemeyer, 2nd edn. Revised and Expanded. Series: Masters of Architecture. Stroyizdat, Moscow (1986). https://archive.org/details/1986_20220614
21. Gombault, A., Selles, D.: Company profile: louvre abu dhabi: a radical innovation, but what future for french cultural influence? Int. J. Arts Manage. **20**(3), 83–94 (2018). , Special Issue: Culture and Media: The Attention Challenge (SPRING 2018). http://www.jstor.org/stable/44989739

Author Index

O. Gervasi et al. (Eds.): ICCSA 2024, LNCS 14813, pp. 465–467, 2024.
https://doi.org/10.1007/978-3-031-64605-8

Printed in the United States
by Baker & Taylor Publisher Services